Massachusetts Historical Society

Founded 1791

WINTHROP
PAPERS

VOLUME III

1631-1637

The Massachusetts Historical Society

1943

Published at the Charge of the Frederic Winthrop Fund

THE MERRYMOUNT PRESS, BOSTON, MASS., U.S.A.

PREFACE

THE contents of this the third volume in the series of the *Winthrop Papers*, covering the years 1631–1637, offer new and eloquent testimony in substantiation of the claim made at the time the first volume appeared in 1929: that the publication of the Winthrop manuscripts in their entirety and in chronological sequence would be "the most important contribution of original material ever made to earliest New England history." Much in the following pages has long been familiar to scholars; much has hitherto been unknown. But until now it has not been possible to make even the old yield its full contribution to the history of the years concerned.

This was a time in which economic, social, religious, and political problems tested in manifold ways the strength and integrity of the new colony. The Antinomian controversy and the war against the Pequots were perhaps the sternest of these trials, certainly the most spectacular. But no one can read these pages without realizing anew that the life and character of an individual and of a society are molded no less surely by the humdrum events that make up the greater part of life for the greater part of the people.

* * *

There is in this volume but one radical departure from the editorial policy laid down in Volumes I and II: the piecemeal publication of Governor Winthrop's Journal concurrently with the letters and other manuscripts has been abandoned. Instead it is the expectation that the Society will at some later date publish a new edition of the entire Journal comparable to its edition of Governor Bradford's history of Plymouth, issued in 1912.

It is a fixed policy of this series to reduce footnotes to a minimum. Since these volumes are not designed for the general reading public, it seems proper to assume that the users have advance familiarity with the subject. In the case of biographical notices the attempt is made to give only the most accessible sources of information.

The manuscripts are printed in their entirety except that endorsements are included only when they (1) further identify the writer or the recipient, (2) add to the factual information in the body of the document, (3) establish dates, (4) indicate the length of time the document was in transit from writer to recipient, (5) supply information about ship movements.

The style of editing conforms to the system established for the series (see *Winthrop Papers*, I. ix–xi) except where the original manuscripts are unlocated and unavailable for checking. In the latter cases, the style of the previous printed version has been retained unless otherwise stated in a footnote. The editorial *sic* has been used only where the extremely unusual spelling in the original might otherwise be interpreted as an error in proofreading.

ARTHUR MEIER SCHLESINGER
For the Committee of Publication

JULY 1, 1943

CONTENTS

Papers designated by an asterisk are now printed for the first time.

vii

1633

ILLUSTRATIONS

LIST OF ABBREVIATIONS

B.M.	British Museum.
Collections	Massachusetts Historical Society, *Collections* (Boston, 1792–).
D.A.B.	*Dictionary of American Biography*, Allen Johnson and Dumas Malone, Editors, 20 vols. (New York, 1928–1936).
D.N.B.	*Dictionary of National Biography*, Leslie Stephen *et al.*, Editors, 63 vols. (London, 1885–1900).
L. and L.	*Life and Letters of John Winthrop*, Robert C. Winthrop, Editor, 2 vols. (2nd ed., Boston, 1869).
N.C.	"The Letters of Roger Williams," John R. Bartlett, Editor, *Publications of the Narragansett Club*, First Series, VI (Providence, 1874).
Proceedings	Massachusetts Historical Society, *Proceedings* (Boston, 1859–).
Savage, 1825	John Winthrop, *The History of New England from 1630 to 1649*, James Savage, Editor, I (Boston, 1825).
Savage, 1826	The same. II (Boston, 1826).
Savage, 1853	The same. 2 vols. (Boston, 1853).
Twichell	*Some Old Puritan Love-Letters: John and Margaret Winthrop, 1618–1638*, J. H. Twichell, Editor (New York, 1893).
W. Au., W. 1, 2, 3, 4, 7A., 12, 13, 15, 17, 65	Manuscript volumes of Winthrop Papers in the Library of the Massachusetts Historical Society.

WINTHROP PAPERS

Volume III

1631–1637

WINTHROP PAPERS

ACCOUNTS OF JOHN WINTHROP, JR.[1]

March 10, [1629/30]. Received of mr. Harwood tres[urer] for the Comp[any] 30*li*

Paid mr. Revell towards the powder 40*li*[2]

March 11. Paid mr. Covels man for shot as by the acquittance vpon his bill which mr. Pinchen hath, appeareth 92*li* 10*s*

To mr. Ray for my brother Henry for holland, and lockrum 3*li* 19*s*

To mr. Goldsmyth for my sister Winthrops Coat 46*s* 8*d*

To mr. Preston in full payment 3*li*

my vncle Downing half mr. Brands acquittance for the mony he is to pay into the Ioynt stock. he hath also the license of alienation and fine for Groton land and acquittance for respit of homage all in a blacke box together.

Apr: 6: Received of goodman Pond 10*li* wherof 7*li* 17*s* 6*d* in mony the rest accounted for mault.[3]

---

[1] W. 65. These accounts fill eleven pages at the end of a commonplace book kept by one Arthur Blundefeild, who, according to Robert C. Winthrop, Jr., "is supposed to have been a fellow student of John Winthrop, Jr., at Trinity College, Dublin, or elsewhere."

Preceding these accounts there are five pages of notes by John Winthrop, Jr., on Peter Whithorne (Whitehorne), *The Arte of Warre Written First in Italian by Nicholas Machiauell and Set Forthe in Englishe . . . with an Addicion of Other Like Marcialle Feates and Experiments* (London, 1560–1562, and later editions). On another page appear the following undated memoranda, some of them in cipher:

aurum foliatum	crusibles
spiritus vini	peices of loking glasse
aqua fortis	smalest sort of lens
to sublime salamoniac	cristall
vitra diversum fortis	smal glasses made by the lampe
vitrial hungary	a vice, a polisher and other Iron tooles etc.
sulfur	brasse belloues

There follows a page of undated shipping memoranda:

a hogshead with bookes

a small hogshead of butter Cont[aining] 8 firkins and a halfe

a barrell of bookes [*in cipher:*] my chimical bookes

a pipe 2 fetherbeds and 2 bolsters

a pipe with 2 fetherbeds and 2 bolsters

a pipe 4 blankets: 5 Cloth Carpets: 2 Tapstery Coverlets. a blacke silke gowne and a yellow wastcote of my sister winthrops. a silke yellow pelice and stoole Claps [*sic*] of my sister mary a buffe Jacket. 2 brasse Capestickes 13 peices of peuter of divers sorts etc. a brasse skimmer. a dozen of pillowes wherof 6 are downe: 2 Cushons.

a hogshead of butter, Cont[aining] 10 firkins ½

[2] Cf. *Winthrop Papers*, II. 216. [3] Cf. *Winthrop Papers*, II. 223.

[April] 7. paid to Bulbrooke of Wenham for provisions that he had made of meale etc. for New Engl. 36s 4d[1]

[April] 13. Received of my vncle Gostlin for wood for the poore and others, the summe of 3li 16s and accounted for a years Collection for my father 32s.

Received of mr. Walford for Edward Walford for mony which my father lent him. John Samford received it of him. 5li

Apr: 30: Paid back to Tho: Gilson of Sudbury for his man which was turned backe 4li

May 2. received of my vncle Gostlin which he received of Haxall for mony which my father lent my aunt Painter 4li 10s

A bill from mr. Apleton of Royden for the payment of 30li 4s for 2 Cowes which he is to have in new England: due June 24.[2]

[May] 4. payd my brother Hen: bill for 6li to Roger Mather for mr. Craducke   also payde to him for Goodman Cole for his Clothe 5li   in all 11li

my sister Winthrop had of my mother 5li. she had of me June 4th 30s. she had June 19 20s.

paid my brother henrys bill to mr. Goffe 10s

To my Cozen Clarke for tobacco for him 20s

June 24. lent my brother Forth 4li
   more lent my sister Winthrop 20s

Aug: 28: received of mr. Gurdon 20li for goodman Kingsburye of Asington.

Sept: 2: lent my sister Winthrop 20s.

memorand: that the 18 of Octob: I am to pay to Sam: Burrows thirty pounds.

Sept: 15. paid mr. Peirce 50li vpon a bill from my father.

Item paid more to him and mr. Alerton to buy provisions for my father according to his directions 200li

Sept: 2. delivered John Samford for mr. Nicholson his tythe 50s

the browne biskot waied in the baggs 100½ 2 li. the hogshead   The white biscot waied 100½ [   ] with the bags

payments

	li	s	d
potatoes		20	
mr. Vassall bill from my brother[3]	5		
mr. Bundockes bill[4] of	1	10	

---

[1] Cf. *Winthrop Papers*, II. 223.   [2] Cf. *Winthrop Papers*, II. 309.
[3] Cf. *Winthrop Papers*, II. 295–296.   [4] Cf. *Winthrop Papers*, II. 311.

mr. Revells bill	23	4	
Edward Hopwoods 2 bills	6		
Griffith wallers 2 bills	6	7	
mr. Beechers bill	19		
mr. Strettons bill	2	15	
mr. Craduke for vse of 200*li*	8		
Constables for towne rates		15	
mr. Smith	15		
mr. Wright for fraight	30		
Robert Parkes bill	2	1	
mr. Huggen his vse	4		
mr. Sampsons bill	4		
mr. Lee his yeer of mony	2		
mr. Doyles fine	15		
mr. Hodges fine	56		
[ ]	5		
Stansby about Cristide	20		
John Samfords bills for Corne	12		
for malte	9	8	
another bill of his	3		
another bill of his	3		
vncle Gostlin which I lent him	4		
more	20		
mr. Cradocke	200		
to him for vse more	8	2	
more to him for mr. burrowes	7		
To Thomas Denton for pease 40 bushells	14		
mrs. Knaps bill	10	12	6
mr. Drakes bill	8		
my aunt Branch for 6 quarters[1]	60		
for Fees to the lawyers and writings etc.	10		
laid out at bristol for more things I sent besides what mr. Peirce had	5		
spent there in going and comming in Charges	10		
mr. Ray for holland for my brother H.	3	19	
to mr. Goldsmith for my sister Winth.	2	6	8
to mr. Preston in full payment	3		

---

[1] Cf. *Winthrop Papers*, II. 185.

	li	s	d
to Bulbrooke for his meale	1	16	4
Gilsons bill for his man	4		
To mr. Cradocke my brother Hen: his bill	6		
Goodman Cole for cloth	5		
to mr. Goffe my brother Hen: bill		10	
to my cozen Clarke for tobacco	1		
lent my sister winthrop in June 1630	4	10	
my brother Forth	4		
Paid mr. Peirces bill from my father Sept: 15, 1630	50		
Delivered to him per mr. Alerton to buy provitions at Bristol	300		
Sept: 2: 1630 delivered to John Samford for mr. Nicolson	2	10	
Payd mr. Peirce May 21, 1631, vpon a bill from my father	100		
paid the fraught of the Arabella and Talbot	350		
Paid mr. Stansby for Mrs. Knewstub	20		
Paid mr. Smith the Taylor more	15	10	
Paid goodwife moulton vpon bill	15		
June 12 at Groton 1631	30		
my sister Winthrop	10		
more to her	2		
more my wife to her	5		
Paid mr. Sharpe vpon bill	12	15	
Jul: 2, 1631 paid mr. Huggen vpon bord	100		
my sister Winthr:	10		
more to her	4		
Jul: 18 paid John Samfords bill london	19	18	6
at london	60		
mr. Humphries beife	12		
Tho: Caly for mrs. Sands	5		
for tin ware	3	18	
to Joh. Samford to buy chese	20		
a pair of smiths bellowes		10	
for Iron ware	36	6	
for a Chest		6	
for drugs	17	11	
for seeds[1]	1	6	

---

[1] See bill of July 26, 1631, pages 47–48, below.

to my sister Winthrop	6		
to my mother at london	18		
more paid John Samford	15	14	
delivered him more	10		
paid Sam. Goslin for Cloth	12		
the maids Charges to london	1		
paid my vncle Gostlin for the tooles at braintre other Charges	6		
to my mother more Aug. 2	80		
paid mr. Smith the taylor	18	4	
paid him more for my sister Winth:	3	8	6
paid mr. Kerby for skins	3	17	
paid mr. watson	6	7	
paid John Samford more	4	8	6
given mr. Peirce of london			
deliv: my aunt Downing to buy provitions for my mother	20		
to mr. Burrowes	23	12	
to John Samford when we came from london	20		
paid mr. Childs bill from my father[1]	27	9	
Paid Rich: Raimonts bill from my father	3		
Paid paul Woods bill	4		
paid mr. Goffe by bill from my father at hampton[2]	150		
paid him since	50		
my sister winth: at Sandwich			
sister Ursly had of me	7		
The carrier at severall tymes			
at once he had 30s			
brought with me from London to Sandwich	20		
left with my vncle downing	130		
philip Gostlin to pay	3		
for glasses[3]	5		
Electuarium lenititum[4]	1		
the greate peece	5		
laid out in provisions as per mr. John peerce his bill appeares	221	5	10
paid to mr. willm. peirce	350	4	

there remaines of John Samfords last bill to be paid backe to
    me 1*li* 13*s* out of 18*li* 17*s* which he received of me at
    London, wherof he hath laid out 17*li* 4*s* as per his bill

---

[1] Cf. *Winthrop Papers*, II. 308.   [2] Cf. *Winthrop Papers*, II. 307.
[3] See bill of July 22, 1631, pages 45–46, below.   [4] Cf. *Winthrop Papers*, II. 303.

I gave in my father a bill of disbursements   2930*li*
   and of receipts   2472

receipts

	li	*s*	*d*
Received of mr. Revell for mr. dudlies freight	40		
Received mr. Nuttall per bond[1]	20		
Received of mr. Clarke for mr. Nowell	50		
Received vncle Gostlin	10		
Received of Ridlesdale	10		
Received Smiths bond of Leaven heath	60		
Received of my Cozen Forth	605		
Received of mr. Harwood for Parker	7	15	
Received of goody Hammond to send her husband	7	5	
Received of goodman Pond	7	17	
and 2*li* 3*s* in mault			
Received of mr. Andrewes of bow lane[2]	20		
Received of my vncle Goslin for wood for the poore and others	3	16	
Received of Walford	5		
Received of Sir Drue Deane per bond	80		
Received of my vncle Gosl: for my mother Painter which my father lent her	4	10	
Received of mr. Gurdon for Kingsbury	20		
Received of goodman warren of Colchester per bond for his brother	12		
Received of mr. Waring[3]	2000		
Received of Gregory Stone for warren	20		
Jul: 1: 1631 Received of mr. Clarke for mr. Nowell	70		
Received of mr. Wells[4] of Tarling for Edward Lambe	13	7	
Received of Loverun of essex to send provitions for N: E:	6		
Received of mr. Rogers for provis: for N: E:[5]	3		
Received of mr. Cotton of boston	3		
Received of mr. Smith the taylor	5		

---

[1] Cf. *Winthrop Papers*, II. 321.   [2] Cf. *Winthrop Papers*, II. 306.

[3] This entry relates to the sale of Groton Manor. See *L. and L.*, II. 77–78. See also the references on pages 27, 29, and 32, below.

[4] The Reverend Thomas Welde of Terling, Essex.

[5] For letters of the Reverend John Rogers concerning his gift for provisions to be sent to Massachusetts, see *Winthrop Papers*, II. 316–317; pages 8–9, below.

JOHN BULBROOKE TO JOHN WINTHROP[1]

To the right worshipfull mr. Wintrop in new England this be delivered

TO THE RIGHT WORSHIPFULL MR. WINTROP GOUERNOUR AT NEW ENGLAND, Grace and peace be multiplied vppon yow. I John Bulbrooke your seruant though absent in Body yet present in spirit desirous hartily to remember my seruice to you: in humble manner, desiring God to blesse and aboundantly to prosper yow in all your proceedings: entreating your wor[ship] to remember your promised loue to me your seruant. so desiring to heare from you the next returne and some litle note of your prosperous iourney and of your love towards me so leauing you to the protection of the almighty who has promised to keepe and defend all thos that walke in a perfect way I rest Your seruant in the Lord

JOHN BULBROOKE

[*Ca.* 1631]

I entreate your wor[ship] to remember my harty love to my Cussen Child and his wife, praying God to keepe him vprite in his feare and to send to me some token of their love.

THOMAS GOSTLIN TO JOHN WINTHROP, JR.[2]

To his very loving Cosen Mr. John Winthrop at Mr. Downings house in Peterborow aly in fleetestrete this be delivered in London

LOVINGE COSEN, according to your request I went to lanham[3] and tooke particulers of all your lands there (as neere as I could gather of your tennants) whereof ther is 83 akers or thereabouts, all of the which is Copy saving 3 or 4 akers which is free and houldeth of Mr. Barrow and the house with halfe an aker is also fre but they know not of whome it houldeth Mr. Doyle haue demanded 3 pence the yeere for it but ther have not any rent bin payed because they never knew iustly of whome it held Mr. Harman farmes 20 akers rents 7*li* 12*s* ther is 10 akers of it errable and the rest fennes and ther is a littell tenement vpon the ground Allin farmes where he dwelleth 20

---

[1] W. 11. 88. For earlier references to John Bulbrooke of Wenham, Suffolk, see *Winthrop Papers,* II. 223, 306; and above, pages 2 and 4.
[2] W. 1. 83. Thomas Gostlin, a clothier of Suffolk, married Jane Winthrop, sister of the Governor.
[3] Lavenham, Suffolk.

akers   28 akers of it is erreble the rest fennes saving one aker of medow which
lyeth in a common medow   it rents 20*li* 12*s*   more Allen farmes 20 akers 13
of it erreble the rest medow   it rents 13*li* 10*s*

Mr. Forth farmes one medow of 3 akers   it rents 4*li*   the yeerely rent with
the Lords rent is 45*li* 14*s*   the Lords rent is in all 3*li* 7*s* the yeere, 41*s* 4*d* to
Mr. Hoges, 24*s* to Mr. Doyle, 1*s* 8*d* to Mr. Barrow   and thus with my truest
loue to you my Brother Downing and sister with commendationes to all the
rest of my cosenes and freinds I rest Your ever loving vncle

THO: GOSTLIN

[*Ca.* 1631]

I could wishe that you would not sell any of it as yet   it is thought that the
land that lyeth at masones bridge which Allen last toke to farme will sell for
as much as all the rest. Your Ante remembers her loue to you all.

JOHN ROGERS TO JOHN WINTHROP, JR.[1]

To the w[orshi]pfull Mr. John Winthrop at Groton geue these

LOVING AND GOOD SIR, your letter was exceeding wellcome to me, for I
longed to heare whether my letters and the monyes I sent came to your hand
or noe, and whether imployed to the vse of those poore distressed creatures
our good Brethren and sisters in New England:[2] And now I heare that my
desire is fullfilled, I give you most harty thanks: you haue indebted me much
to you, and I hope you haue ere this, or will shortly make some glad harts of
those that haue felt much hardnes. The Lord in mercy blesse it to them. God
hath bene pleased vntimely (as we may say) to take your 2 Brothers[3] out of
this life, for which I haue bene much grieved: I blesse his name that hath yet
reserved you to be a comfort to your Fathers hart over all his heavy crosses,
and to be a Blessing to the place whither you are intending. I pray be so good
as send me word when you heare of any shipp that is to goe next, for I would
write by any meanes: yea if I have fitt meanes I would send over a Cow or
Bullock or 2. If I were able to travell I had seen your mother and bene with
you once and twise ere this. But I have not bene a mile out of Towne since

---

[1] W. 4. 71; 5 *Collections*, I. 197. For the Reverend John Rogers of Dedham, Essex, father of the
Reverend Nathaniel Rogers of Ipswich, Massachusetts, see *D.N.B.*

[2] See Rogers's earlier letter to Winthrop, *Winthrop Papers*, II. 316–317.

[3] Henry Winthrop, who was drowned at Salem on July 2, 1630, and Forth Winthrop, who was
buried at Groton on November 28, 1630.

my lamenes now this halfe yeer allmost, yet I am forced tomorow to adventure to Assington to see my weak sonne. I pray God enable me to hold out the Journey. my loue hartily remembred (good Sir) I hartily take my leaue and commend you to the grace of God. Your w[orshi]ps in the Lord to his power

JOHN ROGERS

[January, 1630/31]

PRISCILLA PAYNTER TO ELIZABETH WINTHROP
AND MARTHA FONES[1]

To my beloued daughters Elizabeth and Martha I pray you deliuer these

MY DERE DAUGHTERS, I knowe your loue to be such one to another that you will not take it amis that I now kindly sallut you both in on letter giueing you both harty thankes for your louing letters and for your grat loue shewed to your pore sister in this time of her grat affliction which I take as to my selfe and shall euer be riddy to requit it to the utmost of my power I should be right glad to se you once againe before your departuer which if it plase the lord to giue me life and helth I trist I shall this summer   in the meane time I intrate your prayers for me as also the continuance of your loue to your pore sister to whom I pray giue your best aduise ether for her comming to me or staying with you which you shall thinke will give her most content and so with the remembrance of my loue to her and to my worthy sonne your littel one and all with you I command you both to the goodnes of god and rest Your louing mother till death

PRIS: PAYNTER

Feb: 6, 1630[/31]

---

[1] W. Au. 45. Priscilla Paynter, wife of the Reverend Henry Paynter, had as her first husband Bezaleel Sherman and as her second husband Thomas Fones, whose first wife was Anne Winthrop, Governor Winthrop's sister. Elizabeth Winthrop, the widow of Henry Winthrop, and Martha Fones, who two days subsequent to the writing of this letter married John Winthrop, Jr., were daughters of Fones by his first marriage. The sister referred to in this letter is Ursula Sherman, Mrs. Paynter's daughter by her first marriage, who had been engaged to Forth Winthrop at the time of his death in November, 1630.

AGREEMENT ABOUT FREIGHT ON THE *LION*[1]

We whose names are heervnder written havinge severall parcells of provisions and other goods aboarde the Shippe Lyon now rydinge at Ancher in
the Baye of Massachusets,[2] whereof the fraught and other Charges are not
yet cast vpp, doe heerby promise and binde our selues to paye our severall
parts of the said fraught and of all other Charges both ordinarye and extraordinary couveringe the said goods and provisions, accordinge to suche rate
and proportion as shalbe agreed vpon, and sett downe by the Governor and
Assistants or the greater parte of them, the same to be payde within fower
dayes of notice given and demand made thereof. In wittnesse whereof we
have heervnto putt our hands this 14 of Febr: 1631. stilo novo

Jo: WINTHOP Gou[enou]r for [*blank*]

JOHN WINTHROP ON REFORMATION
WITHOUT SEPARATION[3]

*Reasons to proue a necessitye of reformation from the Corruptions of Antechrist which
hath defiled the Christian Churches, and yet without an absolute separation
from them, as if they were no Churches of Christ*

1. And first a Q[uestion] would be demanded, whither Antechrist or the
Antechristian Church hath vtterly nullified the Christian Churches: or whither
it hathe onely polluted them for great Consequence will followe vpon either
side.

And first of the 1: viz: if Antechrist hathe nullified and quite destroyed the
Christian Churches then is it needful that we knowe the tyme when they were
thus destroyed and nullified: and how longe Christs Churches did remaine.

2: If Christs Churches were vtterly nullified then how these Scriptures etc.
can be fullfilled. Dan. 7: 14. there was given him dominion etc: that all
people etc: an everlasting dominion etc. Math: 16. 18.—and the gates of hell
shall not prevail against it. Heb: 12: 28.—we receiving a kingdom which

---

[1] Suffolk County Court Files, No. 4. The document is in the handwriting of Governor Winthrop.
[2] See William Peirce to John Winthrop, Jr., *Winthrop Papers*, II. 317–318.
[3] W. 1. 117; 1 *Proceedings*, XII. 338–341. Robert C. Winthrop, Sr., suggests that this document
is probably related to the controversy arising out of Roger Williams's refusal "to join with the congregation at Boston, because they would not make a public declaration of their repentance for having
communion with the Churches of England while they lived there." 1 *Proceedings*, XII. 337.

cannot be moved.   and divers others, that doe promise the Continuation of Christs Churches to the worlds ende.

On the other side, how shall these Scriptures be fullfilled. 2 thes: 2: 4. where that Antechrist is called that man of sinne, that doth sitt in the Temple of God: but these and such scriptures wilbe more properly brought in, when I shall shewe the Consequence on the other side.

3: If Christs Churches were vtterly nullified, and quite destroyed, then I demande when they beganne againe and where? who beganne them? that we may knowe, by what right and power they did beginne them: for we have not heard of any newe Jo: Baptist, nor of any other newe waye from heaven, by which they have begunne the Churches a newe.

4: If the Churches were quite nullified and destroyed: and that there have none been erected since with newe Authoritye from heaven, then either our outward, visible, and externall badge of our profession, viz: our Baptisme, is not right, or els there is an other power, besides the Churches power, that hathe the Authoritye to Baptize: but we knowe no suche power since the tyme of the Appostles and Evangelistes did Cease: ergo, if the Churches were destroyed, our Bapt[ism] is not right.

But before I goe any further, I must Answer some obiect[ions] against the 2d position: viz: concerning the scriptures that were Cited for Continuation.

ob: The scriptures are to proue the Continuation of the invisible Church and that indeed must Continue. Answ. that it is not the invis[ible] but the visible Churches that are meant by these places is certaine and cleere, and that by this Argu[men]t: That Church that hath the Keyes committed to it, that is the Church that is meant by these scriptures: but the visible Church etc: ergo, The proposition is cleare, math: 16: 18.

The Assump[tion] is thus proved: That Church onely that hath the Keyes, must be able to meet togither, and be able to heare a Complaint, and to give an Answer: but the visib[le] Church is onely able etc. ergo.

The propos[ition] is cleere. math: 18. 17. 1 Cor: 14. 23.

The Assumption no wise man will question, I thinke: seeinge the invisib[le] Church never did, nor can come together, vntill the last daye.

Ob: against the 4th position viz. Concerninge our Baptisme.

1: Ob: that man, that can preache (which is the greater worke) he may allso baptize (which is the lesse): but we see, that manye a man can preache by vertue of a Guifte, that he hathe attained vnto ergo all suche may baptize.

Answ: preachinge is to be vnderstood diversly: but I will speake of it but these 2 wayes, at this tyme: and so take it, either as it is a guifte, or grace, which men by endeauour may attaine vnto, and as the Ap[ost]le Commanded the Cor[inthian] churches (and in them all other Churches) to Couett after, as that 1 Cor: 14: 1, and drives at the same in the wholl chapter. Or els I will take it according vnto that preachinge spoken of Rom: 10: 14, 15. where sendinge enables them to an office of preachinge: and so take preachinge in the 1 sence, and then I denye that either suche preachinge is greater then Baptizinge, or that suche a man, though he preache, may therefore baptize. but take preaching as it is meant in the 2 Consideration (that is as it is tyed to an office) then I grant their sayinge, that he that may or can doe the greater, may doe the lesse, preferinge preachinge to baptizinge: but this later, no man takes to him selfe, but he that is called of God as Aron was. heb: 5. 4.

2: Ob: Baptisme is Baptisme, by whomsoever it is performed: and therefore where water is layd on in the name of the father sonne and holy Ghost, there is true Baptisme. Ans: 1: it is meet to vnderstande what they meane by Baptisme, seeinge the worde signifies washinge, and so take it in the largest sence, then we must grant that which they saye etc: But take Baptisme as it is Gods ordinance, to be that washinge, that signifies our washinge awaye of sinne, by Christs bloud and dothe s[ignify the] same to euerye true beleeuer, and then I saye, that Baptisme is not rightly and truly to be called Baptisme, if it want any of these 4 thinges: viz: a true obiecte, and a true subiecte, a true power, and a true and right Element: nay, I suppose, I might proue it a nullitye if it want a 5 thinge.

Other ob: are made, as namely, they will have Baptisme to be a Concept of their owne braines, that is, they will vnderstande Baptisme in their minde, viz: water and wordes vsed without any subiect: but that and suche other are so vaine, that such ob: are not worthe the Answ:

5: As the Consequence of denyall of ho[ly] scriptures is verye dangerous, so is another fowle Assertion verye offensive. The Scriptures before are denyed or falsified, that doe promise the Continuation of Christs Churches as that of Matt. Thes. Heb. and others: and that foule Assertion, that dothe denye the people of God in England or els where, to be visible Church Christians, and the societyes of them to be visible Church Christians, is verye offensive to all Godly and tender hearted Christians.

I am not vnacquainted with their Offensive Ob: that we make whores and drunkards visible Christians. I Answ: 1: to terme the people in gen[era]l whores and drunkards is evill: for althoughe the most part are ignorant (the more is their sinne and our greife) yet whores and drunkards they are not: weake Christians they are indeed, and the weaker for want of that tender Care, that should be had of them: 1: by those that are sett ouer them to feede them: and next for that spirituall pride, that Sathan rooted into the hearts of their brethren, who when they are Converted, doe not, nor will not strengthen them, but doe Censure them, to be none of Gods people, nor any visible Christians: nay they of the separation have gone further, and denyed them to be visib[le] Christians, whose knowledge in religion is not inferiour to theirs, and their walkinge in Religion answerable to their Knowledge; affirminge such to be worse then the other sorte viz: of the Ignorant. this is the Charity of these harshe spiritts, and that because they will not sinne with them in the point of separation: abusinge those scriptures that doe call vs out of Babell, viz: the Churche of Rome, and all other Consociated Churche estates, whether nationall, or diocesan: and applye suche scriptures to their separation from the particular Congregations, because they partake of a mixed multitude: and either pride, malice, or ignorance, in the most of these Censurers, will not give them leave, to distinguishe betweene Corrupt Churches and false Churches, as they doe terme the Congregations: neither will they putt any diff[erence] betweene the Churches as they are nationall, and appointed by man, and as they are particular Congregations, and appointed by Christ: for so they are, as they remaine particular Congregations, even Churches of Christs owne appointinge, althoughe now they be Corrupted.

Ob: Can the sounde of a Trumpett by K[ing] Edw[ard] or by Q[ueen] Eliz[abeth] make the Churches true that were false in the dayes of H[enry] 8. and of Ma[ry] his daughter, who did maintain Popery, and did force the Churches thereto? Ans: no: but the particular Congregations were as true Churches in the dayes of Q[ueen] Ma[ry] as they were in the dayes of Q[ueen] Eliz[abeth] onely they did differ in doct[rine], and were more Corrupt in Ma[ry]s dayes then of Eliz[abeth] althoughe too muche Corrupt then and now too: But the Corruption of a thinge dothe not nullifie a thinge so longe as the thinge hathe a beinge in the same nature, that it had, when it was in the beste beinge: so is it with the particular Congregations.

Ob: The Churches in England were never true, for they did want a right Constitution at the first, for they were Constituted by Aug[ustine] his worke.

Ans: that is more then they doe knowe, that doe saye so: for some are of the minde, that Jos[eph] of Arimathea brought hither the Gospell, I meane into England and so was a meanes to plant Churches: but these must be lefte to Records: and so I Answ: further, that whether Aug[ustine] or Jos[eph] or any other that God made his Instruments to Conveye the Gospell into Engl[an]d or into other lands, yet, blessed be the name of the Lord, it tooke effecte, that Churches were gathered.

Ob: but they were never rightly Constituted.

Ans: how knowe you that? 1: how doe you knowe, how and in what forme

(I mean) or words, the Churches were, and are to be Constituted, to make them right, or els they are not true? 2: If you could laye downe a forme of words, vnto which all Churches must be tyed, or els they be no true Churches (as I doubt you cannot yet) how doe you knowe, but that they might have that forme, when they beganne, altho it be not recorded? It may fall out in this Countrye, where we now live that Records of everye Churchs beginninge are not kept, neither yet any Record who was the first founder of the Gospell heere: I demande now, if this be a good Consequence of those that shall succeede vs heere in future tymes, if differences of opinion shall arise, the Churches that were planted heere had no right Constitution, for suche an one brought the Gospell hether. Even so deale those men with vs in their reasoninge: but wisdome will rather reason thus, we see the Churches are in the particular and Congregationall forme, althoughe now Corrupted, ergo sure they were so at the first.

Againe, Consider one poore defence, to make their owne Baptisme good, by a wronge meanes: they Reason thus: Israell in the tyme of Apostacie, were none of the Churche of God, yet were they Circumsised, and their Circumcition was [good, so][1] is our Baptisme true, saye they, thoughe doone in a false Church. I could [wish][1] these men to take better heed, and not to be so bould, to runne into one [error to][1] boulster out another, I meane, that to shunne that foule Offence, of [denyinge][1] the Churches now remaininge to be true, and yet will holde their Baptisme they will also call Israell a false Church, with whom the Lord made a Covenant, and helde the same, vnto the Captivitye, if not to Christs cominge in the fleshe, as appeareth plainly by holy scriptures. Againe they ob: Zipporah did Circumcise, who might not doe it yet it stood in forme, ergo, their Baptisme is in forme, by whomsoever it was doone. I Ans: 1: they doe but begge the Quest[ion], when they saye she might not doe it, for it is more then they can tell, seeinge that no scripture doe forbidd it either expressly or by Consequence, that ever yet they could shewe; but if it were. . . .

[*End of fragment*]

[*Ca.* March, 1631]

---

[1] So printed in 1 *Proceedings*, XII. 341. The manuscript is now torn at this point.

JOHN WINTHROP TO THE LORD CHIEF JUSTICE
OF ENGLAND[1]

RIGHT HONO[RA]BLE, Our humble dutyes to your good Lo[rdshi]pp presented: may it please you to vnderstand that whereas one Robt. wright Citisen and merchanttayler of London without our privity was come into N: E: and had setled him selfe in Charles towne, we had intelligence that he was fledd out of England for Treason: wherevpon we Caused him to be apprehended, and vpon examination he confessed to vs that about 2 yeares since he had Clipped some of the Coyne of our sover[eign] Lord the Kings ma[jes]tie and the officers coming to search his house he fledd and so was not taken, but vsed meanes by his freinds to obtaine his ma[jes]ties pardon: but forasmuch as he could produce no Record therof before vs we thought it our dutye to send him over prisoner by this bearer mr. Wm. Peirce master of the Shippe Lyon.[2] So we humbly take leave and rest At your Lo[rdshi]pps Comand for his ma[jes]ties service

[JOHN WINTHROP]

[*Endorsed by Governor Winthrop:*] Copy lettre to Lo[rd] Ch[ief] Justice de Wright March 1630[/31].

HENRY PAYNTER TO JOHN WINTHROP, JR.[3]

To my much respected Sonne Mr. John Winthrop at the howse of Mr. Immanuel Downing at the Signe of the Bishoppe in Peterburrow Court neere Fleete conduit

DEARE SIR, I vnderstand your marriage is[4] paste, and I with my wife doe wish you much comforte togeather in the Lord. I thanke you for your kinde profer of accompanying my daughter Vrsula vnto London, hopinge that my

---

[1] Suffolk County Court Files, No. 4. The Lord Chief Justice was Sir Nicholas Hyde.

[2] This episode is mentioned by Thomas Dudley in his letter to the Countess of Lincoln, March 12, 1630/31, where Wright is described as having been "sometimes a linen draper in Newgate market, and after that a brewer on the Bank side and on Thames street." Alexander Young, *Chronicles of the First Planters of the Massachusetts Bay, from 1623 to 1636* (Boston, 1846), 332–333. Wright's contention that he had been pardoned is confirmed by the records, which mention (November 23, 1629) a pardon "to Robert Wright, late of Southwark, brewer, for clipping coin." *Calendar of State Papers, Domestic, 1629–1631*, 103. The order of the Court of Assistants for his deportation was voted on March 1, 1630/31. *Records of the Court of Assistants of the Colony of the Massachusetts Bay, 1630–1692*, II (Boston, 1904), 10.

[3] W. 4. 45; 5 *Collections*, I. 116–117. For Paynter, see *Winthrop Papers*, II. 196, *n*. 2.

[4] See page 9, *n*. 1, above.

letter and my messenger will finde you boath there. My brother Lance and my brother Harris of Cornewall being my worthy friends and now in London proferred me this courtisye to take the care of her safe conducte, and accompany her home and therefore I haue sente but this one messenger. Glad should we be, and our desire is (pardon the vnreasonablenes of your true hearted friends affection) to see your selfe here alsoe, the rather because your voyage is deferred. My wife is alsoe not without hope that my daughter may get and bring downe a good seruant for her: If it be soe, the Exeter carryer lying at the starre in Bread streete may be spoken vnto as soone as he commeth to London for her riding downe which will be better cheape then the sending of a horse of purpose from hence for a doubtefull vse.

Your horse is now solde for six pounds and six shillings: we coulde neuer bring the price soe high till now, though many haue seene him to buy him and haue offered mony for him.

I pray you directe and help my daughter Vrsula what you may. Remember my heartiest salutations to my good brother and sister Downinge. I desire to heare how long you shall stay in London and whither (if you cannot come vnto us) I shall directe my next letters vnto you.

If you returne shortely home commende our deare affection to your worthy mother and our loving daughters, in which I alsoe rest Your louing father ready to doe you any kindenes in my power.

H. PAYNTER

Exon. March 1, 1630[/31]

JOHN WINTHROP, JR., TO MARTHA WINTHROP[1]

LOND: Mar: 4: 1630[/31]

Thy deare husband John Winthrop

MY DEARE, I cannot write the any long narration of our iorny but in breif both on Wednesday and Thursday we came to our iourneys end as wet as drounded rats but came safe and in good health God be praised   Me thinks I want thy company much already which maketh me much greiued to thinke of a month or six weeks   My Aund Downing expected to haue seene the an[d] chid me because I did not bring the up   She thinketh long to see the   I prethe write to her when thou hast leisure an[d] to my cosen Mary is uery sory thou camest not up   I sen[d] doune some orenges and lemons for

---

[1] W. Au. 57.

the and my mother   I wil wright her word I send them her   Thus with my tru lov remembred I commit the to the God of heauen.[1]

All our freinds heare salute the. heere is none yet come for my sister Vrsula but last weeke there was one mr. Harris asked for her two or thre tymes and he had promised them to goe downe with her. So I rest with my love to all our freinds my sister winthrop sister mary (whose things I will shortly send downe) vncle and aunt Gostlin mr. Lee and the rest of our frends Thy loving Husband

JOHN WINTHROP

—— POND TO WILLIAM POND[2]

To my Louinge Fathere William Ponde at Etherston in Suffolcke giue theis

MOSTE LOUINGE AND KINDE FATHER AND MOTHER, my humble deuteye remembreid vnto you trusteinge in god you are in good hellthe and I pray remembr my loue vnto my Brother Joseife, and thanck him for his kindnes that I found at his hand at London wich wase not the ualleu of fardin   I knowe Louinge father and do confese that I wase an undeuteyefull Cheilld vnto you when I liueied withe you and by you for the wiche I am muche sorrowfull and greueid for it trusteinge in god that he will so geide me that I will neuer offend you so aney more and I truste in god that you will forgiue me for it and my wreightein vnto you is to lete you vndurestand what a cuntrey theis new Eingland is whar we liue   her ar but fewoe eingeines and a gret sorte of them deyeid theis winture it wase thought it wase of the plage   thay ar a craftey peple and thaye will cussen and cheat and thay ar a suttell peple and whareas we ded expect gret stor of beuer her is littell or non to be had and thar Sackemor John waiethe it and maney of us truck withe them and it leyethe us maney tymes in 8*s* a pound   thay ar proper men and clen Jointeide men and maney of them go nackeid withe a skein abought thare loines but now s[o]me of them get eingellishe menes parell   and the

---

[1] The letter to this point, with the exception of the date line, is in cipher.

[2] W. 1. 84; 2 *Proceedings*, VIII. 471–473. According to Governor Winthrop's letter to John Winthrop, Jr., July 23, 1630 (*Winthrop Papers*, II. 307), two sons of William Pond of Edwardstone, Suffolk, came to Massachusetts in 1630. From the same source it is known that one was named John, while James Savage says that the other may have been the Robert Pond who subsequently lived in Dorchester. *A Genealogical Dictionary of the First Settlers of New England*, III (Boston, 1861), 452–453. From the nature of Winthrop's reference to John Pond in the letter cited, it seems likely that John was the writer of the letter printed here. Much credit for the deciphering of this exceptionally difficult manuscript is due Mr. Julius H. Tuttle, former Librarian of the Society.

cuntrey is uerey rockey and heilley and s[o]me champine ground and the
soile is uerey flete and her is s[o]mee good ground and marshe ground but her
is no myckellmes springe   cattell threiue well here but thay giue small stor of
mylck   the best cattell for proffeit is sweines and a good sweine is her at 5*li*
preise and a goote is worthe 3*li* a gadene gote   her is teimbur good store and
ackornes good stor and her is good stor of feishe If we had botes to goo 8 or x
leges to sea to fishe in   her ar good stor of weield foule but thay ar hard to
c[o]me bye   it is hardur to get a shoot then it is in ould eingland   and Peple
her ar subgecte to deicesesse for her haue deyeid of the skurueye and of the
bur[n]inge feuer too hundreid and ode   beseides maney leyethe lame and all
sudberey men ar ded but thre and thee woomen and sume cheilldren   and
prouisseyones ar her at a wondurfule rat   wheat mell is xiiij*s* a bushell and
pese x*s* and mault x*s* and eindey seid wheat is xv*s* and thare other wheat is x*s*
buttr xii*d* a pound and chese is 8*d* a pound and all kind of speyseis uerey der
and allmoste non to be got and if theis ship had not cume when it ded we had
bine put to a woondurfule straighte but thanckes be to god for sendinge of it
in   I resayueid from the shipe a hogseite of mell and the gouerner tellethe me
of a hundreid waight of chesse the wiche I haue resayueid parte of it   I
humbley thancke you for it   I ded expecte too coues the wiche I had non nor
I do not arenestly deseyer that you shoold send me aney becauese the cuntrey
is not so as we ded expecte it   tharefor Louige father I wolld intret you that
you woolld send me a ferckeine of buttr and a hogseit of mault onground for
we dreinck notheinge but walltre and a corse clothe of fouer pound preise so
it be thicke   and for the fraute if you of youer Loue will send them I will paye
the fraute for her is notheinge to be gote withe ought we had c[o]memodeytes
to go up in to the este partes amonckest the eingeines to truck for her whare
we liue her is no beuer and her is no clothe to be had to mack no parell and
shoes ar at 5*s* a payer for me and that clothe that is woorthe 2*s* 8*d* a yard is
woorthe her 5*s*   so I pray father send me fouer or fiue yardes of clothe to
mack us sume parell and Lou[i]nge fathere thoue I be far disstante from you
yet I pray you remembure me as youer cheield and we do not know how
longe we may subeseiste for we can not liue her witheought prouisseyones
from ould eingland   thare fore I pray do not put away youer shopestufe for
I theinck that in the eind if I liue it must be my leueinge for we do not know
how longe theis plantacyon will stand for s[o]me of the marchantes that ded
up hould it haue turned of thare men and haue giuene it ouere   beseides god
hath tacken away the chefeste stud in the land Mr. Johnson and the ladye
arabella his wife wiche wase the cheiffeste man of estate in the land and on
that woold a don moste good

her cam ouer xxv passeingares and thare cume backe agayn fouer skore and od parsones and as maney more wolld a cume if thay had whare withe all to bringe them hom for her ar maney that cam ouer the laste yere wiche wase woorthe too hundreid poundes afore they cam ought of ould eingland that betwine theis and myckellmes wille be hardly worthe xxx*li* so her we may liue if we haue suppleyes euerey yere from ould eingland other weyse we can not subeseiste   I maye as I will worck hard sete an ackorne of eindey wheat and if we do not set it withe fishe and that will coste xx*s* and if we set it witheought fishe thay shall haue but a por crope   so father I pray consedre of my cause for her will be but a uerey por beinge and no beinge withe ought Louinge father youer helpe withe prouisseyones from ould eingland   I had thought to a cam home in theis sheipe for my prouisseyones ware all moste all spente but that I humbley thanck you for youer gret loue and kindnes in sendinge me s[o]me prouissyones or elles I sholld and myne a bine helaf famiuyshed but now I will if it plese god that I haue my hellthe I will plant what corne I can and if prouisseyones be no cheper betwein theis and myckellmes and that I do not her from you what I wase beste to do I purpose to c[o]me hom at myckellmes   my wife remembur hur humble deutey unto you and to my mother and my Loue to mye brother Joseife and to Sarey myler   thus I leue you to the protectyon of Allmytey god

                                                          [*No signature*]

from WALLTUR TOUNE in new eingland
     the 15 of marche 1630[/31]

     we ware wondurfule seick as we cam at sea withe the small Poxe   no man thought that I and my leittell cheilld woolld a liueid and my boye is lame and my gurell too and thar deyeid in the sheip that I cam ine xiiij parsones.

JOHN WINTHROP TO MARGARET WINTHROP[1]

MY DEAR WIFE, I haue small hope that this should come to thy hands, in regard of the longe staye of the shipe heer, so as thou maiest be well onward of thy waye hether before these can come to England: therefore I write little to thyselfe and my sonne and those whom I expect to see heer shortly, if it shall so please the Lorde. And blessed be his holy and glorious name that he hath so far magnified his mercy towards vs, that when so many haue been

---

[1] W. 7A. 50; Savage (1825), I. 380; (1853), I. 456–457; *L. and L.*, II. 59–61; Twichell, 177–179.

layd in their graues since we parted, yet he hath pleased to preserue vs unto this hope of a ioyfull meetinge, that we may see the faces of each other againe, the faces of our children and sweet babes: these thinges I durst scarce think off heertofore, but now I embrace them ofte, and delight my heart in them, because I trust, that the Lord our God, who hath kept me and so many of my Company in health and safety amonge so many dead Corps, through the heat of the summer and the Cold of winter, and hath also preserued thee in the perill of childbirth, and vpheld thy heart in the middest of so many discouragements, with the life of all thy companye, will of his owne goodnesse and free mercye preserve vs and ours still that we shall meet in ioye and peace, which I dayly pray for, and shall expect in the Lords good tyme: who still continues his fauour and blessinge vpon thee and our sweet babes and all thy companye. For our little daughter, doe as thou thinkest best. the Lord direct thee in it. if thou bringest her, she wilbe more trouble to thee in the shipp then all the rest   I knowe my sister wilbe tender of her till I may send for her.[1] bringe Amy and Anne Gostlin with thee if thou canst. if they come not, they will much wronge themselues. they need feare no want here, if they wilbe guided by Gods word: otherwise they can looke to prosper no where. I prayse God I want nothinge but thee and the rest of my family: Commend my Loue and blessinge to them all: and to all my neighbours and freinds, but I haue desired my brother Gostlin to performe that. remember to bringe iuice of Limons to sea with thee, for thee and thy company to eate with your meat as sauce. but of these things my sonne hath direction: so again I kisse thee my sweet wife and commend thee and all ours to the Lord, and rest Thine

Jo. Winthrop

March 28, 1631

JOHN WINTHROP TO JOHN WINTHROP, JR.[2]

To my verye lovinge Sonne mr. John Winthrop at London deliver   if he be come away my brother Downing may open this Letter

My good sonne, The blessinge of the Allmighty be vpon thy soule and life foreuer.

---

[1] Margaret Winthrop decided to bring her daughter Anne, who was born April 29, 1630, a month after the Governor's departure for Massachusetts. The child died on the voyage over. *Winthrop's Journal, "History of New England,"* James K. Hosmer, Editor (New York, 1908), 1. 70. Future references to the Journal are to this edition unless otherwise indicated.

[2] W. 7a. 51; Savage (1825), 1. 380–382; (1853), 1. 457–459; *L. and L.*, ii. 59–61.

Amonge many the sweet mercyes of my God towards me in this strange lande, where we have mett many troubles and adversityes, this is not the least, and that which affords much Comfort to my heart, that he hath given me a lovinge and dutyfull sonne: God allsufficient rewarde thee abundantly for all thy Care and paynes in my Affairs, and for all that Love and dutye thou hast shewed to thy good mother. I doubt not but thou shalt finde it in outward blessings, for thou art vnder the promise of havinge thy dayes prolonged: but I desire especially thou mayest finde it in the manifestation of the Goodwill of the Lord towards thee, and in those sp[irit]uall blessings, which may fatten thy soule.

This shipp stayinge so longe here, I am allmost out of hope that my Lettres should come to thy hands: for though I thinke verye longe till I see you all heere, yet I would rather you stayed, though it were 2 or 3 months, to come with mr. Peirce, partly because of his skill and Care of his passingers, and partly that we might be the better provided of housing etc. to entertain you: for we are much streightned yet that waye, and we have had divers houses burnt, and now within these two dayes, mr. Sharpe and mr. Colburne, both of our towne, had their houses burnt to the ground, and much goods lost: thus it pleaseth the Lord still to humble vs. I doubt not, but he will doe us the more good at the last.

I have written to your vnckle D[owning] concerninge all our businesse fearing you should be come awaye. I have sent the Assignment sealed. I lefte all my bonds and writings in my Cupbord at Groton, or els at London.

Bringe no provision with you, but meale and pease, and some otemeale and Sugar, fruit, figges and pepper, and good store of Saltpeeter, and Conserue of redd roses, and mithridate, good store of pitche and ordinarye suett, or tallowe. bringe none but wine vinegar, and not much of that, and be sure that the Caske be good, store of oyled Calues skins of the largest, and the strongest welt leather shoes and stockins for Children: and hats of all Syzes. if you could bring two or three hundred sheepskins and lambs skins with the wooll on, dyed redd, it would be a good Comodytye heere, and the coursest woollen clothe (so it be not flockes,) and of sadd Colours, and some redd, milstones some 2 foot and some 3 foote ouer, with brasses ready cast and ringes, and mill bills, store of shoemakers thread, and hobnayles, Chalk and Chalkeline and a paire or 2 or more of large steele Compasses, store of course linnen: some birdlime.

When you have cleered all things in England, if you haue any moneye lefte, you may bring some with you, (not aboue 100*li*) and the rest leaue with your vnckle D[owning] or dispose of it as your owne occasions may require.

any wise matt. must have 400*li* and there wilbe much due to your sister Winthrop which were best to be left in England. but you must advise with your vncle D[owning] about these things, for I am so full of businesse heere, as I cant think of mine owne affairs as I should. you must allso consider what you would have for your selfe, and how you would imploy it.

I never had lettre yet from your brother F[orth][1] if he intends to come hether, it were good he solde his lande and payd his sister her 100*li* which he promised when I putt over his lande to him. you shall need bringe no more Cowes for I have enough. The good Lord blesse you and bringe you and all my Company hither in safty   so I rest your lovinge father

Jo. Winthrop

Massachusetts March 28, 1631

I hope the Lorde hathe provided a good husband for your sister Winthrop.[2] mr. Coddington is well affected to her. if he proceed I wish you to further it, for he is a godly man and of good estate.

ANNE HIGGINSON TO JOHN WINTHROP[3]

Worthy Sir, My loue and seruice to yow remembred: wishing your health and prosperity in the Lord: the cause of my writtinge att this time is to giue yow notice how it is with me: I haue 10 Acckers of ground to inclose: and it lieth soe among others ground that I must inclose it or forgoe it: now I am destitute of heelp and menns to doe it: hauing noe man: ther fore I doe desire your aduise in it: allsoe the time comes one to sett corne and if soe bee yow with the rest will alow me a man as my husbands condition was I should be glad to vnderstand your pleassur in it: and further as for the howse I now liue in I doe daly expect when they will call for mony for it: now my desire is to knowe whether yow will build me one or pay for that I ame in: I shall be content with what you thinke fitt: only my desire is to know which yow will doe, and I doe ernestly entreat your wor[shipfu]ll with the rest of the Gentel-men to know what yow intend to doe for the time to come: my prouisiones

---

[1] The Governor had not yet heard of his son's death because the most recent ship to arrive from England had sailed on December 1, only three days after Forth Winthrop had been buried.

[2] Elizabeth, widow of Henry Winthrop.

[3] W. 1. 86; 2 *Proceedings*, vi. 424. Anne Higginson was the widow of the Reverend Francis Higginson of Salem who died in August, 1630. The agreement (April 8, 1629) between the New England Company and Higginson is printed in Sidney Perley, *The History of Salem, Massachusetts*, (Salem, 1924), 109–110.

grows skant: though I husband them the best I cane: allsoe concerning the kine my desir is to know how longe I shall haue them and whether I shall haue half the increase: as was before Agreed uppon by the marchants: soe Sir once more I pray yow to send mee word what yow intend to doe.   in my barrell of mault I found some neatts tongs: if yow pleass I will send them yow with the first messenger I can: soe I beeseech the Lord to bless yow and rest Your Frend to her power.

ANNE HIGGISON

[*Ca.* April, 1631]

[*Endorsed by Governor Winthrop:*] Mrs. Higginson about her Couenants.

MARTHA WINTHROP TO JOHN WINTHROP, JR.[1]

To her very loueing husband Mr. John Winthrop at Mr. Downings house in Fleetstreete these deliver in London

DEARE HUSBAND, My afections toward thee is so great as that I can let slip no ocasion of manifesting the same intreating thee to bee perswaded of my loue to thee notwithstanding my pasions and weaknes which formerly haue caused thee to thinke the contrary   I haue sent up thy box this weeke and because it was not full I let Bes Web put in her goune for next weeke shee cometh up   Thus with my loue [to] thy self and all our freinds I rest beeing in great hast and send thee a kiss   Thy faithfull wife

MARTHA WINTHROP

teusday night [*ca.* April 5, 1631]
   diliuer this to my aunt downing

JOHN WINTHROP, JR., TO MARTHA WINTHROP[2]

To my loving wife Mrs. Martha Winthrop deliver In Groton

Thy louing husband John Winthrop

MY DEAREST HART, I receiued thy sweete letter wherby thy loue doeth manifest its true desire and greate diligence to manifest itselfe without the

---

[1] W. Au. 58. With the exception of the superscription, the date, and the postscript, this letter is in cipher.

[2] W. Au. 59; *Proceedings of the American Antiquarian Society,* L. 83.

omission of the least and sodainest occasion offered to him who needes noe glasse of uerbal expression to mak[e] i[t] appeare and shine forth before his eies or put him in remembrance of its former splendor but as he enioyeth the sweetnesse of thy loue being present with the, so recreateth his thoughts with the sweete memory of the same in thy absence: my dere, thou needest not feare but I am fully perswaded of thy loue, nor thought the contrary, although thy clouding of thy loue sometime hath suddenly darkened my mind with greife and sadnes:[1] but my deare, let us beare with one an others weaknesses an[d] seeke to cherish loue by al menes, for that wil make our condition sweete houeuer[2] Send John Robinson on Monday in the morning or if this letter come not to you till monday, then send him a tuesday morning betimes, to hitcham to mr. Kemtons, and desire them to cause theire tailor to take measure of mrs. Penelope Nanton, for a Gowne, and let him stay there till it be done, and let him bring away the measure with him and doe thou put it vp safe in a letter and send it next wednesday to my aunt Downing. let it be done with out faile for my aunt Downing hath promised my lady Nanton, and I have promised her, to doe it certainly, therfore prethe doe not thou faile to see it done. I hope to be downe my selfe before this letter come to thy hands but if I should not remember my duty to my mother, and my love to my sister winthrop and sister mary   tell thim that my cosen Barfoots sonne is deade.

[JOHN WINTHROP]

[*Ca.* April 8, 1631]

JOHN ENDECOTT TO JOHN WINTHROP[3]

RIGHT WORSHIPFUL, I did expect to have beene with you in person at the court, and to that end I put to sea yesterday and was driven back againe the wind being stiffe against us. And there being no canoe or boat at Sagust I must have beene constrained to goe to Mistick and thence about to Charles town, which at this time I durst not be so bold, my bodie being at this present in an ill condition to wade or take cold, and therefore I desire you to pardon mee. Though otherwise I could have much desired it, by reason of many

---

[1] In the original manuscript the spelling is "sadned."

[2] The letter to this point is in cipher.

[3] Original not located; Thomas Hutchinson, *A Collection of Original Papers Relative to the History of the Colony of Massachusets-Bay* (Boston, 1769), 50–52; *The Hutchinson Papers* (Prince Society, Boston, 1865), I. 55–57. For Endecott, see *D.A.B.*

occasions and businesses. There are at Mr. Hewson's plantations 5 or 6 kine verie ill and in great danger, I feer they will hardlie escape it, whereof twoe are myne and all I have, which are worse than any of the rest. I left myne there this winter to doe Mr. Skelton a pleasure to keep his for him here at Salem, that he might have the benefit of their milk. And I understand by Wincoll that they have been ill tended and he saith almost starved. Beside they have fed on acornes and they cannot digest them, for that they vomitt exceedinglie and are so bound in their bodies that he is faine to rake them and to use all his skill to maintaine life in them. I have willed him to be there till he can bring them to some strength againe if it be possible. And I have given him malt to make them mashes of licoris and annis seedes, and long pepper, and such other things as I had to drench them. I could wish when Manning hath recovered his strength that you would free him; for he will never doe you or Mr. Hewson service, for when he was well he was as negligent as the worst of them. Mr. Skelton, myselfe and the rest of the congregation desire to be thankfull to God and yourselfe for your benevolence to Mr. Haughton's child. The Lord restore it you. I prevailed with much adoe with Sir Richard for an old debt heere which he thought was desperate, to contribute it, which I hope I shall make good for the child. I think Mr. Skelton hath written to you, whome he thinks stands most in neede of contribution of such provisions as you will be pleased to give amongst us of that which was sent over. The yeele-potts you sent for are made, which I had in my boate, hoping to have brought them with mee. I caused him to make but two for the present, if you like them and his prices (for he worketh for himselfe) you shall have as many as you desire. He selleth them for 4 shillings a pieece. Sir, I desired the rather to have beene at court because I heare I am much complayned on by good-man Dexter, for striking him.[1] I acknowledge I was too rash in strikeing him, understanding since that it is not lawfull for a justice of peace to strike. But if you had seene the manner of his carriadge, with such daring of mee with his armes on kembow etc. It would have provoked a very patient man   But I will write noe more of it but leave it till we speak before you face to face. Onely thus farre further, that he hath given out if I had a purse he would make mee empty it, and if he cannot have justice here he will doe wonders in England, and if he cannot prevale there, hee will trie it out with mee heere at blowes. Sir, I desire that you will take all into consideration. If it were lawfull to trie it at blowes and hee a fitt man for mee to deale with, you should

N. B.
J. P. REFERENCE.

---

[1] *Records of the Governor and Company of the Massachusetts Bay in New England*, Nathaniel B. Shurt-leff, Editor, 1 (Boston, 1853), 86.

not heare mee complaine; but I hope the Lord hath brought mee off from that course. I thought good further to wryte what my judgment is for the dismissing of the court till corne be sett. It will hinder us that are farre off exceedingly, and not further you there. Mens labour are precious here in corne setting tyme, the plantations being yet so weak. I will be with you, the Lord assisting mee, as soone as conveniently I can. In the meane while I committ you to his protection and safeguard that never failes his children, and rest Your unfeigned loving friend to command

JO: ENDECOTT

SALEM, the 12th of Aprill, 1631

MARTHA WINTHROP TO JOHN WINTHROP, JR.[1]

To her much respected Husband Mr. John Winthrope at Mr. Downings howse in flet street neere the conduit giue this with speede

Thy faithfull wife Martha Winthrop

DEARE HUSBAND, I reiceiued a letter from thee to day wheirein thou sentst me word that John Robinson was comeing and this is Tuesday and hee is not come yet   My mother aduiseth me to goe up now   My Uncle Gosling saith that hee shall bee at more leisure now than if I stay longer to come up with mee   Therefo[re] if John Robinson come this weeke I would faine hear from thee to know why John came not doune and what is becom of Bes Webs cloaths and a Bible that my sister Ursula sent to litell Martha which[2] wee haue not yet receiued   Wee receiued a port mantle on Monday with things from my sister Ursula by Jeruese who saide hee had no thing ellse   Send word what carier you deliuered them unto   To day I receiued a letter from thee by good man Freinch and am faine to make hard shift to get this letter sent   I am so straitned of time that I canot manifest my loue as I wold but I send thee sweete loue a hundred kises and bid thee good night.

[MARTHA WINTHROP]

[*Ca.* April 12, 1631]

---

[1] W. Au. 58. This letter is, with the exception of the superscription, in cipher.
[2] The spelling is "whidh" in the original manuscript.

JOHN WINTHROP, JR., TO JOHN WINTHROP[1]

To the right wor[shipfu]ll my much honoured father John Winthrop Esqr. Governour of the mattachusetts deliver In New-England

LONDON Aprill 16: 1631

SIR, My humble duty remembred vnto you, may you please to vnderstand that, since my last letters,[2] which I sent by mr. Allerton, wherin I wrote you word that we had not yet any Chapman for your land, we are come this last weeke to an agreement about it, with one mr. Warren a grocer of this Citty an acquaintance of Goodman Piper, and Goodman Lambert, and by them procured to deale for it   he hath but newly carried the writings to his Councell, and therfore we have noe certaine answere whether he will goe through but expect this next weeke, and I hope I shall have occasion to wright you of the conclusion of it before this ship (the Freindship) shall sett saile from Barstable. the price we have agreed for is 4200*li* wherof 2000*li* to be paid at midsommer, the rest at six and six monthes my mother to continue in the house till the next spring. since mr. Gurdon broke of we have had 3 or 4 about it but none would offer above 4000*li*. I have paid mr. Gurdon 200*li* of his six hundred wherof 100*li* I borrowed of my vncle Downing, and 100*li* of mr. Kerby. another 100*li* I must pay him as soone as I can procure it and the other 3 hundred I shall have till midsommer paying vse for it.

when this ship went first out (which was soone after Christide of which and their comming backe mr. Hatherly the bearer hereof can better informe you) I sent with it diverse letters and a dedimus potestatem, to acknowledg a fine, with advise in my letters of the reason we were forced to a dedimus for a new fine. I give mr. Hatherly directions to enquire out those letters and dedimus and receive them of the m[aste]r of the ship or whom else mr. Allerton delivered them to but least those letters should miscarry I will againe set downe wherin theire councell find your fine and deed to the feoffees defective they haveinge not power to give assurance of the whole estate to the buyer. the former fine couvering most of the land by the name manner, now they say that whatsoever hath beene severed from the manner heeretofore by any Joynters that can not passe vnder the name of manner, therefore we were forced to take out a new dedimus for you to acknowledge a fine in New-England, which was done whilst we weere agreed with mr. Gurdon for it, and therfore made to him: but it is as good though now we sell it to another.

---

[1] W. 1. 85; *L. and L.*, II. 71–73; 5 *Collections*, VIII. 28–30.
[2] See *Winthrop Papers*, II. 325–327.

we sent an other dedimus by mr. Allerton, and reserve one still to be sent by some other ship when there be occation having taken out 3 lest one or other might miscarry. they can make noe full assurance of your land till they receive backe one of them therfore desire they may be sent backe with the first.

we now expect with longing to heare from you of your health and welfare, and of the Company with you, and are much greived that we have beene hindred from our intended voyage this spring. my mother brothers and sisters and all our friends at Groton are well I received letters from them this weeke, but they know not of this occation of wrighting to you for I knew not of it my selfe till yesterday: we are all well heere save my aunt Downing who hath still a quartaine ague but goeth abroad vpon her well daies: my wife remembreth her duty to you: my vncle and aunt Downing remember their love vnto you. thus desiring your praiers and blessing I commend you to the tuition of the allmighty and humbly take my leave. Your obedient Sonne

JOHN WINTHROP

The Spaniards hath a mighty fleete prepared to goe against the Dutch at Farnambuco, who are very strong there, and have sent out strong fleets also. you will have the newes of france in my vncle Downings letters by mr. Allerton: the french kings brother is with the Duke Lorraine. The King of Sweden prevaileth in Germany   he hath lately give Tilly an overthrow with a small army against his mighty army. some say he received some light wounds in pursuite of Tilly and had his horse slaine vnder him. The Duke of Bavaria is dead, and the Protestant princes have appointed a diet at Lipsia, it is hoped they will doe something for the palsgrave. Corne was once risen heere to 14 and 15s a bushell, but now is fallen to 11 and 12s. we have had hetherto a very seasonable tyme, and likelihood of a very fruitfull yeare.

MARGARET WINTHROP TO MARTHA WINTHROP[1]

To hir very louinge daughter mr[s]. Martha Winthrop these deliver

LOVINGE DAUGHTER, I am sory that time did so preuent me, as I could not right to thee by the caryer, but haueinge nowe another mesenger I must needs right a word or to, thought I haue no matter of wayte to impert to you, onely an intercorce of loue betwene vs which will take all ocasions to shewe it selfe, wheare it finds good entertainment. I doe very much and often, wish[2]

---

[1] W. 1. 83; *L. and L.*, II. 76.
[2] The word in the original manuscript is "which."

for my deare sonne and your selfe, for my owne comfort, but in regard of his manyfoulde imployments I must the more paciently beare his longe abcence I think now the time the longer the nearer it aproches, for newes from new ingland. I shalbe the more ioyfull when it comes if it be good, or if it be bad the more oppressed with grefe. I hope I shal heare shortly when your horsses shall come vp, if my sonne haue [*torn*] setled his busines, but I thinke he cannot [*torn*] much before [*a whole line torn*] he can heare, he may come downe and bringe you and goe up againe, but I shal leaue it to his own descresion. I thank god we are all heare in health. my daughter winthrop is much imployed in hir surgurye and hath very good succese my cosin Anne is gone home to hir mother, and so my companye is lese in the parler you had neede com home to helpe to increace it againe. my daughter Mary I thinke liked hir coote well   I am shure I did and thanke you for it. I am now shortned in time which makes my pen rune fastter then my wit. and thus with my best loue to thy good Husband, my brother and sister Downinge thy owne selfe all the rest of my frends I commite you to god   Your louinge mother

MARGARET WINTHROP

[*Ca.* April 20, 1631]

Deane and Sam and Anne remember thear respect as well as thay can.

MARGARET WINTHROP TO JOHN WINTHROP, JR.[1]

To hir much respected and very louinge sonne mr. John Winthrope at mr. Downings house neare fleete condite, these be delivered

MY GOOD SONNE, I am glad to heare of thy welfayre, and hope shortly to be refreshed by thy presence, which I much desyre. I hope thou wilt be that welcome messenger that will bringe me good tydings from a far countrye, which wil make our meetinge the more comfortable. I receiued thy louinge letters this weeke and thank thee for it. I feare mr. warren will doe as the rest haue done when he hath confered with his counsell, and yet in my conceyte he is the most likely man of any yet. this daye I received a letter from my brother Tyndall, who remembers his loue most kindly to you and your wife. thinkinge you had bine at home, he sent to know what newes from N: E: and to knowe whether thear ware any thinge doen conserninge the land. he hath ocasion to be at Londone this terme. you may if you thinke fit aquaint him

---

[1] W. Au. 52; *L. and L.*, II. 77.

with your prosedings with mr. warren. I thanke the lord we are all heare in resonable god health. I pray tell my daughter I thanke hir for hir letter, and my boyes inkehorne. I rote to hir the other day by Samwell Goslinge and desyre to be nowe excused haueing other ocasions. I shal haue some other opertunitye are longe, and thus with my louinge affections remembred to thy selfe, thy sweet wife, my brother and sister Downinge all my cosins and frends I leaue thee and commit thee to god, rest thy very louinge mother

MARGARET WINTHROP

Aprill 29, [1631]

your sisters and brothers remember thear loue my brother and sister Goslinge remember thear salutations   all the rest of your frends desyre to be remembred.

EMMANUEL DOWNING TO JOHN WINTHROP[1]

*To his verie loving brother John Winthrop Governour of the plantacion
in the Mattachusetts Bay*

MY GOOD BROTHER, your last lettres which cam this passadge with mr. Peirce (though they brought the newes of mr. Johnsons and some others death) haue much refreshed my hart and the myndes of manie others, wel-wishers to the good worke you haue vndertaken, for much more was feared, then the good lord through his mercy hath laid vpon you, in that soe few haue dyed, and that now there is hope you wilbe able to subsist and proceede to lay the foundacion of a plantacion, whereas yt was the Iudgement of most men here, that your Colonye would this winter be dissolved partly by death through want of Food, howsing and rayment, and the rest to retorne or to flee for refuge to other plantacions, but blessed be God that hath maynteyned his owne Cause and preserved you alive to helpe further forward this great worke.

I am glad you haue begunn to remove and plant some what higher vp the river into the land among the woods I meane at watertowne   It is my dayly prayer that the lord would give me leave to goe vnto you, which I hope wilbe next spring, vbi animus, ibi homo. you haue my hart, and I doe mynd nothing for this world more then to prepare for my goeing vnto you and when I shall see the lords providence opening my way I shall make litle stay here. I thank

---

[1] W. 2. 17; 4 *Collections*, VI. 39–40. For Downing, see 4 *Collections*, VI. 33n.

you most kindely for your lettres booke and plotts. tis tearme and I haue had yet scarce tyme to pervse your lettres and plotts; I must be troublesome to you about my Cattle and Corne whereof my Cosen Winthrop writes vnto you. I pray excuse me that I write noe newes herein for I haue not tyme, but this rest assured of that you may be secure from any trouble from Spayne or France for they haue theire hands full here   soe with my Comends to all my freinds with my wives and my dayly prayers for you I rest yours

E. D.

30 Apr. [1631]

JOHN WINTHROP, JR., TO JOHN WINTHROP[1]

To the right wor[shipfu]ll my much honoured father John Winthrop Esqr. Governour of the Massachusett deliver in New-England

LONDON Aprill 30, 1631

SIR, My humble duty remembred vnto you, may you please to vnderstand that mr. Peirce with all his company arrived heere in health and safety yesterday being the 29th of this present, by whome I received the Joyfull and welcome newes of your health, and welfare to my great Comfort. your letters were the sesonabler to give satisfaction to many, that they were of soe fresh date, and brought relation of a winter wholy passed. my vncle Downing is very well satisfied with your reasons you give him for the Country   we had once made an agreement with some merchantes and Captaine Cleyborne[2] for to deliver 100 tunnes of Indian wheat from Virginia to you, which they had covenanted to deliver before or soone after harvest, the Copy of which agreement I thinke mr. Humfries sent over by mr. Allerton, which was intended but hath not yet beene sealed by vs. my vncle Downing mr. Humfry and my selfe were the vndertakers in it, but now the ship having delaied her setting forth so long so as we could not see it possible to be delivered so soone, we have broken of that covenant, and my vncle Downing and my selfe doe covenant with them for fourty tunne, wherof 20 is for your selfe the other 20 is for my vncle Downings owne accompt which if it be delivered vnto you he desires you to keepe his 20 tunne safe till you heare further from him. mr. humfry will likewise send twenty tunne and mr. Cottington 20, likewise mr. Cradock 20, and others, but we shall wright you particularly therof by the

---

[1] W. I. 85; *L. and L.*, II. 73–75; 5 *Collections*, VIII. 30–33.
[2] Captain William Clayborne of Northampton County, Virginia. 2 *Proceedings*, III. 4–5.

ship that bringeth it, which is the Affrica, wherof Capt: Cleyborne is Commander. he and the merchantes that set him out offer vs to bring what corne we will for fish, and for this would take fish of you if you could provide it for them   this Corne we vnderstand they buy of the Natives there for trucke. there is great store all alongst the coast, from a little to the sothward of you to florida and beyond etc. and to be had for toyes, beads, Copper, tooles, knives, glasses and such like.

Concerning your land I can add little to that I wrote about a fourtnight since, which I suppose will come to your hands with these by mr. Hatherly. we expect all the Feoffees in towne together this weeke, then I thinke we shall make a full Conclusion, with mr. Warren, or breake of: our occasions requiring monies for the satisfying of such monies as are owing and the want of full power in the Feoffees for the giving of assurance in the whole, and the vncertaintie of the tyme of the returne of the fine from you, puts vs vpon much disadvantage in the sale. mr. Peirse is very earnest to have vs goe over this summer, and we are all as earnest, and desirous to goe, but I feare it wilbe so long ere the fine I sent to you doe returne, that it wilbe too late in the yeare.

my mother, brothers and sisters, and the rest of our freinds at groton are well   we heard from them this weeke, they have yet scarce the letters from you. I sent them away yesterday as soone as I received them. my wife hath beene heere with me awhile but is now going downe againe having acknowledged satisfaction to the Court of Aldermen for her portion. she remembreth her duty to you. I should be larger and write of other things but I feare the ship may be gone, or my letter otherwise miscarry before it commeth to mr. Hatherly, for day is past which they apointed to be gon, but I would howsoever adventure these that you might vnderstand of the receipt of yours, and those other particulars. Thus with my duty againe remembred desiring your praiers and blessing I commend you to Gods protection and rest your obedient Sonne

JOHN WINTHROP

my vncle Downing desireth you to buy 6 goats for mr. Sewell and three sowes: the goats he hath agreed for at 40s apeice and the sowes at 30 shillings apeice, and to deliver them all to goodman Perkins for mr. Seawell.

For Cowes my vncle Downing doth referre it to you, whether you thinke he shall need have any more. for mr. Allerton is to deliver him six etc. he and my aunt remember their loves to you   she is not yet ridd of hir ague, but on her well dayes goeth abroad, having 2 daies well and one sicke, etc.

the bill which you sent from mr. John Dillingham of 9li will not be paid for his kinsman to whom he sent it refuseth to pay it, and tells me he knoweth not what is become of his brother.

Postscript   for those goats and sowes which my vncle Downing desires you to buy for him to be delivered to Goodman Perkins for mr. Seawell, he desires you not to give above the prises before written for soe he giveth to mr. Allerton for those he is to deliver him, and thinketh you may have them so at Plymouth.

MARGARET WINTHROP TO JOHN WINTHROP, JR.[1]

MY DEARE SONNE, blessed be our good god who hath not fayled us, but hath given vs cause of most vnspeakable ioy, for the good newes which we haue hard out of n: e: mr. wilson had bin with me before thy letters came to my hands, but brought me no letter. he speakes very well of things thear, so as my hart and thoughts are thear allready. I want but means to carye my bodye after them. I am now fully parswaded that it is the place whearein god will haue us to settle in, and I beseech him to fit vs for it, that we may be instruments of his glorye thear   this newes came very seasonably to me, beinge possessed with much greefe for thee hearing how things went conserninge thy wife ǵointer, but now I have cast of that and hope god will turne all to the best. if thou canst but send me ouer when mr. wilson goeth back, I shalbe very very glad of his companye. if thy manyfould imployments will not suffer the to go with me I shalbe very sory for it, for I would be glad to carry all my company with me, but I will not say any more of this till I heare from thee, how things may be done. I pray consider of it: and giue me the best counsell you can. mr. wilson is now in london and promised me to com and see you. he can not yet perswad his wife to goe, for all he hath taken this paynes to come and fetch hir. I maruiell what mettell she is made on. shure she will yeald at last, or elce we shal want him excedingly in new england. I desyer to hear what newes my brother Downinge hath, for my Husban rit but little to me thinking we had bine on our voyage, and thus with my love to thy selfe my daughter and all the rest of my good frends I desyer the lord to blesse and keepe you and rest Your lovinge mother

MARGARET WINTHROPE

[*Ca.* the first week in May, 1631]

I receiued the things you sent downe by the caryer this weeke and thank my daughter for my bande   I like it well. I must of nesessity make me a

---

[1] W. 7A. 52; Savage (1825), I. 382–383; (1853), I. 459–460; *L. and L.,* II. 85–86.

goune for to weare euery day, and would haue one bought me of some good stronge black stufe, and mr. smith to make it of the ciuelest f[as]hon now in vse. if my sister Downing would plese to giue him some directions about it, he would make it the better.

MARGARET WINTHROP TO JOHN WINTHROP, JR.[1]

To hir very louinge sonne mr. John Winthrope at mr. Downings house neare fleet Condite these deliver Londone

LOUINGE SONNE, I can saye little of any businesse haueinge not yet hard how you and the Feeffees will agree with mr. warren   I beinge not able my selfe to know, what wilbe the best corce to take for my voyage, doe refeer my selfe to you and the rest of my frends, to be gydeed by your good counseles. my will is readdy, to goe, as sone as may be with any conueniency. I am glad that thy selfe and the rest of my companye are willinge to acompanye me. we shall al ioyne together I hope, and be of one minde, to suffer what god hath layed out for vs, and to reioyce together. I reioyce much to heare that mr. cottington beares such good affections to my daughter; I trust theare wilbe a further prosedeinge. I haue heard him very well reportted of, to be a religious man, and one of good meanes. mr. wilson had some speach with me aboute it, and did very much desyre to knowe hir vertues. I gaue hir the best commendations that I could. I shall dayly expect his cominge. he shalbe very welcome. my brother Tyndall was with me the last weeke, and tolde me he would be in Londone on tuseday, and so I did not send to him, knowing he would be gone. I send vp your horse this weeke, and thus with my loue to my brother and sister Downinge, your selfe and wife al the rest of my frends, I commite you to god and rest Your Louinge mother

MARGARET WINTHROP

[*Ca.* May 17, 1631]

I pray tel my daughter I thanke hir for hir letter and would haue ritten to hir but that I hope to see hir shortly at home

as sone as I had ritten these mr. cottington came to see vs but would not stay all night   he hath not yet made his minde knowne to my daughter, but is gone to Sudbury to mr. willson   I doe veryly beleeue it wilbe a mach, and that she shalbe very happy in a good Husband. commend me to my brother goslinge.

---

[1] W. 1. 87; *L. and L.,* II. 87–88.

MARTHA WINTHROP TO JOHN WINTHROP, JR.[1]

To hir very louinge Husband Mr. John winthrop at mr. Downings house in fletstrete
neare flete condite these deliver

MY SWEETE HUSBAND, I came safe to Groton upon Teusday at noone
thankes bee too God and in this litle time haue much wanted thy company:
since my coming I heard such strange newes: it is credebly reported all over
the countrey that thou wert taken up at the court like a very boy and the
reason was 1. because wee were neere a kine 2ly becaus wee maried without
consent 3ly because I was under age with soe many surcumstanses has made
my mother and all of them beeleve it and to mend the matter my Uncle
Gostlin came and tould my mother that shee could not goe too New Ing.
because of that and that she and the rest must starve and I must haue 60
pound a yeere ioynter with many more such like words which made them all
very sad and it was that newese which made my mother write of going withowt us   I have a great deale of newes to write thee bu[t] time will not
permit   I comend thee thearfore to God with my owne love and rest yours
thy faithfull wife

MARTHA WINTHROPE

comend mee to all our freinds with thee   all our freinds heere are in health
and remember theare loues unto thee   my mother would pray thee to send
downe a bottle of sallet oyle.

teusday night 1631 [*ca.* May 24]

MARGARET WINTHROP TO JOHN WINTHROP, JR.[2]

To hir louinge and much respected sonne mr. John Winthrop at Mr. Downings in
fletstrete neare flete condite these deliver

MY DEARE SONNE, Since it hath pleased god to make a waye for me, and to
giue me incoragement for my voyage, and vpholds my hart that it faynts not,
I doe resolue by his assistance to cast my selfe vpon him, and to goe for N: E:
as spedyly as I can with any conuenience   thearfore, my good Sonne, let me

---

[1] W. Au. 60; *Proceedings of the American Antiquarian Society*, L. 82. This letter, with the exception of
the superscription, the postscript, and the date, is in cipher.
[2] W. Au. 54; *L. and L.*, II. 86–87.

intreate thee to take order for our goeinge as soone as thou canst, for winter wil come on apace. yet I doe not knowe howe wee can goe wel before haruest by resone of our provisions of corne. I did heare from my brother Tyndall whose counsell is for to stay till the springe, but I hope to breake through that, and geete his good will. I did speake with mr. wilson, who was very desyrus to knowe when we went, but then I could not tell howe things would falle out at London and could not resolue him. if he goe it must be without his wifes consent, for she is more auerce then euer she was. if he goe not it will disharten many that would be wiling to goe. I haue bin constrayned to send to the tenants for rent wantinge monye but haue receued but a little yet this weeke thay promise to paye. thay complayne of the hardnesse of the time, and would be glad to be forborne, but I tell them that my nesessityes requires it, so I hope to gette in some. I thank god my daughter came home safe, and is very welcome. I should haue bine very glad to haue seene thy selfe, but I knowe that thou art full of businesse. I heare my sister Downinge will come doune   I pray tell hir from me she shalbe very welcome which wilbe hir best inter-tainement   so shall mrs. Downinge, if she pleas to bringe hir, and thus with my best affections to thy selfe brother and sister D[owning] I commit you to god   your louinge mother

MARGARET WINTHROP

[*Ca.* May 24, 1631]

JOHN READING TO JOHN WINTHROP[1]

To the right worshipfull John Winthorpe Esqr. Governour, At Charles-Towne in Newe England deliver

SIR, one Mr. Hueson[2] hath bene often with me to write to you. It seemeth Mr. Johnson had some Cowes of his (six as he sayth) of the deliuery of Mr. Endycott, without any authority to sell them. In Mich[aelm]as Tearme last he acquaynted me with his dislike of the Bargen, and euer since he disclaymes it, and tells me he wrote as much to Mr. Johnson, and this morninge he shewes me Capten Endycots letter that he had no authority   And the scope

---

[1] W. 2. 185; 4 *Collections*, VI. 577–578. John Reading was a lawyer of the Inner Temple. *Calendar of Inner Temple Records*, F. A. Inderwick, Editor, II (London, 1898), 155. He has hitherto not been identified because of the misreading of his signature as "John Bradinge." Another letter of his, with that signature, is printed in *Winthrop Papers*, II. 318–319.

[2] Thomas Hewson, a merchant of London and an adventurer in both the Massachusetts Bay Company and its predecessor, the New England Company.

of all is he desires he may haue his Cattell agayne, to which you are best able to giue answere. I can giue none.

We are at a stand here about Mr. Johnsons executorship. you write he made a will there to conferme this here.[1] How can this then be proued as his last? You write you haue sent it over, John Drake sayth he copyed it to that purpose, But none can be heard of. I beseech you Sir let not your great occacions there cause an vtter neglect of the Credit and honour of that worthy gent[leman], who liues still in the harts of many worthy Chr[istia]ns here and I doubt not but he doth liue as freshly there in your harts. I pray Sir send ouer his will as soone as you can, And let his engagements be discouered if any were. It would be a great dishonour if his debts should not be payd   And who dares meddle till they know all. I wrote lately to Mr. Dudley to the same purpose   So I hope hath Mr. Holled.

The lord keepe you and prosper your designes. Your

Jo: Readinge

26 May 1631

JOHN WINTHROP, JR., TO MARTHA WINTHROP[2]

To my loving wife Mrs. Martha Winthrop deliver In Groton

Thine whilst mine owne John Winthrop

My deare wife, I receiued thy louing letters and am uery glad to heare that thou diddest come safe to Groton   For those reportes thou wrightest of let them not trouble the   Thou maiest maist [sic] satisfi them that it is al false but I prethe doe not tel any that I doe not meane to pay the fine of fiue marke for I feare it may by the same tatling tonges be spread abroad and come to some of the aldermans ears with additions   I hope to see the the beginning of next weeke which I thinke longer then ten time the time when thou art with me   Farewel my deare God keepe us and send us a merry meeting.

I send the heerwith a handred and twenty kisses an[d] as many more   My loue remembred to my sister Winthrop and Mary   I must haue a horse meete me on Monday.

[John Winthrop]

London May 28, 1631

---

[1] The earliest known will of Isaac Johnson is printed in *Winthrop Papers*, ii. 49–56. For a discussion of Johnson's later wills, see *ibid.*, 49, *n.* 2.

[2] W. Au. 57; *Proceedings of the American Antiquarian Society*, l. 83. This letter, with the exception of the superscription and the date line, is in cipher.

HENRY PAYNTER TO JOHN WINTHROP, JR.[1]

To my worthily respected Sonne Mr. John Winthrop at the howse of Mr. Emanuel Downinge at the signe of the B[isho]p in Peterburrow Courte neere fleete conduit these

WORTHY SIR AND MY DEERE SONNE, I am very thankefull vnto you for your kinde letter this Weeke; but the newes of your soe sudden going awaye, makes vs all sad for the presente because we cannot be certayne that we shall be able to get vp vnto you, that we might comforte our hearts togeather in one meeting agayne before your departure. Yeat write once more I praye you, where and at what very tyme (if it be possible) you take shipping: and when our worthy sister and you shall be in London. Who knoweth how the Lord in his good providence may dispose of our occasions, and guide our iourney that waye.

I am not a litle troubled that my hudled hasty lynes were soe broken and obscure to occasion your mistaking in soe many particulars. 1. It was much agaynst my minde to be altogeather soe troublesome vnto you about the Lady Modye,[2] and now your busines is multiplyed, I desire but onely what standeth with your leasure, and I thought a word from you might the rather move her: You know there is a band for 100*li* vpon my wife in your hand aboute it: and this was the mony I meante in my letter   and the 2 mistake I am very sory you are not payed. We haue both of us now written very effectually vnto her. she made a kinde of promise to Edward Searle and therefore should be willing he might goe to her againe. but I would not include the letters in his but in yours. I should hope you might intreate Mr. White of White fryars out of terme to speake to her, seeing her howse is but in fetter lane, as I haue desired him by letter, and shall agayne by the nexte. And 3. I mentioned not that mony as if I doubted of the disposall for 125*li* of it was aduentured, the rest bestowed in Corne and sente with particular directions for the disposing of it; neyther shall we in these partes be backward to further the plantation in any thinge we may as opportunity may be offered hereafter (I know noe one place better affected toward it) but vsed it onely as a rash inducemente to gette some more particular informations from you touching the state of the place. The rather because I intend God willing to write by you, and hereafter to write you, and who knoweth who may alsoe come at length vnto you. but now I will not be ouertroublesome but contente me with my daughter

---

[1] W. 1. 87; 3 *Collections*, IX. 231–232.
[2] Lady Deborah Moody. For a biographical sketch, see *Essex Institute Historical Collections*, XXXI. 96–102.

Winthrops generall reporte in her letter that you haue very good newes from thence, and your resolution for the iourney assureth me. The Lord in mercy keepe you and my good daughter, with all your company our deere friendes and bring you safe to that place, and prosper you in it. I shall be ready to retourne you answer to your nexte letter, and soe write to your good mother. We are in health, and intreate your prayers for vs all and namely for Your father vnfeignedly affected towards you

HENRY PAYNTER

[*Ca.* June, 1631]

URSULA SHERMAN TO JOHN WINTHROP, JR.[1]

To my worthy and uery louing Brother mr. John Winthrop at Groton in Sufoke deliver

from EXETER June 18, 1631

MY WORTHY AND BELOUED BROTHER, I am tolde by my mother and she shewed mee a letter, which you haue very kindly written to my father, that you will repaye certayne mony that was taken up in London, by reason of my troubles occasioned by gods prouiedence in that my so much Desired match with your Deerest brother,[2] which the lord othewise ordarred, and broght his estate into your hands, the lord prospar it unto you and yours. I shall truly praye for you and Desire your prayers may be before the lord for mee who am lefte to passe through the miseryes of a trublesome pilgramage. I thanke you for the continuanc of your loue. my father and mother ar uery kinde unto me and will not be wanting I know in thare loue, but though the lord should greatly Increase your estate by the losse of my Deerest frieand and the lessening of my poore porsion and laying other Hindrances apon mee, yeeat shall I neuer think my loue ill settled upon one that loued me So Deearly, though he could leue me nothing but his prayers for me and the Intrust I haue in your loue, whoes kindness is so clearly manifested like the kindnesse of ruth to the leuing and to the dead. the 30 pound you writt of was taken up of my unkle talley, besides which the 10 pound my fathers man brought with him and the 5 pound of mr. Brinscely and 8 pound from my unkle Downing goeth out of that som of 50 pound in his hands which my father Paynter was willing my mother should add to my porsion which was but 2 hundred and 50 pound before for your brother. and now that is all sp[e]nte exeptting uery littell, but

---

[1] W. Au. 55; Savage (1825), I. 383–384; (1853), I. 460–461; *L. and L.*, II. 83–85. See *Winthrop Papers*, II. 223–224.

[2] Forth Winthrop.

in this I do submitte my selue patiently to the will of god, and take it as the least part of that great affliction. I do not mention anye of this to pr[e]sse you good Brother, nether ar you bownd but as the consideration of gods Dealing, boeath with you and your brother, and mee, shall moue you. your promiseses ware your kindnes   I could not disuurue [deserve] them, forlorne and Dessolate as I wase. yeeat thay ware comfortable in that case, and I still thank you and pray the lord to reward you. the mare I confesse I should Desire to gett Downe if it might stand with your good liking. I hope to ridde to Sutton upon her shortly. mr. Brinscely knowes how to send har downe by the carryer. I am ashamed to put all thes thing in letters which your well knowen loue and redy kindnes would preuente me in if I could but see you, nay hath preuented. my father and mother desires to see you all if it be possable, though they haue lettell hope by resoan of my fathers Imployments. praye remembar my unfayned loue to my worthy sister your wife and my sister Elizabeth Winthrop   praye scertifie her that I reseaued har louing letter and excuse me to har that I haue not now written to har. I should be uery thankefull, if you would be please to lett me here from you the mesingar of your wellfare being allwayes wellcom and much reoiysing the hart of mee your euer louing sister

URSULA SHERMAN

My mothar remembreth har loue to your selue and your wife and thankes you both for your kind tokens you sent har by mee. she desires to be execused for not writtin unto you at this time.

THOMAS CALEY TO JOHN WINTHROP, JR.[1]

To my very louing and approued kinde Friend Mr. John Winthrop at Mr. Downings in Fleet street be these delivered in London

Emanuell

GOOD SIR, I haue desired a good while to haue spoke with you, but could not neither at home nor at London: The busines about which was this. Whereas there was not a Cow deliuered in New England to my Vncle John Gosse, he doth desire in his letter that my mother would send him so much as it commeth to: either in cloth, in money, or butter and cheese. Now I haue sent vp halfe a red cloth to my brothers Chamber, desiring that it may be sent among your clothes, and that you wold be pleased to cause it to be safelie

---

[1] W. 4. 71; 5 *Collections*, I. 198–199.

delivered to him: my mother had thought to haue bought 4 or 5*li* worth of butter and cheese and sent him but that your goods are sent away more suddenly than we are aware of: So as if we can not conueniently send it, if you please to let him haue either 5*li* in money or in such necessaries as he stands in need of, my mother and my selfe shall acknowledge ourselus much bound vnto you. And for the other fiue pound if you thinke so fit, if you please to deliuer it to my brothers Chambar before you goe (if I do not see you my selfe which I hope I shall this next weeke or the weeke after) my mother dothe resolue to bestow it on him, and it may be it may do him more good another yeere: either in money or some such commodities as he shall write for; Thus wishing you all health and happines in the Lord and a prosperous voyage and a comfortable meeting with your father in N. E. I commit and commend you and all your affayres to the safe tuition of our good God and most loving father, who neuer fayleth his and desire to approue my selfe to be Your Faithfull and intire Friend in all well wishing of the best good

Thomas Caley

Little Waldingfield this 5th of July 1631

WILLIAM DWIGHT'S BILL TO JOHN WINTHROP, JR.[1]

Soulde to Mr. John Perce the 9th daye of Julie 1631 these perselles followinge

	li	s	d
30 bushelles and a halfe of oatmill at 7*s* the bushell	10	13	6
Receaued the som of tenn poundes and thirteen shillinges and six			
pence in full for this 30 bushelles and a halfe of oatmill by me	10	13	6

William Dwighte

[*Endorsed:*] Mr. Winthrops bill For oatmeale 10*li* 13*s* 6*d* Full paid.

INVOICE OF GOODS SHIPPED ON THE *LION*[2]

1631. An In voyce of all the goodes thatt are laden a boord of the good shipp called the Lyon: this 15th of July: for the proopper accountt of the Wor[shipfu]ll Mr. John Wintroop as the pertticulers in the margen will apeere.

---

[1] W. 1. 88.   [2] W. 1. 88.

		hh	ba	k	fer
	Item 5 hogedes of peease No. 1:2:3:4:5	5			
	Item 2 hogedes of butter No. 1:2	2			
	Item 2 mattes with Iron woork att	1			
	Item 24 hogedes of meall No. 1 to 24	24			
22th day	Item 8 hogedes more att	8			
	Item 1 bondell of lether att	1			
	Item 2 hogehed of beeffe att	2			
	Item 2 Buttes of this mark	4			
	Item 3 ferkines more			1	1
	Item 1 troncke in a matt		1		
23 day	Item 1 Cheste of Candells att		1		1
	Item 1 bondell of spittes and andeyrs				1
24 day	Item 5 ferkines more att				5
	Item 2 trunckes att	2			
	Item 11 hoghed more att	11			
26 day	Item 2 longe Caske with Cheesse	2			
	Item 3 hoghed more att	3			
28 day	Item 2 Cabells att	2			
	Item 5 Coylle of small Roopes		1		1
	Item 13 hogedes more att	13			
	Item 3 barelles of this mark		3		
	Item 2 harnes Barrells att		2		
	Item 3 half hogedes more att	1	0	1	1
	Item 2 baylles No. 1: No. 2: att	2	1		
	Item 3 Chesse Caske att	1	2		
	Item 1 Cheste att	1			
	Item 1 baskett att			1	1
	Item 1 payre of smithes belos		1		
	Item 2 small trusses att				1
	Item 6 longe saes and 2 Crosses				1
	Item 2 longe Chestes att the	2	1		
	Item 1 bondell of shouells att			1	1
	Item 2 halfe Barrells att		1		
	Item 2 hampers att		2		
	Item 2 hogedes of vineger att	2			
	Item 1 barelle of pouder att				1
	Item 1 Ronlett of oylle			1	
August 1	Item 1 greette packe with beeding	4			

	hh	ba	k	f
Item 1 ferkin more att				1
Item 1 small Ronlett att				1
Item 1 small troncke att				1
Item 1 Casse of boottells att				1
Item 4 Chestes att	1	4		
Item 1 matt with goodes att		1		
Item 4 pipes att the tonedge of	8			
Item 1 troncke att		2		
Item 1 longe packe att	1			
Item 3 Chestes att	2	2		
tonn 31	1	1		1

1631. More goodes shipped a boord of the good shipp called the Lyon this 2 day of August 1631 for the prooper accountt of the Wor[shipfu]ll Mr. John Wintroopp as the perttickelers in the marge will apeere.

	hh	ba	k	f
Item 3 hogedes more	3			
Item 4 halfe hogedes	2			
Item 1 Ronlett and a ferkin				2
Item 1 Cheste att	2			
Item 4 tronckes att		4		
Item 1 barrell att		1		
Item 1 halfe Barrell			1	
Item 1 Barrell att		1		
Item 2 Barrelles of pich		2		
Item 2 Barrell of tarr att		2		
Item 2 ferkines att				2
Item for a seeutte of small saylles	2			
tonn 3	3	1	1	4
31	1		1	1
35	2		1	
1	2			
ton 34			1	

more for the beeding in the gonrome [gun room?] and maney small boxes and tronck:

EDWARD CLARKE'S BILL TO JOHN WINTHROP, JR.[1]

July the 15th 1631 A noat of Caske deliuered to mr. Persse

	li	s	d
Item deliuered to the bridghouse 6 hogshedes quarter bound for pease	01	04	00
1 hogshed quarter bound			
3 hogshedes full bound at 18s the tonn and 7 hogshedes quarter bound at 16s the tonn	02	01	06
more 2 butes for butter	00	16	00
For puting in 8 hedes and setan 7 houpes one butter	00	01	03
For 1 hogshed that was filed at dice key with pease quarter bound	00	04	00
For 2 hogshedes full bound that was filed with bookes and Cloth	00	09	00
More 1 hogshed quarter bound 2 barelles and 1 rundelit of 4 gal. 2 Chese Caske	00	15	00
For 2 hogshedes quarter bound one for barley and one otes and 1 barell for barley	00	10	06
For 3 Chese Caske	00	07	06
setan 10 houpes one a barell of reyssones and putin the hed	00	01	00
For sponinge a rundelit of Lemon water	00	00	02
For 5 hogshedes for meall full bound at 18s the tonn	01	02	06
For 2 halfe hogshedes with Coueres and Irones over them 3s the Iron worke and 7s the 2 Caske	00	10	00
More 2 halfe without Coueres 3s 4p apece	00	06	08
More for houpinge and naylinge of soop firkines	00	00	08
For puting in a hed into a barell of shoues and setan 2 houp	00	00	04
For 2 hogshedes for pease quarter bound	00	08	00
For 1 rundelit of 6 gall.	00	01	02

Reseued this 4th of Agust 1631 in full of this bill the some of eyght poundes and eyghtteen shilinges I say raseued by me

EDWARD CLARKE

[*Endorsed:*] Mr. Winthrops bill for Cask from Mr. Clark for 8li 18s Full paid.

---

[1] W. 1. 88.

JOHN LING'S BILL TO JOHN WINTHROP, JR.[1]

Bought of Jno. Ling the 16 July 1631

	li	s	d
2 hog. wine vineger Full gaige at 47s per hog. is	04	14	00
Swete oyle 1 Rund. at 9 gall. 5 pints at 5s 4d per gall. is	02	11	04
For hooping of the 2 hog. with Sn. marke and boisterus hoopes 5s 3d	00	05	03
For the oyle Rundlet 20d	00	01	08
For nayles and Sponing of the hog.	00	00	06
For Cartage and portage	00	01	03
	07	14	00

Rsd. in Full Seuen pounds Twelue shillings per me

JOHN LING

Moer bought dito			
1 Rundlet Swete oyle at 2 gall. 6 pints at 5s 4d per gall. is	00	14	08
For the Rundlet and portage	00	01	04
Redy Money	00	16	00
	7	14	00
	8	10	00

Rsd. in Full xvjs per me

JOHN LING

For Mr. Jno. Perce

[*Endorsed:*] Mr. Winthrop for oyle and vineger 7li 10s Full paid.

BILL OF JOHN STEWARD, JR., TO JOHN WINTHROP, JR.[2]

The 22 July 1631

Bought of John Steward Junior at the Signe of the Princes Armes in Leaden hall streite as follows

	li	s	d
Imps. An Infernall glasse	0	3	0
1 greate Receauer	0	3	0
1 greate boult head	0	2	0

---

[1] W. 1. 89.   [2] W. 1. 89.

	li	s	d
4 gallon Bodyes	0	8	0
4 pottle Bodyes	0	6	0
7 small Bodyes	0	3	6
1 gallon Retort	0	2	0
7 small Retorts	0	3	6
2 pottle Retorts	0	2	6
1 quart Retort	0	0	8
1 gallon head	0	3	0
1 pottle head	0	2	0
1 quart head	0	1	4
4 small heads	0	4	0
20 wt. boult heads	0	10	0
1 wt. Ovall	0	1	0
3 parting glasses	0	2	6
2 greate glasse baysons	0	3	0
2 midle glasse baysons	0	1	6
2 small glasse baysons	0	1	0
5 glasse funnells	0	1	6
12 halfe pt. glasses	0	1	0
3 ds. of Vialls	0	2	0
1 ds. of marmelaites	0	2	0
1 morter and pessell	0	5	0
4 ds. of Jam glasses	0	4	0
6 nest of melting potts	0	1	0
6 round melting potts	0	3	0
12 calsining potts	0	4	0
6 Earthen Retorts	0	3	0
2 greate Juggs	0	3	4
3 ds. of Thum glasses	0	2	0
1 midle peece	0	1	0
2 cupping glasses	0	0	6
2 sewgar chest	0	4	8
a basket	0	0	8
	5	2	2

[*Endorsed by John Winthrop, Jr.:*] Bill of glasses.

ROBERT HILL'S BILL TO JOHN WINTHROP, JR.[1]

Bought of Robert Hill gr[ocer] dwelling at the 3 Angells in lumber streete the 26th July 1631

		s	d
1 ʒ Alisander seeds at 2d			2
1 ʒ Angelica seeds at 4d			4
1 ʒ Bassill seeds at 3d			3
1 ʒ Buglos at 2d			2
1 ʒ Burradg seeds 4d			4
1 ʒ Burnett 3d			3
1 ʒ Beets at 2d			2
1 ʒ Bludwort seed 2d			2
1 ʒ Carduus benidictus 6d			6
1 ʒ Colewort seeds 3d			3
1 ʒ Cullumbine seeds 3d			3
1 ʒ Cresses seed 3d			3
8 ʒ Cabedg seed 2s per li.		1	
1 li. Carrett seed 12d per li.		1	
½ ʒ Charnill seed 3d per ʒ		o	1½
½ ʒ Cicory seeds at 3d per ʒ		o	1½
½ ʒ Clary seeds at 3d per ʒ		o	1½
½ ʒ Corn sallett at 2d		o	2
2 ʒ Culiflower seed 2s 6d per ʒ		5	
½ ʒ dill seed 3d per ʒ		o	1½
½ ʒ endiue seed 3d per ʒ		o	1½
1 ʒ fennell seed 1d		o	1
½ ʒ sweet fennell 1d		o	1
1 ʒ hysopp seed at 2d		o	2
½ ʒ hollihocks seeds at 2d		o	2
1 ʒ louadg seeds 2d		o	2
3 ʒ lettice seed 2d per ʒ			6
½ ʒ Lang de beefe at 1d			1
1 ʒ leekes seeds at 3d		o	3
½ ʒ mallow seed at 1d		o	1
½ ʒ marigold at 2d		o	2
1 ʒ sweet maioran at 8d		o	8

[1] W. 1. 90.

		s	d
1 ℥ pott maioran at 4d		0	4
½ ℥ munkhoods seeds at 3d per ℥		0	1½
½ ℥ maudlin seed 2d		0	2
1 ℥ nipp seed 2d		0	2
1 li. new onyon seed at 2s 8d		2	8
4 ℥ parsley seed at 16d per li.		0	4
1 ℥ pursland seed at 4d		0	4
½ ℥ popey seed at 2d		0	2
8 ℥ pompion seed at 2s 8d per li.		1	4
1 li. new parsnipp at 20d		1	8
8 ℥ Radish seed at 12d per li.		0	6
½ ℥ Rockett seed at 4d per ℥		0	2
1 ℥ Rosemary seed at 8d per ℥		0	8
1 ℥ Sorrell seed at 2d		0	2
1 ℥ winter sauory at 6d		0	6
½ ℥ summer sauory		0	2
1 ℥ spynadg at 2d		0	2
½ ℥ stockielliflower 3d		0	3
3 ℥ skerwort seed 3d per ℥		0	9
1 ℥ Thyme seed 6d		0	6
½ ℥ Walflower seed at 4d per ℥		0	2
for orradg seeds 1d		0	1
flower of the sonne		0	1
Tansy seeds		0	2
violett seeds		0	2
½ ℥ walflower		0	2
½ ℥ hartichockes 2s per ℥		1	0
	£1	6	0

[*Endorsed by John Winthrop, Jr.:*] bill of garden seeds.

EDWARD KEDDEN'S BILL TO JOHN WINTHROP, JR.[1]

1631 July delivered to Mr. John Winthrop per Edward Kedden

	li	s	d
for 106 Cth. 0 10 bolted meall at 16s per Cth.	84	16	00

---

[1] W. 1. 88.

Recs. this 4th of August 1631 the some of eighty and four
pounds and sixteen shillings In full of this byll. I saye Res:
these by me   84 16 00
                          EDWARD KEDDEN

[*Endorsed:*] For Mr. Winthrop Mr. Keddens bill for Meal. 84*li* 16*s* Full paid.

WILLIAM COTTWEN'S BILL TO JOHN WINTHROP, JR.[1]

A note for making of a suite of Cetch sailes for mr. Winthroppe

	li	s	d
For working of 139 yards of French Canvas into a maine saile and 2 bonnetts and fore saile and bonnett at	02	00	03
For working 2 boults and 2 yards of warp Ipswich Cloth into a top saile and meson and sprett saile contayning 66 yards at 2*d* 3 farthings the yard	00	15	03
For 139 yards of Royalls for the making the fore saile and maine saile at 15*d* per yard	08	14	00
For 2 boults and 2 yards of warp Ipswich Cloth to make the 3 small sailes at 26*s* the boult and 10*d* the yard for the 2 yards	02	13	08
Summ is	14	03	02

Rec. the 8 of Agust 1631 of mr. Pearce in full of this bell the som
of forteen pownd per me   14 00 0
                          WILLIAM COTTWEN

[*Endorsed:*] Mr. Winthrops byll for small sayls 14*li* 3*s* 2*d* Paid.

JOHN HUMFREY TO JOHN WINTHROP, JR.[2]

To his worthily respected and assured loving freind mr. John Winthrop at the Dolphin
Mr. Humfries house in Sandwich

DEARE SIR, It much troubled mee I came away so hastilie and unhappilie
finding no so great cause at home my wife yet holding up. I much desired to
see mr. Peirce and you aboard but the will of the lord bee done as it is. I pray

---

[1] W. 1. 90.
[2] W. Au. 56; 3 *Collections*, IX. 232–233. For Humfrey, see *Winthrop Papers*, II. 153, *n.* 4.

you remember mee in the most respective manner to your good mother, your wife and Sister. I hope I shall in no lesse tender manner rem[em]b[er] you to god, then I desire to bee remembred by you. I beeseech you rowle your selves and your burthens and cares on him. the more you trust him and impose in an humble faithfulnes upon him the more you glorifie him and the greater glorie shall you receaue from him. I wish and hope you will have aboundant experience of the inlargment of his grace in you and to you, in which I shall have as much matter of thankefulnes as now of request on your behalfe. I must cast my selfe and mine in an especial manner under him upon your selfe for directing and disposing of my servants and estate assuring my selfe of the reciprocation of that kind respect which in the most unfeigned manner I beare and owe vnto you. I pray you let it not bee burthensome or greiuous to you to doe for him as for your selfe who will bee readie to præfer you in anie thing within his power before himselfe. I must contract my selfe now vnto you, desiring so much the more to inlarge myselfe vnto the god of all grace for you in whome with my most kind respects and love vnto you I rest Your trulie assured and loving

Jo. Humfrey

London August 18th 1631

Mr. Downing adviz[es] by all meanes you should carrie good store of garlicke to physicke your cowes.

EMMANUEL DOWNING TO JOHN WINTHROP, JR.[1]

To his lovinge Cousin John Wynthropp Esqr. at New-England these deliver

Loving Cosen, Yours at your departure from the waterside I receiued and sent lettres supposing they might haue overtaken you there, but coming short they were safe retorned to me againe. of the hundreth and thirty *li* you left with me I paid my Awnt Branch 10*li* for hir last quarteridge; 5*li* for my Cosen Dudlye to my lord Sayes kinsman of whom he borowed yt to beare his chardges hither, and 15*li* more I haue laid out for him in Clothes and some other necessaries. what other chardge I shalbe at to furnishe him I yet know not. I wilbee as frugall as I can therein, and soe I perceive himselfe wilbe   My brother and sister Paynter were at my howse since your departure. they tell me they are in hope to gett the 100*li* of the lady Moodam.[2] I perceive they

---

[1] W. 2. 18; 4 *Collections*, vi. 40–40a.

[2] Lady Deborah Moody. See Henry Paynter to John Winthrop, Jr., *ca.* June, 1631, page 38, above.

hope you will stay till yt be recouered there, otherwise you must write earnestly to them.

I pray lett me know what I am growne in debt there that I may cleare
reckonings with my brother   thus in hast with my love to your selfe and your
wife my Cosens Elizabeth and Mary Winthrop I rest your louing vnckle

EM: DOWNINGE

2do 9br 1631

4to 9br

this morning about 5 a Clock the Queene was delivered of girle which was
presently after Baptised because yt cam before the tyme and was verie sick.

the king of Sweaden Mustered his army after he had retorned from the
pursuite of his victorie to vnderstand what men he had lost and found his
army to be 25000 men, soe he found 7000 more then when he begann the
battle; he hath 3 other armyes ioyned to him whereof 20000 are sent to subdew Bavaria, and 20000 into Sileatia and the rest for the setling of the Palsgrave in his Countrye, and himselfe with his 25000 men are gone to Frankford
vpon the Meyne which if he takes he is to be king of the Romanes, by the
Emperiall law; he was within 5 myles when this newes cam from him, and the
generall opinion is that the Citty dares not refuse his first Somons.

JOHN HUMFREY TO JOHN WINTHROP, JR.[1]

To his worthy and much beloved mr. Jo: Winthrop Junior at Boston

DEARE SIR, True love will fasten upon a small occasion and the least
opportunitie to have such fruition of the partie loved as our distance will
affoord; so that I doe and may well want a head and time sutable to the
affections and heartie desire I have to powre out my selfe unto you. Though
wee yet cannot in possibilitie heare of your comfortable arrival, yet I waite
upon the god of all mercie and comfort, and kisse and embrace the comfort
thereof afar of. The mercie I know will bee so apprehended by you, yours and
all of us that must challenge a share and interest in you, that (I hope) it will
engage us and manie more in improving such means further to improve ourselves times and talents to his glorie who strengtheneth us (by so greatly
desired favours) in our reioycings to his service, and the sincere obedience of
his will in all thinges. Sir, I presume I neede not so much excite you to a
zealous contending to improve your pace and reachings out to perfection, by

---

[1] W. I. 91; 3 *Collections*, IX. 233–237.

the mercies you have receaved, as I neede (by soaking a little upon the mercies in and to you and by you to others) to raise up some affections and expressions answerable to my true desires. And great neede I find hereof, having so much experience of my flashie hart, that sometimes I am enforcd directly, sometimes by way of reflection to trie whether I can helpe my spirit in this duty, as now. It is a well knowne truth (oh that I could know it effective in meliorem partem) that those mercies to ourselves or ours which leave us not better, they certainely doe much worse, for as a christian cannot stand at a stay (for non progredi est regredi) so there is besides other sinnes, the capital guilt læsæ maiestatis in not walking answerable to favours received. The smart of this, Hezekiah David and manie others of gods dearest servaunts have found with the sad experience of. And indeede what follie is it for a man to bee so iniurious to himselfe, that when hee knowes thankefulnes and fruitefulnes under mercies receaved as they open gods hand more largely toward him, so they qualifie him more to a disposednes to receave and still to get more sweete in receaving (for there is an influence and sap in everie mercie which if the lord withhold, it is but the huske or as the sedement of the mercie wee enioy) the spirit and the quintessence thereof, being of infinitely greater vertue and vigour. And againe in deliverances what is it to scape the beare and to fall into the paw of the lion, what to avoide the snare and to sinke into the pit, what is it to enioy the utmost that created nature can affoord in this world, and to loose (by resting herein) the creator of nature and of all comforts. (For saith hee I the lord create the fruite of the lips etc. thence flowes peace to him that is far of and to him that is neare.) Hee can reach us at what distance soever yea and will in riches of mercie to accept our least (if sincere) services, and to fetch us in, if belonging to his election of grace how far remote soever, and on the other side his hand can easilie find out his enimies where ever they thinke vainely to shrowde themselves under anie false refuges. But oh the depthes of his wisedome and goodnes unto us whome by faith hee hath made heires of the promises, what hath hee seene in us that hee should deigne an eye to behold us; but that hee who hath the treasures of all happines in himselfe should account us his peculiar treasure, tender us as the apple of his eye, should make us his owne, and provide for us all good thinges (grace and glorie) and as an overplus those inferiour comforts of this life, what hart can conceave or tounge of men or angels expresse the vastnes of this unlimited depth of love and goodnes which is without bottome or bancke. So that wee may well sit downe in a holie amasement, and wonder, and then out of the impressions of his goodnes cast about and thinke what shall wee render to the lord for all his goodnes unto us. Trulie these thoughts had neede to take up our best intention, not onely as they are the best and cheefest fruite of saving grace in us, but as they are (as I said before) the shortest and most expedite way and meanes of elevating us into a higher degree of grace glorie and all manner of happines here and hereafter. Wee mani times groape after happines in manie yea anie other wayes which is to seeke the living among the dead, these fresh springing waters (which onely flow from under the sanctuarie) in dead and standing puddles. Wee exceedingly abuse ourselves, yea and abase our noble condition to stoope in a beggerly manner to borrow or seeke anie comfort in these sublunarie vanities, with the neglect of that fountaine which puts what ever fulnes there is in these cisterne or broaken pit comforts; god is our roote our foundation, our father our fountaine rocke and magazine of all precious thinges, and how much to blame are wee when wee seeke to build upon a weaker foundation, that have one so firme, to draw sap from brambles that may from him; to come with cap and knee to the servant whereas his master is our father, to drinke of corrupted streames that may have immediate accesse to the well head, and to patch up a few comforts which yet (though wee prostrate ourselves to manie) will not make a garment large enough to cover the nakednes of the least part of our manie defects and our large-sp[r]eading indigencie When as in him alone wee may have infinitely more then all that is contained within the circumference of the creature can affoord. Let us then resolutely conclude with the Prophet it is good to drawe neare to god, yea so to draw neare as by our communion with him to draw all from him, to bee wholie unto him, to acknowledge him in all our wayes as the great reward to good and rewarder of evill that so according to his never failing promise he may establish all.

But it is time to recall my selfe least these meditations carrie mee beyond my time, and make mee and themselves burthensome unto you. I desired a little bout with you and I conceave I could not have it more proffitablie then by helping my selfe up the Mount with you. Now the good lord reveale himselfe everie way unto you, shine upon you with a loving countenance breath a blessing upon all your holy endeavours, sanctifie you throughout in your whole soule bodie and spirit, continue you a blessing with your familie to this worke of god, and at the end crowne all your holie and faithfull labours with him selfe who is the fulnes of glorie   To his grace I commend you and all yours, wife, mother, sisters all, to whome I desire in particular to be remembred in the bowels of the tenderest affection in Christ Jesus in whome I am Your most assured and trulie d[torn]

Jo: Humfrey

London Nov: 4th [1631]

If in anie thing my people have neede of your love, and you can steede them and mee by your direction and helpe I doe not so much desire as [*torn*] upon you though I doe both.

[*Endorsed by John Winthrop, Jr.:*] Mr. Humfrey recd. May 1632.

[*Memorandum by Winthrop on the superscription leaf:*] Mr. Vassall, Cozen Forth, Mr. Humphry, Mr. Kerby, my vncle Downing, Aunt Downing, Cozen Clarke, Mr. Howes, Vncle Gostlin, Sir Archisden, Mr. Gurdon, Mr. Jacye, Mr. Robt. Gurdon, Mr. Richard Saltenstall, Father Painter, Mr. Chambers, Sir Hen: Mildmay, Dr. Wright, Robt. Gelston, Cozen Mary Downing.

EDWARD HOWES TO JOHN WINTHROP, JR.[1]

To his louinge frind Mr. John Winthrop at his fathers house in the Machassetts Bay these deliver at Boston in New Engeland

CHARISSIME J. W., Health to you and to all the Israell of God; as this doth testifie my life and health, soe let it my harte and minde. perswade yourselfe that all the water betweene vs shall not be able to wash away my former professed loue to you and the place where you are; and to the persons with you, to whome I am obliged in a neuer to be cancelled bond. The bookes Mr. Gurdon hath fetcht away, and the Luna is at your service; soe is both the books and Sol et quodcunque sub sole habet vel habebit me tuum.

I heare your mothers vnkle is dead, and hath left her an 100*li* in his will   heare is a mutteringe of a too palpable seperation of your people from our church gouernement. allas, alas, it is not any outward will worship that god requires, but god being a spirit ought to be worshiped in spirit and truth. there are many guifts by one and the same spirite yet not all giuen to one man.   let euery man, as the guift is giuen continue in his callinge, one to rule another to convince another to exhorte, one the guift of healing, another guift of tongues etc. the eyes cannot performe the office of the hand nor the eares of the tongue etc. hence you receiued your being; and best being; in striuinge soe sodainely to be better, may proue to be starke naught. thus in rude termes I haue exprest my mynde out of a tender regard of the weaknes of your infant state. Children suck the brests of theire mothers, stronge meate is for stronge men; I pray god account you and preserue you all as worthy stones in buyldinge his newe Jerusalem, and that ye may be conformable to

---

[1] W. 2. 163; 4 *Collections*, VI. 472–473. For Howes, see *Winthrop Papers*, II. 226*n*.

the head stone Christ Jesus, whoe make ye wise to the salvation of your owne soules, your generations after you and the poore heathen with you; that ye become not a prey to the spoyler, and your children turne heathen, vncessantly shall pray Your

E. Howse

I hope my interest in you may procure a shorte relation of your arivall, of your present beinge, and some direction for the disposinge of my selfe my estate and affaires here. Vale in Christo.

E. H.

Peterborough Court, 9° Nouember 1631

I haue sould all and meane to followe Deo iuvante.

FRANCIS KIRBY TO JOHN WINTHROP, JR.[1]

To his very lovinge and much respected frend mr. John Winthrop Junior this deliver in noua Anglia in Charlton per a frend whom god preserue

Laus Deo in London 26° 10bris 1631

My very louinge and no lesse loued friend, harty salutation to your selfe and second selfe with my respect to your good father and mother for whom as also for the rest of your company I do and shall daily implore the aid of the almighty; we haue taken notice of very boisterous winds we had immediately after your departure from our Coaste (res est soliciti plena timoris amor)   We haue no hope to hear from you vntill the returne of mr. Peirce from virginia whom we expecte siccis faucibus.

I desire to acquaint you with such occurrents as may be newes to you whether foreine or domesticall. I received a letter dated in August last from Newfound Land in the bay of Bulls aboord the William and Thomas rideinge there to take in fishe and is bound for Genoa. my frend writeth that the ships Company goeinge on shore to cut timber did accidentally set that woody Contry on fire which had then burnt 20 miles alonge and that they had no likelyhood to quenche it vntill rayny wether come.

Captain Bruton who was imployed by my Cozen Moris Thomson[2] and

---

[1] W. 1. 92; 3 *Collections*, IX. 237–239. For Kirby, see 4 *Collections*, VII. 13*n*.

[2] Morris or Maurice Thompson was the son of Robert Thompson of Watton, Hertfordshire, and with his brothers, George, Paul, and William, lived for a time in Virginia. In 1639 Morris Thompson was engaged in the fishing trade at Cape Ann, and Governor Winthrop wrote that it was hoped he "would, ere long, come settle with us." *Journal*, I. 310.

company for the trade of beuer in the riuer of Canada is now ariued heere haueinge been since at St. Christophers for a freight of tobacco. he hath brought in heer about 3000 li. weight of beuer, and they are now hasteninge to set forth a small ship only for that riuer hopeinge to be there before Captain Kerke whom (I hear) is to fetch his men from Quibeck and yeild vp the Castle againe to the Frenche this next somer.[1] For German newes, you shall vnderstand that Swedens kinge hath been very successfull. the duke of Saxon who all this while hath been a neuter is now forced to take vp armes and craue the aid of Sweden, for Tilly did set vpon his cheife towne called Lypswicke and tooke it, but kept it not many daies before he with the helpe of the kinge regained it and gaue him battle about 2 eng[lish] miles from Lipswicke, slew about 15000 of the imperialists tooke much munition and with the losse of about 6000 of their owne, since that he hath taken Norenberghe and Frankford and lefte soldiers in them bothe. We hope that god will make Sweden an instrument for the fall of Antychrist. I find noted in the margin by the Geneua translaters Revel: 17. 16 that diuers nations as the Gothes, Vandals and Hungarians who were subiect to Rome shall rise vp to destroy the whore. Sweden is king of Gothes and Vandals. A little of Greenland newes because it may make some what for your encoragement who may sometime possibly aduenture vpon discouery where bread is not alwaies to be had, for therin you may see it is possible to liue without bread by gods blessinge vpon the fleshe of beares and foxes etc. 8 English men wintered there in the latitude of $77\frac{1}{2}$ and are returned home all in good likeinge. they liued from August vntill June without bread or other prouisions then what they killed and the fritters or rather fragments of the whales out of which they had tried oile and cast them to the dunghill the somer before. they lost their passage by reason of misty wether while they were on shore to kill venison.[2]

---

[1] On February 26, 1630/31, Sir William Alexander, David Kirke, and others, adventurers in the Company of Canada, represented to the Admiralty that about three years before, the King granted them a commission to plant colonies on the St. Lawrence, "to displant those who were enemies in those lands, and to trade with the natives." Being informed that several ships were bound thither, particularly the *Whale* of London, Richard Brewerton and Wolston Goslyn, masters, "contrary to that commission and greatly to the petitioners' prejudice," they prayed that the vessels might be stayed or sufficient assurance given that they would prosecute no such voyage. The Admiralty directed Lord Dorchester, Secretary of State, to examine those against whom the complaint was made and to prohibit their going if it appeared they had any intention of so doing. Three days later a warrant was issued to stop the sailings in question. *Calendar of State Papers, Colonial, 1574–1660,* 128.

[2] The story of these men is given in *Gods Power and Providence: Shewed, in the Miracvlous Preservation and Deliverance of Eight Englishmen, Left by Mischance in Greenland Anno 1630. Nine Moneths and Twelve Dayes. . . . Faithfully Reported by Edvvard Pellham* (London, 1631).

Thus with my earnest praiers to the almighty for you all I rest Your euer lo[uing] frend

FRA: KIRBY

[*Endorsed by John Winthrop, Jr.:*] Mr. Kirby recd. Jun: 1632.

EDWARD HOWES TO JOHN WINTHROP, JR.[1]

CHARISSIMO AMICO, Setting asside all vowes and protestations of my continuing amitie which would seeme but rather complements then true harted Loue, I salute you with good newes in my mouth; that God hath not forgott to be gracious to his church beyond the seas but hath heard the sighs and grones of his servants yea the blood of his saints hath cryed loud for vengance; and wrath since your departure hath come downe furiously vpon the enemies. I need not instance in particulars, for I dowbt not but the fame thereof is at this day the talke of all the world; yet to satisfie you a little fullier then by word of mouth, and that your worthy father with all my louinge frinds may reead at large the workinge of our God in these latter dayes, here I haue sent you the Swedish Intelligencer[2] which speakes wonder to the world withall I haue sent you your Archymedes and an Almenack with a booke or two of other newes besides; Mr. Dudly went away soe sodainely from vs in the begining of Christmas that I could not take my leaue of him as I would. I desire earnestly to heare of your healthe and welbeing; Thus Mr. Allerton staying for my letter I abruptly conclude with my loues to all my frinds I rest Your louing frind

E. HOWES

[*Ca.* January, 1631/32]

HENRY JACIE TO JOHN WINTHROP, JR.[3]

To his very worthy and much respected friend Mr. John Winthrop junr: Son to the Right Worthy Governour of New England at Boston there these be delivered with a Book   Leav these with Mr. Huison at London Stone, whom I desire to convey safely

KIND SIR, I humbly salute you and yours in the Lord.
We eagerly covet to hear of your safe arrival, yours with your good com-

---

[1] W. 2. 164; 4 *Collections*, VI. 477–478.
[2] *The Swedish Intelligencer* was entered in the *Stationers' Register* January 9, 1631/32.
[3] W. 2. 159; 3 *Collections*, I. 235–240. For Jacie, see *Winthrop Papers*, II. 87, *n.* 2.

pany, for we have good hope that we shal hear wel when it shall be, (it may be before your receipt hereof,) both in regard you were garded with so many prayers, and so many Angels (as if you had heard and seen would much have rejoiced you and so may do in greatest perplexities you have been are or may be in:) and also we hear this day from Mr. Huison (at London stone) that some that came lately from your coasts saw your ship com'd within 3 days saile of your desired haven. It would be very acceptable to this house if you writ to some of them, and if you pleased to send over also some of your Indian Creatures alive when you may best, as one brought over a Squirrel to Bures another some other creature, one a Rattlesnake Skin with the rattle.

I have herwith sent to John Sanford[1] a note of the winds ever since [you] went til after your arrival in N. E. the Patterne wherof I sent before your going to Jo. Sanf[ord] desiring his noting also. I pray you desire him to send back a copy of his, that so we may compare (for I have a copy of this) how they agree or disagree. I have not time now to write to him, no not to your worthy fa[ther] the Governour, nor to Mris. Winthrop nor others to whom I would gladly. I pray you excuse me to them.

The affairs beyond sea in Germ[any] ar almost beyond credit, how soe weak a king as Sweden sho[uld] go on and prosper and subdue stil so much against the mighty Emperour and Spains forces, maugre all their mallice and their holy fathers Curses. Our affairs at home ar almost as lamentable, as I h[ave] writ (and want time to reherse) to g[oodman] Firmin, and g[oodman] Child. The plague having been lately at Colches[ter] the B[ishop]s[2] visit was propria persona at Keldon,[3] wher with much gravity and severity he inveighed against the pride in the Ministry, that they must have their plush and satin and their silken Cassoks, and their bandstrings with knots; if every knot had a bel at it, it would be a goodly show, saying if any would informe him of abuses in the ministry by drinking etc. he would severely censure them. Mr. Cook there being comanded to attend him in his chamber, got a black riband to his rufe, which he so plaid upon O what a show it would make if it were of carnation or purple etc. He was very pleasant thus sometimes: by both which he drew the most people to admire him and applaud his proceedings. There he excommun[icated] Mr. Weld, who had been suspended above a month, and requiring Mr. Rog[ers] of Dedham to subscribe there (no law

---

[1] John Sanford was chosen in 1634 to be cannoneer at the fort in Boston, where he had already done two years' service. In 1636 he was appointed "surveyor of the ordinance and other ammunition." *Records of Massachusetts*, I. 125, 179.

[2] William Laud, Bishop of London.

[3] Kelvedon, Essex.

nor Canon so req[uires] I take it) he refused. He told how he had borne with him, and shewd how he must needs suspend him and so proceed if he reformd not to do all accor[ding] to Canon after a month to excom[municate] him, and then after a month to deprive him of the ministry, (so lying open also to a writ of excom[municato] capi[endo]) as was read in the Canon. Mr. Rog[ers] said if he would rather now put him by for altogether. He said no, he would proceed according to law. So suspended him. Mr. Shepherd he charged to be gon out of his Diocesse as one that kept Conventicles.[1]

Colchester men would have had his admission of Mr. Bridges of Emanuel for their lecturer in Mr. Maidens steed. He was angry and said When you want one you must go first to Dr. Gouge, and to Dr. Sibs and then you come to me, I scorn to be so used. Ile never have him to lecture in my Diocesse that will spew in the pulpit (it seemes he had preached on this I will spew thee out of my mouth.)

At Braintree (whither he went thence) Mr. Wharton Mr. Marshal and Mr. Bruer and others were spoke to after the Bishop had looked in his book opening it before them. He 1 commended them for parts and paines and their lives, and then charged them with Non Confor[mity] al denied it. Mr. Mar[shall] said he was misinformed. Ay but said he do you conforme always? He ans[wered] he did somet[imes] but not alwa[ys] he was much employed in preaching and in catec[hising] the youth. The B[ishop] ans[wered] your prea[ching] I like wel and your Catec[hising] wondrous wel but I mislike your answers, (which he spake angerly) you wear the Surpless sometimes, and then you lay it aside from you for a long time, and what say your people then?

These good men canot abide these ceremonies, and if they might they would never use them: But to avoid the Persecution of these Bishops that would fetch them up to the High Comm[ission] therefore these good men ar fain to stoop to them sometimes. Thus they will say, etc. So enjoining them to conform and seek the peace of the Church they escaped. Mr. Car of Twinsteed being cald Mr. Allen stood up and said (trembling as he spake, as he did at Bury when he informed against his Sudbury peo[ple], sitting with heels as high as their head) that many of his peo[ple] of Sud[bury] were enterteined by him, etc. The Bishop took him up therefore sharply if he admitted any to the Commu[nion] not of his own parish, or if any such came to hear him and he forbad them not, he would take a Course with him.

---

[1] For Thomas Shepard's account of this episode, see *Publications of the Colonial Society of Massachusetts*, XXVII. 369–370.

He said he hoped to join with his bro[ther] of Norw[ich] for refor[mation] there also. Now York being dead (on whose tombe he appointed should be indelibly ingraven, Hic jacet Samuelis Harsnet, quondam vixit indignus Episcopus Cesistrensis, indignior Norvicensis indignissimus Eboracensis, in his wil, therein protesting against the Genevensians) Winchester Dr. Neal to York, Durham to Winches[ter], Coventr[y] and Litch[field] Dr. Morton to Durh[am], Roches[ter] Dr. Bowls to Coven[try], our Norw[ich] Dr. White to Ely who is dead, Oxford Dr. Corbet to Norw[ich], that Rev. Dr. Linsel to Roch[ester] or Oxf[ord].

The Kings Attorney Sir Ro[bert] Heath is removed. Mr. Noys is put by the K[ing] into his place, who is very just in it. Tis said W[illiam] N[oy] for his book laid him down about 5 or 7 or 8 peeces. He asked what he meant 20s was due and would no more. Some usd to pay 5li I think. And hearing his man scraping with his foot at the door he came and asked what he gave him. He told a peece. He ans[were]d 2s was his due, he should have no more.

But I forget myself; tis near one aclock, I must bid you a good night. Yet a word more with you before I take my leave, for I know not when I shal talk with you thus again. Wher I left before. Mr. Nat. Ward being cald whose silencing was expected and charged with rejecting the Cerem[onies] and Common Pr[ayer] book, he answered (as tis said) ther is one thing I confes I stick at, how I may say for any that *dy in sure and certain hope*, or that *we with this our bro[ther]* etc. Upon this the Bishop to resolve him made a large explic[ation] and so he escaped then. Mr. Wels[1] after Excomm[unication] coming into a Church where the Bishop was visiting the Bishop spied him and cald him and asked him if he were on this side N. E. and then if he were not excom[municated]. He said yes. And why here then. He hopd he had not offended. But he would make him an Exam[ple] to al such. Take him Pursivant. The Pursivant called Mr. Shep[herd] and said he would rather h[ave] Shepherd, but he escapd,[2] and Mr. Wels by a bond of 100 marks others bound with him, and so fled to Bergen. Either he or Mr. Hooker was abated 40li in the forfeiture.

Mr. Bruer the last Terme had 22 Art[icles] against him, and 6 or 7 Additionals, these devised by Ja. Allen as Mr. Bruars late Sexton confesseth in anguish of Consc[ience]. I would write more as I could write too much such as I joy not in writing, but you more safely heare than I write it.

I beseech you Sir consider our Condition and provoke others to it some in

---

[1] Thomas Welde, first minister of the church at Roxbury.
[2] For Shepard's account of this episode, see *Publications of the Colonial Society of Massachusetts*, XXVII. 370–371.

the General, for some would make the worst of things to your disparagement though tis more their own shame. accept of what I have writ in scribling after midnight hast and let me hear of your receipt hereof, and of your welfare and yours and al your liking of the Country as you may. The L[ord] our good God and Gracious Fa[ther] be with you al as he wil be with al his in Christ in whose armes and sweet embracings though tost in afflictions I leave you, resting At your service to be used in him

HEN: JACIE

Jan. 9, 1631[/32]

My Bro[ther] Tho. desires to hear whe[ther] Mr. Win[throp] the Gov[ernour] have employment for him, he is yet willing to come if he may do him service. he can shoot wel and is content to endure what he can and to work etc. if it may be for his bettring in outw[ar]d estate. Me thinks I repent I have writ ought about him, for I would not have him to cumber you. Jo. Sanford knows my mind about him. I pray you desire him to write to me, with the Note of Winds.

If I can I wil send you herewith a book of the *Morning Star* tis cald, of that great star 1572 in the north, (in 63 of latitude and I think 53 of longitude which is Finland of which Sweden is the great Prince) which Ticho Brahe in his Spiritual book on that Star, pag. 800 and so forward shews not to be an ord[inary] comet, but a *new* star, the forerunner of happy changes to the Churches esp[ecial]ly beginning about 1632 as he calculates, from one that should come from such a place of longitude and latitude, applying it to the K[ing] of Sweden.

In this book he stands not so on the Anagram Gustavus Augustus, nor that saying that tis said appals the Emperours wisemen Te debellavit adversus Devs: Why or how Devs, tis said Sved, and relates many passages of the late victories.

[*Endorsed by John Winthrop, Jr.:*] Received these June 1st: Mr. Wilson arrived the last of May.

HENRY JACIE TO JOHN WINTHROP, JR.[1]

To his Worthy good friend Mr. John Winthrop junr. in New England these be delivered

GOOD SIR, I salute you in the Lord.

Hearing that as yet the ship towards N. E. is not yet set forth I adventure

---

[1] W. 1. 92; 3 *Collections*, I. 240–242.

this 3d week to send some thither, having sent one letter to you, and ano[ther] with a packet to the Worthy Governour the 2 last weeks to be conveighed by Mr. Huson.

Since my last weeks letter we hear its questioned whether Col[ogne] have yelded to pay 300M*li*, yea whether it have yelded Tho we hear it confirmd that Mentz hath (I mean to that renowned Instrument of God, the K[ing] of Sweden) and Openheim and Worms, and Creutznach. and also that he hath taken Frankendel, wher is a strong Castle, and it was strongly fortified. We hear he lost about 4000 men therby.

We hear the Spanish Ambassador being at Rome, affirmed that the K[ing] of France had assisted the K[ing] of Sweden which though the French ambas[sador] there denied that he knew any such thing, the Cardinals would needs have the Pope excom[municate] the French K[ing]. But he would not til he might see it further proved, and that K[ing] answer for himself. hereupon tis said was a great faction there, insomuch that the Pope fled to a strong hold in France. tis said so.

A book of the Northern star (by Dr. Goad) was sent you to go herewith.[1] ther ar now added to that book in print Verses in Latine (2 or 3 leaves) dedic[ated] to our K[ing] by Mr. Gil jun. in London, Bac[helor] in Div[inity] in Comend[ation] of the K[ing] of Sw[eden's] proceedings, relating part, and encouraging our K[ing] in assisting that Way. We have heard of some exploit done by the Marq[uis] Hamilton. Magdenburgh that was cruelly used by Tillies forces and a great part of it burnt (for which we hear was solem procession in Hungaria by the Jesuits procurement and casting the pictures of Luth[er], Calv[in] and Beza into a pit with fire which they cald hel, when suddenly G[od] sent such Thunder and lightning, that kild 3 or 4 hundred that day or the next as we heard) we heare its now beseged by the Duke of Saxonies forces, who joind with Sweden about Sep. 6 Neer Leipsich. Bohemia and Moravia is subdued by them for the most part (many countrymen revolting from the Emperor to them). Mr. Harrison of Sudbury molested by meanes of Mr. Allen, Mr. Warren, Mr. Smith of Caundish and Mr. Steward (the most favourable) sate in Commission about him, and now by his conforming more then ever he did, he yet preacheth at Sudbury.

Sir Arthur Herries of Essex was buried about the 8th of Jan. instant, for whom Dr. Aylot made many Eng[lish] verses which ar much applauded,

---

[1] *The New Starr of the North Shining vpon the Victorious King of Svveden* (London, 1631). The third edition or issue of the work (London, 1632) contains the poem by Alexander Gill, Jr., which Jacie mentions in the next sentence of his letter. No other evidence than this letter has been found for attributing the authorship of the book to Thomas Goad.

expressing his life beyond sea and here, his 2 wives and 12 children, his faith-fulnes to the Country and K[ing] etc. Mr. Hudson of Capel is departed and his bro[ther] is in his steed as I have writt. I pray you good Sir let me have Exchange of News from you, of your Comm[odities] and Disco[veries] etc.

Your good Company is remembred at table here in drinking oft in a week, besides more solemnly. We hear you do not drink one to another, ergo not to us, but remember us in a more serious sort. Remember us stil, for this land and corner have great need. The Grace of Our God be with you all. Yours in him to use

H. J.

As[SINGTON] Janu. 23, 1631[/32]

[*Endorsed by John Winthrop, Jr.:*] Mr. Jacye recd. May 1632.

THOMAS ARKISDEN TO EDWARD HOWES[1]

To his much deseruing Freind Mr. Edward Howes at Mr. Downings in Fleet streete by the Conduit these deliver

It was the 29th day of this Month befor I arriued at Cambridge hauen and I am agayne bound for Suff[olk] within this day or two   the occasion of it is this   Mr. Jacy who is Mr. Gurdons Chaplain vnexpectedly was sent for into his owne Country and it will be about six or seauen weekes befor he returns wheruppon I being then in Suff[olk] was earnestly requested to supply his place whervnto I did assent. I knew it would be some trouble to me but being in some respects obliged to them I dared not to shew my selfe soe disrespectiue of them as to giue a deniall   Mr. Gostlin with all his family are in good health   I preached at Groton the last Lords day being ouerswayed with their entreatys: I preached alsoe at Waldingfield parua the same day but at night hauing beene vnaccustomed to such exercises I was almost quite tyred. I receiued your letter   I am glad to heare of that newes wherof you writ vnto me. I haue not heard as yet from Anthony. If you please the intercourse of our writing neede not be hindred   there is one goodman Gifford who cometh weekely to spread Eagle   it is not far from the Bull   he vseth to come by Mr. Gurdons: Our Colledge is now about inlarging our Colledge with the addition of a new building   the charges of it will come to a 1000*li*   they haue the

[1] W. 1. 93; 3 *Collections*, IX. 239–240. For Arkisden, see *Winthrop Papers*, I. 141, *n*. 52; II. 300, *n*. 2; *D.N.B.*

money out the Colledge treasury: I pray remember my seruice to Mr. and Mrs. Downing giue them many thanks from me for their kindnesses to me: remember [my entire affection to Mrs. Mary]¹ my hearty loue to all the rest Thus alsoe not forgetting my obligement to your selfe I alway remain in all readines to gratify your kindnes

T. A.

From CAMB. Jan. 30, 1631[/32]

[*Endorsed by Edward Howes:*] This lettre is from Mr. Arkis[den] I pray view the other and if you thinke good seale it vp and deliuer it according to the superstition [*sic*] of it; otherwise lacerate or inflame it as you please.

THE GOVERNOR AND ASSISTANTS OF PLYMOUTH TO THE GOVERNOR AND ASSISTANTS OF MASSACHUSETTS²

To our Wors[hipfu]ll good freinds mr. Winthrop Gouer[nour] of the Massachusetts and the rest of the Counssell ther

GENTLEMEN AND WORTHYLY BELOUED FREINDS, We haue now at length returned an Answer to your letter dated the 26 of July (The reason we haue so longe deffered the same, is because we haue had no courte till the last month being Januarie) The sume wherof is this: that we are willing to curesponde with you in this, or any other neborly course, so fare as may no way be prejudicall to any, or swarue from the rules of equitie. how fare mr. Winslow expreste that agreement you intimate we know not (seeing he is absente) but our meaning, and former practiss, was and hath been, only of shuch as come to dwell, and inhabite, whether as seruants, or free men; and not of soujournours which come but for a seasone, with a purpose to returne yet if any abuse should grow hereby, we shall agree to any good order for the preuenting or redressing of the same; prouided the way be left open for pore men to releue ther wants, And for mutuall help to both plantations. We haue therfore giuen warning in open courte to all our people; not to receiue any as seruants, or other dwellers with them, but to aquainte vs first therwith that

---

¹ The words in brackets are crossed out. This was apparently done by Edward Howes, to judge by the similarity between the ink used for the cancellation and that used by Howes in adding the note to Winthrop which is printed after the text of Arkisden's letter. "Mrs. Mary" is probably Mary Winthrop, the sister of John Winthrop, Jr.

² Boston Public Library; *Bulletin of the Public Library of the City of Boston*, Fourth Series, 1 (April–June, 1919), 92–94. The body of the document is in William Bradford's handwriting.

we may inquire of ther certificates or dismisions, but we haue sett no penealtie vpon it as yett, because we hope ther shall be noe need   if ther be we haue libertie to punish shuch things at our discretions; if that will not serue; when we vnderstand what penealtie you apointe in the case, we shall doe the like, or that which shall be equivelente vnto it. As for the instances you giue we find that John Philips when he came was sick and if he had not been by some receiued to house he had been in danger to haue perished. he aledged he was sent by his maister to seeke a seruise, yet as a seruente he was not entertained by any; till his maister came and sould his time, (not to him that gave him house roome) but to him that would giue most, so he had no cause to complaine. for John Pickworth he came but as a soujournour to worke for a few weeks, in which time he goote a wife, and so is longe since returned duble, and hath no cause to complaine, excepte he hath goot a bad wife. Richard Church came likewise ass a soujournour to worke for the present; though he is still hear residente longer than he purpossed; And what he will doe, neither we nor I thinke him selfe knowes. but if he resolue here to setle we shall require of him to procure a dismision; but he did affirme to vs at the first, that he was one of mr. webbs men, and freed to goe for England or whither he would, the which we the rather beleued because he came to vs frome wessagasscusett upon the faling out with his parttner; for others intimated, we know none, (thoug we haue inquired) but they had a dismission either to come hither, or goe for England. Now ther are diuerce goone from hence, to dwell and inhabite with you, as Clement Brigges, John Hill, John Eedy, daniell ray, etc. the which if either you, or they desire thir dismissions; we shall be redy to giue them; hopeing you will doe the like in the like cases, though we haue heard something otherwise. Thus with our prayers to the Lord for your prosperity, as our owne, and our harty salutations vnto you all we rest your assured louing freinds

PLIM: feb. 6, 1631[/32]

WILLIAM BRADFORD *Gouer[nour]*
MYLES STANDISH
THO: PRENCE
SAMUELL FULLER
JOHN ALDEN

EDWARD HOWES TO JOHN WINTHROP, JR.[1]

To his very louinge frind Mr. John Winthrop at the Gouernors house these deliver in Mattachusets bay in New England

GAUDIUM MEÆ VITÆ, As the feare and Loue of God is the begininge of true Wisdome: soe the vertue deriued from that wisdome maketh Loue eternall, which vertue in you hath kindled such a fire of true Loue in me, that the greate Westerne Ocean cannot quench, but maugre all opposition it shall be with you wheresoeuer you are; while the possessor thereof hath beinge: I am and must be yet confined within the lymitts of my natiue soyle, because Gods tyme is not yet, but when the tyme is accomplished that I must departe, whoe shall resist his will? Mr. Arkisden and I doe now and then enterchainge letters. he in his last promised to send letters for N: E: but I haue not yet heard of him this three weekes. Mr. Lee is come from St. Christophers very poore   he hath lost all his tyme and voyage. I here he hath a desire to goe for N: E: his wife and hee are come from Groton; Common Garden neere the Strand is converted to a market Towne with a church in it   about 50 brick howses are buylt alredy   a wonder that a plantation should be made betweene the Court and the Citty that should extend it selfe to the skirts of either. I here it must be called Bedford Berry, it lookes more likely Ba Bell, I pray God it proue to Be Better; I could say more; but here is enough to contemplate on. Neuer was knowne more buyldinge of howses and repairing of churches, yet weekely some poore or other dye starued in the streets. here hath binn some lately executed for Quoyninge Siluer and Gold. Other newe I haue not instant, but there is expected greate good or eivell this sommer in these parts of the world; God will haue his worke done by vs, or vpon vs; I haue not yet attained to the perfection of the medicine   I doe much want my beloued frinds helpe and company; she hath more patience then I, and a more quick apprehention to discerne;[2] I cannot expresse the strainge condition I haue bin in euer since I lost both your companies, and had it not bin for the good of the Plantation; and for your sake; I should haue vsed my best Retoricke to haue perswaded her to staye here; I thanke God I am yet and I hope to continue (for many yeres) a single man, vntill I may enioy her, whome my harte may loue as it selfe; Thus desiringe you to remember my humble service vnto your father

---

[1] W. 1. 93; 3 *Collections*, IX. 240–241.
[2] See the letter from Margaret Winthrop to Martha Winthrop, page 29, above, in which Elizabeth, the widow of Henry Winthrop, is said to be "much employed in her surgurye."

and mother my much honored frinds, with my respectiue Loue to your selfe, your wife, your sisters both, not forgetting my qondam bedfellow James, with the rest of my louinge frinds; I rest yours till death

E. H.

7° Martij 1631[/32]

I pray tell gooddy Scarlets sonne the letter he sent his mother, I found lately in our house, which I intend god willing to gett conveyed this weeke to Karsey in Suffolke by some Clothier.

[*Written on the superscription sheet:*] Mitte mihi litteram per primum nuntium quæso.

THE COMPANY OF HUSBANDMEN TO MEMBERS IN NEW ENGLAND[1]

Grace and pese be mullteplyd for eure

from LONDON 8 march 1631[/32]

CRISTEN BRETHEREN, mr. Crispe John Cermen John Smith and the rest of our Sosiate: Wee as members of the sam bode send gretinge in the nam of our lord and Safiour Jesus Crist: hopinge and wishinge your hellth as our one: and as at this tim wee all are thainkes be vnto god   mane thinges we haue to wright vnto you of but our tim hath bin so taken vp with fordringe, hillpinge and providinge thinges fittinge for these our bretheren that are now to com vnto you, that wee shall not posible exprese, or put that to incke and paper which wee desiared, but wee hope they will relate vnto you anne thinge matteriall that wee forget to wright: and furst let vs not forget to reme[m]ber you of yours and our dute that wee return humble and harte thainkes vnto all mighte god, that hath filld the hart of our reuerent paster so full of selle, of loufe and extreordenare affection towards our pouer sosiate, that not with standinge all the oposition, all the suttell persawations of abundens of oposers that hath bin sturd vp against vs partly through sellfe loufe not affectinge this genarall serfetud and partly through that vntimly brech of our brother cermen: yet he remayneth constent, perswadinge and exortinge: yee and as

---

[1] John Davis MSS., M.H.S., 1; 4 *Collections*, VII. 91*n.*–94*n.* For the Company of Husbandmen or the Plough Company, see 4 *Collections*, VII. 88, *n.* 2; *Journal*, I. 65. This is undoubtedly the letter which Stephen Bachiler (referred to in the letter as "our reuerent paster"), writing to John Winthrop on June 3, 1633, said he was enclosing. See below, pages 101–103 and 122–124.

much as in him lyeth, constrayinge all that lufe him to joyn together with this sosiate; and seinge the cumpane is not able to bere his charges ouer, he hath straynd him sellfe to prouid prouision for him sellfe and his famally and hath dun his vttermost indeuer to hellp ouer as mane as posible he can for your further strainketh and incurigment: and allthough it may be if he had stayd one yer longer, you mayt haue better bin prouided to haue receued him, yet through his gret car of all your good, will by no mense stay longer from you. o let vs neuer forget this unspakeable marce of god towerds vs: wee hope the lord will mak him an espeshell instrement to vnit you all together in tr[e]w loufe vnto god, and vnto one another which will be our strongest wallse and bullworkes of defens against all our enemise; and wee hope you will not forget to shew your loufes vnto him and to tak nottes of the charges he is now at, and to apoint for him or his as he shall desier such shares or parts of shares as shall belong vnto him for the charges he is now at, and that his man seruent and his mayd saruent may be receued as members of the cumpane and haue such shares or parts of shares as is in that case prouided for euer membr   as for his naibours that now cum with him, they proumise all to joyne with you, but becase they do desier furst to see how you agre together in loufe, they are not joyned to our bode, and therfor wee haue toak no pertickuller nottes of them nor therse desiaringe you to do it ther if they joyn with you: and the lord of his merce grant that ther may be no ocation one your parts but that they may joyn with you   Mr. Dumers promise is allso to joyn with you if ther be anne resen for it. the lord vnit you all together if it be his will: then shall you put to sham and silanse mane that do now shamfulle ris vp against vs   Thomas Jupp hath allso sent you a pledg of his one cuminge in du tim his Eldest Sonn vpon his last 20*li* in goods and monese disburst for the Cumpanes vse   ther is allso Nathanell Harrese which wee haue sent you vpon a new adventure of ten pounds by his father whoe is now sargent of the roall and a member of our cumpane   ther is allso John Smith sunn of Frances Smith miller vpon a new adventer of ten pounds by one John Asten mellman and ther is nathenell mereman vpon the adventur of petter wouster beinge now mad vp ten pounds all which beinge members of the Cumpane, acordige to ther yers and adventures   wee desier you to recefe them and emply them   2 of them are vere able to work, and wee hop will be willinge   wee desier they should be put vnto it acordige to ther abillets and the other 2 allso acordige to ther strainckte wee desier they shulld be em- plyed   ther is allso Ann Smith our brother John Smiths wife and hur daughter; shee beinge incuriged by mr. dumers promise to giue hur hur pasige in part hath resolued to cum vnto hur husband whom wee can not deny and haue put hur in vpon the oalld adventur of Mr. Dy for hur sellfe and hur dauther.

all these are cuminge in the whalle with mr. dumer   they are all furnished with bedinge and aperell vere soffeshently and beinge all able to labor wee hope will be hellp full to the cumpane   ther is allso one Thomes Payn of sandwige experensed in the makinge of sallt which hath braught in ten pounds and cumeth in the William and Frances whom wee desier you to recefe as a member of the cumpone only in regard he hath a wife and 4 small chilldren which he desierth to be transported 12 month hense: wee haue only conditionly receud him that if betwen this and that tim you do find that he will not be a mor hellp vnto the cumpane: then his charge will be hindarns beinge he can bringe in but 20*li* mor for his wife and 4 chilldren that then he haueinge sarued the cumpane one wholl yer for his pasige, the Compane shall pay him his ten pounds again and so let him shift for him sellfe.

sum prouisions for these wee haue sent you: what prouisions you ellse want wee desier you to tak of mr. Dumer and send vs ouer your Comodetes: that wee may pay both for that and sum oulld dets which wee haue mad hard sheft for vnto this tim   pray necklect not but by what mesenger so euer Mr. Thomes master of the William and Frances doth send ouer his letters to haue his Fraight payd let vs by the sam mesinger if not befor recefe sum goods from you for wee wer constraynd to mak vse of the tunige mone of 20 pasingers to pay oulld dets tell a sertefecat be sent ouer: the goods you shall recefe in the William and Frances that is the cumpanes is 4 hogshds of pese which cost cask and all 6*li* 5*s* 0*d*   the caske as markt with 2 plouse markt one one hed wher as all ther go[o]ds haue 1 plou one ech hed and

	li	*s*	*d*
12 yards of brod cloth at 5*s* 6*d* cumes vnto	3	6	0
200 yards of list at 7*s* 6*d* per hundred which lest wee think may be good to mak indin briches or blankits I pray send woard if it be a comodete worth sendige anne mor	0	15	0
1 fryes coat 1 payr of briches boath at	0	19	0
	5	0	0

these thinges are packt vp into hogseds amonkst sum of mr. Bachellers thinges and sum thinges of Thomas Juppes which he hath sent vpon his pertiquller adventur   so soun as you can sell them ther is to the valle of ten pounds ad mone as you shall see by his pertiquller letters mr. hardige hath sent allso a persell of comodets vpon his pertiquler as by his letter you shall recefe derection   wee gaue you nottes by mr. Allertun and wee hope you haue long since receued it that wee haue had much ado abought our patten and that ther was one bradshaw that had proquired letters patten for a part as wee soposed of our former grant; and so wee think stell but he and Sir Fardinando think it is not in our bouns: he was frustrat of his furst purpose of cuming ouer but is now joyned with 2 vere able Captens and marchants which will set him out and wee sopowse will be ther as soun as this shipe, if not befor   wee can not posible relat vnto you the labur and truble that wee haue had to establishe our former grant: mane rufe words wee haue had from Sir Fardineando at the furst and to this houer he douth afferm that he never gaue consent that you should haue aboufe forte mills in lenkth and 20 millses in bredth and sayeth that his one hand is not to your patten if it haue anne mor   whe haue dun our good wellse and haue proqured his loufe and mane promases that wee shall haue no wronge: wee bestoud a suger lofe vpon him of sum 16s prise and he hath promisd to do vs all the good he can   wee can proquer nothinge vnder his hand: but in our heringe he gaue order vnto mr. Aires to wright vnto Capten Neyle of pascatoway that bradshew and wee maight be bounded that wee mayght not truble ech other and hath giuen the Capten comand to serch your patten what it is you haue vnder my lords hand and his. wee ned not counsell you what to do in that case only wee giue you nottes of it: desierige god to derect you that no just ocation may be giuen one our parts to be euell spoken of.

   wee gaue Sur Fardingand this resen whey wee desierd so larg a patten: becase that the grettest part of it was not habetable beinge rocke wer no man could life and he ansored wee should not dout but be allowed enofe for vs all and in the best part of it acordige to our desier: but if wee should haue so much as wee say they haue granted vs then do wee includ difers of ther former plantations which they neuer intended   this conterfers must be ended betwen your sellfes and such guferners of thers of pimequed as they haue apointed: wee will pray to god to derect you and to hellp you: this besenes doth requer the astens of all of you to joyn together in one   wee hope the lord in marce will so dispose of it.

	li	s	d
wee haue sent in the Whalle 70 ston of ocum at 10d and the carig	2	19	8
3 C wayt of rassell all charges cost	1	14	0
1 Ferken of flouer of 5 peckes and a ferken of pese	0	14	0

   ther is allso a vere pour Yorksher man is nam is John banester   he hath mad such extreordenary mone to com ouer that mr. bachellr and mr. Dumer hath had sum compasion and payd for his pasage   if you thinke you be able to receue him and do so think good of it wee then do desier you to let him be the cumpense saruent and put him to such emplyment as you thinke good and vpon such conditions as you shall see mit: goodman Tamage and his wife tak it vere vnkindly that you should kip his mollt and not let his sunnes haue a small quantetie of plattewer at his requst to be payd at return: how you will answer this vnkindnes wee know not   we would desier you to giue no ocations of such vnkindnes   her is now the people them sellfes com vnto you: wee asuer you they be vere honest playn doun right dellinge people   if they find you louinge and kinde and vp wright towerds them then will you haue ther cumpone   if not I pray consider you will not only lise them but wounder- fully discurigment it will be vnto diuers others for tim to cum: it may be vpon furst fue you may sopose them to be a charg in regard the men louck aged and the chilldren younge but yet wee sopose they haue porfessd to bring it for to anser that wee refer the acount to tak of them if they do joyn: and by the next ship you shall haue our acount for the wholl yer   and so the lord proteckt you and defend you now and euer. your louinge brethern

John Dye
John Roch
Grace Hardwin
Tho. Juppe

THOMAS ARKISDEN TO JOHN WINTHROP, JR.[1]

To the w[orshipfu]ll and his much respected freind Mr. John Winthrop the younger these be delivered in N. England

Worthy Sir, It is not the latitude of place were it 90 degrees in the merid- ian line nor the longitude of 360 being the whole length of the worlds æquinoctiall girdle that can ecclipse the sun of true affection among faythfull freinds: The Moone being in a diameter line farthest from the sun shines brighter than when they are both neere together and soe ought love among them whom affection hath vnited in a Constellation of freindship: Sinc I have noe better token to send you in requitall of all your favours I pray let these rude lines find intertainment at the poale of your acceptanc as proceeding from the Zenith of my best devotion to you ward, and shall ever tend to the Nadir of my vtmost indevours: Let me intreate you to cause these letters to be delivered according to their severall superscriptions: As for any news I haue

---

[1] W. Au. 61.

none to relate vnto you but that which I suppose you shall heare by others that come over   therfor being much straitned for time I make bould to be silent: Thus wishing the happines and prosperity of your selfe and of the whole plantation I ever rest Salutis tuæ desideratissimus

THO: ARKISDEN

From CAMB. March 20, 1631[/32]

EDWARD HOWES TO JOHN WINTHROP, JR.[1]

To his worthy frind Mr. John Winthrop the yonger at Boston in Mattachusetts Bay or else where these deliver in N: England

Salus in Salvatore nostro

OPTATISSIME AMICE OPTIME, I cannot but vpon all occasions salute you with myne indeared Loue and respects; these lettres from mr. Arkisden I receiued very lately   I was affraid they would haue bin left behind. accordinge to your appoyntment and vpon my desire, I thought good to entreate you to acquaint me with some particulars of your Contrie; vizt. howe farre into the Contrie your planters haue discouered, 2 what riuers, Lakes, or saltwaters westward, 3 howe farre you are from Hudsons Riuer and from Canada by land, 4 what are the most vsefull comodities to send ouer to traffick with ThIndians, or amonge your selues; 5 what kind of English graine thriues with you and what not; and what other thinge you please; daringe not to trespasse any farther upon your gentle disposicion, only be pleased to send a map or some discription of your land discoueries. For you know well the cause of my desire to know New England and all the new world, and alsoe to be knowne there, yet not I but Christ, in whome I liue and moue and haue my beinge. My m[aste]r hath sent my most honored frind your father, a sword in a walk-inge staffe which he forgatt to mention in his letter. Mr. Winslowe hath it; whoe I doubt not will deliuer it. Thus concludinge with our last and freshest newes here inclosed which my mrs. sends to your father I take my leaue to rest Yours and euer yours

E. HOWES

26° Martij 1631 [1632]

[*Endorsed by John Winthrop, Jr.:*] Edw. Howes recd. Jun: 1632.

---

[1] W. 1. 84; 3 *Collections*, IX. 242.

EDWARD HOWES TO JOHN WINTHROP, JR.[1]

To my much esteemed frind Mr. John Winthrop the yonger these deliver at Boston in New England

WORTHY SIR, Vpon the 23th of march last past with greate Joye I opened your letter, but with sorrowe and greife read the same, consideringe the affliction God had layed vpon you. Your letters all I my selfe disperst into the contrie, and deliuered the rest according to the superscriptions, only Dr. Ayleworth I cannot as yet find out; The receipt of morter you shall here receiue, vizt. One man he buylt with this mixture; 2 loads of wast soapashes, one loade of lyme, one loade of loame, and one loade of Woolwich sand, tempered together. An other man vsed only loame and soape ashes tempered together instead of morter, whereby he layed the foundations chimnies and theire tunells etc. of aboue threescore howses in london and the suburbs. I am about to procure all Platts workes to be reprinted, or else I would haue sent you my Jewell house of Arte and nature.[2] I am crediblie informed that Clay, otherwise called loame and horse or Cow dunge tempered together will make an exceeding stronge bindinge morter; I conceiue the manner of buyldinge in Ireland, vizt. to frame the howse and reare it, then with loame and strawe tempered together, to daube both outside and inside to a foot thicknes or more, to be very stronge and warme; I was lately tolde that in Italy men vse to temper ox blood and claye together, with which they make floores or walles smooth and glisteringe, and with all that it is very stronge and bindinge; I like well the old English and still Irish buyldinge where the roome is large and the chimney or herth, in the middest. certainely thereby ill vapour and gnatts are kept out, lesse firinge will serue the turne, and men had then more lusty and able bodies then they haue nowe. I will relate vnto you a pretty and plesant Jest of a fellowe in Suffolke, whoe hauinge a shrewish wife made as though he were a wearie of his like; and went away from her. It was coniectured by all, that he had made away with himselfe for he could not be found nor heard of in almost a whole winter, and where thinke you this fellowe was all this while, he had made him a howse in his woodstack and buylt it soe artificially with bavins, that it was a farre better and warmer cabin than Diogines Tubb.   it seemes he had plotted the busines before hand, and had conveyed there in provision before hand, or else he had some boy or servant of his councell whoe conveyed provision vnto him, for the waye in was

---

[1] W. 2. 163; 4 *Collections*, VI. 474–475.
[2] Sir Hugh Platt, *The Jewell House of Art and Nature* (London, 1594).

at the topp, and so artificially archt ouer and hollowed vnder, that it was
hard for either wind, frost, snowe, or could to trouble him; Nowe if one man
could make this shift of his owne invention, surely some amonge you if they
haue neede, may vse of the like or some other better, for I heare you haue
wood enough; methinks the southerne or westerne side of a hill, might with
small charge be made an habitable place for good people, like the boothes
against the Tennis court at Whitehall, especially if it be a Rockie and steepe
hill. I hearinge of a ship redie to set forward for your coast could not but
ymparte my minde vnto you concerninge this busines   Thus with my wonted
loue and louinge salutations to you and all the rest of my friends I rest Your

E. HOWES

26° March 1632

My letters by Mr. Dudley and Mr. Winslowe are more large, and the
sodaine departure of this ship euen tomorowe, causeth me thus to break of
abruptly. Vale in Christo.

I have sent you by this ship the oyle of vitrioll, that you left behind you.
It is directed to your father because of the more safe conveyance thereof. it is
in a litle double voyall, bound vp in 2 or three course papers.

This afternoone I receiued a letter from John Samford, wherein I vnderstand there is greate hopes of Jo: Sagamore, to be civilized and a christian;
I conceiue it were very good, to bestowe respect and honor vnto such as he
(petty kings) by giuing them a scarlet coate I meane a red coate to weare;
or some other vestment in token of his place and dignitie, which other
Sachems (of greater command then he) hearinge and seeinge, may thereby
be allured to loue and respect the English in hope and expectation of the like,
or in theire conceite more glorious clothinge and soe you may thereby discouer further into the land haue more frinds and allies, and by the blessinge
of god, it may be a greate meanes of civillizinge the meaner sorte; and after,
the revealinge Christ vnto them; for it is a rule in warre, to aime to surprise
and captiuate greate ones, and the lesse will soone come vnder, soe winn the
hartes of the Sachems and you win all. The wise man saith; guifts blinde the
wise; howe much more them that are ignorante and simple, as I thinke all
the natiues are. The more loue and respect you shewe to the Sagamores and
Sachems the more loue and feare shall you gaine from the common natiues.
I could wonderfully enlarge my selfe vpon this and the like subiect, but that
tyme and tide tarrieth for noe man. I haue one thing more to ymparte and
then I shall conclude.

*A receipt of a wholsome and savorie drinke for such
as are sick, weak, or cannot drinke water*

℞ 5 or 6 gallons, or quantum placet of water, put to euery gallon a pinte of white wyne and a pretty quantitie of potatoe Rootes, which I suppose you haue good store of, and after 2 or 3 dayes standinge, drinke out halfe, and fill it vp againe with fresh water, and the second drinke wilbe better then the first. Probat Mr. Thomson.

This drinke Capt. Drake vsed very often to drinke of in his voyage about the world, and one of the voyage lately told it to me, with the manner as afforesaid.

E. H.

[*Endorsed by John Winthrop, Jr.:*] Ed: Howes Jun: 1632.

EDWARD HOWES TO JOHN WINTHROP, JR.[1]

*To his worthy frind Mr. John Winthrop the yonger at the Massachusetts Bay
these deliver in New England*

Such is the force and effect of true Loue (my beloued frind) that it acounteth noe paines too much, and all tyme too little, in performinge the offices, and duties, of deserued respect: I hauinge sent some bookes to James Downinge with a letter dated the 3 of Aprill, beinge incited thereunto by his father; your demerritt clamed parte of my paines, and soe greate a parte, that had I not written by mr. Wilson vnto you my selfe would haue exclaimed against my selfe, and at the barre of conscience haue adiudged me a traytor to the bond of amitie; and lyable to the liuinge death of a Turtles solitarines that hath lost her mate; I knew not of mr. Wilsons going ouer till within this two dayes, Soe that I had deliuered a packett of letters vnto mr. Humfries to be sent by this Ship vnto you, one whereof was a letter vnto your selfe another to your beloued wife another to your sister Eliza: and two to James with your oyle of vitrioll you left with me; I hope God will send all in safety vnto you; and retorne vnto vs ioyful newes of your recouery; and of your perfect health; In James lettre I mentioned 2 or 3 thonges of a horse hide that I sent you I pray you comtemne not the meanesse of my conceit but consider that I hearinge your father writt for Shoemakers thridd, I sent you those for a tryall, therefore let not the servilenes of the worke preiudice your good opinion of me but knowe my aimes is and euer was at the generall good of your whole

---

[1] W. I. 94; 3 *Collections*, IX. 243–244.

plantation; which I hope to liue to see, and see to flourish and to remaine till tyme shall haue an end with me. Your assured

E. Howes

3° Apr: 1632 12° hor: noctis

I sent your honored father a booke of bookes among those to J[ames] D[owning] if he haue them alreadie, yet my good-will is nere the lesse, if they should not be soe welcome as I desire I beseich him to excuse my boldnes, for my hart is still as vpright to your worke as euer, as soe till death shall continue (Deo iuvante).

I haue heard diuerse complaints against the severitie of your Gouernement especially mr. Indicutts and that he shalbe sent for ouer, about cuttinge off the Lunatick mans eares,[1] and other greiuances; well, I would and doe desire all things might goe well with you all. but certainly if you endeavour in all mildnesse to doe gods worke, he will preserue you from all the enemies of his truth; though there are here a thousand eyes watchinge ouer you to pick a hole in your coats, yet feare not, there are more with you then against you, for you haue god and his promises which if you stick to, be sure all things shall worke together for the best. when you haue leasure spare me two or 3 wordes of your minde in what Caracter you please, that I may solace my selfe with your contentation, or helpe to beare the burthen, if not redresse your greiuances and soe I leaue you to God with my respectiue salutations to all my frinds.

my father mother and sister desired to be remembred vnto you.

[*Endorsed by John Winthrop, Jr.:*] Ed. Howes, June, 1632.

EDWARD HOWES TO JOHN WINTHROP, JR.[2]

To my much esteemed frind Mr. John Winthrop the yonger at the Massachusetts Bay these deliver New England

Noble frind, I hauinge the 14th of this Aprill receiued of Mr. Barker a letter from your sister myne approued frind, and mr. Drake callinge this morninge to see if I had any letters, (he preparinge to goe for Pascataway and

---

[1] The allusion is to the case of Philip Ratcliffe, sentenced to be "whipped haue his eares cutt of fyned 40*li* and banished out of the lymitts of this Jurisdiccion, for vttering mallitious and scandalous speeches against the gouernment and the church of Salem. . . ." *Records of the Court of Assistants*, II. 16. See also *Journal*, I. 64.

[2] W. I. 94; 3 *Collections*, IX. 244–245.

soe to you) I thought good, to let you vnderstand hereby that god hath still lent me life and health, the same I hope of you. I pray you thanke your sister for her remembringe of me (mr. Arkisden thinks you haue all forgotten him) and tell your sister I shall endevour to obserue and performe those good instruccions she sent me. I accidentally this morninge or rather by providence lighted vpon my bookes of the ordringe of silkewormes which I could wish with you for I heare you haue store of mulberie trees, doe but send for them if they wilbe any way proffitable or desirable I will with all convenient speede send them; I haue lately come to my hands (made by an excellent scholler and a linguist)—a prophet hath small honour in his owne Contrie—an English written Accedence and grammer of such a rare method that it is admirable to conceiue, which hath beene in obscuritie at least this 14 yeares, and by a speciall prouidence come to my hands I hope for the good of N: E: and the speedy bringinge of English and Indians to the perfect vnderstandinge of our tonge and writinge truly, and speaking elegantly. alsoe I haue of the same mans invention a booke of Characters, grounded vpon infallible rules of Syntax and Rhetorick. I would gladly print them that they might be the better dispersed amonge my frinds with you but that I doubt the mallice of some euely minded may hinder, or take them from me. if you thinke good I will send you some of the cheifest grounds and rules for a tryall; I conceiue it sufficient to teach the Indian children only to read English and to knowe none other, because they may not imagine there is the same confusion of tongues amonge Christians as there is amonge them. mr. Drake stayes soe that I cannot enlarge   Thus with my continued respects and Loue to you and all my frinds I remaine Your loueinge frind till death

E. Howes

Peterborough Court 20th Aprill 1632

[*Endorsed by John Winthrop, Jr.:*] mr. Howes: by mr. Drake August.

HENRY JACIE TO JOHN WINTHROP, JR.[1]

*To the Worshipful, his very good Friend, John Winthrop junr. Esqr.
son to the Cheef Governour of N. E. at Boston there*

Dear Sir, I humbly and most heartily salute you in the Lord, as also your loving Yokefellow, not forgetting the other Mris. Winthrops, your pious Mother and Sisters, to whom I pray you excuse me, for I want time to write.

---

[1] W. 2. 159; 4 *Collections*, vi. 454–457.

How affayrs go here, may better be related then written. Neither have I time
to write the late passages of that worthy Swedish King: And besides I have
not the late Corantoes to send you any of them, as I would: (for they ar of late
as true as ordinary letters) yet seing like as cold waters to a weary soul, so ar
good News from a far Countrie, Pro. 25. 25. I haue therfore sent you the best
Corantoes we have in the house, that have things of most importance, though
some of them long since, yet may be News to you, of another world. After you
have perused them, I pray you send them according to their superscriptions.
This I adde. After Tillie's encounter with Gustavus Horn a brave Swedish
Commaunder, a messenger that came from the Archduchesse must needs
speak with our K[ing] his message was to certify his Ma[jes]tie that
Gust[avus] H[orn] had lost 10000 men, which Sir Isaac Ashly presently
crossed, who being newly come from the K[ing] of Sw[eden] said such a
report came at 1 to the K[ing] of Sw[eden] which made him very sad for 2 or
three hours: then came a post to him from Gus[tavus] H[orn] to certify him
that the said Gust[avus] had lost 3 or 400 of his men, but had cut off 2
Regiments of the Enemie, and routed another. This being towards Bavaria,
the K[ing] of Sweden sent thitherward a great Armie, which hath greatly
spoiled a great part of Bavaria, making that as the seat of the Wars. Thereabout the Lord hath given that king divers great Victories. about 8 weeks
since we heard that our K[ings] Ma[jes]tie had a letter wherein was declared
how the Forces of Tillie being encamped on the River Donaw, the Sweds
came so hotly on them, that they were forced through the River, to escape,
to Dunwerken in Bavaria. The K[ing] of Sw[eden] having lately took a bridge
neer, came upon them thereby quickly, and drove them out of the Town
which yelded to him. tis said the K[ing] routed the Armie, took al his munition
and ordnance, and took 3000 prisoners. Ag[ain] we hear since, that Tillies
forces being entrenched strongly by Donaw, and some othir forces within a
few dayes were to joine with him, against the Sweds. Sweden seing their was
no adventuring on the Land's side, profered 10 dollars a peece (1.20s) to his
Finlanders to lead the way over the great water, which some of them did, and
but 3 of al drowned. Yet Tillie subtilly hath an ambushment against him,
which the K[ing] of Swed[en] perceived, and seemd as if he did not, set his
ordnance to follow the foot and horse: which being come to the place, and
the Ambushment appearing, the horse turne aside one way the foot ano[ther]
and leave them before the mouth of the Canon to play on them.   So routed
the Armie. Of late the K[ing] of Swed[en] hath had his horse twice kild
under him. Yet God preserved him.

    The last news we heard was, that the Bores in Bavaria that slew about 300 of the Swedish forces, and took about 200 prisoners, of which they put out the eys of some, and cut out the tonges of others, and so sent them to the K[ing] of Sw[eden] which caused him to lament bitterly for an howr. Then he sent an Army and destroyed those Bores about 200 or 300 of their Towns. Thus we hear.

Great stir is among the Turks, bec[ause] of the Emperour of them putting a Viseir Basha to death, by an other Basha, which caused a mutinie, the partic[ulars] I cannot, nor have I time to relate. Mr. Gurdon with Mrs. G[urdon] and their sons and dau[ghter] were al wel lately, they having ben now a fortnight at London, and to stay about a 14 day more.

One Mr. Milburn that sets forth a Prognos[tic] under the name of Sofford, s[ays] on the 3d of Octob[er] next wil be a fearful Ecclise of the Sun in New Engl[and], about a quarter before 4 in the afternoon is the midst of it, with us not seen, being about 8 at night with us. So he accounts. He desired me to write to some in N. E. to observ it, so should the Longitude be more perfectly known of N. E. I shal send you his observ[ation] of it: I pray you observe it and send me yours, which I shal returne with his, if you please. In great hast, I take my leave, resting Yours in the L[ord]

H. JACIE

[Ca. June, 1632]

Dr. Taylor of London dying, hath given (we hear) 20s yeerly for a yeerly sermon to be as a memorial of Leipswich.

Mr. Nath[aniel] Rog[ers] desires to have his best respects remembred to the Cheef Governor (as I also) and to Mrs. Winthrop and your selfe.

[Endorsed by John Winthrop, Jr.:] Mr. Jacy received Sept: 20: 1632. of the Eclipses.

JAMES WALL TO JOHN WINTHROP, JR.[1]

To his much Respexted Frend mr. John Winthrope sonne to the governer wors[hip] in newe Ingland giue this with all speed

WITHAM IN ESSEX this 20 of June 1632

SIR, I mad bould to write to youe at your going to newe Inland, but I

---

[1] W. 1. 95. James Wall is clearly the passenger in the Winthrop Fleet of 1630 whose name in the Governor's provisional list was deciphered by Savage (1853 edition, II. 416), as "Mr. Ball." Wall did not remain in Massachusetts, as appears from the letter Governor Winthrop wrote to John Winthrop, Jr., on July 23, 1630. *Winthrop Papers*, II. 306.

knowe not whether you ressevved it or noe for I am vnsertane of it: the substance of my writing was to intreat your Favor to be a Frend for me to the governers worship your Father, that he would be pleased to releue me in my wrongs that I sustaind when I was ther and more sence I cam from thenc. when I was ther your Father knoweth howe greatly I am wronged in the over rating of my goods, besids the bed I shuld a lien on was pout done into the hould so I could not haue it and it was reated at 30 or 40*s*, and I payd att least 20*s* for beds For want of my owne which the master of the shipe mr. becher knoweth well anof. the wrong that I haue sustained in over reating of my goods and bed came to much more then can be demanded of me, and though I never dennied payment of any, yeet I referr my selfe to the mersy of your Father. I vnderstand your Father the governer haue stayed my bever ther. if he would be pleased to showe me that Faver that he would use his athorryty to geet it in and send it to mr. Tho. Chambers hands of london or any other mans hands whom he shall think Fite I will pay any thing shall be demanded of me from your Father. I am wonderfully wronged in new Ingland, I think more then I should amongst those that knowe not god, as in my beaver my Censman Samuell hosyer knoweth, as sum denneth great part of ther deate in bever others will not pay he knoweth all. if your Father would be plesed to assist him with his authorrity to get it or els I shall be wronged of it and thay will not pay it, so my poore wife and Childrin must smart for it. also one mr. John Dillingham of yor plantation that had many goods and all the Cowes I was to reseue, and he owed me mony but would not speak me when he was here in Ingland, though he was with in 2 miles of my houghs and spok with som of my Censmen and doeth deetaine part of my deat, pretending that my Cowe he had of me was not worth his mony, when he took my lot and payd not one peny more then I payd. in this I hope your Father will be pleased to feech him to pay his deats being so well able as he is whom I could proue his estat is beter then three times so good as mine is, though he plead poverty, as I am informed. I am informed that the governer will mack men pay ther dewe deats. ther is behind still of his deat 5*li*, besids the great Charg in Jurniing after it to get that I have in. I would intreat the governor your Father to tack that of him, which he oweth me still, as 5*li* on the true deat and 5*li* in Chargis, and I humbly craue the governers Faver that that is my dewe in bever and mony he would be plesed to forse them to pay me and to send it to mr. Tho. Chambers of london for me, and what mony shall be short of that yor Father will haue I will repay afore I tack any goods from him. thus with my humble duty and Sarvis to your Father and your selfe hoping of yor prosperyty and helth craving yor prayers I rest macking over bold with yor patiens Committing yee all in to the hands of the allmity Yours in all Sarvis to command tell he seace to be

JAMES WALL

This I pray sho me that Faver to write to me a feawe words of an answer and what your Father the governer will doe.

[*Endorsed by John Winthrop, Jr.:*] James Wall Recd. Sept: 17.

JOHN HUMFREY TO JOHN WINTHROP, JR.[1]

To his worthily respected good freind mr. John Wrinthrop iunior at Boston or else where in Mattachusets Bay

DEARE SIR, I sent you a wavd'e sword as a pledge of my love by goodman Greene passenger with mr. Grant. I pray you doe mee such loving offices as occasion may inable you further to oblige your allreadie engaged freind especiallie put your father in mind to answer two particulars of his letter from mee, which you may see and so know how to bee helpful to mee therein. I pray you commend my kind respect to your good wife mother and sister   So leaving newes and busines to other letters which I know are full of satisfaction in that kind with much respect I rest your trulie loving and much desiring

Jo: HUMFREY

LONDON June 21th 1632

[*Endorsed by John Winthrop, Jr.:*] mr. Humfries. recd. Sept. 17 per mr. Peirse.

FRANCIS KIRBY TO JOHN WINTHROP, JR.[2]

To his very kind and much respected frend mr. John Wynthrop the younger at the Mattachusets in New England this deliver per mr. Peirce whom god preserue

Laus deo in LONDON 22º Junij, 1632

MY KIND AND MUCH RESPECTED FREND, I hartily salute you hopeinge of your good health the recouery wherof I desire siccis faucibus to hear of. You shall god willinge receiue per this bearer mr. Peirce 2 great drie fats marked as in the margin [I.W.]

At the motion of my brother Downeinge I willingly Condescended (if not

---

[1] W. I. 95; 3 *Collections*, IX. 245–246.   [2] W. I. 96; 3 *Collections*, IX. 246–248.

boldly intended) my selfe to be a third partner with him and you in this parcell of goods, which is such wares as your father gaue advise for, And I haue endeuored to get good and as good Cheap as I Could. the Cloth was provided by my brother Downing and mr. Smith the tayler, and it is such as master Winslow did buy heer to trucke with the natiues. for the rest of the wares if they be not well bought I only must be blamed. You shall find in one of the fats a book sent by my br[other] Downeinge to his son for his direction to keep a marchants booke and therin also some letters you shall find, and 2 paper bookes for the keepinge of this partable account, the lesser for a memoriall wherin you may write as you shall buy sell or barter, and the broader may serue to post it into by way of Debitor and Creditor if you be so skilfull. but for my part I shalbe carefull to keep all things right and straight heer though in a more rude and playne method for want of skill. The Comodity to make returne of I suppose will be beuer, it beinge almost the only Comodity of that Contry and therin your skill may be lesse then mine a word therfore of direction will be requisite. Note that there is great difference in beuer although it be all new skins for some is very thicke of lether and thin of wooll, which is best discerned by layeinge your fingers on the middle or backe of the skin. 1 pound of deep wooled skins may be worth 2 li. of thin wooled skins. Mr. Peirce brought a parcell for his owne account which was much of it of that bad sort   he offered it to mee for 12s per li. and I hear he hath now sold it for 11s or 11s 6d at most   also note that the old Coates are better by a third part then new skins are, partly for that they generally dresse the best skins for that purpose, partly for that the lether is thinner and so consequently lighter by dressinge, and partly for that the Course haire is in part worne of from the wooll. but I pray be carefull that you take not old worne otter skins or Coates for beuer, for they ar nothinge worth if they be so much worne that the glossy top haires are decayed, but ther are some good otter skins in Cotes 5 or 6 skins in a Cote, which are sowed together with the tailes on and beinge not perceiued to haue been worne but by the soyleinge of the lether and beinge very black and glossy may be worth 50s per Coate or 10s per skin. you may know the otter skin from the beuer partly by the Fabricke, for the otter is more longe though the tayle be of, and the wooll is more short and of euen haire the glossy haire not much exceedinge the wooll in lenght, but the Course glossy haire of the beuer doth more ouertop the wooll and is more stragleinge and more wild. I haue sent you some paternes of old otters for your better information.

For newes, the most is of the successefull kinge of Sweden who hath now taken all Bauaria. Ingelstad did hold out the longest but is now lately taken.

Also the prince of Orange hath gotten a stronge towne in Gelderlant Called Venlo a towne of great Consequence for that through it the Spaniard did convey all his provisions vp into Germany. also he hath taken the halfe of a towne in Cleuelant Called Mastich, but not the other halfe it beinge diuided (as it seemeth) by a riuer. and this taken with some difficulty, for Graue Ernste was slayne there and some other Comanders of the Hollanders. I earnestly desire to receiue a letter from you of the Contry and your Condicion there, which I shall receiue I hope per mr. Peirce if not before. I pray remember mee to your second selfe your good father and mother your sisters bretheren my Cosen James with all the rest of mine and your frends. We must intreat you to take Care of these goods and dispose of them. you may imploy my Cosen James in it so far as you thinke fit, but as yet I thinke he is vnfit to take the sole Charge of them. I pray make no bad debts, but rather keep them till you can haue mony or comodity for them.

[Francis Kirby]

The 2 driefats containe as followeth

	li	s	d
400 paire of shoes cost 2s 4d per paire is 46li 13s 4 but the shoe-maker abated in the whole 0 15 0 so we paid for them	45	18	4
18 li. shoe thrid at 1s per pound did cost	00	18	0
5000 large hobnailes at 2s per thousand cost	00	10	0
10000 midle sort at 18d per thousand cost	00	15	0
10000 small sort at 1s per thousand cost	00	10	0
16 peeces of Cloth wherof 1 is white and 15 Colourd cost all they containe about 13 yeards in a peece and is about 3li 4s per peice or 5s per yard	51	00	0
20 li. of Browne thrid and black at 2s per li. cost	02	00	0
2 paper bookes cost	00	02	0
2 fats with nailes to head them cost	00	15	3
paid for cartage to the water side	00	01	2
paid for freight to mr. Peirce	06	00	0
	108	09	9

[*Endorsed by John Winthrop, Jr.:*] Mr. Francis Kirby received Septemb. 17 per mr. Peirce.

[*Memorandum by John Winthrop, Jr., on the superscription leaf:*] Sandever or Sal alcali. In barrells. a barrell of sope ashes. ¼ of 100 tinne: ¼ 100 Copper.

FRANCIS KIRBY TO JOHN WINTHROP, JR.[1]

To his very lovinge and much respected frend Mr. John Winthrop the yonger at the Mattachuset in New England this deliver per amicum quem Deus conseruat

LONDON·this 22th of June 1632

Lo[VING] AND KIND FREND, Salutacons etc: you shall receiue per this ship 2 fats marked as in the margin, which is goods partable between your selfe, my bro: Downinge and my selfe   they containe 400 payre of shoes 16 peeces Clothe with some other things, of which I haue written you at large per Mr. Peirce yet least that letter should miscary I thought it not amisse to write a word or 2 per this bearer my Contry man Nash who is imployed in my Cosen Moris Thomson his buisines. Thus with my harty praiers to the almighty for you all I rest Yours at Comand

FRANC: KIRBY

BILL OF LADING[2]

Shipped by the grace of God in good order and well conditioned by me Francis Kerby of London in and upon the good Ship called the lion of London whereof is Master under God for this present voyage William Peyrce and now riding at ankor in the riuer of Thames and by Gods grace bound for New England To say two dry fats of goods being marked and numbred as in the margent, and are to be delivered in the like good order and well conditioned at the aforesaid Port of Mattachuset bay (the dangers and adventures of the Seas only excepted) unto John Winthrop the yonger or to his assignes, he or they paying fraight for the said goods, at foure pounds per ton with primage and Avarage accustomed. In witnes wherof the Master or Purser of the said ship hath affirmed to three Bils of Lading all of this tenour and date, the one of which three Bils being accomplished, the other two to stand void. And so God send the good ship to her desired Port in safety. Amen.

Per me ROB: REEUE

Dated in LONDON this 22th of June 1622 [1632]

[*Endorsed:*] Reeced this 22th of June 1632 of Mr. Frances Kerbey the som of

---

[1] W. 3. 5; 4 *Collections*, VII. 13.
[2] W. 3. 5; 1 *Proceedings*, III. 27–28. The original is a printed form filled out in manuscript.

six pound and is in part of paymentt for the fraight of thes goodes I say Reced in per me Rob: Reeue.

[*Endorsed by John Winthrop, Jr.:*] Bill of lading per mr. Peirse ship Sept: 17: 1632.

EDWARD HOWES TO JOHN WINTHROP, JR.[1]

To the wor[shipfu]ll his worthie frinde Mr. John Winthrop the yonger at the Massachusetts bay these deliver in New England

MOST NOBLE FRIND, Can a ship passe from our porte and you expect not letters by it, or shall you receiue letters from others and none from me; farre be it from me at any tyme to frustrate your expectations; it being the dutie of loue, to be alwayes operatinge towards the beloued; I neede not name you the North Starre towards which the compasse of myne endevours constantly inclynes, for you partlie knowe it, and the sequell of my life (God sparing vs both life) shall confirme the truth. Although I was ample in my last lettre; giue me leaue to vent the aboundance of myne affection in this defectiue character of expression; True it is, I about a fortnight since writt a letter for you, but some malignant spirit, knowinge thereof hath stolne it from me as I conceiue it being not endorsed to see to whome it was and what was in it, and now is ashamed to restore it. therein was nothinge but common newes, and therefore I lesse care for the losse. The shipp beinge thus sudainely departed vpon the end of This Trinity Terme I could not relate the particulars of my other letter; in breife my father and mother and sisters remember them to you and I would request the fauour of you to present my humble seruice to your honored father and mother, and my respectiue loue and due respects to you and your best beloued, and to Mr. Dudley and his beloued, and to my Quondam frind Mris. E., desiring for shortnes of tyme to haue leaue to be remembred alsoe in particular to my louinge frind John Samford and his true loue and to the rest of my frinds I rest and remaine Yours as you knowe

E. H.

Caput corui vidi, Lac Virginis quoque vidi, finem denique non ausim videre. Notitia misterij datur, potestas tamen operationis non datur mihi.

There is a tyme ordained for all things, etc. Crede et habebis.

[*Ca.* July, 1632]

[*Endorsed by John Winthrop, Jr.:*] Mr. Howes: Recd: Octob: 12: 1632.

---

[1] W. 2. 164; 4 *Collections*, VI. 478–479.

ROGER WILLIAMS TO JOHN WINTHROP[1]

*For the right Wor[shi]pfull John Wintrop Esqr. Governour of the English
in Massachusetts*

PLYMOUTH

MUCH HONOURED AND BELOVED IN CHRIST JESU, Your Christian acceptation
of our Cup of cold water is a blessed Cup of wine, strong and pleasant to our
wearied spirits. Only let me craue a word of Explanation: among other pleas
for a young Councellour (which I feare will be too light in the ballance of the
holy One) you argue from 25 in a Church Elder: tis a ridle as yet to me whether
you meane any Elder in these New English churches, or (which I belieue not)
old English, disorderly functions, from whence our Jehovah of armies more
and more redeemed his Israell or the Levites who serued from 25 to 50:
Numb: 8. 24: or my selfe, but a child in euery thing (though in Christ called
and persecuted euen in and out of my fathers howse these 20 yeares) I am no
Elder in any church, no more nor so much as your worthy selfe, nor euer
shall be if the Lord please to graunt my desires, that I may intend what I long
after, the Natiues Soules: and yet if I at present were, I should be in the dayes
of my vanitie neerer vpwards of 30 then 25: or whether Timothie or Titus be
in thought etc., at your leasure I craue interpretation. Sorry I am since
Rationalls so much circumround and trouble you, that *bestiale quid* (and mine
especially) should come neere you: but since the Lord of heaven is Lord of
Earth allso, and you follow him as a deare child I thanckfully acknowledge
your care and loue about the cattell, and further entreate if you may (as you
giue me incouragement) procure the whole of that second, and let me know
how and how much payment will be here accepted, or in mony in England.
The Lord Jesus be with your spirit and your dearest one (and mine) in their
extremities   to you both and all the S[ain]ts our due remembrances. Yours
in all vnfeyned and brotherly affections

ROGER WILLIAMS

[*Ca.* July, 1632]

The brethren salute you.

You lately sent musick to our eares when we heard you perswaded (and
that effectually and successfully) our beloved Mr. Nowell to surrender vp one
sword: and that you were preparing to seeke the Lord further: a dutie not so
frequent with Plymmouth as formerly: but *Spero meliora.*

---

[1] W. 2. 95; 4 *Collections*, VI. 184–185. For Williams, see *D.A.B.* For the occasion of this letter,
see *Journal*, I. 83.

JOHN WINTHROP TO JOHN WHITE[1]

To his Rever[en]d and verie loving freinde Mr. Jo: White Minister of the Gospell
in Dorchester deliver

REVER[EN]D AND WORTHYE SIR, I salute you in the Lorde, beinge muche comforted to heare of your healthe, and in the hope at lengthe to see and enioye you heere that you may reape some fruite of all your labours, Care, and coste bestowed upon this worke of the Lorde.

I wrote to you by the last returne, how I had vndertaken to paye them of Dorchester for Jo: Gallop and Dutche their wages, which Mr. Ludlowe did accompt to receive parte heere and parte in England, so as I mervayle you should have any further trouble about it. I have allso payd Jo: Elford the remainder of his wages being xi*li* and other arreares heere, so as I thinke there is now nothing to be demanded for suche reckonings: I have disbursed above 300*li* for the Companyes engagements heere but I have some Cattle, and olde kettles etc. for it, and I hope more then enoughe to satisfie me.

I have muche difficultye to keepe John Galloppe heere by reason his wife will not come. I mervayle at the womans weaknesse, that she will live miserably with her children there, when she might live comfortably heere with her husband. I praye perswade and further her comminge by all meanes: if she will come let her have the remainder of his wages, if not, let it be bestowed to bringe over his children, for so he desires: it would be above 40*li* losse to him to come for her.

The Surveyer of our Ordinance[2] is now returned home   we were lothe to parte with him, but his longing after his native Countrye would not be stilled: he hathe received of me xii*li* 10*s* for a yeare and quarter service and 5*li* I procured him from the Court (thoughe I am forced to disburse it)   his diet he hath had of me with his lodging and washing all the tyme he hathe been heere. yet if his passage be payd he will not have above 8*li* lefte, which will not suffice to apparrell him, and carrye him into Germanye. I praye Sir, make vse of your old facultye, to helpe him with some small matter more for his better accommodation.

John Gallop hath written to some of your neighbours for 12 doz. of Cod lines, if he provide them and bringe them to you I praye deliver him this bill

---

[1] Public Record Office, C. O. 1/6: 63; 1 *Proceedings*, v. 126–127.
[2] His name is given both as Jost and Joist Weillust. *Records of Massachusetts*, I. 83, 97. He is probably the person referred to as "Mr. Eustace" by Edward Howes in his letter to John Winthrop, Jr., of March 18, 1632/33. See page 112, below.

inclosed, if not I desire you to furnish vs so farre as this bill will goe and some codd hookes also.

Thus earnestly desiring your prayers, and longinge for your presence I commende you to the Lord and rest Yours assured in the Lords worke

Jo: WINTHROP

MASSACHUSETS July 4, 1632

I would sende salutations to my brother and sister Painter but feare they are dead for I have written divers Letteres to them, but never received anye.

[*Bill Enclosed in the Above Letter*]

BROTHER DOWNINGE, I praye paye vnto this bearer by the Allowance of Mr. John White of Dorchester twelve pounds: it is for fishing lines to be sent me into newe England. so I rest Your loving brother

Jo: WINTHOP

MASSACHUSETTS in N: E: July 4: 1632

JOHN WINTHROP AND JOHN WILSON
TO JOHN STOUGHTON[1]

To our Reverend and right worthy freinde Mr. Doctor Stoughton these deliver

REVEREND AND WORTHY SIR, We may be bould to let you knowe (vpon certaine intelligence which hathe come to vs) that we have hearde (with much ioye to our hearts) of the disposition of your thoughts towards vs, or rather towards the Lords worke begunne heere, for the spreadinge of the Gospell in these westerne parts of the world. Withall we have taken notice of that good reporte you have amonge the Saints, and of those Gifts the Lorde hathe furnished you with for this service: Wherevpon we thought good to let you vnderstand, and to give you what firme Assurance we may, of our stronge desires towards you: We meane not of our selues onely but of the Church of Boston whereof we are, and althoughe we dare not presse you with impor-tunitye of Arguments (being conscious of our owne unworthyness of so great

---

[1] Public Record Office, C. O. 1/6: 67; 1 *Proceedings*, v. 128. John Stoughton, brother of Israel and Thomas, was a graduate of Emmanuel College, Cambridge, and received the degree of Doctor of Divinity in 1626. He was rector of Aller, Somerset, 1624–1632, and curate of the parish of St. Mary Aldermanbury, London, 1632–1639. John Venn and J. A. Venn, *Alumni Cantabrigienses*, Part I, IV (Cambridge, 1927), 121. For the Reverend John Wilson, see *D.A.B.*

a blessing) to come into N: E: and helpe vs: yet we assure you, it would muche adde to the Comforte of our selues, and our incouragement in the hope of muche successe in this waye the Lord hath sett vs in, if it may please him to sende you vnto vs, by the returne of this bearer, with a minde so prepared, as vpon your discerninge the state of our Congregation, and the Affections of our people towards you, and our acquaintance with you, and knowledge of your abilityes, you might be ioyned to us in the Office of the Ministerye. Now (good Sir) we beseeche you, that this may suffice, to perswade your hearte this motion proceeds from the truethe of our desires towards you, and the apprehension of our owne want of suche helpe as the Lord hathe enabled you to afforde vs. And for all other matters which you shall desire to be informed of, to receive satisfaction from this bearer Mr. Peirce, our most faithfull freind and brother in Christ, till whose returne (by the good providence of the Lorde) we shall sitt downe and expecte your resolution: in the meane tyme we crave the helpe of your prayers, and so Comendinge you and all yours to the Lords most iust and holy disposinge in this and in all your occasions, with most hearty salutations we take leave and rest Yours truely in the Lorde

Jo: WINTHROP
JOHN WILSON

BOSTON IN MASSACHUSETTS IN N: E: October 1632

THOMAS ARKISDEN TO JOHN WINTHROP, JR.[1]

To his much respected and worthily esteemed Freind Mr. John Winthrop the younger at Boston in the Massachusates these be delivered in N. England

Emanuel

Plinius secundus a Gratiano cordato suo amico vehementi nec minus potenti desiderio adamatus, perditum illum diem sensisse[2] fertur, quo gratulandi, redamandique officio haud perfunctus fuerat, præclarum sanè amoris nec non adfectus ardentissimi exemplum omnium amicorum imitatione prosequendum. at væ mihi infælici non est nostræ fælicitatis tam quotidiani amoris, gratitudinisque (vtcunque cum Plinio tibi (amice dignissime) plus debeo) in apricum proferre. interiecta quippe loci distantia obstat, occurrit, impedit. At quid si quotidianum exhibendo amorem succumbo opportunitati? hoc mihi in solatium quotidianum referendo promptissimo non succumbo

---

[1] W. 1. 96.
[2] The word in the original manuscript is "sentisse," or possibly "sentiisse."

animo. Caput enim hoc meum tango et testor neminem esse, me vno, tui amantiorem (parcas quæso nimiâ si vsus sum familiaritate) neminem deuotiorem, nihil quoque tua consuetudine mihi contigisse gratius, nihil tua (meminisse dolet) discessione fuisse grauius. O quam libentius[1] possem (lachrimosi instar turturis) fletus gemitusque effundere, sed me comprimo. Leuius fit patientia quicquid corrigere est nefas: Magni beneficii loco duxi quod ad me literas dare non dedignatus es. Deo Opt: Max: maximæ habentur gratiæ qui se clementem adeo et benignum vobis ostendit. Non equidem invideo sed vt tua totiusque coloniæ vestræ fælicitas conduplicetur indies obnixè peto: Patri tuo dignissimo matrique amantissimæ quam potes officiocissime ex me salutem dicito. Me etiam vxori sororibus cæterisque nostris amicis, nominatim Mro. Dudleio jun: commendatum diligentissimè curato: Te tandem alijs mihi negotijs incumbentibus valere jubeo. Tuæ fælicitatis salutisque desideratissimus

THO: ÀRKISDEN

Datum CANTAB: Octob: 19 1632

Magister Caly te amoris titulo salutatum habet.

EDWARD HOWES TO JOHN WINTHROP, JR.[2]

LONDON primo Nouembris 1632

SIR, Yours of the 19 of September I receiued this euening, and could not let slipp to giue you intelligence of the receipt, though this be the third by this ship vnto you, my loue is soe intire vnto you that all the tyme I bestowe for you I thinke too little; I thanke you for your resolucion concerninge the silke wormes; Mr. Wigens whome I thinke you knowe, hath fullie resolued me thereof. as for your Cement it is a rare and a strainge request, but shall not be thought impossible, by me to be answered. I haue here sent a very necessary instrument for great ordnance[3] for John Samford. if you please to bestowe a little looking thereon you may quickly informe him in the vse thereof. the notches shewe the diametre of the bores, W. P. the weight of the pouder due to euery piece. L. L. the length of the ladle B. L. the weight of the bullett etc. the other side shewes the seuerall names of the ordnance.

I pray thanke James for his letter of the 18th of Sept. last, and for his

---

[1] This reading for this word, which is obscurely interlined, is doubtful.
[2] W. 2. 164; 4 *Collections*, VI. 479–480.
[3] In the margin: "[torn] 6d price."

wiuinge instruccions. Thus with my loue remembred to you your wife sisters brothers and all our frinds I committ you to Gods protection and rest Tuus dum suus

EDWARD HOWES

EMMANUEL DOWNING TO JOHN WINTHROP, JR.[1]

To his very louinge cossen Mr. John Winthrop at the Mattachusetts these deliver in New England

COSEN WINTHROP, I am very glad to heare of your health and welfare and well likinge of the plantation; Though the tyme be soe busie with me, and that I had but a very shorte warninge of this shipps suddaine goeinge yet I chose rather to write a little, then not at all, and being tired out in writinge to your father, I was glad to haue helpe to write vnto you.[2]

I thanke you for your advice about my cattell. I cannot here prouide such seruants as I would of a sodaine therefore for the present I haue agreed with Mr. Dillingham to take my Cattell and keepe them winter and sommer for the third of the increase, yet with this condition the bargaine is made, that vnlesse my brother Winth[rop] doe approue thereof, its not to stand; and for my swyne I was to haue of Mr. Allerton, being 4 Sowes, Mr. Dillingham will fetch them and put them out, to be kept for me, for halfs. concerning myne owne particular account with my brother Winthrop, I must needs referre it to my next writinge, for I haue bin all this sommer in the Contrie and came home but iust to the Terme and did not dreame of this sodaine going of this shipp, but made account to haue had tyme to consider thereof after this terme. But concerninge my brother Winth[rop's] monies receiued by me, I haue here inclosed sent you the true accompt, of the last 700*li* paid by Mr. Warren I directed my brother Kirby to receiue 500*li* because of his better leisure then myne, for the paying out of the same, accordinge to your occasions, which you may perceiue by the accompt, for a good parte of it is made by him, the rest is laid out by my selfe.

As concerninge Mr. Goffe he refuseth to receiue his monie according to my brothers last direccions, sayeing there is much more due vnto him. I praye send me ouer this acquittance signed and sealed by your father and your selfe with whome I am in parte agreed. For my sonne James I am sorrye to see

---

[1] W. 2. 19; 4 *Collections*, VI. 40a–40e.
[2] This letter is in the handwriting of Edward Howes.

that he writes a worse hand and more nonsence, in his last letters, then in the letters I receiued a yeare since   I doubt there is noe hope of his attaininge to any learning therefore if he hath a mind to husbandry, or may be fitt to truck and playe the marchant, and his likinge stand there vnto, I would gladly knowe it, that accordingly he might spend his tyme therein, for I thinke the tyme lost that he goes to schoole, and therefore take him from schoole, and let my brother Winthrop ymploye him as his seruant as he shall thinke fitt. I sent my brother Winthrop a letter written at the Hage from the germane lately come from you[1] by Mr. Humfreys conveyance. I sent my brother Winthr[op] a staffe with a rapier in it, and a pistoll you left behind by Mr. Winslowe.

The Plymouth trucking howse that was robbed was done not by the French but by some English theire names I knowe not;[2] Concerninge the keepinge of your cattell in the winter, I suppose, had you vnderwoods as we haue in England, you should need howse none but such as you would vse about your house for milke.

I haue written to my brother Gostlyn to prouide you men and maid seruants against the springe. My brother Gostl[in] I suppose cannot come ouer this yeare, neither is his wife willinge vntill he hath prouided a stock of cattell.

The cloth you desire from him will not be sent vntill the springe, neither could it be made ready against this shipps going for we had scarce a weeks warninge of it.

For Newes? Sergeant Finch Recorder of London is dead and mr. Littleton in his place; Judge Haruie and Judge Whitlock are dead, and Sir Robert Bartlet and Sergeant Crawley in theire places. Sir Thomas Wentworth the president of yorke is going Deputie into Ireland where Sir Franc: Angier is lately dead, and one Mr. Ratcliff of Grayes Inn a kinsman of the Deputy is named to be M[aste]r of the Roles there; my father in Lawe Sir James Ware[3] is lately dead. We haue had here a very vnseasonable cold summer, soe that the corne in the north parts did hardly ripen this yeare; about whitsontide last there was many sore Stormes, whereby many sheepe and lambes were killed. the Staffordsheire men doe very much complaine of the vsuall burninge heath growing and not cut downe in theire contrie, alledginge that it is the cause of much Raine amongst them; and if there come a parliament they intend to preferre a bill to preuent the burninge of theire contrie in that kinde.

I haue sent you some bookes of newes. I would haue sent you more but

---

[1] I.e, Jost Weillust. See above, page 87, n. 2.
[2] See William Bradford, *History of Plymouth Plantation, 1620–1647* (Boston, 1912), II. 134–135.
[3] See 4 *Collections*, VI. 40d.

that by direction from the Lords, the printers were restrayned from printinge any more.

In the lowe Contries there is great hope that the states of Holland wilbe lords ouer the 17 Prouinces very shortly for diuerse Lords and Townes haue revolted from the Kinge of Spaine and joyned themselues to the States. For the Kinge of Spaine will not be able to maintaine his warre there; being depriued of his wonted passages through Germany and France.

The Kinge of Spaine, as is generally beleiued stands nowe at a lower ebb then when Q[ueen] Elizabeth dyed. his necessities hath put him vpon strainge exegents for monie. the Spanish Inquisicion hath seised vpon many rich men, and burnt them for Heritiques whereby theire Kinge hath gott all theire estate. the Kinge hath alsoe seised vpon the treasure and plate of diuerse manasteries in Spaine to support him in his warrs.

The Kinge of Sweden goes on very prosperously and carries all before him in Germany. there is newes lately come that he hath ouer throwne the duke of Fridland the Emperours Generall, which if it be true, he will make a shorte worke of the warrs in Germany.

You haue a litle bird in your contrie that makes a humminge noyse, a little bigger then a bee. I pray send me one of them ouer perfect in his fethers in a little box.

I praye excuse me for not writinge to my Cosen Dudly and thanke him for his kind letter. remember my loue to his father and mother himselfe and his wife my cosen Feaks and his wife, Mr. Pincheon, Mr. Wells, Mr. Wilson and theire wiues, and I pray tell James D[owning] that he writt such a scriblinge nonsence letter, that I am ashamed to answere it. Thus with my harty loue to your selfe and your good wife, I take leaue and rest Your very louinge vncle

EM: DOWNINGE

Nouember the xxith 1632

Mall remembers her to you and your wife, and her cosen Feaks, and her cosen Dudly, and his wife; soe doth the scribe.

[*Endorsed by John Winthrop, Jr.:*] My vncle Downinge. Recd. Feb: 23: 1623 [1632/33] These letters per the ship Mr. Trevore master, Mr. Hatherly, merchant, arrived at new-Plymouth.

EDWARD HOWES TO JOHN WINTHROP, JR.[1]

To his worthilie respected frind Mr. John Winthrop Junr. at the Mattachusetts in New England these deliver

DEARE FRIND AND MOST NOBLE SIR, Deare because fewe the like to me, and truly noble beinge one of the Lords Worthies, your letter of July last was much welcome, in that it brought tidings of your recouery, and your thriuinge in the wildernes of N: E: I cannot as yet satisfie your desire in sending ouer to John Samford as I would, for you would wonder what discoragements the diuell putts in most mens mouths against your plantations, some that you are all comminge home, others that you are all gone or goinge for Virginia. for my parte I shall and will by gods leaue endeauour to continue towards you and the worke semper idem; here inclosed you shall find a booke of the probabilities of the N: West passage,[2] not in the 60 or 70 degree of N: latitude, but rather about the 40th. I sore suspect the Hollanders will haue the glory and benifitt of the passage about Hudsons R. yet God the Author and Finisher of all good works will (I belieue) that all shalbe for the good of his Saints. I heare the french haue this summer transported a company of priests and Jesuits and such vermine to Canada; but how longe they will staye there, it is a question. I conceiue the land to cold for theire hott natures.

The vernish for clothes to keepe out wett, I cannot yet learne, but as soone as I can, the next shipp after shall aquaint you with it; As for my vsuall characters they are that wherewith I conceiue you haue bin formerly acquainted vizt. Mr. Arkisdens, whoe hath sent you a letter here inclosed in John Samfords. I though[t] good to send you his character for feare you should haue forgotten it, as thus

A a b c d e f g h h i k l m n o p q r r

f s t u w x y z

---

[1] W. 2. 165; 4 *Collections*, VI. 480–483.

[2] Sir Dudley Digges, *Of the Circvmference of the Earth: Or, A Treatise of the Northeast Passage* (London, 1612). The identical copy of this work mentioned here is now in the Society's library. The word "Northeast" in the title has been altered, in manuscript, to read "Northweast" and the

they are approued of in Cambridge to be the best as yet invented, and they are not yet printed nor comon. you may abreuiate them thus, c. for Christ, ɥ. God, . Jesus, ∩ king, ∪ lord, ⊙ people, etc. / stands alwayes for the, /˙ for thee, ⟩ for w. or wh.   a little vse will make perfectnes; send me word whether you like it and I will send you more direccions.

I thanke you Sir, for remembringe soe farre of when Mr. Saltonstall was with you; by your meanes and good words of me to him, I haue obtained a most singular sweete frind of him. Euer since Michelmas last, haue I had inward familiaritie with him; he perswadinge me it was your desire that I should imparte my selfe vnto him, on your behalfe, and for the good of N: E.   I had enlarged myselfe, but that my m[aste]r called me to write vnto you for him; wherein you shall heare most of our latest newes; I praye you remember my humble seruice vnto your noble father, my most honored frind, and his right vertuous wife, and thanke him, for that he hath bin pleased to regard the good will of his poore seruant, in sending him a letter of encoragement, which was more welcome to me, then any guift besides; remember my loueing salutations to your Sister Feakes and her husband though vnknowne   thanke her for her lettre and tell her that I went with hir brother in lawe to Mr. Kirbys and procurde in my m[aste]r his absence, the monie vpon the bill of exchainge; remember me alsoe to your brother Dudley and his louinge wife, and all others to whome you please to recommend my loue. Thus though in the last place; yet not in the least place, my harty loue and affections to you and your best beloued remembred, with daylie prayers for your healths and prosperities, I rest Tuus ex animo et adyto

EDWARD HOWES

From the INNER TEMPLE this xxiiith of ixber 1632

---

date in the imprint has been changed from "1612" to "1632." Howes inscribed the following on the verso of the title page:

"Happie thrice happie should I be if this little treatise should add any thinge to your knowledge, Invention, or Industrie, to the atcheiuinge of that Herculean worke of the Straits of N: England, which I am as verilie perswaded of; that there is either a Strait, as our narrow seas, or a mediterranean Sea, west from you. The dutch O the dutch I doubt will prevent your discouerie, for they are the nearest, of any that haue not as yet discouered it. But doubtlesse there is a man, (or shalbe) sett aparte for the discouerie thereof, therby to comunicate more freely, more knowingly, and with lesse charge, the riches of the east with the pleasures of the west, and that the east and west, meetinge with mutuall imbracements they shall soe loue each other, that they shalbe willinge to be disolued into each other; and soe God being manifested in Christ through all the world, and light shininge in thickest darknesse, and that palpable darknesse being expelled, how great and glorious shall that light appeare. Which God of his mercy hasten to accomplish."

Howes also inserted the following in a blank space on the first page of the Preface: "To the right noble and worthy Religious and vertuous gent[leman] Iohn Winthrop the yonger all health and felicitie." At the end of the Preface appears in manuscript "yours E. Hows."

I haue bespoken Instruments for John Samford but could not gett them made redie against this shipps departure; he shall haue them, the next springe (God willinge) perhaps I may bringe them my selfe; but noe more of that, I meane to come vnlookt for, but not I hope before I shalbe welcome. The terme is nowe in the full heate thereof, and therefore I hope you will excuse such defects you find in this expression of my Loue and soe I leaue you to god.

A little more here I send concerninge Dr. Fludd, written in greate haste. Seale up James Downing lettre and giue it him.

EDWARD HOWES TO JOHN WINTHROP, JR.[1]

WORTHY SIR, Here I haue sent you a taste of the famous and farre re-nouned English man of our Tymes Dr. Fludd,[2] whoe as you may remember published a booke in defence of the weapon salue before you went ouer, but that is nothinge in comparison of these here menconed, which are all folio bookes, and full of brasse peices, the like I neuer sawe, for engines, fortifica-cions, and a touch of all opperatiue workes, as you may conceiue by the titles; yet let me tell you this, that the titles, nor my penn, is not able to expresse, what is in those bookes, as they are, noe more then you in a map of a sheete of paper, can exactly describe the riuers, creeks, hills, dales, fruite, beasts, fishes and all other things of your contrie; for I thinke it almost imposible for man to add vnto his macrocosme and microcosme, except it be illustration or comment, and that hardly too; his bookes are so bought vp beyond sea, we can gett none brought ouer. Fetherston, the Latine warehowse, nor all London, could within this moneth, shewe these all together to be sould. I layd out all this last longe vacation for them at Hills in Little Brittaine; whoe laid out for them for me and brought them me home compleat as here you see the titles which I could with all my harte wish the bookes themselues were in your hands as certaine as any thing you haue.

I had nowe sent you a catalogue of the marte bookes, but that I would not take any mans busines out of his hands. The iiii*li* xii*s* I had deliuered to Mr. Kirby ere nowe, but that he said he had none vse of it vntill the springe; he called to me for it, about a weeke since, when I not dowbting it, had lent it out, but I gaue him then xx*s* and haue since receiued xx*li* out of which I intend to pay the remainder as soone as I can goe to him, or see him; I had though[t] there with (by your leaue) to haue purchased Dr. Fludds works for

---

[1] W. 2. 165; 4 *Collections*, VI. 483–485.
[2] Robert Fludd. See *D.N.B.*

you for I doubt within this xii month they will hardly be gotten for x*li*. Vale
in Christo. Your assured faithfull frind in life till death

EDWARD HOWES

the xxiiiith of Nouember, 1632

Printed at
Franckfurt

Opera R: Fluddi, Medicinæ D[octo]ris

A[nn]o 1619
{
Vtriusque Cosmi maioris silicet et minoris Metaphisica phisica
atque Technica, in duo volumina secundum Cosmi differen-
tiam diuisa.

Tomus primus

De Macrocosmi Historia in duos Tractatus diuisa, R: F.

1. *Macrocosmi*

Tomus primus de Macrocosmi Historia, in duos tractatus.
1. Tractatus primus habet xiii libr.
}

A[nn]o 1628
{
2. Tractatus secundus de naturæ simia seu Technica Macrocosmi historia in partes xi diuisa.
}

2. *Microcosmi*

A[nn]o 1619
{
Tomus secundus de supernaturali, preter naturali, et contra
naturali, Microcosmi Historia in Tractatus tres distributa.
Authore R: F.
Tomi secundi tractatus primi,
Sectio sécunda de Technica, Microcosmi Historia, in portiones
vii diuisa.
}

A[nn]o 1621
{
Tomi secundi, Tractatus secundus de præternaturali vtriusque
mundi Historia, in iii sectiones. R.F.
}

A[nn]o 1623
{
Anatomiæ Amphitheatrum effigiæ Triplici more et conditione
varia disignatum.
Monochordum Mundi Symphoniacum, seu replicatio ad
Appollogiam Johannis Kepleri.
}

A[nn]o 1626
{
Philosophia Sacra et vere Christiana, seu Meteorologia
Cosmica.
}

A[nn]o 1629
{
Medicina Catholica seu Misticum Artis medicandi Sacrarium
in Tomos diuisum duos.
}

Sophiæ cum moria certamen, in quo, lapis Lydius a falso
structore Fr: Marino Mersenno, monacho, reprobatus etc.
Ro: Flud.

A[nn]o 1629 Sumum bonum, quod est per Joach: Frisium. $\begin{Bmatrix} \text{Magiæ} \\ \text{Cabalæ} \\ \text{Alchymiæ} \\ \text{Fratrum Roseæ} \\ \text{crucis verorum} \end{Bmatrix}$ veræ $\Bigg\}$ subjectum.

FRANCIS KIRBY TO JOHN WINTHROP, JR.[1]

To his much Respected frend mr. John Winthrop the yonger at the Massachusets in New England this deliver

LONDON this 25th of Nouemb: 1632

GOOD SIR, I received your longe expected and very welcome letters (dated the 2 July) about the last of August. I am glad to heare of your safe ariuall, your health, and good likeinge of the Contrie. I wrote you per mr. Peirce who departed this Coast in July last by whom I shipped to you 2 drifats of goods to the value of 110*li* or therabout as per those letters will appear. it was partable between my brother Downeinge, your selfe and my selfe   most of it was shoes and Course Cloth to trucke, such as my brother Downeinge had aduise for. I hope you haue receiued them ere this time. we expect mr. Alerton shortly by whome we hope to hear of mr. Peirce his ariuall with you.

I haue shipped in this ship Caled the William mr. Tryvore beinge master and mr. Hatherly cheef marchant, 2 square Cases of deale with the glasses accordinge to your direction, together with 2 hogsheads and 1 barell of your fathers with such goods as your father wrote for as per my bro[ther] Downeings letters to him will appear. the glasses with Cases Cost in all 1*li* 16*s* 11*d*   the freight will make them dear to you. if the freight be paid hear it shall all be put together vpon your fathers account and you may allow it vnto him. I doubt not but you will agree vpon the diuision of it. for the Catalogue of bookes from Frankfort I haue sent you that of Autumnall mart 1631. the next is not to be had the third not yet come by reason of Contrary wind but I shall send it god willinge by the next ship, and so likewise herafter. for your mony of Ed: Howes I haue receiued part and the rest he saith he will pay to mee shortly. I hear not any thinge of that from mr. Goslin yet. I should be glad to heare that these glasses came whole and safe to your hands. I haue written glasses on the outside of the Cases that they in the ship may be the more Careful of them sed quales sunt nemini dixi. I pray let mee receiue a

---

[1] W. I. 97; 3 *Collections*, IX. 249–250.

letter from you by euery ship, although it be but 2 lines it will be very acceptable.

Postscriptum 28º. I have now receiued all your mony of Edward Howes which maketh in all 4*li* 12*s* for the bookes and Cariage of them. it is now generally reported that the kinge of Sweden is slayne. we haue little other newes, what is I doubt not but you haue it at large per my bro[ther] Downe-ings letters and Ed: Howes. mr. Hatherly telleth mee that I must pay the whole freight before hand and that he will haue for the 2 Cases as much as 3 hogseds which at 4*li* per ton is 3*li*   if you will not haue the freight put all together vpon your fathers account and the Charge of shippinge it (which can not be knowne soone enoughe for my bro[ther] Downeinge to send account of it per this ship) then I pray write me your mind per the first and I will diuide it and put to your particular account. I pray remember mee to your good father and mother, your good bedfellow, your sisters, brethren, James Downeinge and the rest. Whom all I commit to the protection of the almighty and rest Yours at Comand

FR: KIRBY

[*Endorsed by John Winthrop, Jr.:*] Mr. Kirbye recd. feb: 23. 1623 [1632/33].

FRANCIS KIRBY TO JOHN WINTHROP, JR.[1]

To his very lovinge and much respected frend mr. John Winthrop the yonger
this deliver at Boston in the Masachusets bay in New England

Laus deo in LONDON 27º 9bris 1632

MY GOOD FREND, harty salutations etc: These may let you vnderstand that I haue shipped in the William of London per Mr. Hatherly 5 peeces of goods that is to say 2 hogsheads and 1 barrell with goods of your fathers as per my brother Downeings letters will appeare and 2 short Cases of deall boords according to your direction with glasses, of which I haue also written you more at large in another letter per this same ship. We desire to heare of Mr. Peirce his ariuall with you per whom I also shipped to you 2 great drifats of goods to the value of 100*li* and vpwards. I haue receiued yours only of the 2 July. I haue little newes to write, only of a great battell fought between the Kinge of Sweden and the imperialists neer Leipswich, greater then that there about 12 months since, for diuers haue written that were slayne of the im-

---

[1] W. 1. 97; 3 *Collections*, IX. 250–251.

perialists about 40000 and of the Kings about 20000, but some write that the kinge is slayne in the battell, others that he is sore wounded and that Walestein is fled and Papenham slayne. When I knowe more certainly I will write you per the first oportunity in the meane time let vs hope the best:

To your good father, mother, your second selfe, sisters, brothers, and to my Cosen James Downeinge salutem meis verbis dic. Thus with my harty praiers to almighty god for the Continuance of his fauors to you all I rest tuus dum suus

Fr: Kirby

EDWARD HOWES TO JOHN WINTHROP, JR.[1]

To his most respected and worthy Frind Mr. John Winthrop Junr. at the Mattachusetts these deliver in New England

Sir, I though[t] good not to lett passe the aquaintinge you with any thinge that might concerne you or the plantation, though I be neuer soe straightned in tyme. this day being the 27th of Nouember and the last but one of the terme I coming home at noone met 4 men there; that came as they said from Capt. Masons and the Bristoll plantation.[2] I askt them what newes. Lambert as I take it his name is, m[aste]r of the ship, said your father and you and all were well when he left you but he going vp to deliuer a letter to my m[aste]r from your father as I conceiue, I fell into discourse with one of the other a most egregious knaue, whoe would giue none of you a good word but the gouer- nor he was a good man and kept a good table but al the rest were Heriticks and they would be more holy then all the world, they would be a peculiar people to God, but goe to the diuell, that one man with you being at confession as he called it, said he beleiued his father and mother and auntestors went all to Hell, and that your preachers in their publique prayers, pray for the gouernor before they praye for our kinge and state, and that one of the Pascataweyans vowed that if he should heare your minister saye soe he would stabbe him in the place where he spake it; and that you should haue all your throats cutt by the Indians ere it be longe, for they haue killed some Rebbells and would make an end of the rest, for that you are a people not worthie to liue one Gods earth that you neuer vse the Lords prayer, that your ministers marrie none, that fellowes which keepe hogges all the weeke preach on the

---

[1] W. 2. 165; 4 *Collections*, VI. 485–486.
[2] Piscataqua (Dover, New Hampshire).

Saboth, that euery towne in your plantation is of a seuerall religion; that you count all men in England, yea all out of your church, and in the state of damnacion   but I beleiue and knowe better things of you; but here by you may partly see howe the diuell stirrs vp his instruments where his kingdome is soe mightily opposed he setts vpon you with all [h]is might and maine, and would haue you to be like himselfe but he that is with you, is greater then he that is against you; accept this as the token of my goodwill, though I am sorrie to expresse it in these vile and diuelish repetitions, it is to make you the more vigilant and circumspect.

The Kinge of Sweden I heare is slayne; my other newes you shall haue at large in a letter dated the xxiiith of this moneth. I haue deliuered all your monie to Mr. Kirby   Thus in great hast being the last daye of the terme I rest Yours as I haue bin

EDWA: HOWES

xxviiith ixber M.D.C.XXXII

Salute all my frinds againe. Vale optima salute.

THE COMPANY OF HUSBANDMEN TO JOHN WINTHROP[1]

To the right wor[shipfu]ll the worthy Gouernour at Mattachucetts John Wynthropp deliver in New England per our good Frend Mr. Allerton whose voyage God prosper

Grace mercy and peace bee multiplied

From LONDON the first of Desember, 1632

RIGHT WORS[HI]P[FU]LL SIR, Wheras ther hath come ouer from new England of late divers reports of the harch dealeinge of Master Dummer against our lovinge Breathren Bryan Binkes, Petter Johnsonn, and John Smith, in that hee hath not only taken from them that which was left them for there maintenance by the Company, but alsoe retained that which wee sent, And doe keepe in there hands all that is there left of the Companies and retaine it, contrary to that order that wee sent ouer by Master Allerton; And whereas wee haue received the day before the wrightinge heareof, one Letter from John Smith which doth for the most part iustifie that which wee haue heard, and alsoe another from Mr. Batchellor not denyinge the same, And haveinge received incoragment by divers, that there is Justice to bee had, Wee therefore

---

[1] John Davis MSS., M.H.S., 1; 4 *Collections*, VII. 94n.–96n. For other letters in this volume relating to the Company of Husbandmen, see pages 67–71 and 122–124.

appelle vnto you for Justice; There is other Letters sent in this Shipp which were written 3 weekes before this, wherin wee dyd by all the pouer wee haue command them to deliver our goods backe againe, to bee disposed accordinge to the order of the Company: But beinge now certified that Bryan Binkes and Petter Johnsonn are gone to Vergenia accordinge to the Companies order: Wee desire you that whatsoeuer is there left of the Companies estat, should bee theire sould and returned into England, either by Billes of Exchange or in marchantable goodes, vnto John Dye dwellinge in Fillpott Lane or vnto John Roach, Grace Hardinge, or Thomas Juppe, dwellinge in Crooked Lane; Those thinges that are there of the Companies to our knowledge are these. First there is the 6 ordnance with there Carriges 4 Ankers and Cables which stand vs heare in England in littelle lesse then   160*li*   0*s*   0*d*
There is alsoe a parsell [*torn*]izion sent by Mr. Allerton   30   0   0
A parsell of pease   13   0   0
And a parsell of broade Cloth and a Coate and list   5   10   0
And a parsell of plate waire of Thomas Juppes owne perticu-
ler adventure   11   16   8
And a parsell of Master Hardings goods   16   0   0
There was a parsell of the Companies goods ventured by one
Muzze   10   0   0

There is much other goods there of the Companies, which wee cannot give you notice of. Wee desire you to call John Smith to account by his owne letter hee hath 20*li* worth of the Companies estat, which although wee desire not that it should be presently taken from him, Because wee pitty his poore estate, yet wee leaue it vnto your wise Consideration to order or to dispose towarde the payment of Master Batchellor if you see fitt, vnto whome wee doe ough 60*li*, it was sumthinge more, but the rest we haue layd out for him in his frayt, to the vallewe of 7*li*: wee therefore desire that hee should bee payde 60*li*: There is goods allsoe to the vallewe of 40*li* as wee are informed that Mr. Dummer hath taken from Bryan Binkes and Peetter Johnsonn, ther is alsoe the ould shipp, and divers debts oughinge vs, which wee intreate you to call John Smith to account for; And forasmuch as [t]her is oughinge 200*li* by the Company in London vppon bond vppon our Securitie and is yearely a great burden vnto vs: Wee desire you therefore that our goods may not bee there retained any longer, for the debts vppon bond the Companys goods must paye, allthough wee lose all; lett them not dishoner god, and disgrace Religion; Heare hath binn a greate deale of Complainte, and much eivell sirmizinge of the dealeinge of our Brethren departed to Vergenia: but we wish we may haue noe worse from thence: Wee haue faire account, and good reason for what they did, And for profitt or losse, gods will bee done. Wee hope wee shall find that that part of our estate carried away to Vegenia shalbee as well improued for all the Company, according to that proporsion, as they will improue ther owne in new England that doe soe surmize of there Brethren: Time will try all things.

Wee desire you farther to take Notis that when Master Batchellor dubled his adventure, and made his adventure vpp 100*li* it was vppon condition, that wee and Master Dummer should doe soe likewise. Wee at London did duble our adventures, and wee received alsoe 40*li* of Master Dummer, for his duble adventure: Yet after some farther consideration Mr. Dummer sent his mony into the hands of a freind, that would not deliver it vs without bond to paye it againe. Now Mr. Dummer promiseinge as well as wee to duble his adventure, and to bare a part of losse if it soe fell out, as this inclosed letter will testifie beinge the letter of his owne hand sent with the mony: wee desire to referr our selves vnto you, there to judge what is fitt for him to haue: If to venture it as wee are constrained to doe, then at the end of the termes of yeares, wee shalbe countable; At the least we think he should bare a part of losse as well as wee: This hopeinge that out of your pious mind and [*torn*] are to execute Justes betwene vs, you wilbee pleased to take this paynes fo[r] vs, to put an end vnto these Controversies there, which is a greater greife vnto vs then all those other Croses that hath befallen vs; There was in all 14C*li* in jointe stoke. Of this but the vallewe of 250*li* caried to Vergenia, according to your praiseinge when you payde Carman. Wee leaue all to your Christian wisdome; the Lord direct you and soe wee rest Your Christian Frends for ourselues and the rest of the Companie of Husbandmen

JOHN ROBINSON	JOH: ROCH
SAMEL BINCKES	GRACE HARDWIN
ROGER BINCKES	THO: JUPPE
NATHANIELL WHETHAM	JO: CRISPE
HENERY FOWKES	JOHN DYE
BRIAN KIPLING	

[*Endorsed by Governor Winthrop:*] Plough Comp: [*and in another place:*] The Comp: of Husb[an]dmen [*and again:*] Roch, Hardwin etc.

JOHN HUMFREY TO JOHN WINTHROP, JR.[1]

To his worthyly respected mr. Jo: Winthrop iunior

DEARE AND DESIRED SIR, I cannot but write though I can but barely tell you I am thankefull for you and trulie yours   newes of all occurrences and the sad turning of thinges I know you have from abler handes. In a word I beeseech you pardon and accept my unfaigned affection in this hastie salute, you have my hart to which I set my hand   Your lovingly obliged

JO: HUMFREY

LOND: Dec: 3, 1632

In consideration of my short letter I hope my brother Gunner hath paide you with 2 long.

[*Endorsed by John Winthrop, Jr.:*] Mr. humfries recd. feb. 23.

FRANCIS KIRBY TO JOHN WINTHROP, JR.[2]

To his good frend mr. Jo: Winthrop iunior this deliver

LONDON this 3 of 10ber 1632

KIND SIR, Yours of the 19th 7ber per mr. Fogge I received wherby I vnderstand of Mr. Peirce his arivall (deo gratias). as for the returne of that comodity per Mr. Peirce we do not expecte it so sodenly, sat cito si sat bene, and whether the profit shall be more or lesse it shall giue content to the new marchants, when it cometh; the successe wherof we must commit to the providence of the almighty. your inclosed I delivered to mr. Chambers, also those into flitstreet. I haue written you more at large per mr. Hatherly who is[3] now redy to go to Grauesend. With this I enclose the Catalogue of the last vernall mart, the last Autumnall is not yet to be had. Thus with mine my wiues my bro[ther] and sister Hills harty salutations to yours I rest in hast Yours

FR: KIRBY

[*Endorsed by John Winthrop, Jr.:*] Mr. Kirby recd. Feb. 23.

---

[1] W. 1. 98; 3 *Collections*, IX. 252.
[2] W. 1. 98; 3 *Collections*, IX. 251–252.
[3] The word in the original manuscript is "his."

JAMES HOPKINS TO JOHN WINTHROP[1]

To the right wor[ship]full Mr. John Winthrope the worthie and carefull Governour
of the Colonie in New England giue this

WORTHIE AND WORSHIPFULL SIR, it [torn] my soule much to heare of your
worthie carriage [torn] your government. I like it as well, that the wicked
speake euill of you, [torn] the good commend you; the differinge reportes
agree to set foorth your praise. The magistrate beinge the minister of god for
the vpholdinge of the good, and punishinge and suppression of the badd, if he
doe his office well, must needes haue wicked mens mouthes open against him,
as good ones will speake for him. Blessed be god whoe hath called you to the
worke, and assisted you in it; he guide you still, and as he promised to be with
Joshua, as he had bene with Moses, not failinge nor forsakeinge him, even
soe I hope (and shall earnestly desire it) he will be with you, and carrie you
through your worke; only (as was sayd to him) be stronge and verie couragious, be not afraid nor dismayed, but obserue to doe accordinge to gods lawe,
turne not to the right hand or to the lefte, that soe you may prosper. Weake
wicked men wearie of your plantation, send Achans packinge, for they will
hinder you in your prosperous succeedinges. Your first goeinge was hard and
fatall to many of your companie, partly through wante of experience, not
knowinge how to furnish your selues for such a voyage; but god surely had an
ouerrulinge hand, by hard beginninges teacheth people to cleue the closser
vnto him, to seeke the more earnestly to him, and to know, that they can doe
nothinge but by his helpe. But now god goeth alonge most favourably with
them that haue followed you; as if he should say, I did but trie your mettall
how your faith would beare a discouragement, and now I see you clinge to me,
and are carefull to walke with me in courses pleasinge to me, I will magnifie
your plantation, and doe you good. This I hope god intendeth, for out of hard
beginninges haue come greate matters; the famous kingdomes of Judah and
Israell came of a Syrian readie to perish, forced downe into Egipt to soiourne,
kept vnder 40 yeares in the wildernes etc. All plantations were meane at the
first, yet by continuance of time, the world is peopled by that meanes, and
when thinges are come to some perfection, it delighteth people to looke backe
to their founders, and they glorie in their worthie interprises. Some are famous
for discoueries, some for plan[ta]tions, others come into their labours and
grow great, yet he that brake the yce neuer wantes his honour; soe shall it be

---

[1] Miscellaneous MSS., Bound, M.H.S. The Reverend James Hopkins, B.A., Peterhouse, Cambridge, 1600/01, M.A. 1604, was Vicar of Great Wenham, Suffolk.

with you, whoe could neuer haue advanced your name by any worthy actions, as you are like to doe by this; whose honour shall not be like that of heathens [and pa]pistes whoe haue taken great paines to fill the [   ] with sup[erstiti]on and wickednes, even till they haue ouerchardged [   ] that it hath spued them out; but you shall be like Moses and Joshua not only famous for carrie-inge a people into a good land through many hard adventures, but for plant-inge of gods worshipp in an heathenish place, wherby such a blessinge came vpon the verie land, that it was made the fertilest land vpon earth, though naturally montanus and rockie. I hope you shall carrie a blessinge to your land, and the naturall inhabitants of it, which shall be your honour. If you can first civill the natiues, and then bringe some of them to know god, if you prepare a place of refuge for gods banished ones, you shall haue cause to reioyce that euer god honoured you with this interprise; and this I hope you shall. I promise my selfe much of this plantation, for I can not thinke, but god will honour them, that are soe carefull to honour him. Israell euer flourished whilst gods pure worshipp was vpheld amonge them; That plantation must needs prosper, where god (as I may say) hath an adventure. You haue the countenance and protection of our kinge, as you are his subiects, and goe forth by his license, and shall the kinge of heaven denie his protection vnto you, whoe are his servantes, and haue vndertaken this voiage (as we hope) by his license, and for the inlargeinge of his kingdome? Doubtles (as Azariah sayd to Asa) god is with you while you be with him; therfore I shall desire the Lord to blesse your noble interprizes, and to giue you a large vnderstandinge heart, to goe out and in before the people which daily thrust themselues vnder your winge, that all enemies that desire to speake evill of you, may be ashamed, when your vpright carriage shall be able to giue them the lie. Sir I am so well affected to your plantation, that if I can not enioyce my libertie upon gods tearmes as I haue done, I haue a purpose to make my selfe a member of your plantation, and when I come, I hope I shall not come alone; I pray god direct vs, that we may doe that which shall be pleasinge in his sight, that we may haue him come alonge with vs, as he hath done mercifull by others in that kind. But if our peace be continued (which we desire for the good of our land) the[n] we hold our selues tied heere, and dare not breake loose till god sett vs loose. Thus I have made bould (worthie Sir) to testifie my loue and respect to you, acknowledgeinge my selfe much beholdinge to you for your kind remembrance of me in Mr. Wilsons letters. I forbeare [torn] busines and his 500li fine for [torn] church windowes, alsoe the busines of the [torn] are put in trust to buy in Impropriations, [torn] hard put at, and may be in great daunger. Alsoe [torn] of all the hither part of London bridge to the [torn] open place.

Alsoe Mr. Prinne his imprisonment [in] the tower for writinge (as is thought) a new booke. I suppose that you haue friends about London, whoe will informe you of them. Mr. Gurdon of my towne, and his wife remember their loue to you, and to Mrs. Winthropp. My selfe and wife remember our service and respect to you both alsoe. I pray god to keepe you, guide, blesse, and prosper you that you may goe out and in before the people whoe are come vnder you, soe as god may haue glorie, they benefite, and your selfe much comfort and honour, which I comfortably hope for. In much hast I take my leue of you, restinge Your worshipps wellwisher

JAMES HOPKINS

WENHAM Febr: 25, 1632[/33]

THOMAS ASHLEY TO JOHN WINTHROP[1]

To my worthy and much respected frend Mr. John Winthrope the Elder in new England whome God preserve

WORTHY SIR, if this Missive safely arryve att Winthropin itt wyll fall vpon a fortune thatt I wyll nott envye; and yett shall I have an happinesse, thatt I much desire; for then wyll ytt faithfully present yow and your selfe with myne harty Salutations. some happy occurrences have acquainted mee with your well-being, and I should rejoyce to bee certayne of your safe-being: for my feares conclude the Salvages dilligent to sute an opportunytye to their Natures. I am as sorry to heare many reportes blemyshe the hopes of your plantation, as I am pleased to bee wytnesse of severall desires to place yow att Grotton; and had I the casting vote, yow should bee there againe, without being sea-sicke; did I suppose yow would ether bee served here, or would bee served by mee, yow should have a warrant Dormant, vnder myne hand and seale to commaund mee, butt in regard thatt the first stand out of all probabyllytye, ceremonious offers shall nott crowd into this manuscript. I doubt nott, but thatt yow sing the Songes of Syon in a strange land, and thatt yow have brought forth thatt Peace yow travaild with, which I wyshe multyplyed to yow, to the height of all comforte; lett our mutuall prayers meete att the throne of grace; and so in confidence that no Gulphe shall parte vs, when wee must departe, I wyll rest, tyll my long Rest Sir Your truly loving frend

THO: ASHLEY

March the 6th 1632[/33]

---

[1] Suffolk County Court Files, No. 5.

JOHN BLUETT TO JOHN WINTHROP, JR.[1]

To the wor[shi]p[fu]ll and his reverend good friend mr. John Winthropp the younger at Boston in New England giue this

GROTON March the 14th 1632[/33]

GOOD SIR, Soe it hath pleased the Almightie to dispose of us: that both Sea and land hath separated our bodies; yet I may truly say for my parte, it shall not seuere my affections; my loue still remayneth and soe I hope shall doe soe longe as god giueth me a heart to praye: I cannot remember you, nor your worthie father my reverend good friend, without teares; yet when I heare of the good hand of God vpon you, I cannot but prayse him on your behalfe; and humbly beseech him daylie more and more to enlarge your tentes, and increase your seede: Pardon my bouldnesse in writeinge vnto you. I could doe noe lesse haueinge soe fitt a messenger; for whom I wish and desire a true convertion: I pray you remember my humble duetie and service to mr. Winthrop your father to mris. Winthrope your mother to mris. Winthrope your sister in law mris. Marie and to your loveing wife: my loue to Mr. Wilsonn and his wife, my ancient acquaintance goodman Childe and Martha Dogget the wife of goodman Firmyn. my louinge commendations to John Sampford, goodman Pease and his company and to Anne Chambers, John Biggs, my schollers Thomas French and John Clarke: I pray god blesse them all, and graunte vs all a happie meeting in heaven, in earth ther is noe hope thereof. As concerninge any thinge in our nation you may haue relation by worde of mouth, which will spare writeinge, neyther can I say any good therof, but may complayne of badd tymes, and great feare of worse. God in mercy prepare vs for tryalls what it shall please him to put vs vnto: and daylie adde vnto your comforts to the enlargement of his kingdome and glorie: Soe in all most loueinge and due respect had and remembred both on my parte and my wives vnto you all, we humbly take our leaues and commend vs all to the protection of Almightie God. Most loueinge vnto you in the Lord,

JOHN BLUETT

---

[1] W. 4. 72; 5 *Collections,* I. 199–200. John Bluett had been steward of Groton Manor.

HENRY PAYNTER TO JOHN WINTHROP, JR.[1]

To my deere and most respected Sonne Mr. John Winthrop at Boston in Newe England

DEERLY RESPECTED, AND MY LOVING SONNE WINTHROP, We receaued from London a letter from my worthy Sister your mother that came well to our hands, and another from your kinde selfe which was soe washed and the writing scoured oute that the greatest parte of it was soe white and cleane with the salte water (as I suppose) where the lynes had bene, as if it had not bene written vpon: but that some few lynes and endes of lines and words in some places appeared whereby we perceiued in parte that you wrote of your good health and your well beinge. It seemeth to come in that ship which was cast away (as we heare) and to beare date in October.[2] Neither I nor my wife had time at present to write vnto you and your good mother and our beloued daughters as we desire but I hope shall shortely performe it. We are full of ioy to heare of your health and the goodnes of the Lord our gracious God towards you all, and the good successe of that hopefull plantation. I desire you to take notice of Mr. Cogan and Mr. Hill and Mr. Pinny our pious and louing neighbors and good friends that now come vnto you, and to shew them loue for our sakes. they haue bene kinde vnto vs, and they are worthy of respecte and welcome for theire religion and other good partes and abilityes, whereby you will find them I doubt not very industrious and profitable members of the plantation.

In my letter to your honoured Father is inclosed one from a godly gentlewoman and a deere frinde of my wifes, concerning some goods of Captaine Levet her deceased husband due vnto her and her children. And boath my selfe and my wife doe earnestely intreate you to put him in minde therof in meete oportunityes solliciting him to call for Captayne Endicotte and Mr. Conant to examine them aboute it and to doe for her what he can to helpe her to her right. I doubte not but you may alsoe doe her good and further this busines; If you shall write vnto vs what is done herein we shall be very thankefull vnto you. The sooner it is gone aboute the more hope of findinge it out.

This letter commeth vnto you by James Woodyeates and his Wife who boath were sometime our seruantes. Elizabeth Webbe knoweth them well. they can informe you of our affayres. Sam: Fones and John Sherman are like

---

[1] W. 4. 46; 5 *Collections*, I. 117–118.
[2] For the shipwreck of Peirce's ship, in which Winthrop's letter to Paynter was dispatched, see *Journal*, I. 100.

to proue good schollers etc. You shall heare from us more hereafter God willinge. How glad should we be to see each others face once agayne in this life, if it might be the will of God. Pray for us, as we doe for you publikely and priuately. Remember our seruice to my worthy sister, and our dearest loue to my good daughters, your beloued and her sister Feake. litle know you how much your and theire louing lines doe glad the heartes of vs boath which are intirely affected towards you all. The Lord our God keepe your heartes vnto himselfe and prosper you, as your soules prosper, and grante you peace all the dayes of your life: and cease not to pray for Your louing father

                                                        HENRY PAYNTER

EXON. March 14, 1632[/33]

[*Endorsed by John Winthrop, Jr.:*] Father Painter July 27 per Waimouth ship.

EDWARD HOWES TO JOHN WINTHROP, JR.[1]

WORTHY SIR, Your lettres by mr. Allerton and mr. Pierse I receiued; as for the Cement I knowe none as yet worth sending the receipt vnto you. the lettre I receiued by mr. Pierse was so rinsed with sea water I had much adoe to reed it; I thanke you hartilie for them; and that in the midest of your greate ymployments you willbe pleased to remember your poore and vnworthie frind. Sir I am glad and exceedingly reioyce at your prosperitie, and the prosperitie of the whole Collonie, and that it hath pleased god (to shewe his pouer and mercie vpon you all, in a wonderfull manner, beyond the expectation of the great ons of this land) in deliueringe you not from a Spanish pouder plott, nor an accounted invincible Armado; but from a Spanish like French Infection,[2] which was like to haue tainted the haylest and best man amongst you yea all of you, as may appeare by the writtings and lettres written with myne owne hand, and sent to your father my honored frind; In briefe I hope herein the Diuell hath vented all or most of his mallice against your state; Oh the goodnes of our Lord god that hath wrought such

---

[1] W. 1. 98; 3 *Collections*, IX. 252–257.

[2] In the margin: "Are those infectors like to escape the like shame and punishment. noe we hope to pendere Gardiner ere longe etc. vide, tace." Sir Christopher Gardiner, together with Thomas Morton and Philip Ratcliffe, "set on," as Governor Winthrop said, by Sir Ferdinando Gorges, had, on December 19, 1632, petitioned the Privy Council against the Massachusetts Bay Company. An adverse report on the petition was rendered by a committee of the Council on January 19, 1632/33. Charles M. Andrews, *The Colonial Period in American History*, 1 (New Haven, 1934), 408–410. See also *Journal*, I. 101.

goodnes as you shall enioye, out of soe apparent evills as you had like to haue felt; but I leaue to comment vpon this subiect (though I could a longe tyme) leaueinge it for you whoe I knowe will not spare whole dayes and nights to meditate thereof. Sir I am the more sensible hereof, in regard I was a daylie and houerly auditor and spectation of all the passages, which hath caused me to take it into consideration; that your plantation hath need of some hartie and able frinds to back you vpon all occasions, which must remaine here; and haue frinds at Courte;[1] I though not soe able as I could wish (if God sawe it good) yet as hartie as the best, consideringe mr. Humfries preparation for departure, and my masters desire and resolution to be with you, haue betaken my selfe now at last to the studie of the Lawes, and to that purpose haue admitted myselfe as a studient of Cliffords Inn by St. Dunstans Church in fleete streete, and am about to purchase a chamber there; not that I meane absolutely or presently to leaue my m[aste]r but to enable my selfe to liue when he is gone, and to retire my selfe in the vacation tyme to my studie which shall euer tend to the vtmost of my poore abillitie to the good and welfare of your plantation and state.

I haue since heard, that some of your noble and best frinds desire, that you might haue a Councell here estab[l]ished of some choyce frinds; to stand and answere for you vpon all occasions It becomes you nowe to knowe your selues to be statesmen; and to studie state pollicie, which constists principally in *Prevention* of euills and inconveniencies; if it please you to peruse any bookes of that subiect, I shall endevour to fitt your turne; and send them by the next ship.[2]

I haue heard by mr. higinbothom and others that your ministers preach one against anothers doctrine; which I conceiue to be a great scandall to your societies, and if not reformed in tyme, may proue as fatall as the Congregations of Ainsworth and Johnson,[3] which in theire owne dayes begann, flourisht, and came to nothinge; but I am perswaded better things of you; and hope your differences are but ceremoniall matters; I beseich you sir to excuse me if out of the aboundance of my hartie affections for your welfares, I transgresse the bounds of ordinary matter. You knowe God is a Jealous God; and desires integritie of harte; he is a spirit, and wilbe worshipt in spirit and

---

[1] In the margin: "You had bin vtterly ouerthrown had not god, as it were wrought a miraculous deliuerance; for it is in diuerse mouths that you are, and your plantation and planters hath often lately bin preached against at Pauls Crosse etc. vide, tace."

[2] In the margin: "God giues vs the meanes to worke by; if we reiect the meanes, we reiect the good will of God Etc."

[3] Henry Ainsworth, teacher, and Francis Johnson, minister of the English Separatist church at Amsterdam.

truth; I would have you feare nothinge more then securitie, and carnall confidence; I meane the most parte of you.

I haue heard of many of your collony, that saye with the Pharasie *Stana further off I am more holy then thou*; Gardiners relation hath too much, but not all that I haue heard, they cannot be content to talke largely, but write[1] to their vtter Ruine (if they take not heed) for tyme to come, for let them be assured, theire letters will come to light that write against our state ciuill or ecclesiasticall, and the Starchamber hath punishments for such lybellers, and a longe arme to reach them, and god will not defend them that resist the higher powers;[2] Sir I verilie perswade my selfe you haue many of weake Judgments amongst you, on whome it were good your ministers took a little paines, that they might be rectified; I sawe lately a sentence of your owne writinge vizt *Canis dum captat* etc.[3] which may not vnfitly be applyed to them, whoe medlinge with shadowes to them, other mens matters; nay state matters; loose theire substances; and sometymes drowne themselues irrecouerablie; As the Dog did; I haue not heard from Mr. Eustace[4] the Germaine since he went hence. I feare much he is slayne in the last great Battell with the King of Sweden. I shewed him many kindnesses to win him to retorne but he said he would not retorne except he sawe a letter from the Gouernors owne hand, with promise of increase of his wages; I haue sent Mr. Samford the Instrument and sight ruler the Germaine bespoke for him; together with a booke to teach the vse thereof, namely Smyths Arte of Gunnery   at folio 58[5] there the same Instrument is to be seene; I haue likewise sent him Nortons Practise of Artillerie[6] chosen by the german for him; and alsoe diuerse platformes of the latest invented forts and fortifications; for new bookes I writt to you of Dr. fludds works and sent you a cattalogue of them by Mr. Hetherley; there is a booke lately come out of mathematicall conclusion and recreations[7] which I bought purposely for you but mr. Saltonstall hath borrowed it, and is now at mr. Gurdons to marrie mrs. Merriall;[8] albeit I haue sent you two

---

[1] In the margin: "a letter hath bin seene from one of your planters, whoe tearmeth England to be babell and Sodome, and that it should shortly fall, etc. I am promised coppies of 2 or 3 of such lettres; which I intend to send you that you may belieue it; and inflict some punishment on the offenders, that others may beware."

[2] In the margin: "Exempli gratia Rochell. vide, tace."

[3] In the margin: "fabula at vera."   [4] See above, page 87, *n*. 2.

[5] Sir John Smith (Smythe) published two books: *Certain Discourses Concerning Divers Sorts of Weapons* (London, 1590) and *Instructions, Observations, and Orders Militarie* (London, 1595).

[6] Robert Norton, *The Gunner, Shewing the Whole Practise of Artillerie* (London, 1628).

[7] *Mathematicall Recreations*, entered in the Stationers' Register November 14, 1632.

[8] Richard Saltonstall and Muriel Gurdon, daughter of Brampton and Muriel (Sedley) Gurdon, were not actually married until June, 1633. *Ancestry and Descendants of Sir Richard Saltonstall* ([Boston], 1907), 12.

other bookes vizt. Malthus Fireworks,[1] and the Horizantall Quadrant[2] full of new devices; which I present to your kind acceptance; and because I knowe you are tam Marte quam Mercurio; I haue sent you a short weapon you make call it an Irish Skeyne or knife or what you will; together with a small sawe and steele hammer, and a bodkyn and a forke all in one Case.[3] the vsefull applycation of each I leaue to your discretion.

Mr. Arkisden is at Mr. Gurdons   he presents his seruice to you but hath written soe lately to you and being constrained to be very studious at this tyme he desires excuse; yet I haue made bold to send you here inclosed his last letter written to me that you may perceiue he is both well and thriues in his studies etc.

We keepe the strictest Lent that euer was; we haue not one bitt of flesh in the house as your cosen Mary Dow[ning] can informe you. I thought good to advertise you of a discourse I lately heard, that the Leprosie is caused by eating too much fish; for in Scotland where they eate much fish there is more Leapers then in all Europ besides; as it is said.

We haue a Mountebank does strainge feates and cures here openly on Tower hill vpon a stage, and in Comon Garden, and in St. Bartholmews   I bought x*s* worth of his stuffs for the m[aste]r of the wards; and alsoe a paper or two more for your good father vizt his antidotes against poyson etc. which you shall receiue of your cosen Mary.[4] I pray present them vnto him as a small testimonie of my humble seruice and willing mind to appeare before him in a greater good; as god shall fitt and enable me   Remember my humble seruice likewise to Mrs. Winthrop your good mother; Mr. Audley of the Courte of Wards desired me to remember him to Mr. Gouernor Winthrop and often asketh me howe he doth; I should be glad to bringe the old Batchelor to bestowe 1000*li* or 2 on your plantation for he can very well spare it; I perceiue he hath a mind to doe good, but it must be in a course wherein he may haue some certaine proffitt in recompence of his costs; Mr. Fabian Mr. Paise and Mr. Windouer, alsoe desire to be remembred and aske me often howe your father and his companie thriues; generally all that knowes him wishes him well; and the most prophanest that I heare speake of

---

[1] Francis Malthus, *A Treatise of Artificial Fire-Works* (London, 1629).

[2] Richard Delamaine, Sr., *The Making, Description, and Use of a Small Portable Instrument Called a Horizontall Quadrant* (London, 1631).

[3] In the margin: "they are bound vp with halfe a dozen kniues for mr. Samford, in Mrs. Maries chest."

[4] In the margin: "there is a paper about euery one to shew the vse of them."

him, doe but pittie him; for selling soe good an estate here; for want and penurie in N:E:[1]

It is the opinion of all straingers that knowe you not that the most of you are starued, and the rest are cominge home againe;

I haue my mothers good will nowe to goe ouer when I will;[2] My father and she and my sisters desires to haue theire kindest Loues remembred vnto you and to your good wife and sister Feaks soe doth the scribe, as alsoe to your sister Dudley and her husband your two Brothers and mr. James Dow[ning] and all other my louinge Frinds   I committ you to the Lord almighties tuition and rest Yours euer assured

EDWARD HOWES

18º Martij 1632[/33]

I conceiue you were best to direct your lettres for me to my masters or at my fathers house neere Lincolnes Inne in Chauncery laine; for my m[aste]r is about to remoue his dwellinge very shortly into the strand neere the m[aste]r of the wards.

Vale in Christo, Vide et Tace.

EDWARD HOWES TO JOHN WINTHROP, JR.[3]

To my approued louinge frind mr. John Winthrop the yonger at Boston
these deliver in Mattachusets Bay

LONDON March 25, 1633 post horam 10am noctis

SIR, Although I haue bin very large in my lettres dated the 18th of this instant, yet can I not chuse but let loue breake forth a little more, euen nowe when the ship is vnder sayle. Yours of the 29th of September I received per mr. Allerton and thother of the 24 of October 1632 I received per mr. Peirse. Your Cosen Mary[4] sent away her Trunke a fortnight agone, to the Shipp without my knowledge, soe that I am much straightned for place to stowe the things I intended to haue sent ouer; I lent her my Sea Chest to put her other things in, but can hardly haue roome to putt in my lettres. the Chest I desire mr. Samford may keepe for me vntill I come ouer   There are honest men about to buye out the Bristoll mens plantation in Pascataque, and doe purpose

---

[1] In the margin: "none wishes him euill, but all well."
[2] In the margin: "it was since my admittance."
[3] W. 1. 99; 3 *Collections*, IX. 257–258.
[4] Mary, daughter of Emmanuel Downing.

to plant there 500 good people before michelmas next. C[aptain] Wiggin is the cheife Agent therein[1] There was presented to the Lords lately, about 22 of C[aptain] Indicutts lawes;

You haue bin at the Ile of Rue, and at Rochell, a poore people that lye nowe in the dust, had they bin aliue nowe, theire harts would haue leapt within them to see howe theire kinge fauours the Protestants. Faelix quem faciunt aliena pericula etc.

Ad Populum. God is the God of loue, and loue is patient, be not too hastie, a slowe pace goes farre; I could wish my selfe with you but for ½ an hower, to expresse my mind, my feare I meane, but the only wise God I hartily and humblie beseich, make you wise in all things, that you may ioy the heart of your euer vowed

E.H.

I haue sent you a booke of the Lawes established for Virginia[2] (by your cosen Mary) I pray you present it to the view and pervsall of my most honored frind your noble father, together with my humble seruice to him and your good mother.

Sir I pray present my louing respects to my reuerend and worthy frinds mr. Wilson and Mr. Weldd And excuse me to your sister Feakes my louing frind that I writt not vnto her; I pray thanke her for the lettres she sent me dated the 4 of July 1632 I had not a lettre by mr. Pierse from any one but from you and that hardly to be read; I pray send me a description of the Discouery of Patowneck if you haue it and what other nouelties you shall thinke fitt.

Mr. Rich: Saltonstall is retorned vnmarried. I saw him by chance last night at Sir Richards. Vale in Christo.

E.H.

26 Martij 1633

[*Endorsed by John Winthrop, Jr.:*] Mr. Howes per mr. Rose June 1633.

---

[1] Lord Say and Sele and Lord Brooke bought out the Bristol men's share, designating as their agent Thomas Wiggin, who had previously been at the settlement as the agent of a group of Shrewsbury investors. Thomas Hutchinson, *The History of the Colony and Province of Massachusetts-Bay*, Lawrence S. Mayo, Editor (Cambridge, 1936), II. 92.

[2] Since no printed edition of the Virginia laws appeared between *For the Colony in Virginea Britannia. Lawes Diuine, Morall and Martiall* (London, 1612) and *The Lawes of Virginia Now in Force* (London, 1662), it is likely that Howes's "booke" was a manuscript copy of the revision of the laws adopted by the General Assembly in September, 1632.

FRANCIS KIRBY TO JOHN WINTHROP, JR.[1]

*To his very lovinge and much respected frend mr. John Winthrop iunior
this deliver at Boston in New England*

Laus deo in LONDON 26º Martij 1633

MOST LO[UING] FREND, Yours of the 24 Octob: per mr. Peirce I receiued
but it hauinge suffered shipwrack on the Coast of Virginia it was hardly
legible. I am very glad to hear of your welfare with the recouery of your
second selfe from her late sharp fit of sicknes. I vnderstand how you haue dealt
with mr. Pinchen for the Cloth which bargain is not amisse, but may produce
reasonable profit if he deall well with you in the Condicion of the beauer that
he shall deliver to you, which you shall easily discerne if you remember my
instructions in those letters to you per mr. Peirce. for the shooes your father
wrote to my brother Downeinge that they ar most of them Calues lether, sure
I am that I paid for neats leather and they were waranted to mee for such
and still he doth stand to Justifie the same still and saith if I can procure a
certificate vnder the hands of mr. Cottington and mr. Nowell that they were
not all neats lether I shall haue recompence to my Content, therfore I pray
let them be veiwed by some that haue skill. his name of whom I bought them
is mr. Jo: Rodson in Gracechurch street. I hope ere this time you receiud the
2 great glasses per Mr. Hatherly in the William who went hence in Decemb:
I receiud the 4*li* 12*s* of Ed: Howes, also now 5*li* of mr. Gosslyn   I receiud
none of my bro[ther] Downeinge for you, neither had I any occasion for it
seinge I can not find all the things you wrote for. sope ashes ar not to be had
for ther ar none come of late yeares out of the east, they beinge now out of vse
with the sope-boylers who vse only potashes. I haue sent in a paper a little
potashes for a paterne. for old musket barrels I can find none that will be
sold by waight vnles it be some very smal and short peeces and of that ther is
no quantity to be had for other that ar past vse they peece them vp againe
and make them saleable and will not sell them by waight.

I haue enquired concerninge ruffe barils vnbored. musket bore ruffe vnbored may be had for 8*s* per barill 4 foot longe of 2 inche bore 4 foot longe
ruffe and vnbored 16*s* or thereabout   I perceiue it is not vsuall with them to
forge any so big which causeth to aske so dear, for they muste make or alter
some tooles for the purpose and so must be paid extraordinary vnles they
make a great many; I pray if you send for any write me iustly what lenght

---

[1] W. I. 100; 3 *Collections*, IX. 258–260.

and in euery respect your mind very playne, least I do you a displeasure against my will. I pray excuse me if I haue mistaken any things in this your comission for the incke is washed of in many places of your letter, so that I do but guesse at your meaninge, and if I haue erred in buyinge what you intended not it is *error amoris, non amor erroris.* I hear ther is one at Wappinge that can forge barils of 2 inch bore but I haue not yet spoken with him; and he forgeth small ordnance. I haue sent you heer inclosed the Catalogue of the Autumnall mart 1632. all the former I haue sent before. I haue no newes to write you. ther hath not been any great exploits done in Germany since the death of the Kinge of Sweden. how it fareth with our republique and of the occurrents in Court and Contry is safer to be related by those that come to you then to be committed to paper. your frends heer who ar members of your plantacion haue had much to do to answer the vniust complaints made to the Kinge and counsell of your gouernment there. I vnderstand that you ar an assistant and so haue a voice in the weighty affaires of that Comonwealth. I know I shall not need to aduise you that the prayeinge for our kinge be not neglected in any of your publique meetings, and I desire that you differ no more from vs in Church gouernment, then you shall find that we differ from the prescript rule of gods word, and further I meddle not. I haue sent you (in this ship wherin my cosen Ma[ry] Downeinge and Su[san] and mr. Codington ar) all the things you wrote for except old musket barils and sope ashes, if I be not mistaken in readinge your letter. the particulars you shall find on the other page. they ar packed with other goods which I bought for your father at my bro[ther] Downeings instance, in one great long Chist and one little barrill   also ther ar directed to your father 2 tronkes and a little trusse which my Cosen Mary Downeinge knoweth how to dispose of. mr peirce will be redy about the last of may, as I suppose per whom I entend to write although I haue no buisines more then si vales bene valeo. I desire to be remembred to your second selfe, your father, mother, brethren and sister, also to Mrs. Feake and thus for this present I commit you to the almighty his protection and shall euer rest your assured lo[ving] frend

FRA: KIRBY

	li	s	d
Sandiuer 2 li. and Soda 8 li.	0	5	6
stone blewinge 14 li.	0	10	0
brimstone 1 C waight	1	3	4

	li	s	d
Copper ¼ C	1	10	4
Tin ¼ C	1	8	0
Canarie seeds 3 pintes	0	0	9
	4	17	11

paid before for the glasses and the Charge of packing them
and for 3 Catalogues of bookes

	li	s	d
	1	18	5
	6	16	4

receiud in all	9	12	0
paid in all	6	16	4
I rest indebted to you	2	15	8

You shall receiue for your father in the same Chist and barrell which my bro[ther] Downeinge will put to his account 2 dosen Howes, 20 li. white Coperas, 6 shorlinge sheep skins, 30 lamb skins, 1 dosen sithes, 1 hatchell for hemp with 2 other little tooles of iron vsed about the streiteninge of the teeth when they ar bowed and driueinge them out. other tooles ar none vsed about dressinge hemp vnles some beetles of wood or such like which to send from hence wer but to Charge you with vnnecessary freight. euery Contry hous-wife can direct your Carpenter to make them.

1 hachell for flaxe with 2 brushes, 6 felling axes, 20 sutes of Canuas, 20 suites of Cotton, 10 dosen Irish stockings.

[*Endorsed by John Winthrop, Jr.:*] mr. Kerby received June per mr. Rose his ship. mony to mr. Howes. otter skinnes.

FRANCIS KIRBY TO JOHN WINTHROP, JR.[1]

To his much respected frend mr. John Winthrop iunior this deliver

March 26, 1633

MOST LO[UING] FREND, I receiued your letter (which had first been washed in the sea) per mr. Peirce whom it pleased god to preserue though with the losse of the ship and all the goods on the Coast of Virginia. I haue sent you in this ship such thinges as you wrote for packed with other goods of your fathers marked as in the margent in one great long Chist and 1 little barill, also ther ar 2 trunkes and 1 little trusse of Canuas directed to your father, of which

---

[1] W. 1. 99; 3 *Collections*, IX. 261–262.

my Cosen mary Downinge will giue further direction. I haue written you in another letter of the same date and in the same ship more at large of many particulars; what the occurrents ar heer you shall vnderstand per your frend mr. Cottington who cometh in this ship. the old musket barrils ar not to be had, neither sope ashes. I haue sent the sandiver, soda, stone blewinge, brimstone, Copper, Tin and Canary seeds. the quantity, price, and account you shall haue in my other letter of this date more at large specified. I desire to be remembred to your consors tori; and to your good father and mother and the rest, for whom as for my selfe I shall daily pray for both temporall and eternall felicity and Thus in hast I rest your ever lo[uing] frend

FRANC: KIRBY

[*Endorsed by John Winthrop, Jr.:*] mr. Kerby per mr. Rose his ship.

WILLIAM HILTON TO JOHN WINTHROP, JR.[1]

To the wor[shipfull] mr. John Winthrope the younger at aguawam giue these

PASCAQUA Aprill 18th 1633

SER, There ariued a fishing shipe at Pascataque about the 15th of this presant moneth where in is one Richard Foxwell whoe hath Formerly liued in this cuntery   he bringeth nuse that there were tow shipes making ready at Barstaple whoe are to bring passingers and catell For to plant in the bay he hath leters For mr. wearom and diuers others at Dorchester which hee intends to bring in to the bay so soone as possible he can   like wise he heard From mr. Alerton whoe was making ready at Bristoll For to come For this cuntery   other nuse he bringeth not that I can heare of onely Mr. Borowes purposeth to come For this cuntery From london   and soe desighring you to conuey thes leters in to the bay with what convenency you can desighring the lord to blesse you in your lawful designes I humbly rest Your wor[ship's] ashured to com[mand]

WILLIAM HILTON

Ser I purpose eare longe be if the lord will to see you.
The masters name of the shipe is John Corbin of Plimouth.

---

[1] W. I. 101; 3 *Collections*, IX. 232–263. Hilton, who had come to Plymouth in 1621, had moved, sometime before 1627, to Piscataqua, where his brother Edward had already settled. Savage, *Genealogical Dictionary*, II. 423.

JOHN WINTHROP TO WILLIAM BRADFORD[1]

SIR, vpon a petition exhibited by Sir Christo[pher] Gardner, Sir Ferd[i-nando] Gorges, Captaine Masson etc. against you and vs; the cause was heard before the lords of the priuie counsell, and after reported to the king.[2] The success wherof maks it euident to all, that the lord hath care of his people hear. The passages are admirable, and too long to write (I hartily wish an opportunitie to Imparte them vnto you being many sheets of paper) But the conclusion was (against all mens expectation) an order for our Incouragmente; and much blame, and disgrace vpon the Aduersaries; which calls for much thankfullnes from vs all. Which we purpose (the lord willing) to express in a day of thanks-giuing, to our mercifull God. (I doubt not but you will consider, if it be not fitt for you to Ioyne In it) who as he hath humbled vs by his late correction, so he hath lifted vs vp by an abundante reioysing, in our deliuerance out of so desperate a dan[g]er, so as that which our enemies builte their hopes vpon to ruine vs by, He hath mercifully disposed to our great aduantage, As I [s]hall further acquainte you, when occasion shall serue.

[JOHN WINTHROP]

[*Ca.* May, 1633]

WILLIAM HILTON TO JOHN WINTHROP, JR.[3]

To the wor[thy] and his much respeckted Frend mr. John Winthrop gouernor
at aguawam giue these

SER, my duty and respeckt remembred to you and to mrs. Winthrope   These are to serteyfie you that after a short yet sumthing a teadeous Jorny it pleased the lord that I ariued at my habetatyon the saterday after my departure From you   I praise the lord I am in good health with mr. Leueridge and the rest of our good Frends with vs   Ser I must remaine your debter For that kindenes I reseaued From you   I pray you remember my dutyfull respect to

---

[1] Original not located; Bradford, *History of Plymouth*, II. 142–143; *Hutchinson Papers* (1769), 52–53; (1865) I. 57–58. For Bradford, see *D.A.B.*

[2] A copy of the report of the Council is printed in Bradford, *History of Plymouth*, II. 114–145; *Hutchinson Papers* (1769), 53–54; (1865), I. 58–59. From the entry in Winthrop's Journal (I. 100–101) it appears that the news of these events reached Boston in May, 1633.

[3] W. I. 101; 2 *Proceedings*, x. 361–362.

your good Father   I am amoungst other his loue and kindnes to mee much
bound to him For his louing counsell to mee in his last letter For the which I
most humbly thanke him   Ser presuming vpon the goodnes of your loving
and kind disposison make bould to serteyfie you of that which I aprehend
may stand with the good of you and your neighbors with you seeing the extreordenary conuenience that your plantatyon hath aboue any in this land
that I haue seene For the keeping of Swine   I inquired what quantety of
swine were kept there   it was answered mee but a smaule quantety and that
it was determened that there shuld not many bee kept there intemating that
it was thought that the plumes and clames might proue a greter beenefit
which cannot bee nor any way the 100 part so benefisiall   this winter I haue
had the benefit of 10 hoges eauery hog worth 7 or 8 pounds beauer   I was
constrayned the winter was twelue moneth to Feed them all winter yet it was
with such meate as was not any way costly beeing but huskes of indean corne
now the maner of ordering them John maning is able to serteyfie you   now
For the preseruing of your Corne From them vntill you can Fense your grounds
aboute your houses you may set your corne very conuenetly on the oposit
side of the riuer and you shall Find that if you pracktis the breeding of swine
with the beenefit of the Iland you may with a smaule charge in short time
raise sum hundered of pounds yerely by them as you may gather by the pre-
portyon of my stocke in that behalfe whoe haue not any such coueinecy as
you haue   Ser I pray you pardon my bouldnes herein For my eror herein
is out of loue in that I desigre the good of you all both For speretuall and
temporall things   I knowe that mens labors cannot bee had at easie rats
vntill corne and porke with the like prouison bee plenty   if I were with you
I thinke I could answere all your obiecktyons and showe you a way that you
might keepe them at an easie rate   I am affred I haue bin teadeous vnto
you and therefore desighring the lord to blese you and yours I humbly rest
Your wor[ship's] Asurd to command

WILLIAM HILTON

[*Ca.* May 1, 1633]

    Ser mr. Leueridge desigreth to be remembred to you though vnknowne.

STEPHEN BACHILER TO JOHN WINTHROP[1]

To the Right Worship[fu]ll my very loueing Frend and our Gouernour
at his house in Bostone these

The wisedome of Gods spirit direct and guide
you in all your affaires, now and for ever. Amen.

RIGHT WORSHIP[FU]LL AND MY LOUEING FREND MR. GOUERNOUR, I haue
sent you this inclosed letter from our Company at London to that part of our
Company which was then supposed to be here, the last yere,[2] to certifye you
that the 4 hogsheds of pease (which are assigned to my brother Wilson, in
the right of the youth that is with him[3]) do no way belong to him but to me
and the rest of our Company, and to speake the truthe to me only and
properlye by reason of the Companies debt vnto me; which all that I haue
(by your favour) seazed on will not countervayle my debt by a great deale,
in case I could sell the goods presently, which I know not how long they will
lye and [torn] worse and worse before they will make any satisfaction to me.
The goods which are looked after for the boye came not in the ship, wherin
these pease came, but (as I take it) in the Whale, if any were sent. besides,
these pease comming with my goods in the William and Frauncis (the ship
wherin I came) with the 12 yards of cloth mentioned in the letter, and 200
yards of liste etc. I payde both for the Tunage of it to the ship m[aste]r, and
for the carryage of them from the ship to New Towne. the cloth also and the
liste I tooke into my keeping, and weare of it; and wraping vp the letter
amonge many others forgot to seaze vpon these pease, till within these 8 or 9
dayes reading over the letter for some other occasion, I light vpon that passage which mentioneth the pease and the clothe and liste etc. whervpon I
demanded of my wife what became of these pease mentioned? She answered,
certainely they are the pease which lye vnowned at New Towne, whervpon
I sent to compare the markes of the letter, with the markes vpon the pease
hogsheds, and found them perfectly to agree, and there vnderstood, that the
pease (for want of an owner) were by your authority committed to my
brother to be disposed of in right of his servant: and that this day (being the
3 of this 4th moneth) my brother sent me this message, that forasmuch as

---

[1] John Davis MSS., M.H.S., 1; 4 *Collections*, VII. 88–98. For a biographical sketch of Stephen
Bachiler, who was at this time minister of the church in Lynn, see 4 *Collections*, VII. 88*n*.
[2] See letter of March 8, 1631/32, from the Company of Husbandmen to members in New
England, pages 67–71, above, and also the Company's letter to Winthrop, December 1, 1632,
pages 101–103, above.
[3] John Smith, son of Francis Smith, miller. See *Records of Massachusetts*, I. 98.

these pease were assigned to him by the autho[rity] of your worship and the Court, (thoughe he sawe the contents of this letter the last weeke) he would sell them, and stand answerable for the monny that they yelde. My request therefore is vnto you, that forasmuch as the pease do cleerely appeare to be no goods of the boyes, but to belonge to our Company: and that I lay claime to them (as to the rest) not in respect of my adventure, but for the debt of (neere) an hundred pownds which I lent the Company in as good gould as can be waighd with scales, and that I haue payde both for the Tunage and portage of them: and only thoroughe forgetfullnes lefte them thus longe, and diverse other circemstances of reason which I forbeare for tediousnes to vrge— that you would be pleased to prevent the withhoulding of them from the right owners, at least to stay the sale of them, forasmuch as I haue disposed part of them, and the residue are exceedingly wanting in myne owne congre- gation: who vpon the vnderstanding of the busynes thus comming to light haue ben earnest with me for them: and I accordingly haue graunted their requests. There being equity in all that I require (as I trust will appeare vnto you vpon the sight of that passage in the letter) I trust I shall not doubt of your vprightnes towards me, and betweene my brother and me: whose care for his servant I do much approue, tho I cannot see the meanes which he vseth to recouer his servants doubtfull goods, to be so right as I could wish. for my parte, were it my case as it is his, I should easyly yeld vpon the sight of such evidence as I conceave doth appeare, that the goods can no way be- long to him. one thing more, wheras I vnderstand, that you put the last day of this weeke apart, for enquire of God to discover a great and difficult secret, we will by Gods grace assist you vpon that day in like manner. And thus with my loue service and Christian respect vnto you (with myne and my wiues harty Salutations to your blessed and beloued yokefellowe) I cease any further to trouble you; and rest, at your Service and commandment, in Christ his moste vnworthy servant

STEPHEN BACHILER

[June 3, 1633]

Sir, I vnderstand since the writing of my letter, that it is conceaued that the goods of the boye came wholly or in parte to me, which if it may but probably appeare I will make 7 fould Satisfaction. Verely it is not so, nether did I (but my wife) meddle with my owne goods, and my wife sayth (from Mrs. Smyth of Watertowne) that the boyes father and an vncle of his or some such frend did adventure 10*li* into [the] Company with the boy. so that I cannot conceaue how any such goods should be ex[*torn*]d, but for my parte I

HENRY JACIE TO JOHN WINTHROP, JR.[1]

To the Right Wor[shipfu]ll his much respected good friend, Mr. John Winthrop junr.
Esq. son to the Right Worthy Governour of New England these

The Lord make his face shine upon you and be gracious to you,
and to the whole Plantation, and grant you Peace in Christ Jesus

KIND SIR, I received your loving letter bearing date Jul. 4. (1632) by
g[oodman] Bruise of Boxford, (who came safely from your coasts to ours he
s[aid] in 3 weeks and 3 dayes.) I humbly thank you for your so large Relations
of your affaires therin. Wheras both you and that Right Worthy Governour
had wished my furtherance to boyes and yong maids of good towardnes, for
your service, I haue enquired, and found out some few. But they desiring
some knowledge of the maintenance, and good conveyance, etc. I spake to
Mr. Gosling, who could say nothing in it, but would enquire of Mr. Downing,
and afterward he said Mr. Downing would undertake for no more but a boy
and a maid or 2 for Mr. Governour, but no more. I pray you therfore Good
Sir write over to either of them that there may be good Satisfaction in these
following particulars, and I shal not be wanting in endeavours for your best
furtherance. Vizt. What shal be the most of their employment there, whether
dayrie, washing, etc. and what should be the Wages, and for how many yeers
tyed, whether apparel found, who should provide for theire shipping over,
their iourney thither, their diet while they stay for the wind or ships setting
forth, and provision in the ship besides ship diet, (for tis said that must be,
or it wil go very ill with them.)

   She that was Mary Bird, of late the wife of g[ood]m[an] Bigsby of Hadleigh, now a good widow being poor (whom Mr. Governour knows) desires
if she could to come to you hers[elf] and she would gladly have her 2 daughters, the one about 16 y[ears] old, wel desposd, I hear, the other yonger, to
serve M[istre]s Winthrop the Elder, or you. so a maid or 2 about Ass[ingt]on,
and some others. Goodman Choat with his wife, and good[man] Boohan
(such a name) an honest simple poor man a lock smith of Sudbury, and
G[oodma]n Bacon, with his good wife of Boxford (having divers yong children) desire to have their service humbly rem[em]bered to Mr. Governour
and desire his kind rem[em]brance of them to pity their poor Condition here,
and when he can, to send for them, as it pleased him to say he would. They
ar fild with the contempt of the proud, and their spirits ar ready to sink and
faile in them.

---

[1] W. 1. 102; 3 *Collections*, 1. 242–246.

I send you herewith a note of the judgement of a Goldsmith in Norwich my good friend concerning that litle thick peece which is in it, and another lesse peece, which he returned to me (I having had them of one that had them from New England and thought them better mettle then he judges) with other glassie peeces of that which he counts to be of the same mettle, wherby you may better judge of the same ure if you see the like, and not count it better then it is.

I have now received another letter from you. I thank you kindly for it. in it you mention your readines to have observed that ecclipse that I (with Mr. Milburne) writ about, but the cloudines hindered. But you have writ the Calculation of another, about which as soon as I can I shal send to the said Mr. Milborne, that you may have his calcula[tion] also and judgement of the same. I was gone down to Yorkshire when your last letter came to Suffolk, being writ to and desired to come to a place there about 9 miles SSE from York. its called Aughton, wher a Godly Minister was lately for about 12 or 14 yeers. and I conceive as my Chri[sti]an friends do also that God hath cald me to go thither, where now I am, but not certaine how long I shal have freedome to be here. Armen[ian]ism doth much spread, esp[ecial]ly in York. (B[ishop] Neal is now their Arch B[ishop]) and Dr. Cousins Deane. Commaund is given in York, tis said from the K[ing]s Ma[jes]tie that the Chancels be kept neat and comly, ergo the Seats to be removed thence into the body of the Church, (as its enjoined at Hull and Beverley by Dr. Cousins). Much renueing old Customs, setting Tables Altarwise, Genuflexiones ad nom[en] Jesus, solemme processions (as tis cald) observing wedn[esday] and fryday prayers, and other such th[ing]s that ar counted most for order and decency, and keeping unity in Confirmity in al such th[ing]s in the Church. Popery much encreaseth: in many places in Yorkshire ar swarms of p[a]p[ist]s. in Durham County and Northumberland many ar known to go as openly to a masse, (where such and such ar fam'd to be priests) as others to a sermon. Many p[a]p[ist]s grow very insolent to boast over protestants therabouts. O pray for us, that God would root out all Idolatry and superstition and every plant that he hath not planted, and that he would uphold his Gospel in the power and purity of it, notwithstanding our sins, as he yet doth in divers places. I often think I shal yet see you againe before I dy. the L[ord] direct. Our King in his progresse toward Scotland to be crownd there (and establish conform[ity] tis said in a Parli[ament]) came safely to York on fryday May 24. He is exceeding greatly commended and extolled for his Courtisie and affablenes, and his Piety. it was a very rainy day so that he came into York in a Coach: and sent word afore he was sory he could not so come in, that

mother, sisters and brothers, also to my nephew James Downeinge, and my neeces Mary and Su: who I hope ar safely ariued with you ere this time. Although I haue little else to write but salutacones, yet I thought it not meet to neglect any opertunity of writeinge to you. I hope you haue receiud the goods I shipped in the Mary and John per Mr. Collier wherin I sent all the things you wrote for but sope ashes and old musket barreles, which were not to be had, also to your father were shipped all the things he wrote to my bro[ther] Doweninge for, but only shorlinge sheep skins, 100 which now I haue bespoken and will be dressed within 6 weekes by which time I thinke another ship or 2 will be ready. I heerwith send you the catalogue of this vernall mart 1633 packed with some small things which my sister Downeinge sendeth, and I am still in your debt some monies which I expect aduise from you how to dispose of. the some I wrote you in an accompt per Mary Downeinge. for newes we haue little only we heare from Germany that a great battell was fought neer vnto Nice, for it was about to be beseiged had not this battell prevented it, wherin the Duke of saxony got the day, but with the losse of his generall Arneham: but the aduersary Walestein was slayne there with a great number of his Comanders also we hear that the prince of Orange hath taken Rhyne Berck. Thus for this time I comit you to god and rest Your euer lo[ving] freind

FRANC: KIRBY

LUCY DOWNING TO JOHN WINTHROP, JR.[1]

To her louinge nephew Mr. John Winthrop at Boston present thes

June 22th 1633

MY GOOD NEPHEWES AND NESES, your loues and deserts challeng many expressions of my loue and thankfullnes to you all againe: much more then to euery of you a seuerall letter: I must confess you haue not straitned your loues to me as I am forced to doe my thankfullnes to you: yet beleeu thes feew words wish you as many hapyneses as you can be capable of: I simphathise with you in all your joyes: I am afflicted in your sorrowes: I wish hartilie that I knew wherin to be seruisable to you: I pray wherin I maye spare me not: for to my power I desier to be imploied for your goods: but a good scribe I shall neuer be: and I am now taken of by a suddaine imployment   last night

---

[1] W. 4. 3; 5 *Collections*, I. 8. Lucy Downing was a sister of Governor Winthrop and the wife of Emmanuel Downing.

ould msr. Gurden came to me to desire my house for his logdinge and his daughter is heer to be maryed the next week to Sir richard Saltinstalls sone: the youngest daughter: next spring they intend for new eng: I am allmost blinde. Your Louinge ant

LUCIE DOWNING

EDWARD HOWES TO JOHN WINTHROP, JR.[1]

To his highly esteemed Frind Mr. John Winthrop Junr. at Boston present these in New England

Salus in Christo Domino

SIR, Although I haue written vnto you alredie by this shipp per Mr. Atherton Haugh and hauinge soe largely exprest my loue to you per your Cosen Mary Downinge, yet I could not chuse but as it were seeke newe matter of loue and respect; you shall receiue here inclosed a lettre from Mr. Kirbie, and in a bundle of Clothes for your Cosen Mary marked with M: D: you shall find from him a cattalogue of the last Marte bookes; and from your poore frind an exact and large and the latest discouery of the N: West passage made by a painfull and industrious gentleman Capt: James[2] as a remembrance of my obliged loue; I writt to you by the last shipps of your vncles remouinge his dwellinge into the Strand or the Covent Gardein. he hath (and my Mrs.) bin very hott vpon the remoue lately but I haue in parte if not altogether, altred theire purpose and advised them not to remoue vntill it be to plant themselues in N: E: which I hope wilbe next springe; my m[aste]r hath caused me to put off my chamber in Cliffords Inn againe; and would haue me take his partners parte in the Temple. we are to buyld them new this sommer: my m[aste]r said lately, he had rather be buylding at Boston in N. E. but whie should I trouble you with these impertinances, only that you may knowe where to send to me if my m[aste]r should remoue to you but before that tyme I hope to see you here. tis certaine your vncle Gostlyn and Aunt will goe ouer with theire family in the Springe; and if you come this winter to vs, its very likely you may perswade your Aunt Dow[ning] to goe with them, for your vncle D. he could wish himselfe there nowe; he is neuer better nor merrier then when he is talkinge of N: E: Your 100*li* with your

---

[1] W. 2. 166; 4 *Collections*, VI. 487–490.
[2] *The Strange and Dangerovs Voyage of Captaine Thomas James in His Intended Discouery of the Northwest Passage into the South Sea* (London, 1633).

vncle Paynter were worth the comming for, and your promise of comminge ouer were worth the performance. it may be you may prevaile that I may goe with you   there is not a question but if the Lorde sees good to send you to vs, he will aboundantly content your paines; I haue heard of 200*li* which was giuen to your mother which is in the hands of your vncle Tindall, thats worth the fetchinge too; I question not the safety of it, but I conceiue it were better to be ymployed in N: E: then in Old; and I heare of some lands bought in Suffolke almost a yeare since, I haue heard my m[aste]r say he neuer saw the conveyance, but I haue not heard your vncle Down[ing] speake of any rent he hath as yet receiued; perchance you may deeme me too bold, to medle with that I haue nothinge to doe with; but I conceiue you my frind to be (Alter idem) and what concernes you concernes me, either to pertake of your Joye or sorrowe. There is a pretty youth, brother to Sarah your Sister Feaks maide that hath much desired to spend his dayes in N: E: he is a pretty good clarke and as I heare hath liued a year or two with a Common law Attorney; this youth (his name is John Sandbrooke) my m[aste]r thought good to preferre him to your worthie father, to whome he is bound for fiue yeares; my m[aste]r told him before he bound him, that he must follow old Adams trade; which he freely consented vnto. my m[ist]ris was intreated by his father (who hath noe other sonne but he) to write to your father about him; and I speakinge of writing to you, he intreated me, to procure you to take a little notice of him, and encorage him in goodnes; I neede not advise you to take a man or boye, for I knowe you are able enough to knowe what is best for your selfe; and for ought I knowe you may haue diuerse Indian boyes, which are or may be in tyme Necessary seruants: Before I end, I must not forgett to put you in minde of one that is cominge to you whoe hath deserued exceedingly of your father and the plantation, many wayes; he dis-couered (vnder God) our Enemies plotts, and helpt to prevent them;[1] he hath alsoe dispossest our Enemies of theire hope Pascataque and intends to plant him selfe and many gracious men there this sommer. noe doubt but this may be and wilbe by diuerse in this shipp reported to you; but out of the mouth of diuerse witnesses the truth is confirmed. I haue and you all haue cause to blesse god that you haue soe good a neighbour as Capt. Wiggen. I could spend my dayes in shewing my respects to you. Mr. Arkisden is very well and hath bin steward of his colledge; and is nowe in the very Acte of commencing master; Mr. Saltonstall and Mrs. Meriall Gurdon are to be

---

[1] Captain Thomas Wiggin. Governor Winthrop attributed the failure of the schemes of Sir Christopher Gardiner and his allies in part to "the good testimony given on our behalf by one Captain Wiggin." *Journal*, 1. 99.

married next weeke here in towne, et signum perderit pudicitiæ fertur in domus thalamo nostri; For my parte I am as farre from marrying as euer I was. Yet I should be loath to goe to N: E: without one; Thus with my humble seruice to your noble Father and good Mother and my due and respectiue loue to your louinge wife and your selfe; and my salutes to your sister Feaks, and Sister Dudley, and theire husbands; and to my louinge frind Mr. Samford and his wife; remember me alsoe to your cosen Ma[ry] Dow[ning] and Susan and James: not forgetting your brothers; and all the rest of my louinge frinds. With most hartie wishes and prayers for all your healths and prosperities, and grace and fauour with the Lorde Christ, to whose guidance and keeping I committ you and rest Yours as you knowe

E. Howes

Inner Temple the 22th of June 1633

The harts of all Gods people here are all bent towards your Syon, and from all parts of the land they are goinge vp by flocks to *New Salem* Jerusalem to worship; helpe me to you with your prayers; or if the lorde see good that I may to his glorie suffer here.

EDWARD HOWES TO JOHN WINTHROP, JR.[1]

To the wor[shipfu]ll his assured frind John Winthrop esqr. Junr. at Boston in the Mattachusets Baye present these in New England

Sir, This is the fifth or sixth lettre to you since I received any from you, the post it may be hath lost your packett. I hope you will not say I haue bin a niggard of my paper and paines, if they all come safe (as I wish they may) to your hands, and as it is said nulla dies sine linea, soe I may say nullum tempus sine occasione, theres noe tyme but it offers occasion of loue and seruice towards you. I was requested by Mr. Sandbrooke (whose only sonne he hath sent as seruant to my noble frind your worthy father) to write to you to shewe some fauour to the ladd; as alsoe that Mr. Gouernour will be pleased to consider that he is sent to him, with all or most necessaries as alsoe his passage paid for by his father; I told Mr. Sandbrooke that he need not doubt but it would be taken notice of, and remembred when his sonne comes out of his tyme: It much reioyces our hearts here that the lord sends forth such store

---

[1] W. 2. 167; 4 *Collections*, vi. 490–493.

of labourers into his viniard; they flock to you euen from Dan to Bersheba; from Plymouth to Barwick.

Sir Hugh Platts Engine that you and I haue bin often hammeringe about, to boyle in wooden vessells is now come to light, and I hope wilbe with you as soone as this letter: my m[aste]r hath bin at the cost of making one, and wee tryed it in our Parlor   it will doe verie well, but it being in its infancie, had need of such mature Mathematitians as your selfe to bringe it to perfect proportion and strength. now you haue the hint and waye of it, facile est addere.

You shall alsoe receiue in this shipp 3 woolfe doggs and a bitch with an Irish boy to tend them.[1] for the doggs my m[aste]r hath writt sufficiently, but for the boye thus much. You haue bin in Ireland, knowe partlie the Irish condition. this is a verie tractable fellowe, and yet of a hardie and stout corage; I am perswaded he is very honest especially he makes great conscience of his promise, and vowe. I could wish (for as much as I haue seene by him) you would take him to be your seruant, although he be bound to your father for fiue yeares; At his first comminge ouer he would not goe to church; nor come to prayers; but first we gatt him vp to prayers and then on the lords day to catachise, and afterwards very willingly he hath bin at church 4 or 5 tymes; he as yet makes conscience of fridayes fast from flesh; and doth not loue to heare the Romish rel[igion] spoken against, but I hope with gods grace he will become a good convert. Converte gradatim. Sir, I dare boldlie saye it is as much honor for you to winn this fellowes soule, out [of] the subtillest snare (Romes pollitick Relig[ion]) of Sathan; as to winn an Indians soule out of the Diuells clawes; pardon my zealous boldnes for I doubt not but you shall enioye abundantly the sweete fruits of your labours this waye; As for his fittnesse to be a member of your church; its well if the Lord worke it in 3 or 4 yeare, yet he can doe it sooner if he please; The fellow can reede and write reasonable well which is somwhat rare for one of his condition; and makes me hope the more of him.

Concerninge the vernish for clothes and the Ceament for Earthen vessells; I conceiue the vernish nowe in vse is not that which Sir H: Platt speakes of, or if it be, it is very little or not at all vsed here in Towne, in rany wether or in winter which makes me doubt of the device. As for the Cement, I am told by the most profound Artist and naturallist here in this cittie that he can make such a Cement out of an Animall, but he would not teach it at any rate, and if he should make any, it would be deare, soe that I doubt (if all

---

[1] See *Journal*, I. III.

be true as he sayes) the Cure wilbe worse then the disease; it would not quitt cost to make it if we knew it. This Dr. for a Dr. he is, braggs that if he haue but the hint or notice of any vsefull thinge not yet invented, he will vndertake to find it out, Except some few which he hath vowed not to medle with, as Vitrum maliabile, perpet. motus, via proxima ad Indos, and Lapis philosi: all or any thinge else he will vndertake, but for his priuate gaine, to make a monopolie thereof, and to sell the vse or knowledge thereof at too high rates.

As for other newes we haue little. Mr. Davenport hath left London; and its said Mr. Nye will follow him, some say they bend theire thoughts towards your Plant[ation]   I know not how longe it wilbe ere I shall see you. I doe longe to see N: E: but the Lord sees that I am vnworthie and vnfitt to come amonge you as yet, otherwise then in some few scrawles of paper; remember vs as we doe you in our prayers, and present my humble seruice to Mr. Gouernor and your good mother   present my loue and respects to your selfe and your second selfe, together with all our good frinds with you whome God preserue and so I take leaue and rest Yours as he would be or should be

EDWARD HOWES

Quinto Aug: hora 12ª noctis 1633

Sir, I am willed per my m[aste]r to acquaint you that Mr. Sewall had deliuered to his vse in N: E. one of my m[aste]r his Cowes, for which he was to pay 15*li*, whereof my m[aste]r cannot gett a penny, therefore he desires that notice might be taken, that Mr. Sewall hath a Cowe of his vnpaid for, which he desires may be restored againe, if Mr. Sewall will not haue her; but herein let there be nothinge done, vntill Mr. Gouernour heares from my m[aste]r.

FRANCIS KIRBY TO JOHN WINTHROP, JR.[1]

To his much respected frend Mr. John Winthrop the yonger
this deliver at Boston in New England

LONDON 6º Augustij, 1633

Although (most lo[ving] frend) I haue not any thinge to write which may be worthy your paynes to read it; yet can I not omitte this or any other oportunity to write, hopeinge therby to oblige you to write to mee by euery oportunity likewise. I received no letter since that per Mr. Peirce. I should be

---

[1] W. 3. 6; 4 *Collections*, VII. 15–16.

dwell in this winter and it is uncomfortabl for us to liue thus I think thou hadest beter come home this winter for thear is no likelihoud of obtaining a minister this winter.[1]

i send 4 leters that came by mr. grant   the peices you writ for are not ready but i will send them as soone as i can   i have many things to write but at this time i am forced to breke of by reason of the speedy returne of the mesinger   thy faithfull and obedient wife

MARTHA WINTHROP

thursday [*ca*. October 31, 1633]

prethee loue make hast home.[2]

HENRY JACIE TO JOHN WINTHROP, JR.[3]

To his Worthy friend Mr. John Winthrop, sonne to the Right Worthy Governour of New England

WORTHY SIR, If you knew how ioyful a thing it was to me to receive (the last night) though but one letter from your so renowned plantation (vizt. from Ephr: Child) I am perswaded you would have added to my ioy by a line or two. Before this his letter yours dated Octob. 21, 1632 concerning the moones ecclipse Octo. 17, was the last I received thence. A copy of that I sent to Mr. Milburne, from whom I expected to have received more in that kind about ecclipses, and directed him how to send to you. I received none since from him. Our estate here in particular in General you may better hear from the honest bearer John Firmin, then by my letter. The Lord hath been merveilous in his mercies to this our land; and we have dealt shamefully unthankfully with him: and therefore if he proceede to deal wonderfully in his judgements against us, as he threatned to do with Israel Isa. 29. 13–15, that the Wisdome of the wise sh[all] fail them, and the seers he covered etc. It were just with him. We have not feared when he hath oft shaken the rod, nor turned to him when he hath smitten us, except fainedly, and then to our sins againe. Yea even to spiritual adultery, defiling the mariage bed, and yet say wiping our mouths, What evil have we done: who dare charge us therewith, name him that we may make him smart for it, as some have, others do, and more are likely. I read lately a large letter from Archb[ishop] Grindal of Cant[erbury] to Q[ueen] Eliz[abeth] from whom commaund was

---

[1] The letter up to this point is in cipher.   [2] This postscript is in cipher.
[3] W. 2. 160; 4 *Collections*, VI. 457–459.

comming to him to forbid exercises, and cause fewer preachers in regard of Contention etc. He writ, God forbid his tongue should be an instrument of publishing that was so to Gods dishonour. We have no power against the trueth, but for the trueth. How it is for the Sab[bath] you shal heare. What wil become of us God knowes: we had need stand as much in the gap as we can, tho we be not without some danger for it. Blessed be God, there are divers such in this cold Climate of Yorkshire, yea and in Northumberland, people, ministers, gentlemen, and here some knights also. Pray for us deare Sir and desire your ministers to do so in publick, though I conceive they oft do so. God is not yet departed, he walks sometimes in our Gardens, and makes some dead herbs to live and blossome, both elder and yonger in these cold seasons. The God Alsufficient be amongst you, and perserve you that you may be al of one mind according to trueth, that you having salt in your selves may be at peace one with another Mar. 9 end, that you may deny your selves, and your own reasonings, in humility condescending one to another so far as may stand with a good conscience, considering one anothers weakenesse to cover it in love, avoiding needles disputes, causing strife, rather then edifying Heb. 13. 9. I desire al your prayers for me to the God that heareth prayer, that he that hath called me here to the ministery, and given desires of doing his work faithfully and syncerely, $\epsilon\nu$ $\pi\alpha\rho\rho\eta\sigma\iota\alpha$ and humility would direct me in al things to do his wil, and keep my selfe pure, and uphold and blesse me and my endeavours, as he hath given me cause of praises to him in this behalfe. Blesse his holy name with me, who rejoice with you in his great kindnes towards you, and hope I shal no longer live, then I abide Your and New Englands faithfull friend so far as I am able

HEN: JACIE

AUGHTON Dec. 17, 1633

My best respect and heartiest love remembred to al my deare friends with you, richer and poorer, for I am straitned in time. I can write no more now thither.

EPHRAIM CHILD TO JOHN WINTHROP[1]

To the right Wo[rshi]p[fu]l Mr. Wintrop at Boaston these be delivered

RIGHT WO[RSHI]P[FU]L AND MUCH RESPECTED, being carefull least by any miscareag of mine I should [*torn*] procure your dislike, I thought it not

---

[1] W. 4. 57; 5 *Collections*, I. 165–166. For Ephraim Child, see 5 *Collections*, I. 165n.

amisse to comit vnto your consideration the present ocasion, that may breed some dislike in you off me.

the last night late goodman pease sent your seruant henry Kingsbury for a payre of bullocks. I went this morning with him to looke them but could not find them, so he went without them. I perceiuing that there was a purpose not only for present to vse them but altogether to take them and the rest home, your wo[rshi]p, hauing in time past fatherly intimated to doe me good, which in a larg measure you haue don, but further in this particular putting me forward apon this corse of plowing, and I now hauing indeauored my selfe vnto the period of preparation of the thing intended, as in furnishing my selfe with a maire necessarie for such a corse with all other impliments necessary vnto such ocasions, as plow cart with yoakes and cheynes and Iron workes vnto the disburstment of much monie, doe conceiue that it canot but tend to much disaduantag and losse, besides taking me off cleane from my former intended corse, which I haue this 12 months been ploding apon doe therefore humbly desire your wor[shi]p, that I may not at the pleasure of any belonging vnto you except your selfe, be at such comand as apon an instant to breake off my practises of this nature, which howeuer as yet you may conceiue it to be an vnprofitable corse for your wor[shi]p to part with your cattle for so litell benifitt. yet I doubt not but that in a short time both your selfe and others shall comend off it not only to be good in generall, but such cattle as of yours are in mine hand shall be as benificiall as you can espect, and thus desirous to exscuse myselfe of not coming being busily imployed apon necessarie ocasions, I doe humbly craue a word or two for answer vnto my request which is, that what I shall doe in this case, and for either going to help in any imployment for carting or plowing with our draft at your apoyntment at your farme, I will be willing at all times, or otherwise to giue you a part of the thing I shall doe acording to your content. only vntil such times as I can furnish my selfe with a plow teame, let me not be weakened noe more then your loue toward me will afford, and that your cattle may not be required at the wills of such as may hapily fayle in care towards me. Yours in all humble respect

EPHRAIM CHILD

[*Ca.* 1634]

RICHARD SALTONSTALL, JR., TO JOHN WINTHROP, JR.[1]

To his worthely endeared Mr. John Winthrop junior deliver N. England

DEARE SIR, The best thing that I have to begg your thoughts for at this præsent, is, a Motto, or 2, that Mr. Prin hath writt, vpon his chamber walls, (in the Tower.)

Carcer probat amicos, detegit inimicos, excludit mundum, includit deum; alit virtutes, extinguit libidines, edocet temperantiam, cohibet luxuriam, mortificat carnem, sanctificat hominem, ingenerat gratiam, thesaurizat gloriam.

Psal: 61. 3. Deus est turris etiam in Turre. Turris libertatis, in turre angustiæ; Turris consolationis in turre tristitiæ; turris quietis in turre molestiæ; Turris fælicitatis in turre miseriæ; Turris honoris in turre dedecoris; Turris splendoris in turre obscuritatis; Turris securitatis in turre perturbationis; Turris salutis in turre perditionis; Turris spei in turre desperationis; Turris gaudij in turre afflictionis; Turris pacis in turre belli; Turris protectionis in turre periculi; Turris vitæ in turre mortis; Turris gloriæ in turre perpessionis; et in turre peccati, turris Gratiæ.

Turris	protegendo, consolando, eripiendo,	a malis; in malis; contra malos, inter malos,	semper, abundanter, vbique,	Fortissimè Suavissimè Gratiosissimè

Citò, tempestivè, sapienter, optimè;

Arctari non potest qui in ipsâ dei infinitate incarceratus spatiatur. Mortalium procul dubio beatissimus qui mundi exul, christique captivus turri: Turris christianos fideles fictè incarcerat, verè liberat. Nil crus sentit in nervo si animus sit in cælo; nil corpus patitur in ergastulo, si anima sit in Christo.

I have nothing els (being in great hast) but my best love, which is (as my selfe) alwayse yours:

RICHARD SALTONSTALL junior

[*Ca.* 1634]

[*Endorsed by John Winthrop, Jr.:*] Mr. Saltonstall wherin Mr. Prinne his motto in the Prison.

---

[1] W. 3. 68; 4 *Collections*, VII. 251–252. For Saltonstall, see 4 *Collections*, VII. 251*n*.

THOMAS OLIVER TO JOHN WINTHROP, JR.[1]

To the Right Wor[shi]pfull his very loving frend Mr. Winthorpe
at Agawam thes be delivered

The good sperit of god posses your precious souls

RIGHT LOVING BROTHER IN THE BEST BELOUED, my deare loue and servis Remembered to you, and your beloved on: with many thanks for many kindneses Reseved from you both. the good lord shew mercy to your souls againe: the great ioye that wee haue in the ordinance of Christ is mixt with sorow that our souls should faire so well, and you our dear bretherin and sisters should want the same. We may pity your state for the Present: but help you we Canot by Reson of the sharpnes of the time, but we trust our good father will suply your wants, and be as a litle sanctuary to you for the present and giue a duble suply in the end and so fill your souls with such a measure of that precyous grace of faith in beleeving, that our good father that brought you to that Place will send after you in his time, for those that serv him shall lack nothing that is good: this time of the want that your souls stands in for the present: will move you to mak a precious acount of it, when it Coms, which we do ernestly desire you may haue to the sweet Content of your souls: my wiffe Remembers here dear loue to you both: the good lord be with you both and gard your bodys by his angels, and gide your souls by his good sperit. yours truly to Comm[and] in the lord

THOMAS OLIVER

BOSTON this 3 of the first moneth 1634 [N.S.][2]

JOHN WINTHROP TO JOHN ENDECOTT[3]

The things which will cheifly be layd to his charge are these. 1: that he chargethe Kinge James with a solemne pub[lic]k lye. 2: that he chargethe

---

[1] W. 1. 104. Thomas Oliver, a native of Bristol, came to Boston in 1632. He served as selectman, 1634–1638, and was a ruling elder of the First Church.

[2] It would seem as if the correct date for this letter must be January 3, 1634 (N.S.). Oliver must either have used New Style dating or have made an error in the year. In March, 1634/35, John Winthrop, Jr., was in England, not in Ipswich. Furthermore, his first wife died in July, 1634, and there is evidence that his second marriage, which occurred in England, had not taken place by March, 1634/35.

[3] W. 1. 103; 1 *Proceedings*, VII. 343–345. The occasion for this communication to Endecott was Roger Williams's "treatise," written during his sojourn at Plymouth, wherein he attacked the validity of the royal patent for "these parts." Upon Williams's return to Massachusetts Bay the powers that

bothe Kinges and others with blasphemy for calling Europe Christendom, or the Ch[ristia]n world etc. 3: for personall application of 3 places in Rev:[1] to our present Kinge Charles. 4: for concluding vs all heere to lye vnder a sinne of vniust vsurpation vpon others possessions: and all these to be maintayned and published by a private person etc:

For the first: it was no lye of Kinge James, but the Trueth: for his people were the first, that discovered these parts: but admitt he had been mistaken: was it ever knowne, that a true Ch[ristia]n did give his naturall Prince the lye? was he not the Lords anointed?

For the 2: that it should be Blasphemye to saye Christendom or the Ch[ristia]n worlde: and for a subiecte heervpon to charge his Prince with Blasphemye is too great presumption: are not things often named from the better parte, as the Electe are called the worlde in 8 places at least: as God loued the worlde, reconciled the world etc.? Again all Israelites (good and badd) were called the Circumcision and the people of God etc: to distinguish them from the Heathen: so may all baptized ones be called Christians to distinguishe them from the Turks etc: in which respecte to be baptized and Christned were all one: because Baptisme was the first pub[lic]k badge whereby a Christian was distinguished from a Pagan: and so in the dayes of Constantine and Jovinian and other godly emperors, the Arians, manichees and other Heretiks were called Christians and that without Offence to the most orthodoxe: who tooke it in no other sence than as baptized ones, to distinguishe them onely from the Pagans, who were the Com[mo]n opposites to them all: therefore I am perswaded it is no Blasphemy (when I would distinguish a nation, that professeth the Faith of Jesus Christ (be it in trueth or not) from other nations which professe him not) to saye they are Ch[ristia]ns: neither is it any more Contradiction (as he would make it) to saye a Ch[ristia]n worlde, or a heavenly earthe, than to saye an heauen vpon earthe or a worldly sanctuarye: Heb: 9: 2. for if he allowe not allegoryes, he must condemn his owne writings and speeches, seeinge no man vseth them more than him selfe: and this verye treatice of his, exceeds all that ever I haue read (of so serious an Argument) in figures and flourishes. For the 3: the first place which he applies to our Kinge is Rev: 16: [14] the spiritts of Deuills going forth to the kinges of the earth, which is all one, as if he had sayde, that the Deuill had

---

be felt it necessary to take official cognizance of this document, and the Governor and Assistants, meeting at Boston on December 27, 1633, gave order, after "taking advice with some of the most judicious ministers," for Williams's appearance at the next General Court. Endecott was not present at this meeting, and Winthrop, as he states in his Journal (I. 117), wrote Endecott "to let him know what was done, and withal added divers arguments to confute the said errors. . . ."

[1] In the margin: "Rev: 16: 13, 14, 17: 12. 13. 18: 19."

Thus hoping of your good health, with our dayly prayers to God for you and the whole plantation, I shall ever rest, Your true hearted Friend

Jo: Downyng

Layer Marney Feb. 28, 1633[/34]

I pray good Mr. Wintrop let me entreate you to enquire out the man who should have the inclosed letters. it seemes he dwelleth neare new Plimouth, he is a friend of myne. you shall commaund me a greater kyndnesse, if the man will write backe I pray lett him inclose his letters in yours to me.

I pray good Sir when you see my Cozen James Downyng, my Cozen Marie, and my cozen Su: commend me kyndly to them all. Tell my cozen Marie that I will not forgett her, her token shalbe restored at the last, she shall have a letter from me next month.

[*Endorsed by John Winthrop, Jr.:*] mr. Joseph Downing received July: 1634.

LONDON PORT BOOK ENTRY FOR THE *JONAS*[1]

v Martij 1633[/34]

In le Jonas of London Jon Crowther m[aste]r versus New England. John Wenthorpe Esquier gouernor etc. j chest Iron Bare value v*li* xs j chest apparell value 1s j truncke with shirts and other made linen value xxxs j barr of xv stone beefe value xxxs j muskett, j foulinge peece powder and shott value 1s j firkin butter cost xxs Free per lic. Regis.

LONDON PORT BOOK ENTRY FOR THE *RECOVERY*[2]

vij^mo Martij 1633[/34]

In le Recouerye of London Wm. Wildye m[aste]r versus New England. Jon Winthorpe Esquier gouernor and Comp. halfe a ton Iron ij barr pitche and tarr v smale Rundletts grocerye wares cost iiij*li* iiij C wht yron potts j C xij*li* brass kettles v trunks j packe of houshould stuffe and prouisions cost xxx*li* v chests j case glasse for windowes cost x*li*, x Iron backes for Chimneys j hhd ij Rundlette of xx dozen tallowe candles ij C wht of birding shott of lead vij Cases j Rondlett of ij hhds Aquavitae j Corslett j bag of j C wht Copperas iiij hides Free per lic. Regis.

---

[1] Public Record Office; *Proceedings*, XLVII. 179.
[2] Public Record Office; *Proceedings*, XLVII. 180.

LONDON PORT BOOK ENTRY FOR THE *REFORMATION*[1]

vij^mo Martij 1633[/34]

In le Reformacon of London Thomas Graves m[aste]r for New England.

John Winthorpe Esquier gouernor etc. vj trunks xx smale paq'tts v Chestes of xl yards perpetuannes xvj yards baies v C xliiij ells Canvas xij doz knit woollen hose xxij dozen yrishe stockinge Apparell value xxvj*li* yron worke and Edge tooles value j C xij*li* haberdashers wares value xiiij*li* iiij barrels and a halfe powder v C wht birdinge shott of lead absq. subss. etc. per lic. Regis.

In the Reformacon prd.

Idem John etc. C hhdes xxx firkins of lix quarters wheat meale xlviij quarter mault xvj quarters oatmeale xij quarters pease xxxvij firkins butter and suett xxxvij C wht Cheese iij hhdes vinegar xvj dozen Candles xxiiij muskets and fowlinge peece absq. subss. etc. per lic. Regis.

LONDON PORT BOOK ENTRY FOR THE *JONAS*[2]

xij Martij 1633[/34]

In le Jonas of London Jon Crowder m[aste]r versus New England.

John Winthorpe Esquier etc. prd. j C iiij hhds xvj barrells of lx quarters wheate meale xvj quarters pease xxx quarters mault xx firkins butter v hhds glasse for windowes other necessaries value xl*li* ix hhds Iron workes value xl*li* v hhds grocerye wares and other prouisions value lxiiij*li* x hhds and chests tooles for smithes and other necessaries value xl*li* xviij Chests xxiiij hhds Apparell houshold stuff bedding etc. per lic. Regis.

LONDON PORT BOOK ENTRY FOR THE
ELIZABETH BONAVENTURE[3]

xij^to Martii 1633[/34]

In le Elizabeth bonaventure of London Tho: Coitmore m[aste]r for New England.

Jon: Winthorpe Esquier etc. prd. xlij hhds ij killderkins of xliiij quarters

[1] Public Record Office; *Proceedings*, XLVII. 180.
[2] Public Record Office; *Proceedings*, XLVII. 180.
[3] Public Record Office; *Proceedings*, XLVII. 180–181.

wheat meale   viij hhds of viij quarters mault   iij hhds of iiij quarters oatmeale   iiij hhds of iiij quarters pease   xvj firkins butter   x ferkins suet
v C wht   ij firkins tallowe Candles of xxx dozen   xxx Chests divers killderkins   x packs Apparell houshold stuff and Iron wares value xxiiij*li*   j hhd
sweet oile   j tonn Iron potts   ij C sheepskyns tawed for the prouision of
divers passengers   per lic. Regis.

JOHN STRATTON TO JOHN WINTHROP, JR.[1]

*To the wor[shipfu]ll and his much honored freind Mr. John Winthrop Esqr. att his
house theis hast and deliver in Aggawaam per Jno. Gallopps boate*

In BOSTON this 17th of the first
month Called March, 1634 [N.S.][2]

RIGHT WORTHY SIR, with much respect your health desyred   Concerning
my goeing to Virginia itt goeth not forwards for for my owne part I haue nott
any thing worth the advancing in goods to such a Charge as will bee neces-
sarilie made vpon the Voyage. And Mr. Mayhewe will he saith doe any thing
to further mee in accommodation of a planter butt liks nott the Course [to]
Virginia. I purpose god willing to bee at Aggawaam the latter end of the
weeke when wee shall haue tyme to relate all passages. I knewe nott of Jno.
Gallops Comming till this present day   I professe I have made enquiry for
Course Cloath for shirts And Could nott gett any And more ouer nott goeing
the voyage I haue nott a penny [of] Monney to procure itt butt haue spoke
to [the] Governor   he tells me he knoweth not of any butt if he sends you
any I will al[   ] itt if yow requyre itt butt my misvnderstanding Mr.
Mayhewe (for he tells me whatt he ment to doe was nott in way of trade to
virginia) is twyce tenne pounds out of my way putting of my ser[van]t Consydering the Course Mr. Mayhewe now proiects butt I Confesse itt is nott a
100 parte soe troublesom to mee to thinke of itt Consydering thatt I haue
assigned to your selfe. I haue nott yett I professe hade one farthing for my
Cannoa or peice nor will now vppon any rates parte with them   Soe with
my service to Mrs. Winthrop and loue to my sister I Committ yow to gods
tuition And shall euer rest Yours faithfullie to bee Commanded

JOHN STRATTON

---

[1] W. 1. 105. John Stratton, son of John Stratton of Shotley, England, was born about 1606.
He came to Salem about 1631 and in 1638 was settled in Charlestown. Charles H. Pope, *The
Pioneers of Massachusetts* (Boston, 1900), 439.

[2] From the context of the letter it seems unlikely that it was written in March, 1634/35, at
which time John Winthrop, Jr., was in England.

I haue putt my sister a suite of Moyheare to making att Goodm. Frenches shee were best gett the taylor to take her Measure and send per Jno. Gallop.

LONDON PORT BOOK ENTRY FOR THE *ELIZABETH* [1]

xxvj^to Martii 1634

In le Elizabeth of London Wm. Stagg m[aste]r for New England.

Mathew Cradocke j Hd of iiij C yd. goods Cotton vi dozen of Irishe stockings xxx paire shooes j barrell of ij bushells of hemp seed ij bushells of flaxe seed ij spem Iron per lic. Regis.

LONDON PORT BOOK ENTRY FOR THE *ELIZABETH* [2]

xxviij^mo Martii 1634

In the Elizabeth of London prd.

Jon: Winthorpe Esquier gouernor etc. j hhd yron tooles value ix*li* j barrell of vj bushells salte j barrell honny j hhd of grocerye and haberdash. wares value vj*li* x*s* ix*d* j barrell of iij C wht promes j quarter pease in Caske j barrell of iiij bushells wheat meale j hhd vinegar ij Chests Apparell and beddinge. j barrell of dd *C* pewter j hhd with trenchers dishes and other houshold stuff value i*s* j dryfatt of beddinge and old linnen value v*li* j case of ij dozen plaine felt hattes j Case windowe glasse ij hhds j fatt iiij barrells iiij Chestes j truncke of beddinge and wearing Apparell and Iron ware for theire private prouision all value xxx*li* d^l hhd vinegar j fatt of vj C wht kettles j fatt of vj wht fryinge pans j tte of v dozen Irishe stockinge lx paire knitt woollen stocking ij dozen whalebone bodyes j C and d^l wht pewter absq. subss. etc. per lic. Regis.

EDWARD HOWES TO JOHN WINTHROP, JR. [3]

To my very good frind Mr. John Winthrop at Agawom these present in New England

WORTHY FRIND, Yours of June August and September I haue receiued since my last to you as alsoe the otter skinn you sent me for which as for your

---

[1] Public Record Office; *Proceedings*, XLVII. 181.
[2] Public Record Office; *Proceedings*, XLVII. 181.
[3] W. 2. 167; 4 *Collections*, VI. 495–497.

many other reall fauours I most hartily thanke you; according to your direction I haue receiued 55*s* 2*d* of Mr. Kirby which I haue laid out for you as may appeare by this inclosed; for Dr. Fludds workes there is since more come forth of him, as by the back of my accompt. I haue sent you only a taste of him, in two volumes; I conceiue they are well drest for your Pallate; I haue bin held in hand at Mr. Fetherstons shop by his men, euer since 8ber, to be furnished with all those bookes you writt for, and now am forced to buy them where I can find them; I can gett noe others but what I haue sent you vntill next Marte.

As for your Quodling slipps I hope against Mich[aelma]s next I shall haue some to send you, for now tis noe sending them. I haue made bold to putt a few other bookes to fill vp spare roome in the box; whereof one is the Contrie farme which I suppose you haue alreadie. if you haue, be please then to let Mr. Samford haue myne, or whome else you please. if you haue it not be pleased to accept it as a pledge of my constant loue and respects to you. Thus much concerninge your box of bookes which you shall receiue of Mr. Dillingham directed to you and marked with ☿. you shall haue me more large in my next either by Mr. Humfries or before in the meane tyme be pleased to present my respect to your best beloued and to your selfe and euer comand Your true though poore frind

EDWARD HOWES

29° Martij 1634 from our new howse in Lincolne's Inn feilds by the lyon Tauerne neere Princes streete

Sir, a very good frind of myne, Sir Symon Harcourts brother desired me to convey this inclosed to his frind by some trusty hand; I pray let me make bold that at best leasure by one of your seruants or otherwise it may be deliuered to Mr. Coggeshall.

I haue not had leasure to visit Mrs. Waterhowse as yet, at Easter next if not sooner I intend to present your respect vnto her. Vale in Christo.

[Enclosure in the preceding letter]

Rec. of Mr. Kirby 55*s* 2*d*

    The bookes I haue sent you March, 1634

    2 Catalogues of Printed bookes

	li	*s*	*d*
Dr. Fludds Macrocosme in 2 volumes	1	10	0
Isagoge Phisico Magico etc.	0	1	6
Petrus Galatinus de Arcanis Catholicæ veritatis	0	10	0
Phillippi Grulingij Florilegium	0	2	0

These are parte of them you writt for.

I haue here alsoe sent you a few others which if you like not I pray send them againe or any of them.

Mercurius Rediuiuus per Norton	0	2	6
The Rarities of Cochinchina[1]	0	1	0
Wingates Logarithmes	0	4	6
An English Grammer	0	1	0
The gunners Dialogue	0	2	0
Bedwells Messolabium	0	1	0
The box to put them in	0	0	10
Carrying them to the warehowse	0	0	8
	2	17	0

The rest I cast in to the bargaine for you and your fancie to make merry withall.

29º Martij 1634

Integrum Morborum Misterium siue Medicinæ Catholicæ Tomi Primi tractatus secundus, in sectiones distributus duas. Quorum Prior generallem
morborum natura, etc. Vltima, Vniuersale medicorum siue ægrotorum
depingit Catoptron: etc. Francofurti Aº 1631. Authore Ro: Flud alias de
Fluctibus.

This is a new Booke and is now betweene 20 and 30*s* price. Dr. Fludd is of
farr more esteeme beyond sea then at home.

---

[1] Christophoro Barri, *Cochin-China: Containing Many Admirable Rarities and Singularities of That Countrey* (London, 1633). The copy which Howes presented to Winthrop is now in the Society's library. At one time it was said to have contained the name "E. Howes" on the title page. 4 *Collections*, VI. 497*n*. No trace of such a name is now visible, but the title page does bear Winthrop's catalogue number.

LONDON PORT BOOK ENTRY FOR THE *ELIZABETH*, THE *JONAS*, AND THE *SEAFLOWER*[1]

xxxj^mo Martij 1634

In le Elizabeth of London for New England.

John Winthorpe Esquier etc. prd. xxv hhds vij barrells   v killderkins   viij firkins   iiij Chestes   iij Hd. of viij quarters wheate meale   iiij quarters mault   iij quarters pease   xij bushells oatmeale   viij firkins butter and sewet   vj C et d^l Cheese   ij hhds vinegar   Grocerye wares value 1s   Iron workes value 1*li*   houshold stuffe, apparell for prouision of passengers going thether absq. subss. etc. per lic. Regis.

In le Jonas of London for New England.

Idem Jon: etc.   lvj heifers   viij mares   lx quarters oates   iiij quarters mault   v barrells pease of iiij quarters per lic. Regis.

In the Seaflower of London Henrie Morgan [master] for New England.

Idem Jon: etc. prd. xviij Colts   xv heifers   lx quarters oates   xj quarters mault   xj quarters barley for prouision of the men and Cattle by the waye. per lic. Regis.

LONDON PORT BOOK ENTRIES FOR THE *SEAFLOWER*[2]

ij^do Aprilis 1634

In the Seaflower of London prd.

Jon: Winthorp etc. prd. xxvj hhds iiij barrels, v kilderkins   vij firkins   iij Chestes   iiij trunckes of xv quarters wheat meale   vj quarters mault   iij quarters pease   iij quarters oat meale   ix firkins butter and sewet   vj C wht Cheese   xvj bushells salt   ij hhds vinegar   windowe glasse value xl*s*   Iron wares value xxvj*li*   fishing instrumentes value viij*li* with bedding etc. for provision for the passengers absq. subss. etc. per lic. Regis.

Eodem ij^do Aprilis 1634

In le Seaflower of London prd.

Jon: Winthorpe Esquier governor etc. ij hhds iiij tte of iij C l ells normandye canvas   xj dozen loome worke quofies value xxx*s*   ij C paire knit

---

[1] Public Record Office; *Proceedings*, XLVII. 181–182.
[2] Public Record Office; *Proceedings*, XLVII. 182.

woollen xiij dozen Chilldrens woollen stockinges   Cl Cotton and flannel wastcoates value x*li*   lx Chilldrens wastcoates value xl*s*   ij dozen shirts and smockes value l*s*   vij dozen shooes   xlv dozen Irish stockings   j barrell pitche   j barrell tarr   ij C wht tard Cordage for the plantation per lic. Regis.

LONDON PORT BOOK ENTRY FOR THE *PLANTER*, THE *TRUE LOVE*, AND THE *ELIZABETH AND DORCAS*[1]

Quinto Aprilis 1634

In the Planter of London Nico. Tracey m[aste]r versus New England

John Winthorpe for prouision for the passengers   iiij butts   lxx hhds   xxxiiij barrells   xviij kilderkins   lij firkins of xlvij quarters of wheate and meale   xxiij quarters malt   viij quarters oatmeale   xvij quarters pease   xlviij firkins butter   xij firkins sewet   xxiij C wht Cheese   xxv gallons Civett oile   viij hhds vinegar grocerye ware value liij*li*   xlviij bushells salt   xvj coarse blankets value iiij*li*   Iron workes value xl*li*   haberdashers wares value xxx*li*   Crooked lane wares value iij*li*   windowe glass value iij*li*   xxviij dozen candles   iiij C wht roughe lead   Certain necessaries with houshould stuff and apparell per lic. R.

In le Planter prd.

Jon: Winthorpe etc. for prouision for the planters there   xj hhds xvij chestes   xvij trunckes   xij tte of v dozen plaine felt hattes   xviij lxxij ells Canvas   xlv dozen shooes   ij C xx paire knitt woollen stockings   xxvj dozen Irishe stockings   Iron workes value liij*li*   Cl muskettes   v barrell powder   xl gallons Aqua vita   x ps. Jeane Fustians   iij C ells lockromes   iiij barr. pitch and tarr   iij C wht tard Cordage per lic. Regis.

In le Trewloue of London Jon: Gibbs [master] for New England.

Idem Jon: etc.   xxiij heifers   xxv quarters meale   xij quarters pease   xij chestes apparells   vj firkins butter   xij barr. oatmeale   xxiij hhds mault   iij tte xij troncks apparell   ij hampers Iron wares and pewter   xx quarters oates absq. subss. etc. per lic. Regis.

In le Elizabeth and Dorcas Anto: Watts m[aste]r for New England.

Idem Jon: etc.   j C hhds. of j C quarters meale   lx hhds of xl quarters pease   xx quarters oat meale in bag   xij quarters pease in barr   xxx firkins butter   xiiij firkins nailes   x firkins vinegar   xxj chestes apparell beddinge and stone wares   viij Rundletts vinegar   v Rundletts oile   iiij Rundletts of

---

[1] Public Record Office; *Proceedings*, xlvii. 182–183.

iiij C wht sugar   x cases of lx gallons stronge waters   iiij bundles sawes   j butt sacke   xij tronckes apparell and worne linnen   vij quarters mault   vj C wht lead wrought   j bundle shouells spades and spittes   ij mill stones   xxxv C wht wrought Iron   three grindlestones   xxxij heifers   xj mares and Colts   x goates   l quarters oates   iiij quarters mault   iiij bundles bedding   j tte of j C paire knitt woollen hose   ij packes made clothes and bookes vj trunckes apparell and bookes for prouision for the passengers absq. subss. per lic. Regis.

LONDON PORT BOOK ENTRY FOR THE *NEPTUNE*[1]

x^{mo} Aprilis 1634

In le Neptune of London John Vamell m[aste]r versus New England
Jon: Winthorpe Esquier etc. for the planters   ij hhds sacke   j halfe hhd muscadel   j halfe hhd veeneager   ij barr: of j quarter meale   j firkin butter   j firkin of iij dozen candells   j barr: of ij bushells pease   j Rundlet of vj gallons wormwood wine   j Rundlet of vij gallons Aquavitae   j Rundlet of j gallon sweet oile   j barrell wooden dishes and platters   ij beds   ij trunckes iiij boxes of linnen Clothe and wearinge apparrell   j birdinge peece   j mare absque subss. per lic. Regis.

FRANCIS KIRBY TO JOHN WINTHROP, JR.[2]

To his much respected frend Mr. John Winthrop the yonger at Agawam or else where in New England this deliver per amicum quem deus conseruat

LONDON this 11th of Aprill, 1634

LOVINGE AND KIND FREND MR. WINTHROP, I wrote at large lately per mr. Graues of 1 fat and 1 hogshead shipped in mr. Crouther the Jonas per mr. Graues his aduise himselfe beinge not able (as he said) to take it in vnles he should leaue out some of his passengers goods. I haue inclosed bils of ladeinge to your father. since the date of those your letters I haue paid the freight primage auarage and all other Charges, the freight beinge 3*li* 15*s* at 3*li* per tun prim[age] and auarage 3*s* 6*d*   I haue lefte nothinge for you to pay. I pray forget not to put to account what Charge you haue been at with the tripartable goods.

---

[1] Public Record Office; *Proceedings*, LXVII. 183.
[2] W. Au. 63; 3 *Collections*, IX. 266–267.

I thinke I haue sent you very neer the value of your third of the beuer that you sent in returne. I haue now sold it but the mony will not be due before michael[mas] next, about which time I hope we shall receiue some more beuer from you for the partable account. I do not perceiue my bro[ther] Downeinge to be forward to ioine with you in the fishinge trade. I haue intreated him to write you a resolued answer which I haue not from him yet, and as I wrote you before, my resolution depends vpon him, without him nothinge therin, with him halfe so much as hee so that my part may not exceed 40 or 50*li* at the most. I haue disbursed for this goods with the freight and other Charges 44*li* 4*s* 3*d* if I mistake not. You shall find euery particular mencioned in my letters per mr. Graues, also euery seuerall rug and paire of blankets hath his price written vpon it. The 24 Coates Cost you about 13*s* 7*d* per Coat, besides the Charge vpon them; I and my wife and my bro[ther] and sister Hill desire to be remembred to your second selfe, your father and mother, my Cosen James, Mary, and Su: Downeinge and the rest yours and my frends. The bearer herof mr. William Alford skinner is an honest man well knowne to mee and also to mr. Cotton of Boston. I desire you to be acquainted with him and to shew him what kindnes you can without preiudice to your selfe. he is come with his family to plant amongst you. Thus for this time I Commit you to god and rest your lo[ving] frend

Franc: Kirby

My bro[ther] Downeinge sendeth the greatest part of his estate in Catle this year videlicet sheep and Cowes   I thinke it were not amisse for you to take some of his Cattle vpon such termes as mr. Dilingham hath done, seeinge you haue other imployment for your stocke.

LONDON PORT BOOK ENTRY FOR THE *PLANTER*[1]

xj^mo Aprilis 1634

In le Planter of London prd.
John Winthorpe etc. for the planters   j tte v chestes j barrell j killderkin of Iron worke value x*li*   xxviiij paire knitt woollen stockinge   xxiiij*li* Rice   v bushells wheat meale   v chestes windowe glasse value v*li* goods welche Cottons   CL yrds baies absque subss. per lic. Regis.

---

[1] Public Record Office; *Proceedings*, xlvii. 183.

ELIZABETH KNOWLES TO JOHN WINTHROP[1]

To the wor[shipfu]ll Mr. Winthropp Governor of New England deliver these with trust

WORTHY SIR, my humblest seruice to you remembred with my prayers for your health and prosperity. theis are to certify you that my husband when he came home to me told me that my brother Robert Mills did leaue but 46*li* which he hath receiued; which I doe much marvel att; my husband is now comeing to liue with you againe in new England; and I would entreat and desire you for gods loue to be pleased to write me word whether there was noe more then 46*li* and whether my brother James Dauies did not receiue any part thereof as in the behalfe of my childe   Soe Comittinge you to gods protection I rest your dayly beadswoman

ELIZABETH KNOWLES

14th of Aprill 1634

EDWARD HOWES TO JOHN WINTHROP, JR.[2]

To his much esteemed frind John Winthrop esquire at Agawom present [torn]

WAOBRETAHOY STITRA AGAWOM SAGAMORE, Aus Neost flourigreathinnog obuor whoinatreid meagniedra olfa wortinthienag,[3] giue me leaue in plaine English the second tyme this springe to present my vnfeigned respects to you in a few lynes. I sent you per Mr. Dillingham soe many of the bromoiklets[4] you writt for, as I could procure for the present, but I am promised the rest this sommer, and then by the next followinge they shalbe conveyed to you; The noelwo frudrinnamcle I writt to you of is mourcah ilmaportouvoend wiheeproeloaf I haue speinato yaoduir tohie frogrimoe haetrie ionacoltois-teud.[5] I haue learnt two devices to kill wolues, one is with peices of spunge laid couertly in such flesh or garbage they feede on; the other is certaine

---

[1] W. 1. 105. Elizabeth Knowles is probably the woman of that name whose husband, John Knowles, was in 1638 given administration of the estate of Robert Bills. Mrs. Knowles was, at the time of her marriage to Knowles, the widow of Ephraim Davies. *Records of Massachusetts*, 1. 235.

[2] W. 2. 168; 4 *Collections*, VI. 498–499. The passages in this letter which are in code are read by taking only the alternate letters.

[3] "Worthy Sir Agawom Sagamore, As not forgeting our wonted maner of writing."

[4] "Bookes."

[5] "The new furnace I writt to you of is much improved, whereof I haue sent you the forme here inclosed." The furnace is the contrivance mentioned previously in Howes's letters of August 5 and August 13, 1633, and in Emmanuel Downing's letter of August 13, 1633.

peices of stronge wyer twisted together ether 4 or 3 or 2 peices and the ends
to be bowed and fyled sharpe and beards cutt in them like fish hookes (thus
🪝); and them put within theire meate. There is one alsoe here in towne that
makes very good Shanlota prestheir waidtoh Vortimnoe agnud cloimnoan
Ebafretah[1]   I am verie much abashed that I haue not all this while procured
you the salue and plasters you writt for   you partlie knowe my nature I had
rather effect any busines with ten men, then one woman, yet your intrest in
me, might be sufficiently effectuall to mannage a farre more weighty busines;
and assure your selfe, I will ere longe comaund my selfe in that perticular;
As for the Quodling apple slipps I spake to Mr. Humfries once or twice about
it, and he sayd he would see for some. I hope he will bring some ouer with
him; and yet I doubt it because it is soe forward in the yeare   Thus with the
continuance of my respects, loue and seruice to you and your best beloued I
take leaue and rest Yours as God shall enable me

EDWARD HOWES

From our new howse in Lincolnes Inn feilds neere princes streete the 18th of
Aprill 1634

WILLIAM FORTH TO JOHN WINTHROP, JR.[2]

*To the Woo[rshi]p[fu]ll his very Lovinge Cosene Mr. John Winthrop the younger
giue thes in Nue Englande Per henerye Brygth*

COSINGE WINTHOP, vnto yow and to my good Cosinge yower wyffe I wishes
all health and happenes in Christe Jeses   I was verrye glayd to heare of yowr
good health by this baere henerye Bright as all so that yow doo lick so well
of that place wich god have Caleyd yow unto   I am sorowefull to here that
god have not it bleseyd yow with yowr Cheldren but I hope hee will in his
good tyme untell wich tyme yow much wate with pachones his good will and
plsuer. Sir I have in my handes A Deyde wich yower Father and granfather
mayd of the landes in groten ware in they Convayde them vnto them selfe for
tearme of lyfe and after a good parte of them vnto yow and to the ayres males
wich landes as I heare sinces Ar solde ware for I woolde intret yow for to write
vnto me weether I shall kepe the written or Deliuer it vnto mr. warene or to
aynne other or I shall kepe it still   and thus with my Dayle prayres vnto god

---

[1] "Salt peter with Vrine and comon Earth."
[2] W. 1. 106. William Forth of Nettlestead was the son of William Forth of Hadleigh, whose
niece, Mary, was the mother of John Winthrop, Jr. The Henry Bright who was the bearer of this
letter married the writer's half-sister.

men asked Howland if he should kill him allso, but he forbade him saying he feard there had been too many killed allready: the pinace being then driven on shoare and in danger, the Pl[imouth] men saved her, and putt one of their own men into her to carry her homewards toward Pasc[ataqua]   vpon the reporte of this we were muche greived, that suche an occasion should be offerd to our enemys to reproache our profession and that suche an iniurye should be offered to those hon[our]able persons who for loue of us and for furtherance of our beginnings here, had so farre eng[aged] themselv[es] with vs, so as we wrote to them to knowe the truethe of the matter, and whither they would advowe it: the wrote to vs againe relatinge the matter in effecte as I have expressed, with iustification of the facte etc: yet declaringe their sorrowe, that it had hapned so sadlye, otherwise then they intended: but they did not doubt but their Grant would beare them out: vpon this, we refuse to holde communion with them, till they give better satisfaction, and havinge the said Alden before vs, at a gen[era]l Court, we took security of him for his forthcoming and wrote to them what and wherefore we had done it: and upon their answeare, that themselves would doe iustice in the Cause, we remitted him to them, as having no iurisdiction in it, to trye it ourselues. All that we ayme at is that they may come to see their sinne and repente of it: which if they shall doe, I would intreat you to intercede with the Lords for them, that the iniury and discourtesy may be passed by, vpon such satisfaction as they can make.[1] I can think of nothing more at present to acquaint you with: so desiringe the continuance of your care and prayers for vs, as we wish and reioyce in the successe of your like vndertakings to the Southward I take leaue and rest Yours ever to be Commanded in the Lord

Jo: Winthrop

Boston Massachu[se]ts N: E: May 22, 1634

heere are 6 shipps lately arived with passengers and Cattle, most of them came in 6 weekes space   we have setled a plantation 20 miles to the north-ward, neere Merimacke. Mr. Parker is to be minister there.

JOHN WINTHROP TO THOMAS GRAVES[2]

Mr. Graves, I praye bringe me a paire of mill stones peake stones seaven foote broade and of thicknesse answearable. they are for a windmill and vpon

---

[1] See *Journal*, I. 137.
[2] Original in the possession of Robert Winthrop, Esq.

sight heereof this shalbe sufficient warrant to my brother Downinge to deliuer you monye for them. so I rest Your loving freind

Jo: WINTHOP

MASSACHUSETTS N: ENGLAND June 5, 1634

Mr. Pincheon desires you to bringe him six Chalder of sea coale.

[*Endorsed in another hand:*] Mr. Downing in Lenckoun end felds, by the goulden Lions touer.

THOMAS MAYHEW TO JOHN WINTHROP[1]

To the wor[shipfu]ll John Wynthropp this deliver in Boston

SIR, I doe hereby Request your wor[shi]pp to deliuer this bearer That hempe yow spake of for Caulkinge the pynnase: And I doe farther Intreate yow to lend mr. Craddock the hellpe of your teeme a day or two to hellpe Carry the timber for buillding the mill at watertowne. I haue sent vnto mr. Doomer I hope he will afford me his hellpe; that with the hellpe of our owne wee may doe it in two daies; the reason I desire to haue it donne with such expedition is for that the Cattell must be watched whillst they are about it; In regard they will be from home and soe doubtlesse otherwise woulld stray or at least Runn home: I will at any time yf your wor[shi]pp haue occasion in the like kind fullfill your desire: the time wee intend to goe about it is the second or third day of the next weeke. Thus Ceaseing farther to trouble yow at present, saluteinge you with all due Respecte, Committing you to the lords protecion, I rest Your worshipps to Commaund

THOMAS MAYHEW

MEADEFORD the 22th of the fowerth Moneth June 1634

I shall gladly pay for it yf you think good as willingly as to afford the like hellpe: its but hallfe the work concernes mr. Cradock or me: he is indeede partely Content I shoulld doe it my sellfe.

---

[1] W. Au. 63; 4 *Collections*, VII. 30–31. For Thomas Mayhew, see 4 *Collections*, VII. 30n.; *D.A.B.*

LONDON PORT BOOK ENTRY FOR THE *PHILIP*[1]

xix^mo Julij 1634

In le Phillip of London Rich: Hussy m[aste]r versus New England
John Winthorpe etc. of the Plantacon of matchechusatts baye   xxvj
Colts   xj heifers fre per lic. Regis.

JOHN WINTHROP, JR., TO JOHN WINTHROP[2]

*To the right wor[shipfu]ll my much honored father John Winthrop Esqr.
deliver In Boston*

SIR, I have cast up the account of the remainder which is yet behind of the goods that Mr. Kirby sent over   it amounteth to 44*li* 14*s* whereof the 3d parte deducted there remaineth 29*li* 16*s* to be returned for England, which is to be equally divided betwixt my uncle Downing and Mr. Kirby: I pray be pleased to send a bill for the said 29*li* 16*s* to Mr. Kirby to be received of my Uncle Downing with directions to him to pay himselfe his owne third part: I have to this purpose written to Mr. Kirby to receipt it and sent him a full account of all things. I understand that a Virginia pinnace hath brought over many Goats. If you please I would desire you to buy some of his Goats for some of those trucking Coats if he will exchange, they may be valued I think at about 20*s* a Coat etc.   it may be he would take all the other things. they stand in above 44*li*   I thinke they may be vallued altogether at about 6o*li* or dearer if his goats be deare.

I received some Corne by John Gallop, I thanke you for it. I understand by him that you would have bought some English meale for me, but I pray doe not for if you please to send me Corne my men shall beat it if I cannot have some ground, only I desire to have 2 or 3 bushell ground if it can be, because I have borrowed some on condition to pay in meale againe: If any pinnace come I pray be pleased to remember us with some munition ordinance muskets Carbines pikes and such as are to be had. thus with my duty and my wifes to your selfe and my mother saluting my brothers Cosens and freinds I humbly take my leave and rest Your Obedient son

JOHN WINTHROP

AGAWAM July 20, 1634

---

[1] Public Record Office; *Proceedings*, XLVII. 183.
[2] Original not located. The text as given here is taken from a copy in the handwriting of Charles Deane.

LONDON PORT BOOK ENTRY FOR THE *GRIFFIN*[1]

xxj^mo Julij 1634

In le Griffen of London Thomas Babb m[aste]r versus New England
Jon: Winthorpe Esquier Gouernor etc. for the passengers   xvj butts   ij
Ciiij   xxiiij hhds   xlj barrells   xxx killderkins   liij firkins   lxix Chestes and
troncks   xxiiij tts and packes of Ciij quarters wheat and wheat meale   xx
quarters Danske Rye   lxvj quarters mault   xv quarters pease   xxij quarters
oat meale   xxxvj C wht Cheese   j Cxvij firkins butter and suet   x hhds
vinegar   ij hhds sider xxiiij   j barr: salt and Grocerye wares value i*li*   haberdashers wares value j C ij*li*   vj C foote windowe glasse   fishinge instruments value xv*li*   xxxv ells canvas   lxx ells lockromes   xvij C wht birdinge
shott of lead   v barr et d^l gunpowder   Certen other necessaries value ij C
x*li* absq. subss. etc. per lic. Regis.

In le Griffen of London prd.
Idem Jon: etc. for the planters   xxiiij yrds sale clothe   ix C ells norm.
Canvas   Cxl ells spruce Canvas   v C ells lockromes bed tikes value iij*li*   xxij
paire coarse blankets   xij dozen Yrishe stockinges   xl dozen mens and xiij
doz. woemens shooes   vj dozen Chilldrens shooes   Cviij pares bootes   Cert.
ps. and remnants stuff cost lv*li* packt cum alijs absque subss: per lic. Regis.

JOHN WINTHROP TO SIR SIMONDS D'EWES[2]

*To the right wor[shi]p[fu]ll Sir Simonds Dewes Knight at Lavenham in Suff:
Leave this with Mr. Gurdon or with Mr. Rogers of Dedham*

MUCHE HONORED SIR, Yours per Wm. Hamond I received, acknowledging
my self so muche bounde to you, that you are pleased to take all occasions to
manifest your good will to our Colonye, and to myself in particular: that I
would gladly have bestowed much paynes in Satisfieing your desire concerninge the estate of our Countrye and Affaires, and I did hope vpon the discharge of my place, to have good leysure to that end, but our new Governor
(my brother Dudly) dwelling out of the waye, I am still as full of Companye
and business as before. But for the natives in these parts, Gods hand hath so
pursued them, as for 300 miles space, the greatest parte of them are swept

---

[1] Public Record Office; *Proceedings*, XLVII. 184.
[2] Harleian MSS., B.M., 388, fo. 188; *Publications of the Colonial Society of Massachusetts*, VII. 71–72.

awaye by the small poxe, which still continues among them: So as God hathe hereby cleered our title to this place, and those who remaine in these parts, being in all not 50, have putt themselues vnder our protection, and freely confined themselues and their interest within certain Limitts.

For your counsell of Conforminge ourselues to the Ch[urch] of E[ngland] though I doubt not but it proceeds out of your care of our wellfare: yet I dare not thanke you for it; because it is not conformable to Gods will revealed in his worde: what you may doe in E[ngland] where things are otherwise established, I will not dispute, but our case heere is otherwise: being come to clearer light and more Libertye, which we trust by the good hand of our God with vs, and the gratious indulgence of our Kinge, we may freely enioye it: so desiringe you to excuse my brevitye, and to continue your good will towards vs, I commend you with your good Lady and all yours to the gratious protection and direction of the Lord, and so I take leave and rest at your service in the Lord

Jo. Winthrop

Boston N: E: July 21, 1634

JOHN WINTHROP'S FINANCIAL STATEMENT
TO THE GENERAL COURT[1]

The Accompt of John Winthrop, Esq. late Gouernour

Whereas by order of the last generall Court Commissioners were appoynted viz. Roger Ludlowe Esq. the Deputy Gouernour and Mr. Israell Stoughton gent. to receave my accompt of such things as I haue receaved and disbursed for publique vse in the time of my Gouerment In all due observance and submission to the order of the said Court I doe make this declaratory accompt ensueinge.

First I affirme that I never receaved any Monyes or other goods comitted to mee in trust for the Comonwealth otherwise then is hereafter expressed.

Item I acknowledge I haue in my custody certaine Barrells of common Powder and some match and drumeheads, with some things belonging to the Ordinances: which Powder, being landed att Charles Towne and exposed to the Iniury of the weather, I tooke, and bestowed first in a Tent which I made of myne own broadcloth, (being then worth viij*s* the yard, but in that service

---

[1] Manuscript records of the General Court, Massachusetts Archives; *L. and L.*, ii. 120–122; *Records of Massachusetts*, i. 130–132. For Hutchinson's comment on the occasion for this financial statement of the Governor, see *History of Massachusetts-Bay*, i. 40.

much spoiled)   after I removed it to my store howse att Boston, where it still remaines save that some of it hath bene spent in publique service and fyve barrells deliuered to Dorchester and foure to Rocksbury, and three barrells I solde to some shipps that needed them, which I will allowe Powder or money for. the rest I am ready to deliuer vpp to such as shalbe appoynted to receave them.

I receaved also some meale and pease from Mr. White of Dorchester in England, and from Mr. Roe of London, which was bestowed vpon such as hadd neede thereof in the seuerall Townes, as also x*li* gyven by Mr. Hewson. I receaved also from Mr. Humfry some ruggs, freese suits, shoes and hoose, (the certaine valewe whereof I must knowe from himself) with lettres of direccion to make vse of the greatest parte thereof as giuen to helpe beare out my charge for the publique. I paid for the fraight of theis goods, and disposed of the greatest parte of them to others, but howe I cannot sett downe. I made vse also of two pare of carriage wheeles which I will allowe for. I hadd not medled with them but that they lay vselesse, for want of the carriages which were lefte in England.

For my disbursements I haue formerly deliuered to the nowe deputy a Bill of parte of them, amounting to neere 300*li* which I disbursed for publique service dyvers yeares since for which I haue receaved in Corne att vj*s* the bushell (and which will not yeild me above iiij*s*) about 180*li* or neere soe much.

I disbursed also for the transportacion of Mr. Phillips and his Family, which was to be borne by the generall, till he should bee chosen to some particular Congregacion.

Nowe for my other Charges by occacion of my place of Gouernour it is well knowen I haue expended much, and somewhat I haue receaved towards it, which I should haue rested satisfyed with but that being called to accompt, I must mencion my disbursements with my receipts, and in both shall referre myselfe to the pleasure of the Court.

I was first chosen to be Gouernour without my seekeing or expectacion (there being then dyvers other gent[lemen] whoe for their abilityes euery way were farr more fitt)   being chosen I furnished my selfe with servants and provisions accordingly in a farr greater proporcion than I would haue done, hadd I come as a private man or as an Assistant onely; In this office I contynued foure yeares and neere an halfe, although I earnestly desired, att euery eleccion to haue bene freed. In this tyme I haue spent above 500*li* per annum of which 200*li* per annum would haue maintained my Family in a private condicion Soe as I may truely say I haue spent by occacion of my late office above 1200*li*. towards this I have receaved by way of Benevolence from some Townes aboute 50*li* and by the last yeares allowance 150*li* and by some provisions sent by Mr. Humfry as is before mencioned about 50*li* or it may be somewhat more.

I also disbursed att our comeing away in England for Powder and greate shott 216*li* which I did not putt into my bill of charges formerly deliuered to the nowe deputy etc. because I did expect to haue paide myselfe out of that parte of Mr. Johnsons estate which hee gaue to the publique but findeing that it will fall farr shorte I must putt it to this accompt.

The last thing which I offer to the consideracion of the Court is that my Longe continuance in the said office, hath putt mee into such a way of vnavoydeable charge, as wilbe still as chargeable to mee as the place of Gouernour will be to some others. In all theis things I referre my selfe to wisedome and Justice of the Court: with this protestacion that it repenteth mee not of my cost or labour bestowed in the service of this Comonwealth: but doe hartyly blesse the Lord our god, that hee hath pleased to honour mee soe farr, as to call for any thing hee hath bestowed vpon mee for the service of his Church and people here, the prosperity whereof and his gracious acceptance shalbe an aboundant recompense to mee   I conclude with this one request (which in Justice may not be denyed mee) that as it stands vpon record that vpon the discharge of my office I was called to accompt, soe this my declaracion may be recorded also: least hereafter, when I shalbe forgotten, some bleamishe may lye vpon my posteritie when there shalbe noething to cleare it etc.

JOHN WINTHROP

Sept. 4th 1634

CERTIFICATE OF MARRIAGE[1]

the 10th day of the 8th month called October 1634 Edmond Hubberd senior,[2] and Sarah Oakeley[3] widow did ioyne in marriage before mee, and others   witnes my hand per me

INCREASE NOWELL

---

[1] W. I. 107.

[2] Edmund Hobart, Sr., father of the Reverend Peter Hobart of Hingham.

[3] The widow of the Reverend John Lyford, who played an important part in Plymouth Colony.

JOHN WINTHROP TO JOHN WINTHROP, JR.[1]

To my lovinge sonne Mr. John Winthrop deliver At Mr. Downinge his Chamber
in the inner Temple lane London

MY DEAR SONNE, I hope the Lord hath carried you safe to E[ngland] with our most deare mr. Warner,[2] and the rest of our good brethren and freinds. there is nothing befallen since your departure, but mr. Peirce came from Naragansett 3 days after, with 500 bushels of Corne onely: At the Court it was informed that some of Salem had taken out a peece of the Crosse in their Ensigne, wherevpon we sent forth an Attachment to bring in the partyes at the next Court, where they are like to be punished for their indiscreet zeale, for the people are generally offended with it. mrs. W. was at first very much affected with her husbands departure but she is now well pacified. I intend to sende this Lettre by Captain Vnderhill, who hath leave to goe see his freinds in Holland. if he come to you, he can inform you of all things here. As I was writinge this, Rich[ard] came in and tould me the dogge had killed an olde woulf this morning in our neck: she made more resistance then both the former. I have many things to write to you about, for such necessaryes as are to be provided and sent over, but this occasion is suddain, and I cannot think of them: but shall write more largely by mr. P[eirce] if the Lord will. your selfe know what wilbe needfull, and therefore may consider accordingly. remember Coperous white and green: and 2 or 3 li. of Paracellsus plaister, and some E: indian Bezoar, store of sayl clothe, nayls, Cordage, Pitche, tallow and wicke, steel spades and shouells, 2 hand sawes and small axes the best of all what euer they cost: Commend vs to all our good freinds where you become, mr. W. and the rest, your vnckles Ants etc: advise mr. W. to keepe close by all newes, and make haste back. the good Lorde blesse and prosper you that we may see your face with ioy. your mother etc. salute and blesse you farewell

[JOHN WINTHROP]

Nou: 6, 1634

---

[1] W. 7A. 53; Savage (1825), I. 384–385; (1853), I. 462; *L. and L.*, II. 123–124.

[2] Winthrop undoubtedly means the Reverend John Wilson, who had returned to England on the same ship with John Winthrop, Jr. Since Winthrop considered that Wilson was "like to be troubled and detained" in England (*Journal*, I. 145), he quite naturally avoided using his correct name. He subsequently refers to him in this letter as "Mr. W." Similarly, the "Mrs. W." refers to Wilson's wife.

JOHN ENDECOTT TO JOHN WINTHROP, JR.[1]

To my Deare and right Worthie Friend John Winthrop Junior Esqr. deliver

DEAREST SIR, I writt vnto yow by Mr. Babbe wherein I gaue you full commission to sell my howse. And I doe by theise second it againe, desiring you to sell it to an honest man, else not to sell it. The price I writt was 250*li*, what aboue you can. And if you see good you may abate some of it. I haue giuen order to Thomas Read, who is now in England, to finde out a Chapman if hee can as also to Mr. Peters in Holland, and haue written to him to make you acquainted with their proceedings that there be no wronge don to any. If god should so order that you can sell it I pray you do so much as to certifie soe much by letter to Mr. Peters in Holland who is at Roterdam. There is no newes heere, all your Friends are well: We had the greatest snow fell the xxixth of the 9th moneth that I haue seene yet since I came into the Land. The Crosse is much stood for, and I ame like to suffer in it. The Lord his will be done. My wiefe remembers her loue to you and Mr. Williams.[2] The good God bring you back againe in saftie to vs. To whom I committ you and rest Your assured loving Friend and brother in the Lord Jesus.

JO: ENDECOTT

SALEM the 8th of the 10th moneth 1634

I haue written to Mr. Revell concerning my howse   it may be hee will buy it. If you please you may speake with him.

JOHN WINTHROP TO JOHN WINTHROP, JR.[3]

To my dear sonne mr. John Winthrop at the house of mr. Downing in Lincol[n]es Inn field near the Golden Lyon Taverne London deliver

MY GOOD SONNE, The Lorde blesse thee ever.

I wrote to you by Captain Vnderhill, who went hence in Mr. Babbs shipp, since which tyme heere arrived a shipp from Barnstable of 200 tun mr. Packers master. she brought about 20 passingers and 40 Cattle. she lost but

[1] Essex Institute; 4 *Collections*, VI. 131–132.
[2] Possibly John Wilson is meant. Endecott would have had the same reason as Winthrop for avoiding the use of Wilson's name. See above, page 175, *n*. 2.
[3] W. 7A. 54; Savage (1825), I. 385–387; (1853), I. 463–465; *L. and L.*, II. 125–127.

2 and yet was 17 weekes outward bound, whereof 5 in Ireland. she now returnes empty with mr. Peirce, by whom I send these.

All things continue as when you lefte vs, onely mrs. Warham is dead, and mr. Hookers younge sonne (who died of the small pox which are very rife at Newtowne) and 2 men of our towne Willys and Dowtye and 2 ladds were cast away in a great Tempest at N: E: on friday Nou: 21, in the night, betweene Noddles Island and Boston, in a small boat which they had ouerladen with wood   my selfe and diverse others were in the same Tempest, not without some perill, but the Lord preserved vs. mr. Sewalls boat was then in the Coue at the head of Cape Anne and broken to peeces, but the men and goods saved. The pestilent feaver hath taken away some at Plimouth, amonge others mr. Prence the Governour his wife, and mr. Allertons wife. we mett the last week to consider about the businesse of the Ensign at Salem, and have written a lettre to my brother Downing wherin vnder our hands we signifie our dislike of the Action, and our purpose to punish the Offenders.

I wrote to you in my former lettre about diverse things which we should have need off which I will heere insert allso with addition of some others.

The Pekods sent 2 Embassyes to vs: the first tyme they went away without answeare: the next time we agreed a peace with them (for friendly Comerce onely which was that they desired, having now warr with the Dutch and Narrigansett) vpon these terms viz: that they should deliver vs those men, who killed Captain Stone etc:[1] and surrender vp to vs their right in Conecte-cott, which they willingly agreed vnto, and offered vs a great present of wampompeag and beauer and otter with this expression, that we might with parte thereof procure their peace with the Narigansetts (themselues standing vpon termes of honor, not to offer any thing of themselues).

Winter hath begunne early with vs: the Baye hath been frozen all ouer, but is now open again: and we had a snowe last weeke much depth in many places: it came with so violent a storme, as it putt by our lecture for that day. I wish that in your return you would observe the winde and weather everye daye, that we may see how it agrees with our parts.

mr. Warde continues at your house this winter, and mr. Clerk (to give him content) in his owne. mr. Cl[erk] finds much fault with your servants John and Sarah, and tells me they will not earne their bread, and that Ned is worth them all.

Spades and shovells.

Felling axes, and other small axes.

---

[1] See *Journal*, I. 118, 140.

nayles of 6 10 and 20.

peircer bitts.

Sithes for grasse, and two brush sithes.

Coperas white and greene.

Emplastrum Paracellsi 2 or 3 li.

Emplastrum dominion.

Trading cloth good store, if mony may be had.

Browne thredds and haire buttons and a h[ogs]h[ea]d of twine for herring netts.

Shoes 2 soled stronge, and the best Irish stockins, and washe leather stockins.

stronge cloth suits, vnlined and linen suits of Canvas.

Suet, tallow, and wick.

A Carpenter, and a husbandman, and a ropemaker, and a Cooper.

Some muskets.

Store of Brimstone.

A Brake for Hempe.

bring the more of all necessaryes because this is the last we shall have without Custom.[1]

If my brother Tindale would lett you haue 100*li* you may give him assurance of so much in Cattle heer to be presently sett out for my wife and her Children, with the increase or for 200*li* if he will.

Commende vs to all our good frends, your Ant Dow[ning] and vnkle G[ostlin] and Ants those at maplsted, Graces, Assington, Groton, Charterhouse: Sir Rich: S[altonstall] and his sonne etc. and all the rest as you have occasion, mr. Kirby, etc., and mr. Howes and make haste back: and if there be any matter of importance, write by the first fishing shippes. direct your lettres to Capt. Wiggin, or mr. Hilton. your mother and the rest are in health (I prayse God) we all salute you. the good Lord direct keep and blesse you farewell my good sonne

[JOHN WINTHROP]

December 12, 1634

---

[1] Cf. the provision in the Massachusetts Bay Company Charter whereby freedom from customs duties was granted for a term of seven years.

JOSHUA HOYLE TO JOHN WINTHROP, JR.[1]

To his most respected Mr. John Winthrop in England or wheresoeuer these

GENTLE MR. WINTHROP, not to protract or prologize, my maine buisinesse at this time is to correct the crudity of a few vnhatcht verses vpon your sudden departure: and first of all a mis-take of pen vpon meere hast and oblivion in the nineteenth.

> *Et transmundanis celerem te sospitet oris.*
> *Haud aliter volucri transactus verbere longa*
> *Sæpiùs argutus percurrit stamina pecten.*

So in the five and twentith, for *Cumque,*

> *Atque tuis noster Zephyris occurrerit Eurus.*

Then to the second part prefix (if you please) this title, with some other addition, or change;

Ad regionem ipsam, et Indos

> *Fœcundi latices Nympharum, alveique salubres*
> *Quas Merimacus aquas, quas Mystica flumina torquent*
> *In mare præcipites diris exosa chelydris:*
> *Primus et ignota portus Masachusis arena,*
> *Celsæ vbi consurgunt aliæ Bostonidos arces;* or
> (*Fama est hoc etiam Bostonida litore condi.*)
> *Quique facem praefers nautis etc.* and after,
> *Pande sinus, gremioque Salem deterge madentem,*
> *Ac tandem fessos secura sede recondas.*
> *Nulla lues pecori: pestis, rabidique leones*
> *Absint; flamma vorax, frugibusque inimica locusta*
> *Absit: et Hispanos procul his arceto superbos*
> *Litoribus; mare ne exundet: ne naufraga puppis:*
> *Tempestivus agros ac rura redintegret imber:*
> *Copia, paxque suis certatim dotibus, ornent:*
> *Persuade indigenis.*

these to stand according to this my last Will and Testament.

---

[1] W. 4. 74; 5 *Collections,* I. 204–205. For Joshua Hoyle, Professor of Divinity at Dublin University, see *D.N.B.*

Remember my humble service and deerest respects to your worthy parents vnknowen; and Reverend Mr. Cotton flitted out of the world and yet still in Boston whose praiers I much desire to enioy: and to your fellow-traveiller Mr. Wilson, whose friendship I am sory the Kernes have intercepted. Keepe sufficient privacy. The infinite God be with vs all. Amen. Yours euer

JOSUA HOYLE

Ex eadem mensula, Decemb. 26, [1634]

THE COMMISSION FOR FOREIGN PLANTATIONS TO THE OFFICERS OF THE PORT OF LONDON[1]

To our louing Freinds the officers of the Port of London or any 1 of them

After our harty commendations whereas it appeareth that greate Numbers of his Maiesties subiects haue bin and are euery yeare transported into those parts of America, which haue bin graunted by patent to seuerall persons; and there settle themselues, some of them with ther families and whole Estates, Amongst which Numbers theire also many idle and refractary humors, whose only end is to liue as much as they can without the reach of authority, We hauing according to the power wherwith we are Intrusted by his Maiesties commission for matter of plantations seriously considered how necessary it is for diuers Weighty and important reasons to take carefull and effectuall order for the stopping of such promiscuous and disorderly parting out of the Realme, doe therfore in his Maiesties name expresly charge and command you the officers of that port not to suffer any person being a subsedyman to imbarke himselfe in the port or any the members thereof for any of the said planta-tions, without Licence from us his Maiesties commissioners, nor any person vnder the degree of a subsidyman without an attestation from two Justices of the peace liuing next the place where he dwelt last or where he dwelt before, if he hath dwelt but a while there, That he hath taken the oath of Supremacie and Allegiance, and the like Testimony from the Minister of the parish of his conversation and Conformity to the orders and discipline of the Church of England. And we do in like manner charge and command you to returne to vs every halfe yeare a particular and perfect list of the names and qualities of all those that haue in the meane time imbarqued in that port or

---

[1] W. 4. 164; 5 *Collections*, I. 481–482. Cf. the Commission's earlier order of February 28, 1633/34, *Acts of the Privy Council of England, Colonial Series*, I. 200–201; *New England Historical and Genealogical Register*, IX. 265–266.

the members thereof for any of the plantations before mentioned, in the performance of all which you are in no sort to faile, as you will answer the neglect thereof at your perills   And so we bid you hartily Farewell. Your louing Freinds

	W. Cant.	Fra: Cottington
From Whitehall	Tho: Couentry	Ed. Dorsett
the last of December 1634	Portland	Tho: Edmonds
	Arundell	John Coke
	Surrey	Fr: Windebanke
	R. Ebor.	H. Vane
	H. Mandiuill	

Ent. John Dickenson

[*Endorsed by John Winthrop, Jr.:*] The lords lettre to the Ports about passengers goeing to Pl[an]t[ation]s.

ESSAY ON THE ORDERING OF TOWNS[1]

As the most magnificent structure aboundently bewtefyed, with noe lesse speculatiue ornaments then with dilectable curious conceites for humane contentments: yet the same wanting its due proportion, declyneth the principall of its worthy Commendacions. Soe in all pragmaticall imployments, the Fownedacions to be disposite, that the perædifications (with much wisdome in weighty matters) may orderly be proceeded in: is a thing necessarely Required. The Geometricall delineacion of the dimension belongeth only to the Circumspicution of the personally present. Only a fewe things a farre of may be thought fittinge briefly according to your proposicion.

First. Suppose the Towne square 6 miles euery waye. The Howses orderly placed about the midst, especially the Meetinghouse, the which we will suppose to be the Centor of the wholl Circomferance. The greatest difficulty is for the Imployment, Improuement of the parts most remote, which (yf better directions doe not arise) may be thus.

The wholl being 6 miles: the extent from the Meetinghouse as the Centor, wilbe vnto euery side 3 miles: the one halfe wherof being 1500 paces rownd about and next vnto the sayd Centor, in what Condicion soeuer it lyeth, may

---

[1] W. 4. 163; 5 *Collections*, 1. 474–480. The handwriting of this anonymous and undated document has not been identified.

first beginnings, for in likelyhoode ther may be neede enough: And that thus, for the better expedicion according to the necessety, Seing fewe haue wholl draughts sufficient for a plowe, diuerse may joyne together to make an wholl draught: And soe to sett soe many plowes aworke as all the beasts fitting in the towne may be Imployed, and that by the skillfullest men in the towne: wherby euery mans turne, one after an other, may be speedely serued, at convenient rates, and that sine expilatione, the common Exprobration of the wholl Newe England. I wold I could exempt Newe Towne: but I hope wisdome shall be Iustefyed both of her Children and in her Children; ther is good vse to be made of the voyce of an enemy, to quicken the watch of the Citty.

When the number of the Inhabitantes are rightly resolued vpon: then it may be necessary that the wholl towne be set out into portions, by dooles, as may be thought fitting, without more afterinlargments. For though ther be none expectacion of sudden incloseing, yet it will be such a Goade in the side of the Industrious to drawe in and make the spediest and best imployment of his knowne proportion: that others will of necessety be drawne on by his good example, to their much benefit and compfort on euery side. For as it is an Axiome in all science to doe a thing, first Perite, then Expedite, so it is most necessary in all Plantacions which haue soe many dependances but especially amongst Christians whoe for the improueing most precious tyme in all things to the best, are bownd with the suerest Ligaments. And though in the Interim it must lye common: yet he that knoweth the benefit of incloseing, will omit noe dilligence to brenge him selfe into an inclusive condicion, well vnderstanding that one acre inclosed, is much more beneficiall then 5 falling to his share in Common. As also by this meanes shall noe man make waest of timber but vpon his owne portion, soe assigned out vnto him: though for the present (only concerneinge the feede vntill it be fenced in) it lyeth in common.

One thing more I am bould to suggest vizt. That concerning Swampes and such Rubbish waest grownds within Compas of the wholl towne, which harber Wolues and such noyesome beasts and serpents may be suppressed, and gradatim at some generall charge become of all the lowe growne stuffe cleered: which may be well soe performed. Or rather it may be soe conveniently ordered, that vnto euery mans Lot, ther may according to the contents by the acre be given, an answerable proportion, with an iniunction, that euery such parte must within 2 or 3 yeares be w[holly] of such harboring stuffe (by cutting downe) cleered, and [torn] for euer maynteyned, which by a dilligent hand may without [torn] be accomplished: And the benefit will soon be perceived.

It is a thing not vnnecessary to be considered, but well performed. For howe much damage other plantacions haue susteyned and may still expect by such rauenous vnsatiable creatures hath ben too much experimented, haveing also begonne with greate beasts, and shall we thinke that in tyme they will not fall vpon men. And why shold such a thing be neglected, seing soe many lawes and practises (as of our owne soe) of many other nations are gonne before vs, wherby we might be Incoraged: First to depriue them of all their harbours, then of the heades of soe many as shall come within our Compas, which may without greate difficulty be performed. Rewards haue generally ben ordered, and ought in all such Cases still to be given.[1] The lawe of Dracho gave one tallent for a yong wolfe, and 2 tallents for an old Wolfe. The auncient Rewards of our owne cuntry have ben diuerse, and some greate, which I thinke are well knowne. And it hath in some other Cuntries ben accounted a shamefull misery to induer the tyrany of such spoyleing beasts without laboring for Resistance and Revenge. Therfore in Lumbardye be-yonde the Alpes, yf a Wolfe came but into the cuntry: presently the Bells are runge, and themselues armed for Resistance, neuer giveing ouer vntill they haue killed or expelled him the wholl cuntry. much more might be spoaken of this but I am allredy too long. only thus much more: that I haue often hearde (by seemeing credible men) that Wolues are much more increased since our Nation came then when the Indians possessed the same, and a Reason rendred, that they were dilligent in destroying the Yonge. And is not this a dishonor vnto our Christian newe Common wealth: to the very name of our nation yf not to the nature of our proffession.

Thus haue I ben ouer long to soe smale purpose in answering your desier for a litle improuement of my single pore tallent which I shall euer desier to be imployed vnto better inlargement, yf any smale advantage might any wayes proceede from it. In the meane tyme I rest assuered of your curtious acceptance: And soe for the present I take my leave, humbly intreateing of you, one peticion amongst your fervant supplications, even for me, the vn-worthiest of all the vnworthy: vnto which the Lord Allmighty (your ever guider) may ever saye Amen. Amen.

[*Ca.* 1635]

---

[1] A bounty established by the General Court on November 9, 1630, for the killing of wolves was repealed November 7, 1632, and reëstablished September 2, 1635. *Records of Massachusetts*, I. 81, 102, 156.

ALICE DANIELL TO JOHN WINTHROP[1]

To the Right Worshipful and worthily respected Mr. John Winthopp senior
these deliver Boston

DEARE AND WORTHY SIR, my humble and due seruise remembered to your selfe and your deare yoakfellow together with my constant requests to the lord of wisedome and grace to perfect his worke in you and by you to the prayse of his owne grace: I made bould som months since to present your wor[shi]pp with a few lines touching the Cattell that mr. Skelton left with mee: and since that time I haue Received a letter from your selfe: and by direction of our beloued mr. Endicott from your self haue taken a true coppy of those writings which mr. Endecott presented to you soe neere as possible can bee desiring rather to charge my selfe than to doe the least wrong in any kind; which Coppy I haue here sent: as allso mr. Skeltons Will: desireng to lay all things naked before you as the lye: now I beeseech you worthy Sir: though I haue the Cattell in a compleate number: yet the charge of the keeping hath beene much to mee: as allso diuers debts of mr. Skeltons wherof som are payd and some are not: now this I know that since mr. Skeltons death I am out of purse of my owne money laiyd for the cattell and the keep-ing of the house (as som freinds are able to Relate) the some of 25*li* and better almost 26*li* besides all that I haue made of the milke: which I hope was put to the best advantadge: and as I haue intimated the losse of the cattell in the accompt soe allso there remayneth since mr. Skeltons death but onely one Bull calf: and for the Cowes there are but two that haue taken the season of breed: and one of them will not com till the latter end of the sommer   many cattell were brought into the towne this yeare and our bulls fayled much: And whereas you were pleased to expresse that you saw not your selues ingaged for the keeping of the children: there is noe ingagments by mee: your selfe knoweth how the Couenant Runneth: if mr. Skeltons will bee disanuld which is the ground of my ingagement: I beeseech you then consider vpon whom shall it ly: now since I haue seene the lords hand calling mee to this busines I haue had triall euery way both of vnderstanding and care how to order things for the best: thus knowing your care and indeauour to please the lord

---

[1] Suffolk County Court Files, No. 6; 2 *Proceedings*, x. 109–110; *N. E. Historical and Genealogical Register*, xxv. 320. For Alice Daniell, see *N. E. Historical and Genealogical Register*, xxv. 318–320.

in all things I Rest leauing these to your godly and wise consideration Yours
vnfeinedly to command in the lord

ALICE DANIELL

[*Ca.* 1635]

SIR JOHN CLOTWORTHY TO JOHN WINTHROP, JR.[1]

WORTHY FREINDE, I shall request you, when you are freed from the distractions which a werisom jorney may perhapps afford; to consider of these
particulers.

Fyrst whatt cowrse you and your good freinds together can propose for the
transmission of yonge children, vppon tearmes of aprentishipp on the conditions I have spoken to your selfe off, or any other way, as the Lo[rd] shall
dyrect.

2 To prouide for your seruant, when you speak with your Yorksheire
freinds, for the sending of twoe mares very good to your country of Goshan:

3 To bestow a word on your frind thats your skinner for a beauer coate; itt
must bee made very large; and to the length of the calfe of the leg:

4: I request a bever hatt of the best sort:

Either Mr. Francis Allen Jeweller who dwelles over against St. Dunstons
Church, or Mr. Burnett who dwells att the Golden Fleece in Lumbert Streete
will geiue you notice of som Irish merchants that may be bound for Dublin;
by these be plesd to dyrect your Lettres etc. to Mr. Lake merchant in Dublin
in the Castle Streete. I remaine your affectionate frind and seruant

JOHN CLOTWORTHY

ANTRIM 5th Jn: 1634[/35]

JOHN LIVINGSTONE TO JOHN WINTHROP, JR.[2]

KILLINSHIE 5th Januar 1634[/35]

MR. WYNTHORP, Hast to bee at my charge wes the reason why I come
away so abruptly th'other day. I could have been glad to have had more
tyme, and so to have been more refreshed with yowr company, But I hope
the tyme may come when wee may see one another in that land where a great
part of my heart is already. I have made bold to send some letters that yow

---

[1] W. 4. 73; 5 *Collections*, I. 203–204. For Clotworthy, see 5 *Collections*, I. 203*n*.
[2] W. Au. 83; 5 *Collections*, I. 206. Livingstone is mentioned by Governor Winthrop in his Journal
(I. 127). For a biographical sketch, see *D.N.B.*

may cause bee delyvered as you go along. To three I have writen somwhat concerning yow, To Johne Stewart in Air to Mr. David Dicksone in Irvin, and to James Murray in Edinborough, To whom if yow bee pleased yow may showe yowr self and give some information how maters goes beyond Seas They are men religious and wyse, with whom yow may be free and who (I dare promise) will communicate what yow impart to them only to such and so much as yow shal think fitting. The lord whom yow serve is with yow, wilbee with yow and guyd yow the way that yow are going which shalbee the prayers of him who is Yowrs in the trewest respects

Jo: LEVINGSTONE

HENRY JACIE TO JOHN WINTHROP, JR.[1]

To the Worsh[ipfu]ll John Winthrop esq. in York

DEARE SIR, How much am I endebted to you for your great paines and love, which hath endeared you yet more unto me: If I should heare it turnes to your hurt any way, I must needs sympathize with you.

One or 2 Questions came not to my mind, which I would entreat by you to be resolvd in, vizt. seing such a company of Christians have foreintended such a one to be their Minister, and he to accept it, Whether in their fast they desire Gods directing in their choise (when they have no other fit to be chosen) or its only for Gods blessing his paines etc. Also Whether they use imposition of hands, or by whom, and when. And whether any imposition on the Elder, and by whom, or on the Deacon.

Now Sir since your going to york, I have found H. Kingsburies letter (which I could not light on) the bookes he desired me to procure him were these 3. 1 A Treatise of Faith. (I suppose The Doctrine of Faith by Mr. Jo. Rogers would be as useful for him, and about the same price.) 2 Perkins Principles. 3. The sweet Posie for Gods Saints (2*d* a peece, the 1 about 18*d*.) He writ he would pay for them. We shal be further indebted to you if you can procure the Map, the Pattents Copie, the Model of Charity,[2] (also what Oath is taken) Mr. Higgisons letter, and the Petition to our Ministers for praying for them, made at their going, which is in print.[3] Which of these you

---

[1] W. 1. 59; 1 *Proceedings*, XVIII. 300–301.

[2] "A Modell of Christian Charity," written by Winthrop on board the *Arbella* (1630). It is printed in *Winthrop Papers*, II. 282–295.

[3] *The Hvmble Reqvest of His Majesties Loyall Subjects, the Governour and the Company Late Gone for New England; to the Rest of Their Brethren, in and of the Church of England* (London, 1630). It is reprinted, among other places, in *Winthrop Papers*, II. 231–233.

can best, with your letter, give to Mr. Overton Stationer in Popes head Alley, my good friend, and receive money of him for them, or for writing (giving him this note) that he may send them by York Cariers either to the now L[ord] Majors, or to Mr. John Penrose Attorney, for me. But I pray you resolve me those Ques[tions] now (for I suppose you ar not gone from York.) Remember my kind respect and love to Mr. Downing, Mr. Robt. Gurdon with Mrs. Gurdon and Mr. Edward Gurdon, and to Mr. Huison at London stone if you see him (from whom I have had letter though I have not seen him) Also in Essex and Suffolk. I am now posted. The good Lord be with you. Yours in him

HEN: JACIE

[*Ca.* February, 1634/35]

I pray you Mr. Overton repay to this my friend what he hath laid out for me, and I shal see that you be repaid, either as formerly, or by my Bro[ther] Thomas Jacie, servant to Mr. Elwis in Drury lane a litle beyond Qu[een]s street.

And direct your letters etc. for me, to be left with the Lord Major of York, for so is Mr. Hodshon now.

I received your letter and compasses etc. remember me kindly to Mr. Peck. Yours

H. JACIE

PRISCILLA PAYNTER TO JOHN WINTHROP, JR.[1]

To my beloved Sonne Mr. John Winthrop at Mr. Downings neere the Lion taverne in Lincolnes Inne fields by Princes street end deliver in London

MY DERE SONE, your letter cam to my hands whin I was full of sorowe so as I could not then wright for it plased god that uery weeke to take from me my dere daughter mary fones to my husbands and my grat grife and to the grife of all those that knewe her swete and louely disspossion: conserning the paymant of those monys you wright of I doe not well understand: you demand of my husban one hundered pound for which you say you haue his band: you desier to know wether he hath payed ursula thirtie pound: we layed out aboue

---

[1] W. 4. 27; 5 *Collections*, I. 71–72. For earlier correspondence dealing with the subject matter of this letter, see Henry Paynter to John Winthrop, Jr., *ca.* June, 1631, pages 38–39, above; Ursula Sherman to John Winthrop, Jr., June 18, 1631, pages 39–40, above; Emmanuel Downing to John Winthrop, Jr., November 2, 1631, pages 50–51, above; and Emmanuel Downing to John Winthrop, Jr., June 18, 1633, page 129, above.

fiftie pounds and out of her portion but why we should paye her thirtie for
that I see no reson: it is true ther was on hundered pound due to your dere
wife which was to be payed her out of those depts which wear due to mr.
fones as will apere by the deede of gift to your wife   the monys that shuld
haue payed this, we haue receiued but fiftie pounds of it as yet: forty 5
p[ound]s more is in my lady mouddes hands which if you will be earnest with
her for it I mak no dout but she will pay it forth with and the other 50 pounds
I will pay presently, if you will be peased to giue vp my husbands band: I
shuld much reioyce to see you here if it might be and if it were as conuenent
for me to trauell as for you, it should not be long before I would see you and
then would ther be a quick disspaich of this buisnes which other wayes will
require many letters and much mistaken of on naother, for in your first letter
after your brothers death you wrot that my husband should take no care for
it if you could sell his land   for respect to vrsula, your father in his letter
wrot that you had giuen her 60 pounds or above which shee neuer knew what
way unles it ware ment in your sayed letters   yet if you wright that you will
except of 50 pound and of 20 more when it shall be receiued of my lady
moody you shall receiued the 50 pound before you goe away at the hands of
my vncle tally vpon conuenant warning from you as I hop   I shall intreat
him by letter vpon your deliuering vp the band to him who I know will doe
his vtmost with you for the rest from the lady   thus desiering your answer
and the presenting of my best loue to your selfe my worthy brother and sister
downing I rest your louing mother

PRIS: PAYNTER

[*Ca.* March, 1635]

SIR JOHN CLOTWORTHY TO JOHN WINTHROP, JR.[1]

MY DEARE FREINDE, Herinclosed I send you a casement through which I
thinke you may much more securely impart your minde then any other way;
you will finde at euery corner of the paper a little noch of this length ——,
you must cause those noches to bee iust putt on those due places on the letter
I haue written; and then you may reade my secrett minde;[2] the rest being

---

[1] W. 12. 9.

[2] The "casement" used by Clotworthy and Winthrop is a sheet of paper 7½ inches by 11⅜
inches, with rectangular slits of varying lengths cut in such a way that when the "casement" is
superimposed on the letter, only those words constituting the message can be read through the
openings. The results obtained by the use of this device can be seen from the illustration facing this
page.

this side vppermost;

now hauing ... fully in ... formed my ſe ... ſe

of ye ſtatue w ... wee mainly d ... doing I oft, Ioe ... now kindy

giue yu notice, ... twee are most ... led to ... ſend off yt chat

the ... you most off all ... and, & ... as ye giuing no ... notice,

hath by Gods hel ... alya, the ... ſpedy dyly ... grace for

he guiding off ... ſuch a quan ... tity as ... yu ſhall ſend ... this ſuch

... ing for, giue ... rimous war ... ming ... k full by ... endeauours tho

... utions for me ... ey gticular ... otherwiſe our

... yh neuer ... or ſee ... ous, may pro ... he little ... hialpfull

... thinke it bet ... t yu find ... one yu hath ... ſkill in

Sparing the ... epe for ſuch ... t Voyage har ... ſhall not

want for any gai ... tion ye country ... affordeth ... k weg,

will allſo ... contribute our ... beſt ſkill y ... muſt giue

yu notice, yt tha n ... ſtorma wea ta ... ure had hath ... much

impouriſhed all ... chattell, & ſpirit ... most, if not ... all of our

fodder, ſoe ... as the new t ... hay will bea y ... quiſtion of y

ſort, yu muſt ... truſt into ... now ſt nott to beou

ble y w whatt hath ... formerly pai ... betwixt ſs ... y deſire you

to ſend froe ... towre Cowes ... & comaund ... ſom off

ſtruant to keepe ... them, I ſhall be ... thankfull to them

for there ... cares & paines; ... y ſame y ... yu remembe

whoſe diſcourſe wee ... had of y maxes ... twos off a ... princi

ſhall breake ... for my ſelfe, ſitt y ... ſame courſe ... yr bester

for yr ſelfe beī ... for mee, y ... wholly vimiſh ... my ſelfe to you

diſpoſition, beiny ... fully confide ... of y fauours &

good furthwande ... in this d ... ſigne y ... gladly

would heare ... of y ſafe comeing to lon ... vpon & whatt you

can ſay of y ſhip ... whwas att or neve ... with m Scotte

couered; soe when you doe write, gett paper somwhatt larger then your casement, and pinn the casement to the paper, then make your corner marks;
soe shall I be able to reade itt iust as you write; I had written in the way wee
agreed on, butt I fownd itt, in my iudgment, more tedious, and less secrett;
you may carry your casment allwayes aboutt you in a paper booke, don vpp
in an other sheete of paper, to keepe itt from breaking. I thought meete to
tell you, that som off our freinds where I last saw you thinke fitter to send
there —— in a —— of ther owne then trouble you; they hauing noe partners
before; butt I presume to cast my selfe on your favoure; and hope allsoe you
will pardon mee; I long to heare from you; and hope very shortly to be
satisfied; Mr. Allen the bearer hearoff will healpe to send your Lettre to mee
very safely; allsoe one Mr. Burnett a mercer at the Golden Fleece, in Lumbert-
Streete, as I remember hee dwells there; he sends vsually letters to the Pri-
mate; lett yours to mee bee inclosed in a backett to his Lordship and then
allsoe they will bee safely conveyed to mee; whatt other conueniencie you
meet with, lay hold on; and your Lettres will bee as heartily welcom as they
are earnestly expected, by your affectionate freind and seruant

Jo: De-gleba-digna

[*Ca.* March 6, 1634/35]

I pray present my seruis to mr. Hall   I thanke you vnfeignedly for vsing
my horse, butt I take itt vnkindly (if I could doe soe, any thing that you doe)
that you made not vse of the other allsoe for Mr. Hall; I pray send my coate
hatt etc. by the fyrst.

SIR JOHN CLOTWORTHY TO JOHN WINTHROP, JR.[1]

Reade this side fyrst.[2]

Dublin 6 Martij $\frac{1634}{1635}$

I now hauing fully enformed my selfe off that part[ic]uler which wee
mainly douptd off; doe now herby geiue you notice, that wee are enabled to

---

[1] W. 4. 75; 5 *Collections*, I. 206–208.
[2] This letter and the one on pages 195–196 were written to be read with the use of the "casement"
mentioned in the letter from Clotworthy immediately preceding. In the printed version given here,
only the words which appear through the openings have been retained. However, to give the full
flavor of the original, there is quoted here the first sentence as it stands in the original, those portions
which are covered by the bars of the "casement" being printed in italics: "*Ass* I *intend* now hauing
my minde fully en*larged and con*formed my *serious p*elfering *surly* off that partuler which *I heard* wee

send off that chattle you most off all neede, and ass you geiue notice shall by Gods healpe vse spedy dylygence for the prouiding off such a quantity ass you shall send shipping for; Geiue timous warning and full dyrections for euery particuler otherwise our endevours though neuer soe serious, may proue little healpfull.

I thinke itt best if you send one that hath skill in preparing sheepe for such a voyage   hee shall not want for any prouition the country affordeth, and wee will allsoe contribute our best skill. I must geiue you notice, that the storme wee haue had hath much impourished all chattell; and spent most, if nott all of our fodder, soe ass the new hay will bee the prouition of the sort you must trust vnto   now Sir nott to trouble you with whatt hath formerly past betwixt vss I desire you to send for me fower Cowes and commaund som off your seruants to keepe them. I shall bee thankfull to them for there care, and paines; I presume you remember whatt discourse wee had of the mares twoe off a principall breede for my selfe. lett the same course you take for your selfe bee for mee. I wholly remitt my selfe to your disposition, beeing fully confident of your favour and good furtheranse in this designe. I gladly would heare of your safe coming to london and whatt you can say of that ship which was att or nere Leith in Scot[land].

I am a sharer in that wee are building, yett willingly wowld I haue a part in that greate ship soe bee you resolue conserning hir. of this I exspect to heare by the fyrst. ass for those fyshing boats wheroff one of our friends gaue you a memorandum, I gladly will be a partaker in that way allsoe soe bee you send a ship this sommer into Ireland for the sheepe by whom I may send seruants, to imploy in whateuer shall bee most nedfull. of these I can write butt a word, and more were needless, to such an one as yourselfe: I desire to heare from you and if you resolue to send hyther this sommer, if then you will com and sett forth hence; it will bee noe small furthering of the proiect. Letts bee instant with the Lo[rd] in begging his councell, and then we may the more resolutely goe on, in hope of a blessing; I forbeare to send ouer money vnto you, vntill I heare whither you will sett vss on worke here. if nott, ther shall bee present payment made to you there. I expect from you a word of whatt is amongst you there and shall inuite you to itt, by geiuing a tast of our procedings [   ]¹ this greate [   ]¹ butt [   ]¹ itt pleaseth soe

---

mainly *disputing her* douptd off: doe *ass her can* now herby *see butt fyrst* geiue you notice, *the snow fall* that wee are ena*bricated to* bled to *the booke which* send off that chat*mantle and stockins* you most off all *gett a pedding* neede, and *musterd* ass you geiue no*thing to entice,* hir *when shee* shall by Gods *heede and* healpe vse *hast make* spedy dyly*ght for that* gence for *which you say her ans*the prouiding off *a capers* such a quanda*ry butt* tity ass *itt clen* you shall send *the anchor* shipwrack *kept such a pupping* for."

¹ Obliterated.

ass those who are nott strong in frinds had neede walke very streightly, for thers nothing falls to the grownd   the church heere is tenderly prouided for, and hath fine new clothes   wee want no addition that the witt of man can inuent, to make the worship off God pompous in outward butt penurious in the inward part; In a word, all things further a calling; remember vss, soe shall we you.

Jo: DEGLEBADIGNA

You will receiue the casement wherby you may reade this letter, from Mr. Allen an honest Goldsmith, dwelling ouer against St. Dunstons church Fleet streete.

[*Endorsed by John Winthrop, Jr.:*] Sir John Clotworthy to be read by the casement which is in it.

WILLIAM WILSON TO JOHN WINTHROP, JR.[1]

To his Loueing And much respected Friend Mr. Wintropp these be delivered

WORTHY SIR, I haue writtin to yow to Dublin afore, thinking to haue spoaken with [you] my selfe againe, but yow were gone afore my man came to Dublin. Nowe my Deseire is, that yow would be pleased, to writ vnto me, how Doth all thinges goe with yow in England; And what newes yow here out of Newe-England, And weather Mr. Plume Doth goe to New England or noe, And whoe else goes out of them partes; And wheare Doe they take shipping And wheather is Mr. Wales returned back or noe, for we here, he is blowne back from sea   also I p[r]ay Direct your letter to me, by the next messenger to Mr. Wales his house, or to Mr. Robt. Duttin his house, in fishamble streete in Dublin, with all the relacion yow can. Thus with my loue unto yow leaueing yow And yours to gods protection, I remaine And am Your assured loueing Friend

WM. WILSON

Dublin vj° Mar. 1634[/35]

I pray if yow see Mr: Wilson deseir him to writ unto me.

---

[1] W. I. 107.

THOMAS READE TO JOHN WINTHROP, JR.[1]

To the Wor[shipfu]ll John Winthrop esquire

Roterdam th 7 Mearche 1635 [N.S.]

DEARE SIR, I cane not chooes but trobell you withe thes feaue leynes to let you for to vnder stand that I should a bean very glad for to a spoke withe you at london but the shipes coming a way so sone that I could not inquier you ought (thoe I was at deyveres places to heare of you)   touching Mr. Endecots house I thinke he dead wryt to you a bought it in the letter wiche I brought[2]   I ould in treate you that you ould not sell it wryt ought be fore I speacke withe you for I had all moste sould it be fore I came a way by his order but I hope for to se you heare be fore feaue deayes be peast for my father[3] hath writ to you all for to come hether   we should be glad of your Company to ouer desyered porte   if so be that you doe not come soddonly I preay let me heare a word or to frome you what youer resolushons ar abought the viege. I thinke for to be in England with in this forte nyte at the furtheste but I hope for to se you heare or for to heare frome you be fore that teyme   thus in great haste I comeit you to Ceaper of the Isrell of god and rest Yours to com[mand] to my pouer

THOMAS READE

EMMANUEL DOWNING TO JOHN WINTHROP, JR.[4]

To his loving Cosen John Winthrop Esqr. at mr. Gostlins in Groton hall Suffolke deliver

MY GOOD COSEN, mr. Sheapheard was with me yeasterday, to enquire of your estate; whereof I could give him noe account. he prayed me to write vnto you thereof, and desires that you would retorne an answeare thereto this weeke, if you come not your selfe speedyly back. he would know your present estate in possession, and what in future you expect from your father, for this wilbe demaunded of him, before he can conclude any thing for you. And yts good reason you should satisfie him herein, because noe man that

---

[1] W. 3. 29; 4 *Collections*, VII. 113–114. For Reade, see 4 *Collections*, VII. 113*n*.
[2] See the letter of John Endecott to John Winthrop, Jr., December 8, 1634, page 176, above.
[3] His stepfather, Hugh Peter.
[4] W. 2. 22; 4 *Collections*, VI. 42–43.

knowes you not, will parte with his Child till he know how shee shall be provided for to live in the world[1]

this day my brother Kirby cam to me to tell me that mr. Atwood the leather seller was with him, to give him notice that you should walke waryly and close because there be some that laye wayte to Attach you. Mr. Winsloe lyes still in prison, and is like soe to continew, for I doe not heare when the lords will meete againe for plantation buisines.

I doe heare there will goe at least 20 ships this yeare to the plantation. there is one at the Custome howse apoynted to receive Certificats and give discharges to all such as shall goe to the pl[an]t[ation].[2] some that are goeing to N. E. went to him to know what they should doe. he bad them bring him any Certificate from Minister Church wardens or Justice that they were honest men and he would give them theire pass. they asked him what subsedy men should doe. he answeared that he could not tell who were subsedy men, and would dischardge them vpon theire Certificates. soe with my love to yourselfe my brother Gostlyn and his wife I rest Yours whilest I am

EM. DOWNINGE

25 Martij 1635

SIR JOHN CLOTWORTHY TO JOHN WINTHROP, JR.[3]

I will not touch vppon what I writt in my last to you only for the chattle which you soe much want, and wee can soe conueniently spare, I meane our best sorts of sheepe; I dare not continue my former aduice, of sending for any this summer, because ther can nott bee such store sent, as is needfull, and I feare after thers notice taken of any thatt goe from these partes ther will bee restraint after. soe as many as you can prouide shipping for, against the spring, I will soe prepare this next winter, that I hope few or none shall miscary; and those that goe must away together, that before the state cann send to inhibite, wee may haue dispacht a competent number, iff nott all that wee prouide; ass I writt before soe now againe I thinke itt will bee requisite

---

[1] At some date between Downing's letter and Winthrop's sailing for Massachusetts on the *Abigail* in August, 1635, Winthrop married Elizabeth Reade, daughter of Edmund Reade of Wickford, Essex, and Elizabeth Cook Reade. The latter, after her husband's death, became the wife of Hugh Peter.

[2] See the order of the Commission for Foreign Plantations to the officers of the Port of London, December 31, 1634 (pages 180–181, above).

[3] W. 4. 76; 5 *Collections*, I. 208–209. This letter, like Clotworthy's letter of March 6, 1634/35 (pages 191–192, above), was written so as to be read through a "casement."

to send a man who hath had experience in transporting and is somewhatt skilld in sheepe all healpes will bee little enowgh; iff the Lo[rd] please to furnish that blest land with this commodity from this wicked land; I shall almost thinke itt was the chiefe end for which itt was made; I wonder that I heare noe worde from you sythense your departure; my last will geiue you notice what particulers I most desire to heare off; good Sir bee not over-sparing in your relations; I thinke itt will nott be nedfull for mee to write now to Sir Richard Saltingstall presuming that you will impart this to him, and that I shall heare from either off you the resolution off you both; lett me heare whatt is donn with Mr. Winslow, and whither the byshop we heard off and gouernour hold for your nott ass yett polluted land.[1] With such trash, God bee your dyrection.

[JOHN CLOTWORTHY]

[*Ca.* April, 1635]

[*Endorsed by John Winthrop, Jr.:*] Sir John Clotworthy to be read by a casement.

JOHN SPENSER TO JOHN WINTHROP[2]

To his Honorable Friend mr. winthrop att Boston thes deliver

SIR, Understanding that it is yowr pleasure to let out yowr dayrie till yowr Sonns retorne I desire to hire two of them and shal be content to imbrace yowr termes, and shal resigne them when mr. winthrop requires it: and wheras I am accidentally disappointed of the vse of my Steeres, I entreat yow that yow would giue mr. Clark alowance to let me worke gentlie yowr Steeres which ar at Ipswch wil otherwise grow wild for want of manageing, wherwith and the rest of my Cattle and Seruants I shal be ready to drawe yowr Sonns Hey and wood together this Summer: or els if He retorne late I shal be willing to winter some of his Cattle if I may know before hand that I may get pro-vision for them And so with my respect to yow and mrs. winthrop with thanks for yowr great and no way deserued kindnes I rest yowrs to my Power

JO: SPENSER

[*Ca.* April, 1635]

---

[1] See *Journal*, I. 130, 152; Bradford, *History of Plymouth*, II. 199; Hutchinson, *History of Massa-chusetts-Bay*, I. 47–48; *The Autobiography and Correspondence of Sir Simonds D'Ewes, Bart.* (London, 1845), II. 118.

[2] W. I. 107. John Spenser settled in Ipswich in 1634, became a freeman of the colony on September 3 of that year, and subsequently moved to Newbury. His name appears frequently in the

MARY WRIGHT TO JOHN WINTHROP[1]

To the Wor[ship]full my very much esteemed cosen Mr. John Wintervp the Ellder these

Worthy Cosen, I ame very glad to take this ocation to evidence My Respectts to you allthough at this disstance   I would It ware In Me to doe It by any Reall performance   How Joyfull and willing I should be you should then know   I send this by one Mrs. Knight for whose sonn I once Made bould to writt to you In his behalfe, which now I beceech you give Me leave to do as much for the Mother home you will finde In sumė Measuer worthy the fauour don: and if In ould England I may wittnes My thankfullnes I shall not be backward.

I craue your thoughts for vs heere that live In the Midest of a sinfull land   the lord teach vs how to walke In vprightnes before hime.

With My best Respectts and service to your selfe and My good Cosen your Wife I ever ame Your Most Respecttive freind and Cosen

MARY WRIG[HT]

Char. May the 15, [1635]

ANNE TYNDAL TO MARGARET WINTHROP[2]

Louing aunt, I am bolde to present my duty to you in these few lines being the best token I haue to xepres my loue to you   I beseach you xecept them thou sorri to send them by my preti cosen whcih wee are all loath to part with all   it hath peased god to take to of my brothers my eldest and yongest[3]   I thanke god wee are all weell   with my selfe my brothers and sister present their duty to you and to my deare uncle and loue to all my cosens and praying god to blesse you and yours and send you all health and happiness I rest Your loueing cosen

A. T.

[*Ca.* July, 1635]

---

records of the General Court as representative both for Ipswich and for Newbury. He returned to England in 1638, having lost favor in Massachusetts because of his siding with John Wheelwright in the controversy of the preceding year. Savage, *Genealogical Dictionary*, IV. 147.

[1] W. 4. 30; 5 *Collections*, I. 80–81. For Mary Wright, see 5 *Collections*, I. 80n.

[2] W. Au. 61. Anne Tyndal was the daughter of Deane Tyndal, Margaret Winthrop's brother, and Amy Weston Tyndal.

[3] Francis and Deane Tyndal.

AGREEMENT OF THE SAYBROOK COMPANY
WITH JOHN WINTHROP, JR.[1]

Articles made (betweene the right hono[ra]ble the Lord Viscount Say and Seale, Sir Arthur Hesilrige Barronet, Sir Richard Saltonstall Kt., Henry Laurence, Henry Darley and George Fenwick esquiers on the one part and John Winthrope the younger esquier of the other part) the 7th of July, Anno Domini 1635.

First that we in our owne names, and the rest of the Company, doe by thes presents constitute and appoint John Winthrop the younger, Gouernour of the riuer Conecticut in New England and of the Harbors and places adioyninge for the space of on whole yeare, from the tyme of his arriual ther. And the said John Winthrop doth vndertake and couenant for his part, that he will with all conuenient speede repaire to those places and ther abide as aforsaid for the best aduancment of the Companies seruice.

Secondly that soe sone as he comes to the bay he shall indeauour to prouide able men to the number of fiftie at the least for makinge of fortifications and buildinge of houses at the Riuer Conecticut and the harbor adjoyninge, first for ther owne present accommodation and then such houses as may receiue men of qualitie which latter houses we would haue to be builded within the fort.

Thirdly That he shall imploy those men accordinge to his best abilitie for the aduancment of the Companies seruice especially in the particulars aboue mentioned duringe the tyme of his gouernement, and shall also giue a true and just account of all moneys and goods committed to his managinge.

Fourthly That for such as shall plant ther now in the beginninge he shall take care that they plant themselues either at the harbour or neare the mouth of the riuer, that thes places may be the better strengthned for ther owne saftie, and to that end, that they also sitt downe in such bodies together, as they may be most capable of an intrenchment, prouided that ther be reserued vnto the fort for the mentenance of it on thousand or fiften hundred acres at the least of good ground as neare adioyninge theruunto as may bee.

Fifty that forasmuch as this seruice will take him off from his owne imployments, the Company doe ingage themselues to giue him a iust and deue consideration for the same.

---

[1] W. 4. 165; 5 *Collections*, I. 482–483.

In witnes whereof wee haue heare vnto interchangeably subscribed our names.

> W. Say & Seale
> A. Hesilrige
> He: Laurence
> Ric: Saltonstall
> Geo: Fenwick
> Hen: Darley

ARTICLES OF APPRENTICESHIP[1]

This Indenture witnesseth that Thomas Goad son of John Goad cittisen and skiner of London deceassed doth put himselfe apprentise to Mr. John Winthrop Esquer inhabitting in America neare Mattachushets bay and with him to dwell after the manner of an aprentyse for the tearme of fower yeares from the day of the date heareof   hee shall not absent himselfe from his sayd maysters service neyther day nor night   hee shall not haunt nor vnlawfull nor forbidden places nor play at cards or dyce or any other vnlawfull games, nor wast or consume any of his sayd maysters goods nor suffer them to bee wasted by any other, but in all things shall behave himselfe as a faythfull aprentise ought to doe, and the sayd mayster shall fynd him sufficyent meat, drinck and apurrell with due correction and good education affording him the pryviledges of the country in as ample and as large a manner as any other aprentyse may or can bee capable off, in witnes wheareof wee have interchangable put our hands and seales this seaventh day of July 1635

> Thomas Goad

Read sealed and delivered in the presence of vs
> Em: Downing
> Franc: Kirby

JOHN WINTHROP TO SIR SIMONDS D'EWES[2]

To the right wor[shi]p[fu]ll Sir Simondes Dewes, knight

Sir, I received 2 lettres from you the one written longe since and putt backe in the Hope: by the other I vnderstande your good Affection to our

---

[1] W. 13. 98.
[2] Harleian MSS., B.M., 388, fo. 188; *Publications of the Colonial Society of Massachusetts*, vii. 72–73.

Plantation whereof you desire we should tast the fruits: blessed be the Lord who hath inclined your heart thus towards vs for good, and blessed be you of the Lord for it. According to your direction I spake with Hamond, who tould me that he bestowed part of your mony in vinegre to have made Sturgeon, which being putt aborde the Richard, was forced back again, and so by stoping and putting abord another shippe suffered much loss: I spake with Mr. Trerice the master of the same shippe who affirmed that of 12 hogsh[ea]ds of vinegre there was lost by leakage about 3 hogsh[ea]ds: Old Hamonde came allso before the Governor (Mr. Haines) and other of vs and affirmed that there came no benefite of your mony but losse, so that howsoever by the bonde we might have compelled them to have payd the whole 30*li* yet respecting the losse which (by Gods providence) hapned in the adventure, we were content to take the principall, which the old man hath vndertaken to pay, which when we have received it shalbe bestowed vpon some publ[ic] worke: in the meane tyme the Governour and Assistants returne you thanks by me.

For our Condition heere, the Lord is pleased still to continue health and peace to vs: and so to increace our numbers (there have come about 30 shipps this summer allreadye) as we are putt to rayse new Colonys about 100 miles to the west of vs, vpon a very fine river and a most fruitfull place, onely shipps cannot come neere by 20 legues: Mr. Hooker is like to goe thither next yeare not for any difference between Mr. Cotton and him and soe reporte for they doe hould a most sweet and brotherly Communion togither (though their iudgments doe somewhat differ about the lawfullnesse of the Crosse in the Ensigne) but the people and Cattle are so increaced as the place will not suffice them: The passingers this yeare (through the Lords speciall providence) and their Cattle are come with such speed and safety as no sickness hath been among them nor above 2 persons miscarried and very fewe Cattle. I might further enlarge but indeed I am so full of business as I can scarce gett leysure to scribble these fewe lines   I desire you to beare with me, and to continue still your goodwill towards vs, and your prayers for vs, and so with my Love and due respecte to your self and your worthy Lady I commend you to the Lord and rest At your service

                                                                Jo: Winthrop

Boston in New Engld. July 20, 1635

PHILIP NYE TO JOHN WINTHROP, JR.[1]

To his much assured loving Frend Mr. John Winthrop the yonger deliver these[2]

Sir, I haue sent you by this bearer an Instrument vnder the gentlemens hands so many of them as were in towne, with whom authoritie was left to do any act in the name of the rest. my request vnto you is that you would subscribe the inclosed paper and inclose it in a letter sealed vp directed to me, and deliuer it to this bearer Alexander Winchester Mr. Vanes Man, who will retaine it vntill I com or send it by a safe hand. I promised the Gentl[emen] that there should be somthing to this purpose, therefore I desire it may without fayle be thus dispatched   I would haue it inclosed and sealed because it is not fitt that any but those of vs here should take any notice thereof, therefore neither Mr. Vane nor his man nor any with you knoweth any thing of this passage, because it is the Gentlemens desire you might haue all the advantages the busines will afford for your comfortable and creditfull going on in this project, which I hope the lord will bless to whome I leaue you with my rembrance to your wife and rest Yours in Jesus Christ

PHILIP NYE

From the Cowes this July 28, [1635]

I haue sent the other 1000*li* by Mr. Peirce to be deliuered to your Father for you.

EDWARD HOPKINS TO JOHN WINTHROP, JR.[3]

To the Wor[shipfu]ll his much Respected freind Jno. Winthropp the younger Esqr. att Boston or elcewhere in the Massechusetts Bay in New England, or in his absence to the Wor[shipfu]ll Jno. Winthropp the Elder att Boston aforesaid deliver Per the Shipp Batchler whom God preserve

LONDON the 16 of August 1635

Mr. Jno. Wintropp

Sir, My best respects premised etc. you may please to vnderstand I haue

---

[1] W. 4. 76; 5 *Collections*, I. 210–211. For Nye, see 5 *Collections*, I. 210*n*.; *D.N.B.*

[2] Beneath the superscription there appears in the handwriting of John Winthrop, Jr.: "for Marsilius Ficinus."

[3] W. Au. 85; 4 *Collections*, VI. 325–329. For Edward Hopkins, see 4 *Collections*, VI. 325*n*.; *D.A.B.* The text of the agreement between Hopkins and four members of the *Bachelor's* crew is appended to a copy of Hopkins's letter in W. 1. 109.

now cleared of from hence the North Sea Boatt in whom (God sending her to you in safety) you shall receave these particulars following

	C.	q.	lb.
14 piggs of lead weighing	40	0	22
80 barrs of Spanish Iron w[eigh]tt	20	2	19
52 barrs English Iron w[eigh]tt	20	2	19

20 hoggshedds of meale no. 11 to 30

14 Barrells of pease no. 1, 2, 4, 5 to 15

a Barrell of oatemeale no. 16

A Barrell of Butter no. B and 6 firkins of Butter no. 1 to 6

4 hoggsheds and 5 Barrells of Iron ware, the particulars I send you herein-closed

A Bundle of Sythes Cont[aining] 3 dozen

2 Bundles of Shovells and Spades

A packe of linnen Cloth No. A Cont[aining] 320 ells of Roane Canvas for sheetts being 13 pieces, and one piece of narrower Cloth Cont[aining] 87 ells

8 flocke beds, 25 Ruggs, and 40 Blanketts

6 grindstones

3 Barrells of pitch and 2 Barrells of Tarr

4 Scrues and one barrell of Iron things that came from Holland, the particulars I haue nott yett receaved   it is marked RS

2 small Cables for shallops weighing 3 C. 1 Q. 6 lb. and 2 C. 0.11 lb. of lesser Cordage

Iron worke for 2 draw Bridges as foll[ows]

    62 Staples

    40 Staple hooks for a porcullis

    4 Chaines

    10 Boults

    4 Plates

    8 Chaine Claspes

    4 vnder hinges

$23\frac{1}{2}$ yards of redd flagg stuffe for Serieant Gardeners[1] vse and some small lines that came from holland and a wheelebarrow.

I intended to haue laden much more in this vessell, and had putt aboard other things but was forced to take them out againe, by reason she was too much pestered, butt what is wanting now you shall have per the True Loue Mr. Gibbs who will be ready I hope to sett saile within 14 or 20 dayes in

---

[1] Lion Gardiner.

whom such Servants as are provided by the gentlemen are to be shipped, butt what their nomber will be, I yett know nott.

I herewith also send you the particulars of the furniture of this Barque, the Bachler, that you may know what to require from the Ma[ste]r. There are some small things as dishes and such like belonging to her nott here mentioned Butt the things omitted are of noe great value. I haue hired the ma[ste]r and all the men (whose names and wages I shall afterwards expresse,) eyther to remayne in the Cuntrey to saile the barque there or to be returned home in some other Shipp, as you shall find most convenient. I cannott say much for Ma[ste]r nor men to incourage you to keepe them yf you can provide your selfe of others that are fitting for the Imployment. It was nott easy here to gett any att this tyme to goe in soe small a vessell, and therefore I was forced to take some, that otherwise I would nott haue medled withall. The ma[ste]r is able enough, but savours nott godlinesse yett hath a desire as he tells me to continue in the Cuntrey.   yf you keepe them there I have vndertaken they shall haue their wages paid them att 6 monthes end from their clearing att Gravesend, butt for my owne part I rather incline to haue them sent home; and yf you determine this, the sooner you doe itt the better for they will be in pay vntill their arivall here   yf the Shipps that goe from thence want any men, you may happily gett some allowance for them, wherby the charge may be somewhat abated, Butt it is left to your discretion to doe herein as you shall iudge most advantageous to the Company. Serieant Gardener and Wm. Job his workem[aste]r with the Serieants wiefe and his mayd come over in this Barque. if you require it of them both Gardener and Job can shew you their covenants with the Compa[ny] whereby you may in part perceave what to require of them and what to performe to them. they are all to be att the Companies charge for matter of diett. The Serieant hath receaved of me beforehand towards his first yeares wages 30*li* sterling and Wm. Job hath received 15*li*, the M[aste]r also of the barque hath receaved 8*li* before hand towards his wages, all which you are to deduct, when you pay them any more.

The wages to be paid the Ma[ste]r and his Compa[ny] are as foll[ows]

	li	*s*	*d*
To Jno. Webber M[aste]r of the Barque	4	10	0 per month
To Ric. Baker M[aste]rs mate	2	00	0 per moneth
To Jno. Brikin Carpenter	1	11	0 per moneth
To Jno. Sherlocke	1	6	0 per mo.
To Jno. Harman	1	5	0 per mo.
To Jno. Hall	1	2	0 per mo.

	li	s	d	
To Robt. Sherley	1	0	0	per mo.
To the boy	0	12	0	per mo.

The Charge att present for soe small a vessell is very great but I hope (God sending her thither in safety) shee may be sayled with fewer men whereby the charge will be lessned   I haue given to the ma[ste]r of the Barque 5*li* starling to pay the men their halfe pay att Gravesend, which will be onely for one weeke, and to disburse otherwaies as the occations of the shipp shall require   he is to giue you an Account of the disbursing of the same and what shall nott be layd out, to deliver to you. Soe nott having elce att present I take my leave resting Yours in what I may

EDWARD HOPKINS

Att my comming to Gravesend to cleare of the Shipp there 4 of the Mariners vizt. Brikin, Sherlocke, Harman and Hall came to me and tould me they would nott goe the voyage vnlesse they might be free vppon arivall of the Shipp there to dispose of themselves to any other imployment, and haue their wages paid them att the discharge of the Shipp. Wherevppon being putt to some streights, I was in a manner constrayned to yeeld to their desires, and vppon second thoughts, I conceave to noe disadvantage to us, as you may perceave per the inclosed agreement, the originall whereof vnder their hands, I haue given the Ma[ste]r, that if they putt into the West Cuntrey and offer to leave the Shipp he may haue something to shew to constraine them to the Contrary for now you are left free from taking any care to send these backe to England, and they are bound Nottwithstanding, yf you offer them as much wages as others doe, to serve you yf you stand in nead of them, which yett I hope you will nott, the ma[ste]r, his mate, one mariner and the Boy sticking to the former agreement, who with small helpe more will be able I conceave to saile the barque in the Cuntrey. you may perceave per the agreement that I haue paid 30*s* to these men in part of their wages before hand. Yours as before

EDW. HOPKINS

18º August 1635

GRAUESEND this 18th the August 1635

It is agreed betwixt Edward Hopkins of London Merc[han]tt and Jno. Brikin Carpenter Jno. Sherlocke Jno. Harman and Jno. Hall who ar now shipped in the Bacheler of London Bound for New Ingland as f[oll]oweth Vizt.

That vppon ariuall of the sayd Ship in New England aforsaid and discharge of the goodes now laden by the said Edward Hopkins aboard her the Wages of the aforesaid men shall be paid them by the said Edward Hopkins or his Assignes after the rates hereafter expressed And it shall be then free for the said Brikin Sherlocke Harman and Hall to dispose of themselues to any other imployment vnlesse the said Edward Hopkins or his assignes giue them as much wages as they Can haue elcewhere And it shall be free likewise for the said Edward Hopkins or his Assignes to refuse the further seruice of the aforesaid fower mariners But may at his or their pleasure vppon payment of the aforesaid wages discharge themselues fully of them

Ther seuerall wages is as followeth.

To Jno. B[r]ikin 31s per month to whom is paid 5s before hand

To Jno. Harman 25s per month to whom is paid 10s before hand

To Jno. Sherlocke 26s per month to whom is paid 10s

To Jno. Hall 22s per month to whom is paid 5s before hand

Vnderwritt by
JOHN SHERLOCK
JOHN HARMAN
JOHN BRIKIN
H I the marke of JNO. HALL

BILL OF LADING[1]

I Jno. Webber Ma[ste]r of the good Shipp called the Bachler of London, Being bound for the Massechusetts Bay in New England, doe acknowledge to haue Receaved into the sayd Shipp from Edward Hopkins of London Merchant these goodes following vizt. fowerteene piggs of lead, eighty Barrs Spanish Iron, fifty two Barrs English Iron, twenty hoggshedds of meale, fowerteene Barrells of pease, one Barrell of oatmeale, one barrell and six firkins of Butter fower hoggsheds and six Barrells of Iron ware one packe of Lynnen Cloth, one Bundle of Sythes, two Bundles of Spades and Shovells six grindstones, three Barrells of pitch, two Barrells of Tarr, two small Cables and other Cordage for Shallopps, fower Scrues and other loose Iron worke for Iron bridges with small packs of bedds, blanketts, and Ruggs.

All which goodes are to be delivered (the dangers of the Seas excepted) vnto Mr. Jno. Wintropp the younger or his Assignes, att Boston in the Masse-

---

[1] W. I. 110.

chusetts Bay in New England: In wittnesse whereof I haue herevnto putt my hand the 17th of August 1635.

JOHN WEBBER

[*Endorsed:*] Mr. Webbers ingagement.

EDWARD HOWES TO JOHN WINTHROP, JR.[1]

To my much honored frind Mr. John Winthrope at Ipswich present these in New England

MY MOST DEARE FRIND, In hope and confidence of your safe ariuall together with your best beloued whome I salute as your selfe, I knowe you expect a lettre. though I haue but small matter to write of, I dare not frustrate your expectations. I haue bin 2 or 3 tymes since with the Dr. and can gett but small satisfaccion about your queries. I doubt he hath some preiudicate conceipt of one of vs, or both; yet I must confesse he seemed verie free to me, only in the maine he was misticall. this he said that when the will of God is you shall knowe what you desire, it will come with such a light, that it will make a harmonie amonge all your authors, causing them sweetly to agree, and putt you for euer after out of doubt and question. To discerne the fratres scientiæ I cannot as yet learne of him. I am very shortlie to take my Jorney soe that I must here breake of, hauing other occasions and noe matter of importance to acquaint you with all, I rest Yours as you knowe

E. H.

21º Aug. 1635

I thinke I shall helpe you to one of the magneticall engines which you and I haue discoursed of, that will sympathize at a distance.

SAMUEL READE TO JOHN WINTHROP, JR.[2]

To my very loving brother mr. John Winthrope esqr. present these in New-England

LOVING BROTHER, We cannot but marvell that we haue received not one word from you, nor any in your shipe, seing we were (as you might haue conceived) still in hope to heare from you. we knew not how to send but

---

[1] W. 2. 168; 4 *Collections*, VI. 499–500.
[2] W. 4. 77; 5 *Collections*, I. 211–212. Samuel Reade was the brother of Elizabeth Reade, second wife of John Winthrop, Jr.

hearing that the shipe was at Plymoth we sent thither but received noe
answeare; least therfore you should thinke us forgetfull of you, as you are of
us, and therfore silent, I take hould of the opportunity to salute you; and to
rejoyce with you for my sisters deliverance from sicknes soddenly come and
gone; and alsoe for my fathers[1] escape out of cruell hands   we heare if you
had stayed but 2 dayes longer my father would scarcely haue avoyded them,
for they had taken an extraordinary cunning course for his attachment; as
we are informed by letters out of the cuntry. all your freinds with whom I
haue any acquaintance are in health   mr. Downing his sonn is come over
and going into Holland but I haue not seene him yet.[2] pray let us heare from
you howe comfortable a voyage you had and what my father will doe. I wish
you all good in soule and body from the author of all good to whose protection
I commit you with my loue to my sister, and my due respects to your father
and mother and all our good freinds   I shall ever remaine I hope as I am
Your truly loving brother

                                                      SAMUELL READE

LONDON the 21 August 1635

FRANCIS KIRBY TO JOHN WINTHROP, JR.[3]

                                          LONDON this 25 August, 1635
   LOVINGE (AND NO LESSE LOUED) FREND MR. WINTHROP, You shall vnderstand that I haue shipped in Mr. Bab the thinges bespoken at the plummers
and a little barill of shot brought to mee per Ed: Howes, all contained in
one firkin marked with your marke. I haue heer inclosed the plumbers bill of
parceles wherby you may know what is in the firkin, also Mr. Peirce his bill,
which I haue paid the rest of, my whole disbursement beinge 3.12.6 which
is more (I fear) then I shall make of your horse, for we pay 1s per night for
hay which maketh horses a bad Comodyty, but I will doe what I may therin,
and when he is sold I will write you an accounte. I desire to be remembred
to your second selfe, my Cosen Tho: Goad your seruant, also to my frends at
Boston from whom I haue heard per my Cosen James who ariued heere
about 10 daies since.

                                                      [FRANCIS KIRBY]

---

   [1] His stepfather, Hugh Peter, who came to Massachusetts on the *Abigail* with Winthrop, arriving
in Boston about October 6, 1635. *Journal*, I. 160.
   [2] Interlined: "to day I shall 24 august, 1635."
   [3] W. 3. 6; 4 *Collections*, VII. 16.

ROBERT BARRINGTON TO JOHN WINTHROP, JR.[1]

To my very good Freind Mr. John Winthrop Junior at Boston or elcewhere deliver

SIR, The bearer heerof being sent ouer among other seruants for the vse of the common stock, I shall entreate you for my sake to shew him what fauour you may. I hope you shall finde he will deserue no less. I thinke he is one that truly feares God; and you shall finde him able to take paines. I pray haue a speciall Care of his spirituall good. I beseech you commend me to Mr. Peters and desire him from me, (though not much knowne to him) to doe the like, and I shall thinke my selfe much beholding to you both. thus commending you and this busines to the blessing of the Lord I rest Your assured freind

ROBT. BARRINGTON

HATFEILD BROADOKE Sep: 4th 1635

JOSHUA FOOTE'S BILL FOR IRON IMPLEMENTS[2]

Bought of Joshua Foote 15th September 1635

	li	s	d
1 Coopers Axe	0	3	6
1 Coopers Ades	0	1	10
1 headding knife	0	1	8
2 howells	0	3	0
2 pair Compasses	0	2	4
1 round shaue	0	1	2
1 spock shaue	0	1	4
1 Crowes Iron	0	0	7
1 vise	0	0	7
2 brick trowills	0	2	8
2 tilling trowills	0	2	0
2 stone Axes 19½ li.	0	8	1½
1 brick Axe	0	2	6
15½ li. Spanish stell	0	7	9
16 li. fle: stell	0	10	8
1 doz Nayling hamers	0	14	0
4 Nayling steacks 43½ li. at 4½d per li.	0	16	3½
1 Cuntry bag and Cords	0	0	8
	4	0	8

---

[1] W. 4. 77; 5 *Collections*, I. 212. For Barrington, see 5 *Collections*, I. 212n. [2] W. I. 108.

[*Endorsed:*] Mr. Hobkins his Note: 4*li* 0*s* 8*d*.

[*Endorsed by Francis Kirby:*] The Contents of a Bundle of Iron Instruments shipped in the true loue Mr. Gibbs.

SIR ARTHUR HASELRIG AND GEORGE FENWICK TO JOHN WINTHROP, JR.[1]

To his most Worthy frende john Winthrope the younger Esq:

Sir, You shall receiue from Mr. Hopkins a perticular of what is sent.[2] Therin you shall finde our Constancie, and Care. our dependance on you is greate, wee neede not expresse it, your abilitie to performe your vndertakeing we doubt not, your integritie to goe on with the woorke we suspect not. only our request is, that (with what speede possible may be) fitt houses be builded.

We write this (as we hope) to Congratulate your ariuall, and to incourage your forwardnese, in a woorke of such exceedinge Consequence. Wee shalbe happie to liue to see you   howsoeuer our best desires are yours and wee Your truest seruants

A. Hesilrige
Geo: Fenwick

Lond: This 18 of Sep: 1635

EDWARD HOPKINS TO JOHN WINTHROP, JR.[3]

To his worthy freind Mr. Jno. Winthropp the younger Esqr.

London the 21th of September 1635

Mr. Jno. Winthrop

Sir, My best respects premised etc. I herewith send you both a Copy of my letter sent per the Bachler, wherby you may perceave what was laden aboard her, as also a particular of whatt I haue laden aboard this Shipp the true loue together with a bill of lading for the same, soe that I shall nott nead to adde much more for advise att present, only you may please to know that

---

[1] W. Au. 86; 4 *Collections,* vi. 364. For Haselrig, see *D.N.B.;* for Fenwick, see *D.A.B.* Both were active in the affairs of the settlement at Saybrook.

[2] See letters of Edward Hopkins to John Winthrop, Jr., August 16, 1635, pages 201–205, above, and September 21, 1635, immediately following.

[3] W. 2. 132; 4 *Collections,* vi. 329–330.

the hoggshedds of meale now sent from no. 11 to 30, are somewhat better then eyther those 20 in the Bachler, or the other 10 aboard this Shipp, also of the 2 Rundletts of oile no. A is the best, of the barrells of powder no. 41 and 42 are fine powder for musketts and fowling, the rest is for the ordinance. all the Irons for the Cariages are nott all yett fully fitted, butt whatt is now wanting shall come per the first att Spring which I conceave willbe as soone as any vse willbe made of them; there is besides the bedds that are packt vpp, a dozen bedds and a dozen of Coverletts putt aboard for the vse of the Servants in the Shipp. Mr. Gibbs hath also a new cable or hawser weighing 4 C. 3 q. 5 lb. which after it hath beene vsed in taking the ordinance out of the Shipp he is to deliver to you. There is also 2 drumms and 4 or 5 trunks with the Servants apparell in them, which are nott included in the bills of lading. Butt Edward Bush[n]ell cann tell you what they are, as also the particulars contayned in them.

I likewise herewith send you a list of the Servants names that are now shipt. Edward Bush[n]ell hath all their Covenants they are bound some to Mr. Ny some to my selfe and some to Edward Bush[n]ell, butt wee assigne them all over to you. I will write noe more concerning them butt will referr my selfe to their advise who vndertooke the providing of them. I had as great care as I could in the provisions now sent I hope they willbe answerable to expectacion; the Irons for cariages no. 36, 37 and the 2 hoggsheds of woodden ware no. 50, 51 are packt vp in malt. I send noe cheese because you seemed to haue noe desire to itt Soe nott having elce att present I take my leave resting Yours to Commaund

EDW. HOPKINS

Edward Bush[n]ell was imployed by Mr. Ny in buying some things for the Servants, and att making vp of accounts with him. I find we are indebted to him 3*li* which he desires to haue in the Cuntrey.

More he saith he hath laid out in these occasions, of which he can give noe account at present about 4*li* besides some tooles he bought the prise whereof he remembers nott; butt he is honest, and will doe noe wrong.

[*Memorandum by John Winthrop, Jr.:*] Plaster of tarras.
Plaster of Pareis.
3 bills of exchange of 30*li* to be payde
to Rich: Baker.
Drummes: silke ancients, trumpets etc.

PHILIP NYE TO JOHN WINTHROP, JR.[1]

To his much honoured Frend John Wynthrope the yonger Esquire deliver these

LONDON 7ber this 21th

WORTHY SIR, We haue sent you som servants but not so many as we purposed   the reason is this   some of the Gentlemen of the North who lay som 3 or 4 Monthes in London transacting these affaires did thinke that their would haue been no notice of their purposes and therevpon assumed to send vs vp servants but when they came down found the Countrie full of the reports of their going   now those two (being Dep. leuetenants of the shire) did not care to moue any further in sending vp of men for feare of increasing the reports; my lord Brooke likewise that vndertooke for xxtye failed likewise and sent vs not one. our gentlemens minds remaine the same, and are in a way of selling off their estates with the greatest expedicion.

You haue one Edward Bushnell the bearer hereof a godly man and so is his wife a gratious woman. I would intreat you to take speciall notice of him as a man you may both for his parts and pietye trust in your weightiest affaires, and his fittest imployment besides the labour of his hands (to which in many faculties you will find much reddines and forwardnes in him) will be to ouer-looke som of the yonger sort and trayne them vp according to their capacities. the widow Bristow that cometh with him is likewise a godlye woman an excellent huswife fitt for all domestike imployment and a great paynes taker. som of our husbandmen likewise are not only godlye but very skilfull. but of euery mans parts and disposicion you shall more fully vnderstand of Edward Bushnell who the better you know him the more vsefull you will judg him. The lord prosper in your hands this hopefull busines, and strengthin your hands to this happie vndertaking   I pray remember me to Mrs. Wenthrope, and my service to your worthy Father. Yours in Jesus Christ

PHILIP NYE

---

[1] W. 4. 78; 5 *Collections*, I. 213–214.

HENRY LAWRENCE TO JOHN WINTHROP, JR.[1]

*To my Worthy Freinde Mr. John Winthrop the Yonger att Agawam
or elsewhere in New-England*

SIR, My fayth makes mee willinge to outrunne my intelligence in congratu-
latinge your safe arriuall in New-England, for God hath alreddy shewed
himsealfe so gratious in the conductinge of those who haue gone your way,
as we may at laste venture to truste him without any farther tryall. Yet I
shall be glad vpon the first occasyon to haue the certayne knowledge of it
from your sealfe that my thankefulnes may haue both a greater bottom and
buildinge then now it can. The greate busines God hath cast vpon you, the
great truste that is reposed in you, and the expectation that is iustly raysed
of you, ar weights I assure mysealfe sufficient to carry you on in all faythfulnes
and diligence to the prosecution of that seruice. But that we may not bee
wantinge either to you or oursealues we take it to bee our parte to putt you
in minde of that which we ar assurd you forgett not, our owne serious
desires and your answerable ingagement in this worke, of which we ar sure
this att least may come, that by aduising you to do what you do alreddy we
shall both prayse you for so doinge, and testify our owne acknowledgment
and approbation of it. I shall remember you now butt of [*torn*] thinges. One
is the place of our pitchinge wherein (if in any thinge) we ar peremptory for
Connecticutt, it beeinge as you know and so continuinge, the ioynte resolution
of vs all that nothinge but a playne impossibility could diuerte vs from that
place which in many respects we conceiud moste aduantagious both for the
securinge of our freindes att the bay and our owne personall accommodations.
Another is the time of your goinge vp, which wee assuredly expect shall bee
this winter, for which reson we haue sent a farther supply of such men and
prouisions as we could, and thought fitt for the present, of which you shall
receiue intelligence from Mr. Hopkins; A thirde which will inforce this 2d is
that forti[fi]cations and some conuenient buildinges for the receipt of Gentlemen may go hande in hande, for there ar like to come more ouer next
Summer both to be wittnes of what you haue done, and to thanke you for it,
then you ar yett aware of. Other thinges I shall leaue to your owne wisedome
and the directions giuen you, earnestly beseechinge God that he would farther
suggest such thinges to vs all as may be most for the glory of his greate name,
and (which in this designe we espetially ayme att) the good of his churches.

---

[1] W. 4. 78; 5 *Collections*, I. 214–215. For Henry Lawrence, one of the signers of Winthrop's
commission as Governor of the Saybrook settlement, see *D.N.B.*

I desire to haue my loue and seruice presented to Mr. Winthrop your father, to whom thoughe I haue not seene his face, his owne worth hath causd that I am no stranger. Next your sealfe I desire to bee affectionately remembered to Mr. Peter. I rest Your assured Friende

HE: LAWRENCE

Septemb: 22th 1635

EDWARD HOPKINS TO JOHN WINTHROP, JR.[1]

LONDON the 24th of Sept. 1635

SIR, I wrott you per this conveyance of the 21th present, and sent you the particulars of what I laded aboard this shipp. I haue nott any more to add att present, but onely to convey the inclosed, which I hope may meett or ouertake the shipp in the Downes.

I desire you willbe pleased (yf opportunity serve) to give notice per the first, of the receipt of these things, and to advise whatt supplyes you shall stand in nead of att spring; for I hope by that tyme, the gentlemen's stocke willbe increased, and they therby better inabled to affoard such accommodacions as shallbe necessary for the furthering of the businesse then now they were, for I know through streights of tyme and meanes, many things are now omitted, which the state of the Plantacion will soone call for. Soe nott having elce att present, with my best respects to you and yours, desiring the same may be presented to Mr. Peter, I take my leave, resting Yours in what I may

EDWARD HOPKINS

RECEIPT OF JOHN WILSON[2]

Receyued by me John Willson this 13th of october at the handes of William Peirse by appoyntment of mr. Hugh Petter the some of on hundred pounds which is a part of Certayne moneys Committed to my Chardg by mr. ney:[3] at London: 100*li*

JOHN WILSON

---

[1] Original not located; 4 *Collections*, VI. 331.

[2] W. I. 110.

[3] Philip Nye. See the postscript to his letter to John Winthrop, Jr., of July 28, 1635, page 201, above.

EDMOND FREEMAN TO JOHN WINTHROP, JR.[1]

To the Worshipfull my very good frend Mr. Winthorpe the yonger

Sir, I desire you to be pleased To retaine for us mr. Geeres part and my part of the provicions left of the vndertaker which you haue bought of Henry Troute   Oure part is the eight part which I do desire you to retaine in youre hands. yours to vse

EDMOND FREEMAN

The fift of November 1635

MARY DOWNING TO EMMANUEL DOWNING[2]

Worthy Sir, Deare Father, The continuall experience that I enioy of your tender love and care to a child, though I confesse an vnderseruinge one (yet) your love emboldens mee to present my humble duty and respect I owe and shall render with my might and power to your selfe soe longe as it pleaseth the Lord to continue my life. I haue found soe much your love and see that neither time nor distance of place doth diminish or blast the same, which I confesse and desire to acknowledge as a great mercy and the cheife comfort for a temporall, that I have to solace my selfe withall; Father I trust in him who hath the harts and the disposinge of them in his hand, that I haue not provoked you to harbor soe ill an opinion of mee as my mothers lettres do signifie and give me to vnderstand, the ill opinion and hard perswasion which shee beares of mee, that is to say, that I should abuse your goodnes, and bee prodigall of your purse neglectfull of my brothers bands and of my slatterishnes and lasines. for my brothers bands I will not excuse my selfe, but I thinke not worthy soe sharpe a reproofe, for the rest I must needs excuse, and cleare my selfe If I may bee beleived. I doe not know my selfe guilty of any of them. for myne owne part I doe not desire to bee myne owne iudge, but am willinge to be iudged by them, with whom I live and sees my course, whether I bee addicted to such thinges or noe   for my habitt, it is meane, for the most as many seruants, and if I had not had money which I had for some thinges here I might have wanted many necessaries which I

---

[1] W. 1. 110. Edmond Freeman of Pulborough, Sussex, who settled first at Lynn and then at Sandwich, and Dennis Geere (Geary) of Galmer, Sussex (mentioned in this document), who settled at Lynn, were fellow passengers of John Winthrop, Jr., on the *Abigail*.

[2] W. 4. 30; 5 *Collections*, I. 81–83. Mary Downing, daughter of Emmanuel and Lucy Downing, and her sister Susan came to Boston in 1633, five years in advance of their parents.

could not have bin without, except I should have made you a scoare here,
which I was not willinge to doe: I writt to my mother for lace not out of any
prodigall or proud mind but onely for some crossecloathes, which is the most
allowable and commendable dressinge here. Shee would have mee weare
dressings which I did soe longe as they would suffer mee, whilest the elders with
others intreated mee to leaue them of; for they gave great offence and seeinge
it hath pleased the Lord to bringe mee hither amongst his people, I would not
willingly doe any thinge amongst them that should be displeasinge vnto them,
but for myne owne part since my sendinge for thinges gives such offence I will
be more sparinge in that kind hereafter but leave it to the Lord to deale with
mee accordinge to his mercy earnestly desireinge him to give mee an hart to
bee content with my porcion, knowinge that nothinge can beefall mee but that,
that hee hath appointed   I may take that verse in the 106th Psalme 17th verse,
fooles because of their transgressions and their iniquities are afflicted soe I
thinke that iust it is, whatsoeuer affliction shall come vnto mee. Deare Father
I am farr distant from you, and know not how longe it will please the Lord
to continue it soe, but howsoever I desire to rest satisfied with his will and doe
earnestly desire to submitt my selfe in all duty and obedience as belongeth
vnto a child to your selfe and my mother, as if I were with you. Father I
perceive by your lettres that you would very willingly to have mee change
my condition which I must confesse I might soe may with divers if the Lord
pleased to move my hart to accept any of them, but I desire to wayte vpon
him that can change my hart at his will. thus with my humble duty to your
selfe and my mother craving pardon of you both and of her If I have given
her any offence, and soe desiringe your prayers to him, who is able to give
wisedome and direccion to me in all thinges I rest: Your obedient Daughter
till death

MARY DOWNINGE

BOSTON, 27th of Novemb: 1635

[*Endorsed by Governor Winthrop:*] Cosin Ma. Downinge to her father.

NATHANIEL WARD TO JOHN WINTHROP, JR.[1]

SIR, I receiued your loving Letter in Mr. Halls behalfe: I was neuer against
his having a lott amongst vs nor to my remembrance haue spoken anythinge

---

[1] Essex Institute; 4 *Collections*, VII. 24–26. For Nathaniel Ward, first minister of Ipswich, see
D.A.B.

to hinder him, only the company that he brought to towne and his manner of cominge before the towne knew any such thinge was obserued and disliked. I neuer heard sillable of that yow mention in your letter concerning a mayde in Ireland till the tyme of opening your letter att that instant Mr. Dudley was telling me of it. I dare not beleeue empty rumours aganst any man: I am and shalbe tender of young and hopefull men, and ready to incourage them. I am bold to say I am and haue bene and shalbe so whateuer is reported to the contrary. our Towne of late but somewhat too late haue bene carefull on whome they bestowe lotts, being awakned therto by the confluence of many ill and doubtfull persons, and by their behauiour since they came in drinking and pilferinge; I pray if you speake with Mr. Hall advise him to suffer no priuate drinking in his howse, wherin I heare lately he hath bene to blame.

The reasons which moue our freemen to be very considerate in disposall of lotts and admission of people to vs are thes: First we conceiue the lesse of Satans kingdome we haue in our Towne, the more of Gods presence and blessinge we may expect. 2ly we haue respect to the creditt of our Church and Towne, from which we heare there are too many vniust detractions in the bay to serue their owne ends. 3ly we consider our Towne as a sey or port towne of the land remote from neighbours and had neede to be strong and of a homogeneous spirit and people, as free from dangerous persons as we may. Lastly, our Thoughts and feares growe very sadd to see such multitudes of idle and profane young men, servants and others with whome we must leaue our children for whose sake and safty we came ouer, and who came with vs from the land of their nativity their freinds and many other comforts which their Birthright intitled them to, relying vpon our loue wisdome and care to repay them all in this wildernes either in Specie or Compensations: but I must Confesse it sinks vs almost to the graue to looke vpon the next generation to whome we must leaue them and the fruite of our adventures labours and counsells: we knowe this might haue bene easily prevented by due and tymely care of such as had the opportunity in their hand, and if it be not yet remedied we and many others must not only say with greif we haue made an ill change, euen from the snare to the pitt, but must meditate some safer refuge if God will afford it, but I hope he will cause light to shine out of darknes and glorifie his strenght in the weaknes of men, and do that which seemes to be past all doing. We haue our eyes upon yow magistrats to helpe vs, and now Good Sir giue me leaue with patience to tell yow, as I did before yow went to England, that your absence hath bredd vs much sorrowe, and your still going from vs to Connecticote doth much discourage vs. I feare your tye or obligation to this state and in speciall to this towne is more then yow did well consider when yow ingaged your self another way, and I feare your Indeauours that way will not be operae ac spei pretium. I am in a dreame att least not awake if it be the way of God for so many to desert this place turning their backs vpon vs and to seeke the good of their cattell more then of com[monweal]th, and my thoughts are that God doth iustly rebuke our state by the losse of so many men vessells and victualls in a tyme of dearth, for their facility in giving way to their departure: for your part we looke and long for yow here and are in a misery for the want of yow. The Lord bring yow in his season and in the meane tyme afford yow his presence and blessing where euer yow are: and so I rest Your wor[shi]ps in all truth of loue

NATHL. WARDE

IPSWICH Dec: 24, [1635]

I forgett not my due respect to your Father mother and wife.

I heare Mr. Coddington hath the sale and disposall of much prouision come in this shipp. I intreate yow to do so much as to speake to him in my name to reserue some meale and malt and what victualls els he thinks meete till our Riuer be open   our Church will pay him duely for it. I am very deestitute. I haue not aboue 6 bushells corne left and other things answerable.

BARTHOLOMEW GREENE TO SIR RICHARD SALTONSTALL[1]

To the Right Worshippfull and his most lovinge Mr. Sur Richard Saltonstall Knight at his house in whitt streete london

RIGHT WORSHIPPFULL, my humbell Serves is remembred. hauinge soe fitt a mesenger I canot but right a word or tow   this is to certifie your worshipp this mesenger was at Canaticoatt and can tell you how the case stands   for my parte it is a greefe to me but the truth is I canot nor could not do no mor in it   I did vse the best consell and did vse wat meayns I could in the busnes for your good but mr. whitt comision was to be one side of the river, mr. stilles one the other[2] and after I had vsd meyns when mr. whitt and mr. stills went

---

[1] W. 4. 79; 5 *Collections*, I. 216–217. For Greene, see 5 *Collections*, I. 216n.; for Saltonstall, see *Winthrop Papers*, II. 153, *n.* I. This letter was presumably sent over to Winthrop by Saltonstall in his letter of February 27, 1635/36. See pages 229–230, below.

[2] Marginal note by Saltonstall: "They were to plant on that syde of the Ryuer New Plymouth trading howse was buylt."

and could not get a man to go by no meayns and as soonne as I hurd the
went not forward in the busnes I put myselfe vpon it agayne and at last got
a man to go to measur it out at a dear ratte and when he came ther ther was
not ground neather for medow nor ariball or pastur gronds that would geue
your worshipp content that the men darst not laye it out   the shuld a done
your worshipp ronge in the same seinge that dorchester men had taken vp
the best place befor and plimmoeth men sente a letter[1] to discharge our men
for medellinge with it sayinge it was ther right: for I conseaue that mr. ludloe
was the cheffe man that hinderd it   he was the onli man of dochester that
sett downe ther   I hope that this barer mr. woodcock man[2] will sertifie you
how it is   I haue riten manie letter for this purpose   other things I haue
bine large in letters   I am loath to be tow trobellsome to your worshipp in
the lik expresures   mr. hooker hath expressd some thinge that waye   the
lord direct you and advise you for the best and further your ofrings for his
glorie and your good and all ours   thus with my Serves agayne I commit you
to the only wise god and rest your poor Servant to the vtter most of my power
to command.

BARTH. GREENE

from WATERTONE this 30 of December 1635

[*Endorsed by Sir Richard Saltonstall:*] Md. that this letter be sent to Mr. John
Winthropp our Gouernour at Conectacutt with Fr[anci]s Styles his Relation.

LORD BROOKE TO JOHN WINTHROP, JR.[3]

To his worthie Freind mr. John Winthrop Esqr. these deliver in New england

GOOD MR. WINTHROPPE, I am informed by mr. Woodcocke that hee sent
ouer the last yeare to Connectucut at the least 20 seruants, to impale some
ground whereon they might improoue their industry to his aduantage and
wherein hee might feed some store of sheep which (I take it) now are there; but
hee was preuented by the Dorchaster men though his carpenter had first sett
downe uppon the place. I beseech you take care that hee bee prouided for.
his demandes I leaue to his owne expressions, you shall receaue them with this
Letter. as farre as I cann iudge of them they are moderate and iust and whilst

---

[1] Marginal note by Saltonstall: "Mr. Brewsters precept to my carpenter Francis Styles." For
Bradford's account of the controversy, see *History of Plymouth*, II. 216–224.

[2] Marginal note by Saltonstall: "Jo: Dauis."

[3] W. Au. 92; 5 *Collections*, I. 240–241. For Lord Brooke, see 5 *Collections*, I. 240n.

they are so I doubt not but they shall find you their freind yet shall I esteeme what you shall doe in this case as done to my selfe who will rest alwayes Your louing freind

R. BROOKE

[*Ca.* 1636]

I haue written to mr. Fenwick and intreated him to recommend this to mr. Hooker but least hee should bee uppon his way homeward before my letter come I must intreat that fauour from you and what respect hee shal show to mr. Woodcocke in this busines as hee will bee able to repay it by his industrious, affectionate fidelity towards your plantation so shal I take it for a fauour done to myselfe, and it cannot but rellish well here, where yet I assure you the ouer hasting of the Dorchaster men doth not sauour so well as I could wish.

BILL TO JOHN WINTHROP FOR TAILORING[1]

	li	*s*	*d*
Item for Mr. Adam one sute of aparell	0	4	0
Item for Mathay Watters a Coote	0	1	2
Item for one dayes worke for darneckell[2] of the Chamber	0	1	0
Item for Mr. Adam a westcoote	0	0	10
Item for Mr. Adam a sute	0	3	6
Item for Mr. Adam a wescoote	0	0	10
Item for 2 men 2 wescootes	0	2	0
Item for John Sambrock a geirkin	0	2	0
Item for Josias Firmin a sute	0	3	0
Item for himselfe a sute	0	4	6
Item for Josias Firmin a payer of breches	0	1	2
Item for your Worship a payer of stockins	0	1	2
Item for Mr. Steaven a westcoote	0	1	2
Item for William Freman a Coote	0	2	0
Item for John Sambrocke a Coote	0	2	0
Item for Mr. Adam and Mr. Deane each of them a payer of mitten	0	1	0

---

[1] W. 1. 106; 2 *Proceedings*, XIII. 59–61.

[2] This word is a variant of "dornick," a "coarse damask usually employed for making curtains and hangings." *Dictionary of American English*, II. 799. One illustration (1648) given there has the spelling "darnicle." A "danakell Coverlette" is listed in the inventory of Lionel Chute's estate, Ipswich, 1645. *Probate Records of Essex County*, I. 48.

	li	s	d
Item for Henry Kinsbury a sute	0	4	6
Item for John Sambrocke a payer of breches	0	1	8
Item for Josias Fyrmin a sute	0	3	6
Item for mending of his Worshipes Cap	0	0	6
Item for mending Mr. Adams breches	0	0	3
Item for Mr. Adam and Mr. Deane 2 wescoots	0	1	8
Item for Mathay Watters a payer of bodys	0	1	0
Item for Josias Fyrmin a payer of sliuers	0	0	6
Item for Robart Scarlit a sute	0	3	0
Item for the Frenchman a payer of breches	0	1	6
Item for Mr. Deane a sute an Coote	0	5	6
Item for Mathay Watters a sute	0	2	4
Item for 2 dayes and a halfe worke for your wife	0	2	6
Item for Mr. Deane a payer of mittens	0	0	6
Item for Worship a mufe	0	0	6
Item for your wife a mufe	0	0	6
Item for your Worship a wescoote	0	0	10
Item for Allen the frenchman a sute	0	3	6
Item for Joshua a sute	0	3	6
Item for John Tinker a payer of sliuers	0	0	6
Item for John Tinker a payer of briches	0	1	6
Item for the Frenchboy a sute	0	3	0
Item for Josias Fyrmin a sute	0	3	6
Item for footing a payer of stocking for John Tinker	0	0	6
Item for mending of his breiches	0	0	3
Somme	3	19	4

Receaued in parte of this bill one peck of salt a quart of trayne oyle 3 thousen of eallwiues 8 pound of leade and 3 pound of butter.

[*Ca.* 1636]

[*Endorsed by Governor Winthrop:*] Famelyes [?] Bill.

MARY DUDLEY TO MARGARET WINTHROP[1]

To my deare and very loving mother Mrs. Winthrop at Boston these be delivered

DEARE MOTHER, my humble dutie remembred to you. It reioyceth me to heare of your recoverie out of your dangerous sicknes, and should be glad to heare how your health is continued to you by a letter from your selfe, for I haue not heard from you a long time which troubleth me, though I haue sent you three or foure letters to you: I thought it convenient to acquaint you and my father, what a great affliction I haue met withal by my maide servant, and how I am like through god his mercie to be freed from it; at her first comminge to me she carried her selfe dutifully as became a servant; but since through mine and my husbands forbearance towards her for small faults, shee hath got such a head and is growen soe insolent, that her carriage towards vs especially myselfe is vnsufferable. if I bid her doe a thing shee will bid me to doe it my selfe, and she sayes how shee can give content as wel as any servant but shee will not, and sayes if I loue not quietnes I was never so fitted in my life, for shee would make me haue enough of it. If I should write to you of all the reviling speeches, and filthie language shee hath vsed towards me I should but greiue you. my husband hath vsed all meanes for to reforme her, reasons and perswasions, but shee doth professe that her heart and her nature will not suffer her to confesse her faults; If I tell my husband of her behauiour towards me, vpon examination shee will denie all that shee hath done or spoken: so that we know not how to proceede against her: but my husband now hath hired another maide and is resolved to put her away the next weeke.

Thus with my humble dutie to my father I rest your dutifull and obedient daughter

MARY DUDLEY

[*Ca.* January, 1635/36]

JOHN ENDECOTT TO JOHN WINTHROP[2]

WOURTHIE SIR, I ame sorrie to heare of your affliccion in this visitation of God, though you know that whom he loueth he chastiseth   let that comfort

[1] W. 4. 25; 5 *Collections*, I. 68. Mary Dudley was the daughter of Governor Winthrop by his first wife, Mary Forth, and was the wife of the Reverend Samuel Dudley, son of Governor Thomas Dudley.

[2] W. 3. 39; 4 *Collections*, VII. 156–157.

you, and you will see through Gods goodnes towards you that it will turne to good and you will say with that good kinge and prophet it is good for mee that I was in trouble. The Lord sanctifie this his hand to you. I haue sent you of all I haue or what I can gett: viz. Syrup of violetts Sirrup of Roses: Spirit of mints: Spirit of Annis as you may see written vppon the seuerall vialls. I haue sent you Mrs. Beggarly[1] her vnicorns horne and Beza stone I had of Mr. Humfry who is sorry also for your exercise. I haue sent you a Be[z]oar stone, and mugwort and organie if you should haue neede of it   they are both good in this case of your wife, and also I haue sent you some Galingall root. Mrs. Beggarly knowes the vse of it. If the fitt of the mother come verie violently as you write, There is nothing better to suppresse the rising of it then sneezing: a little pouder of tobaccou taken in her nose I thinck is better then Helibore. If I knew how or which way in this case to doe her good I would with all my heart, and would now haue come to you but I ame altogether vnskilfull in theise cases of weomen: Mr. Humfry and his lady remember them to you. I came from thence last night at 12 of the clock at night for I was from home when your letter came. Mrs. Williams doeth the like and if you please to tell Mrs. Beggerly that all her famly are well. My wiefe remembers her heartie loue to you and your wiefe and Mrs. Feake. The lord in mercie looke vpon you and send you comfort from aboue and strengthen you in patience and in humilitie to vndergoe his hand to whom I comitt you and rest Yours vnfeigned

                                                                    Jo: ENDECOTT

[*Ca.* January, 1635/36]

Your man parted heere halfe an hower after seauen in the morning.

· ·

MARY DUDLEY TO MARGARET WINTHROP[2]

To my Deare and loving mother mrs. Winthrop at Boston these

DEARE AND LOVINGE MOTHER, My dutye remembred being glad to heare of your health and recovery out of your great and dangerous Condition being in part sencible of that sorrow which you sustained by your vntimely travel: I haue of late been very ill of the tooth-ach but am now as well as formerly my Condition will permitt   I must make bold to trouble you for some things I

---

1 See *N. E. Historical and Genealogical Register*, xxxv. 318–320.
2 W. Au. 78; 5 *Collections*, I. 64.

shall stand in need of intreating you send by Henry Kinsbury or any other Convenient messenger 5 yards of flowred holland for a wastcott and tape to bind it an ele of fine holland and some fine thred: I intreat you would be pleased to provide me a mayd against the first weeke in may: myne is then to goe away   I am vncertaine of when my time of deliuery is   I desire your prayers and my fathers for me that god will deale mercyfully with me as I haue had experience of his goodnesse towards mee   my Children are well and my sister Winthrop   I desire to heare from you so soon as you can   pray remember my dutye to my father, and soe I humbly take my leaue and remain Your dutyfull daughter

MARY DUDLEY

Jan. 15, 1635[/36]

CHURCH COVENANT[1]

Wee who through the Exceeding riches of Grace and patience of God doe yet continue Members of this Church, being now Assembled in the holy presence of God, and in the name of the Lord Jesus Christ after humble Confession of our manifold breaches of covenant before the Lord our God, and Earnest Supplication of pardoning mercy through the blood of Christ, and deep acknowledgement of our great unworthynes to be owned as the Lords Covenant people; Also acknowledging our inability to keep Covenant with God, or to performe any spirituall duty vnlesse the Lord Jesus do enable vs therevnto, by his Spirit dwelling in us: and being awfully sensible, that it is a dreadfull thing for sinfull dust and ashes, personally to transact with the infinitely glorious Majesty of Heaven and Earth: We doe in humble Confidence of his gracious assistance, and acceptance through Christ Each one of us severally for our selves, and Jointly as a church of the living God, explicitly renew our Covenant with God, and one with another in manner and forme following. That is to say.

Wee doe give vp ourselves unto that God whose name alone is Jehovah, Father, Son and holy Spiritt, as the one only true and living God, and vnto

---

[1] W. 1. 112; *L. and L.*, 11. 138–141. The handwriting of this document has not been identified. Winthrop made the following entry in his Journal under the date February 25, 1635/36: "The distractions about the churches of Salem and Sagus, and the removal of other churches, and the great scarcity of corn, etc., occasioned a general fast to [be] proclaimed, which, because the court was not at hand, was moved by the elders of the churches and assented unto by the ministers. The church of Boston renewed their covenant this day, and made a large explanation of that which they had first entered into, and acknowledged such failings as had fallen out, etc."

our Blessed Lord Jesus Christ as our onely Saviour, prophett, preist, and King over our Soules, and onely mediator of the covenant of Grace; promiseing (by the helpe of his Spiritt and Grace) to cleave vnto God as our cheife Good, and vnto the Lord Jesus Christ by faith in a way of Gospell Obedience as becometh his Covenant people for ever.

Wee doe also give vp our offspring vnto God in Jesus Christ, avouching the lord to be our God, and the God of our Children, and our selves, with our children to be his people, humbly adoring this Grace of God, that wee and our offspring with us, may be looked upon as the Lords.

Wee doe also give up our selves one vnto another in the Lord, and according to the Will of God, freely covenanting, and binding our selves to walke together as a right Ordered Congregation, and church of Christ, in all wayes of his worship according to the holy rules of the word of God: promiseing in Brotherly love, faithfully to watch over one anothers Soules, and to submitt our selves to the discipline and government of Christ in his Church, and duely to attend the Seales, censures, or whatever Ordinances Christ hath comanded should be observed by his people according to the order of the Gospell.

And whereas the lord our God hath of late brought us vnder very solemn and awfull dispensations of his holy providence, even so, as in some sort, to remove this Candlesticke out of its place; wee must needs confesse before him, that he is righteous, and that by our transgressions against the Covenant, we have deserved all the evill that is come vpon us. Particularly, Wee from our hearts bewaile it before the Lord, that wee have loved Christ no more, and the world with the things and vanityes thereof so much, as also, that wee have no more loved one another with a pure heart fervently. [Wee must moreover confesse, that some amongst us have been visibly guilty of that Sin of Pride in apparelling themselves or their children, otherwise then doth become their places, and those that professe Godlines. And that some amongst us have been Guilty, in respect of that too common, and prevailing Sin of Excesse in drinking. Wee desire to be ashamed before the lord our God this day, that ever such evills should be found amongst us or in any of us][1] and humbly apply our selves to the throne of Grace for pardoning mercy: and as an Expedient to reformation of these, and what ever evills have provoked the Eyes of Gods glory, amongst us. Wee doe subjoine vnto our Church Covenant a further engagement whereby wee doe as in the presence of God promise.

1. That wee will (by the helpe of Christ) endeavour every one of us, to re-

---

[1] These brackets are in the original manuscript and seem to indicate that the subject was still under consideration; or, perhaps, that the words were stricken out.

forme his owne heart and life, by seeking to mortify all our Sins, and endeavouring to walke more fully, firmely, and closely with God, then ever wee have done, and to uphold the power of Godlines, and that wee will continue to worship God in publike, private, secrett; and this (as God shall helpe us) without formality, and hipocrisy, and more fully, faithfully then heretofore to discharge all covenant dutyes, one towards another in a way of church Communion.

2. Wee promise (by the helpe of Christ) to walke before God in our houses, with a perfect heart, and that wee will vphold the worship of God therein constantly, both in respect of prayer and reading the Scriptures, that so the word of Christ may dwell richly in us, and that wee will doe what in us lyeth to bring up our children for Christ, that they may become such, as they that have the Lords name put vpon them by a solemn dedication to God in Christ, ought to be; and that therefore we will Catechise them, and exhort and charge them to feare and serve the lord, and endeavour to sett an holy Example before them, and be much in prayer for their Conversion and Salvation.

3. Wee doe further engage (the Lord helping of us) to keep ourselves pure from the Sins of the times, and in our places to endeavour the Suppression thereof. Whether those Sins mentioned, or any other scandalous transgressions, against the first or second Table, and that we will make Conscience to walke so as that we may not give occasion to others to sin, or to speake Evill of our holy profession.

Now that we may observe, and keep this sacred Covenant, and all the branches of it, inviolable forever, we desire to deny ourselves, and to depend wholy upon the power of the eternall Spirit of Grace, and vpon the free mercy of God, and meritt of Jesus Christ; and where we shall faile, there to wait vpon the Lord Jesus for pardon, and for acceptance, and for healing for his names sake.

[*Ca.* February, 1635/36]

OWEN ROWE TO JOHN WINTHROP[1]

LONDON, the 18th February 1635[/36]

WORTHY SIR, I have received yours dated the 10th December, 1635, being very glad to hear of your wellfare, it doth somewhat rejoice my hearte when I

---

[1] Original not located; *Hutchinson Papers* (1769), 59; (1865), 1. 65–66. For Owen Rowe, the regicide, see *D.N.B.*

consider and think what you enjoyne: my hearte is with you. I shall I hope be glad if the Lord make mee a waye which I hope hee will that I may come, see your and behold the bewttye of our God in those gouernings of his in his tempel: Sir, it dyd glad mee to see that you had not forgott mee and more that you would be pleased to take the paynes to wryte to mee. Sir, I have now put off my trade, and as soone as it shall please God to send in my debts, that I may paye what I owe and cleare things so here that I may come away without giving offence, I am for your parte, the Lord make mee a cleare waye: now Sir, seeing you have mee in your thoughts, help forward that Mr. Ransford may be accomodated with lands for a farme to keep my cattele, that so my stock may be preserved; for I conceive I have lost neare £500, as Mr. Willson can certifye you: thus not doubting of your love he rests Who is yours to command

OWEN ROWE

SIR MATTHEW BOYNTON TO JOHN WINTHROP, JR.[1]

To my verie worthy friend John Winthorpe the younger Esqr: att Boston in the Massachusetts Bay in New England present this

SIR, Mr. Jacye deliuer'd a letter to me which was inclosed in a letter to him selfe, which had like to haue miscaried after itt came to his hand, he nott understandinge by the superscription to whom you had directed itt, and in this doubtfulness comminge to enquire of me if I knew of anie such gentleman in Yorkshire or Northumberland that had made anie such aduenture itt fell into his thoughts that the letter was intended to my selfe, and that the direction was purposelie made soe obscure for preuention of discouerie in case the letter had miscarried, and theyrfor he intreated me to read the letter, and to consither itt: and then, I did (prima facie) discerne that itt was to my selfe. The reasons why I relate all these circumstances are these, first to shew you that letters are in uerie great dainger of miscarriage by such obscure directions and secondlie though they fall butt into the handes of friends, yett I had rather haue the free enioyment of my owne thoughts and purposes to my selfe then that all should lye open to theyr eyes: Sir I beseatch you mistake me nott: for I infer nott from hence that I conceyue anie fault in you att all, for I know well, the cause of this proceeded from my owne tenderness, butt onelie to aduertise you of the inconuenience which I finde and the dainger of miscariage which may arrise this way: this is all I meane, onelie to intreate you

---

[1] W. 3. 40; 4 *Collections*, VII. 162–164. For Boynton, see 4 *Collections*, VII. 162n.

that for better certaintie, as alsoe that my owne brest may be the sole Cabinett of my affayres (which I desire nott to communicate with anie butt your selfe and your worthy Father: nor that anie other should haue anie intelligenc from you of anie thing that concernes my owne particular) theyrfor that you would be pleased to direct your letters to my selfe well seald   onely this if itt please you inclose them in a letter directed to Mr. Henrie Darley att the signe of the Lamb in Grays Inn Laine because it is a knowne place and he will deliuer them to me: for the Cowes, my desire is to preserue the increase by all the [means] that may be for I shall bringe ouer a greate Familie and if itt were possible I would be soe well furnished with that I might haue Beeues to kill as soone as I comm: What charge you haue beene att with them hitherto with them I will thankfullie returne you upon the receypt of your noates of disbursments: Sir I doe acknowledg my selfe exceedinglie obliged to you for all your paines and care for me. giue me leaue I pray you still to repose my-selfe upon you; your trowble is like to be the greater because I haue soe few acquaintance in your Contry, butt my thankfulness shall be the greater if euer I haue an opportunetie to express itt:

I intend (if the Lord giue leaue) for ought I yett know, to send ouer a care-full and a painfull godlie seruant, if not two, besides somm sheepe from Holland and Goates from hence: I pray you if the seruants comm lett them haue your best helpe and direction, and when the sheepe or Goates comm lett them be carefullie disposed of for I feare whether my seruants cann comm att the same time: I desire to heare from you as often as possibly you cann how my stocke prospereth and I shall long to heare how they haue increased this yeare.

I pray you aduertise me what course I shall take for prouidinge a house against my comminge ouer, where I may remaine with my Familie till I cann be better prouided to settle my selfe; and lett me haue your best assistance and withall I pray you lett me receyue aduice from time to time what provitions are most commodious to be made theyr or to be sent from hence that soe I may make the best aduantage of my time before I comm, as alsoe what things will be moste expedient for me both for my necessarie use and benefitt theyr to bring ouer with me when I comm: Thus confidinge in your loue I rest Your euer assured friend

MATT. BOYNTON

LONDON From Pauls Allie in Red-Cross streete Feb. 23th 1635[/36]

Sir I haue remooued my Familie out of the Contry and ame now constant-lie att London.

HERBERT PELHAM TO JOHN WINTHROP[1]

To the wor[shipfu]ll and his very loveing Cosen John Winthropp Esqr.
at his House in Boston this deliver

LOVING COSEN, I returne yow many thanks for your great love and hearty
intertaynement of my Brother   the ten pounds you desired me to pay for his
board I payd to your brother Downing, and think it litle enough if not to
litle as things are with [you] for the present, and must acknowledg my selfe
your debtor for your Care and paynes with him. the account yow sent I have
perused and cast it up together with my disbursment and those of Sir Richards Saltonstalls which I have added to myne haveing repayd him what he
layd out for stones 10*li* and Brasse, and fraught of the stones with some other
small things as when I send yow the accompt will appeare, soe that if I be not
mistaken the accompt will be somewhat over, but for the present I conceive a
mistake in the Casting up of your account, which because I could not tell How
to rectifie I resolved by mr. Downings advise to send yow backe your owne
Coppy, and to keep an other my selfe, which his man hath written out for me
soe that when yow se your owne hand you may be the better able to sett it
straight. I have sent over some frute trees and some grape Cuttings, the best I
could gett. if you like any of the grapes yow may take what yow please of
them. I pray advise what I were best doe with my trees   I shall be larger
next time. remember me kindly to my Cosen your wife   soe with my hourely
prayers I rest your ever loving Cosen

                                                                    H. PELHAM

Feb. 23, 1635[/36]

MARY DUDLEY TO JOHN WINTHROP, JR.[2]

To my Deare and Loueing Brother Mr. John Winthrop at Boston give this

DEARE AND LOUEING BROTHER, my Loue remembred to your selfe and my
Deare Sister. I am sorry that I shall not se you before you take your Journey
to Coneticott but I wish you a prosperous viage: I giue you many thankes for
your many tokens that you sent me which will doe me a great pleasure being
I had but a little suger ith house and remember my Duty to my father and

---

[1] Massachusetts Archives, CCXL. 19; *Hutchinson Papers* (1769), 59–60; (1865), I. 66–67. For
Pelham, who came to Massachusetts in 1638, see *Winthrop Papers*, II. 315, *n.* 4.
    [2] W. 4. 23; 5 *Collections*, I. 65.

mother and pray thanke my father for my parsnips and pray my mother to
send me as much cloth as will make John 3 shirtes and that as you write
about Jhon Davis I haue sent to him to do it   So haueing nothing more to
say I rest Your truly Loueing Sister

MARY DUDLEY

IPSWICH Feb. 26, [1635/36]

tell my mother John is well and send the cloth as sone as she can.

SIR RICHARD SALTONSTALL TO JOHN WINTHROP, JR.[1]

*For my worthy Good Freind Mr. John Winthropp Gouernour of the Plantations at
Conectecott Ryuer in New England these deliver per Fr[anci]s Styles whom God preserue*

GOOD MR. WINTHROPP, Being Credibly informed (as by the inclosed[2] may
appeare) that there hath beene some abuse and injurie done me by mr. Ludlowe and others of Dorchester[3] who would not suffer Frances Styles and his
men to Impall grounde where I appointed them att connecticut Although
both by patent, which I tooke aboue foure yeares since, and per posession,
Dorchester men being then vnsettled, and seekeing vp the Riuer aboue the
falls for A place to plant vpon, butt findeing none better to their likeing, they
speedily Came backe againe and discharged my worke men, Casteing lotts
vpon that place, where he was purposed to begine his worke, Notwithstanding he often tould them what great Charge I had beene att In sending him
and so many men, to prepare A house against my Comming, and Enclose
grounde for my Cattle, And how the damage would fall heauie vpon those
that thus hindered me, whom Francis Styles Conceiued to haue best right to
make choyse of any place there. Notwithstanding they resisted hime slighteing
me with many vnbeseeming words such as he was vnwilling to Relate to me,
but will Justifie vpon his Oath before Authoritie, when he is Called to itt.
Therefore wee haueing appointed you to be our Gouernour there; the rest of
the Companye being sencible of this Affront to me would haue signified there
minde In A generall letter vnto you, but that I tould them sithe itt did Con-

---

[1] W. Au. 87; 4 *Collections*, VI. 579–581. There are two other originals of this letter: one, without
date but endorsed by John Winthrop, Jr., "Sir Richard Saltonstall 1636," is in the possession of
Mrs. R. M. Saltonstall and was printed in 2 *Collections*, VIII. 42–43; the other, bearing the date March
30, 1636, is in the possession of the Connecticut Historical Society and is printed in *N. E. Historical
and Genealogical Register*, LI. 66–67.

[2] See Bartholomew Greene to Richard Saltonstall, December 30, 1635, pages 217–218, above.

[3] Windsor, Connecticut.

cerne my selfe In particular and might perhaps breed some Jealousies In the
people and so distast them with our Gouernementt, wherevpon they Advised
me write vnto you to Request you with All speed and diligence to Examine
this matter and if (for the substance) you find itt as to vs itt appeares, by this
information heerewith sent you that then In A faire and gentile way you giue
notice to Dortchester men of this greate wronge they haue donne me etc; (Being the first that to further this designe sent my pinnace thither At my owne
great Charge of almost A thousand pounds which now Is cast away by theire
detaineing her so long before she could vnlayd and for which Iniustice I may
require satisfaction as also for my prouisions which cost aboue fiue hundreth
pounds and are now (I heare) almost all spent by this meanes and not any
palling as yet sett vp att that place where I appointed them, which had I but
Imagined they would haue thus greedily snatched vp all the best grounds
vpon that Riuer my pinnace should rather haue sought A pylate At new Plymouth then to haue stayd ten days as she did In the Bay to haue giuen them
Such warneing thus to preuent me) and lett them spaire as (I am tould) they
may very well forth of that great quantity they haue ingrossed to themselues
so much as my proportion Comes too and if they haue built any houses therevpon I will pay them theire reasonable Charges for the same   But I pray you
either goe yourselfe with some skillfull men with you or send Sergieant Gardiner and some with hime to sett out my grounds (1600 akers) where It may be
most Conueniant betweene Plimouth Trucking house and the falls[1] according
to my directions giuen both to the maister of my pinace and to Francis Styles
which I thinke they will not now denie me vnderstanding what Charge I am
att (with others of the Companie) to secure this River mouth for the difence of
them all wherin I hope you will negclect no meanes according to our greate
trust reposed In you   thus beseeching the Lord to prosper the worke begun I
Commend you with All our affaires vnder your Charge to the gratious direction and protection of our good God In whome I am Your most assured loveing freind

RIC: SALTONSTALL

WHITEFREYERS the 27th February 1635[/36]

pray you commend me After yourselfe to your good wife and Sergieant
Gardiner with his fellow Soldier whom I purpose God willing to visitt this
summer if he will prouide A house to receiue me and mine att my landing.

---

[1] In the margin: "I had Rather haue it towards N: Town becawse I purpose to buyld there and
Joyn with mr. Hooker."

PROPOSED ORDER OF THE GENERAL COURT[1]

A consideration for this present Gen[eral] Court That it may be ordered to preuent future inconveniences of vnnecessary multiplication of Ch[urch] societie and disturbanc both to State and Ch[urche]s and for the maintayneing the Maiesty honour and Credit of gods holy Ordinances amongst vs, That hencforth noe persons in this Jurisdiction shal in any way Embody themselues into Ch[urch] Estate without consent of the G[eneral] Court and approbation of neighbour Churches, And that there shalbe noe ministery or Ch[urch] Administration entertayned or attended by the Inhabitants of any Plantation in this Colony distinct and seperate from and in opposition to that which is openly and publiquely obserued and dispensed by the setled and approued Minister of the place except it be by approbation of contry and church And that noe person liueing vnder an Orthodox ministery shal ioyne in Church society in another Plantation vnles they remoue their habitation thither where they ioyne in relation or procure the approbation of the Gen[e]r[a]l Court to the proceeding.

[*Ca.* March, 1635/36]

[*Endorsed by Governor Winthrop:*] presented to the Court but did not passe in this forme.[2]

HUGH PETER TO JOHN WINTHROP, JR.[3]

To my frend and son Mr. John Winthrop yonger these deliver Boston

DEERE SIR, By these you may vnderstand that I haue receiued your letters and am glad our busines goes on, though I am very tender of your personall aduenture in the busines, in which I pray be very carefull by all meanes. You know many have an interest in you. for my part I neuer meant lesse then to goe with you, but Gods hand hath bin and is vpon mee more and more in the weaknes of my body, which declynes dayly. for the nayles at Salem there are diuers very much rusted, and so are the clinchers. for the things in the Barke I pray bee carefull of, these are they I thought you should not haue carryed with you, because I feare that our frends will alter their purposes when they

---

[1] W. 5. 208.   [2] Cf. *Records of Massachusetts*, i. 168 (March 3, 1635/36).
[3] W. 2. 50; 4 *Collections*, vi. 93. For Peter, see *D.A.B.*

come. I am sorry for the short prouisions in the bay, it is so all ouer. Helpe Lord! and I hope hee will helpe Salute honest Mr. Garddner and the rest my hart is with you and your iourney, and my prayers shall follow you.

For those things which concerne the Generall, I shall communicate to Mr. Humfry who is home for this Court. I doe not know how too send these nayles you write. there is also 20 or 30 barres of iron left and some meale. to carry too many things thither as guns etc. may not be so advantagious for ought I see. The Lord doe you good abundantly. I am yours euer frend and father

H: PETER

[*Ca.* March, 1636]

HUGH PETER TO JOHN WINTHROP, JR.[1]

For my deer and louing Sonne Mr. John Winthrop iunior these deliver Boston

DEERE HART, Mee thought I broke from you too abruptly last day. My hart is with you: I can say no more but this streighten your accounts and in them bee curious, leaue your mind for mee about your Ipswich busines in writing; and if you will send 20*li* to Mr. Endecot you may seale it vp and send it by this bearer I am buying goates. Salute all yours. tell your wife I will not bee long from her. The blessing of heauen bee vpon you and him who is Yours whilst any thing

HU: PETER

SAGUS, 2d day [*ca.* March, 1636]

Leaue things with your father in some order for feare of the worst, whom with my [your] mother I pray salute from me vnfaynedly.

EMMANUEL DOWNING TO JOHN WINTHROP, JR.[2]

To my verie loving Cosen John Winthrop, the yonger, esqr. at Boston deliver

MY GOOD COSEN, I haue received 3 letters from you, the first of the 9th of 9ber thother 2 of the 12 and 15 of Jannar. Thanks be to God for your safe arivall after soe tedious a passadge.

I hartilye thank you for the kynde offerr of your howse, but because I can-

---

[1] W. 2. 49; 4 *Collections*, VI. 91.
[1] W. 2. 22; 4 *Collections*, VI. 43–44.

not yet resolve of my coming this yeare, I pray dispose of yt to your best advantadge. I am advised not to make choyse of any place for my selfe vntill I come there.

I haue sent you butter, suett and other things by this shipp, for the particulars thereof I referr you to my wives lettres. Sir Arthur Hesilrigg refuseth to deall for Capten Endicotts howse, because as he sayth, the merchants telleth him, the howse is theirs, and built with theire monie etc. as I wrote vnto himselfe; Your mother Peters hath paid me 40*li*, which I haue laid out for you and almost as much more: shee entends to pay you the rest soe soone as shee can possiblie, which I feare wilbe nere Christide 'ere shee can performe yt. I perceive shee stands verie well affected to you, but as yet cannot doe as shee would for you.

I hartyly thank you for the manie good directions in your letters to me, And for my brother Gostlyn if possiblye I can I will helpe him over, and the rather because his goeing may cause my wife more willinglie to listen therevnto. shee feareth much hardshipp there, and that wee shall spend all, ere wee be setled in a Course to subsist even for foode and rayment. I pray in your next write hir some encouradgement to goe hence vnto you.

Tom Goade sent his letters out of Spayne which I haue received and delivered, but himselfe is gone with that shipp into the Streights, soe I hope he will prove a Sea man. Ben Gostlyn is like to prove a propper Sea man, he is retorned out of the streights and gone to Sea againe. his master vseth him like a sonne, and the youth would not change his Course of life for any other. so soone as he shalbe out of his tyme, he entends to see New England.

having written more at lardge to my brother Winthrop whereto I referr you, with my love to your selfe and second selfe leaving you and your occasions to the blessing of our good God I rest Yours assured

EM: DOWNINGE

1° Martij 1635[/36]

SAMUEL READE TO JOHN WINTHROP, JR.[1]

To my very louing brother mr. John Winthrope esqr. at his fathers house in Boston or else where these present in New-England

DEARE BROTHER, When letters came to my hands from my father and my brother Thomas Reade, I doubted not but to haue found one from you; but

---

[1] W. 4. 79; 5 *Collections*, I. 217–218.

ther was none, wherfore I began to suspect, that mine came not to your hands; in defect wherof let these shew that I am not altogether forgetfull of your selfe nor yet of her my deare sister, whom I heare in wedlocke you haue made great; the lord grant you the fruition of your hopes, to the glory of his name. your letter of atturny I haue delivered to mr. Downing, who will deale with my brother William Reade about the 50*li*. we wonder we haue noe certaine information whether my father Peter intendeth to stay with you, or to returne. it is necessary it should speedily be determined of, that his church may know how to dispose of themselues. mr. Davenport supplyeth his place yet. mr. Hunt I hear is goeing into the Isle of Providence. the glasmen will not undertake to goe ouer, till there be claye found out fitt for them in the country: least they should be a burthen to those that transport them, or elce liue miserably; for they haue not wherwithall to defray theire owne charges ouer. I forbeare to write newes, because the passengers can relate it more fully. here is much talke of a gouerner to be sent ouer, but the lord being your protector, why should you feare, into whose fatherly tuition I commit you; with my due respects to all my well respected freinds knowne and unknowne, being least unmindfull of your selfe and my litle sister, I take leaue and remaine Yours in what I may

SAMUELL READE

LONDON March 5, 1635[/36]

THOMAS HEWSON TO JOHN WINTHROP[1]

To the Right worr[shipfu]ll and his Respectted Frend Mr. John Wintrope Senior in New England with trust deliver

LONDON this 7th March 1635[/36]

RIGHT WORR[SHIPFU]LL, I am full sorry my respect and care and cost vpon the plantation of a Colini in new England is so slighted and little regarded haueing formerly maid over all I had to you in trust for me by a letter of attorney and your self writting so often you would gett francis Johnson to send me an accompt and let him and Captaine Indeco deall like honest men and truly maike it appeare what is becomde of those goods of myne receiued ashore out of the ship Tho: and Willam Mr. Willam Bundox m[aste]r of her as by a tru copy I sent to you vnder Captaine Indecot and francis Johnsons

---

[1] W. 4. 80; 5 *Collections*, I. 218–220. For Hewson, see 5 *Collections*, I. 218*n*.; Frances Rose-Troup, *The Massachusetts Bay Company and Its Predecessors* (New York, 1930), 114–115.

hand and I intreat you deliver for me to Willam Hudson of boyston all such writtings as I sent to you by your son mr. John when Mris. Wintrop came to you   I intreat you deliver them to him ether to copy and giue you them againe or you will let him haue them for my use   also I desire an accompt from you of all passages since you receiud any goods of myne and how you paid me because thes things I have had from you is very imperfitt and no accomptant I can get can tell how to profitt it being so improperly sett down and so I shall find some yet not paid for my servants, not yet paid me   I humble desire you let Daniell Hardwicke be fre and at liberty this somer about June or July   I know ther libertys ar mor pleasing and he being a stranger and the rest at liberty it is my request   I hop you will grant it and let me humble request one accompt from you because no accomptant I can get to profitt thes particulers I haue from you. Againe I desire answere from you of that parcell of shows sent to you in aprill 1633 from hence per Willam bundocke   you receiud them and I requested you deliver one fourth part to Willam hudson another to mr. oldam another to mr. Conant another to my brother in law Tho: Wincoll and desired you order them to sell them and bring beaver to you for them and the same somer I had beaver from Willm. hudson for his and yet nothing from them nor no letter from you in a yeare and mor to my best Remembrance   maike my case your owne   me thinketh better dealling should be offered to so well a willer as I haue bene to new england and not to be so grosely wronged as I am   Delays breadeth Divers Dangers   be pleased answere me effectually and advise me what to do and what you will do   I haue written to my Brother Gurdon of Ass[ingt]on in Suffock and desired him writ to you effectually to afford your assistance to helpe me to what is detained from me and also ether you will procure from Captaine Indeco 2 cows for Willam hudson of boston at 15*li* per peace for me to pay heare or els you will deliver him 2 as good as the best of the six mr. Johnson had and you paid me for them about a yeare or two after heare   Do you thinke mr. Johnson was of so base a dispossion if he had liued he would a kept my Cattle sould at a vnder value by him had no right to a done it and did it for his owne base by ends. assure you self if this reasonable request be denied me I shall not pase it so over; neither standeth it with the Creditt of mr. Johnsons frends to swallow such Guggions   wrongs will provoke words when writting will not serve I feare not but procure a comanding power in what I request if it be denied me   Therfor lett me intreat answere as pleaseth, and howsoever I shall rest your Frend to vse

THO: HEWSON

LUCY DOWNING TO JOHN WINTHROP, JR.[1]

DEAR NEPHEW, I am much satisfied to hear of your safe ariuall and my neeces in N: E: and doe hartilie thank you for our kinde inuitation thither: and your care of our acommodations: but I confesse neither when you weer heer: not yet am I conuinct, that wee are like to see new E: this year: nor doe I wish to abuse your so precious affections with procestinated hopes: concerninge your commands: 1. Your mother peters desires my neeces clothes maye staye till she goes ouer to you, because she hath some to send her, both from hence, and from holland. allso she hears my neec is with childe and therfore she cannot be well fited att present: for many younge weomen grow much of ther first child for the other things you shall receiue acordinge to your directions, and this inclosed note: You shall allso receiue a large box with linine and pewter wich I desire you to conceall the donor therof if you chance by the marks, or such like, to discouer whence they come: and that for 2 resons: first the partye would auoide ielozie of another that hath none sent him att this time: 2 theer are more to come to you from the same place: and she would not have thes wich are noe part of them to preuent the other: allso I pray impart not any thinge of them to your mayd that went ouer with you: whoe came out of hollan: not that theer is any wronge done heerby, be confident of that: as you shall fullie vnderstand very shortlie: but I pray obserue thes directions to preuent iniuries:

I should much maruill your seruant goad and you wear so sudinlie parted, but that I knowe your man richards base qualities, and that he hath exstreamlie abused both you and himselfe in his words and carigd hear: as mrs. peters, myselfe, and diuers other frinds of yours can witnes, apon my owne knowlegde, and my brother gostlin and my brother hill. he tould my brother hill he had as good send thom goad to the gallows as with you: and villified and sleighted your seruis to my sister and him: and profest him selfe would not be perswaded to goe backe with you apon noe intreatie: it would be very prolix to perticuler things in this kind to you but be conuinct this far, that if you would not harbour a man guiltie of this foornamed vice of detraction to you, swearinge, drunkenes in a frequent manor, and so much whoredome as steallinge into a womans bed vnknown to her, allthoughe she denyes it: then I pray reiect all trust in him, for apon my creditt thes things are true of him. the woman her selfe came to me to complaine of him, whom he frighted in this manor: and his doged speaches of you makes many of your frinds fear you

<hr>

[1] W. 4. 3; 5 *Collections*, I. 8–10.

maye be liklie to haue a mischiue by him, att one time or other, if you haue to doe with him   and a man that went ouer with you in the abigall, and from thence into Spaine with thom goad and is now in London tells my sister hill that richard did cosen thomas goad of all such things as my sister furnisht him with for his iournie: and I perceiue my sister takes it somwhat vnkindlie you afforded her not a word why you parted with him: I thank you for your dayntie token, and all those moste affectionat respects wich I shall euer highlie vallue, allthough meanlie requite. I pray present my best respects to my neec, prayinge her prosperitie, and all our good frinds with you, my Dutch cosen msr. humphries msr. cotten and all our kindred and frinds att your commands. the polsgraue and his brother the sight of them takes me sudainlie of.

L. D.

March 8, [1635/36]

LADY MARY EDEN TO JOHN WINTHROP[1]

To my loueing freind Mr. Wintrop in Boston in New England giue these

Mr. Winstropte, I receiued a letter from you which I take very kindly, and if you would write mee some news it would bee very wellcome to mee for I know you will write nothing but the truth and wee heare news some good and some bad. I would desire you to send mee worde whether wheate and rye and mislin will grow in New England: my cosin Fernly which is married to one Mr. Norton is amongst you and I wonder that I haue not heard from them   I heere there were 2 shipps taken by the Turke and I am afraide that they were in one of them   pray send me worde whether they are with you soe with my kind remembrance to you I rest Your loueing freind

Mary Eden

From Patiswick hall in O: E: March the 10th 1635[/36]

---

[1] W. 4. 31; 5 *Collections*, 1. 83. For Lady Eden, see 5 *Collections*, 1. 83n.

BILL OF WILLIAM PYNCHON TO JOHN WINTHROP, JR.[1]

Mr. John Winthrops Bill of Parsells of his cloth and other things
Bought of William Pynchon of Roxbury 17 March 1635[/36]

	li	s	d
37 y. ¼ cloth at 8s y.	14	18	0
36 y. ¾ at 8s y.	14	14	0
38 y. ½ at 8s y.	15	08	0
54 y. at 8s y.	21	12	0
40 y. at 7s 6d y.	15	00	0
29 y. ¼ at 8s y.	11	14	0
41 y. at 6s 8d y.	13	13	4
25 y. ¼ in 2 peeces at 6s 8d y.	8	8	4
35 y. ¼ at 8s y.	14	2	0
35 y. ¼ ½ at 8s y.	14	3	0
15 y. ¾ at 6s 8d y.	05	5	0
38 y. ½ at 8s y.	15	4	0
36 y. at 8s y.	14	8	0
35 y. ½ at 8s	14	4	0
11 y. at 8s y.	04	8	0
	197	1	8

More Bought of him the day aboue said

2 doz. looking glasses at 2s 4d doz.	0	4	8
3 quart potts at 4s peece	0	12	0
4 doz. Jewes harpes at 12d doz.	0	4	0
4 doz. of steele aule blades at 16d doz.	0	5	4
1 doz. of porengers large	0	10	6
1 doz. occomy spones at 6s 6d	0	6	6
15 howes large at 2s peece	1	10	0
	3	13	0

---

[1] W. 17. 15. For William Pynchon, see *D.A.B.*; Samuel E. Morison, "William Pynchon, The Founder of Springfield," *Proceedings*, LXIV. 67–107.

JOHN HUMFREY TO JOHN WINTHROP, JR.[1]

To the wor[shipfu]ll his much respected freind John Winthrop iun: Esq.
gov[erno]r of Conecticot

DEARE SIR, You had received ere this an earnest expression of my m[as-
te]rs desire to have brought or (at least) sent mr. Gardiner over to Marblehead, (had it beene but for one halfe day,) had not the snow intercepted his
designes. You know and apprehend more then my selfe the importance of that
place; which supposed, there are manie as important considerations concerning the place of his setling; least that in one, wee precipitate him, the place,
and whole countrie (by it) into greater adventures then is meete. I sadly with
him apprehend much usefulnes (if not necessitie) of your lending us one night
before you goe. Let it be where you will at my house, Marblehead or Salem.
The foundation of his future course and comforts depend much upon it You
may thence be set over to Scituat, or be returned as you please. You may accompanie mr. Peirce, and so beare out betweene you a full understanding and
conclusion what to determine upon. With my best respects love and service to
you all respectively I rest Your trulie loving

Jo: HUMFREY

March to SAGUS 20th [1635/36]

MARY DUDLEY TO MARGARET WINTHROP[2]

To my very Deare and Loving mother Mrs. Winthrop give this at Boston I pray

DEARE MOTHER, My duty remembred to you and my father. I haue ocasion
at this time to trouble you by reason that my maid is to goe from me at may
day and I am onprovided of one. now I pray you to send me some cloutes and
a paire of sheetes and pillow-beeres as soone as you can for I doe not know
how quickly I shall need them, and I pray you to send me 2 calfes bages for
my Cheese. I am much troubled that I haue not heard either from you nor
my father. I should much reioyse to heare from you by a few lines that I ame
not forgotten of you. what wages you agree for my husband will be willing to
stand to. Thus ceasing further to trouble you I rest Your dutifull Daughter

MARY DUDLEY

IPS: March 28, [1636]

W. I. 113.   [2] W. 4. 24; 5 *Collections*, I. 65–66.

JOHN WINTHROP TO JOHN WINTHROP, JR.[1]

To my verye loving sonne mr. Winthop iunior Gouernour of Conectecott deliver

SONNE, I went to Tenhils this morning with your mother and your wife to have seene Goodman Bushnell: but the Lord had taken him away half an houre before we came there: so I made haste downe to sende you notice of it: but the shipp was vnder sayl before I came, which gives me no tyme to write further to you: for I must send the boat prestly after her. you shall receive of mr. Hodges the key of one of his Chests where the seeds are, the key of the other cant be found, so you must break it open. there is in one of them a rundlett of honey, which she desires may be sent to her against she lye down   she desires you to take an Inventory of all he hath there. we are all in health I prayse God for it   your two men you left sick, your wife and mother and all of vs salute you and your good Company   the Lord blesse and prosper you. farewell my good sonne.

[JOHN WINTHROP]

this 28 of the 1 mo. 1636

SIR WILLIAM MARTIN TO JOHN WINTHROP[2]

SIR, I ame glad to heare of Mr. Nortons safe arriuall, and should haue bene more glad if it had bene at the baye. I hope he will setle with you; his abilityes are more then ordinary, and wilbe acceptable and profitable to the churches. I haue receiued Prats exposition from Mr. Downing; and in the mayne I finde litle difference therin from his letter.[3] I should be glad to be truly informed by you what you conceiue of the soyle, and meanes of subsistance, And whether that exposition agrees with the truth of thinges. I ame sorry to heare of Mr. Williams seperation from you: his former good affectiones to you, and the Plantationes were well knowne unto me and make me wonder now at his proceedinges. I have wrote to him effectually to submit to better Judgments, and especially to those whom formerly he reverenced and admired, at least to keepe the bond of peace inviolable. this hath bene al-

---

[1] W. 7A. 55; Savage (1825), I. 387; (1853), I. 465; *L. and L.*, II. 151.

[2] Miscellaneous MSS., Bound, M.H.S.; *Hutchinson Papers* (1769), 106–107; (1865), I. 119–120. Sir William Martin was of Woodford, Essex.

[3] For the episode of John Pratt and his letter wherein he "affirmed divers things, which were untrue and of ill report, for the state of the country," see *Journal*, I. 165. His answer or "exposition" is printed in *Records of the Court of Assistants*, I. 109–111.

wayes my advise; and nothing conduceth more to the good of Plantationes; I praye shew him what lawfull favoure you can, which may stand with the common good. He is passionate, and precipitate, which maye transporte him into error, but I hope his integrity and good intentiones will bring him at last into the waye of truth, and confirme him therin; In the meane tyme I praye God to give him a right vse of this affliction. Thus leauinge him to your fauourable censures, and you all to the direction and protection of god, with my best respects to you and yours, I signe me Yours affectionate

W. M.

March 29, 1636

[*Endorsed by Governor Winthrop:*] Sir Wm. Martin.

GEORGE PHILLIPS TO JOHN WINTHROP, JR.[1]

To the worthy and deseruedly respected Mr. John Winthrope iunr.
gouernor for the plantation at Quinticuke these deliver

WORTHY SIR, I am bold to write a few lines vnto you and therby to request a great matter at your handes, wherunto I am encouraged from the vprightnes of my Conscience in presenting the motion vnto you and further by the wayght of the matter both in necessity and profit that I truely apprehend to attend the Cause   The summe is that you wold be pleased to sett downe with that plantation begonne there by Watertowne[2]   The necessity of it is, the weaknes of a company without a head cannot well sway and guide it selfe but is subiect to many errors distractions confusions and what not, which in our vndertakings in this part of the world cannot but proue dangerous to the cause of religion, dismal to the Common state, both in generall and particular, and disturbance if not destruction to the church estate which wee desire may there be established and prosper: The profit wilbe (I am resolued through Gods mercy) not onely the preuention of the former euills, but very great aduantages to the glory of God, much furtherance of his prayse in many thanksgiuings, and the prosperous and peacable estate of that people and soe of all the rest. I had spoken vnto you here but was discourged by the sence of mine owne disabilities to performe any thing that might be satisfac-

---

[1] W. Au. 89; 5 *Collections*, I. 123–124. For Phillips, see 5 *Collections*, I. 123*n*.; Henry W. Foote, "George Phillips, First Minister of Watertown," *Proceedings*, LXIII. 193–227.

[2] Wethersfield, Connecticut.

tory on my part to such a fauour if you shold be pleased to yeeld it Were I not
conscious of mine owne weaknes I shold be exceedingly importunate if not
impudent in pressing my request in this case, but mine owne infirmity makes
mee (though litteræ non erubescunt) ashamed and therefore to say little but
leaue this to your louing Consideration and the blessing of God All I will
say is that you wold take this in good part and beleeue mee it proceeds from a
free and sincere heart And with the tender of my humble respect and true
loue vnto you I shal not cease to pray to God to blesse you in whom I remayne yours in all Christian duty and affection

GEORG: PHILLIPS

WATERTOWNE the 29 of the first moneth, 1636

MARY DUDLEY TO MARGARET WINTHROP[1]

DEARE AND LOUING MOTHER, My duty remembred to your selfe and my
Deare Father hopeing of your wellfare as all we are I shall make bold to
trouble you with a few thinges as I do allwayse on thinge is that you take
some paines in providing a maid for me for the first of may my maid is to goe
away from me: on that should be a good lusty seruant that hath skille in a
dairy and for what wages you shall agree that my husband will be willing to
stand too and I would intreat you to send me word as soone as you can and
I would pray you to send me a childs chaire for I can get none made heear
and goodman Buttons Boat shall calle for it a fortnight hence: John begins to
brake out with heat I would pray you to send me that that you think fitt will
do him good: he hath tow teeth allready So haueing nothing else but my
Loue remembred to all my friendse I rest Your Dutyfull and obedient
Daughter

MARY DUDLEY

[*Ca.* April, 1636]

I do desire that you wold please to get Margarett Steele released from Mr.
Simkins to come and liue with me for my maid is to goe away from me the
first of may or els to gett me some other mayd which is skilfull in the Dearie to
come to me to Ipswich the first weeke of May.

---

[1] W. 4. 24; 5 *Collections,* I. 66.

RICHARD SALTONSTALL, JR., TO JOHN WINTHROP, JR.[1]

To the wor[shipfu]ll his assured loving freind Mr. Winthrop Gov[ernou]r at Conectecote

DEAR SIR, I am bould to troble you, and entreat you in my fathers Case; whearin your love to him; and authoritie, and wisdome, to direct and helpe, or (indeede) rather to overpower injurious oppositions, shall make mee your bond-man. You know how all things goe. The lord direct and prosper all your affayres; to whose guidance and gratious protection I commend you, and rest Yours vnfaynedly

RICHARD SALTONSTALL

[*Ca.* April, 1636]

My great hast cravs pardon for my brevitie and abruptnesse.

MURIEL SEDLEY GURDON TO MARGARET WINTHROP[2]

To my much respected worthy freind mrs. Winthropp the eldere at Boston give this

MY MOST DEAR AND MUCH RESPECTED FRINDE, I rejoyc to hear of your recovery, for my daughter had wrote to me of your weaknes which made your lettar the more wellcom to me; the Lord continew your helth to the comfort of your good husband, and the furthering of that great worke which the lord hath called you unto. You say you shall not nede to informe of any thing consarning the countrey: having so many othar friends: I may say to you, so wright all the rest, that wee hear but very littell, but what we hear from thos which come ovar from you, and thay for the most parte diffar so much ayther in ther spech or in judgment, though we thinke well of them: that thear is littell satisfacttion to be had from what they speake: but you have so many come to you from us I am sure you shall be informed of such prosedings as will greve any christien hart to hear: that in so short a time so many of Gods faithfull ministers should be silinced: and that which is wors; many that semed to be zeleous doe yeld obedence to the inventions of men: it will be a hard matar to chous the good and lav the evill: I did thinke befor it had come to this haith that we should have been providing to come to you, but now I

---

[1] W. 3. 68; 4 *Collections*, VII. 252–253.
[2] Original not located; *Publications of the Colonial Society of Massachusetts*, VIII. 202–203. Muriel Sedley Gurdon was the daughter of Martin Sedley of Morley, Norfolk, and the second wife of Brampton Gurdon of Assington, Suffolk.

see that my husband in regard of his many years rathar thinke he hath a calling to suffar hear then to remove himselfe: the Lord teach us what his will is and giv us harts to submite truly unto it and his holy Spirit to carry us throwe I give mr. winthrup and your selfe many thanks for your care of my sonne Edmound I did hope he would have bin of mor euse to have ben imployed by you then it seme he was. the weaknes in his hands grew upon him not long befor he went from us. we ded hope the Sea would have been a good meanes to helpe it: but I rathar fear he is worse: my husband is desirous to give satisfaction for the charge he hath put you unto and with many thanks for your love and care: thus desirous to have my best respect tendred to mr. winthrup and your selfe I becech the Lord to keepe us all stedfast to the ende. your Asured frind

MERIELL GURDON

ASINGTONE this 4 of Aprell [1636]

JOHN WINTHROP TO JOHN WINTHROP, JR.[1]

To my very lovinge sonne Mr. Winthrop the yonger Governor of Conectecott

SONNE, I wrote vnto you by the Rebecka of the death of Bushnell and sent the keye of his Chest, that you might take out the seeds and inventorye his goods and havinge this opportunity by mr. Oldhams Pinace I thought good to Certifie you how things are with vs here, but I shall not need to write muche because this bearer can inform you of rest. mr. Allerton is come here: but his pinace neere spoyled: she laye 10 dayes vpon a rock, and beate out all her kele: and being mended another storm came, and beate out all again   he is come home without provisions: so is mr. Mayhew, who yet gave 6 hhds. of Bread but he was forced to take aboard 40*li* worth of trading commodytes. The Indians have killed so many of their swine in these parts, that there is no pork to be had.

We were at Dorchester last fryday at the gathering of the new Churche there, but the partyes were most of them founde so weake as the ministers present advised them not to ioyne till they were better fitted, which they agreed vnto.

your wife and all ours are in healthe (I prayse God). they all salute you, but the cominge of this bearer is so suddain as none could write: your sicke ones begin to mende.

---

[1] W. 1. 113; *L. and L.*, 11. 151–152.

So much in hast, with my love and blessinge to you: and salutations to all with you, I commende you and your affaires to the direction and blessinge of the Lord and rest Your lovinge father

J: W:

This 4 of the 2 mo: 1636

forgett not to send me some Saltpeter: for I thinke it hath saved one of our mens lives.

SIR NATHANIEL BARNARDISTON TO JOHN WINTHROP, JR.[1]

To the Wor[shipfu]ll his assured loueing Freind John Winthropp Junior Esqr. in New England these deliver

GOOD MR. WINTHROP, Yours of the 12 of January I receaued and thanke you for your kind remembrance therin   I sent to your frind Mr. Hopkines to desyre hym to take order for the transporting of your boy and Mear to you who returned me answar that the boy he would prouide for (who I intend to send to you if I cann when I heare from Mr. Hopkines agayne) but for the Meare the custum for hir would come to six poundes besides all other charges and therfor was vnwilling to medle with hir   I intend therfor to sell hir for you and returne the mony for hir by hym about September next God willing, if in the meane tyme I heare not to the contrary from you. I haue written to your father which I intended to haue done by you but was prevented by your vnexpected sodayn departure whear in I pray you to excuse me to hym   so desyring you to remember my best loue to hym and your mother with Mr. Cotton Mr. Hooker Mr. Wilson Mr. Welde Mr. Ward with the rest of our all good frindes and acquaintances beseeching them to pray for vs as we doe for [them] wee all hear salute you beseeching the good Lord to be with you and to prosper you in all your wayes to his glorey. I rest Your euer most assured loving frind

NATH: BARNARDISTON

KETTON Aprill 5th 1636

---

[1] W. 2. 179; 4 *Collections*, VI. 545–546. For Barnardiston, see *D.N.B.*

JOHN WINTHROP, JR., TO JOHN WINTHROP[1]

To the right wor[shipfu]ll my much honored father John Winthrop esqr.
deliver In Boston

PASBESHAUKE[2] Apr: 7, 1636

SIR, My humble duty remembred to your selfe and my mother with my love to my brothers and all our freinds with you: I suppose you have heard of our arrivall at Teeticut and oportune meeting with our vessell. Concerning that place I conceive it is not above 22 or 24 miles from mount Wooliston or Dorchester mill the Cuntry thereabouts very fertyle and rich ground and so all downe the river for 30 miles together (for so farre we went downe before it grew wide into Saceames harbour) a ship of 500 tunnes may come vp about 10 or 12 miles in the Narrow river. There is noe meadow nor salt marsh all the way, neyther could I see any in all Narigansett bay and as farre as I could perceive there is more marshe vpon Charles River and misticke then all the Naragansetts neere the sea. I was vp with Canonicus at his great Citty. there be many wigwams but they stand not together as I have heard reported. The ground there seemeth to be farre worse then the ground of the massachusett being light sandy and Rocky yet they have good Corne without fish; but I vnderstand that they take this course they have every one 2 feilds which after the first 2 yeares they lett one feild rest each yeare, and that kepes their ground continually in hart. The first of this month we sett sayle from Nariganset and in the afternoone, about 6 a Clocke arrived heere: for this place I have not yet seene any thing that I should be able to wright of it. mr. Gibbons can fully informe you of all things.

thus craving your prayers and blessing I commend you to the Almighty and rest Your obedient Sonne

JOHN WINTHROP

I am informed by mr. Ludloe that Dorchester plantation[3] hath lost 2500*li* in cattle this winter, besides other townes.

I pray be pleased to remember to receive 2 barrells of peas of mr. Allerton a hogshead of porke of Capt. Lovell, and if mr. Mayhew hath bought the pro-

---

[1] W. 2. 171; 4 *Collections*, VI. 514–515.
[2] The Indian name for the point of land at the mouth of the Connecticut River that was Winthrop's stopping place.
[3] Windsor.

visions at the East, I should desire 5 or 6 hogsheads peas and as much bread I have but one turkey which as they say proves to be a Cocke.

I send you backe by mr. Gibbon the booke you wrote your receipts in.

SIR MATTHEW BOYNTON TO JOHN WINTHROP, JR.[1]

To my uerie worthy friend John Winthorpe the yonger esqr: att Ipswidge present this

SIR, I haue now accordinge to my former intendment sent ouer two seruants tenn Ewe sheepe and a Ramm. I haue directed them to your father because, I suppose, you will be eare this, att Connecticutt. Twentie Goates I haue alsoe sent with them and a Bucke: I haue written to your Father to entreate him that they may be conueyd to Ipswidge, as soon as they may conuenient-lie be remooued without dainger, because I perceyue by your letter that the Cattle are theyr: Sir you know what neede theyr is that seruants should haue eyes ouer them espetiallie when they are att soe far a distance from theyr maister, tho I hope the menn be honest, yett I pray you that you hauinge occasion your selfe to be absent, you will be pleased to intreate somm Friends of yours att Ipswidge that they will both aduise them and examine them and direct them. I pray you lett me haue notice from you of what you shall con-ceyue shall be expedient for me to send ouer for my prouision: I would be glad to heare from you as often as you cann, and how you like of the Contry aboute Connetticutt, and how our businesses goe on theyr. I writt to you by the first shipps that went from hence this yeare, that I intended by all meanes to preserue the increase of my cattle and now I haue for that purpose sent ouer these seruants: I intend (God willinge) to send ouer by the next Shipps that comm twentie Goates more, which I haue alreddie bought, and would haue sent them now, if I could haue gotten them caryed as I was promissed, butt after disappoynted: I haue noe more to say, butt to giue you hartie thanks for all your loue and kindness which shall euer deepelie engage Your trewlie louinge and assured friend

MATT. BOYNTON

LONDON: From Pauls Allie in Red Cross streete Aprill 8th 1636

---

[1] W. 3. 40; 4 *Collections*, VII. 164–165.

SIR MATTHEW BOYNTON TO JOHN WINTHROP, JR.[1]

To my uerie worthy friend John Winthorpe the yonger Esq: giue this in New England

Sir, I haue none, upon whom I cann relye, butt your selfe, beeinge, as you know, a strainger in your Contry and to those that are theyr. I ame theyrfor the more bould to entreate your helpe, which I hope you will nott onelie pardon, knowinge how I ame necessitated theyrunto; butt alsoe that you will be pleased to afford me your best assistance, my businesses now increasinge, both in regard of stocke, which I haue now sent ouer, and of seruants, as alsoe of the good increase (I hope) of those Cattle which I had before: and theyrfor itt beeing soe, as I suppose, that somm other occasions haue, eare this, required your remoouinge to Connetticutt, soe that I cannott hope for the benefitt of your owne eye upon my seruants, to whose trust alone itt is uerie daingerous committinge soe great a charge: for experience tells me that seruants (tho of the best sorte) will neglect, or lett slipp manie aduantages for theyr m[aste]rs profitt, if they be nott somm times called upon, and except they know that theyr doeings are obserued, by those that haue authoritie to call them to accompt: theyrfor Sir I intreate you earnestlie, that you will be pleased to interest somm friends of yours (in what place you shall thinke fitt, that the Cattle and other stocke of sheepe and Goates shall remaine) that are both able to direct and such as you may be assured will be carefull to obserue and rectifie what they shall see att anie time to be amiss: els, I know, I shall sustaine much loss; and discouragement from future aduenturing: butt I ame uerie confident of your helpe herein, hauinge alreddie had good testimonie of itt: for which I desire I may haue anie occasion whereby I may express the trew than[k]fulness which is reallie acknowledged to you by Your euer assured friend

MATT. BOYNTON

LONDON: From Pauls Allie in Red Cross streete Aprill 13th 1636

I haue sent by this Shipp 23 Goates and two seruants.

---

[1] W. 3. 41; 4 *Collections*, VII. 166–167.

MATTHEW ALLYN TO JOHN WINTHROP, JR.[1]

To the Worsh[i]pp[fu]ll Mr. John Wintropp esquier at the mouth of the Ryver of conecticutt deliver these

WOR[SHIP]FULL SIR, My love and service be preferred to you   these are to signifie to you that I have a desire to have a lott at the mouth of the Ryver that may be fitt to sett a howse vppon to receave the goods and such other allotmente of lands to yt as your wors[hi]pp shale judge meete for mee   I knowe not but I may have occasion to live in yt my selfe   your wors[hi]p I beleeve knoweth I have bine at Charge in keping the possession of yt but I having receaved such Curtesie from your wors[hi]pp this request being a thinge that lyeth in your power to frend mee and wrighte mee I doe not question butt your worshipp will order yt soe that I shall bee accommodated comfortetablely   I desire your worshipp would be pleased to send mee a woorde or two what you allott mee that I may send servants to bulde vppon yt   thus craving perdon for my bouldnes I reste Leaving your worshipp to the moste safe protection of the Allmightie and remayning your Loving Frend to his power to bee commaunded

MATHEWE ALLYN

This 16th of Apprill 1636 From NEWE TOWNE[2]

SIR WILLIAM SPRING TO JOHN WINTHROP[3]

To my Euer Honored and faythfully Beloued Freind John Winthup Esqr. att his house att Boston in New England

MOST BELOUED AND STILL HONORED FREINDE AND BROTHER: itt is your charrety and not my words that I rely vppon for my fayrest and best Excuse of my seeming neglect and faylings of the dues of loue, yett that you may not bee vnknowing of truths giue mee leaue to tell you, I haue I verely suppose much ill happ for some of my letters and remembrances sent vnto you, for else I know in your last I had from you I should haue found mention of theire

---

[1] W. 10. 63. Matthew Allyn first settled in Cambridge and went to Connecticut with Hooker, settling at Windsor, where he died in 1670. He was a prominent figure in the early days of Connecticut, serving as deputy, magistrate, and assistant in the colony government and as one of the commissioners of the United Colonies. Lucius R. Paige, *History of Cambridge* (Boston, 1877), 479.

[2] Hartford, Connecticut.

[3] W. 2. 180; 4 *Collections*, VI. 551–553. For Sir William Spring, see 4 *Collections*, VI. 551n.

ariuall, seeing they had surely bin with you long before the date of yours to mee, if I could haue hope that you had them att all. But my last I hope better of, sent by my cossin Gurdon that they haue saluted you and still lett you know how desirous I am to liue in your brest and hould the place I had wont, though I could justly complaine of some accidents that (full ill against my will and hope) might in some construction render mee less deserving your continuing goode Opinion then I hope I deserue: But I avoyde those thoughts that may any wayes mooue mee to a Jelousy of that loue I soe much couett: these lines come now by a meanes which my Brother Barn[ardiston] (now with mee) hath found out, but my time of warning is verry short and difficult for my Enlargment, yett such times and oportuneties are soe scarse as I may not nor will willingly pretermitt any that I cann lay hould of: Neyther is the time with vs heere soe free and sure to vs, as that I dare write you what I think and would you knew, neyther doe I euer expect a time for itt till wee meete in the hauen after our storms are passed: You that are vnder lee I hope forgett vs not that are yett in the storme, nor wee you (as wee may) for the encrease of Gods Blessings: for my particuler you want not a constant memory in my vnworthy servises; I would I were as able as desirous to enlarge my Hart to you: As touching your mention of my kinsman[1] and his estate I haue I hope before this time satisfied you, how my affections and abilities stand inclined towards him, though happely soe farr short of his Expectation (I am sure of his demands) as that I cann hardly beleeue I haue any way satisfied him: My cosin Gurdon did vndertake to returne a token for mee towards him, when I neyther had the liberty to write to him nor your selfe: I could much complaine of my ill success with him, in that (hauing disburst euen that which I assure you I haue since wanted for neerer Occasions, and to which I am more Bound) I haue giuen him or my selfe eyther soe little Comfort or Content in itt, as that I reape noe fruites but lamentable Complaynings, Immoderate demands and some vnkinde expostulations, and in generall giues mee cause to judg that nothing I eyther haue done or cann doe, is inough, or to any purpose: Itt almost discoraged mee for altogether, seeing hee writes to mee as if I had none else to respect, or att least not as to one that would bee, (as heeretofore) free in my charety, if I did not plainly foresee, that except I doe prejudice my selfe and my neerer duties and Occasions, (which are farr otherwise then hee conceyues of mee) I cannot come neere the 100 part almost of his requirings: Hee poore man is ignorant of our condition generally and mine in particuler heere now, and minding himselfe only, forgetts his

---

[1] Sir William Spring's nephew John settled in Watertown in 1634.

freind and his first terms and promises with mee, when could I haue prevayled I had stayd him vntill his strength might haue bin better to vndertake what hee would attempt too headily, and wherein (without my then forwardnes in a way beyond ordenary and his owne Expectation) hee had fayled of all hee aymde att: But I haue writt a few lines to him, and send them heereinclosed presuming of your fauor to lett them bee deliuered to him, wherein I forbeare these particulers purposely, for I desire rather to pitty him then provoke him. what I would haue done for releife this Spring I profess I could not for meanes I could learne none to send by nor now more then this letter: I hope amongst other you finde mee in the matter of seade you writt for God prosper itt: I cann now noe more both for paper and time: vnto that God that disposeth all things by his Will and Wisdome and that to the best for those hee loueth you are dayly commended, and entreated to commend Your faythfull frend and Brother

WLLM: SPRI:

Aprill 16th 1636. From PAKENHAM yett.

To yourselfe and all and euery of yours I hartely tender my best affections: farewell farewell:

[*Endorsed by Governor Winthrop:*] Sir Wm: Springe. Recd. this by Mr. Babbes ship.

EDWARD REVELL TO JOHN WINTHROP[1]

To the wor[shi]p[fu]ll and my worthie good freind John Winthroppe Esqr. in New Englande these present New England

WORTHIE SIR, That kinde respect and fauour yow pleased to shew vnto me, whiles yow was a magistrate of Justice in this our ould England, and I a poore seruant with your deere assosciate and my good Mr. maister Gurdon, doth much encourage me to write two lines vnto yow wherein I desire with all thanckfull acknowledgment to remember my humble seruice vnto yow, with my prayers to god for a continuall supplie of blessinge, to be powred vppon yow and the rest of that christian companie whom it hath pleased the lord to select and sett aparte for the aduanceinge (I doubt not) of his glory, and your eternall welfares; whose tender bodies goods and estates haue not

---

[1] W. 4. 80; 5 *Collections*, I. 220–222. Edward Revell, as it appears from Governor Winthrop's endorsement of this letter, was at one time clerk to Brampton Gurdon.

beene thought too deere to be exposed to the danger of the merciles waues, soe as our good god might haue a church established amongst poore heathens, and Indians, that neuer yett knew him; manie prayers haue beene and are continually sent vpp to the throne of grace, by your deere fellow breethren in this our poore land for a good successe vppon your godly vndertakeings; the benefitt whereof I trust the lord will make manifest amongst yow. Manie of my good freinds in Darbishire my natiue Countrey (where now by gods proui- dence I liue) haue beene and are yett takeinge their Journey vnto yow, whom I trust yow shall haue cause (for the most parte of them) comfortably to enter- taine; amongst the rest there is this voyadge one Mr. Flinte both an able man in estate, as alsoe an honest godly man, who with diuers others accompanie- inge him, (togeather with one Richard Griffen a man of very rare parts,) are willinge to take their liues in their hands, not accountinge their estates too deere to parte withall soe as they may helpe to sett forward this godly enter- prise so considerately vndertaken; and as wee doe heere (to all our comforts through gods blessinge) with soe much hope of good successe hithertoo con- tinued; lett me be soe bould I humbly intreat you, to craue your countenance and respect for their kinde intertainement, and acquaintance with yow. I trust neither of these two good christians will frustrate my expectacion, nor faile in some sorte to gaine your fauour. there is amongst some seruants Mr. Flinte taketh ouer with him, one James Farren (the bearer hereof,) a plaine youth, but borne of honest christian parents, neighbors in the same towne, where I liue, whose wellwishes and prayers I know are not wanteinge for a blessinge vppon your good proceedings; I pray yow be pleased alsoe to take notice of him, and as ocation shalbe offerred and his indeauours sutable to your good likeinge lett him haue your respect and fauour which I know wilbe a great comfort and incouragement vnto him, in the absence of his deere and tender parents, whose care haue hithertoo beene expressed (to their poore abillityes) in his good and honest educacion. I hope good Mrs. Winthroppe with your sweete children are in good health. Yett what alteracions it hath pleased the lord to make since I saw them, I am ignorant of. much I should reioyce to heere of the welfare of your family in generall; we haue in most parts of this land a great mortality amongst children which dye of the small pockes, and it is feared this summer that the sicknes wilbe very great amongst vs, the tymes haue beene of late soe vnseasonable. the lord in mercy prepare vs for a stroake, for longe hath this nacion beene treasureing vpp wrath, which justly may be feared eare longe will fall full heauie vppon vs. Thus worthy sir hopeinge yow will excuse my bouldnes, I leaue yow and all that belonge vnto yow to the good blessinge and proteccion of the allmighty, who is onely

able to reward and crowne all that paines and trauell yow haue taken to promote his glory, with longe life and manie happy dayes heere; and a crowne of
glory for euer hereafter restinge euer to be Your seruant and welwisher in the
lord whiles I am

EDW: REUELL

CHESTERFEILD DARBISHIRE Aprill 20th 1636

[*Endorsed by Governor Winthrop:*] Edward mr. Gurdons Clark.

THOMAS MAYHEW TO JOHN WINTHROP, JR.[1]

SIR, touching my Journey to Ile of Sholes to buy 80 h[ogs]h[ea]ds of prouis-
sion when I came I fownd noe such thinge as vnto me for trueth was reported.
to procure 8 h[ogs]h[ea]ds of bread I was fayne to lay out one hundred
pownds in Ruggs and Coates vnnecessaryly: and for pease I got but 1 h[ogs]-
h[ea]d and ½, whereof I sowed certaine bushells: had things beene free at the
coming in of this vessell I woulld haue had a greater Share of what she
brought yett I confesse as matters hath beene carried, I haue not ought
against that which hath beene donne. I doubt not but that Mr. Peeters hath
remembred yow: your father told me that he had shippt in the blessinge one
h[ogs]h[ea]d of beiffe in lieu of that deliuered vnto Mr. Louell. I shall confer
with Mr. Wynthropp when more victualls com in how wee may steede yow
assure your sellfe my hellp yow shall not want. I haue made out th[e] accompt
betweene vs   Concerning the bermuda voyadge, and accompting the pota-
toes at 2d the Corne at 9s per bushell the pork at 10li per h[ogs]h[ea]d
orrenges and lemons at 20s per C wee two shall gaine twenty od pownds: Now
that accompt cleared and the Cattell wintring paid for there will not be much
coming vnto yow of the 80 od pownds I borrowed of yow. I shalbe ready at any
time to advance soe much mony to steede yow with thankes yf your occassions
shall require it. I salute you respectyuely with my Loue. I commend yow to
the guydaunce and protecion of the lord Jesus and doe rest in som hast Yours
assuredly loueing and readyly to be comanded

THOMAS MAYHEW

MEADEFORD this 22th of the 2d moneth 1636

---

[1] W. 3. 12; 4 *Collections*, VII. 31–32.

WILLIAM PYNCHON TO JOHN WINTHROP, JR.[1]

To the Right Wor[shi]pfull Mr. John Wintrop Gouernor at Conettecot deliver

ROXBURY 22 Aprill 1636

MR. WINTROP, my respectiue loue remembred: being glad to heere of your safe ariuale: and of your comfortable hopes of a good proceedinge: my desyer is to see you but because I desyer to hasten back I shall not now find tyme to see you I thinke: But I will hasten to setle myself there as soone as I can and then I shall see all the plantations: It pleased god by his prouidence to bring home the Blessinge before Mr. Allerton could be ready for vs, and so we haue agreed with your Father Mr. Gibbons for the fraight of 16 Tunns of Goods at 35*s* to the riuer mouth: and also It is further agreed that if ther a faier wind will giue way we must haue our goods deliuered at New Towne[2] or Water Towne[3] at such further prise as shall be iudged by the medle prise of carrienge goods vp the riuer: and I doe earnestely intreate you to be a meanes to hasten them vpp, if by any meanes the wind will serue: for it will greately helpe to promote our worke hauing so few hands to helpe vs and so once more I pray further vs what you can: I haue but 4 peeces of cloth loose being 4 speciall good peeces at 8*s* heere but fraight and venture will be 6*d* in a yard more: so if you please you may haue them: or at least I pray lay them vpp safe for me: also the Contentes and cullers of the cloth are

> 1 violet 35 y.
> 1 russet shagg 37 y. ¾
> 1 murry 35 y. ½
> 1 russet 35 y.

so markd also on the cloth

If you accept of them, send me word by my seruant, because else I may sell them to some of New Towne or Dorcester.[4]

Also if you haue any further Councill or aduise to giue me about plantation or the like write me 2 or 3 words: also you shall doe well to inquier and take carefull informations about the Indians killing 2 of our men that a course of iustice may be taken so as may be cleere to all that the course is iust: and so if our goods be landed with you doe vs all the kindnesse you can with howse-

---

[1] W. 2. 146; 4 *Collections*, VI. 369–370.   [2] Hartford.
[3] Wethersfield.   [4] Windsor.

roome: and so Jehouah blesse you in layeing a good foundation in all your vndertakinge for the publike. Your euer assured faithfull Freind

WILLIAM PYNCHON

I pray remember my harty loue to Mr. Gardener, and to the rest with you.

JOHN WINTHROP TO JOHN WINTHROP, JR.[1]

*To my verye lovinge sonne mr. Winthrop iunior Governour of the new Plantation
vpon Conectecutt deliver*

SONNE, Blessed be the Lord who hath preserued and prosperd you hetherto.

I received your lettres by the Blessing which arrived heere the 14 of this present: and is to returne to you with mr. Pincheons goods, so soone as she can be laden: by her I shall (God willinge) write to you of other things which I may now omitt. your wife and all our famyly (I prayse God) are in health. I thinke you will haue no lettre from her till the Blessing come. It hath been earnestly pressed to haue her goe to Virginia for mr. Mavericke and his Corne, but I haue no heart to it at this season, being so perillous both to the vessell (for worms) and especially the persons: I will never haue any that belonge to me come there, if I can avoyde it: but mr. Mayhewe hath taken order the Rebecka shall goe, if she can be mett with.

The Lord in much mercye sent vs a shippe the 12 of this present with provisions, but she had putt in at Pascataqua and sould much there: for she brought onely 39 h[ogs]h[ea]ds of meale: 25 of pease: 8 of otemeale: 40 of malte and some Beiefe and prunes and Aquavitae, and 18000 of [*torn*]. My brother Peter bought it all: and devided it amonge all the [*last third of the page mutilated*].

Q[ueen] of Boh[emia] her eldest sonne is in England, and no speech of any stoppe of shipping hether: nor of the General Governour, more then diverse yeares before. this shipp came in 8 weekes from Dartmouth, and saith, there had not been an Easterly winde in England 14 weekes before.

For home newes, the general Court hath ordayned a standing Councell for life: and quarterly Courts to be kept at Ipswich: Salem, Newtowne and Boston: and 4 Courts in the yeare at Boston for greater Causes, and for Appeals. mr. Allerton is returned, but had a very ill voyage: his Barke lay 10 dayes vpon the rock and beate out all her keele: and so the 2 tyme, mr. Mayhew and he could gett but little provisions and at extreme rates: but 6 h[ogs]-

---

[1] W. 7A. 56; Savage (1825), I. 388–389; (1853), I. 465–467; *L. and L.*, II. 152–155.

h[ea]ds of Bread, and some pease. I can get but one Barrell of pease of mr. Allerton, which I will sende you. some porke they brought but so leane as I haue not seene the like salted: the Indians killed vp all their swine so as Capt. Lovell had none, but you shall haue Beife in stead of it. I have sent to Ipswich for your Cattle and your servant, for it wilbe great losse to keep them there. I will take the others from mr. Mayhew so soone as grasse is vp. [*Last third of the page mutilated.*]

I sent you 2 Lettres lately: one by mr. Hodges, and the other by mr. Oldham, wherin I certified you of the death of goodman Bushnell: one whom you will misse aboue all the rest: I had him down to Boston to doe him what honor I could at his buriall. your Carpenter and the other fellowe (who I think truely feares God) are recovering and I hope shalbe able to come to you in the Blessing. I praye sende me some Salt Peter, for I suppose it was a meanes through Gods Blessing to save one of their liues, being farr spent in a feavor.

I purpose to sende you some milch goats and swine. The prunes I suppose you may sell such of them as you cant spende. The Butt cost 10*li* and should weye neere 1000 li. The Aquavitæ was putt aborde by my brother Peters order, without my Appointment. it cost 22*li*. what you will not spende of it, you may sell to the Dutch for profitt enough.

I sent you two Lettres by mr. Tilly. Your Brother Steph: was desirous to come to you: if you have any imployment for him you may keepe him, otherwise you may returne him back.

This Shipp is bound for the Ile of Sable. if you will sende the Blessinge with her, she may be heere tyme enough a month hence: but 2 things I feare. 1: that heere wilbe no men nor provisions to sett her forth with: the 2: that bothe of them will not be of sufficient strength against the Fr[ench] for this Shipp hath not aboue 14 men: neither would I send any of ours without taking leave of the French. I think the Bark goeth away in the morning: therefore I heere end with salutations to all our frends with you mr. Gardiner and his wife etc. your mother salutes you: your wife writes: the Lorde in mercy preserue guide prosper and blesse you in all your wayes   farewell my good sonne.

mr. Hooker and his Company intend to set forth three weekes hence.

[JOHN WINTHROP]

This 26 of the 2 mo: 1636

This night we heare of a shippe arrived at Pemaquid and of 24 shippes vpon the Seas bounde hither.

MARY DUDLEY TO MARGARET WINTHROP[1]

To the wor[shipfu]ll my deare mother Mrs. Winthrop
at her house in Boston these present

DEARE MOTHER, After my bounden duty I still continue to be a troublesome suter to you, in the behalfe of a mayd. I should hardly haue made so bold to iterate my request, but such is my nessecity that I am forced to craue your help hearein as speedily as may be my mayd being to goe away vpon may day and I am like to be altogether destitute. I cannot get her to stay a month longer, and I am soe ill and weak that I am like to be put to great straits if I cannot get one by your meanes. I doe not doubt of your care hearein, but yet I make bold to put you in mind, lest you should conceiue my need to be lesse than it is. my husband is willing to stand to what you shall thinke meet to giue   I desire to haue my duty and thankfullnesse presented to my father, for the wheat he sent me by the pinace I haue not yet receiued it but by my letter I perceiue there is some for me. I intreat you would be pleased to send those thinges that I formerly writ for. I am ashamed of my boldnes in this and other requests, but the constant experiance of your loue and boundty to me makes me still presume on your favour: I desire the mayd that you provide me may be one that hath been vsed to all kind of work, and must refuse none   if she haue skill in a dayrie I shall be the gladder. my Children are well, and my husband who desires to haue his duty and service presented to my father and you. thus intreating your acceptance of these scribled lines I humbley take my leaue, Your dutifull daughter

MARY DUDLEY

April 28, [1636]

JONATHAN BREWSTER TO JOHN WINTHROP, JR.[2]

To the Woor[shi]pp[fu]ll John Winthrope Gouernour of the Foorte in Cunnitecutt
Riuer deliver these

WOOR[SHI]PP[FU]LL SIR, This is, (If I maye make soe bould with you) that you would be pleased, as to lett some of your servants to be a meanes of sending two hogsheads of provisiones marked ST, which lyes at the Riuers

---

[1] W. 4. 25; 5 *Collections*, I. 67.
[2] W. 3. 21; 4 *Collections*, VII. 66–67. For Brewster, see 4 *Collections*, VII. 66n.; Bradford, *History of Plymouth*, II. 218, n. 2.

mouth, by any vessell that comes vp the Riuer, eyther to Watertowne[1] or Newtowne[2] or this plantation. And if my brother Oldam be at the Riuers mouth, I suppose if he knowes that it is myne, he will doe me that Curtesye.

Thus fearing I am ouer bould with your Woorshipp heerin, with my duty remembred to your selfe, I take my leaue And Rest Yours to vse to his poore power

JOHNNATHAN BREWSTER

MATTAINUKE[3] this 30th Aprill 1636

MURIEL SEDLEY GURDON TO MARGARET WINTHROP[4]

To her much respected freind Mrs. Winthrop the elder at Boston giue these

MY DEARE AND WORTHY FRIND, I acknowledg my selfe so much indebted to you for many formar kindneses, and now in a great mesur for my sonne[5] that is with you; which I fear hau not ben so eusefull as I had hoped he showld: in regard of the weakenes in his hands for I canot hear that he doth any thing recouar, but is rathar wors which makes me to thinke he might haue sume begenings of the scuruy befor he went and may be now increased: I hau sent him sum good quantity of consarue of scuruy grass and sum surup of lemons in hope it may doe him good I desir that if you or any othar showld haue caus to thinke that to be his grefe then [*torn*] he might hau any thing giuen him for the helpe of it and [we] shall be accountable for it: I shall be most glade to hear of any grouth of grace in him how soeuar it shall please God to dele with his body; but I desir to waight upon him in faith who is all sufisinte: I am sur it is hapy for him that he is remoued from this place, wher all is a declining nay I may say all good strongly aposed: I would wright to you how, in sum particluars, but that you hau sum so uery able to informe you a coming to you: our deare ministar mr. Rogars for one and many othar worthy parsons: oh the heauy condition of this land that doe parte with such as showld hau ben the pilars to uphowld it, but I desir that my selfe and othars may rejoice at the grouth of gods church with you the strongar you grow I trust the mor powar your prairs shall hau for the rest of gods children that are left hear behind: I hau sent you a small remembranc not having any bettar thing at this time it is a ferkin of great otemeale and sixe dried nets

---

[1] Wethersfield.　　　　[2] Hartford.

[3] Matianuck, the site of the Plymouth trading house in what is now Windsor, Connecticut.

[4] W. Au. 88; 5 *Collections*, I. 84–85.　　　[5] Edmund Gurdon.

toungs. thus with all due respect remembred to mr. Wintrupe and your self, with my lou remembred to all your children I becech the lord to keepe you and us allwais in his fear I rest Your euar loving frind[1]

MERIELL GURDON

ASINGTON this 5th of May [1636]

FRANCIS KIRBY TO JOHN WINTHROP, JR.[2]

To his much respected frend Mr. John Winthrop the yonger this deliver

LONDON this 7th May 1636

DEARE FREND, Yours of the 14th January I receiud and did deliuer the inclosed to Mr. Kepler, but haue not yet provided the things you wrote for, but I pray blame not Mr. Kepler nor my selfe, the cause beinge in the primum mobile; that should set vs on worke, vidz: the want of your mony which my bro: Downeinge can not receiue. the other things for which you wrote to my sister Downeinge I hope will be with you longe before this letter, they were shipped in the Susan and Hellin. I am sory that Tho: Goad did not proue a fit seruant for you, he is not yet come home to London but we haue had letters from him where he is in Spayne. Thus desireinge you to remember mee to your second selfe and the rest of my frends with you I rest Your lo[ving] frend

FRA: KIRBY

I paid for the fother and plumbers tooles	1	10	0
for the firkin to pake them in and headinge it	0	1	0
paid Mr. Peirce Charges about your beefe and lead and suche like	2	1	6
	3	12	6
I received for your horse of your vncle Goslin after I saw that I could do no better for hay was at 1s the night	2	0	0
The rest I shall receiue of my bro: Downinge	1	12	6

---

[1] The spelling in the original manuscript is "fring."
[2] W. 3. 7; 4 *Collections*, VII. 17.

JOHN WINTHROP, JR., TO JOHN WINTHROP[1]

QUINETICUT May 16: 1636

SIR, John Wood being returned without any Corne I shall now desire that I may be supplied by the first shipping that arrive with any store of provisions with 10, or 12 hogsh[eads] of meale 5 or 6 hogsh[eads] of peas 2 or 3 barrells of oatmeale 2 hogsh[eads] of beife. for if we should want I see noe meanes to be supplied heere, and a little want may overthrow all our designe.

I send home the Bacheler, and desire your helpe for her disposing. I must of necessity have her returne heere for I may shortly have much vse of her: but I desire they may goe for shares and victuall them selves, which John Wood, and his company are willing to doe. I cannot find that the miscariage of his voyage was through his default but Contrary winds therfore I am desirous he should and that Company goe still in her, so they will goe for shares and victuall themselves. the Blessing I would sell if any will buy her at 160 or 150*li* she Cost 145 besides some new saile, and rigging and a new Cable above 20*li*. the Cable is speciall good. except you should foresee any occasion that she should rather be kept still: or if their be imployment to Sable for her: but if she continues still to goe vpon any designe I desire she should goe likewise for her share the men to find themselves, otherwise I would have her laid up at Boston till further occation. the men I desire should be discharged as soone as ever they Come ashore, and their wages paid them: I thanke you for the bread you sent. you write of 800 but there is not above 300 and an halfe at most delivered, besides 100 they keepe still aboard the rest I cannot learne what become of it but that it hath beene wastfully spent: they had besides halfe an hogshead of bread of their owne which was likewise spent and they were but [*mutilated*] eleven persons they say most of that tyme. [*Mutilated*] for they pillaged her the tyme they had her to Salem pittifully that she hath neyther blockes nor braces nor running ropes, which the Bolt[2] Will sayth that mr. Holgrave cutt them of he saw him. therfore I have agreed with John Wood Fredericke and George to take her to thirds. thus with my duty remembred I rest Your obedient Son

JOHN WINTHROP

---

[1] W. I. 114; Savage (1825), I. 389–390; (1853), I. 467–468.
[2] This reading is doubtful.

LUCY DOWNING TO MARGARET WINTHROP[1]

To my dear sister mrs. margret winthrop att Boston present this new england

MOSTE DEAR SISTER, ther is such a distance betwixt my letters, and my memory is so short that I maye fear troubleinge you with totaligie, but in a waye of thankfullnes I am sure not to writ superfluouslie. your fauors doe so aboundantlie exceed the vtmost extent of my expressions: and are so frequentlie repeated. I haue littill news to impart to you, but I hear they are well att chensy hows. mrs. fowle is dead of a consumtieon: my sister gostlin god be praysd is very well abroad againe. but they are very like to lose msr. Lea. the bishope of norwige, whose name is wren doth impose a hundred and 32 articles to the clergy in his diocess, some wheerof they fear will put by both Msr. Lea and diuers others, wich thought themselues very conformable men: msr. gourden is questioned for not bowinge and knellinge att buriall prayers. sir hary millmay and my lady are in towne: and well and doe earnestlie wish your wellfear: msr. arksden is maryed. my lord carliell is buried as statelie as he liued: I should be very glad to see my dear brother and your selfe and all our good frinds with you, but wee can not yet bringe all ends together. I doupt not but he that apoints the end apoints the time and means:

I pray present our due respects to every frinde of ours with you as you haue opertunietie   I send stufe for mary and susan downinge suposinge they maye haue need of it in time, if not yet. wee wish it weer in our power to doe you any seruis hear, and I should be very glad of it: wee are in much fear of both famine and plauge   wee haue had noe raine hear this 6 or 7 weekes. god make vs wise ere his decree be irreuocable   Yours affectionatlie

LUCIE DOWNINGE

May 19, [1636]

GEORGE FENWICK TO JOHN WINTHROP, JR.[2]

To his much respected freind Mr. John Winthrope, Gouernor, at the mouth of the Riuer of Conecticute thes

SIR, I will not now spend tyme to tell yow how well your freindes in England take your care and paines in ther occasions. I hope ere longe to doe it by mouth. I arriued heare thre dayes agoe, where I shall rest myselfe awhile

---

[1] W. 4. 4; 5 *Collections*, I. 10–11.   [2] W. 4. 81; 5 *Collections*, I. 223–224.

and then intend to take my iourney towardes yow, and soe to goe one further in discouering the countrie accordinge to your aduice who I vnderstand by your letter to Mr. Vane now gouernour hath mad the largest and furthest inquirie your selfe. in the meane tyme I would intreat yow to goe one with the worke yow haue in hand in as frugall a way as can stande with securinge the place, and for the intimation yow giue of your vncertaintye of continuance, if it can stand with your owne occasions it wilbe much desired for my cominge shall not dissolue your commission, neither will I appeare other then a stranger   therfor I pray yow proceed to procure what shalbe for your comfortable continuance ther, and if in any thinge I can contribute to it I will not be a wantinge   my cominge from London was very sudden soe that we had not tyme to send prouisions   I expect by the next ship a good quantitie with spades and some such other things as yow wrot for. She was sett downe to goe off 10 dayes after our departure. I hope she may be heare befor I come from hence   if yow can haue any opportunitie of writinge informe me what way, and in what maner, and with what prouisions and company it wilbe necessarie to come   I haue with me two case of pistols 6 carabines and 10 halfe pickes, which I did conceiue would be of most vse for trauellinge in the countrie. if your experience hath found other thinges more vsefull, I pray yow certifie me of them. Soe with my hartie loue and well wishes recomended to yow I comitt yow to the safe protection of our gratious God and rest Your louveinge freind

GEORGE FENWICK

BOSTON, May 21, 1636

Time not permitting me now to returne any other answer to your letters then what this Gentleman hath writ to you: I shall only let you know that your resolution to keepe the fort intire within itself [torn] necessary [torn] you must not care though it be displeasing to some. By Mr. Hodges I shall write fully to you if the multitude of affayres which vnexpectedly came vpon me since the country haue called me vnto office do not hinder me. Thus recommending you to God I rest your truly louing freind

H: VANE

MARY DUDLEY TO MARGARET WINTHROP[1]

MOSTE DEARE MOTHER, my duty remembred to you: after my accustomed manner I make bold still to trouble you for such thinges as I want. I intreat you woud be pleased to send me 3 or 4 yards of fine buckrom and an ele of fine holland for Bigims for my child and some pines small ones and other sort and some Sugar. I am ashamed to be thus continually troublesome to you but your readinesse to fulfill my desires imboldens me thus to do. dwelling so farre from the bay makes me the oftener troublesome to you but my appoligie is needlesse.

I humbley thanke you for those thinges you sent my and for you vnde-serued loue continually manifested towards me which can neuer be requitted by me but in loueing you back againe and shewing that duty and respect I owe you wheneuer occasion shall be offered. thus intreateing your favorable acceptance of these poore lines I humblye take my leaue Your dutyfull daughter ti'l death

MARY DUDLEY

[Ca. June, 1636]

pray remember my duty to my father

I pray you to send me some sope   I can get none in this towne, and some fruit. My child growes but not very fast.

JOHN HAYNES TO JOHN WINTHROP, JR.[2]

To his much esteemed freind John Winthropp Esqr. Governour of Conectecott River lett these bee delivered

SIR, Oportunity offeringe it selfe I gladly salute yow with my best wishes. I am to solicite yow in the behalfe of my Neighbours and frinds of this Towne beinge vnwillinge to enterprise any thinge without your aprobation and good likinge; the businesse in A word is only this, wee takinge into consideracion the hazard of our goods that wee haue sent and shall send to the mouth of the River for want of somme shelter, would entreat yow, that A lott may be granted vs, with leave to build A howse in somme convenient place neare the River and forte that ther wee may haue one resident to take care and chardge

---

[1] W. 4. 26; 5 *Collections*, I. 69.
[2] W. Au. 88; 4 *Collections*, VI. 354. For Haynes, see *D.A.B.*

of our goods, as alsoe that sixe Acres of planting ground may bee added ther-
unto that the party ther abidinge may not bee altogether without employment. presuminge of your readynesse to condiscend to my request haue sent
one to that purpose. not havinge further to trouble yow for the present, with
mine and my wiues kindest remembraunce to yow, wishinge all good successe to your vndertakings rest Yours in all good offices

Jo: HAYNES

[*Ca.* June, 1636]

Sir, Conceauing there can come noe prejudice to you by this motion, I
salute you.

H: VANE

ISRAEL STOUGHTON TO JOHN WINTHROP, JR.[1]

[Torn] *Wenthrop Gouernor in Connecticott Riuer these present*

Grace and Peace be with you in Christ Amen

Sir, Vnderstanding of Newtownes Motion for some conuenient place for a
warehouse for the present and future benefit of their towne,[2] where both they
and we shall perpetually haue speciall need of it for vnlading goods at the
mouth of the riuer: We your neighbors of Dorchester[3] are bold in like manner
to request your fauor in that particular; And tho we haue not obtayn·d
letters from Mr. Vane etc. as they haue, (time not permitting vs) yet we
trust the equitie of the case, and paritie of the cause (ours being the same
with Newtownes) will moue you (without other arguments) to shew vs in
this point like fauor as they: and we trust we shall be ready in all points to
testifie our thankefullnesse, and such other seruice as in equitie we are bound,
either for matters that concerne the publike state, or your owne particular
person. For the particular place or the quantitie we desire it may be according
to the aduice of this bearer our brother Mr. Tilley, whome we request to
accomplish this Matter with you, and according to your direction. Only this
we desire so much inlargment as may possible be afforded Considering it is
for a whole townes occasions: and now a good quantitie is but a small matter
to you to grant but it may be of great benefit to vs to receiue. And when you

---

[1] W. 1. 108. For Stoughton, see 5 *Collections*, 1. 274*n.*
[2] Hartford. See the letter from John Haynes to John Winthrop, Jr., immediately preceding.
[3] Windsor.

may do so great a benifit to so many with so little preiudice to your selfe we trust you will not be wanting.

The truth is I conceiue a matter of such importance for we indwellers that my selfe intended, (before I heard of others) to make a Motion to you in particular for my selfe, for some small portion, resoluing if you would shew me that fauor to count my selfe no small debtor to you for euer: and besides to be publiquely benificiall for it, as you in discretion should judge meete. So if you please together with the Townes Motion to heare mine and add a little the more therto as particular to my selfe and to declare it to Mr. Tilley that I may Challenge it as my owne I will by gods assistance doe as I haue aforesaid: And Continew my true respect to you and prayers, for you, and for your happie proceedings in all your waighty occasions   So for present I take my leaue Resting Yours in all due Respect

ISRAEL STOUGHTON
intrusted for the towne of Dorchester

[*Ca.* June, 1636]

ADAM WINTHROP TO JOHN WINTHROP, JR.[1]

To his dere and louinge brother Mr. John Winthrop liuinge at conekticot
giue thes with spede

LOUINGE BROTHER, The thoutes of youer loue and kindnes to me youre vnworthy brother does st[ir me] up to writ vnto you, as I cold doe no les but it wold haue bene a sine of grat vnthankfullnes and disregard of so much kindnes wich I wold be very loth to doe: much blaming my self for my neklegens and slouthfullnes that I haue not writen to you allredy: desiring now by my dobell [*illegible*] for to amend my formar neklegens: louinge brother we haue hard ofen of your well fare wich did much rejoyses us and will doe I hope more and more: Thare haes com grate store of shipes this yeare all redy to the nombar of fourten and but litell neues only this that the viese admarall of the kinges flet as thay war riding in the temes amaking meri the ship sodenly sunke and a grat many of the men ware drouned:[2] Allso the king gaue the sitsens too or thre brase peses of ordinans wich thay for to gratify

---

[1] W. 1. 122; 5 *Collections*, VIII. 220–221. Adam Winthrop, son of John and Margaret Winthrop, was born April 7, 1620, and came to Massachusetts with Governor Winthrop in June, 1630.

[2] The *Anne Royal*, which sank in the Thames on April 9, 1636, with "divers men drowned and some women, the master's wife being one." *Calendar of State Papers, Domestic, 1635–1636*, 364, *et passim*.

the king again made a grat meting in the feldes and hauing grat store of poudare thar pouder was fired and did bloue oup 30 of them that war killed and diues more hurte.

louing brother I shuld be very glad to see you hear if it ples god   if not I shuld be very glad if I myght hear from you if it be not to much trubell to you in the multeteud of your busnes: I shall be very willing and glad for to doe any busnes for you hear the wich does ly in my power: I desiar that you wold exept this as a small token of my loue and mindfullnes of you

and so I rest your loueing brother till deth

ADAM WINTHROP

[*Ca.* June, 1636]

I pray you remember my lou to mister gardner and his wife and to all the rest of my frindes.

My brother Dean does remember his loue to you.

ELIZABETH WINTHROP TO JOHN WINTHROP, JR.[1]

To her very louing and much respected [blot] *husbond Mr. John Winthrop Gou[ern]or of Conitecot this deliuer*

MY DEAREST BELOUED, I can not[2] but I must bee trobboll some to the with these my poore lines, which are to sartifi the that I haue recaueed thy letter which doeth not a lettell reioces my harte to see that thee Lord hace bene so pleesed to geue the thy halte and life that soo thou mayest despach thy besnes to retorne home againe so soone as thee Lord shall se it fetting for truly I fare my time is neeare then thou thinkest it bes[3] and thearfor let me intreate the that thou woldes not bee unminde of me in thy praieres to the Lord ouer greate God of Heauen before wohe wee must all appeare at the iugmente seeate of christ   I thinke thou shoueds doo wall to write to my mother if thou caneast not come with the next   but littell doest the thinke how much it wold refreach my haui and sad sparet to see thy deare face againe   I pray come

---

[1] W. Au. 67; 5 *Collections*, I. 85–86.

[2] The word in the original manuscript is spelled "mot."

[3] Elizabeth, daughter of John Winthrop, Jr., and Elizabeth Winthrop, was, according to the records of the First Church of Boston, baptized on July 3, 1636. *Report of the Record Commissioners of the City of Boston*, IX (Boston, 1883), 4. A statement in the Boston records (*ibid.*) that she was born on July 24 is obviously incorrect, as can be seen from the letter of Adam Winthrop to John Winthrop, Jr., July 3, 1636 (page 283, below), and those of Robert Feke and Elizabeth Feke to John Winthrop, Jr., July 5, 1636 (pages 287–288, below), all of which make mention of the infant daughter.

away so sone as thou canest and so I rest commetting the to God I rest thy eauer loueing and kinde wife to comande in whatsoeauer thou plesest so long as the Lord shall bee plesed to geue me life and strenge

ELIZEBETH WINTREP

[*Ca.* June, 1636]

I thanke the for my basket but I haue gau it to my mother for she was in loue with it

WILLIAM PYNCHON TO JOHN WINTHROP, JR.[1]

To the Right Wor[shi]pfull Mr. Jo. Wintrop at the Riuer mouth

June 2, 1636

MR. WINTROP, my deere loue and affekeon rembred with thanks for your care to send away my goods: which I haue Received and also paid all the fraight: but 3*li* doth still remaine dew to you: I am now preparing to goe to the Bay and haue setled vppon a plantation at Agawam: and cannot [*torn*] Towne without both sid[*torn*] for the best ground at Agawam [*torn*] incombred with Indians that I shall loose halfe the benefit thereby: and am compelled to plant on the opposite side to auoid trespassing of them: so when I see you I shall talk more.

I Received the letter: and think it a pore shift for the Indians of long Island to lay all the fault vppon a Pequat Sachem: so Jehovah blesse you Your most louing Frind

W. PYNCHON

I haue no good pen. I Received the wampam you sent.

AWARD OF WILLIAM PEIRCE AND BENJAMIN GILLAM[2]

BOSTON in New england the 28th of the 4th mounth called June: 1636

Wheras Will: Peirse and Beniamyn Gillham were requested to arbitrat the worth or valleue of Joshua Winsor[3] his service for fower yeares and nine

---

[1] W. I. 114; *Proceedings*, XLVIII. 38–39.

[2] W. I. 115. For Peirce, see *Winthrop Papers*, II. 262, *n.* 2. Benjamin Gillam was a ship-carpenter in Boston. Savage, *Genealogical Dictionary*, II. 255.

[3] Winsor subsequently went to Providence. He was one of the signers of the "Civil Compact" of Providence and also signed the "Combination," July 27, 1640. *The Documentary History of Rhode*

mounthes dew to his maister Will. lomice of Redrise neare London, he now by
his owne consent put ouer to the Wor[shi]p[fu]ll John Winthrop Esqure of
Boston deputy Gou[ernor] with him to serve out the forementioned tyme
from this day till the sayd tyme aforesayd be fully compleat: we do award vnto
his former maister to haue for his sayd tyme payd him the some of five pounds
of currant money of england and the sayd Mr. John Winthrop is to find him
meat drink and cloaths, with lodging convenient, for his tyme of his service.

WILL: PEIRSE
the mark of BENIAMIN X GILLHAM

JOHN WINTHROP TO JOHN WINTHROP, JR.[1]

*To my verye lovinge sonne mr. Jo: Winthrop Governour of the plantation
vpon the mouth of Conectecott deliver*

SONNE, Mr. Hooker went hence vpon teusday the last of maye by whom I
wrote to you, and sent all your Lettres with one from England, and all such
newes as came to hande. and with that Company viz. by Tho. Bull and a
man of mine owne I sent 6 Cowes, 4 steeres and a Bull: I lefte it to James and
Tho: Skidmore to sende such as might be fittest both for travayl and for
your vse. I now send this by the Rebecka, in which you shall finde such provisions as are here expressed on the other side. mr. Fenwick of Grays Inne
(one of those who imploy you) hath written to you by mr. Hooker, and intends about a month hence with my br[other] P[eter] to be with you. The
gentlemen seeme to be discouraged in their design heere: but you shall knowe
more when they come to you.

I received a very loving lettre from my Lo[rd] S[ay and Sele] wherin he
expresseth a great deale of satisfaction in your proceedings: but sayth withall
that those vp the River have carved largely for themselues, which he thinks
they will after repente when they see what helpes they have deprived themselues off. The Shippe which went to Ireland for sheep lost all ther sheepe
being 500, and so bare vp when she was neere this Coast. Capt. Mason is
dead, and thervpon all their designes against vs are (through the Lords great
mercy) fallen a sleepe. but of all these things you shall heare more fully when

Island, Howard M. Chapin, Editor, I (Providence, 1916), 97, 110–115. See also *ibid.*, 137, 196; 3 *Collections*, x. 39–40.
    [1] W. 7A. 57; Savage (1825), I. 390–391; (1853), I. 468–470; *L. and L.*, II. 155–157.

my other lettres come to you. here are come for you from my sister Downing
diverse Chests of Commodytyes, and many firkins of butter and suett, which I
have bestowed till I heare what you will haue done with them: heere is a great
glutt of all provisions, so as they are not like to sell in haste. we had 9 peeces of
Ordinance to the Rebecka her side, but all the means could be vsed could
not gett one into her. Sir Math: Boynton hath sent more Cattle and 2 servants. I intend to sende his servants to Ipswich to provide for them against
winter, for heere is not haye to be had. his Lettres to you come by mr.
Hooker. Sir A: Hazelrig hath refused my brother P[eter] his billes, which is
great damage both to him and mr. Endecott.

I pray deliuer this Lettre inclosed to Jo: Friend: and if he paye you the
mony deliuer him his bill (which is heere allso inclosed) if not, I pray return
it to me again.

Heere was an anvill with a beck horn at the end of it, which I thinke was
carried to Con: if it be, I pray send it back for it is challenged.

I paid mr. Garsford of Salem 5*li* for a Buffe Coate for mr. Gardiner, which
you must remember to putt vpon his accompt.

Your wampompeak I put off for 30*li* to be payd in England for the provisions I send you.

Solling and his wife will [come to] you by the next, [if you] heere not to
the contrarye. I know not what to write [more] on the suddain. I think your
wife writes, but she is now at the Garden with my Cousin Mary. The Lord
blesse and prosper you: your mother salutes you   farewell

[JOHN WINTHROP]

Provisions sent in the Rebecka

	li	s	d
A h[ogs]h[ea]d of Otemeale			
2 h[ogs]h[ea]ds of meale	8	2	
5 Casks of pease	10	8	
7 barrells of beife	14	14	
a h[ogs]h[ea]d of porke which my br[other] P[eter] putt in	14	7	7
a frayle of figgs which I send to your self (in the bar[rel] of Reysons)			
2 kilderkins of Butter putt in by mr. Peirce for Sergeant Willes			
I have payd for them 7*li* 4*s* 4*d* which he is to pay you			
a barrell of Reysons of the sonne: (the figgs are in the ende that			
hath your marke in black leade) about 2 C. at 45*s* the C.			
which is about 4½*li* [illegible]			

4 bar[rels] of meale
a Rundlett of sacke of [*blank*] gallons
Biskett in 2 great Bagges at 30*s* the C.

this 10th of the 4 mo: 1636

JONATHAN BREWSTER TO JOHN WINTHROP, JR.[1]

To the wor[shipfu]ll John Winthrop Gov[e]r[nou]r at the mouth of the river Coniticutt

Haveing 4 dayes agoe had occasion to send my man who hath the Indian Language to a place called Munhicke, distant from the Pequents 12 myles, partly vpon busines of my owne, and partly to discover the Proceedings of the Pequents, as also there present abode in great secrecy, the sachem thereof called Woncase, sent me word that vpon the 23d of May last, Sasocuse, cheife sachem of the Pequents, with his Brother Sacowauein, and the old men held consultation one day, and most part of one Night, about cutting off of our Plymouth Barke, being then in their harbour weakely manned, who resolving therevpon appoynted 80 men in Armes before Day to surprise hir: but it pleased the over Ruleing Power of god to hinder them, for as soone as those bloody executjoners arose out of Ambush with their canoes, the deserned her vnder sayle with a fayre winde returning Home: which Act of theirs (circumstances considered) is intolerable for vs to putt vp.

I vnderstand likewise by the same messenger that the Pequents have some mistrust, that the English will shortly come against them, (which I take is by indiscreet speaches of some of your people here to the Natives) and therefore out of desperate madnesse doe threaten shortly to sett both vpon Indians, and English, [j]oyntly. Further by the same Sachem, (whom I have found faithfull to the English) I am enformed that Sasocuse with his Brother, vpon consultation with their own men, was an actor in the death of Stone,[2] and thes men being 5 of the principall actors alive, 3 living at Pequent, and 2 at Ma ham le cake: his Brothe[r] Sacowauen with another of his men cheife actors in the Death of the 2 last vpon the Iland.

I am Informed also by the Dutch that this weeke into the River from Manhatas that 2 English men that dwells there went in a canoe to Long Iland to looke for goods that was cast away, in the Barke that came forth of the

---

[1] Yale University Library; 4 *Collections*, vii. 67–68.
[2] See *Journal*, i. 118.

Bay, who noe soone landed neare the wracke, but was sett vpon, and immediately one slayne.[1] the other recovering his peice killed one Indjan, and presently recovering the slayne mans Peice shott another, who recovering his canoe gott safe againe to Manhatas.

and vpwards of 2 yeares agoe the Pequents confessed that if our Barke had but stayed 6 houres longer in their Harbor, they had cutt hir off, or at least had attempted it. Yours in all love, and service

JONATHAN BREWSTER

PLIMOUTH HOUSE IN CUNITECUTT this 18th of June, 1636

JONATHAN BREWSTER TO JOHN WINTHROP, JR.[2]

To the Woor[shi]pp[fu]ll John Winthorpe Gouernour of the Forte in Cunnitecutt Riuer deliver these

WOOR[SHI]PP[FU]LL SIR, Your last kyndnes with them formerly doth much oblige mee to you, to requite you according to my poore ability In the meane tyme I rest my selfe humbly thankefull vnto you for the same, being sorry I was not home when as your men came to my house. Sir: as yett I haue noe intelligence from Plymouth concer[n]ing the busynes you spoke to me off, exspecting daily, which as soone as I heare, I will certifye you of their myndes. Furthe[r] Sir I thinke it convenient to certifye you concer[n]ing the Pequents, who continewes still in theyr blody mynds towards the English. For this weeke hauing occasion to send my man to Mauseicke the Sachem therof sent me woord that vppon the 23th of May last they purposed to cutt off our Barke, after shee had done trading with them, who for that end appointed 80 men in Canoes suddainly in the night to surprise her. But by gods overuling power at the very instant, our men had a fayre wynd and soe vnknowen to them escaped the danger And further there is reported there that shortly they intend an e[n]vasion both of English and natives in this Riuer. therefore Sir it is, as I take it, necessary that you give notice to bootes as they passe vp and downe, not to be too secure, for I will assuer you, if you please but to examine some bottes they haue not a gunn in theyr boote, and if ther be any you shall fynd them vnservisable. As also of which I haue complaind of, many people gooes ouer land vnarmed to the harteing of the enemie, As thoughe we were soe stronge our selves, or the enimy soe weake as that it is

---

[1] William Hammond, Jr.
[2] Miscellaneous MSS., Bound, M.H.S.; 1 *Proceedings*, v. 38–39.

Cowardize to feare any thing, whenas in wisdom all thinges considered neither of both is true. Thus much for present to your Woorship least I should be tedious   And with Remembrance of my duty to your selfe I take my leaue and rest Yours to be commanded

JOHNNATHAN BREWSTER

From PLYMOUTH HOUSE this 18th June 1636

LONDON PORT BOOK ENTRY FOR THE *PHILIP*[1]

20 June 1636

In the Philip of London, master, Robert Huson for New England. John Winthorpe for the Plantation 13 barrel small band pitch, $4\frac{1}{2}$ cwt. Raisins, 10 cwt. prunes, 5 cwt. sugar, 2 hhds. of vinegar, 38 iron pots and Kettles cost 6*li* 13*s* 4*d*, iron work value 40*li*. 250 ells of Vitrii canvas, 200 ells packing canvas, 600 ells coarse linen cost 8 pence an ell, several remnants of stuff cost 26*li*, 5 ordinary yard broad sayes, 40 goads Welsh cottons, 14 gross Sheffield Knives, 14 dozen pair shoes with other things.

EDWARD HOWES TO JOHN WINTHROP, JR.[2]

LONDON 21º Junij 1636

FIDELIS AMICUS, Since I receiue yours of the 9th of Nouember and the 6th of January I saluted you with a few lines but in regard of theire farre Jorney, and the dainger of miscariage in the passage, my loue to you constraines me to acquaint you with some generall and particuler affaires, namely that the plague sword and famine looks with a gashly aspect vpon germany and other our neighbour nations, and begins to peepe vpon vs soe frightfully, that mens harts faile them for feare, and many 1000ds runne they know not whither. tis reported that about 57000 people haue left this citty and suburbs within this 3 moneths. I thanke my God he hath taught me to turne to him and not to hide my selfe, or runne from him: I haue resolued to trye it out here. The Dr. I haue not seene since last Sommer; I doubt all is not gold that glisters like it, and he that would learne to distinguish, may pay too deare for his knowledge. I thinke there is not any thinge that the Dr. hath or knoweth, but

[1] Public Record Office; *Proceedings*, LI. 283.
[2] W. 2. 168; 4 *Collections*, VI. 500–501.

a frind of myne neere home enioyes as much; I could wish you with him, or he with you, for a moneth or two; but seing the Diuine Prouidence hath disposed it otherwayes, I hartilie desire you to be fully content with your allowance, and thanke God; whether you haue more or lesse, let it be all one to you; let not what God doth, trouble you; but what you doe contrarie to God; I pray present my best respects to your father and mother, and to Mr. Humfries when you see them, and to your dearest, and your selfe etc. praying for the prosperitie of the whole Church of God amonge you I take leaue and rest Yours assured

ED: HO:

WILLIAM GOODWIN TO JOHN WINTHROP, JR.[1]

GOOD SIR, I am requested by our neighbores the Dutchmen to mind you of what you willed me to tell them viz. that if they thought Good to call to you as they went out with ther sloope (and did desire so much of you) you would then giue them answer in wryteing to ther protest   the Sirgion is now going to ther plantation and meaneth to Come to you about it and desired me to signifie So much vnto your worship, which is all I haue to you at this tyme thus with the remembrance of my servis I end and rest Yours

WILL: GOODWIN

SEKIOGE, June 22th 1636

I suppose you here by our bretheren of the ariueall of our pastore and if your request for healp be as it was you may be pleased to send vs word.

EDWARD HOPKINS TO JOHN WINTHROP, JR.[2]

To the Wor[shipfu]ll his much respected freind John Winthropp the younger att Boston or elcewhere In New England deliver

SIR, My last was per the Peter Bonadventure, wherin I gave you notice what goodes I had laden aboard that Shipp consigned to you, to witt, 2 hoggshedds, wherein are Irons for cariages, 20 hoggshedds of meale, 8 hoggshedds of oatmeale, and 8 hoggshedds of pease. att present you may please to vnderstand, I have put aboard this Shipp the Phillip 4 small pieces

---

[1] W. Au. 89; 4 *Collections*, VII. 44–45. For Goodwin, see 4 *Collections*, VII. 44*n*.
[2] Yale University Library; 4 *Collections*, VI. 331–332.

of ordinance which were bought by Mr. Lawrence and Mr. Fenwicke in Holland and 4 cariages to them, as per the bills of lading inclosed you may perceave. I have also laden aboard another Shipp which may be ready in 14 dayes, 10 hoggshedds of oatmeale which I was incouraged to buy in regard I had it above a shilling in a bushell cheaper then the markett. But of this I shall write you more per that Shipp. In the meane tyme with my best respects to your selfe I rest Yours in what I may

EDW. HOPKINS

LONDON the 22th June 1636

EDWARD WINSLOW TO JOHN WINTHROP, JR.[1]

To the Wor[shi]pp[fu]ll his much respected Friend Joh: Winthrop Esqr. these be delivered Coneetacut

NEW PLYM. the 22th of the 4th moneth [1636]

WORTHY SIR, I perceived by a letter of Mr. Brewsters of a mocion of yours to him to procure you hay for an 100 beasts. We had a purpose to haue sent some cattle thither but so discouraged by him through the injurious dealing of his intruding neighbours as we feare there will not be long living for man or beast, but if you please to make vse of our right my Brother shall sett your servants to worke in our names and by our order, and affourd them what ever personall helpe shall be thought meet to the utmost of our power. What we shall yet doe I know not but will know ere long, and if new England will affourd no Justice, will appeale further; but God forbid we should be put on such extremities: But were it not for Christs cause in that our profession may come to suffer by it we would not be satisfied with the tenth of our demand but would hasten another way: These oppressors deserue no favor, their pride would be taken downe tis pitty religion should be a cloake for such spirits. News I suppose I cannot send more then you heare. I haue now written to your Government and exspect answere ere long. I thanke you for the good office you endeavoured when you were aboue but sorry to heare how little effect your words tooke with them. God in time I hope will shew them their folly. In the meane time and ever God direct you in all your proceedings. Be you kindely saluted and all that feare God with you who in mercy preserue you and them So prayeth Your assured Friend

EDW: WYNSLOW

---

[1] W. 2. 89; 4 *Collections*, VI. 162–163. For Winslow, see *D.A.B.*

JOHN WINTHROP TO JOHN WINTHROP, JR.[1]

To my very lovinge sonne mr. Winthrop Governour of the new Plantation vpon Conectecott deliver

SONNE, I wrote to you by mr. Hooker and sent you withall the lettres out of England, and 6 Cowes, 4 steers and one Bull. I wrote since by mr. Hodges in the Rebecka, and sent many provisions as by my lettre did appeare, since which tyme the Wrenne came in, and one brought me your lettre, but being very busy with diverse friends I desired him to come to me again at diner but I never heard of him since nor of any other of that vessell: so as I knowe not what they intend to doe with the claye you sent. the potter saith that you sent formerly is very good. I shall take order with him about your store etc: I have spoke with mr. Wilson and mr. Cottington for mony but can gett none. I will sende you what I haue or can borrow by Jo: Gallop (10*li*) and some weather goats. The Batchelor is to come to you next weeke with mr. Peirces goods and the lighter with some Ordinance [*torn*] Mr. Peirce his pinnace. mr. Fenwick, my broth[er] Peter etc: set forth on horsebacke on the 27 of this month, and will expecte your shallop at the vpper townes to carry them downe the river, and so will goe in mr. Peirce his pinnace to Long Iland Hudsons river etc. I would have sent you some shipp beere but mr. Fleming hath provided a butt brought in John Gallop. Goodwife B. is delivered of a daughter and abroad again in a weeke. your wife grows bigge but as liuely as any woman in the house God be praysed.

I doe not send you George because they are speaking of putting off servants etc. I suppose when they come to you, they will consider of the wid[ow] Bushnell, and of the other wid[ow] at Tenills, w[idow] Briskow, who hath been sick ever since you went abroad and is a great burden to vs.

We heare that Scilla Noua[2] is at the W: Indies but we heare nothing of the Pied Cowe.

I must ende with remembrance of mine owne and your mothers loue and blessinge to you and to Stephen. farewell my good sonne.

[JOHN WINTHROP]

23 of the 4th mo: 1636

---

[1] W. 7A. 58; Savage (1825), I. 392–393; (1853), I. 470–471; *L. and L.*, II. 157–159.

[2] Captain Peter de Sallenova, who had been in the colony the previous year and had been consulted by the General Court in connection with the proposed expedition against the French at Penobscot. *Records of Massachusetts*, I. 160.

I sende you 2 small sugar loafes by J. Gallop.

mr. W: debt is 310*li*. I shewed him his Bill with all the severall somes, and of whom he received them. I have layd out since you went in provisions etc. and for Seam[en]s wages neere 200*li*.

Jo: Gallop hath a pair of stockings for Stephen and shoes and stockings for Hen: Smith.

Serieant Willes 2 kilderkins of B[utter] coste 7 4 4 at 7*d* the li. if you have more pease and beife then you need, you may sende back some.

if you write into England sende your lettres by the first returne, and I shall convey them.

I have taken order with mr. Coggeshall [for] mr. Oldham etc.

JOHN WINTHROP TO SIR SIMONDS D'EWES[1]

To the righte wor[shipfu]ll Sir Simonds Dewes, Knight, at Stowe Langthon in Suff:
To be left with Mr. Gurdon at Assington in Suff:

SIR, The benefite which we have received from that which you were pleased in your kindnesse to bestowe upon our plantation, calles upon me to give you accompt therof and to acquainte you further with our estate heere. As soone as I vnderstood your minde in it, I acquainted the Governour and the rest of the Assistants with it, and calling Hamonde before vs, and finding by such evidence as he produced that parte of that 30*li* he received of you miscarried by the waye,[2] and that his estate was not able to answere what might be required of him, we thought fitt to accept of 20*li* whereof he hath payd 10*li*; but the other 10*li* is now desperate, for yonge Wm. Hammonde goeing with all that his father and he could make and borrowe to trade in Virginia for Corne, the vessell was caste awaye vpon Longe Iland and 7 persons drowned: Hamonde escaped on shore, but was killed by the Indians and one other with him: whereby the olde mans estate is wholly overthrowne. It hath been observed that God hath allwayes crossed us in our trade with Virginia: Diverse of our people went thither aboue halfe a yeare since, but haue not been yet heard off: there was a verye great mortality last winter: about 60 masters of Shipps and other Officers died there; but our people (I prayse God) have their healthe well heere. Sir Hen: Vane his sonne and heire is our Governour this yeare, a godly gentleman and of excellent parts. heere haue been allready

---

[1] Harleian MSS., B.M., 388, fo. 191; *Publications of the Colonial Society of Massachusetts*, VII. 73–74.
[2] Cf. John Winthrop to Sir Simonds D'Ewes, July 20, 1635 (pages 199–200, above).

11 English shipps and 4 Dutche, most of them were but 5 weeks in their passage. my tyme is short and I haue many letters to write, so as I cannot enlarge: my love and due respect to your self and Lady remembered I rest At your seruice

Jo: WINTHROP

BOSTON N: E: June [24],[1] 1636

ABRAHAM SHURT TO JOHN WINTHROP[2]

To the Wor[shipfu]ll John Winthrope Esquire at Boston deliver Recomended to a freinds Conveyance

PEMAQUID the 28th of June 1636

WOR[SHIPFU]LL, My dutye remembred with my prayers for your health ettc. Sir some 10 dayes past I wrote you by Mr. Allerton to which I referr me. Now you may be pleased to take notice that Richard Foxwill cominge from the french at Pennobscott spake with a boate of ours (draylinge for mackrell) and tould them that Wm: Hart had him comended vnto me, and that I should looke to my selfe for that the french were gone to the Eastwards to fetch more helpe to take this plantation and others and that they had left but five men at Pen[nobscott] and withall that he had an English heart although he were with them: wishinge his freedom from them and that he knowes a meanes to take Pennobscott with five men without losse of bloud. This the master and purser of our shippe tould me; cominge hither for my Lettres for England. Here comes natives from thence and sayes that they will remove to some other parts they are soe abused by them. me seemes they should not leave such a small crew at home neyther blason their intents. It is lamentable that a handfull should insult over a multitude. We must feare the worst and strive our best to withstand them. They wrote vnto me of desired freindship and amitye with mutuall correspondence: and they pretended the same at their beinge here, A franciscan Fryar insinuatinge vnto me that Mr. Comander and Mr. Donye desired nothinge but fayre passages betwixt vs, and that he was sent purposely to signifie so much vnto me. This is the relation that I heare from them which I conceive you would willingly be acquainted with-

---

[1] Owing to a tear in the original manuscript, only the "4" of this date remains. In view of Jonathan Brewster's account of the episode on Long Island given in his letter to John Winthrop, Jr. (pages 270–271, above), it is reasonable to suppose that this letter from the Governor was written on June 24 rather than on June 14.

[2] W. 2. 183; 4 *Collections*, VI. 570–571. For Shurt, see 4 *Collections*, VI. 570n.

all. I haue not elce to inlarge at present doe comitt you and your affayres to
the guydance of the almightye. Your Wor[shi]ps in all service

ABRAHAM SHURT

LUCY DOWNING TO JOHN WINTHROP[1]

MY DEAR BROTHER, Wee are nowe moste iustlie for our great vnworthynes,
by the correctinge hand of our father and god banisht the citty: yet hitherto
by his gratious prouidence preserud and moste louingelie cherished by many
kind frinds in the country, amongst whom I may not pass by in silence sir
hary millmay and my lady, whoe haue and doe still desire to expres themselues to vs, far beyound our expectations, for they would haue vs to be wholly
with them; but wee haue diuided our selues and georg and Joshua are at
maydstone in Kent at schoole, the master hauinge taken a hows there, and the
other 3 are at my brother gostlins where wee nowe are for a fewe dayes if god
pleas, and then wee intend for shrubland: nowe could I present to your vewe
howe acseptable your so affectionat leter is to me, it is like the ouerflowings of
nilus, wich inricheth the land and firtileth it for a year after: allso I am much
obliged to your loue for your sesonable caueats, and I wish you that expresion
of my acseptation of them, that my affections maye therby be redresed from
all adequat obiects, and incited and fixed apon that one thinge wich only
makes vs hapy, and can neuer be lost, and that I am confident is your principall ayme in thes your sweet admonitions. but for your 2 ayme wich concerns our abode: for ould enlan and London, whoe that knowes them can
deny the desireablenes of them, as they are in them selues: and for my owne
part, changes where euer irksome to me: and the sea much more: but the
cheefe incitement of our stay hear, and that wich justifies all others is: that
god doth nowe as gratiouslie and gloriouslie howld forth Christ, and the word
of reconcilliation to vs nowe hear: as hath bin knowne in England, in my
poor obseruation; but I cannot say that the doctrin of sanctification is now so
frequentlie prest and taught, as wee haue known, and could wish it. wee are
apt to forget that whome he justifies he sanctifies: that lesson is too harsh for
our pallats: but truly Christ doth so gratiouslie now salute vs, and wee so
nicelie receiue him, as might make vs half fear theer wear a farwell concluded
in it: especiallie his faythfullest mesingers beinge intertained as they are in
some places, and the word and saboth so clipt. but mans greatest extreamitie

---

[1] W. 4. 5; 5 *Collections*, I. 14–17.

gratiousest opertunitie, and his power wee cannot doupt: and I
but hear are many more to seek him faythfullie now then wear in
promise of Christ: but secret things belonge to god. but for our poor coun-
tryes sake, and the infinit souls therin, that know not the right hand from the
leeft, in good and euill, I shall euer pray that his mercy maye still be exallted
hear ouer all his works: and I doupt not but the soules of all his shall be safe,
in the worst of times and euills: and for such of his, as he pleaseth to call to
other places (in his time) both the end and the means shall concure to effect
his will: and the fainted hartedest woman shall then find courage sufficient for
the work, and her loathnes shall not hinder it: but I must then deall plainlie
with you, and let you know, that many good people hear, and some that
vnderstand new engl. resonable well, both by sight and relations of frinds that
are able to iugd, they doe much fear the country cannot afford subsistance
for many people, and that if you wear not supplyed of incomes from hence
your liues would be very misserable: and I must confes my obseruation cannot
confute there opinnions in this, for I hear not of anny such commodities from
thence yet, as can furnish your nessesities, much less inrich you: and our
sauiour sayth, it is a more blesed thinge to giue then to receiue: and euery
mans experience will teach him what wants are: but my dear brother I fear
all that I haue hitherto writen will but confirme your opininon of my loathnes
for new en. but let it not doe so, for wear there noe other thinge to induce me
thithire, but your single selfe, I could not want a hart thither: and as far as I
can vnderstand my self, could I deuide my life, and that it wear a thinge
aproued by god, I could willinglie spare a good share of my life, to enioy your
sosietie the rest of it: allthoughe it wear in a condition somwhat inferiour to
what I now haue: yet from exstremities good lord deliuer me, for I haue litell
confidence of my self in such cases: but if wee see god withdrawinge his ordinances from vs hear, and inlarginge his presence to you thear, I should then
hope for comfort in the hazards of the sea, with our litell ones shrikinge about
vs, and that Daniells pulls should be better to vs with a Christ, then all worlds
of plesures without him: and in such a case I should willinglie rather venter my
chilldrins bodyes, and my owne for them, then there soulses but otherwise I
cannot see but it weer an effect of diffidence rather then of fayth, to leap callings, estates, conueniences, and all till wee are forced from them by some com-
pulsion. but now you may saye I take to much apon me, I am but a wife,
and therfore it is sufficient for me to follow my husban. for that let me answeer you, that what I say to you, by way of caueat I haue obiected to him.
that I will not deny, for I thought it my duty but that I was euer peremptory
against his goeing: or that I euer knew the time that he might haue composed

his ocasions fit for such a change with promise of comfort to himse[...]
lie, or satisfaction to christian frinds, if my will had not bine his h[...]
this I vtterly deny whoe euer affirms it, and therfore I desier you both t[...]
cuse and to credit me so far: and allthoughe of my selfe, I durst not, if I wear
in his case, allter my condition, but apon thes terms yet if he likes to goe apon
other grounds, if god giue me life and abillities I shall endeuor to be with you
as sone as I maye: for I should promise my selfe much fellicitie in such a societie: and the satisfaction of leauing my chilldren vnder such means for there
soules, and so littell bad examples as I hope will be there yet, wear a great
abatement to my nowe cares: but good maners commaunds me to forbear
your further trouble at this time, for it is noe pleasinge work to read my scrib-
illinge: the god of all good preserue and prosper my indeared brother, and all
yours, and if it may stand with his glory, that owre eyes maye yet once againe
behould each other in the land of grace: or ells willinge submission to his will:
and the kingdome of glorie: I would writ you news, if I had any good, but
such as it is I suppose my husban will beter furnish you with it then I can.
sir hary millmay is much worn with exstremitie of the gout   wee leeft him in a
sore fit a week since, and he takes it not kindlie that he hath noe letter from
you. he thinks it answeres not the confidence he did put in you. my lady receiued hers when wee wear thear: my brother Gostlin and sister are allso
troubled they hear not from you. If any one hath done them any ill offices to
you, I presume it is causles for I am confident they would be glad of any opertunitie to serue you: so would your vnworthy sister

LUCIE DOWNINGE

[Ca. July, 1636]

THOMAS HOOKER TO JOHN WINTHROP, JR.[1]

To his much Honored and worthy freind Mr. John Wynthropp Governor at the mouth of the river of Conitticut these

WORTHY SIR, Your letter coming but late this evening immediatly before
your servants were returning, I am forced to shorten these few lynes: Your
charge and advise is seasonable and so exceeding vsefull, that I should be
much awanting in my duty to God, and that due respect I owe vnto your self,
if I should not help forward the execution of so good a work. I haue observed
in my life tyme that want of prudence and providence hath occasioned the

---

[1] Yale University Library; 4 *Collections*, VI. 387–388. For Hooker, see *D.A.B.*

most of hazards that befall men in ther life. I desire that we may not preiudice the Lords care he hath had of our preservation, and our owne comforts: for the way is open and easy in my apprehension to prevent any pretended evill, if we be faythfull to attend Gods way. I heard but this day how likely the trade is to miscary, for want of care in setling of it. If you be pleased suddaynly to advise that a course may be taken by the mutuall agreement of all the plantations, and that execution may be speedy and through for the accomplishment of it, it may yet be recovered, but delay will breed a vtter and irrecoverable decay. The good Lord blesse you in your way and work: which he wisheth who is Yours in all due respect

T: HOOKER

[*Ca.* July, 1636]

[*Endorsed by John Winthrop, Jr.:*] mr. Hooker 1636.

GRIEVANCES OF THE SERVANTS AT SAYBROOK[1]

To THE RIGHT WORSHIPFULL, master fenix and master peters our masters as we vnderstand and master leftenant gearner being preasant which is your debate we desire to make bold with your patienc to take theess wordes in to your consideration   we desire to lete you understand what nesesaries we desire to have as we ar seruants to you   first we hav liued a great while without the meanes of grace and salvation we being ignorant and scarse know any thing of the way and hav great need of teaching   the end of our coming was the hope some of us for to haue the meanes in a more frequent and gloriouse way then we had in our natiue contrie and likwis it is your chardg to se it performd as we to desire it.

and also we desire for other nesecari comodities that be long to seruants as for our washing and lodging as our couenants rune   hitherto we hau mist of it as we ought to hau had it as we hau been promised shirtes from on rainy day to another and here hath been many Rainy Dayes sines we hau been promised them but we hau been put of still from on day to another and so we shall be still if you do not tak some cours for us.

I hope this enough to let you vnderstand the whole   many other thinges we could Rite as for our diet our bread that is taken away our brakfast and our bere and so most of our diet is peass porig   so thess thinges that we hau de-

---

[1] W. I. 116.

sired here be performed in your part we hope the lord will incline our hartes and afactiones vnto you   we seing your loue and afacktion to us it will make us goe on Chearfuli and faithfulli in our places and calling wherein we hope the lord hath sete us in.

thess thinges not being performed with the whole consent of the companie we are resolued not to be content without them.

[*Ca.* July, 1636]

[*Endorsed by John Winthrop, Jr.:*] Servants at Saybrooke their pro.

SIR HENRY VANE TO JOHN WINTHROP, JR.[1]

For his Worthy and much respected freind Mr. John Winthrop the Yonger
Gou[ernou]r of Connetticut

MR. WINTHROP, For as much as it hath pleased God to send Mr. Fenwicke into this country And to call me to a distinct charge and care ouer the matters of this Plantation; I shall no way interest my self in the matters of Connetticut any further then as a publike person of this Body. so that in all these matters I shall wholy referre you to Mr. Fenwicke who accompanys these lines to you. That which for the present I haue to commend to you is a busines that concernes not only this state but all the English upon the Riuer, that is to say a cleare examination of the Pequots proceedings and such expression of our minds to them as in this case is requisite. To this End we haue thought fitt to send you a commission and to recommend to your consideration certaine instructions which containe the summe of our thoughts in that busines.[2] And farther we do desire you to lay downe so much Wampum there as the Pequots sent vs and we shall see you repayd heere: your Father will write to you what quantity it is of. For the skins we shall send them by some of the Barkes that go to you. The oppertunity of Mr. Fenwick and Mr. Peeters being with you may somewhat aduance this worke and therfore I beseech you let not the occasion slip. As for other matters that concerne the mouth of the Riuer and those that liue in the vpland, if you acquaint me with them I shall giue you my aduise and assistance for establishing thing[s] according to Justice and the Equity of the cause. Your owne wisedome is such I know as to lay vp such obseruations

---

[1] W. 2. 186; 4 *Collections*, VI. 582–583. For Vane, see *D.N.B.*
[2] The commission and instructions, dated July 4, 1636, are printed below, pages 284–285.

by you as may be for the benefitt of the Gentlemen: and may giue them some returne of their great disbursements: as also for counsell and direction how to setle things at the Riuers mouth, in All which you may be helpfull to Mr. Fenwicke who is a stranger to those parts and so I doubt but you wilbee. Thus In hast I rest Your affectionate freind

H: VANE

BOSTON 1 of the 5th Month 1636

I haue sent you this paper inclosed to acquaint you with what intelligence we haue receaued: what your knowledge can further adde: I am silent in.

ADAM WINTHROP TO JOHN WINTHROP, JR.[1]

To his very louinge brother Mr. John Winthrop liuinge in conekticot riuer
giue this I pray

LOUINGE BROTHER, I haue reseued your leter whar in you did express a grat dell of loue vnto me; for wich I can not but thanke you that you wold take the payns to writ vnto me your vnworthy brother: the considarachon of this does sture me to lay hould of the first operteunyty that is ofred to me for the writing vnto you and sending you the thinges that you sent for: wich is the bacheldor at your desiar I haue sent a turke koke and a hene wich ware brout doun from mistick all so ferkin of lime wich you did send for all so sum turnupe sede I did ask henry kinkgesbery whether he had bout any gotes for mr. jase he tould me he had boute non becas that there was som com from ingland for him: and those he wold haue boute but that thay ware both dere and apt to dye furdor word the tould me he wold send you thare of.

conserning shipes wich won did writ about thare haes com 15 allredy 4 duchmen 6 londonars grate shipes besides other west contrymen: the duch shipes brout shep and other catall grat store and buter and chese: my sister is brout abed of a dafter thankes be to god and is well I pray remember my loue to my brother steuen and mr. gardner and his wife and all the rest of my frindes, and so I rest with my loue remembred to you and thanking you for all your kindneses your louing brother whill deth

ADAM WINTHROP

Jeuly the 3, 1636

---

[1] W. Au. 66; 5 *Collections*, VIII. 219–220.

COMMISSION AND INSTRUCTIONS FROM THE COLONY
OF MASSACHUSETTS BAY TO JOHN WINTHROP, JR.,
FOR TREATING WITH THE PEQUOTS[1]

For John Winthrop iunior esqr. gouernour of Quenecticut

Whereas it so falls out by the good Prouidence of God that the place of your present residence is neare adioyning vnto certaine of the Natiues who are called the Pequots, concerning whom we haue diuers things to enquire and satisfy ourselues in; Our Request to you therefore is and by these Presents we do giue you full power Authority and Commission to treate and conferre with the sayd Pequots in our Names and according to the instructions to these annexed, as if we ourselues were present. And to make Report backe agayne vnto vs of the Issue and successe of the Whole before the next Generall Court (which God willing is intended in the beginning of the 7th Month). Thus recommending you and your affayres to the blessing of Allmighty God Wee Rest Your Louing Freinds

H. VANE *Gov[ernou]r*
Jo: WINTHOP *Dep[u]t[y]*

MASSATUCHETS the 4th day of the 5t Month 1636

*The Instructions which are recommended to John Winthrop Junr. Esqr.
in his Negotiation with the Pequots*

MASSATUCHETS Month 5. 4. 1636

1 To giue notice to the Principall Sachem that you haue receaued a Commission from vs to demaund A Solemne meeting for conference with them in a friendly manner about matters of importance.

2 In Case they slight such a Message and refuse to giue you a Meeting (at such place as your self shall apoynt) then you are in our names to returne backe their present (which you shall receaue from vs) and to acquaint them with all that we hold ourselues free from any peace or league with them as a People guilty of English Blood.

3 If they consent and giue you a meeting as aforesayd that then you lay downe vnto them how vnworthily they haue requited our friend[shi]p with

---

[1] Miscellaneous MSS., Bound, M.H.S.; 3 *Collections*, III. 129–131. Cf. Sir Henry Vane to John Winthrop, Jr., July 1, 1636 (pages 282–283, above).

them: For as much as that they haue Broken the very condition of the Peace betwixt vs by the not rendring into our hands the Murtherers of Captn. Stone (which we desire you once agayne solemly to require of them) As also in that they so trifled with vs in their Present which they made proffer of to vs, as that they did send but part of it and put it of with this as to say the old men did neuer consent to the giuing of it, which dealings sauour so much of dishonour and neglect, as that no people that desire friend[shi]p should put them in Practise.

4 To let them know what credible relation hath beene giuen vs, that some of the cheif of them were Actors in the Murder of Mr. Hamond and the other vpon long Iland; and since of another English man there: And of their late determination to haue seized vpon a Plimouth Barke lying in their Harbour for trade: as by the more large descriptions of these things which we also send vnto you will more distinctly appear. Of all these things we desire you to take the relation from their owne mouths, and to informe vs particularly of their seuerall answers: giuing them to vnderstand that it is not the Manner of the English to take reuenge of Injurys vntill the Partys that are guilty haue beene called to answer fairely for themselues.

5 To let them know that if they shall cleare themselues of these Matters, we shall not refuse to hearken to any reasonable proposition from them for confirmation of the peace betwixt vs. But if they shall not giue you satisfaction according to these our instructions or shalbee found guilty of any of the sayd Murthers and will not deliuuer the Actours in them into our hands, that then, (as before you are directed) you returne them the Present and declare to them that we hold ourselues free from any league or peace with them and shall reuenge the blood of our Countrimen as occasion shall serue.

H: VANE *Gov[ernou]r*

Jo: WINTHOP *Dep[u]t[y]*

WILLIAM PYNCHON TO JOHN WINTHROP, JR.[1]

To the Right Wor[shi]pfull and my worthy Freind Mr. John Wintrop at Quinettecot Riuer mouth deliver this

ROXBURY July 4, 1636

DEERE AND WORTHY FREIND, My true loue remembred: I sent you a few lines by land and now againe by sea to assuer you that I forget you not: and

---

[1] W. 2. 147; 4 *Collections*, VI. 371–372.

the name of your good health is good newes vnto me: I suppose the former parsell of cloth is neere all gonn and therefore I haue sent you a smale parsell more: the best that euer came to Quinettecot: the contentes are as followeth viz:

33 y. of Tauny: plaine wool	
39 y. ¾ Tauny shagg	
38 y. ½ liuer cullor shagg	} 225 y. at 8s—90li os od
38 y. murry shagg	
37 y. ¾ murry shagg	
38 y. of liuer culler shagg	

all thes at 8s per y. better cloth by much then any I see heere in the Bay.

I pray accept my bill of exchang to you by Mr. Peeter for 63li: and as for the fraight of the Blessing formerly I haue a perfett account of it: but I haue not mett with Anthony Dike to confer my notes with him.

And as for the fraught of the Batcheller I shall mak vpp the Tunag with Mr. Gose at Watertowne[1] for thither I haue conditioned that she must deliuer our goods: I asked Leiftenant Gibins before I would hier her if she might goe as far as Watertowne and he confidently affirmed she might and that there is water enough: therefore I pray giue all the furtherance you can.

Also I received a parsell of course wampam from you but I could not trade any of it because others were furnished with plenty of better: But if you will send me a parsell of a 100 or 200 fathom of fine white wampam I shall accept it as beuer: If you sell not this cloth keepe it in good condition and I will take it againe.

As for vsing ould traders to trade for you it is not the best way for your gaine: for they know how to saue themselues but a trusty man that neuer was a trader will quickly find the way of trading and bring you best profitt.

And so the god of peace be with you euer. Your euer louing Freind

WILLIAM PYNCHON

---

[1] Wethersfield.

Wentrope esquer at Kanufticott give this

BROTHER, I salute you in the lord rememberinge my ... vnto you. I thanke you for that you would take the paynes to write to vs. I confess wee are to blame that wee haue not write to you all this tyme but I soppose that you knew our occasions and Distrachtions wee have bin in by reson wee weare all together vnsetteled you would then excuse vs and beare with vs for it. assure your selfe it is not for wante of loue to you or vnmindfullness of you. you write to vs to knowe our minds which wen I received your letter I did not knowe my owne mynde, but sence it hath pleased god wee are resolued agayne for Knufticott, and therefore I haue nowe sent my man to mowe grass their for to winter my cattell their, and to gett what houseinge hee can their thoughe never soe meane for a shelter, tell I come thether my selfe. I purpose god willinge in the springe to come their my wife and fammeley. I should bee glad to here that you will sett downe theire towe that yf god plese wee maye inioye your compayneie their to dewell which I doe profess would bee a greate comfort to mee yf god soe please to dispose of it. your wife and dafter was lately verie well last thursdaye I saw them boeth your wife I meane for a woman in hir case lately broght to bed, and soe with my prayers to god for a blessinge vppon you and all your affayres I take my leaue and Rest beinge in haste, Your truly louinge Brother

ROBARTE FEKE

WATTERTOWNE this 5th July 1636

ELIZABETH FEKE TO JOHN WINTHROP, JR.[2]

*To the Worshipfull my very Louing brother John Winthrop Esquire
att Connefticote deliver*

DEAREST BROTHER, I reioyce with you and blesse god for the safe deliuery of my sister and the welfar of her and your daughter; I receiued A Letter from you for which I thanke you that you continue your Louing remembrance of vs; my husband doth remember his loue to you   we are now fully

---

[1] W. I. 115; 2 *Proceedings*, v. 8n.–9n. For Robert Feke, who married Elizabeth Fones Winthrop, the widow of the Governor's son Henry, see Henry W. Foote, *Robert Feke, Colonial Portrait Painter* (Cambridge, 1930), 19–26.
[2] W. Au. 46.

Resoulued to goe to dwelle att connefti
pose you will sett downe thare att watt
and expected their   we do now send our ma
to winter them their; and to prepare some ho
forced now to pich on some place and we thinke In this
to inioye your company   if our desire had not bin cheifly to ha
you we had chosen Concord for to dwell in   I exspected your retourne to vs
longe ere this; otherwise I should haue writen to you of a testimony of my
vnfaned loue as also to haue desired your aduice   I hop to see you hear
shortly   in the meane time I present to you my reall loue and remain Your
euer Louing Sister

ELISABETH FEKE

July 5, 1636

LONDON PORT BOOK ENTRIES FOR THE *WILLIAM AND JOHN*[2]

8 July 1636

In the William and John of London, master, Rowland Langrum for New England: John Wenthorpe esq. for the Plantation at Massachusetts Bay in New England one single serge, 36 yards of flannel, 250 goads Welch cottons, 100 goads Northern cottons, 240 yards ruggs for beds, 7 pair of blankets, 2 cwt. of wrought iron, 200 ells of vittry canvas, 36 pair of canvas breeches cost 45*s*, 19 cotton waistcoats cost 40*s*, 108 pair woollen stockings, 3 dozen children's woollen stockings, 40 goads Manchester cottons, 200 yards of Norwich stuffs cost 20 pence a yard, 4 yard broad perpetuanoes, 8 pieces of Tregar, 20 dozen of shoes, 3 dozen of boots 50 gallons of Aquavitae, 150 yards coarse linen for breeches cost 7 pence a yard, 2 tons of cast lead, 5 cwt. of currants, 17 cwt. of raisins, 1 cwt. of figs, 50 lbs of pepper, 20 doz. of Irish stockings packed in divers parcels with other goods, 10 pieces of double sayes.

12 July 1636

In the William and John of London, master, Rowland Langrum for New England: John Wenthorpe esq., one single serge, 26 yds. of flannel, 211 goads of Welch, and 100 Northern cottons, 108 pair men's woollen stockings, 40 goads Manchester cottons, 200 yards Norwich stuffs cost 20 pence a yard, 4 yard broad perpetuanoes, 50 gallons Aquavitae, 2 tons of Cast lead and 10 Double bayes.

---

[1] Wethersfield.   [2] Public Record Office; *Proceedings*, LI. 283.

14 July 1636

foresaid: John Wenthorpe esq. 50 goads of Welsh

or breeches cost 5 pence a yard, 4 yard broad

ingle serges, 2 pieces single bayes, and one

Elizabeth Ff

Robert Feke to Jc

To the wor[ship]full John

Lounge and Kinc Res

best respeckts

[1636]

HN WINTHROP, JR.[1]

no. Winthrop the younger Esqr. att

the Wm. and John

To th

Sir, N.   as per the Peter Bonadventure, in w   to   u 42 hoggshedds of severall
Commodit   vised to which I desire to be referred
att present   erstand I have laden aboard this Shipp the
Wm. and Jn   us of oatmeale more (which I gave you some intimacion of the   per the inclosed bill of lading you may perceave. I mett
with this parcell vppon reasonable tearmes otherwise I should not have gone
soe farr in disbursements for that account, being out of cash for it. I had
thought when I made the former provitions that a farr greater summe of
mony would have been sent in, according to promise otherwise I would have
disposed of that which came to my hands somewhat different from what I
did, and have disbursed part of it in provitions of other kinds, but I lived in
a dayly expectacion of more Supply, which fayled me hitherto, and now the
sicknesse comming into the Citty hath scattered the interested into severall
parts, soe that I much question whether any more willbe sent this yeare.
Since the former mentioned by the Peter, I wrott you breefly per Mr. Babb,
by whom I sent you 3 small pieces of ordinance, and cariages to them. I am
now bringing my owne occasions to a head and intend (god willing) the first
of the next Spring to come away: I have not elce att present to inlarge, but
will take leave and rest Yours in what I can

EDW. HOPKINS

July the 14th 1636

1 W. 2. 133; 4 *Collections*, VI. 332–333.

BILL FOR EQUIPMENT FOR THE *DESIRE*[1]

Anno 1636

The ship Desire or the owners therof are debitted to account of the bark Warwick or her owners for theis particulers following taken by order of the Gouernour Winthrope

	li	s	d
Per 3 falkons and one falkonet poy. 38 C. 3 q. with the old Carradges at 10s 6d per Cwt.	21	5	10
Per an old poupe lanthorne 5s and a small croe of Iron 2s 6d		7	6
Per 2 spindels for vanes 18d a pump bolt and a wooden brake, all		2	2
Per a small anker stock 4s a pistoll barrell 6d and 3 small takell hooks 12d all is		5	6
Per a Copper funnell 6s 2 spung staves a rammer and a ladell all		11	0
Per 11 falkon shott 4s a small bell 3s		7	0
Per a small anker estemed at	2	0	0
	24	19	0

Per me

WILL. PEIRSE

[*Ca.* August, 1636]

[*Endorsed by Governor Winthrop:*] Mr. Peirce for Barke Warwick.

EDWARD HOWES TO JOHN WINTHROP, JR.[2]

To my verie louinge frinde Mr. John Winthrop the yonger these present at Conectecut with trust in New England

MI CHARISSIME, Yours of the 9th of Nouember, and of the 6th of January last I haue receiued, and haue since sent you two lettres, which I hope will kisse your hands before this. The manie obligations where with you haue tyed me to you being soe pleasant and delightfull, doe constraine me to sue, to be more fast tyed. I cannot discouer into terram incognitam, but I haue had a kenn of it shewed vnto me. the way to it is (for the most parte) horrible

---

[1] W. 1. 112; Savage (1853), 1. 230n. In Winthrop's Journal (1. 187) appears the following entry under date of August 26, 1636: "A ship of one hundred and twenty tons was built at Marblehead, and called the *Desire*."

[2] W. 2. 169; 4 *Collections*, VI. 501–504.

and fearefull, the daingers none worse, to them that are not destinati filij; somtymes I am trauelling that way but the Lord knowes when I shall gett thither, soe many flattering foes are still in the way to preuent me, and diuerte my course. I thinke I haue spoken with some that haue bin there. I am informed that the land lyeth where the sunn riseth, and extendeth it selfe southward, the northerne people doe account it noe better then a wildernes; and the spies that they haue sent out to discouer and view it, haue reported as much: for they knew it was in vaine to reporte better of it.

Deare frind I desire with all my harte that I might write plainer to you but in discouering the misterie I may diminish its maiestie, and giue occasion to the prophane to abuse it if it should fall into vnworthie hands   in many things you haue sympathized with me, and whie not in this? after the hint of a thing, facilius est addere. Let me make a Quere. was the bodie made for the soule, or the soule for the Bodie? was the house made for man or man for the house? doe or did the true louers of wisdome, studie more for the bodie, then the soule? did they not know the man? the bodie is but our seruant, and shall our studies for it take vp our endeuours as for [*torn*] is it not spirituall fornication and adulterie to cast the eye of our mind and harte vpon sensualitie, or any sensible good as to lust after it; must not the fiue kings be vanquisht and hung vp, before Israell can enter into the rest of the Lord; which rest I wish vnto you, and rest Yours

ED. HO.

4º Aug: 1636

I pray let me not be forgotten of any frind, whome you thinke worthie to be put in minde of me; but salute them in my name as if I had named them vnto you.

I haue not seene Dr. E: since last sommer: our frinds at the old house are all well and are nowe either at Graves or Groton; your aunt D[owning] hath bespoken a black marble grauestone for your grandsire and grandmother; there dyed in and about London of the plague this weeke 181. There is great mortallity in our land in diuerse places, and in other places beyond the seas, and in Germanie there is a great famine. Prince Thomas the King of Spaines brother, hath ouer runn all Pykardy and burnt 100 villages in 4 howers. he threatens that his next attempt shalbe vpon Paris it selfe; the commons of France begin to mutinie against the gentrie, and the spaniard where he comes doth reape the Frenches Corne for them, and they themselues in some places haue burnt theire standing corne rather then the Spaniard should haue it. my hartie affections salute you and your best beloued. Vale Christo.

3° Sept. 1636

This lettre hauing lyne written a moneth in my hands, I was about to can-
cell it, because I could not send it, but vpon second thoughts I spared it. The
Falcon is safe come to vs, but not one lettre to me in it, as I heare of. I mett
with one of Captaine Wiggins seruants that came ouer, whoe told me of such
things he knew. I doe much applaud your resolution to plant Conectecut.
fortifie the mouth meanely well, but except you can find a place there naturally fortified, in the water as Venice, or on the maine as Douer, bestow not
too much cost and paines vpon it; rather goe vp further (leauing a garison
belowe). learne by reports and your owne obseruation where (on that Riuer)
the natiues haue liued longest and healthfullest and in greatest aboundance,
though it be 50, 60, or 70 or more miles vp in the land. if any be there, gett
theire good will, if possible you can to sitt downe with them or by them.
howesoeuer be as neere as may be, soe it be a place comodious for trade and
husbandrie, and not easilie surprized by an enimie. But you may say its easie
to sitt vpon a Cushion and direct, but difficult to performe. I doe not speake
of ympossibilities, but giue caution for a good begining and foundation, that
hereafter it may not be said *Pœnitet*, or had-I-wist: A busines wel begun is
plesant and hopefull The best wilbe therefore to begin with God, which I
doe not doubt but you will and seeke his directions, howe and where you may
lay a foundation for a Cittie of Peace, to the honor of his great name; in your
religious cohabiting together; And soe that you may prepare and prouide
conuenient and comfortable dwellings and portions for your future generations, that they may haue cause to blesse God in theire harts, for your labours
of loue.

I shall not need to request of you some knowledge of your plantation, and
howe farre you haue discouered the riuer, and howe you like it, and what
newes of the Lake, and howe farr you are from the Dutch, and from Boston; I
am perswaded you will acquaint me with that which you thinke is fittest for
me, and reserue for me the rest vntill a seasonable tyme. Only this I would
gladly see a Mapp of the longe Iland and the coast from Cap Cod to Riuer
Hudson [when] you haue one to spare. My father and mother salutes you
with theire loue, and soe doe my sisters. your Brother Dr.[1] was wel lately, he
was with me. there dyed this last weeke in and about london of all diseases
855, and of the Plague 536, besides aboue 100 in Westm[inster] and Contrie
parishes adioyninge, but howe many 1000 amonge vs are dead in theire sinns
I knowe not, yet noe doubt we haue a remnant that haue not bowed theire

---

[1] Dr. Samuel Reade, brother of Winthrop's wife.

knee to Baal. for my parte I doe as much as in me lyes commend and committ my soule to God in wel-doeing, and ventre my bodie amonge the liuing and dead. But I doubt I haue bin too tedious and troublesome, it's my loue to you constraineth me to write the more, because we cannot speake together. I hope your remotenes from the Bay will not hinder the entercourse of lettres be-tweene vs.

SIR MATTHEW BOYNTON TO JOHN WINTHROP[1]

To my uerie worthy friend John Winthorpe Esqr. att Boston in New-England giue this

SIR, I desire to express that thankfulness to you which your continewed kindnesses require of me: with which beeing soe well acquainted though un-knowne to your selfe itt may be soe much a stronger engagement, nott onelie to moue me to acknowledg them butt to striue to deserue them wherein I assure you I will nott fayle howsoeuer I may comm shorte, in that which may be worthy of your acceptance:

I haue here-in[c]losed sent somm letters, which I desire you will doe me the fauour by the first conueniencie you cann, to send to my seruants: Sir I shall alwayes continew as I ame exceedinglie engaged Your assured and thankfull friende

MATT. BOYNTON

August 26th 1636

Sir, Amongst the rest here is one letter to mr. Fenwicke which I beseatch you if cann conuenientlie conuey to him.

SIR WILLIAM SPRING TO BRAMPTON GURDON[2]

GOODE COSIN, I thank you hartely for this your Courtesy of sending these letters and all other your goode Wishes and affections expressed to mee and mine: yett this your letter comes to mee att such a time, as I assure you I am scarse fitt or att leysure to returne you soe decent and fitt an Answer as I would, for though I am I prayse God reasonable well yett att the Instant I am in a Phisicall vndertaking which will not permitt mee hardly this liberty but vtterly denies mee any farther to Enlarge myselfe to you or to our Deere frend

---

[1] W. Au. 91; 4 *Collections*, VII. 167.
[2] W. Au. 90; 4 *Collections*, VI. 554–555. This letter was forwarded by Gurdon to Governor Winthrop. See Gurdon's letter to Winthrop immediately following.

in N: E: as I desire, touching whome (I perceyue by the hast of this returne now sudden and heeretofore vnknowne to mee), I cannot (as the Case is now with mee) write to him as I would and were most fitt. I shall pray you therefore to lett him know my honest and just Reasons and Excuse heerein written to you, And withall whereas I perceyue hee hath farr beyond that proportion (which by you I did signifie I was Content to bestow on my kinsman)[1] disburst neere 20*li*, but in Certainty I yett know not what, though I confess considering my former disbursments, and soe many charges as I dayly meete with amongst others of his kin[d]red and mine that must haue releife from mee, I finde my selfe in those charges to haue runne a higher streyne then my owne priuate Cares and necessary Occasion will well allowe. Yett when I know what my goode Freind hath certainly disburst (as I expect by his promise shortly to bee inform'd by a letter from himselfe) I will take order that hee shalbee noe looser for his disbursments past, hoping that (as hee sayth) that debt beeing payd, hee will subsist of himselfe, who I assure you hath Cost mee deepe, And to whome (considering the many more that dayly draw from mee) I am not able to doe more. In the meane time vntill I receyue perticuler Information of what itt is, espetially att this extreame sudden I cannot tell what to send: I haue receyued Mr. Downings receipt of 5*li* disbursed by you for mee towards the leade, which 5*li* I send you heare by your seruant reseruing the note of receipt, I should be gladd to see or heere of the receipt of our disbursment in N: E: whether I pray Commend mee most hartely to our Deere and worthy freind, and acquaint him fully with the perticulers of this letter, on my behalfe and excuse for not writing now to him, which is to mee att this time impossible: and pray him to lett mee enjoy his loue and promise to write perticulerly to mee next time, and I shall (if god please) apply my selfe to his satisfaction: forgett not I agen and agen entreate you to signifie these things to him: nor to continue your loue and prayers for and vnto Your faythfull Freind and louing Cosin

WLLM: SPRING

PAKENHAM 29 of August 1636

My wife with mee returne our true loues to you and my Cosin and all yours, and doe commend you all to the goode mercies of God as wee desire the like from you [at] all goode times.

[*Endorsed by Governor Winthrop:*] Sir Wm. Springe, Answ:

---

[1] John Spring of Watertown. See Sir William Spring to John Winthrop, April 16, 1636 (pages 249–251, above).

BRAMPTON GURDON TO JOHN WINTHROP[1]

*To my muche honerred frend Mr. Jhon Wenthrop at Boston in Neu England,
be thes I pray*

MY WORTHY GOOD FRIND, I haue resayued your letter of the 24 of Jeun. I reioyes to hear of godes mersy expressed to your plantatyon in genrall and to yow and yowers in the perticuler I thancke yow for your care of my sonn. I hoped his passing by sce and then the chang of ayer would haue so changed his weacke body to a more abule body for the performans of that which his years and statuer mought exspect. I haue before now found fault with him for his so bad writeng, but I now impeut it to the weackenes of his Joyentes so as he is not abule to gyed his pen as heartofore. He writ better 4 years past then he doo now. I doo perswad him to put him selff to soum suche exersyes as may infors his sweatteng the which I thincke should be especyally good for him as I now fyend his condecyon I may fear he is to burdensoum to you but by Godes helpe I am verry welling to macke good any thing for his charge as you shall desyer. Sir scins I resayued your letter I went to Jhon Brand and found his sonn Joseff with him for so I desyred. When I had sheued Joseff your not of the perticeuler layenges out and the not of the goodes scent his brother Ben-iamen, he tould me he could say nothing till he had loked in his bocke at London, [*torn*] as he tould me he should be gone thether and after he had veued his bocke he would writ to yow. I shall not slacke to put him in mind to geu satisfaccyon. I scent my sonn Brampton to my cosen Ryes to acquayent him as yow desyred. vpon saterday last I resaved a letter from Jarmen Pyen which informed me a ship was to goe doun to grauesend the later end of this wecke that is goeng for N. E. which caused me to hast a man to Sir W. Spring to acquayent him so muche as conserned him in your letter. his answer is in desyreng me to exceus him to yow but I am contented to scend you his owen letter the which may geue yow the best satisfaccyon.[2] he is now in parly and I hope it is concleuded for a mache with his sonn and Sir Hamund Strange dafter. he is to haue 4000*li* at the lest with a hansoum well bred gentelwoman. It hathe faulne out verry hard with the shipe whear in Mr. Nathl. Rogers imbarked him selff his wiff who locke for at the end of 7bur and 4 children and 3 other pore fameles out of this towen won is Robinson that liued in Lit[tle] Waldenfeld with his wiff and 6 children thay went abord at Grauesend the

---

[1] W. 2. 181; 4 *Collections*, VI. 559-561.
[2] Cf. the letter from Sir William Spring to John Winthrop immediately preceding.

furst of Jeuen and haue euer scins ben houereng to the Ile of Wite and this day Mris. Crane their scister and Mris. Rogers mother in law tould me her husband had a letter from them from Plimworth writ on saterday scen[nigh]t this will fall exceding heui to dyuers in the ship who had mad som prouicyon for thear liuelyhod in N. E. thay will be inforsed to spe[nd] it before thay goe and all for want of a constant Est wind. thay haue had the wind for a day or 2 and then brought backe agayen. thay haue had dyuers feruent prayers to geue them a good wind but the tyem is not yet coum for god to haue the prayes of it. my sonn Saltonstall doo dayly expect his coummeng. I haue not time now to writ it to him whot this day I hard I pray thearfore doo him word of it, and thus praying god to kep vs in his treu fear with my wiffes and my best respect to [you] and to Mris. Winthrop in all treu affeccyon remembred I rest your euer asseured louing frend

BRAMPTON GURDON

ASSINGTON this 30 of August [1636]

I sheued Sir Nathanyele your remembring of him.

ROGER WILLIAMS TO JOHN WINTHROP[1]

[Torn] *much honoured Mr. Wintrop Deputie Gov[erno]r these*

MUCH HONOURED SIR, The frequent experience of your loving eare ready and open toward me (in what your Conscience hath permitted) as allso of that excellent spirit of wisedome and prudence wherewith the Father of Lights hath endued you, embolden me to request a word of private advise with the soonest Convenience, if it may be, by this Messenger.

The Condicion of my selfe and those few families here planting with me, you know full well: We haue no Pattent: nor doth the face of Magistracie suite with our present Condicion: Hietherto, the Masters of Families haue ordinarily mett once a fortnight and consulted about our common peace, watch, and planting; and mutuall Consent hath finished all matters with speede and peace.

Now of late some young men single persons (of whome we had much neede) being admitted to freedome of Inhabitation, and promising to subiect to the Orders made by the Consent of the Howseholders, are discontented with their estate, and seeke the Freedome of Vote allso, and æqualitie etc.

---

[1] W. 2. 96; 4 *Collections*, VI. 186–188.

Beside, our dangers (in the midst of these dens of Lyons) now especially, call vpon vs to be Compact in a Civill way and power.

I haue therefore had thoughts of propounding to my neighbours a double subscription, concerning which I shall humbly craue your helpe.

The first concerning our selues, the m[aste]rs of families: thus

We whose names are here vnder written, late Inhabitants of the Massachusetts (vpon occasion of some difference of Conscience) being permitted to depart from the Limits of that Pattent, vnder the which we came over into these parts, and being cast by the Providence of the God of Heaven, remote from others of our Countriemen amongst the Barbarous in this towne of New Providence, doe with free and ioynt Consent promise each vnto other, that, for our common peace and wellfare (vntill we heare further of the Kings royall pleasure concerning our selues) we will from time to time subiect our selues in Actiue or passiue Obedience to such Orders and Agreements, as shall be made by the greater number of the present Howseholders, and such as shall be hereafter admitted by their Consent into the same Priviledge and Covenant in our ordinarie meeting. In witnes whereof we herevnto subscribe etc.

Concerning those few young men, and any who shall hereafter (by your favourable Connivence) desire to plant with vs: this

We whose names are here vnder written being desirous to inhabite in this Towne of New Providence, doe promise to subiect our selues in actiue or passiue Obedience to such Orders and Agreements as shall be made from time to time, by the greater number of the present Howseholders of this Towne, and such whome they shall admit into the same fellowship and priviledge. In witnes whereof etc.

Hietherto we chose one (named the officer,) to call the meeting at the appointed Time: now it is desird by some of vs that the Howseholders by Course performe that worcke, as allso gather Votes and see the watch goe on etc.

I haue not yet mencioned these things to my neighbours but shall as I see Cause vpon your lo[ving] Councell.

As allso, since the place I haue purchased 2ly at mine owne charge and engagements the inhabitants paying, (by Consent) 30s a piece as they come vntill my Charge be out for their particular Lots: and 3rdly, that I never made any other Covenant with any person, but that if I got a place he should plant there with me: my quære is this.

Whither I may not lawfully desire this of my neighbours, that as I freely subiect my selfe to Common Consent and shall not bring in any person into the Towne without their Consent: so allso that against my Consent no person be Violently brought in and receaved.

I desire not to sleepe in securitie and dreame of a Nest which no hand can reach. I cannot but expect changes, and the change of the last Enemie Death, yet dare I not despise a Libertie, which the Lord seemeth to offer me, if for mine owne or others Peace: and therefore haue I bene thus bold to present my thoughts vnto you.

The Pequts heare of your preparations etc. and comfort them selues in this that a witch amongst them will sinck the pinnaces by diving vnder water and making holes etc. as allso that they shall now enrich themselues with store of guns but I hope their dreames (through the mercie of the Lord) shall vanish, and the Devill and his lying Sorcerers shall be confounded.

You may [please] Sir to take notice that it is of maine Consequence to take some Course with the Wunnashowatuckoogs and Wusquowhananawkits, who are the furthermost Neepnet men for the Pequts driven from the Sea coast with Ease, yet there secure and strengthen themselues and are then brought downe so much the neerer to you. Thus with my best respects to your lo[ving] selfe and Mrs. Wintrop I rest Your Wo[rshi]ps vnfeigned, praying to meete you in this Vale of Teares or hills of mercie aboue

R: WILLIAMS

[*Ca.* September, 1636]

ROBERT RYECE TO JOHN WINTHROP[1]

Whereas abowte 12 moneth synce came forthe a boocke in defence of the orthodoxall doctrine of the church of Englande against Sabbatarian noveltie,[2] whereat many began secretly to murmure, for that it was bytter and dyd overthrowe the tenents of the church of England in that poynte which none durste publickly oppose, bycawse many defended it so earnestly at the lengthe abowte whitsontyde laste there was scattered abroade a very lytle treatise of 16 leaves in 4to entyteled a briefe awnswere to a late treatise of the Sabbath daye, digested dialogue wyse betweene 2 divines A and B, withowte the name of any awthor.[3]

These 2 divines meetinge and conferringe of this boocke, the one of them thowghte it a verye dangerous boocke to the awthor, if it mighte be well ex-

---

[1] W. 2. 154; 4 *Collections,* VI. 398–409. For Ryece, see *Winthrop Papers,* I. 357, *n.* 35.

[2] Francis White, *A Treatise of the Sabbath-Day. Containing, A Defence of the Orthodoxall Doctrine of the Church of England, against Sabbatarian-Novelty* (London, 1635).

[3] Richard Byfield, *The Lords Day, the Sabbath Day. Or, A Briefe Answer to Some Materiall Passages, in a Late Treatise of the Sabbath-Day: Digested Dialogue-Wise betweene Two Divines A. and B.* (London, 1636). This has also been attributed to William Prynne.

amined before competente judges bycawse as he sayeth it overthroweth the doctryne of the church of England in the poynte of the Sabbathe for the very tytle is *A defense of the Orthodoxal doctrine of the church of Englande agaynst Sabbatarian Noueltye*. These divine shewe that the boocke is dedicated to the Archbishop of Cant[erbury] by whose direction, and that accordinge to his ma-[jes]tyes sacred comande he sett vpon this woork bothe for the preventinge of mischeefe, (as he sayeth in his Epi[st]lle dedicated to the Archbishop) and to setle the K[ings] good Subiectes, who of longe tyme had byn dystracted abowte Sabbatarian questions. Nexte of all these devynes doe shewe, that the awthor can have but smalle thankes for his labor, when as the K[ing] who is the defender of the faythe of the church of England hathe often solomly protested, and that in his publicke declarations in printe, as at the dissolvinge of the parliamente, and declaration before the 39 Ar[tic]les *that he wyll neuer suffer therein the leaste innouation*. So agayne one of them alledgeth there adversary is a greate Scholler deepely learned a Reu[eren]de father of the church his Judgemente muste be taken for an oracle. Accordinge to that in a late boocke established by auct[horiti]e as the Communion boocke expounded by Reue[1] page 20, sayeth, that the holy fathers in God the Bishops are to be guydes in divinitie, vnto the wholle clargie of inferior order, vnto whose godly Judgements in all matters pertayninge to Religeon all owghte to submitte them selves, bycawse the fathers in the church now and allwayes doe in the greate mistery of Godlines comprehende which the common people do not, and some thinges which the ministers of the inferiour order do not apprehende, so that wha[t]soeuer thay delyver, muste be beleeved as sownde rewles. And heere the divines take occasion to speake that wee lyve in a learned age, that wee denie the popes infallabyllytie, or that it can convaye it selfe as from the heade, and so confine it selfe within the veines of the body of the prelacye; or that a Rochett can confine this grace ex opere operato. Then thay saye thay had neede to vindicate not only the doctrine of the church of England which is by this boocke cleane overthrowne, but also those calumnious and odious tearmes which he geveth to those whose opinions he impugneth in this treatise, as venemous Serpents, noysome tares, pestilente weeds, vncleane beastes and novell Sabbatarians.

Now to shewe how the doctryne of the church of England is overthrowne in this poynte of the Sabbath these divines say that the doctrine of the church of Englande concerninge the Sabbath is moste cleerely sett downe in the boocke of homylyes vnto which all mynisters do subscribe, and by 39 art[icle]s is

---

[1] Edmund Reeve, *The Communion Booke Catechisme Expounded* (London, 1635).

comended as whollsome necessary etc. Heere the severall places are alledged
at large, and then observeth owte of them these conclusions as 1 That all
Christians are bownde in conscience of the 4 Com[mandment] to keepe the
lords day holyly. Secondly, that by force of the 4 Com[mandment] one day in
7 is perpetually to be kepte holy. Thirdly, that the keepinge of the lords day is
grownded vpon and commanded in the 4 com[mandment], and so is not of
humane institution. Forthely That the lords daye is and may be called our
Christian Sabbath daye, therefore it is not Jewish so to call it. 5ly that this
daye is wholly to be spente in holy reste and dutyes of sanctification, and therefore no parte of it owghte to be spente in vayne pleasures and prophane
sportes, all which conclusions the adversarye overthroweth by this boocke.
The adversary to this sayeth that this position (to wytt the 4 com[mandment]
is properly and perpetuallye morall, and is for qualytie and obligation equall
to the other 9 com[mandments] which for many yeeres hathe reigned in
pamphletts, pulpitts, and conventicles, (and is entertayned as an oracle by all
suche as eyther openly professe, or do leane to the desciplinarian faction) is
destitute of truthe. These woords compared to the homylye ar fownde quite
contrarye.

The divine sayeth that the 4 com[mandment] determynes expressely the
tyme and daye for the Sabothe and Service of God. The keepinge of the
Lords day is grownded vpon the equitie of the 4 Com[mandment]. The tyme
for this resteth in no mans pover to determyn but only in Gods.

The adversary sayeth the particular forme and circumstances of restinge
are prescribed vnto vs by the precepts of the church our Spirituall actions
are tawghte by the Evangelicall lawe; our modification, limitation in respecte
of rytes, forme, place, duration, gesture, habytt etc. are prescribed by the lawe
of the church and so pag. 270: It was in the free election of the church to appoynte what day or dayes or tymes shee thowghte good for religeous dutyes,
etc.

The devines saye that the 4 com[mandment] prescribes a certayne proportion of tyme and a fixed daye consecrated by God hym selfe vnto his solemne
and sacred woo[rshi]p, which in that very respecte is perpetually morall. The
adversary confesseth naturall equitie in the 4 com[mandment] that some
tyme is to be sett aparte for the service of God, but lefte to the liberty of the
church to determyn and lymytt the speciall tyme when, and how longe, what
portion or proportion is to be allowed, whither one day in 20, or 40, or 100,
or one day in the yeere or but one peece of a daye in suche a revolution of
tyme, and not one wholle or entyre daye muche lesse one wholle daye in

euery 7. And so pag. 98, the 4 com[mandment] in respecte of any one defe-
nite and speciall daye of every weeke was not symply and perpetually morall
but posityve and temporary onlye.

This the divines say is contrary to the homylies even in terminis which saye
by the 4 com[mandment] wee owghte to have a tyme as one day in a weeke
etc. and this appurtayneth to the lawe of nature as a thinge moste godly moste
juste and needefull for the settinge forthe of gods glory, and therefore owghte
to be retayned and kepte of all good christian people. No sayeth the adversary
one day in the weeke was but posityve and temporary only.

But the divine leavinge to presse the adversary any more with auctorytie of
the church observeth these reasons and growndes owte of the woords of the
commandimente. Remember the Sabboth daye to keepe it holy, which
woords are the very morall substance of the 4 Com[mandment]. The Lo[rd]
sayeth not Remember to sanctefye some conveniente and sufficiente tyme as
the church shall thinke fytt. The com[mandment] prescribeth a certayne
and sett tyme, yea a daye, the sabbath daye, one daye in the weeke, which is
the Sabbath daye.

Agayne it teacheth vs what daye in the weeke, the Sabbathe daye is, to
wytt, the Sabbothe day of the lorde thie God: that day in the weeke wherein
the Lorde our God resteth muste be our Sabbath day: So that as the com-
[mandment] prescribes vnto vs a weekely Sabbath daye to be sanctefied: so
Gods precedente and example poyntes owte vnto vs, what or which daye in
the weeke wee muste reste on, to sanctefye it. And this is not only the naturall
equitie, but the very naturall lawe and substance of the 4 Com[mandment]
to prescribe a sett solemne day in the weeke, and not to leave it in the power
of man or of the church to appoynte what tyme thay please.

The Reasons ar these   1 bycawse the com[mandment] expressely lymiteth
one sett daye in the weeke, beinge the Sabbothe day of the Lorde our God.
Now the Com[mandment] prescribinge a sett and fixed daye in the weeke,
what humane power shall dare to alter it into an indefinite tyme? 2 The
seconde Reason whie it is not lefte in the power of the church to prescribe
what tyme men please, bycawse it is Gods prerogatyve as a maister to
appoynte his owne woo[rshi]p and service, so the tyme wherein he wylbe
served. 3 Reason is, becawse an indeffenite tyme muste eyther binde to all
moments of tyme, as a debtte when the daye of paymente is not expressed is
liable to paymente eny momente, or else it bynds to no tyme at all. For if the
lawe of God binds vs not to an expresse determinate tyme, or daye consecrate
to his service: then the not allowenge hym a sett tyme or daye there is no

transgression, if a sett tyme or daye be not observed. For where no lawe is, there is no transgression. Heere he alledgeth sondry remarkable judgements of suche as have profaned and polluted some parte of the Lords daye within 2 yeeres.

Agayne the divines affirme thay have harde the Adversary say in open courte, that a man mighte be iustefyed to daye and condemned to morowe. That there is no sanctification of the Sabbath but reste, reste only. And by-cawse the dyvines woolde not be taxed of a pryvate interpretation of the homely as a factious Sabbatarian noveliste enclined to the disciplinarian fac-tion, he sheweth the Judgemente and vnderstandinge of others which do agree in the same interpretation of the doctrine of our church layed downe in the homylie as Mr. Hooker and Dr. Andrewes from whose woorkes thay alledge sondry playne places withowte exception, so that thay conclude that the lords daye is come in place of the olde Sabbathe daye, and so is become our Sab-bathe daye, and by necessary consequence grownded vpon the 4 com[mand-ment]. And if it be asked Quo Jure, by what righte doothe the Lords daye take the place of the Sabbath daye? It is awnswered owte of the Psalme, God made it so; And Christes Resurrection declared it to be so: and the Ap-p[ost]les observed it so; yea and commanded it so too. After thay shewe it was the tenet of the antiente catholicke church which dyd observe it, and call the lords daye, the Sabbath of the Lorde which thay kepte in place of the olde Sabbath daye.

And bycawse there is a greate clamor of late for applienge the name of the Sabbothe to the lords daye thay proove it may be so called by these Reasons. 1. Becawse it is our Reste daye. 2. The App[ost]les calle it our Reste a Sab-batisme. 3. The very name of the lords daye importes so moche as beinge the lords holy daye as Esay 58: 13: and that day whereon the lorde rested from the woorke of his Redemption, and so sanctefied by hym and to hym.

And so thay showe, that in the sayde homyly, it is called the Sabbathe daye 10 tymes, in one other homylie 8 tymes, and in a 3 homely 2 tymes: And in King James his proclamation 7 of May 1603, twyce.

Then thay come to all recreations on the Sabbath daye, which thay proove vnlawefull, by lawes domesticke, by the Imperiall lawes, by the Edictes and constitutions of famous princes, comon lawes and cyvill lawes, and by all the reformed churches, thowghe the adversary nullefyes them, for no true churches, bycawse thay have no prelates, to putt them in order and governe them, who all calle the Lords daye the Sabbathe daye, for the due sanctifica-tion whereof, they pleade moste earnestly and zealouslye.

In May laste came forthe a boocke allowed by auct[horiti]e, and withowte the name of the awthor entytled *A Coale from the Altar*,[1] or an awnswere to a lettre not longe synce wrytten to the vicar of Grantham against the placinge of the Com[munion] table at the Easte ende of the chancell, and now of late dispersed abroade to the disturbance of the church. Heere I pray you I vnderstande that the vicar of Gran[tham] was deade 6 years synce, and this supposed lettre is sayde to be wrytten at a leaste 11 yeeres synce by the Bishop of Lyncolne one not in the favor of these tymes, but labored by his adversaryes to have all disgrace heaped vpon hym. And the Author of this *Coale from the Alter* is an notable flatterer of the Courte one Dr. Helyn, one that hathe mooche for abrogatinge the olde syncerytie of the Sabbathe.

The Doctor at the firste enterance gathereth that this lettre to the vicar of Gr[antham] shoolde come from a Reu[eren]de prelate of this church which lettre havinge muche discoraged a greate friende of the doctors, who had thowghte to have removed his com[munion] table to the vpper ende of the chancell, vntyll readinge this lettre or Epistell he was wholly discorged, vpon the which the doctor wryteth his opinion of this lettre, and awnswereth every parte of it advisynge his friende to obay the orders now prescribed. Then he gathereth the passages in the Epi[st]le for which it is probably beleeved the Epi[st]le was wrytten by a Reu[eren]de prelate as from a diocesan to a private parish prieste in his Jurisdiction, which when he had made as playne as he coolde, he sayeth that he can not thus beleeve but rather that this lettre was wrytten by Mr. Cotton of Boston, who meaninge one daye to take sanctuary in new Englande, was wyllinge to doe some greate acte before his goenge that he mighte be the better wellcome when he came amongest them. And thus he concludeth that this Epi[st]le was now spreade abroade of purpose to discowntenance the vniformitie of publicke order, to which the pyetye of these tymes was so muche enclyned, And that this discourse or epistell which was so muche sowghte after applawded and scattered in sondrye coppies was so of purpose doone to distracte the common people, and to hinder that good woorke which was now in hande. As towchinge the preamble he had not sayd any thinge, but that there he mett with somewhat, which seemed to cast a scorne vpon the Reverence appoynted by the Canon vnto the blessed name of Jesus.

Then he discendeth to the 3 particulars wherein the vicar of Gran[tham] desyred to be satisfied   1 for the havinge of an altar at the vpper ende of his quier   2 the placinge of the com[munion] table Altarwyse. 3 the fixinge of it in the quier, so as it may not be removed into the bodye of the church. He

---

[1] Peter Heylyn, *A Coale from the Altar* (London, 1636).

sheweth that the Elders of the vestrye, and the vestry doctryne of these dayes, were againste this doctryne: he declared that as the lords Supper may be called a Sacrafize, so may the holy table be called an altar, and sett vp in the place where the altar stoodde. he shewed that the martyrs called the Lords Supper a Sacrifice and many tymes the Sacramentt of the altar. So that there is a Sacrefice Christes propitiatory Sacrefize, and there is an altar, not the Jewysh altar vpon which the Jewes were wonte to offer there burnt offeringes, but the table of the lorde, And there is the Sacramente of the altar, the sacramente of the body and bloodde of Christe.

He sheweth that the papistes calles the com[munion] table sett in the myddest of the channcell an oyster boorde or oyster table, and when this table is fixed in the wall, the Puritane and Mr. Prinne calleth the com[munion] table a dresser bourde; he expecteth that this trymme Epistoler wyll shortly contrary hym, and for the latter parte of dyvine service called the seconde Service, he sayeth there muste be some spare tyme for the mynister to goe from the readinge Pewe and the lordes table, there muste be some tyme reasonable betweene Morninge prayer and the Comunion, yea he affirmeth the wholle frame and fashion of divine Service had byn longe synce cleane loste in Englande had it not byn kepte and preserved in the K[ings] chappell, and cathedrall churches.

He calleth hym an ex[tra]vagante Epistoler, by this you may see of what strayne the epistoler is, for the lorde table was awntiently called an Altar. In Kinge Edwards Raigne the comon people tooke the lordes table sett altar wyse for a dresser, thowghe Bishop Jewell sayeth that the holy table was called an altar only in allusion of the altars of the olde lawe.

He concludeth that the vicar of Gran[tham] might safely holde his 3 conclusions. 1 that an alter maye be vsed in the Christian church. 2 that the com[munion] tablie may stande alterwyse, the mynister officiatinge at the northe ende thereof. 3 That the table may stande constantly in the vpper parte of the channcell close alonge the walle bothe in the fyrste or seconde Service.

Laste of all he alledgeth that in a case of St. Gregoryes church nexte St. Pauls London his sacred ma[jes]tie hathe declared his pleasure, that all Metropolitanes Bishops and Ordinaryes shall require in all the churches commytted to there charges that the com[munion] tables be placed altarwyse, and this he sayeth he faythefully coppied owte of the registers of his cowncell table.

And further sayeth that the com[munion] table is to be placed altarwyse at the vpper ende of the channcell in suche manner as it standeth in the K[ings] chappell and in all colledgiate and cathedrall churches the moother churches (as consonante to the practise of approved antiquitie,) by which all other churches dependinge therevpon owghte to be guyded and governed.

I muste nowe entreate you to goe backe agayne to calle to mynde our Ep[iscop]all visitation in lente laste as you have harde, the strictest that euer was so many good men suspended and removed for not conformitie to the new orders, amonge which a lytle before harvest Mr. Stansby was deprived. thay enquire, whither the Surplyce hathe byn woorne and the signe of the cross vsed at euery tyme the Sacramente is administred, whither the Sacramente of the Supper byn admynistred to any not syttinge, standinge, or leaning vnreverently but humbly kneelinge vpon there knees in playne and open viewe withowte collusion and hipocresye. Doothe the com[munion] table stande at the Easte ende of the chancell where the alter in former tymes stoodde   doothe euery one vse lowly reverence at the name of Jesus? Dothe euery one stande vp at the Ghospell   dooth all the people stande vp and say glory be to the father, at the ende of euery psalme readinge, to beginne the mariadge in the mariadge in the body of the church and then to goe to the com[munion] table: at every mariadge to have a comunion; to kneele at all the collectes, at the Buriall and the comunion: the women to be churched with there vayles, which is begunne in the body of the church and then fynished at the com[munion] table. No Mynister or Lecturer but muste fyrste in his whoodd and surplyce reade all the devine service what so euer befor the sermon, and then goenge into the pulpitt he muste saye his Sermon (for the woorde preache is obsolete)   at the ende he muste goe to the hie altar there to saye the second service and to fynishe all. Is there any vestry meetinges who doe secretly hinder the peace of the church?

By this breviate heere formerly abstracted you may see how the Lords day is kepte heere. Maysters of famylies complayne exceedingly thay cannot contayne there servantes from excursions into all prophane sportes and pastimes on the lords daye; wee haue Judgements daylye vpon suche occasions, but no man regardeth them. It hathe byn well observed this laste Springe heere was very whotte and drye euen in seede tyme and so contynewed of longe tyme that the grasse was so burned vp, that at our vsuall hayseele wee had lytle or no grasse to cutt or to feede our catle. at laste God sente vs rayne, but it was so immoderate and vehimente even in our harvest with suche stronge blastes and stormes layenge moste of the corne flatte vpon the grownde, that not halfe of the corne which came vp coolde be reaped, and that which was reaped is so growne that many feare but doe not knowe what maye heereof prove and ensewe. The plague and infection is come to 536 this laste weeke at London. The Kinge hathe byn very carefull to prevente the infection from dispersenge, for which cawse he adiourned parte of laste Trynitie tearme as from the second retorne called octavis trinitatis, vntill tres trinitatis then next followenge, at Cambrydge no publicke Commencemente, no Barthollmew fayer at London, or our lady fayer in Sowthewoorke, no Styrbrydge fayer, no Ely fayer etc. In all these calamyties wee never wente to God publickly by fastinge and prayer, which was deemed as hatefull as conventicles the frute of the vestry elders there vestry doctryne and the disciplinarian faction; yett at the lengthe vpon the private prayers and fastes of many of Gods deere Servants it pleased the lorde to sende suche an abundante frutefull Mihell Sprynge to the full supply of what so euer was wantynge in our soommer sp[ri]nge that for grasse haye and pasture euery one hathe an aboundante store and supplie. I woolde I coolde wryte vnto you of any lectures contynewed, our hie contempte of the woorde when wee had it abondantly, hathe begoonne this presente famyn, which is feared wyll styll encrease. I haue no more roome so that I can not now goe any farther, only I woolde entreate you remember vs in your prayers. And so after the true contynewance of our beste affection and respecte vnto you wee desyre the allmighty styll to preserve you with all yours. Yours euery wayes as I shoolde be or woolde be

LAWRENCE BROWNE[1]

9 September 1636

I praye you remember the plott or mappe of N. E.

JOHN SMITH TO JOHN WINTHROP[2]

To my verie much Respected good friend mr. Winthrope the Elder in New Ingland these deliuer

GOOD MR. WINTHROPE, I haue by Mr. Downings direction sent you a Coate, a sad houlding coler with out lace. for the fittnes I am a little vncertene, but if it be two big or two little it is esie to amend, vnder the arme to take in or lett out the Lyning   the outsid may be let out in the gathering or taken

---

[1] From a comparison of the handwriting of this letter and that of letters dated January 17, 1636/37 (pages 346–348, below), and April 19, 1637 (page 394, below), it is clear that Lawrence Browne is a pseudonym for Robert Ryece. Cf. Ryece's letters to Winthrop with the signature Thomas Smythe, March 1, 1636/37 (pages 363–365, below), and March 10, 1636/37 (pages 371–375, below). Ryece's use of a pseudonym is doubtless to be explained by the nature of his subject matter.

[2] W. 4. 82; 5 *Collections*, I. 224–225. The Winthrop family had long done business with John Smith, a London tailor. See, for instance, entries in the accounts kept by John Winthrop, Jr. (pages 1–6, above), and the postscript to the letter of Margaret Winthrop to John Winthrop, Jr. (pages 33–34, above).

in also without any preiudice. I haue also sent to mrs. Elizabeth Foanes, for I know not her name now, a pair of sisers and halfe a hundred of nedles for a small token, and also the lik to mrs. Elizabeth Winthrope and to mrs. Marie Downing and her Sister. I intreate you lett them be deliuerd about a week a gone a friend of mine came from Exeter and then Mrs. Foanes that was, now Mrs. Paynter with all hers was in good hea[l]th, as also Mr: Samuell Foanes whoe was then there and verie well. the lord is pleased to lay his hand heauie vpon London at this time there dyeth of the sicknes and other diseases aboue a thousand a weeke and it doth still increase and yet which is worst of all the lord is not in publique sought vnto by fasting and prayrs although at other times the lord hath beene pleased to giue a speedy and gratious answer when he hath bene publiquely sought vnto, soe that we canott but expect some heuier hand to seese vpon vs. the lord in mersie look vpon vs: I pray you remember my servis to good mrs. Winthrope and Mrs. Jo: Winthrope with the Rest of our deare Cristian frinds there with you. I pray you remember ould Ingland in your petitions to the throne of grace its a great hapines that those that are soe far aparte may come soe neare as that by our prayers we may meete at the throne of grace: the Lord in mercie be with you all and Inrich you more and more with all soule rauishing Comfortes, Your louing friend to his pore power

Jo: SMITH in Ould Baly

LONDON Sept: the 10, 1636

[*Endorsed by Governor Winthrop:*] Mr. Smith tailor.

MATTHEW CRADOCK TO JOHN WINTHROP[1]

HONORED AND MY WORTHEI FREYND, With tender of my best seruice I harteley Com[mend] me to you: I haue received your letter of the 25 June by the ship Falcon by which as also by letter from Jno. Jolliff I take good nottice of your loue to me and reddyness to furder me in my occasyons there for which I yeeld you most hartye thankes and dessyre the contynuance thereof as occasyon shall bee. Were my discoragments but of small Consequence I should bee verry loath to bee troblesome. Errors I knowe I haue Comitted maney and great by reposing trust in maney not worthey to bee trusted. Theise

---

[1] W. 2. 63; 4 *Collections*, VI. 122–124. For Matthew Cradock, see *D.N.B.* Cradock did not actually send this letter to Winthrop until February of the following year, at which time he added a postscript dated February 21, which is printed below (pages 348–349).

errors I must suffer for and ame willing to beare, but would bee loath to haue
that which is bad to bee made worsse and affliction added to affliction. Truley
I will yeet hope mr. Mayhewe will geeue mee that satisfaction in all which
may geeue resonable satisfaction to mee and in so doinge I ame confydent he
will doe himselffe a great deale of right. It were to much for me to relate all
passages vnto you and loth I ame to bee therein offensyue to you with longe
discourses but if it bee so that my seruant Jno. Jolliffe doe not Recieyue satisfaction to Content lett me Crave that favour of you as to Read ouer my letters
wrote mr. Mayhewe which I sent him by Jno. Jolliffe and which I nowe send
him by this Convayance. I must Confesse in regard of the length of them it is
to much troble I putt you vnto, and yeet without hearing them Read you can
not my selffe beeing absent vnderstand wherein I fynd my selffe agreyued, or
whether that I propound and desyre to haue done be resonable or not and I
shall not desyre in aught to bee my owne Judge and because I would bee the
less troblesome to you seeing Mr. Peirse had a great hand at his last beeing in
England in my sending ouer so great an Estate thether as I ded last yeere and
was not wanting to haue had me sent as much this yeere I wish that he also
who Is an Intymate well willer to mr. Mayhewe may seey what I propound
and wherein I fynd my selffe agreyued, and if I Cane haue noe other accounts but by calculacion that the same may bee done with Judgment and
vnderstanding and with your approbacion, and then I shall leaue you to
Judge how I haue thryuen and doe at p[rese]nt thryue in Newe England.
oneley bee pleased I pray you if occasion so Requyre to order Jno. Jolliff with
Mr. Pearse to take some paynes to goe to the depth of my buiseyness, and
what Can not appeare by accounts that to Estymat so as may be equall and
Indifferent boeth for Income and expense, and where ought shall appeare
difficult that you would bee pleased to geeue them your aduize for the better
Cleering of it, and withall to cast your eye vppon the Chardges shalbee layd
vppon me by Estymats that the same doe not exceede whereby my loss should
bee made heauier then really it is or ought to bee. had I Receued that Correspondence from N. E. which I might Justley haue expected in the Course
of my dealing thether the publique had beene partaker thereof ere this more
sensybley but I haue not beene so happey, yeet what shall I say　Mr. Mayhew Is approued of all and I desyre he may still contyneue so and I shalbee
harteley glad thereof as realley wishing his good and welffare, but so as my
welfare also may subsist with his; I knowe noe liberty he hath to trade in
aught For himselfe but the Cleane Contrary by our Covenants which my
seruant Jolliff cane shewe you and they exspire not till about June next. the
Reading of those 2 letters afforemencioned will shewe you more then I cane

heere express, and when your selffe shall haue heard and seeyne all, I ame perswaded you can not propound that For me to doe which I shall not bee Reddy to yeeld vnto. For yf Mr. Mayhewe doe realley approoue his Integrity I shall desyre to Contyneue him in my Imployment according to his owne offer by his Letters Receiued by this shippe, and as I knowe him abell for my buiseynes so I ame perswaded when euer wee parte he will not eseley fynd one so willing to doe him good as I haue beene and ame. I doe once more Intreate your Love Furderance and advize in this buiseynes of myne which doeth much Concerne me to haue my affayres there setteled in some good way and so as I may boeth Cleereley seey what Is become of my estate I haue or showld haue there as also howe for the tyme to come I may haue an equall and Fayre carriadg of my buiseynes. I ame harteley glad to heare of the good approbacion of our Newe Gouvernour there Mr. Vane. the sicknes heere weekeley Increasing wee haue noe relacion nowe to the Court beeing in this Respect as banished men from thence so as I make questyon whether it bee knowen there as yeet. howeuer I trust God will Raise vp freynds and meanes to furder and aduanse his owne worke, yea wee may bee Confident thereof, he will neuer forsake vs if wee forsake not him, and if god be with vs wee neyde not feare who Is agenst vs; I will heere Conclude with harty Com[mendations] from me and myne to your selffe and yours and will Rest euer in owght I may Your assured louing Freynde to bee Commaunded

MATHEWE CRADOCK

LONDON, 13 September 1636

Sir, I haue a purpose to apply my selffe to tylledge and incresing my Stock of Cattell, and hauing had Recourse to a plase caled shaweshynn where I heere none comes but my selffe I desyre your Fauour when the Court shalbee moued in my behalfe that I may haue 2000 Acres there allotted to me where I shall Fynd It most Convenyent For mee. I know the orders made heere in Court allowe me maney thousand acres more then euer I Intend to demand or looke after. This my shuite I hope will geeue offence to none and when I shall sett vp a tenement and a teame as I haue heerewith geeuen order thereabout, I hope in a short tyme others will Followe if once a good mynister bee plased there, and I ame perswaded the more English Corne Is Cherished the better it wilbee For the whole plantacion. I once more take my Leaue and Rest Yours

MATHEWE CRADOCK[1]

---

[1] This postscript is canceled in the original for the reasons set forth in Cradock's later postscript of February 21, 1636/37, printed separately below (pages 348–349).

LONDON PORT BOOK ENTRIES FOR THE *GEORGE*[1]

13 September 1636

In the George of London, master. John Saborne [Severne] for New England: John Wenthorpe esq. for the Plantation in New England. one butt of Spanish wine in rundletts, 610 yards of Darnix with thread, 5 pieces of single velures, 9 Irish ruggs for beds, 15 cwt. wrought iron, 11 barrel of head nails, 2 ordinary yard broad sayes, 1 cwt. of pewter, 110 goads of Northern cottons, 4 dozen shoes, 5 dozen Irish stockings, 600 ells Normandy canvas, 400 ells English linen cloth cost 10 pence an ell, 250 ells of Holland cloth, 6 pieces of Treagar, 100 ells narrow Hamborough linen cloth, 20 pieces sack cloth to make sacks, 24 canvas suits cost 20s 6d a suit, 1 ton of cordage, 1 last of small band pitch and tar, 90 yards of frieze, 4 hhds. of vinegar, 10 cwt. of currants, 7 cwt. of raisins, 5 cwt. of prunes, 56 lbs. of pepper, 56 lbs. of West Indies ginger, ½ cwt. of sugar, 4 doz. tallow candles, 30 cwt. of cheese, and 50 firkins of butter with other things.

14 September 1636

In the George of London master John Severne for New England John Wenthorpe esq. for the Plantation there, 870 yards of Dornix with thread, 2 ordinary yard broad sayes, 1 cwt. pewter, 120 goads of Northern cottons, 80 yards of freizes with others.

WILLIAM LEIGH TO JOHN WINTHROP[2]

To his much honoured and respected Patron mr. John Winthrop Esqr. att his House in Boston in N: England giue these

Grace and Peace from Christ, the Prince of Peace

WORTHIE SIR, meruell not though I write not soe often to you, as some others of my place, calling, and Relation to you would haue done. For I am yet (as always I haue bene,) conscious of mine own weaknes, being not able to write to you of anie thing, which others of farr more abilitie then my self write not of to you.

---

[1] Public Record Office; *Proceedings*, LI. 284.

[2] W. 4. 82; 5 *Collections*, I. 226–230. For William Leigh, rector of Groton, Suffolk, see 4 *Collections*, VI. 177n. For the occasion of this letter, see Lucy Downing to John Winthrop, *ca.* March, 1636/37 (pages 352–354, below).

Et quid est acta agere, nisi insipientis verba sapienti proferre?

But least that proverb might seame to take place in me, out of sight out of mind, know that I make more frequent mention of you, and your whole Companie, before the Throne of grace then is to be expressed with pen and Inke; and if my heart deceiue me not, the loue and inward respect of my hart is as entire to you and yours this daye, as when you were personallie present as my patron in this Towne of Groton; and if I knew in what to express it, I must alwayes, (and will) acknowledg a dept of loue due to you.

But me thinks (worthy patron) I heare you saye, what loue can you shew to me, who shew soe little to the people of god vnder your Charge? for whom you must giue account to god; for whose good my soule melteth within me; and soe much the more, because hoping I had left them a zealous, faythfull, true hearted Minister, I heare since my departure, he is become a fearfull time seruer, and a corrupter of those whom he ought to instruct in doctrine, so that it repenteth me that I called such an one to that place, or left him in it?

Louing Sir, the complant is sore agaynst me, and the argument is strong on your side. For if I loue not gods people of whom I haue the Charge from Christ himself in my Ministerie, I cannot respect you that calld me to that charge att the first. For he that loues his freind will keep carefullie the best depositum of his freind. I must quitt my self from this Crime, or yeild the Conclusion agaynst my self. Know therfore (louing Sir) in the words of sobrietie and truth, that my carefullnes for my Charge is as much, (yea more,) then in the daye of your aboad with vs; my diligenc in preaching as frequent, and my doctrine deliuered as sound, and as pertinent to my peoples estate. For witnes to this truth, I appeale to your Brother Downing, who of his own free choyce, came and liued vnder my Ministerie some part of this summer, to whose iudgment, I referr my self, being not a competent Judg in mine own cause.

But you will saye, what euer your doctrine be, you are giuen to be too ceremonious, a great practiser of them, a great preacher for them, as if that were good food for the souls of your people?

Worthie freind, be iealous, (yet with a godlie iealousie) not with a carnall. Accept my defenc, which is in truth and playnnes of heart, as before god. Know I am not more zealous of Ceremonies this day, then when you first called me to Groton. I then wore the Surpliss, lesse frequentlie for your sake; now more frequentlie for my Ministeries sake. Consider of it well; he that iudges he may weare the Surpliss, and yet will not often, because he will not offend one, may he not weare it often, for the good of manie? I will leaue the Conclusion to your self.

Agayne, for preaching for them, (I witnes before Christ, whose Minister I am) I neuer did it, noe not in the least mention, in anie degre.

In a word, I know how to vse thes Ceremonies for the peace of my ministerie and good of my people. But to be zealous of them, to take them into my sermonds, instead of gods word to his people, I neuer did, and resolue by gods grace neuer to doe.

Bountifull patron, if the saluation of your Sisters soule, and the word of truth, be not as pretious in mine eyes, as mine own, lett Christ require it of me. I professe I neuer was a perswader in anie degree, to keep your Sister from comming ouer to you. It cutt me to the heart, when you bad her to take heed to her soule, least by me she should be ledd into by paths; the Lord of his Grace, keep me in the truth, or att least suffer me to perish alone, that I may not be a Factor for Satans kingdome.

Louing Sir, without breach of godlie loue, I must speake what I think, that you iudg of me in your thoughts as one not worthie to be saluted, naye not to be prayed for; my grounds hereof are

1. you make mention of me in your letter, as of one that is fallen from the truth and power of my Ministerie, and as one to be feared, and avoyded for feare of corruption and contagion.

2. you doe not once witnes anie sorrow for this, in respect to me, as if the losse of my soule in that way were noe care to you.

3. you doe not once send me anie salutations in your letter, much lesse anie aduice, or councell, what to doe. The Apostles sayeing to Archippus, Take heed to the Ministerie thou hast receiued in the Lord, that thou fulfill it, would not haue bene vnseasonable.

4. And, which I most meruell att, in you a godly man, that knows that vproars are in our Church, and that gods Ministers, (especiallie such poore ones as my self) are in daynger of taking hurt, by reason of oppression and trouble, yet you express not one sigh for me, nor one petition to god in my behalfe.

Reuerend Freind, what think you of me? haue I soe fallen as not to be pittied? as not to be saluted? as not to be prayed for? god forbid you should soe think of me. Iudg not according to appearanc, eurie thing reported is not true, euerie offenc committed is not vnto death. Be better informed of me for the present, and be more charitable of me, and my fellow Ministers, for time to come.

It were now a thing vnseasonable to tell you, that I was att a poynt to haue lost liuing and libertie both, for continuing to preach on the Holy dayes, a Task taken vp att your Intreatie onely, without anie worldly profitt to myselfe, as you can witness; yet soe it was. For noe fault being found in me, for matter of Discipline, the reading of the Kings Declaration for the Libertie of the Sabbath, was by Authoritie pressed vpon me, the daye limited in which I should read it, the witnesses appoynted, which when I fayled to doe, my Name was called in publique Court, twice, on 2 solemne dayes, and it was bruted, that I was suspended, but by gods only help I stand free this daye from anie such censure. The cause, and onlie cause hereof, my refusing to cease preaching on the Holy dayes. This is the truth; and I leaue it to your iudgment to make the Conclusion.

And now (beloued brother in Christ) I know you passe iudgment on me, by some report of men, not of your own thoughts onelie, who being godlie, may be deceiued in reports, and may slander, which is a sin, and the greater, if from a godlie person. The seruant of god must not walke about with slanders.

My Apologie is, Agaynst an Elder, receiue not an accusation, but vnder 2 or 3 witnesses; lett it be founde confirmed, before iudgment be passed, soe shall wee not easilie err in iudgment.

And I beseech you, iudg of me as of a Brother, vnited to you in the same true f[aith] of Christ, by the bond of the Spirit, and soe iudging, I will conclude with Saint Paull: Lett brotherlie loue continue.

Lett this large letter possess the place of 2 letters, and giue the reading, and I pray you, if you receiue it, acquaint me with the cause of your soe writing, that if it be possible, our creditt in the ministerie may be recouered with your Congregations, that wee maye pray hartilie one for another, in fayth strengthned by loue. I doe truly salute you in the Lord, in the affection of sincere loue, and wish you aboundant prosperitie in spirituall blessings, without the mixture of anie burthen, soe long as may stand with the will of Christ. But expect it not for euer; false Apostls came into the Churches, when the true had finished theire work. Oportet esse hæræses, is to you a known truth. labor to think of it, and to pray for vs now vnder it.

I hartelie salute your louing wife, whose kindness to her Godson, in the Bible she gaue him, and I with her gift haue bought for him, I hope will be a remembrance of her whils he liues. The Lord hath giuen me 3 Daughters to my son.

The Lord is good to vs this daye, in keeping the Sickness from our dwelling; now gods iudgments are abroad, the Lord by them teach vs in righteousness.

My wife saluts you, and my son craues his Godmothers blessinge. all in Groton of your acquaintance are in health; for the particulars I referr you to the letters of others.

The Lord blesse you, and vs, with all spirituall blessings in heauenlie places in Christ for euer. Your louing freind and sometimes your minister in the Lords seruice

WILLIAM LEIGH

Written att my studie in GROTON September 20, 1636

WILLIAM PYNCHON'S MEMORANDUM OF HIS ACCOUNT WITH JOHN WINTHROP, JR.[1]

Reckned with mr. Jo. Wintrop Junior this 23 Sept. 1636

	li	s	d
dew for the fraight of 16 Tunn in the Blessing at 35s per Tunn	28	0	0
dew for 24 Tunn in the Batchelor 45s per Tunn	54	0	0
Received for the payment of 21 sheep	63	0	0
Paid for the passage of my Son Smyth and 3 daughters and 1 maid	2	10	0
for 36 fatham and ½ y. wamp[um] at 10s	18	5	0
	165	15	0
Resting of the first bill	35	1	8

and 10 otter skins and 4 bever skins weighing 3 li. ½

ROGER WILLIAMS TO JOHN WINTHROP[2]

PROVIDENCE the 24th of the 8th [1636]

SIR, WORTHY AND WELLBELOVED, I was abroad about the Pequt busines when your letter arived, and since Messengers haue not fitted etc.

I therefore now thanckfully acknowledge your Wisedome and Gentlenes in receaving so lovingly my late rude and foolish Lines: You beare with Fooles gladly because you are wise.

I still waite vpon your Loue and Faythfullnes for those poore papers and can not but belieue that your Heart, Tounge and pen should be one, if I were Turke or Jew etc.

Your 6 Quæries I wellcome, my loue forbidding me to surmise that a

---

[1] W. 1. 115. Cf. William Pynchon to John Winthrop, Jr., July 4, 1636 (pages 285–286, above).
[2] W. 2. 107; 4 *Collections*, VI. 233–238; *N. C.*, VI. 7–13.

Pharisee, a Sadduce, an Herodian etc. wrote them: but rather that your Loue and Pitie framed them as a phycitian to the sick etc.

He that made vs these Soules and searcheth them, that made the Eare and Eye and therefore sees and heares I lie not but in his presence haue sadly sequestred my selfe to his holy Tribunall and your Intergatories, begging from his Throne those 7 fiery Lampes and Eyes his holy Spirit to helpe the Scrutinie: desirous to suspect my selfe aboue the old Serpent himselfe and remembring that He that trusteth in his owne hearte is a Foole Prov. 28.

While I answere let me ymportune from your loving breast that good opinion that you deale with one (how euer so and so in your Judgment yet) serious, and desirous in the matters of Gods Sanctuarie to vse (as the double waights of the Sanctuarie teach vs) double Diligence.

Your first Quærie then is this:

What haue you gayned by your new found practices etc.

I confess my Gaines cast vp in mans Exchange are Losse of Friends, Esteeme, Maintenance, etc. but what was Gaine in that respect I desire to count losse for the Excellencie of the Knowledge of Christ Jesus my Lord etc. To his all glorious Name I know I haue gained the honour of one of his poore Witnesses, though in Sackcloth.

To your beloved selues and others of Gods people yet asleepe this Witnes in the Lords season at your waking shall be prosprous, and the Seede sowne shall arise to the greater puritie of the Kingdome and Ordinances of the Prince of the Kings of the Earth.

To my selfe (through his rich grace) my tribulacion hath brought some Consolacion and more Evidence of his Loue, singing Moses his Song and the Lambes in that weake victorie which (through His helpe) I haue gotten ouer *the Beast, his picture, his Marke,* and *Number of his Name* Revel. 15. 2. 3.

If you aske for numbers, the Witnesses are but 2 Revel. 11. and how many millions of Christians in name and Thoughsands of Christians in Heart doe call the Truths (wherein your selfe and I agree in witnessing) Newfound practices?

Gideons Armie was 32 Thoughsand: but Cowardize returned 22 thoughsand back and 9 thoughsand seauen hundreth Worldlings sent but 3 hundreth to the Battell.

I will not by prophecye exasperate, but wish (in the black and stormie day) your Companie be not less then Gideons, to fight (I meane with the Blood of the Lambe and Word of Witnes)[1] for what you professe to see.

---

[1] In the margin: "Revel. 12. 11."

To your 2nd: viz: Is your Spirit as euen as it was 7 yeares since?

I will not follow the Fashion either in Commending or Condemning of my selfe. You and I stand at one dreadfull Dreadfull Tribunall: Yet what is past I desire to forget, and to press forward towards the marke for the price of the High Calling of God in Christ.

And for the euennes of my spirit.

Toward the Lord I hope I more long to know and doe his holy pleasure only: and to be ready not only to be Banished, but to Die in New England for the name of the Lord Jesus.

Towards your selues, I haue hietherto begd of the Lord an Euen Spirit, and I hope euer shall as

First Reverently to esteeme of and tenderly to respect the persons of many hundreths of you etc.

2ndly To reioice to spend and be spent in any service (According to my Conscience) for your Wellfares.

3rdly To reioice to find out the least Swarving in Judgment or practice from the helpe of any euen the least of you.

Lastly to mourne dayly, heavily vncessantly till the Lord looke down from Heaven, and bring all his precious living stones into one New Jerusalem.

To your third viz. Are you not grieved that you haue grieved so many?

I say with Paul I vehemently sorrow, for the Sorrow of any of Zions Daughters, who should euer reioice in her King etc. Yet I must (and O that I had not Cause) grieue, because so many of Zions daughters see not and grieue not for their Soules Defilements, and that so few beare John Companie in weeping after the vnfoulding of the Seales which only Weepers are acquainted with.[1]

You therevpon propound a 4th. Doe you thinck the Lord hath vtterly forsaken vs?

I answere Jehovah will not forsake his people for His great names Sake 1 Sam. 12. That is the fire of his loue towards those whome once he loues is æternall like himselfe: and thus farr be it from me to question his æternall Loue towards you etc. Yet if you graunt that euer you were as Abraham among the Chaldees, Lot among the Sodomites, the Kenites among the Amalekites, as Israell in Egipt or Babell, and that vnder paine of their plauges and Judgments yow were bound to leaue them, depart flie out, (not from the places as in the Type) but from the Filthines of their Sinns etc. and if it proue

---

[1] In the margin: "Revel. 5."

as I know assuredly it shall, that though you haue come farr yet you never
came out of the Wildernes to this Day: then I beeseech you Remember that
your selues and so allso many thoughsands of Gods people must yet mourn-
fully reade the 74, 79, 80, and 89 Psalmes, the Lamentations, Daniells 11th
and Revel. 11, 12th, 13th,[1] and this Sir I beseech you doe more seriously
then euer and abstract your selfe with a holy violence from the Dung heape
of this Earth, the Credit and Comfort of it, and cry to Heaven, to remooue
the stumbling blocks, such Idolls after which sometimes the Lord will giue
His owne Israell an Answere.

Sir You request me to be free with you, and therefore blame me not if I
answere your Request, desiring the like payment from your owne deare hand
at any time in any thing.

And let me add, that amongst all the People of God wheresoeuer scattered
about Babells Bancks either in Rome or England etc. your case is the worst
by farr, because while others of Gods Israell tenderly respect such as desire to
feare the Lord your very Judgment and Conscience leads you to smite and
beate your fellow Servants, expell them your Coasts etc. and therefore, though
I know the Elect shall never finally be forsaken yet Sodomes Egypts Amaleks
Babells Judgments ought to driue vs out to make our Calling out of this
World to Christ, and our Election sure in him.

Sir Your 5th is From what Spirit and to what End doe you driue?

Concerning my Spirit as I said before I could declaime against it, but
whether the Spirit of Christ Jesus, for whose visible Kingdome and Ordinances I witnes etc. or the Spirit of Antichrist (1 John 4) against whome only
I contest doe driue me, let the Father of Spirits be pleased to search and
(worthy Sir) be you allso pleased by the Word to search: and I hope you will
find that as you say you doe, I allso seeke Jesus who was nayled to the Gallowes, I aske the way to lost Zion, I witnes what I belieue I see patiently (the
Lord assisting) in Sackcloth, I long for the bright Appearance of the Lord
Jesus to consume the Man of Sinn: I long for the appearance of the Lambes
Wife allso New Jerusalem: I wish heartily prosperitie to you all Gouernour
and people in your civill way, and mourne that you see not your pouertie,
Nakednes, etc. in spiritualls, and yet I reioice in the hopes that as the way of
the Lord to Apollo, so within a few yeares (through I feare though many
tribulacions) the way of the Lord Jesus the first and most ancient path shall
be more plainely discovered to you and me.

---

[1] In the margin: "All these places and abundant more argue Gods forsaking his people in
respect of the visible Kingdome of the Lord Jesus."

Lastly You aske whether my former Condicion would not haue stood with a gracious Heart etc.?

At this Quærie Sir I wonder much, because you know what Sinnes yea all manner of Sinnes (the Sinn vnto Death excepted) a Child of God may lye in, Instance I neede not.

2ndly When it comes to matter of Conscience that the stroke lyes vpon the very Judgment, that the thing practiced is Lawfull etc. as the polygamie of the Saints, the Building of the Temple (if David had gone on) the many false ministries and ministracions (like the Arke vpon the New Cart) which from Luthers times to this Day Gods Children haue conscientiously practiced: Who then can wonder (and yet indeede who can not but wonder) how a Gracious Heart before the Lords awakening and calling and drawing out may lie in many Abominations?

2 Instances I shall be bold to present you with: First, doe you not hope Bishop Vsher hath a Gracious Heart? and 2ndly Doe you not iudge that your owne Heart was gracious euen when (with the poysoned shirt on your back) you etc.?

But while another iudgeth the Condicion faire, the Soule that feares, doubts, and feeles a Guilt hath broken bones etc. Now worthy Sir I must call vp your Wisedome your Loue your patience your Promise and Faythfullnes, candid Ingenuitie etc. My Head and Actions willing to liue (as the Apostle Paul) καλῶς ἐν πᾶσι. Where I err Christ be pleased to restore me, where I stand, to stablish. *If you please I haue allso a few Quæries* to your selfe *without your leaue I will not:* but will euer mourne (the Lord assisting) that I am no more (though I hope euer) Yours

R: WILL:

Sir Concerning Natiues: the Pequts and Nayantaquits resolue to liue and die togeather and not to yeald vp one: Last night tidings came that the Mauquauogs (the Caniballs) haue slaine some of our Countrimen at Qunnihticut. I hope it is not true.

LION GARDINER TO JOHN WINTHROP, JR.[1]

To the Wors[hi]p[fu]ll Mr. John Winthrope Junior Esquire at Bostowne
in the bay these present

Wors[hi]p[fu]ll Sir, I have received your letter whearein I doe vnderstand that yow are not like to returne, and accordinge to your order I have sent your servaunts Robeart and Sara. I wonder that you did not write to me but it is noe wonder seeing that since your and Mr. Phenix departure there hath beene noe provison sent but one the contrary people to eate vp that small now noe store that wee had heare hath come many vessells with provison to goe vp to the plantations but none for vs it seemes that wee have neather masters nor owners but are left like soe many servaunts whose masters are willinge to be quitt of them but now to late I wish that I had putt my thoughts in practice that was to stay and take all such provisions out of the vessells as was sufficent for a yeare. summer goods gods good providence hath not onely brought but allso stayed but if the could have gone I did intent to have taken all the victualls out and kept them for owre necesitie and seeinge that you Mr. Peeters and Phenwicke knowes that it was agaynst my minde to send the Pequitts present agayne and I with theas few men are by your wills and likeings put into a warlike Condicion there shall be noe Cause to complayne of our Fidelitie and indeavours to you ward and if I see that there be not such Care for vs that our lives may be preserved then must I be forced to shift as the lord shall direct. I wish that it may be for Gods glory and all your Credits and proffitts. heare is not 5 shillings of money and noe bevor the dutch man will bringe vs some Corne and rye but we have noe thinge to pay him for it Mr. Pinchin had a bill to receive all the wampampeige we had we have not soe much as will pay for the mendinge of our ould boate. I haue sent your Cowes vp to the plantations with 2 oxen 2 of them we have killed and eaten with the goates a ramm goate was brought from the Manatos but the Enemie gott him and all the greate swine 22 in one day and had gotten all the sheep and Cowes likewise had we not sallid out it was one the Saboath day and there was 4 men with the Cowes with fierlocks for the sheep I haue kept them thus longe and when the pinckes comes downe I hope the will bringe hay for them for I have not hay for them to eate by the way if I should sent them to the bay but now for our present Condicion since Mr. Phenwicke is gone for England I hope you will not be forgettfull of vs and

---

[1] W. 3. 18; 4 *Collections*, vii. 52–56. For Lion Gardiner, see *D.A.B.*

the matter to hearte and intended to raise a sufficient stocke to furnish all the Colony with necessarys vppon the same terms that we intended only requiring that none should trade with enterlopers who perhaps might marr their markett. Sir I am not worthy to advise those that vnderstand more then I can doe yet I knowe lookers on may see more then such as play the game. I conceive the Condition to be very æquæl considering the Gentlemens intention and cannot see how it may be preiudicial to any vnles perhaps to some few that desire to engross Commoditys to sell them at a dearer rate and soe to take away from others the benefite of a good markett enriching themselvs by their necessitys: an olde mischeife which hath proved a mothe to many stats and may be better prevented in the first forming of a state then remedyed afterwards. I know it will be pretended that all manner of restraint is preiudicial to Liberty and I grant the name of Liberty is pretious soe it be Liberty to doe good but noe farther. Now the good which ought to be respected is Bonum publicum not Privatum Commodum. Salus populi suprema lex was wonte to [be] the Rule. now I would faine know what the General shall gaine by making halfe a dosen rich by pinching more then soe many thousands. Sir I conceive the offer made to be such an advantage vnto you if it be entertained as will not easily be recovered if it be neglected; I heare shopkeeping begins to growe into request amongst you. In former age all kinde of retailing wares (which I confess is necessary for mens more convenient supply) was but an appendixe to some handicraft and to that I should reduce it if I were to advise in the government. Superfluity of Shopkeepers Inholders etc. are great burthens to any place. we in this Towne where I live (though we are somwhat reformed that way) are of my knowledg at Charge 1000*li* per annum in maintaining several familys in that Condition, which we might well spare for better employments wherein their labours might produce something for the common good which is not furthered by such as drawe only one from another and consequently live by the sweat of other mens brows, producing nothing themselves by their owne endevours. Sir if I might advise I wish two sufficient men were sent over with sufficient instructions to conclude an agreement with these Gentlemen who are soe well disposed towards you. I should besides thincke it very convenient and almost necessary to sent on for fishing which is the first means that will bring any income into your lande. Two or three good masters that might bring with them each halfe a dosen good boates masters and three or foure good splitters in all would keepe you a good number of boats at sea, and time would soone bring in many of your owne men to be fitt for that employment. I cannot give directions in particular these two that I have named I take to be matters of great importance, which

I desire to recommend vnto you as one whose hearte I know to be soe firmely bent for the common good. If you conceive my intimations suite not soe well with the present Condition of your state let me sustaine noe blame but from your selfe who I know will beleive that any errour of mine in Judgment is not accompanyed with any ill intention. Sir I heartily wishe and pray the prosperity of you all and desire nothing more then to manifest my selfe Yours in the L[ord]

JOHN WHITE

DORCH: Novemb: 16, 1636

EDWARD GIBBONS TO JOHN WINTHROP, JR.[1]

To the Wor[shipful] John Winthrop esquier Junior at boston guife this

LOVING SUR, my tender louf to you remembered; sur I know that you would bee glad to here of the welfare of this plase and these prosedinges: I can guif you but letel lite intow thinges: and that in my one jugment will not bee much benifetiall to the onors there of   the plase is streung anuf with good wach and direcktion to put mani Indianes to the worst   Mr. Gadenor is karefull so far as I am abel to jouge: but worck gowes heuili of hand: and the worck that wos beegun when you ware here louckes ould for want of fenashing: thi find there stomockes to bee good ther bisnis much: but I fere the profit letel and if sum spedi cors bee not taken the burden will bee so heui tha[t] I know not how it will bee borne: and if it should bee kaust up we must cast up the hole reuor and keape our howsis if we kan here: for the indeanes are ueri insolent: the lord direckt this waye: sur I haue inquered for your thinges but can geat but a small passill   I hope you will understand the reson   thus desiering that you would bee plesed to remember us and our ockkasiones to the god and fathor of Crist Jesus my umbell seruis remembered to your father and mother: your wiuf and all the rest I leafe you in the bosum of a wise god to gide you all in all your godli imploymentes and so I rest your pore 22*li* 20*s* deattor or there aboute

ED: GIBONES

from SEBRUCK the 29 of the 9 mounth 1636

---

[1] W. 4. 83; 5 *Collections*, I. 233–234. For Gibbons, see 5 *Collections*, I. 233*n*.

PROPOSITIONS OF THE CHURCH OF BOSTON[1]

Fyve propositions giuen by some of the Brethren of Boston to some of the Brethren
of Newtowne at a Conference betwixt them at Boston

1. That there is no saveing worke of preparation vppon the soule before Reall vnion with Christ, but such as Hypocrits may reach vnto. Joh. 15.5.

2. That in the Act of Justification Faith is not Active but Receptiue. Joh. 1.12. Rom. 4.4.5.

3. Though the soule be convinced by Reason of the worke of God in him, yet it is no sin vnto him vppon that ground not to beleeve: Hab. 2.4. Heb: 11.1.

4. The soule must first see his person accepted in Justification before he can conclude the truth of his Sanctification, Rom. 3.25. Gen. 4.4.

5. The Spirit doth not vse any worke of Sanctification to perswade me by it of the truth of his testimonie. 1 Joh. 5.6.

These were given to them in writing with consent of vs all. but those 15 which they charge vppon vs were not ours but theires; collected and framed in theire owne termes after we were parted; whereas it was our desire againe and againe when we were together to haue writ downe the differences betwixt them and vs that there might be no mistake, which they promised also to do at last and yet contrary to promise they departed away and refused to write, which we gladly would haue done. And yet afterward they forge these thinges which were not spoken by vs. Indeede some words repeated by them we did vse but not as they are expressed by them; and therefore we haue set downe our owne answer to those 15 propositions in our owne words. You may easily iudge what wrong we suffer when they haue left out all our fyve and instead therof haue 15 put vppon vs: and that these 15 should be carried and shewed to the magistrates and Comittees as Tenents of ours which are theire owne yow may iudg how brotherly and Christianly this is done by them.

1. We say that in our Real vnion with Christ, Christ doe apprehend vs first in order of nature, before we receiue him by faith.

2. The second we vtterly deny as being contrary to our constant professed Judgments.

---

[1] W. 1. 121. The handwriting of this document has not been identified.

3. Our Faith in Justification is not actiue but Receptiue as an earthen wall receiues an Arrow that sticks in it.

4. We deny that any of vs said, It is the only vse of the word to worke Faith: But that it doth worke Faith we said it was because God doth vse it as an ordinance.

5. We deny that any of vs said that Faith after Justification is only Receptiue; but we do acknowledge that it is as well receptiue of all that life which it doth convey to the acting of every spirituall worke after Justification as before Justification.

6. This was our true meaneinge: That the soule goeth not out in it owne strength to fetch fresh Supplies from Christ, but as it is acted by the Spirit of God inhabiting in the soule.

7. That the Soule must first see his person accepted in Justification before he can conclude the truth of his Sanctification.

8. Though the soule be convinced by Reason of the worke of God in himself yet it is no sin vnto him vppon that ground not to beleeue; but it is to beleeue vppon a promise of free Grace applyed vnto him by the word and Spirit of God.

9. We do not deny but the Lord hath Commanded the Soule to believe all Conditional promises: but that God hath not commanded vs to build our Justification vppon a Conditionall promise.

10. He that receiueth his first Comfort from a Conditionall promise, and rests thereon, God wil breake his confidence and Comfort if he saue him.

11. In the Covenant of Grace there is no condition required, but what Christ himself vndertaketh to performe for vs.

12. That the Covenant of Grace is made imediatly with Jesus Christ, and in him vnto his Church his mysticall body.

13. We say that a person may be in Christ as a branch in the vine, and may have Sanctification from the bloud of Christ and faith in the name of Christ (though not to receiue Christ) and yet fall away and be damned.

14. We said that Paul, Act. 23.1. Spake of his good conscience as well before his conversion as after (though there was a great difference of the goodnes of it) and if any man may plead right to a Conditionall promise by his Legal Righteousnes, Paul might much more before his conversion.

15. We deny that the only way to try the Spirit is by the Spirit, for we are also to try it by the word: but we sayd that the Immediat Revelation of the Spirit is not vppon any worke of God in vs: but in an absolut promise of free

grace perswadeinge the soule of his interest in Christ, and that this is the infallible certaine evidence of our Justifyed estate.

[*Ca.* December, 1636]

[*Endorsed:*] Propositions of the Churches of Boston to those of Connecticut.[1]

JOHN TYNDAL TO MARGARET WINTHROP[2]

To his much honored Aunt Mrs. Winteroppe these præsent

MOST LOVINGE AUNT, thinke not though I haue bin in an error a long time, I am hardned in it, or intend to make my silence as perpetuall as your fauors haue bin largely bestowed. I confesse they weere soe great that they put my shamefast expræssion soe much out of countenance that it can scarce recouer itts blushinge, much lesse growne soe præsumptuous as to conceiue that it can giue the least satisfaction, yet least you shold thinke this distance shold make mee forget my obligation, I nowe wright and offer the due deuotion of a loyall hart to your imbraces who shall bee neuer truly happy longer then you please to loue him. Your most obedient nephew

JOHN TYNDALE

From MAPLESTEAD MAG: this ii of December Anno Domini 1636

I pray præsent my humble dutie to my vncle, my best respects and humble seruice to my cousins.

THOMAS SHEPARD TO JOHN WINTHROP[3]

To the right Woo[rshipfu]ll Mr. Winthrop dwelling at Boston be these delivered

DEAR SIR, I receiued by your reuerend pastour Mr. Wilson, two of your papers, the first I call your Declaration, vizt. That a man is justifyed by fayth, and not before he beleeueth; the 2d I call your Pacification wherin your

---

[1] This endorsement is written in what appears to be an eighteenth-century hand. It seems more likely that this document is connected with the episode related by Winthrop in his Journal under date December, 1636 (I. 203–207), than with some episode in early Connecticut history.

[2] W. 4. 84; 5 *Collections*, I. 234–235. John Tyndal was the son of Deane Tyndal, Margaret Winthrop's eldest brother.

[3] W. 3. 70; 4 *Collections*, VII. 257–265. For the occasion of the writing of this letter, see the entry in Winthrop's Journal under date December 10, 1636 (I. 201–206, especially 206).

godly endeauour is to quiet and still those tumults, which your wisdom may foresee will arise in the Churches concerning Justification by fayth, as its conceiued by some, and contradicted by others; now it was his desire and your own too as he intimated to me that I would read them ouer, and then come and speake with yow; which I did intend to do, the last Thursday, but that your being with the Gouernour kept me from the speech of yow; and had I had but time this weeke I had came to yow, but being hindred I thought it fit to send vnto yow my thoughts by way of wrighting, vntill we speake together, if so yow thinke fit; when I read the question in your declaration, I did woonder and greaue that I should liue to see the liberty of mens spirits, not only to deny so playne a truth, but that they should abolish the very forme of wholsom woords of truth which the apostle exhorts Timothy to keepe as well as the truth itselfe; in saying a man is justifyed without fayth, when the truth and forme of woords in scripture is that we are justifyed by fayth; and surely it hath not done me a little good to see your spirit contending for the fayth, once deliuered to the Saynts, Jude: 3: and seeking to preuent errours in there beginning; which I earnestly desire of god yow may still doe, both by woord and wrighting; yet its a great scruple in my thoughts (and I leaue it with yow to consider of) whether it will be most safe for yow to enter into the conflict with your pen (though the Lord hath made yow very able and fit for it) or if yow doe, whether then so largely; it being an easy thing for a subtill adversary to take aduantages at woords, or if yow doe wright more breefly, whether yow do not think it most meet to leaue them to the view of some of your freinds, before yow send them to him yow haue to trade withall; I confesse it would be a worke worth your labour, if yow could by woord or pen gather from them the full meaning of there minds wherein they differ from others, but otherwise I much question priuate duells with some kind of spirits; and therefore if yow should thinke it fit in your wisdom to forbeare wrighting for a while, I perceiue it would be most safe for yow; I would also intreat of yow not to send these papers as they are, in regard of some things I haue obserued according to my little time obserued in them; which I haue in faythfulnes yet in respect and submission to your better judgement sent herein vnto yow, not with a spirit to contradict, or to dispute it with yow, (for I am most vnfit) but with an humble desire that yow would be pleased to haue a few second thoughts of some passages, of which some seeme to me to be doubtfull and some others to swerue from the truth; perswading my hart of your sincere loue and respect and readines to see euery truth of Christ, and that if I doe mistake yow will out of your loue be ready to lend me better light; I shall not send yow my thoughts concer[n]ing all that which yow haue written, but according to my time, (which is but little, to be busied in matters of this nature,) I haue pickt out some things which I feare your aduersary may take aduantage at, or your freinds, offence at.

1. In your Declaration, your arguments are very weighty and strong and I wholly and gladly assent to all, only may it please yow to consider of these things which I gleane here and there.

1. In your 5 argument: your woords are out of the parable of the sower; A man must haue an honest and good hart, before the woord can haue any sauing effect; that is as I expound breefly, Before the woord woorke fayth to beleeue to Justification, the hart must be made honest and good, in preparation; which tho it be a truth which for the substance of I haue euer held and would not deny; yet an aduersary will or may take much aduantage vpon the starting of so deepe and doubtfull a question; and may keepe yow off from the pursuit of his errours, by pursuing yow for this, wherin he knowes many of your freinds that would stand by yow in other controuersies, will be agaynst yow in this; and so while yow are about to conuince them of errours, they will proclayme your selfe to hold foorth worse.

2: In your clearing vp that some woorke of god in vs may stand with free grace, yow haue this expression, that Adam did not only loose Gods Image, but himselfe and should haue dyed childles had not Christ purchased a repriuall or vniversall redemption: I grant an vniuersall redemption and saluation in your sence; yet whether Adam for sin should have bin annihilated as your woords seeme to imply, or dyed childles, is very doubtfull; for Adam like the great parlament man of the woorld stood as a generall person; so that as if he had stood all his posterity should not only haue had beinge but blessednes; so (it was the couenant) if he fell, his posterity should not only partake of being by him, but eternall curse and misery by him; for it was not the couenant doe and liue, Sin and yow and your posterity shall not haue a being, but yow shall dy and haue a miserable being.

3: in your discouery of Justice in justification the glory of which god aimes at as well as of his mercy; yow haue this expression, God could not be just, vnles he should make a sinner close with Christ for justification by fayth; (which is thus far true, because tis his reuealed will to haue it soe, and hence tis just it should be soe) yet your proofe is doubtfull because else Esau might accuse god of justifying Jacob, vnjustly, vnles god had this to stop his mouth; Jacob did beleeue, Esau would not: Answ: 1: This answer beares a colour of Arminianism, which I beleeue your soule abhors; 2: this seemes to make fides, qua opus to concur to the satisfaction of Justice, or at least to be part of the matter of our justification, which you know diuines dispute agaynst; 3: in such a way of reasoning why might not Esau reply vpon the Lord agayne, and say he is an accepter of persons, in that when they were both alike, he should giue Jacob power to beleeue, and would not giue any vnto him:

4: in the 9 Arg: That the couenant of grace to wright his lawes in our harts; yow expound to be the law of Fayth. Answ: This is true, in part; but the cheefe meaning of the promise seemes rather to be of our conformity in our renewed Image to the morall law; which god promiseth to wright in our harts, as he writ the law it selfe in tables of ston:

5. In the last argument, as god and man concur to be the meritorious cause of Justification, god and the woord of man to be the instrumentall causes of it, so god and the fayth of man concur as the formall cause of justif[ication]. Answ: 1. this seemes to make fayth no instrumentall cause of our justif[ication] but god and the woord: 2: Diuines haue disputed it out, that as infusion of grace is the forme of Sanctif[ication] so Imputation of righteousnes and grace is the forme of Justification; and then how can god and fayth be the cause of it:

In your Pacification: me thinkes I see the sweetnes of your spirit inclining and deuising for peace and truth if possible; but herein many things (all I cannot name vnto yow) are very doubtfull to me; which I hope yow will see into, and see also a good hand of prouidence that your papers are not sent, as yet:

1. Your 7 Propositions deserue much scaning. Ile note 3 of them only.

Your 2 prop: That all the woorkes of god done in time are but the manifestion of god or declaration of his eternall counsell or manifestation of his Attributes. Answ: Ens primum et ens a primo, differunt tota spec: hence tho the Attributes and counsells of god are manifested in and vpon the creature, as Lux non videtur nisi in opaco; yet it cannot be properly sayd that they are the very manifestation of gods Attributes and counsells; for as Opticks obserue of Light that its not seene vnles it be in opaco; yet we cannot define the Body to be the manifestation of light, tho light be manifested vpon it.

Your 5 prop: Election is of gods free grace, without respect of any thing in the creature; Answ. Tis true nothing in the creature can be a motiue cause or condition of election, antecedenter; but yet it may be and is the effect of election, consequenter; for we are elected not because we were holy, but that we might be holy. Eph: 1: 5: hence in that sence god hath a respect to what he will woorke in the creature, accord[ing] to his free election; for I could neuer tell how to auoyd the dint of Armin[ian] arguments till Dr. Twisse helped me with more cleere light to see his coordination of homo condendus, conditus, lapsurus et rediturus to be the objectum prædestinationis; so that god in election hath respect to the creature beleeuing: i. e. that shall be made to beleeue by him:

Your 7. All the Elect are righteous holy and the sons of god in Christ from all eternity: Answ. Not actually, for then how could they be child[ren] of wrath by nature? but intentionally only in gods decree and purpose.

2: *Your Conclusions*

1 Con[clusion]: That Justification is not as tis commonly taken an act of god absoluing the creature from sin, for that was done before in gods eternall counsell: But a Declaration of it by a woorke in and vpon the creature in time, being righteous before in Christ: and for this purpose yow quote diuerse scriptures, which I thinke not needfull to answer: Answ: 1: There is a 3 fold Justification as it appeares to vs; 1: intentionall in gods decree and secret purpose of election; 2: purchased Justification, which was perfected by on offring of Christ in Redemption: 3. actuall or communicated Justification, which is in vocation and so continues while sin and life continue; now tho I grant God did justify the sinner intentionally from before all woorlds, 2: and that a man was righteous before he had a being, that is meritoriously; yet I see not any ground how it can be sayd a man was actually justifyed or righteous before he beleeued, or how actually clothed with Christs righteousnes, (which garment was made for him in redemption) before he put on the garment by fayth; the considering of this distinction is a thread to lead out of many errours; 2: In your Declaration, yow shewed that fayth did more then declare a man to be justified, but here yow make it only a declaratiue cause of it: 3: Its granted that fayth doth declare our Justification, but it doth more also, which God would haue joyned not separated: 4: To make fayth a declaratiue cause or euidence of our justification, will not bring any pacification (which is your scope) for my selfe haue bin told and tis generally professed, that a man must see his Justif[ication] before fayth can declare it, and when it doth declare it tis but a candle in the sun: but I desire yow to consid[er] the arguments yow produce:

1 Arg[ument]

Rom: 1: 17: The righteousnes of god is reuealed by fayth; 1: Euery act of fayth declares a man righteous: Resp. There seemes to me to be 2 things included in these woords of this verse: 1: that not fayth but the gospell reueales a righteousnes: i: a purchased righteousnes for all them that beleeue; 2: that this righteousnes is not only declared but obtayned and applyed by fayth, and so a man is actually justifyed.

presented my humble duty to my aunt and a trew tender of the
my seruice to yee both I beseech you if you find any curious flow
me with some and in all things commande Your obedient Neph
                                                                      D

[Ca. 1637]

[*Endorsed by Governor Winthrop:*] Sir Drew Deane.

RICHARD ELLIOTT TO THE COURT OF ASSIS

To the Right Worshipfull John Winthrop Esquier Gouernor deli

TO THE HONNORABLE COURT AT BOSTON, I Confesse and Ack
I have sinned against the Great God of heaven and Earth be
fencis which I haue committed   I acknowledge that I haue d
hear and eternall destruction hear after, but hear is my comf
mercifull and desires not the death of any that truely Repe
heauen knoweth that I speake out of a Trobled minde and g
I speake it not because I am hear but I hope the Worke of god
mee for I have made a promise god helping mee to keepe it ne
the like soe longe as I haue to liue   I am not Eloquent neat
what the lord hath putt in to my hart but thus I saie it is goo
am afflicted. I desire not to troble you with many words but
of my sorrow I speake. the lord of heauen make mee an Instr
ing honnor vnto his name as I haue dishonnored it which I
power labore for to doe the lord helpe mee to keepe my vow
poore Sarvant   RIC

[Ca. 1637]

GEORGE LUDLOW TO ROGER WILLIA

WORTHY SIR, It should seeme that there is a mistake; for
to Mr. Coxwell for the goods I had the last yeare of yow; An
paid Mr. Mayhew 8*li* in lue of the 3 goats I should give yo

---

¹ W. 1. 118.
² W. 4. 90; 5 *Collections*, 1. 250–251. George Ludlow, a brother of Rog
admission as a freeman in Massachusetts in 1630, but his permanent plac
Virginia. See *Virginia Magazine of History and Biography*, XXIX (July, 1921), 3

2 Arg[ument]

The same answer will serue for this too.

3 Arg[ument]

If our pardon should be in time then there should be a change in god:
Answ: The frame of the whole woorld was not actually made when he intended to make it for then it should be ab æterno; and yet the actuall making of it doth not make any change in god, or in his counsell; so tho a man be not actually justified ab æterno, but intentionally only; yet our actuall justif[ication] in time doth not make any change in god or his counsell, but rather establisheth gods vnchangeable counsells, in that he is as good in deeds as in his intentions; the execution of gods counsells cannot make gods counsells changeable; amor beneuolentiæ toward the elect is long before amor complacentiæ, which is in time.

4 Arg[ument]

I perswade my selfe when yow consider what hath bin said will appeare to your selfe of no great weight: for our title to Justif[ication] and acceptance, is giuen vs at on instant and for euer; but the fruition of our justification especially in foro conscientiæ is oft renewed; Justification is on continued act on gods part all our life time, and hence we may be oft, nay euery day and moment really pardoned, as well as declaratiuely.

5 Arg[ument]

To this I answer; take 2 beleeuers in Christ they are not more justified on then the other; no farther then on hath more sins pardoned then another; but a hypoc[rite] and a beleeuer, the on may be and I am sure is not only declaratiuely but really more justified then the other, both before god and men.

6 Arg[ument]

To the 6 I answer this place of Mary having much forgiven her prooues euidently that loue justifies and consequently woorkes as well as fayth; because these declare and that sometimes more euidently then fayth (as some thinke) that a man is justified.

7 Arg[ument]

Answ. Not only declare them to be couered, but be a means to lead to Christ wherby they may be actually couered.

Arg[ument] 8

The summe of the verse is this, that Abell offring his sacr[ifice]
manifested to be a righteous person, by some speciall tok[en]
(some thinke fire from heauen) which is a good argument th[at]
obedience flowing from fayth may euidence a mans justifi[cation]
notice from god but cannot prooue that a man by fayth is [made]
righteous:

This is your 3 conclusion and proofes: now the 4 Con[clusion]
you say fayth puts vs not into Christ, nor Christ into vs, s[o the]
whole current of scripture, which without manifest wresti[ng]
sayd; I need not name them; and the proofe of it that fa[ith is the evi]
dence of things not seene; that is not any description, bu[t]
fidei, as Erasmus and Ames notes ag[ainst] the Papists [who would place]
fayth only in the mind: and tis true it is an euidence of t[hem]
all.

Your 5 Con[clusion]

In gods eternall counsell fayth repentance Christ crea[ted all]
things are together, and seeme vnico intuitu; thus I hau[e used a]
playnnes which I hope yow will beare with, sent yow [my]
thoughts of your notes; which yow may please to conside[r]
as whether to send so large answers of your mind or noe [in such]
hast. The god of all grace and peace liue and dwell wit[h]
yow a hart to contend for the fayth once deliuered to t[he saints in]
the L[ord] Jesus

NEWTOWN [*ca.* December 15, 1636]

SIR DREW DEANE TO JOHN WIN[THROP]

For my much honoured vnkle Jhon Wintherop Esqr. gouer[nour]
these deliver

WORTHY SIR, you may receiue more lines but not [more love]
in any mans seruice then you shall alwayse finde in [me]

---

1 W. 12. 117. Sir Drew Deane, born January 31, 1605/06, son of [... son]
of Margaret Winthrop) and Anne Drury Deane, was a graduate of [... He]
was knighted in 1627, became Justice of the Peace for Essex in 1637, [See]
Venn, *Alumni Cantabrigienses*, Part I, II. 25.

---

but I conceaue that there will be some more money due to yow for the goats
more than the 8*li*; And as for the other house watch which yow value at 30 or
40*s* I assure yow it is not sold; and I had left it soe farr vpp the Countrey that
when I came away I could not fetch it; but and please god yow shall have a
returne of it the next Spring; and as for the Cowe and tobacco; the tobacco
I had brought for yow but since my comeing our barke sunck and the tobacco
tooke wett and was spoyled with much more of myn owne, but the next yeare
yf yow please, yow shall have soe much againe; And for the heifore soe it was
that I could not bring her by reason I could gett [*torn*]; And for the present I
cannot sattisfie yow for it by reason of my great losses; but yf yow please (And
the lord blesse me) and my endeavours I will sattisfie yow for the heifer and
the rest in Corne this next yeare; I doe intend god willing to be with yow ere
longe and then I shall better explaine my self vnto yow then now I cann by
writeing; I assure I shall and will deale as fairely with yow as with any; Soe
being glad to heare of hope of your recovery desireing the lord to continue it
with my love and service remembered I shall desire ever to rest Yours truly
to power

[*Ca.* 1637]   GEO: LUDLOWE

[*Note, in the handwriting of Roger Williams:*] mr. Coxall hath a letter of particulars, but in this Mr. Ludlow acknowledgeth 1st an Heifor which was mine
4 yeares since   the increase of her is mine.
  2ndly vpwards of 4 score waight of Tobacco.
  3rdly consideracion aboue 8*li* for 3 goats due to me when they were almost
2 yeare since about 4*li* a goate, as allso their increase.
  4thly an house watch.
  5thly Another new gowne of my wiues new come forth of England and cost
betweene 40 and 50 shillings.

HUGH PETER TO JOHN WINTHROP[1]

To the right Wor[ship]full John Winthrop Esqr. Boston

DEEREST SIR, I cannot let so many dayes and nights passe without speaking
with you, and now I am at it I haue little to say but that I long to haue your

---

presumably forwarded to Governor Winthrop by Roger Williams with the letter printed in 4 *Collections*, VI. 212.
  1 W. 2. 49; 4 *Collections*, VI. 92.

ioyes and peace to continue full; and that much of my comfort is wrapt vp in yours. A little newes I had out of a late letter come to hand out of Eng: which you may tell the Gouern[ou]r from me to make him laugh viz: that there was a fast in Eng: and at Bristow in one Church whilst they were preaching a great Bull broke into the churchyard and a company of boyes followed him with squibs. the people within were taken vp before with thoughts that the papists that day would rise, and had warding all the Country ouer; the Bull and the squibs so wrought vpon their melancholy braynes that one cryes out if I perish Ile perish here, another swounds away, another they are come they are come   Mr. Prichard the preachers wife cryes to her husband in the pul-pit, come downe (husband) come downe the tyme is come, and much of this. At Taunton brimstone was smelt in the church and such another Combustion as when Trestrams boy gote into the fryars Cools. In hast I rest Yours and euer so

H: PETER

SALEM 2d day [*ca.* 1637]

We desire a day of thanksgiuing 4th day sennight. I haue wished this bearer to buy me some bees.

JOHN WHITE TO JOHN WINTHROP[1]

To my honoured freind John Winthrope Esqr. at Boston in New-England deliver

SIR, I much reioyce to heare of the welfare of your selfe and the rest of our freinds vnto whom I cannot but present my hearty affections although God deny me the happines to see your persons. I conceive you doubt not of my vnfeined desire of your good which makes me the bolder to lay open vnto you the thoughts of my soule. The rumors of your affairs which are diversly repre-sented vnto vs according to the different humors of the persons from whom they come, as they give me noe foundation to builde on, soe withal they seeme to me to serve insteed of Jonathans arrows, and to pointe at those things which either men naturally are prone vnto or at least which other men desire to have soe that wish ill vnto your estates, which I know makes you the more careful to cutt of occasion from those that seeke occasion. I presume not to give you advise but desire you to remember that as Liberty is sweet soe it is apte (as it is with sweet meats) to allure men to Excess, which made the wise

[1] W. 4. 90; 5 *Collections,* I. 251–254.

man give that Caveat Prov. 25. 16. Hast thou found hony? eate soe much as is sufficient etc. You are wise to vnderstand my meaning which is noe more but this that if the providence and wisdome of some prevent it not you may be as much endangered by your liberty as we are by our bondage. I cannot insiste in particulars but desire you to have an eye to one thinge that you fall not into that evil abroad which you laboured to avoyd at home to binde all men to the same Tenets and practise in things which when they are well examined will be found Indifferent. I have not leisure to dispute but desire you only to take notice that some of the maine things which are insisted on with you as matters of absolute necessity are esteemed by all godly Ministers that euer I spake withall amongst vs small things as if they be alowable yet at best are and will be found only things of Conveniency. I have seene and pervsed such arguments as are produced to maintaine them which will not hold when they come to scanning. But above all things lett me request you to avoyd that rocke of separation which if you once light on you will finde will shake you in peices. I would not give this intimation but that I see already soe much that makes me exceedingly feare in some whom I forbeare to name a stronge inclination that way which if it hold on will appeare in time. To leave matters of this nature for your civil affairs. The longer you differ fishing and vse of other means that may bring you in some supplys the more you weaken your body and will ere longe make it wholy vnfitt for those remedys which may helpe it now but hereafter will come to late. Againe it is high time that a Magazine out of which needful provisions might be had at a reasonable hand were erected, and shopkeepers made vnvseful who will prove soe many moaths to their neighbours. I highly approve their way that make shopp keeping only an appendixe to some handicrafte. A thirde thinge which I heartily wish to be seriously thought on is the education of youth you have the Low-Contrys a patterne for Industry. I wish I could present you any other for family discipline. A great parte of your body hath ben vnaccustomed to laborious courses who will very hardly be brought vnto them in their age, all the hope is in training vp the youth in time. Sir I know your hearty affections to the welfare of that place and people to which you have ben more vsefull then any other person amongst you which makes me open my hearte soe boldly to you in private desiring you to burne my letter when you have pervsed it.

A worde or too of my private. I heare John Sweet hath overthrowen me in a suite in your Courte: I say me for if my words be the ground of his suite I must and will save the Company harmeles against whom he commenced it. I little thought that fellow who ows his being in that place vnto my selfe and my freinds would have lift vp his heele against me   he knows and I can make it appeare that our kindnes to him hath cost vs a great deale more then he requires. The words that he reports me to have spoken I remember not nor believe that I ever spoke them as they were alledged   But if he would needs have satisfaction is a suite in law the first intimation of ones demande of recompence for a wronge received? This vnkinde passage hath wrought more on me then perhaps it would on the hearte of a wise man, but Sir lett me desire that seing that he hath gone that way to worke he may not add a second wronge to the former to lay that on others which in conscience can be required of none but myselfe. But seing he takes pleasure in suits I believe we shall ere long paye him home in his owne Coyne. A worde more for my neighbour Mr. Wey of this place who hath ben an hearty freind to N. Engl. hath servants in the bay, who as it seems are not soe indifferently respected in their lott as they ought to be   they desire to open their case to you and I know you will doe them right, which I leave to your care and wisdome. Sir I beseech you pardon my boldnes in opening my hearte vnto you. Now the Lord abondantly multiply his blessings on you and guide you in the best waye that you may be a second Mordecay to that people whose welfare with your owne I commend vnto the grace of God resting Yours in the L[ord]

JOHN WHITE

[*Ca.* 1637]

STEPHEN WINTHROP TO JOHN WINTHROP[1]

SIR, I dellivered your Note to Mr. Nowell and he went with me to the men and they have let me have your hoggs, but they demand Large satisfaction for so litell harme   I have not fully agreaed with them but shall delay vntill I speake with you: the Sagamore hath sent you a Goose which I have sent by this bearer: I have not sent you the rest of the Beife yet because I know not your Mind fully, for Allin is coume vp and hath brougt noe other, nor noe direction from you what we should doe, but If you will have it coume downe, I will send it: I have sent downe the tounge. Your Obeidient Sonne

STEPHEN WINTHROP

[*Ca.* 1637]

---

1 W. i. 107.

THOMAS SHEPARD TO JOHN WINTHROP[1]

D[EAR] SIR, I returne vnto yow many harty thankes for your kind acceptance of my letter, though it might haue appeared too playne and rude vnto yow and so deserue your Censure;[2] it hath gladded many of our harts to see your hart and the truth embracing e[a]ch other, euen tho errour for peace sake hath pleaded for entertaynment, which yow haue turnd out of your hart and house and town to vs to burne to death: the hæretick is yet kept prisoner but we intend to see justice executed on him accordinge to your desire. It would be a woorke of singular benifit and vse to wyar-draw by way of question and doubt those hidden misteries which may be the causes of diuision; for I feare there is aliquid incognitionis, which will in time appeare; errour hath bin euer fruitfull, and commonly false opinions which creepe out of doores and appeare in the battayle, are but the stragglers of the great army, which tho they be taken prisoners, yet little good will be done, because they haue a party within which will renew the battayle when occasion serues; there is a kind of religion in the woorld which the author of it calls the Vn-knowing of a mans selfe, which is a mistery I must not open; the god of heauen still fill yow and preserue yow holy and faythfull to his cause and truth euen vntill death: I am in much hast and haue no leysure this day to come to Boston, when I doe I shall acknowledge your loue; thus in great hast I rest,
Yours in the L[ord] Jesus

THO. SHEPARD

[*Ca.* January, 1636/37]

JOHN WINTHROP'S RELATION OF HIS RELIGIOUS EXPERIENCE[3]

In my youth I was very lewdly disposed, inclining unto and attempting (so far as my yeares enabled mee) all kind of wickednesse, except swearing and scorning religion, which I had no temptation unto in regard of my education. About ten yeares of age, I had some notions of God, for in some great frighting or danger, I have prayed unto God, and have found manifest

---

[1] W. I. 140; 2 *Proceedings*, v. 104.

[2] Presumably his letter of *ca.* December 15, 1636 (pages 326–332, above); but see also his letter of *ca.* May 20, 1637 (pages 415–416, below).

[3] Original not located; *L. and L.*, II. 165–174. The text as here given is that of the copy made by Henry Dunster in his Notebook (119–123), which is in the Society's library.

answer; the remembrance whereof many yeares after made mee think that God did love mee, but it made mee no whit the better.

After I was 12 yeares old, I began to have some more savour of Religion, and I thought I had more understanding in Divinity then many of my yeares; for in reading of some good books I conceived, that I did know divers of those points before, though I knew not how I should come by such knowledge (but since I perceived it was out of some Logicall principles, whereby out of some things I could conclude other) yet I was still very wild, and dissolute, and as years came on my lusts grew stronger, but yet under some restraint of my naturall reason; whereby I had the command of myself that I could turne into any form. I would as occasion required write letters etc. of meer vanity; and If occasion were I could write others of savory and Godly counsell.

About 14 years of age, being in Cambridge, I fell into a lingring feaver, which took away the comfort of my life. For being there neglected, and despised, I went up and down mourning with my self; and being deprived of my youthfull joyes, I betook my self to God, whom I did believe to bee very good and mercifull, and would welcome any that would come to him, especially such a yongue soule, and so well qualifyed as I took my self to bee; so as I took pleasure in drawing neer to him. But how my heart was affected with my sins, or what thoughts I had of Christ I remember not. But I was willing to love God, and therefore I thought hee loved mee. But so soon as I recovered my perfect health, and met with somewhat els to take pleasure in, I forgot my former acquaintance with God, and fell to former lusts, and grew worse then before. Yet some good moodes I had now, and then, and sad checks of my naturall Conscience, by which the lord preserved mee from some foule sins, which otherwise I had fallen into. But my lusts were so masterly as no good could fasten upon mee, otherwise then to hold mee to some task of ordinary dutyes, for I cared for nothing but how to satisfy my voluptuous heart.

About 18 yeares of age, (being a man in stature, and understanding as my parents conceived mee) I married into a family under Mr. Culverwell his ministry in Essex; and liveing there sometimes I first found the ministry of the word to come home to my heart with power (for in all before I found onely light) and after that I found the like in the ministry of many others. So as there began to be some change which I perceived in myself, and others took notice of. Now I began to come under strong exercises of Conscience: (yet by fits onely). I could no longer dally with Religion. God put my soule to sad tasks sometimes, which yet the flesh would shake off, and outweare still. I had withal many sweet invitations which I would willingly have intertained, but the flesh would not give up her interest. The mercifull Lord would not thus bee answered, but notwithstanding all my stubbornesse and unkind rejections of mercy, hee left mee not till hee had overcome my heart to give up it selfe to him, and to bid farewell to all the world, and untill my heart could answer, Lord what wilt thou have mee to doe?

Now came I to some peace and comfort in God and in his wayes, my cheif delight was therein, I loved a Christian, and the very ground hee went upon. I honoured a faythfull minister in my heart and could have kissed his feet: Now I grew full of zeal (which outranne my knowledge and carried mee sometimes beyond my Calling) and very liberall to any good work. I had an unsatiable thirst after the word of God and could not misse a good sermon, though many miles off, especially of such as did search deep into the Conscience. I had also a great striveing in my heart to draw others to God. It pitied my heart to see men so little to regard their soules, and to despise that happiness which I knew to bee better than all the world besides which stirred mee up to take any opportunity to draw men to God, and by successe in my endeavors I took much encouragement hereunto. But those affections were not constant but very vnsetled. By these occasions I grew to bee of some note for religion (which did not a little puffe mee up) and divers would come to mee for advice in Cases of Conscience; and If I heard of any that were in trouble of mind I usually went to comfort them; so that upon the bent of my spirit this way and the successe I found of my endeavors, I gave up my selfe to the study of Divinity, and intended to enter into the ministry If my freinds had not diverted mee.

But as I grew into employment and credit thereby, so I grew also in pride of my guifts, and under temptations which sett mee on work to look to my evidence more narrowly than I had done before (for the great change which God had wrought in mee, and the generall approbation of good ministers and other Christians, kept mee from makeing any great question of my good Estate,) though my secrett Corruptions, and some tremblings of heart (which was greatest when I was among the most Godly persons) put me to some plunges; but especially when I perceived a great decay in my zeale and love, etc. And hearing sometimes of better assurance by the seale of the spirit, which I also knew by the word of God, but could not nor durst say that ever I had it; and finding by reading of Mr. Perkins and other books that a reprobate might (in appearance) attaine to as much as I had done; finding withal much hollownes and vaine glory in my heart, I began to grow very sad, and knew not what to doe. I was ashamed to open my case to any minister that knew mee; I feared it would shame my self and religion also, that such an eminent professour as I was accounted, should discover such Corruptions as

I found in my selfe, and had in all this time attained no better evidence of salvation; and I should proove a hyprocrite it was too late to begin anew: I should never repent in truth, haveing repented so oft as I had done. It was like Hell to mee to think of that in Hebr. 6. Yet I should sometimes propound questions afarre off to such of the most Godly ministers as I mett, which gave mee ease for the present, but my heart could not find where to rest; but I grew very sad, and melancholy; and now to hear others applaud mee, was a dart through my liver; for still I feared I was not sound at the root and sometimes I had thoughts of breaking from my profession, and proclaime my self an Hypocrite. But those troubles came not all at once but by fits, for sometimes I should find refreshing in prayer, and sometimes in the Love that I had had to the saints: which though it were but poor comfort (for I durst not say before the Lord that I did love them in truth) yet the Lord upheld mee, and many times outward occasions put these feares out of my thoughts. And though I had knowne long before the Doctrine of free Justification by Christ and had often urged it upon my owne soul and others, yet I could not close with Christ to my satisfaction. I have many times striven to lay hold upon Christ in some promise and have brought forth all the Arguments that I had for my part in it. But instead of finding it to bee mine, I have lost sometimes the fayth of the very generall truth of the promise, sometimes after much striveing by prayer for fayth in Christ, I have thought I had received some power to apply Christ unto my soule: but it was so doubtfull as I could have little comfort in it, and it soon vanished.

Upon these and the like troubles, when I could by no meanes attaine sure and setled peace; and that which I did get was still broken off upon every infirmity; I concluded there was no way to help it, but by walking more close with God and more strict observation of all dutyes; and hereby though I put my self to many a needlesse task, and deprived my self of many lawful Comforts, yet my peace would fayle upon every small occasion, and I was held long under great bondage to the Law (sinne, and humble my self; and sinne, and to humiliation againe; and so day after day) yet neither got strength to my sanctification nor betterd my Evidence, but was brought to such bondage, as I durst not use any recreation, nor meddle with any worldly businesse, etc. for fear of breaking my peace (which even such as it was, was very pretious to mee) but this would not hold neither for then I grew very melancholy and mine own thoughts wearied mee, and wasted my spirits.

While I wandred up and downe in this sad and doubtfull estate (wherein yet I had many intermissions, for the flesh would often shake of this yoake of the law, but was still forced to come under it againe) wherein my greatest troubles were not the sense of Gods wrath or fear of damnation, but want of assurance of salvation, and want of strength against my Corruptions; I knew that my greatest want was fayth in Christ, and faine would I have been united to Christ but I thought I was not holy enough. I had many times comfortable thoughts about him in the word prayer, and meditation, but they gave mee no satisfaction, but brought mee lower in mine own eyes, and held mee still to a constant use of all meanes, in hope of better thinges to come. Sometimes I was very confident that hee had given mee a hungring and thirsting soul after Christ, and therefore would surely satisfye mee in his good time. Sometimes againe I was ready to entertaine secret murmurings that all my paines and prayers etc. should prevayle no more: but such thoughts were soon rebuked   I found my heart still willing to Justify God. Yea I was perswaded I should love him though he should cast mee off.

Being in this Condition it pleased the Lord in my family exercise to manifest unto mee the difference between the Covenant of Grace, and the Covenant of workes (but I took the foundation of that of workes to have been with man in innocency, and onely held forth in the Law of Moses to drive us to Christ)   This Covenant of Grace began to take great impression in mee and I thought I had now enough. To have Christ freely, and to be justifyed freely was very sweet to mee; and upon sound warrant (as I conceived) but I would not say with any confidence, it had been sealed to mee, but I rather took occasion to bee more remisse in my spirituall watch, and so more loose in my Conversation.

I was now about 30 yeares of age, and now was the time come that the Lord would reveale Christ unto mee whom I had long desired, but not so earnestly as since I came to see more clearly into the Covenant of free grace. First therefore hee laid a sore affliction upon mee wherein hee laid mee lower in myne owne eyes than at any time before, and shewed mee the emptines of all my guifts and parts, left mee neither power nor will, so as I became as a weaned child   I could now no more look at what I had been or what I had done nor bee discontented for want of strength or assurance   mine eyes were onely upon his free mercy in Jesus Christ. I knew I was worthy of nothing for I knew I could doe nothing for him or for my selfe. I could onely mourn, and weep to think of free mercy to such a vile wretch as I was. Though I had no power to apply it yet I felt comfort in it. I did not long continue in this estate, but the good spirit of the Lord breathed upon my soule, and said I should live. Then every promise I thought upon held forth Christ unto mee saying I am thy salvation. Now could my soule close with Christ, and rest there with sweet content, so ravished with his Love, as I desired nothing nor feared any thing, but was filled with joy unspeakable and glorious and with a spirit of Adoption. Not that I could pray with more fervency or more enlargement of heart than sometimes before, but I could now cry my father with more confidence. Mee thought this Condition and that frame of heart which I had after, was in respect of the former like the reigne of Solomon; free peaceable prosperous and glorious, the other more like that of Ahaz, full of troubles, fears and abasements. And the more I grew thus acquainted with the spirit of God, the more were my corruptions mortifyed, and the new man quickened: The world, the flesh, and Satan, were for a time silent, I heard not of them: but they would not leave mee so. This estate lasted a good time (divers months) but not always alike, but if my comfort, and joy slackened awhile, yet my peace continued, and it would returne with advantage. I was now growne familiar with the Lord Jesus Christ hee would oft tell mee he loved mee. I did not doubt to believe him; If I went abroad hee went with me, when I returned hee came home with mee. I talked with him upon the way, hee lay down with me, and usually I did awake with him. Now I could goe into any company and not lose him: and so sweet was his love to me, as I desired nothing but him in heaven or earth.

This estate would not hold neither did it decline suddainly but by degrees. And though I found much spirituall strength in it yet I could not discerne but my hunger after the word of God, and my love to the saints had been as great (if not more) in former times. One reason might bee this, I found that the many blemishes and much hollow-heartednesse which I discerned in many professors, had weakned the esteem of a Christian in my heart. And for my comfort in Christ; as worldly employments, and the Love of Temporall things did steal away my heart from him, so would his sweet Countenance bee withdrawen from mee. But in such a condition hee would not long leave mee, but would still recall mee by some word or affliction or in prayer or meditation, and I should then bee as a man awakened out of a dreame or as if I had been another man. And then my care was (not so much to get pardon for that was sometimes sealed to mee while I was purposing to goe seek it, and yet sometimes I could not obtaine it without seeking and wayteing also but) to mourn for my ingratitude towards my God, and his free and rich mercy. The Consideration whereof would break my heart more, and wring more teares from myne eyes, then ever the fear of Damnation or any affliction had done; so as many times and to this very day a thought of Christ Jesus, and free grace bestowed on me melts my heart that I cannot refraine.

Since this time I have gone under continuall conflicts between the flesh and the spirit, and sometimes with Satan himself (which I have more discerned of late then I did formerly) many falls I have had, and have lyen long under some, yet never quite forsaken of the Lord. But still when I have been put to it by any suddaine danger or fearfull Temptation, the good spirit of the Lord hath not fayled to beare witnesse to mee, giveing mee Comfort, and Courage in the very pinch, when of my self I have been very fearefull, and dismayed. My usual falls have been through dead heartednesse, and presumptuousnesse, by which Satan hath taken advantage to wind mee into other sinnes. When the flesh prevayles the spirit withdrawes, and is sometimes so greived as he seemes not to acknowledge his owne work. Yet in my worst times hee hath been pleased to stirre, when hee would not speak, and would yet support mee that my fayth hath not fayled utterly.

The Doctrine of free justification lately taught here took me in as drowsy a condition, as I had been in (to my remembrance) these twenty yeares, and brought mee as low (in my owne apprehension) as if the whole work had been to begin anew. But when the voice of peace came I knew it to bee the same that I had been acquainted with before, though it did not speak so loud nor in that measure of joy that I had felt sometimes. Onely this I found that I had defiled the white garments of the Lord Jesus That of Justification in undervalueing the riches of the Lord Jesus Christ and his free grace, and setting up Idolls in myne owne heart, some of them made of his Sylver, and of his gold and that other garment of sanctification by many foule spotts which Gods people might take notice of, and yet the inward spotts were fouler than those.

The Lord Jesus who (of his own free grace) hath washed my soul in the blood of the everlasting Covenant, wash away all those spotts also in his good time. Amen, even so doe Lord Jesus.

John Winthrop

The 12th of the 11th month 1636[/37] in the 49 yeare of my age just compleat

MATTHEW CRADOCK TO JOHN WINTHROP[1]

Worthei Sir, the greyffe I haue beene putt to by the most vyle bad dealings of Thomas Mayhewe hath and doeth so much disquiet my mynd as I thanke God Neuer aney thing ded in the lyke manner. The Lord in mercy Freey me from this. I absoluteley Forbad Chardging moneys from thence

---

[1] W. 2. 65; 4 *Collections*, VI. 122–124.

or buying aney goods there. I thanke God my occasions Requyred it not but to haue had great Returnes made mee from thence by meanes of goods I sent thether by the direction of Thomas Mayhewe For aboue 5000*li* In the last 2 yeeres and geeuing to much Credditt to his insynnuating practises and the good opynion I by the reports and aduize of maney and more especialley of your selfe ded apprehend of him, but Farr beyond all exspectacion and con-trary to my express order he hath charged me with dyuers somes and geeuen bills in my name which he neuer had order from me to doe and that not for small somes whereof some partyculers are specefyed in the Inclosed which I pray you deliuer my seruant Jno. Jolliff and good Sir lett me intreate your selfe and those in authority there to take some Course that Thomas Mayhew may bee answerable For that Estate of myne which my sayd seruant Can showe you hath Come to his hands   This conueyance is vncerten and ther-fore I shalbee breiffer then I would or my necessety Requyres but by Mr. Peirse God willing I shall Inlardge, but I knowe you may by this seey and apprehend my Case. Bills come dayley almost presented to me of one kynd or other without aney aduize, but from Jno. Jolliffs aryuall he ought not to haue done any thing in my buiseynes without his approbacion and consent but when It shall appeare how he hath dealt by me you and all men that shall seey it I ame perswaded will hardely thinke It Could be possible that a man pretending sincerity in his actions could deale so viley as he hath and doeth deale by me. This buiseynes Is not to be delayed. if he can iustefy his actions it were to bee wished but not possible. Lett me Craue your fauour and the Courts so Farr as you shall seey my Cause honest and just and boeth the Court and your selfe and the whole plantacion shall euer oblige me to be Yours euer to my power

MATHEWE CRADOCK

LONDON 13 January 1636[/37]

JNO. JOLLIFE, Fayle not to send the shipp Rebecka victualled for three Monthes to Virginea to mr. Thomas Steggs with some commoditty such as you shall vnderstand to be there most vendable For vallewe of 120*li* or 150*li* at most. You may Rate all 20 per cent more then what ech Cost per Inuoice sent from hence. leaue the Shipp wholey to mr. Tho: Steggs disposing and if he send ought back in her to you and Rich: Hoare (for so Is our aduize) Followe his order therewith and with the shipp as neere as you Cane: I wish Mr. Jno. Hodges to whome commend me goe m[aste]r in her and that he obserue mr. Steggs order in her further ymplyment. Shee is to bee victualled for three Monthes and to haue all her ordynance belonging to her with other necessaries whereof what all Is I desyre an Inuentory may be sent me and the m[aste]rs hand to it.   Yours

MATHEWE CRADOCK[1]

Jno. Jolliff writes me the manner of Mr. Mayhewes accounts Is that what Is not sett downe Is spent: most extremeley I ame abused   my seruants write they drinke nothing but water and I haue in an account lateley sent me Red Wyne, sack and aqua vitæ in one yeere aboue 300 gallons besids many other to intollerable abuses 10*li* for tobacco etc. My papers are misselayd but if you Call for the coppyes of the account sent me and examine vppon what ground It is made you shall fynd I doubt all but forged stuffe   by Mr. Pierse I shall god willing inlardge, meane while I euer Rest in ought I may Your worships at Commaund

MATHEWE CRADOCK

LONDON 21 Febr. 1636[/37]

ROBERT RYECE TO JOHN WINTHROP[2]

To the very woo[rshipfu]ll hys mooche honored good Friende Mr. Wynthop
at his howse at Boston in Newe Englande geve these

MOSTE DEERE AND CHR[IST]IAN FRIENDE, your moste kynde lettres of the 29 of June 1636, came safely to my handes the 3 of November laste, by which I doe perceyve, you had not then received any lettres from me for this yeere. Sir your contynewall love to Gods church and his servantes, doothe euer make mee so longe as I lyve to be myndefull of you, even with my beste endeavours. and for writinge to you, I wrotte vnto you the 17 of Maye laste accompaned with a Boxe of Boocks, which I sente by my brother Samuell Appleton to be convayed to hym for you. nowe yf thay bee not yett come to your handes as I feare thay are not, for abowte the 8 of this moneth I received lettres from my brother Samuell dated the 19 of October laste by which I perceyve he had not then received my lettres nor sondry other thinges accompanied therewith, From whence I do feare, as many others else doe heere that the Schippe with the passengers mooche Stuffe and goods are all perished by the waye. I wrotte also vnto you the 9 of September laste, which I hope maye be safely come to

---

[1] "That written in the margent was by mistake and should haue bene written in Jno. Jolliffs letter." Matthew Cradock to John Winthrop, February 21, 1636/37 (page 349, below).

[2] W. 2. 153; 4 *Collections,* VI. 394–396.

your hands, and I hope agayne by the nexte opportunitie God wyllinge, to wryte vnto you. I am muche beholdinge vnto you for your lettres and advertisements, beinge very sory I can not now make any requitall agayne   I am styll a bolde petitioner to you, to helpe vs to a mappe of your contry as it is now Inhabited and is ioyned with new plantation of Conetticote and yf wee lyve, wee hope to be very thankefull for the same.

There is a matter wherein I am entreated to wryte vnto you in the behalfe of one Mres. Sarah the wyfe of Mr. Henry surnamed the blacke Henry Coppinger of Lavenham, that whereas now allmoste 4 yeeres synce the sayd Mres. Sarah had owte of the frugallitie of hir owne laborious Industrye, withowte the privitie of hir husbande gathered the Summe of xj*li*, which desyringe to putt it owte for benefyte of hir poore children, yonge Hamonde heere of Lannam then beinge heere, and vnderstandinge of hir purpose, moved Hamonde [*sic*] for the mony promisinge restitution after a yeere with as moche more for the gayne, heereupon, heere more xx*s* was delivered with the mony in good penny woothes of goods, and Wylliam Payne, late of Lanham nowe of N: E: gave then his woorde for the repaymente of the sayd 12*li*, with the profitt thereof arisynge within a yeere, synce which tyme shee never harde of Hamonde, one whitt, but that he is deade,[1] and shee withowte all meanes for hir mony: From whence shee hearinge that you have in Newe Englande all good lawes to recover debttes, entreated mee to wryte vnto you in her behalfe, beinge vnknowne to you, to desyer you to common with olde Hamonde and with Wylliam Payne, abowte this debtte, and howe it maye be recovered. Sir I praye you beare with my bowldenes, you can not doe a more meritorious deede, wee wyll all be thankefull vnto you for it. Newes wee have none heere that good is, all your friends heere are well bothe at Lanham and otherwheare   So remembringe my beste affection vnto you I ende beseechinge the allmyghtye to keepe you in all your wayes and do remayne Yours ever moste bownde in all Christian observance

ROBERT RYECE

PRESTON this 17 of January 1636[/37]

I Thomas Roote now of Lavenham doe wytnes that I harde the sayd Wylliam Payne then heere at Lavenham to geve his woorde in my presence to Mres. Sarah Coppinger, that yf yonge Hamonde dyd not paye the mony agayne to the sayd Mres. Sarah Coppinger, that he woolde then make good and paye the principall which is Aleven powndes. And this can the wydowe

---

[1] William Hammond, Jr., had been killed by the Indians on Long Island. See page 276, above.

Onge, nowe of Waterton in N: E: but then of Lavenham, in whose prescence and in hir Shoppe wytnes

THOMAS ROOTE

I haue seene a lettre of the sayd Wylliam Hamonde dated at Watertowne in N: E: the 4 of July 1635 to Mres. Coppinger, wherein he promised hir by the helpe of God, to be heere in Englande betweene that and Christetyde nexte followenge, and so to pay hir hir monye.

I have seene also another lettre dated at Watertowne the 15 of July laste from William Hamonde the elder to the sayd Thomas Roote to desyer hym to goe to his moother the wydowe Stewarde of Cockefielde, to whom he had signified in a lettre that shee shoolde paye the mony in question to the sayd Thomas Roote for to paye it over to Mres. Cop[pinger] accordingly but the sayd wydowe Stewarde denyed the sayd Roote to paye one pennye of it.

Nowe for that it may be demanded whie the husbande of Mres. Coppinger (who is of sufficiente abyllytie to deale in this buysynes) is not prevye to this matter, that is awnswered, that it is vnseemelye for the wyfe to reveale the husbands defects, who if he knewe of it or coolde fynger it woolde soone spende it as formerly myserable experience hathe tawghte from whence shee is enforced withowte his privitie to seeke to recoover it only for the Supplie of hir owne and hir childrens necessitie. And if it shoolde so falle owte that any wayes paymente heereof be made, then it is humbly desyred you woolde be pleased to sende it to mee for hir. Yours ever and vnfaynedlye

ROBTE. RYECE

MATTHEW CRADOCK TO JOHN WINTHROP[1]

To my Honored and worthei freynd the wor[shi]p[fu]ll John Winthrop the elder Esqr. Boston in Newe England per the George Mr. Jno. Seuerne whome God perserue

SIR, I lyke my Implyments so well there as I desyre to troble my selffe less then I haue done, which hath made mee cross out this Postscript,[2] I not In-

---

[1] W. 2. 63; 4 *Collections*, VI. 121–122. This communication is written at the end of Cradock's letter to Winthrop of September 13, 1636 (see above, pages 307–309), which was, however, not actually sent until sometime after February 21, 1636/37, as is explained in this letter. Because of this unusually long interval, it has seemed best to treat the portion bearing the February date as a separate document.

[2] See the canceled postscript to Cradock's letter to Winthrop, September 13, 1636 (page 309, above).

tending to haue it mooued. god send me some meanes to dispose of that I haue that somewhat may come of it, towards my exceeding great Charge I haue beene and am at, my taxes in publique beeing to be great maney wayes Considering howe my buseynes are there Carryed by mr. Mayhewe. I send you heerewith a letter date the 13 January which I thought to haue sent away then but missed of Convayance. that written in the margent was by mistake and should haue bene written in Jno. Jolliffs letter[1]   That you maye judge of mr. Mayhewes dealings by me I send herewith to Jno. Jolliffe my chardge on him for what hath come meereley to his hands, whereby he Is debtor to me besyds the increase of my Cattell and improuement of my grounds and proffitt by the labors of seruants which if sett against there Chargs and other losses, yeet I should haue there aboue 1150o*li* yf I be well dealt with, and whereas accordingley I gaue order to haue moneys Remitted home to mee; in steede thereof I ame Charged by Tho: Mayhewe without the knowledge of Jno. Jolliffe with great somes, whereas my expresse order was he should doe nothing in my buiseynes without Jno Jolliffs Consent. I must abruptly breake of but doe pray you with your best aduize to Furder me in Aught that may tend For my saffetey. by mr. Pierse I hope to Inlardg, hauing Caused this letter to be Returned me from Plymouth whether I nowe send it to be sent you by the George mr. Jno. Seuerne. Thus with my best Respects I rest Your W[o]r[shi]ps to be Commaunded

MATHEWE CRADOCK

LONDON 21 February 1636[/37]

WILLIAM MUNNING TO JOHN WINTHROP[2]

To the Wor[shipfu]ll and his very Worthy freind and kinsman Mr. Jo: Winthrop senr. at Boston in New Engld. with truste and speed present these

GOOD SIR, I received your late loving lines dated the 12th of Octob: last past about 9 or 10 weeks after: I am right glad to vnderstand by them, of the generall well-fare of your Plantations (which I beseech the Lord to perpetuate

---

[1] See the message to Jolliffe in Cradock's letter to Winthrop, January 13, 1636/37 (page 346, above).

[2] W. 4. 84; 5 *Collections*, I. 235–237. The Reverend William Munning (Munnings) of Emmanuel College, Cambridge, was the son of the Reverend Humphrey Munning, Rector of Brettenham, Suffolk. He was successively Vicar of Good Easter, Essex (1635–1645), Rector of "Preston" (Friston?), Suffolk, and Rector of Chedburgh, Suffolk. Venn, *Alumni Cantabrigienses*, Part I, III. 227. His wife, Elizabeth, was a cousin of Governor Winthrop and also of the Reverend Nathaniel Ward of Ipswich.

to the Praise of his Name) but very sorrie to heare by them of the death of my Brother-in-lawe of whose true-harted sincerity to god and man, I was as well perswaded as of any with whom I haue had so short acquaintance, which Confidence causeth mee (though I bee sorrie) not to sorrow for him as a Heathen without Hope, but rather as a Christian, with good hope that it is well with him now, and shall bee yet better with him at that Day of Refreshing from the Presence of the Lord. Act: 3. Your Relacion of the manner and 2d cause of his death hath fenced mine eares against the false Rumour which I heard since, vizt. that hee with many others was slaine by the Natives. Wee haue noe news heere worth the Relating, Onely wee heare, that the Archb[isho]ps Metropoliticall Visitacion is (once againe) comming downe into this County. What effects it will produce I am not prophet sufficient infallibly to foretell: but (if wee may ghesse by the Proceedings of Pope Regulus[1] in our next neighbour and natiue diocese) it is to bee feared that wee shall haue more Loste Groates swept out of the House instead of the Duste, to the litle laude of our good huswifery. Hee alone can amend All who threatneth to lay Judgment to the Line, and Righteousnes to the Plummett (Isai. 28) that soe hee may give every one his due to an haires breadth; and to Him they that are His must and doe referre their Case.

For myselfe (bycause I beleeue your good affection may make yow willing to heare how and what I doe) I am, (not longe since) remooved from Graces to the litle plat which gods good Prouidence hath layd out for mee at Goodester, where meeting with the Flocke much larger then the Fleece it seemeth to signify vnto mee that the Lord would haue mee take more paines in Feeding then in shearing of his sheepe, tho many Idle and Idoll shepheards are best skilled in the latter of these. Sir, my earnest Request to yow is that yow would please to put vp your Prayers to the Lord for mee, to intreate him, that Hee which hath counted mee faythfull by putting of mee into the Ministry, would giue mee grace not to fayle his expectation in the Discharge thereof; but would vouchsafe to make mee soe faythfull now both to him and his Church, that Hee may finde mee faythfull at the last Day. For former lettres from yourselfe, I can call to minde but onely one before this that I haue received and in both that and this more love and respect then I can challenge as due. I make noe question but lettres from Graces will more fully informe yow how they doe there then time and paper and my present absence from thence will permitt mee to doe; onely I heere that Sir Hen:[2] hath lately had another sore brush with the gowt, but is now vpwards againe.

---

[1] Matthew Wren, Bishop of Norwich.   [2] Sir Henry Mildmay.

season and sanctify all for good. I am bold to enclose a lettre to my
e widdow, for the more certainty of the deliuery. Thus with the tender
of my due respect and seruice to your selfe and Mrs. Winthrop etc. with my
loue remembred to my sister and to all with yow that desire to loue the Lord
Jesus in sinceritie, I leaue yow and yours to him that leaueth none of His and
soe take leaue to rest Your kinsman in all faythfull and vnfained Affection
to command

WM. MUNNINGE

GOODESTER in Essex, Febr: 21° 1636[/37]

JOHN WINTHROP'S NOTES ON A SERMON
BY JOHN COTTON[1]

Mr. Cotton concerning the soules closinge with Christ in a
Conditionall promise, as in that of math: 11th
Come to me all yee that labour etc. and I will give you rest

1: The common error was this that a soule being laden and labouring vnder
sin, thinks that hereby it deserves rest etc. 2: another sorte finding themselves
thus laden yet think that rest is heere offered them and so they take it to
themselves; but such peace will not holde.

2: The right way of closing with this promise is thus: the soule thus labouring vnder the burden of sin, attends to the promise which consists of 2 Conditions, 1 is of its misery, which it is sensible off, and the 2 is of Comming to
Christ or beleeving in him. heere the soul is at a losse, finding it impossible by
its owne strength to beleeve, yet having some support from Christs invitation
of those who come in such a labouring Condition, it hanges vpon the promise
meditating vpon it, sighinge and groaninge and prayinge as it can over it,
with earnest longings after Christ and so wayting for rest. in this way the
spirit of God works Faith in the soul, and therewith it is brought to Christ
and so findeth rest For Faith and Christ come both at one instant Christ lays
holde of the Soul, and works faith [torn] all Faith lays hold vpon Christ at
[torn].

xij 24, 1636[/37]

[*Endorsed by Governor Winthrop:*] Mr. Cotton about the worke of Conversion.

---

[1] W. 1. 116.

MRS. PAULIN TO SEBASTIAN PAULIN[1]

*To his [sic] much beloued Sonne Sebastian Pawlin Drum maior at the Castle
these in New England*

DEARE SONNE, I have ben heartily reyoiced receauing your letter to vnderstand of your health, and that you were so wel prouided to be vnder the
gouvernour in the Castle but because you desire to come for England I haue
gotten a friend to write this inclosed letter to the Gouvernour to intreate him
to giue you leaue to come home with the first shipping   agree with the master
off the ship for your passage at the best rate and cheapest you can, and iff it
pleaseth God to send you saue hether I will see it duely discharged. You complaine off vnkindenesse endured by your Vnkle. I pray God to forgiue it
him, and doe beseeche him to graunt you a happy passage and that I may see
you here shortely in good health. Your father God be praysed is in good
health and your sister. they commend them to you and so do I heartily and
hoping to see your ere long I praye God for your health and rest

Your Very loving mother
R E P

LONDON this 26 of februeary 1636[/37]

LUCY DOWNING TO MARGARET WINTHROP[2]

MOSTE WORTHY SISTER, Thes tedious passages bares vs of all commerce:
further then the vnlimeted wishes of each others hapynes, wich allthough I
haue noe power to procure: yet it glads all my spirits to hear it: and blesed be
god that hath so tenderd you in this infancie of a plantation, when theer was
so small hopes of support or comfort. god still preacheth the life of fayth to
his: and discouers himselfe in the mount. Ohe that thees experiences of his
faythfullnes maye make vs able to doe all things throwhe christ: to liue hapylie
and to dye comfortable: and all knowinge that ouer dayes heare are but a
moment be they sweet or bitter: and when death comes, our liues are hid with
christ in god: and when he our life shall apear, then shall wee allso apear with
him in glory: I hartylie thank you for all the expressions of your loue, and

---

[1] W. I. 118. Sebastian Paulin had been brought over by his uncle Nicholas Simpkin under an arrangement by which the boy was to have been apprenticed to Robert Keayne for ten years. Savage (1826), II. 345.

[2] W. 4. 4; 5 *Collections*, I. 12–14.

The Lord our company. I know not yet how it will pleas god to dispose of vs. sister th in many distractions: my present condition is vnfit for changes: and ooth this plauge and plaugs aproach, and increas, and maye well affright: as beinge the arguments of the allmighties controuersie with vs: and prouocations increasinge to such heyghts: what can wee expect: if the sonne of god must suffer, rather then his Justis be vnsatisfied. Lend vs all your faythfull prayers: knowinge the head is the same, whereuer the members are: and if god pleas to afford vs the presence of each other in this life, I shall hope of much comfort therin. but if he denyes that, and bringe vs together in heauen, wee shall not haue much cause of complaint: I pray present my best seruis and wishes to your freest commands: to whom I am obliged beyound all hope of merit: but may I haue opertunitie of seruinge you or yours, it would be very acseptable to me: and I pray commend my best affections to all my dear nephues and neses and good frinds: intreatinge theer excuse for not wrightinge to them: for a few lines are now a great dayes work with me, beinge far biger and vnapt for acsion then euer I was: I haue more kinde remembrances to you from graces, groton assington, and indeed I am obliged to that family, so much as I maye well admire, but can never deserue the least part of it: allso from cowne, shrubland, maplested. I thank Msr. Tindall and Mrs. Tindall they very noble proferd vs intertainement for the time wee wear from home, with much earnestnes and desires of fauoringe me in any kinde, as I should haue ocasion. I beceech you to doe me the fauor to giue them many thanks in my behalfe for ther noblenes to us: but indeed I dare not venter of the task to giue you acount of all theer louinge wishes and respects to you: for groton if you haue not letters thence this passage, it is partlie my fault: for I was to giue them notice of msr. peerce his goeinge: and I hear my letter lyes att my brother Kerbyes still, and mist passage this week. but I pray be confident, for I dare ingage my selfe for theer faythfull respects to you: and I am of opinnion they may be with you ere years to an end, if things proceed as now they are with them: for indeed they are very sensible of msr. Leas restraint, as well they maye, for he was an vpright and a paynfull pasture of theers, truly careinge for theer soulles: howeuer some body either weakly or wors did abuse both my brother Winthrop and him, in relations of Msr. Lea wich did a littell touch him: yet I confes, he bare it with as much christian patience, and made as good vse of it to himself I thinke, as might be: and I cannot tell but there might be a prouidence in it for his good: for it came straunglie to his vewe: I sendinge the letter to my sister from cowne: he beinge by, and she beinge a very poor clark, desierd him to read it to her: and poor soulle she was so perplext when she heard the passages in it: but Msr.

lea hath well quit him selfe of those asspersions: for he hath leeft but all for the cause: and I haue littell hope, either of him or any in the like condition to be restored: god of his mercy send vs better newes: I thank you for all your loue to owers. I wish they maye deserue it: and that wee might all haue opertunietie to be seruisable. Yours in reallitie rather then in subscription

L. DOWNINGE

[*Ca.* March, 1636/37]

My cosen wright hath a sonne[1]   the queen lookes euery day.[2]

ROBERT GOLDSTON TO JOHN WINTHROP[3]

To the Right Worshipfull his veery good Master, Mr. John Winthrop the Ellder

SIR, Pleaseth it your worthy Exelensy: your poore yet faythfull saruant togetther with my wiffe, remember our humbell scerues to your selffe, and our much deserueing Mris. your wiffe. my dewty I haue too much foregot in that I haue not written to your worship since your departuer from Groten. one cheefe causse was that I hoped that of your Clemensy, you would haue beggune to me. I if I mistake not desiered you would bene pleased to haue maede some Report of the Country to me; some other Reasons I could allege, that weeare too longe heeare to inscerte: thearefore I desier you that of your Beneggnyty you would not judg of my faythfull loyallty towardes you by my neglecct to wright to you: nor yet that I haue Demas lyke imbrased this present world because that I am constraiened to dwell in Mesheak, but yourselffe knowes that Miphibosheth his lambenes kept him from goeing with Daued, though it weere to his great greefe; through his faithlesse saruant Sibie   euen so vnscertayne estate haue tyed me short, so that in bodyly presentes I can not be wheare I would desier to be; but neither the want nor increase of these thinges can clippe the wingges of my ernest and ardent affections, which are dayly liffted vp to god conscerning his Church with you theare in Jewery, and your selfe and yours in a speshall manner, whombe I know to be worthy of dubell honouer, and deutty bind me in an vnuiellabl bond both now and

---

[1] Henry Wright, later Sir Henry Wright, Bart., son of Dr. Lawrence Wright and Mary Duke Wright, is believed to have been born about 1637. At any rate, at the time of his death on February 5, 1663/64, he was twenty-seven years old. Venn, *Alumni Cantabrigienses*, Part I, IV. 473.

[2] I.e., expects her confinement. The Princess Anne was born March 17, 1636/37.

[3] W. 4. 85; 5 *Collections*, I. 237–238. Robert Goldston had been a tenant of Governor Winthrop at Groton. See *Winthrop Papers*, II. 181.

omytte. while the Bishop his chancelor Dr. C[
Justice at Bury, newes was browghte hym that
the laste nighte.[1] is he so, sayd the chancelor
hathe troobled all the contry these 30 yeeres, a[
for x myle rownde abowte that place—the n[
reported; whiles the Bishop was at Ipswiche,
ryde forthe, comanded his servantes to hyer [
worde that all the horses were taken vp by su[
Dedham: Is the wynde at that doore sayde th[
and so not longe after, as the Commissary syn[
from Cant[erbury] vpon the complaynte of [
Dedham: wherevpon the commissary wrotte [
shewenge hym he had commandimente fror[
to stay his lecture now for a whiles the plag[
concourses was daylie encreased. Mr. Roger[
stayed his lecture, and after harvest ended,
moved for renewene of the lecture, the Com[
ysynge very shortely thay shoolde haue liber[
withowte all in all intention, Mr. Rogers sein[
tion wholly to suppresse that lecture, this st[
all his naturall malladies to his vttermost
thinke I am some what teadious, yett byc[
many lettres, and wrytinge but once in a y[
relations from others, yett you are content
vpon I muste further shewe you what furtl[
libells secretly scattered this yeere, but gr[
of thinges, whereof I wyll geve you only the[
you maye iudge what they conteyne. As
to Archbishops, Bishops, Archedeacons an[
cialls and other awdacious vsurpers vpon [
lawes and his loyall subiectes lawfull liber[
all mens knowledge. Item Certayne Que[
the names of Jesus, and to the patrons the[
reasons alledged by Bishop Andrewes and [
mony are breefely examined and refuted;
cleered, and that texte with others acq[
awthorizinge this novell Ceremony, hee[

[1] The Reverend John Rogers of Dedham died

all way to commend you to the blesseing of godes grasse, and doe desier you to remember me though vnworthy that god would of his mersi be pleased to keepe me vndefilled and make me more zeluse: in these poleuted plases and declying tymes Amen. Your saruant to command

ROBT. GOULDSTON

From GROTTEN this Fiurst of March 1636[/37]

Sir I humbly desier you to wright the next Returne so as that I may vnderstand from you, whether the mannewer of Grotten doe giue any thiurdes out of the coppie hould landes. heere is a poore weddow chaleing a right to the thiurdes of the Fallken: and sheut is lyke to be commensed about it, exept it please you to exprese how it is in the premeses.

ROBERT RYECE TO JOHN WINTHROP[1]

MOSTE DEERE AND CHRISTIAN FRIENDE, to satisfie your expectation, and myne owne dewe respecte, (wherein I woolde be loathe to be any wayes defectyve) I praye you to vnderstande that our Allminake makers blasted some 2 yeeres synce with Jupiters Thunderbolte for beinge to curious in there predictions, have ever synce sylently lefte all presages to the event of euery season: yett have many noted sondry strange alterations this laste yeere now paste. The Springe was very hotte and drye burninge vp the grasse, the harveste very wette and dropping and so the weather followinge very variable, which bredde a sore plague bothe at london and in sondrye other places, by reason whereof mydsommer tearme was in parte cutte of and so was Mihel tearme for the moste parte cutte of. This Sommer the K[ing] wente in progresse as I thinke into Shropshiere, where the K[ing] was exceedinge angry for his badde entertaynemente. the Sheerefe had but 10 men and never a gentleman with hym, but euery gentleman was from his howse, and in all places where the K[ing] shoolde lodge the goodman gone, none at home but the wyfe, with abondance of all sortes of victualls and servants. Heere formerly was Benevolences and Shipmony denyed, which some construed was the cawse of euery mans generall absence. Duringe this progresse there was one Bumpsted sometymes a tayler of Mellforde then followenge the Lorde Savadge, and synce followenge a knighte who maried the lords dawghter, was observed to followe the courte, and there apprehended for dyvers evill woords

[1] W. 2. 155; 4 *Collections*, VI. 410–421.

and purposes to the K[ing]. he was comi
resteth.

This Summer the Bishop of Norwiche[1]
visitation in that Diocesse, as euer was se
putte downe, with Sermons in the afterno
ters sylenced suspended and putt from th
readinge the K[ings] boocke[2] for liberty a
littargie now devyded into 2 partes the on
in the other called the seconde service, to
munion table placed now at the Easte
Northe and Sowthe, euery preacher to
seconde service at hie altar, before he go
no prayer but to end all at the hie alter.
municante is to kneele at the rayle now
hie alter   after the comunion euery one
all humble inclyninge reverence to th
wooman in her vayle goeth to the rayle
is there with all solemnitie fynished. no
crowchinge and humble obeysance. A
devotion so many wayes performed
veneration and addoration of that inv
From the communion tables thay are
altars which they adorne with Sylke a
with lightes, in other places with cru
setlinge and Religion in euery place
wiche to lye there at a howse of his w
gar, impatiente to haue there Mynis
rude affrontes to the Bishop and his
sooddayne as afrayde on his owne c
howse almoste halfe way betweene
he had dayly intelligence of all thir
from the courte, he removed agayne
to bee neere the courte. Soone after
pended and depryved mynisters to
that I coolde euer heere, And at th
severitie and extremitie vsed. one

[1] Matthew Wren.
[2] The Declaration of Sports, first issued
to be republished and read in the churches.

respectes, the 4 edition corrected 1636. The Vnbishopinge of Tymothie and Tytus, or a briefe elaborate Discourse provinge Tymothie to be no Bishop (muche lesse any sole or dyocesan Byshop) of Ephesus, nor Tytus of Creete and that the power of Ordination, or imposition of hands belonges *jure diuino* to Presbiters as well as to Bishopps and not to Bishopps only. Wherein all obiections and pretenses to the contrary are fully awnswered and the pretended Superioritie of Bishopps over mynisters and presbiters *Jure diuino* (now moche contended for) vtterly subverted, in a moste perspicuous manner, by a well-wysher to Gods truthe and people. In the yeere 1636. A breefe awnswere to a late treatise of the Sabbath daye digested dialogue wyse betweene 2 Dyvines A and B. A divine tragedy lately acted, or a collection of sondry memorable examples of Gods Iudgements vpon Sabbathe-breakers, and other lyke lyber-tynes in there vnlawefull sportes happeninge within the Reallme of Englande in the compasse only of 2 yeeres laste paste, synce the boocke was published, woorthie to be knowne, and considered of all men especially suche who are guyltie of the Synne, or arche patrons thereof anno 1636.[1] In the ende of which collection is inserted the history of Mr. Prynne pursewed by Mr. Noy a greate favourer of Sabbathe recreations and pollutions, in this manner. Mr. William Noye the greate Gamaliell of the lawe the K[ings] attornye generall as he had a greate hande in compilinge and republishinge the late declara-tion for pastimes on the lords daye (thruste owte by hys, and a greate prel-ates practice, to thwarte Judge Richardsons good order for suppressinge of wakes and revells in Somersetshiere, and the Justices of that Shires petition to his ma[jes]tye for the contynewance of it, and to make waye for a Starre-chamber cawse against Mr. Prinne) he so eagerly persecuted this Mr. Prinne, of his owne profession and Societye (to whom he was formerly a friende in apparance, but an inveterate enemye in trewthe) for his Histrio Mastix[2] com-piled only owte of the woordes and Sentences of other approoved awthors of all sortes, againste the vse and exercyse of Stage playes, Maypoles, wakes, lascivious mixed dawncinge, and other Ethenicke pastimes, condemned in all ages, withowte any thowght or Suspicion of gevinge the leaste offence, eyther to the K[ings] moste excellente ma[jest]y the Queene or State as he averred

[1] All the above "libels" (i.e., brief writings) have been attributed in whole or in part to William Prynne. *The Lords Day, the Sabbath Day. Or, A Briefe Answer to Some Materiall Passages, in a Late Treatise of the Sabbath-Day: Digested Dialogue-Wise betweene Two Divines A. and B.* has also been attributed to Richard Byfield. *A Divine Tragedy Lately Acted* has been attributed in whole or in part to Henry Burton.

[2] For a detailed account of the events which followed upon the publication of William Prynne's *Histrio Mastix. The Players Scovrge, Or, Actores Tragædie* (London, 1633), see the article on Prynne in *D.N.B.*

in his awnswere vpon his oathe. And althowghe this boocke was written 4 yeeres, licensed allmoste three, printed fully off a quarter of a yeere, and published 6 weekes before the Queenes Ma[jes]ties pastorall, against which it was falsely voyced to have byn principally wrytten; dilligently pervsed and lycensed by Mr. Thomas Buckner, the then Archbishop of Cant[erbury] his chaplyn, bothe before and after it came from the presse, entered into the Stationers Hall, vnder the wardens hande, printed, published in 3 aucthorised printing howses, withowte the leaste controwle; and published by the sayd licensers direction, who woolde haue nothinge newe printed in it, as appered vpon oathe at the hearinge; And althowgh Mr. Noye hymselfe (to whom he presented one of the boocks) vpon the firste readinge of it, commended it, thanked him for it, ofte affirmed, that he sawe no hurte in it; and at the hearinge confessed, that the worste and moste dangerous phrase and passage in it, mighte haue a good and fayer construction, and Schollars woolde all take it in a good sence; yett he handled the matter so (by suppressinge the gentlemans exhibitts and defense, wrestinge his woordes and meaninge, refucinge to discover the particulars of his boocke, on which he woolde insyste, thowghe ordered so to doe by the courte, it beinge also impossible to instructe Cownsell how to make a Replye, and by tamperinge vnder hande with some of his cownsell, by no meanes to make any Justification or defence to cleere his innocencye, thowghe the partie earnestly entreated, and gave them Instructions to the contrarye) that the poore gentleman receved censure at laste to be expelled owte of the vniversytie of Oxforde, and lyncollns Inne, thruste from his profession, in which he never offended, Fyned 5000li to stande in 2 severall pylleryes, and there to loose bothe hys eares, his boockes to be there burned before hym, and to suffer Imprisonmente duringe hys lyfe besydes, which sentence thowghte by moste that harde the cawse to be meante only in terrorem, withowte any intention at all of execution, beinge respited for above 3 monethes space and in a manner remitted by the Queene moste gracious mediation, was yet by this Attornyes and a greate prelates Importunitie beyonde all expectation sooddenly and severelye executed, withowte any the leaste mittigation, fewe of the lords so moche as knowenge of it. The gentleman heerevpon is sett vpon the pyllory at Westminster, and thare he lost an eare: Mr. Noye lyke a ioyfull spectator lawghes at his sufferinge, and this his greate exploite he had browghte to passe, which diverse there presente observed and condemned in hym: the gentleman lyke a harmeles lambe, takes all with suche patience, that he not so moche as once opened his mowthe to lett falle any woorde of discontente. Yett the Juste God and Sovereigne lorde of heaven and earthe, who beholdeth mischeefe and spighte, to requite it with and to his Ma[jes]tye hym selfe, his Queene and there Royall progenye, in dashenge them owte of the nomber of Gods electe. Edition 3: Printed at Ipswich An: 1636.[1]

Vpon the 27 of December laste came the Erle of Arondell and Surrey home from his Ambassage to the Emperor Ferdinande the 2 and to the princes of Germany. he tooke his Journy abowte the beginnynge of Aprill and was sente from our K[ing] as Ambassador ex[tra]ordinary vnto the Emperor, abowte the restitution of the Pallatinate, as it was sayd, but in vayne. he had a longe and difficulte Journy, yett entertayned in euery place very respectyvely, especially at Prague in Bohemia, where an Iryshe man recter of the colledge of Jesuites   there our Ambassador was intertayned with a Comedye in this sorte. Mercuries servante as the prologue employed abowte makinge redy of the Theatre for the assembly of all the Gods and Goddesses (there to be pres- ente, for the receyvinge of the Ambassador) falls vpon lytle children, who woolde fayne see the Ambassador of the K[ing] of Eng[land]   he tells them they cannot see hym in the Theatre, vnlesse they wyll congratulate his com- ynge, whom by reason of there yonge yeeres thay can not salute in latyne, but they may performe it in there owne naturall language which was agreed vpon. And so the Gods and Goddesses enteringe Mercury receyves them and places euery one accordingely. Then comes in Astrea complaynes to Jupiter and the rest of the Gods of the wickednes of the woorlde. Jupiter havinge harde all delyvers the woorlde to be ponished by Mars and Vulcane. Here Peace all forlorne seekes vp and downe whare to have a place to be secured from the fury of Mars. Neptune carries Peace over into Englande in a Sea shell. Then Mars devides the Globe of the earthe into dyvers partes and distributes them to the fury of Bellona and other Agents. Heare Ceres Apollo and Bacchus complayne before Jupiter of the infinite calamytie which thay endure from Mars: Jupiter sends them to Neptune. Neptune tells them, that he hathe comytted the Imperiall Govermente of the Sea to Charles Kinge of Greate Brittayne, and that thay muste make sewte to hym to restore peace to the woorlde. Mercury byds Ceres and Apollo to be of good cheere, and wylls them not to dowbte but that K[ing] Charles wyll shortly by his Ambassador Howarde E[arl] of Arondell, reduce peace. Peace affirmeth that shee shalbe restored to hir former habitations, thay doe all gratulate one another, and geve there acclamation to Howard, to whom thay do wyshe and presage all happines etc.

---

[1] There are three known editions of William Prynne's *Newes from Ipswich* in 1636, one probably published in Edinburgh, the others in London.

Sir, this supplimente I have added, but for a lytle refreshenge, vpon the which many do dyversly opyne. Heerevpon Charles Lodovike Cownte Palla-tyne of the Rhene publisheth his protestation againste all the vnlawfull and violente proceedinges against hym and his brotheren.   Particularlye againste the secrett and invalide dispocetions and decrees of the Emperor in the trans-lation of the Electorall dignitie and dominions vpon the Duke of Bavaria. The vnlawfull and vayne election of a Kynge of the Romaynes, where his highnes and the Ellector of Tryers were excluded, and lastly againste the vyo-lente and vniuste vsurpation and possession of the Electorall dignitie, Tytle voyce and Session by the Duke of Bavaria. What this in tyme wyll effecte tys only tyme wyll relate. And so sceasinge further at this tyme remembringe my selfe moste respectyvely vnto you I leave you with all yours to the safe protec-tion of the Allmightie, and do reste Yours allwayes in all true and synceare affection.

THOMAS SMYTHE[1]

This firste day of Marche 1636[/37]   A

If these lettres come to your hands, as I hope they shall and to which ende I wrotte them I pray you advertise mee of the receipte and date thereof.

[*Endorsed by Governor Winthrop:*] Rec. the 22: of June.

SIR WILLIAM SPRING TO JOHN WINTHROP[2]

To my singulerly Esteemed and worthely Beloued Freind John Winthrop Esquier Boston in New England these

MOST WORTHELY ESTEEMED BELOUED FREIND AND DEERE BROTHER, were I as conscious of any willfull neglect of your loue and my due remembrance of itt, and necessary Salutations or Expressions of this kinde, as I am of defect in all (though not voluntary) I should in a kinde of despayre wholly forbeare to putt you in minde of soe vnworthy a Frend. But my hart is vpright with you, though my hand hath neyther bin able to serue my affections nor your

---

[1] As in his letter to Winthrop of September 10, 1636, Ryece uses a pseudonym. That Thomas Smythe was Robert Ryece is certain from a comparison of the handwriting in this letter with that of other letters to which Ryece signed his own name. The identity is further confirmed by Governor Winthrop's endorsement on a later letter from Ryece also signed "Thomas Smythe" (see below, pages 371–375), where there is also an explanation of the "A" that appears here below the signature.

[2] W. 2. 181; 4 *Collections*, VI. 555–558.

merritts in presenting you with requisite Circomstances of Assurance that itt is soe: For not only meanes (or att least the timely knowledg of itt) hath too often beene wanting and preventing to my purposes, But when they haue bin more free and fauorable, I haue wanted power to make vse of them. About New Yeere last I receyued a kind and louing letter from you by one Betts (as I remember) who came hether att a time when I had suffred a fortnights Extreamitie before and was att first not able to see him or to think of any buisines. Yett before hee went away, I came downe a part of the day and as Company and my infirmities would suffer mee, had a little speech with him, who (then hasting away and promising to come to mee att more Conveniency) I hoped should haue bin the meanes of my sending to you and my Coss: Jo: Spring alsoe. hee came agen indeede when I was vtterly vnable to doe or take thought for any thing that way for itt pleased God for 14 weekes I was in expectance of my passage to my last Port. since I am in a crazie vncerteine Condition neuer well though not soe weake as I was. this lost mee the hope of that Conveyance the man telling mee hee was to goe to and by London back to you: I had little meanes (by my sicknes and trobles continuing) to heare or enquire of any other Course, but att our last Assises, where with much adoe I forst my selfe one day, I mett my Coss. Gurdon who promised to send my Letter to you, which now I hope you haue: testefieng my true Loue to you, and by you entreating to haue my just Excuse for not satisfieng the still important and large requests of my kinsman, to whome I haue made bould with you to enclose this letter: Truly Sir the summe and charge I haue bin att to this man is not after the due proportion and regard I ought to beare to my owne affayres, and more neere duties, yett what I haue done hath not bin grudgingly, nor with a scant hand I assure you. I beleeue in true account (which perhaps) hee considers not duely, more then true charrety (which is to looke home first) or right wisdome would commend, and I cannot nor may not prejudice my neerer requisites too much. I haue lately married my Sonne, and abated my meanes largely   I cannot nor (haue not to) doe as formerly, my owne necessary course and children require mee instantly to my vtmost, and mine owne particuler (as noe less the generall) Burthens grow heauy to my present strength, besides charrety had neuer soe many Objects (that may not bee neglected) amongst vs, honest and good men abundance and in abundant wants, dayly somewhat issueth soe from mee and others, and must doe, and other poore kinred I haue too too many that dayly call for helpe and must haue itt. I profess I neuer was streightned before. This Sir for your satisfaction that I am not vnmindefull but vnable (for the present att least) to satisfie him, and I pray you make him sensible of the Equitie and reason of itt if you conceyue itt soe, and if hee contentfully accept of what I haue done, as God shall enable and enlarge mee heereafter I shall not forgett him, but I desire hee spare mee yett: I could not heare by Betts or other of any shipps goeing by Ipswich whether else I had sent something to this purpose: but lately, and now too late as I am tould I heare some goe or are gone: I perceyue by the lettre that you haue for the releife of this kinsman of mine disbursed some summe but what you express not nor haue I had one word to certefie mee thereof from him: What you haue done for my sake, and hee hath not nor can satisfie agen, I will not that you loose but desire you will certefie mee what itt is and I will not fayle (if God please) to satisfie you when I know itt: Soe as hee sees I neglect not to doe for him still more, though in all hee requires and as hee would I cannot: Truly such is my condition att this present as I haue much adoe to hould out thus farr in this labor, still so weake and vnseruiseable I am to my selfe: I must craue fauor to make goode All present defects, and your goode beleife that I haue a will, though att present streightned and prevented, to giue you larger assurance and better testemony of my faythfull affections: Your charrety without asking affords mee I am confident the benefitt of your prayers, Yett I craue them alsoe, and by your meanes euen to bee remembred amongst you as I dayly in my poore way remember you all: Salute all I know particulerly I beseech you that are with you with my harty Loue and best desires of goode: And think of mee still the thoughts of a loving Frend. the less I deserue itt the greater goode itt is in you and the reward shalbee to your owne Bosome, whether I desire to convey myselfe and to liue there, as wee may to hir alsoe that ownes that place spetially my wife and I commend vs, and to all yours, and hartely commend you all to Gods goodenes and Grace: Your vnfeyned louing Freind and faythfully affected brother

WLLM: SPRING

PAKENHAM Mar: j^{mo} 1636[/37]

What my kinsman hath formerly charged you, and cannot himselfe discharg I pray signifie and I shall take care for itt. But yett I must entreate him to spare mee for my more necessary Care and Cost command my first respects and soe after times (if God lend mee life) may afford more liberty and remembrance of him that way.

EMMANUEL DOWNING TO JOHN WINTHROP, JR.[1]

MY GOOD COSEN, Yours of the 24 of 8ber last I received, and doe hartily thank you for your relation of Connecticott, but you wrote not, where your selfe entend to setle.

For your Account the last yeare I laid for you as I then wrote 103*li* 1*s* 2*d* whereof I received last yeare of Dr. Reade 50*li* of my brother Gostlyn 2*li* more since of dr. Reade 50*li*. In all 102*li*. Soe there rests me vpon that account 1*li* 1*s* 2*d*.

For your tooles sent now by mr. Peirce, my brother Kirby had monie from me to pay for them, who I suppose sends you an account thereof, but I haue not yet received from him the particular charge thereof;

Mris. Peters when[2] shee went into Holland, apoynted dr. Read to pay me 50*li* for you, but he now telleth, he cannot receive yt, soe I beleive your mother will take order for your satisfaction when shee retornes, whom I expect here this moneth.

Sir Mathew Boynton telleth me that he entends to pay 30*li* for you at Whitsontyde next.

For newes I referr you to mr. Peirce who knowes how all things goe here. Germanie is now become a most desolate wildernes; there be manie townes beawtifull for buildings but neither man woeman nor child in them; they fynd, as pass by, goodly and rich wanscott roomes, with tables Cubbards and bedsteads standing in them, which they burne, or sett an howse on fyre to dresse theire meate, and leave yt burning next day when they departe. the Country doth soe swarme with Ratts which goe in such troopes as would fright a man to meet them;

The Emperour the French King and K[ing] of Spayne are making great preparation for warrs each against the other   The Sweades haue taken all Saxonie, the Duke is in a Castle beseidged by the Sweeds where tis thought, he cannot scape   thus with my love to your selfe your good wife mr. Peters etc. I leave you and your affaires to the blessing of the Almighty and rest your assured loving vnkle

EM: DOWNINGE

2 Martij 1636[/37]

---

[1] W. 2. 23; 4 *Collections*, VI. 44–45.
[2] The word in the original manuscript is "went."

you are to pay your Father W: 10s for the Currall which I putt into his account before I vnderstood yt was for you;

LUCY DOWNING TO JOHN WINTHROP[1]

To her dear and worthy brother Jhon winthrop esqr. tender this

MY DEAR BROTHER, I receiued your moste kinde letter dated in Octo. and your dayntie fruits wich indeed wear as good as ould eng. it selfe affords in theer kinde: but coming from new eng: and from your selfe, they wear rarities indeed: and wee then beinge att graces, I sent for them thither and sir hary and my lady wear much taken with them: sir hary profest it did much satisfie him, that things did prosper so well with you. nowe to giue you acount of our proceedings since my last to you: wee wear in progres from present after midsomer till part of Januarie, half of wich time wee wear at graces: and in the other half att groton, ason, shrubland, maplested, cowne: and whear not: and blessed be god for it in all those places wee both found all well in health, and wear well all of vs, all that time: exsept James a few ague fits: since my cominge home my self and mayds haue had agues: but I bless God for it: it hath leeft me againe and god hath hitherto moste gratiouslie preserued our famylie from the arrow of pestilence: or any other such sad disasters, as for our sins might moste deseruedlie haue imbitterd our liues, or depriued vs of life, and all comfort ere this: and on the contrary, hath he blest vs with many contents: now I know you wish vs noe less good then that thes cords of loue maye vnite vs to the fountaine of loue: in the firmest bands: but for the great cause, moste suddaine and sad is the change in so short a time: I confess a hart very dead might haue bine much rapt with the gratious light in those parts all that time: and in a way of admiration: god graunt that it may proue a gleeme before a storm, rather then a lightinge before the night of death. in this relation, might I spend more time and spirits then my condition will nowe permit, but I may spare: ill newes selldome wants messingers (in our climat) and what was then put in execution in those parts is at this instant calld apon in essex and but a month limetted for answeer: wich answeer its feard will proue a very fearfull sillence: thes are dayes of tryall. pray that our fayth fayle not nowe: I confess could a wish transport me to you, I think as big as I am, I should rather wish to bring an Indyan then a coknye into the world. but I cannot see that god

---

[1] W. 4. 5; 5 *Collections*, I. 18–20.

hath yet freed vs for that Journie: yet I doupt not but if he call vs to it, wee shall discern prouidence clearlie thearin: and I see more proballitie of the concurrence of things that waye nowe, then formerlie I euer did, both for generalls and perticullers, if god pleas to speare our liues: but maye itt not be more sesonable for one in my condition to breathe my gratefullnes to so faythfull a brother as your selfe for all your surpasinge affections, both to me and myne, and to desire the continuance of your brotherly care of theer best education, wich is a very importunate suit of myne to you, whether I liue or dye, but especiallie if god should preuent my indeuors theerin. george and his father complye moste cordyally for new eng: but poor boy, I fear the Journie would not be so prosperous for him, as I could wish, in respect you haue yet noe sosieties nor means in that kinde for the education of youths in learninge: and I bless god for it he is yet resonable hopefull in that waye: and it would I thinke as wee saye greue me in my graue, to know that his mynde should be withdrawne from his booke by other sports or imployments, for that weer but the way to make him good att nothinge: its true the collegdes hear are much corruptted, yet not so, I hope, but good frinds maye yet finde a fittinge tutor for him: and If it maye be with any hopes of his well doeinge hear, knowinge your preualency with my husband, and the hazard the boy is in by reson both of his fathers and his owne stronge inclination to the plantation sports: I am bould to present this sollisitous suit of myne, with all earnestnes to you and my nephew winthrop: that you will not condecend to his goeinge ouer, till he hath either attayned to perfection in the arts hear: or that theer be sufficient means for to perfect him theerin with you: wich I should be moste glad to hear of: it would make me goe far nimbler to new eng: if god should call me to it, then otherwise I should: and I beleeu a collegd would put noe small life into the plantation: as things are nowe ellswhear wear my scribship answeerable to my desiers of discourse with you I should be as tedious to you, as I am to my selfe, but in good maners I forbear your further trouble att present: and desireinge your prosperity, and prayers for me and myne, and a happy meetinge either in this or a better life Your sister to commaund

L. DOWNINGE

I pray present my seruis to msr. cotten and his, msr. humphryes and his lady, msr. saltinstall and hiss wife, mr. dudlie, msr. willson, msr. haynes and his, and all our frinds.

Mar. 4, 1636[/37]

I forget to tell you how forward wee are for new eng: georg his jointure and myne is sould, and but 3 hundred an 20 pounds would it afford vs: and 2 years day for payment: but the truth is, I sawe them so vnwillinge to doe me right in the assurance: that I feard payment would be more hardlie drawne from them: and somthinge may be better then nothinge.

LUCY DOWNING TO JOHN WINTHROP, JR.[1]

To her beloued nephew msr. Jhon winthrop present this

MY DEAR NEPHEW, good newes I haue none to present you with. all our comfort is, wee haue a god that brings good out of ill: and for ill newes I beinge very weary allready, I will forbear relations of it: I haue indeuord to prouide your thinges with the best care I could, but paynes I could take none: theerfore I shoud be very glad they be to your likeinge. I pray god bless my neec with her nurcery: and send you both comfort, in your posteritie, and in all your labours. I shoulde be very glad to hear of your good sucses in your salt work: we will indeuor to prouide a stoke to share with you, if you pleas to acsept vs: I thank you for all your loue: wishinge opertunitie to doe you seruis. I knowe you wishe vs with you, and wee some times doe the like, but I see it must cost more paynes then so, ere wee meet: mrs. peters is yet in hollan and James downinge with her, but we now daylie expect them   I pray present my seruis to him. mrs. peters and James are now come safe to vs: god of heauen bless you, and send vs a hapy meetinge either in this or a better place your ant that moste truly loues you

L. D.

Mar: 6: 1636[/37]

EMMANUEL DOWNING TO JOHN WINTHROP[2]

For my brother Winthrop

LOVING BRO[THER], Yours of the 29 of June, the 4 of August, and the 24 of 8ber I haue received this yeare, and paide all your bills except mr. Harts who is dead, and his executours haue not yet demaunded the monie. mr. Lucy who imployed mr. Hart sent to me for the monie. my answeare was that if mr. Lucy would give me his bond to dischardge you from Harts executours I would

---

[1] W. 4. 6; 5 *Collections*, I. 21.   [2] W. 2. 24; 4 *Collections*, VI. 46–47.

then pay yt to him. the messenger said, I should haue yt, but I never heard more of him; I haue hereinclosed sent your account. whereas you write that you entend to sell of my oxen and some other male catle, I pray sell what you please and pay your selfe for my childrens being with you;

My Ant Branch is lately dead.

I hartilye thank you for your lardge Information of the state of the plantation; I was thother day with Secretarie Coke who told me that there hath not ben a word of your plantacion at Councell board these manie moneths past;

the 4th of 9ber last at night here was great thunder and lightning with soe terrible a storme that manie steeples and Churches were beaten downe and verie manie howses and trees blowne vp by the rootes, in divers parts of this kingdome;

The Archb[isho]ps officers are now in visitation in Essex. on Friday last they began at Brentwood, where yt was declared to the ministers that eurie on must reade the K[ing]s declaration concerning the Saboth days recreations, or, at the moneths end, be deprived.

The Lord Maior sent his officers to most of the cheife familyes of the Citty to give them warning to kepe the Fasts, Lent Ember weeks, and the vigills;

I was at mr. Rogers of Dedham his funerall, where there were more people than 3 such Churches could hold; the gallery was soe over loaden with people that yt sunck and crackt and in the midle where yt was Joynted the tymbers gaped and parted on from an other soe that there was a great Cry in the Church; they vnder the gallery fearing to be smothered, those that were vpon yt hasted of, some one way some an other and some leaped downe among the people into the Church; those in the body of the Church seing the tymbers gape were sore afrighted, but yt pleased God to honour that good man departed with a miracle at his death, for the gallerie stood and the people went on againe, though not so manie as before; had yt faln as blackfryars did vnder the popishe assembly, yt would haue ben a great wound to our religion. Our freinds in Suffolke Essex and London are all in health.

The name of a Colledge in your plantation would much advantadge yt considering the present distast against our vniversityes. you need not stay till you haue Colledges to lodge schollars, for if you could but make a Combination of some few able men, ministers, or others to read certeyne lectures, and that yt were knowne here amongst honest men, you would soone haue students, hence, and Incouradgement to proceed further therein; what great burthen would yt be to a Minister for the present (till you haue meanes and be better supplyed with schollars) once a week for a moneth in eurie quarter to reade a logick, greke or hebrew lecture or the like.

thus with my love to your selfe my sister and all yours etc. of my freinds in the pl[an]t[ation], with my dayly prayers for you and yours with the prosperity of the wholl pl[anta]t[ion] I rest your assured loving brother

EM. DOWNINGE

6 Martij 1636[/37]

ROBERT RYECE TO JOHN WINTHROP[1]

Particular orders, directions and Remembrances geven in the dyoces of Norwiche vpon the primary visitation, of the Reverende father in God Mathewe Lorde Byshop of that Sea. 1636

(1) Firste, the wholle dyvyne Service be readde (bothe the firste and seconde Service) on Sondayes and holly dayes, and lecture dayes, (if they have any): And that the Communion-Service called the seconde service be awdiblye and distinctly Redde at the Communion table vnto the ende of the Nicene creede before the Sermon or homely. Yett so as in verye large churches the Mynister maye come neerer to reade the Epistle and Ghospell. And after the Sermon or Homely, the prayer for the wholle estate of Christes church: and one or more of the appoynted collectes, at the Communion table lykewyse; and after to dismisse the Congregation with the *Peace of God that passeth*, etc.

(2) That the prayer before the Sermon or homelye be exactely accordinge to the 55th Canon, (mutatis mutandis:) only to moove the people, to praye as there prescribed, and not otherwyse vnlesse the Mynister desyer, to enterpose the names of the 2 vniversities, and of a patron. And no prayer to be vsed in the Pulpitt after Sermon, but the Sermon to be concluded with *Glory to the Father*, etc. and so to come downe owte of the pullpytt.

(3) That the Communion Table (in euery church) do allwayes stande close vnder the walle vp at the Easte ende of the Channcell: The endes thereof Northe and Sowthe (vnlesse the ordinarye geve particular direction otherwyse). And that the Rayles be made before it, accordinge to the Archebishops late Iniunctions, reachinge crosse from the Northe walle to the Sowthe walle, neere one yarde in heighte, and so thicke with pillers, that dogges can not gett in.

(4) That the Lettany be never omytted on Sondayes, Weddensdayes and Frydayes. And that at all the Mynister be in his Surplice and hoodde, when so ever he is in publicke to performe any parte of his priestely function. And that in Readinge the chapters, he leave owte the Contentes, And after the

---

[1] W. 2. 157; 4 *Collections*, VI. 435–441.

lessons doe vse no psalmes or hymnes, but those that are appoynted by the Common prayer boocke.

(5) That the *Gloria Patri* be sayde after euery Psalme standinge vp, and that all the people doe awdibly, make all awnswere in the Lettany, and in all other partes of the Service, as is appoynted by the boocke of common prayer. And to the ende (to leade the common people theerein) that there bee a parishe clarke provyded in euery parishe, that can reade sufficientlye, and have compotente allowance from the parishe. And where there is none, that there bee one forthewith appoynted and chosen accordinge to the Canon.

(6) That the *Quicunque vult* (or Creede of Sainte Athanasius) bee vsed on the dayes by the Rubrick appoynted, in steade of the App[ost]les creede. And that the Mynisters forgett not to reade the Collects, Epistles, and Ghospells appoynted for the conversion of St. Pawle. And for all the holy weeke before Easter for Barnabas daye and for Ashe Weddensdaye, with the commination (also) on that. And also to vse the prayers and Suffrages goinge the perambulation, which is yeerely to be vsed in every parishe vpon the Rogation dayes—vizt. the Mundaye, Tewsedaye and Weddensday nexte before ascension, and at no other tyme. At which it is awntiently enioyned that the Mynister (at some conveniente places) doe in a woorde admonishe the people to geve thankes to God beholdinge his benefites in the frutes of the earthe, sayenge the 103 Psalme, and (as tyme and place shall admytte it) the 104 Psalme. And at any especiall bownde-markes, this or suche Sentences of holy Scripture, *Cursed bee hee that remooueth awaye the marke of hys neighbours lande*. And that returninge at laste to the churche there thay saye the divine Service.

(7) That no man do presume to haue his hatte on his heade in the tyme of Service, and Sermon in the church. And that due and comly Reverence be vysibly doone by all persons presente, where the blessed name of the Lorde Jesus is mentioned. And that euery one of the people doe kneele devowtely, when the Confession, Absolution, Commandiments or any Collects, or other prayers, is readde, both at the tyme of the Communion-Service of the church as also at Christninges Mariages Burialls etc.

(8) That they goe vp to the holy table, at Mariadges, at suche tyme as the Rubricke so directeth. And that the newe maried persons doe kneele withowte the Rayle and doe at there owne charge, (yf the Communion were not warned the Sundaye before) Receyve the holy Communion that daye, or else to be presented by the Mynister and Church wardens, at the nexte Generall for not Receyvinge.

(9) That woomen to be churched come and kneele at a syde neere the Communion table, withowte the Rayle (beinge vayled accordinge to the

Custome, and not covered with a hatt), as other wyse not to be churched; but to be presented at the nexte Generall by the Mynister and Church wardens or any of them.

(10) That warninge be geven by the Mynister for holy dayes and fastinge dayes of the weeke followenge, Immediately after the Sermon or Homelye. And that the Communion for the Sondaye followenge be warned the Sundaye before, Immediately after the prayer for the wholle estate of Christes church. And that as soone as suche warninge be gyven, the seconde of those 3 exhortations (which nexte after the prayer for the vniversall church are sett downe in the Service boocke) be treateably pronownced. After which to followe some of the Collectes appoynted. And to dismisse the people with the *Peace of God* etc.

(11) That when any neede is, the Sycke be prayed for, in the Readinge Deske (and noe wheare else) at the close of the firste service. Excepte it bee the afternoone And then to be doone Immediately after the Creede, vsinge only those 2 collects which are sett downe in the Service boocke for the visitation of the Sycke. That nexte after the mariadge (if there bee any) be begunne in the bodye of the church, and fynished at the table. That the churchinge of women do begynne as soone as the Mynister comes to the Communion table, before the Seconde Service, vnlesse there be a mariadge the same daye: For then the churchinge is not to beginne tyll those prayers appoynted to be sayd at the lords table (for the Mariadge) be ended.

(12) That no Mynister presume to marry any persons, whereof one of the parties is not of his parishe, vnlesse it bee otherwyse expressely mentioned in the lycence; Nor that he marrye any by vertue of any facultye or licence wherein the name of the Archedeacon or officiall is mentioned *sub pena suspensionis*.

(13) That the parishioners be warned by the Mynister and Church wardens to bringe there children to church for Baptisme in due tyme. And if any childe be not browghte before the Seconde lesson, that then the parents be presented for that defawte. And that no Baptisme be administred, (exceptinge in the case of necessetie) but on the Sondaye or holy daye.

(14) That the Fonte at Baptisme be fylled with cleane water and no dyshes, payles or basons be vsed in it, or insteade of it. And that the Mynister admytte but 2 godfathers and one Godmoother for a male childe and 2 good moothers and one god father for a female. And then doe at the fyrste aske them, whither the childe be yett Baptised or not. And doe take it in his armes, and do signe it with the sygne of the crosse when he doothe Baptize it. And after all do admonishe them to bringe yt to Confyrmation when tyme shall serve.

(15) That all Communicants come vp Reverently and kneele before the Rayle to receyve the Communion. And that the Mynister repeate to euery Communicante (severally) all the woordes that are appoynted to be sayd at the distribution of the holy Sacramente.

(16) That no wicker bottles, or Taverne Potts be browghte to the Communion table. And that the breade be browghte in a cleane clothe or Napkin. And that the woordes of consecration, be awdibly repeated (agayne) yf any breade or wyne be vsed, which was not at the firste consecrated.

(17) That the Mynister and Churchewardens of greate parishes, to avoyde confucion and over longe wearienge bothe of the mynister and of the parishioners, doe take order that there doe not come aboove 300 or at the moste 400 communicants, to one Communion, For which cawse thay are warned to have communions the oftener.

(18) That the holy Oblations in suche parishes where it pleaseth God at any tyme to putt into the hartes of his people by that holy action to acknowledge his guyfte of all which thay have to them, and there tenure of all from hym, and there debtte of all to hym: bee Receeved by the Mynister standinge before the table, at there comynge vp to make there oblations. And (then by hym Reverendly) presented before the lorde and sett vpon the table tyll the Service be ended.

(19) That the Mynister doe chatechyze in the afternoone halfe an hower (at the leaste) Immediately after the laste ringinge or towlinge of the Bell for the Eveninge prayer: accordinge to the Questions of the churche Chatechisme only, and standinge in the Readinge deaske.

(20) That the Mynisters readinge deske doe not stande with the backe towardes the Chawncell, Nor to remote or farre from it.

(21) That the Chawncells and Alleyes in the Churche be not encroched vpon by buyldinge the seates. And if any be so buylte, the same to be remooved and taken awaye And that no pewes be made on hie. So that thay which bee in them, cannot bee seene how thay behave them selves, or the prospecte of the church or chauncell hindered. And therefore that all pewes (within) doe not exceede a yarde in heighte be taken downe neere to that Scantlinge, vntill the Byshopp by his owne inspection (or by the viewe of some especiall Commissioners) shall otherwyse allowe.

(22) That none of what ranke so ever keepe any Chaplyns or Schollers in there howses to reade prayers, expownde scriptures, or to instructe the famylies, vnlesse thay bee therevnto enabled by lawe.

(23) Whereas Sermons are required by the Church of Englande, only vpon Sondayes and holy dayes in the Forenoones, and are permitted at funerralls,

that none presume to take vpon them to vse any preachinge or expowndinge (or to holde any suche lecturinge) at any othe tyme, withowte expresse lycence from the Byshoppe.

(24) That euery one (allowed to bee a lecturer) doe reade the devine Service (Fullye) in his Surplice and hoodde before euerye lecture, in the same manner, as is appoynted on Sondayes. And that all lecturers behave them selves modestly in there Sermons (preachinge faythe, obedience, and good woorkes: In all thinges observinge his Ma[jes]ties declaration prefixed before the 39 Articles, and his Ma[jes]ties Iniunctions) withowte intermedlinge with matters of State, or Questions late in difference, not favoringe or abeattinge any Scismaticks or Separatistes, eyther by especiall prayer for them or other wyse approovinge of them.

(25) That the Churchewardens suffer no man (but there owne person, vicar or curate) to preache vpon any occasion in there church tyll he shewe hys lycence, and subscribe his name in there paper boocke (for that purpose) appoynted, and the name of the Bishop who allowed hym.

(26) That there be the same manner of Ringinge of Bells to churche on holy dayes, which is vsed on Sondayes, And that there be no difference of Ringinge to church (when there is a Sermon) more then when there is none, exceptinge the knell for Funeralls.

(27) That no church or Chappell-wyndowe be stopped vp in any parte, nor the Floore (in any parte) vnpaved or vncleane kepte, nor the church any wayes abused, anoyed or prophanned.

(28) That all defawltes (contrary to the premisses heereof) be faythefullye inquired into by the Officialls from tyme to tyme at there Generalls, of whom the Byshoppe wyll require an accownte concerninge the same.

MATH: NORVIC:

Concordat cum articulis,
WILLYELMUS COLMAN, *Registrarius*

Pardon my Boldenes. Yours euer in the lorde.

THOMAS SYMTHE[1]

10 of Marche 1636[/37] C

[*Endorsed by Governor Winthrop:*] Mr. S: his A: B: C:[2] [*also, in another place:*] Mr. R: Answ:

---

[1] Cf. page 363, *n.* 1, above.

[2] The letter from Ryece (also signed "Thomas Smythe") which Governor Winthrop designated as "B" is dated March 7, 1636/37. The major portion of it consists of a copy of William Prynne's

whome I had a full purpose to haue sent you an Antimoniall Cupp[1] which I make doubt whether I shall gett to send by him. Yf I bee not missinformed the vsse thereof (I feare immoderat) was an occasion of shortening Sir Na- thaniell Riches dayes who hath made exchange of this liffe For a better; For the pretence of the Dorchester men I knowe not what to saie. I thincke if the trueth were knowen they rather should bee Indebted to us. I ame shure by sending the Comp[any's] shippe Lyons Whelp[2] for there occasions, the Comp[any] lost much money, besides the burden euer commonley was layd on the Londoners; For my partyculer I protest vnfeynedley to my best knowl- edge I ame out of purse for the generall Comp[any] twixt 3 and 400*li* and haue bene so For maney yeeres. what Recompence I shall haue I know not and It is not fytt aney pryuat man should beare a burden the generall bodey of the Comp[any] ought to beare   I will indeuour to bee further Informed of this buiseynes of theres if I Cane, but I perswade my selffe if aney such thinge were by order of Court the Court bookes there will shewe it and to my best Remembrance they willingley gaue what they had there to goe vppon accoumpt of there Stock Intended: For my buiseynes with Thomas Mayhewe I Referre you to what Is aboue written and what this bearer mr. Peirse will showe and accquaynte you with and what I haue written to our Gouernor to whome Indeede I haue beene larger therein then I Intended. I desyre your his and the Fauour of the Court so farr as my Cause shall appeare honest and just, and I harteley pray you aduize and Furder my seruant Jno. Jolliffe whereby hee may bee in possession of all my estate there and that it may bee publiqueley knowen mr. Mayhewe neither had nor hath power or order to deale Fore me sethence the tyme of John Jolliffs arryuall there otherwisse then what Is done with the knowledge aduize and Consent of the sayd Jno. Jolliffe. It would bee to long to Relate to you my wrongs, and Tho: Mayhewes vniust and Indirect dealings by me in a most high nature, manner and meas- ure if truley knowen and vnderstoode which I doubt not but mr. Peirse will at lardge accquaynte you with and I desyre he may bee imployed in helping to perffeckt my accowmpts with him. I hope by the Next shippe to Intreate a Freynd that Is mynded that way if he do come thether to helpe settell my account and some Course also about my meanes I haue there before all bee Consumed, For insteede of benefitt by N. E. I suffer to extremley in my estate

---

[1] See John W. Farlow, "The Antimonial Cup of the Seventeenth Century," *Proceedings*, LX. 150–160.

[2] The *Lion's Whelp*, sent out by the Massachusetts Bay Company, sailed from Gravesend on April 25, 1629, "with above forty planters out of the Countyes of Dorset and Somerset," arriving in Salem in mid-July. Charles E. Banks, *The Planters of the Commonwealth* (Boston, 1930), 61.

as you will soone perseyue when you vnderstand the trueth of all things. Excuse me I pray you in beeing to troblesome to you heerein. I may not omitt to accquaynt you with one passage touching the generall nameley of one mr. Cleve and mr. Tucker who this last yeere were with me and pretended great good to our plantacion and great Fauour they could haue at Court and desired my approbacion of somewhat they Intended whereto I could say nothing till I sawe what It was, wherevppon they browght me a writing which hauing seeyne I vtterley dislyked and disavowed for hauing owght to doe therein, but taking it to pervsse before I would geeue my answere Caused a Coppy to bee taken which I send you heerewith sence Mooreton[1] from them Came to me on the exchange and mr. Peirse beeing there I hauing noe desire to speake with Mooreton alone putt him of a turne or 2 on the exchange till I Found Mr. Pierse and then Caled him to me and in his presence disavowed to haue aney thing to doe therein, for Moreton would haue had me pay the Chardge or promiss some such matter in taking out somewhat vnder the seale this beeing done one or about the 9 January last vppon the exchange as Mr. Pierse Cane Relate vnto you.

There Is 4 or 5 sommes of 25*li* a peece owing to pryveat men borrowed on the Companies seale whereof there were maney more but It seemes all paid saue theise and theise I wish were paid, the not doing whereof by Ill mouthes Reflects to much to the disparagment of the Companie. take it to hart I pray you For you would and the Companie would if they knewe and heard that I doe and must heare to my greyffe and disdayne of there base languadge of vs. For my partyculer though I beare alreddy euen by that the generall Comp[any] owes me as touched before more then to much, Yeet were I not ouerpressed by my heauey burdens there laded on me by T[homas] M[ayhew] I would stop some of there mouthes if not all though I paid it out of my owne purse, but I ame Forsed otherwise   god forgeeue him that Is the Cause of It. I will heere conclude, beseeching the Allmightey to bless with good suckcess all your Indeuours. I doe thinke mr. Gouernor shall doe himselffe a great deale of Right to Come for England as soone as his yeere is exspired, and I ame to confident if he negleckt it It will exceedingley preiudice him in his outward Estate. I knowe you wish him Realley well   Consider seriouslei of it I pray you and aduize him For his good, wherevnto the Lord direct you and him and so I euer Rest Your Wor[shi]ps assured to be Comanded .

MATHEWE CRADOCK

---

[1] Thomas Morton of Merrymount.

I thinke I shalbee forsed to bee a suytor for some land at Shaweshynne the best of myne as I am Informed neere my house beeing allotted to mr. Wilson and mr. Nowell, therefore pray your furderance wherein shalbee needfull. Yours

MATHEWE CRADOCK

I pray you be plesed to lett mr. Peirse amongst others shewe you mr. Palmers letter of barnstable whereby you will find a strang passadge of Tho. Mayhewes by me. I maruell mr. Hayne would drawe him into such a buiseynes, but mr. Haynes I ame perswaded thought mr. Mayhewes delings to bee others then they will appeare when they are vnmasked.

ROBERT STANSBY TO JOHN WINTHROP[1]

To the Wor[shipfu]ll my much respected frende Mr. Winthrop at his house in Boaston these be delivered in New England

WOR[SHIPFU]LL WORTHY SIR, Your loueinge letter dated Nouemb. 10, 1635 I receiued whereof I wrott you an answere and sent yt by the shipp wherein Mr. Roger of Asington went, but we haue not hard of the safe arriuall of yt at N: E: I know that you haue hard of the great losse at Dedham, by the death of that paynefull labourer Mr. Roger. One Mr. Newcomen sone of hym at St. Peter in Colchester succeedeth hym etc. Your old freinds of the society are all aliue blessed be the Lord although we are all out of worke.

Old Mr. Harison gaue ouer, and desired the B[ishop] to giue him leave so to do by reason of his age.

Mr. Penching preaching att Stoake Clare was desired by the parisheoners to sitt styll leste they shoud haue byne in trouble for hym being soare threatened etc.

Mr. Morgan was inhibited preaching and after that was taken with the num palsy whereof he is not yet perfectely recouered yett had agayne some liberty to preach for a whyle if he had ability of minde and body.

Mr. Lea of Groton is suspended for refusing to reade the Kings toleration on the Sabboth but I lately hard that ther was some hope of his liberty.

Mr. Mott of Stoake and Nayland standeth suspended ab officio et beneficio for refusing the new conformitie as they call yt.

---

[1] W. 3. 3; 4 *Collections*, VII. 8–9. The Reverend Robert Stansby, a graduate of Cambridge University (M.A., Clare, 1606), was Rector of Westhorpe, Suffolk, from 1630 to 1636, when he was deprived. Venn, *Alumni Cantabrigienses*, Part I, IV. 149.

My selfe was depriued of my parsonage July 18, 1636 by our B[ishop] for refusing the old conformity. Many in Suff[olk] left ther places for feare, and many stand excominicated and many suspended, but none was depriued but my selfe I desyre your prayers to know what is the Lord will therein as for other newes, I leave to the passengers to relate to your wor[shi]p. This bearer John Stansby is the nerest kinsman I haue except one being my eldest brothers second sone. I hope that the Lord haue wrought in hym a great change, outwardly yt seameth so, tyme (especially in N: E:) will tell us more. oh how ioyfull shall I be to hear yt to be in truth.

Good Sir if ther be cause putt hym into some employment: he is both willing and able to work in husbandry although he have byne lately a clothyer. I would desyre that he might haue a convenient lott of ground which he, or his frends, comeing after hym might in tyme build on. I would not haue hym any way to be chargabl to you, or yours, for I heare and do believe yt of your liberality to many, and so will not haue my kinsman to be burdensome to you and he haue brought some provision with hym and of a minde to worke for his liueing My wife and I haue our health and haue a cherfull heart I prayse God, and notwithstanding our loss. I do liue with my sonne in law at Mendlesham. We both do hartely salute you and your wife and whol family in the Lord and rest desiring your prayers Your loueing freinde in the Lord

R. STANSBY

March 17, 1636[/37]

LION GARDINER TO JOHN WINTHROP, JR.[1]

To the Worsh[i]p[fu]ll Mr. John Winthrop at Boston Ipsidge or ese where thes deliver

WORSHIP[FU]LL SIR, these are to certyfie you how the lord hath beene pleased to deale with vs this winter. it hath pleased him of his goodnes and mercy to give vs rest from the Indians all this winter butt one the 22th of the last moneth I with tenn men more with me went abou[e] our neck of land to fire some small bushes and marshes whear we thought the enimie might have lien in ambush and aboute halfe a mile from home we started 3 Indians and havinge posibility to have cutt them short we runinge to meett them and to fire the marsh but whylest our men was setting it one fire there

---

[1] W. 3. 18; 4 *Collections*, VII. 56–58.

rushed out of the woods 2 severall wayes a great Company of Indians which
though we gaue fire vppon them yett they run one to the very mussells of our
peices and soe the shott 3 men downe in the place and 3 more men shott that
escaped of which one died the sam[e] night and if the lord had not putt it
into my mind to make the men draw ther swords the had taken vs all aliue
soe that sometime shouttinge and sometime retraightinge keepinge them of
with our sword[s] we recovered a bayre place of the ground which this winter
I had cleard for the same vse and they durst not follow vs any further because
yt is vnder Com[mand] of our great guns of which I hope the have had some
experience as we heare by the relation of other Indians, and your freind
Sacious and Nebott are the cheife actors of the treachery and villainy agaynst
vs.[1] as concerninge my sheep which you writt to me of I tooke order with Mr.
Gibbins about them but If he be not yett come Home I would intreat you
that the may be kept with yours vntill you heare from him. thus Hopeinge
that you will be a meanes to stirr vp our freinds in the bay out of there dead
sleep of securytie to think that your Condicon may be as ours is vnles some
speedy Course be taken which must not be done by a few but by a great
Company for all the Indian haue ther eyes fixed vppon vs and this yeare the
will all joyne with vs agaynst the Pequtt and it is to be feared that the next
year the will be agaynst vs   we have vsed 2 sheets of your lead which was in
square $\dfrac{64}{40}$ foote. I hav writ to the governour to pay you soe much agayne
$\overline{104}$
I haue sent you your bead steed and would haue made a better butt time
would not permit for we watch every other night neuer puttinge of our
Clothes for the Indians show them selves in troupes aboute vs every day as
this bearer can certyfie you more at large. thus committinge you your wife
father and mother Mr. Peeter and the rest of our frends to God I rest Your
asured frend to comm[and]

Lion G[a]rdiner
1636

Seabrooke this 23th of the first moneth 1636[/37]

I men[tione]d that your lead was the one shiet 16 foot longe and 4 brood
the other 10 longe 4 brodd

---

[1] For Winthrop's account of this incident, see *Journal*, I. 208.

16		10
4		4
64		40
40		

104 square foot

THOMAS TAYLOR TO JOHN WINTHROP[1]

To the Woor[shi]p[fu]ll John Wainthropp Esquire deliver in New england per my good frind Mr. George Cleiue: whom God preserue

BRISTOLL the 25th Mrch: 1637

WORTHIE SIR, After my due Respects premised I made bold allthough vnacquainted, to addresse thes few lines vnto yow: which are to giue your Woor[shi]pp to vnderstand that about one yeare since I sent my sonn Humphrie Tayler from london ouer into New england and furnished hem with such necessaries as was then needfull and paid his passage and haue sithence sent hem ouer more for supplye as by the Invoice which my good frind Mr. George Cleive will shew vnto yow may appeare: it notwithstanding all which my sonn doth continuallie pas bills of exchandge vppon me for seuerall soms of monie: how he liueth to spend so much monie I know not: for he neither sendeth me anie accounts nor Returns: and I do much feare that if he showld continew that Cours he would be a means of my vndoing: for prevencion wherof hearing of your good worth and good gouerment in that Countrie haue presumed to make bolde to authorize yow together with Mr. Jno: Humphry and Mr. Cleiue to take such Cours with my sonn for the getting of such goods he hath left into your hands as yow shall find fitt: wherin I humblie craue your best aide and assistance and that yow wilbe pleased amongst yow to dispose therof as it shall seeme best vnto yow for my benefitt: and also to dispose of my sonn as yow shall thinke best the which I will indeavor to requite to the vtmost of my power. I thowght fitt to name Mr. Cleiue in the letter of Attornie because he was heare present and by his aduise made bold with yow also I craue pardon for my boldnes and leaue all to your dew Consideracion and humblie take my leaue resting Your Wor-[shi]ps to be comanded

THO: TAYLER

---

[1] W. 4. 85; 5 *Collections,* I. 239–240.

RICHARD SALTONSTALL, JR., TO THE GOVERNOR, DEPUTY, AND ASSISTANTS OF MASSACHUSETTS[1]

To the right wor[shipfu]ll the Gover[nou]r Deputie and Assistans

MAY IT PLEASE YOUR WOR[SHI]PS, According to the power which was committed to Mr. Nowell and Mr. Mahue aboute my accompt with Mr. Dillingham,[2] they have taken much paynes (which I thankfully acknowledge) and have sett mee in a fayer way to make a full end for my owne perticuler. And by reason of Edward Dillinghams importunitie to have all things ended betweene him and Mrs. Dillingham disceased: that hee might (as it is meete) have that in his owne hand which is due to him by his brothers will; the Commissioners have therfor appoynted a meeting at Meadford, vppon the 3d day of the next weeke to that end: I have therfore made bould at this time (as I thought it my dutie) to acquaint your wor[shi]ps, that Mrs. Dillingham (in her lifetime) did acquaint Mr. Dudly with her mind aboute many things betwixt herselfe and Edward Dillingham (which will need his presence very much) and did rely vppon his direction and counsell; and entreat his help thearin (when as it should have beene ended by Arbitrators of their owne chusing:) I am therfore bould to thinke that [I] am not troblesome to your wor[shi]ps; nor offencive in the least kind vnto any; if I shall entreate thus much; that Mr. Dudly may bee desired to joyne with Mr. Nowell and Mr. Mahue in this behalfe, and if hee cannot bee at leaisure the 3 day of the next weeke; the soonest day may bee appoynted (in regard of Mr. Dillingham) which will suite with his occasions. Your wor[shi]ps to bee commanded

RICHARD SALTONSTALL

[*Ca.* April, 1637]

SIR NATHANIEL BARNARDISTON TO JOHN WINTHROP[3]

To my assured loving frend John Winthrop Esqr. in New England be these delivered

DEARE SIR, These few lines in hast are only to salut you and yours and to let you know that I shall neuer be vnmindfull of you in my best affectiones as

---

[1] W. 3. 68; 4 *Collections*, VII. 253–254.

[2] "The power formerly granted to Mr. Dudley, Mr. Endecot, and Mr. Bradstreete, is granted to Increase Nowell and Thom: Mayhewe, to examine the accounts betweene Mr. Richard Saltonstall, Mr. Apleton, and Edward Dillingham." *Records of the Court of Assistants*, II. 65.

[3] W. 2. 179; 4 *Collections*, VI. 546–547.

allso to certefy you that I have receaued no letter from you or your Sonn though I haue written to you both by Mr. Clarke a minister who I understand is safely ariued with Mr. Rogers as allso of the boy which I sent you, who I desyre may giue you good contentment   I expected to haue hard how you would haue the mare disposed of which acording to your appoyntmend I gaue your sonn whether to be sent you or sould for your vse and to whom you would haue the mony payd   I haue yet kept hir vntill I might know your determination therin as I wrote to your sonn and expected now his answare Blessed be our good God we all heare inioy our healthes in some competent manor though accompined with noe smale trobles whear of I doubt not but you will hear at large by others   it is the portion that the Lord hath ordayned for his in this life who in his superabundant goodnes turneth all thinges to the best of his   euen so be it   so in the rembrance of myne and my wiues best and intire loue to you and all our good frindes with you remembred as if I should perticularly name them I commend you all to the blessed guidance of the Allmighty and rest Your euer most assured loving frind and brother

NATH. BARNARDISTON

KETTON this 4th of Aprill 1637

FRANCIS KIRBY TO JOHN WINTHROP, JR.[1]

To his much respected frend Mr. John Winthrop at his house at Ipswich this deliver in New England

LONDON this 10th April 1637

KIND SIR, I receiud yours dated 28th January and haue delivered the inclosed to Mr. Keflar, and haue receiud the glasses and the water from him and haue packed them carefully in a runled with 5 or 6 pecks of salt, and delivered it abord the Hector to John Wood masters mate who is my Cosen James Downeings aquaintance   I haue made him acquainted with the nature of the water and danger of it. he hath promised to be carefull of it. Thus with my harty praiers to God for the preseruation of you and yours I rest Your lo[ving] frend

FRA: KIRBY

---

[1] W. 3. 8; 4 *Collections*, VII. 18–19.

BRAMPTON GURDON TO JOHN WINTHROP[1]

To my muche honored frend Jhon Wenthrop Esquer geu thes at Boston in N. E.

MY WORTHY GOOD FREND, The last leter that I haue resayued from yow being 24 of Jeuen 1636, I was then glad thearby to hear of your good helthe with all yowers, and so I hope god still continue the same to his glorry. I would I could writ you anithing licke to geue coumfort to eny honest engleshe myend for good to churche or comonwelthe. the hed is scicke and all the memburs out of frame. we haue a trayter a naybur discouerred, the eldest sonn of the Lorde Skinner of Lanham parck, a papest if anithing, a notorious swagerer. when he was in an alhous with Tom Dande Sir Gorge Waldegraus lat clarck (Sir Gorg dyed the sabothe before our twelff scessyons) he eused this spech   I haue spent my forteunes and I will goo to Romm but I would doo sommwhot that I mought be spocke of after we are ded and after this he expressed his desyer to kile the king. he had the licke speche to Harry Copenger the dockters brother, and thes 2 are his sceuerrall acceusers. I will now informe yow of 3 of our new conformetans in this dyesses. thear is won Briges ceurat to Mr. Legat at Barnam Brome near Norwich. he had begot his moters mayed with child who descouerring so muche and bewayleng her selff to him, he aduised her to be content and scylent, and to met him next morning in a feld which it scem is within the libertis of the scitte. she prepared to do as he dyrected her, but agenst his direccyon she tould a sister that she was to goo she knew not whether. the sister desyred to goo with her till she should tacke hors. the currat comming and sceing 2 wemen he would not rid to them but returned, and indeuerred in the euneng to speacke with her blameng her that she had acquayented any with her Jurny   she exceused and sayed it was to her scister. then he charged her not to speacke a word to any but to met him the next morning, and that fore none she was found ded in the plas and as is judgged strangled with her apern string the which lay a rod from her body. it is sayed a shepperd ded sce them thear together yet he deny the murther but confes he got her with child. it is sayed that soumbody had had the eues of her a litele before or after her stranglin. we had won parson Fockes of Erles Some and another parrishe thear near. he had scet vp a fram of a hous vpon ground he pretended right vnto but his aduersary Starling hired won to disquiet his buldeng who with a hachet endeuerred to beat out the vnder bearrens. the parson hearring him he and his man cam feuryously the on

---

[1] W. 2. 182; 4 *Collections,* VI. 561–566.

with a pichforcke and the man with a hege stack mad him to run   thay pur-
seued him and ouertocke him   he strocke him aboue the forhed with the pichforcke which forsed out part of his brayens and after coum the man and gaue
him a blou with the stacke but not so mortale. the crouners quest found this
manslauter, and hear vpon thay had thear tryale, and allthoughe thear
apered muche males befor yet thay wear conuict only of manslauter. this
tryall was this lent assyses before Justes Crock, and thear atended our 2
reuerent docters Godde and Warren. the parson was tried withought the
gayele   the m[aste]r had his preuileg of presthod and thearfore had no
clargy tendred to him so escaped burning. the man now leget but repryued
for his pardon. This man at his tryall tocke the fact vpon him in hop as was
thought that his master would purchas his pardon.

The 3 mongst haue ben this   Mr. Daulton minester at Woluerston being
this somer won of the 60 reuerent men he and Mr. Stansby depryved the
other suspended as you shall hear. B[ishop] Wren perceued won Cole the
ceurat at St. Mary Kye in Ipswich vnder Mr. Sameuell Ward and as is
knouen he the cheff persceceuter of him in hye commicyon for recompens of
his sceruis he ingenryously proceured him into this liueng, this Cole bearryeng
muche mallis to Mr. Dalton and to all his family who had built him a smale
houes heartofore near his parsonag   Mr. Daltons kow would breacke into
the glebe whear she had formerly had intertayenment, his mayed sceing her
m[aste]rs cow in the glebe ran to feche her ought. Cole sceing her he rid to
her and with a krabtre cogele beat her so as for a month all thought she
would not have eskaped with lyeff. our tyem plesing clargy grow exscedeng
bould thay haue wind and tyed with them, and littele or no gras to stay thear
rage. God in mersy stay thear rage. Sir as conscearning my sonn Edmund I
neuer ment he should be burddensoum to yow, and so I writ to yow and I
gaue that order to my sonn and dafter Saltonstall   I mad account when thay
went that I had monis coumming to me for clothe that I scent by Mr. Dell-
ingan. I must tele you I ded maruell when it was furst writ to me that yow
had vndertaken him and that yow wear to haue the profit of his 2 bullockes
which wear licke to yeld no profet but charg till the spring followeng, only I
hoped yow ded geue him soum Imployment to helpe toward his charg. good
Sir so son as I resayued your letter gaue order to pay 20*li* to Mr. Douneng
as the letter dyrected me, and shall wellingly yeld you whot more yow desyer,
and so I haue geuen order to my sonn Saltonstall. I haue had a purpos of
haueng the boy to returne only in this regard, he haue a copyhould tenement
houlden of Do. Warrens passonage at Melford. the boy shall if he liu to mid
7bur be 21 years of age   I would haue him scele it and then returne if God

will in the spring I should be glad to fyend him met to maneg the stocke that I desyer to bestow vpon him, it may be 5 or 600*li* I shall be glad to be aduised for the best conscedring his weack capasyte for the orderring of it. We are scorry to hear of your and Mrs. Wenthropes late callamyte, but we hope God will restore yow dobule coumfort and thus with the remembrans of my wiffes and my treu loue to yow your wiffe and to all the branchis I pray God to kep vs, resteng Your euer asseured louing frend

BRAMPTON GURDON

Thear is a howes in Boxford now shut vp for the infeccyon of the plage.

I latly doo hear that your aunt Winthrop who liued in Suthworck is latly dede. I had allmost forgot to let yow vnderstand that on teuesday the 28 of marche I met at Beury Sir W. Spring he asked how to scend a letter to yow. He promised to scend me a letter by 8 next morning but ded not. he then as allso at our assyses desyred me to desyer you from him to stay your hand in yeldeng so muche to his kinsman as heartofore. I fyend his desyer is to cut of his yearly mayentenans, aleggeng whot he haue don for him and other licke charges that he in other plases goo thorou with. He haue ben in a great scickenes, that haue muche wasted his body. he haue latly marryed his sonn to Sir Hamund Stranges dafter.

Aprele 11th 1637

SIR MATTHEW BOYNTON TO JOHN WINTHROP, JR.[1]

To my uerie worthy friende John Winthropp the yonger Esqr. att Ipswidge in the Massachusetts Bay in New England giue this

SIR, hauinge considered the uncertaintie of my condition and the more, by reason of manie difficulties which I dayly meete withall, my businesses alsoe which are manie beeing yett undisposed of: I haue thought itt nott conuenient to be att anie further charge with my stocke butt ame upon these considerations fullie resolued to lett them out to be kept for me for a third parte of the increase, which I haue heard to be the usuall rate of the Contrie, butt if I be mistaken therin, I refer itt to your selfe to make such an allowance out of the increase of the Cattle, I meane my whole stocke, as you shall iudge to be equall and proportionable: and because theyr will be noe employment for

---

[1] W. 3. 42; 4 *Collections*, VII. 168–169.

my seruants when my stocke is thus disposed of: I will leaue itt to theyr choice, whether they will returne into England, the charge of which theyr passage I will uerie willinglie beare, if they thinke itt conuenient, which notwithstanding I suppose they will nott, (if they understand the condition of things here) or els to make use of theyr liberties for theyr best aduantage in the place where they are: your kindeness in the disposinge of my businesses for me shall much engage Your affectionate and assured friende

Matt. Boynton

London April 12th 1637

I haue sent eyther of my seruants halfe a yeares wages by Mr. Hopkins which I pray you deliuer to them. I haue heard nothing from you nor them since the last yeare: soe that I know nothing how my stocke prospereth: I haue giuen your vncle Downing satisfaction for thirtie pound concerning which you writt to me. I gaue my seruants a yeares wages before hand when I sent them ouer in May last. I haue alsoe intreated Mr. Hopkins to use his endeauoures for the disp[o]sing of my stocke for my best conueniencie, soe that I may be free from anie charge att all in keeping of them and that itt may be alsoe in my power to deliuer them upon occasion of anie present bargain to anie to whom I shall thinke fitt to sell them here att home.

ROBERT STANSBY TO JOHN WILSON[1]

To the Reuerent, my very loueing and much respected freinde Mr. Wilsone pastour of the congregation at Booston these deliver in new England

Reuerent and welbeloved brother in the Lord, I wrott lately to you by my kinsman who came with Mr. Andrews of Ipswich, but now haueing so fytt an opportunity by many who come with Mr. Cutting shipp as I will not lett yt slipp ouer, in token of my loue and desyre to heare of you, and the rather I am willing to putt penn to paper in regard of some thing that haue lately fallen out amongst vs.

Mr. Morgan is now dead and I hope at rest with the Lord. our ministers who haue yet ther liberty are in great danger of losing yt all over the lands Of them I haue lately hard much and so much as I cannot but grieue for yt (yf yt be true not without cause) especially these 3 particulars.

---

[1] W. 3. 4; 4 *Collections*, VII. 10–11.

1. That ther is great diuision of Iudgement in matter of religion amongst good ministers and people which moued Mr. Hooker to remoue now we see that yt is Christ speeche, a kingdome diuided, etc.

2. That many of the ministers are much sleighted with you, insomuch as although you want ministers (as some wright) yet some amongst you worke with ther hands being not called to any place, as Mr. Burdett of Yarmouth etc.

Others laye downe ther ministery and become priuate members, as Mr. Bacheler, Mr. Jenner, and Mr. Nathan. Ward etc. that which grieue me most your selfe much sleighted of whose faythfullnesse, gifts and diligence I and many others haue had so much experience.

3. That you are so strict in admission of members to your church, that more then one halfe are out of your church in all your congregations, and that Mr. Hooker before he went away preached against yt (as one report who hard hym) (and he saith) now although I knowe all must not be admytted yet this may do much hurt, yf one come amongst you of another minde, and they should ioyne with hym.

Good Sir I pray giue a true, playne and longe answere, for I assure you ther is now so much talke of yt, and such certeyne truth of yt, as I know many of worth, for outward estate and abilty for wisdome and grace are much danted from comeing. I wish you well, and much longe for your priuiledges. what the Lord haue determined I know not. I desyre to wayte vpon hym for his direction. My wife and I do hartily salute you and Mrs. Wilson and your familyes and so for this tyme I commytt you to the Lord and rest Your loueing true frend

R. Stansby

Aprill 17, 1637

Old Mr. Hall is yet liueing but silenced. a letter from Mr. Cotton to hym would chere hym vp in his old dayes, but howsoever I pray remember my respect to hym.

I being putt from my parsonage do not well know wher I shall liue: but I pray direct your letter to Mr. Gurdon of Assington.

ROBERT STANSBY TO JOHN WINTHROP[1]

To the wor[shipfu]ll my very good freinde Mr. Winthrop at his house be these delivered in new England

Aprill 17, 1637

Wor[shipfu]ll Sir, and loueing freinde, since I wrott by my kinsman I haue receiued your loueing letter dated Jan. 28, 1636 for which I hartily thanke you, since which I heare that Mr. Morgan is dead and at rest and that your old minister Mr. Lea hath his liberty to preache, but vpon what conditions I know not. I am sory much for your diuisions   we heare great speche of them, and I ame sure that they dant many wise faythfull christians and men of Ability from comeing, fearing lesse a kingdome diuided, and cannot stande and I heare many haue diverted ther thought   but what another yeare may bringe forth the Lord knoweth: things with vs are dayly much worser. I desyre your prayers for old England. I haue wrott more at large to Mr. Wilson. I desyre your worsh[ip] to send this letter to my brother Hubbard with all speede, lesse his goods in Mr. Cuttings shipp should miscary: he will pay the messenger. My wife and I hartily salute you and Mrs. Winthrop with your whol family and so I rest Your loueing freind

R. Stansbye

EDWARD WINSLOW TO JOHN WINTHROP[2]

To his worthy and much honored Friend Joh. Winthrop Esqr. at his howse at Boston these be delivered

Worthy Sir, Your Letter by my wiues sonne I received the 6th day of the last weeke being very sorry mine came so unseasonably to your hands. For answere to yours Our Cowncell having weighty occasions this day to meete and confer about divers businesses which much concerne us I imparted your Letter to the Governor and them, who seeing it impossible for the Governor or myselfe to bee at your Court to morrow requested me to write by the bearer and thereby salute your Governor your selfe, and Assistants   Concerning your present busines we conceiue it will be simply necessary for you to proceed in the war begun with the Pequots, otherwise the natiues we feare

---

[1] W. 3. 4; 4 *Collections*, vii. 12.

[2] Historical Society of Pennsylvania; Increase Mather, *Early History of New England*, Samuel G. Drake, Editor (Boston, 1864), 286–288.

will grow into a stronger confederacy to the further prejudice of the whole English. We are very glad to heare that the Munheges are fallen from the Pequots and brought to a professed war with them knowing their inveterate hatred and desire it may be nourished by all good meanes, who are soldiers as well as the other. These best know the Pequots holds and holes and the fittest instruments can be employed and such a people as will also well accord with the Narrohiggansets. But there is one thing of ill consequence which we heare from Coneetncut vizt. that there are some English there that furnish the enemy by way of trade having made a league with them. If you enquire of mr. Jesop who came in the barke with mr. Harding you may receiue particular informacon thereabout   That this will be ill taken I dowbt not, yet durst doe no other then informe you. Yet let me commend one thing to your consideracion how dangerous a thing it may proue if the Dutch (who seeke it) and they should close by reason of the Pequots necessity: I speake not this as desiring the benefit of their trade, for we are weary of the worke as we are dealt withall. Concerning things Estward, Capt. Standish is returned who reporteth of the Royall entertainement Shurt hath given Dony at Pemaquid. He saith (being Commander Generall) that if he receiue a Commission he must take him, onely six weekes before he will giue him notice, and in lue thereof tis [   ] mr. Shurt hath promised him to informe him of whatever preparacon shall be made or intended against them.[1] He further saith that if his Commission be to take the Grand Bay (yourselues) he will attempt it though he should haue no other vessell then a Canoe. But the English are all his Friends except Plimoth: nor is he enemies to any other. Shurt hath undertaken to furnish him with powder shott yea all manner of provisions, And to that end under a colour of gathering vp some debts is come to make provisions for them till his owne ship come. Tis also reported that Sir Ferdinando Gorges hath written to Saco That the French heere are not sett out nor allowed by the King of Fr[ance] but a base people which their estate disclaime, and therefore stirreth them up to informe both you and us that we might joyne together to expell them. One thing more which I had almost forgotten they haue lost their Gally and a pinnase at Ile Sable and brought away their people who are at Penobscot where they haue built a pinnase of threescore tunne. The last news is this whereat I am most grieved That all the late differences between mr. Wheelwright and your selues in Church and Court are in writing at Richmunds Ile where Turlany shewed him six sheets of paper

---

[1] In the margin: "I report these things from Capt. Standish but as the reports that are familiar in the Estern parts, that you may likewise make your use of them."

full written about them. The Lord in mercy looke upon us and leaue us not to the malice of Satan and wicked men his instruments, but so direct us, by his Spirit as the end may redownd to his glory and our mutuall good.

Sir However I could not come at this sudden warning by reason of our publick occasions and the fowlenes of the latter part of the weeke past yet neverthelesse if you conceiue my comming may be any furtherance in any good accion God giving hea[l]th and ability mine owne occasions shall giue place, and I shall be ready to doe any service God shall inable me. In the meane time and whilest I haue being my prayers I hope shall be to the Throne of grace for you and yours whom I salute in the Lord and rest Yours Assured

EDW. WINSLOW

PLYM. the 17th of the 2d mo. 1637

If now after your Court you haue any desire to speake with me at goodman Stows of Roxbury you shall heare of one that is to come foorthwith hither.

HERBERT PELHAM TO JOHN WINTHROP[1]

*To the Right Wor[shipfu]ll his worthy and much Respected friend John Winthrop Esqr.
at his House in Boston*

LOVEING COSEN, It much refresheth me when I heare from yow but woud more could I have the Happines to see yow. your letter by Mr. Peirce I received and rejoyce in the welfare of your selfe and yours. your frinds of the Ferrers[2] though now removed thence one step neerer yow, are I blesse God in good health from whom yow shall heare by the next I have heere inclosed sent yow a letter from your old friend who sent it to me in the winter and should have sent it to you by the first but sliped the opportunity not being sure of a trusty messenger. your Brother mr. Tindall and his are in good health only he hath at this time occasion of Heavines for the Death of his youngest Daughter who dyed the last weeke of a Consumption we haue no Newes worth the sending to yow. yow heare more dayley from us and of us then I know yow desier. lett us still as we have had soe entreate the Helpe of your prayers. remember my best respect to your good wife my cosen John and his wife thus comitting you and yours and the greate worke yow have in hand

---

[1] W. 4. 86; 5 *Collections*, 1. 241–242.
[2] The manor of Ferrers, acquired by Pelham through his first wife.

to the guideance and direction of him who is able to keepe amongst yow the unity of the Spirit in the Bond of peace which is and shall be the prayer of him that is your ever loveng kinsman

H. PELHAM

April 19th 1637

ROBERT RYECE TO JOHN WINTHROP[1]

To the woo[rshipfu]ll his moste respected good Frinde Mr. John Wrinthrope esqr.
at his howse at Boston in Newe Englande geve these

SIR, this bearer Mr. Fyske[2] beinge one every waye so pious and religeous, needes not my comendations of hym, but the malignitie of the tymes, removinge hym with sondry others of his profession into your partes, hathe required this shorte wrytinge of mee, in his behalfe that what imployement you can procuere hym, I may be thankefull vnto you for it. hee is a graduate and havinge preached mooche seinge the danger of the tymes, he changed his profession of Divinitie into physicke wherein he hathe now laste warde employed hym selfe. he is a good Scholler and an honeste man. I pray pardon my abrupte and sooddeyne writinge. I can stay no longer but after the true remembrance of my beste respecte vnto you I take my leave this 19 of Apryll 1637 and do remayne Yours euery wayes mooche bownde

ROBTE. RYECE

PHILIP FORTH TO JOHN WINTHROP[3]

To the Right Wor[shipfu]ll my Worthie Cossen John Wynthrop Esquier
in New England present theese

WORTHIE COSSEN, my self with all other your Allies and Freinds in Hadleith doe much reioice and prayse the Allmightie for your prosperous successe together with the safetie and good health of all your Famyle and societie these many yeers in New England. the Continuance and Increase of theese wee inuocate and adore the deuine and supreme Ma[jes]tie to bless and crowne with all externall internall and eternall bounties and Fauours: the oppor-

---

[1] W. Au. 91; 4 *Collections*, VI. 397.
[2] The Reverend John Fiske. See 4 *Collections*, VI. 397n.
[3] W. 4. 87; 5 *Collections*, I. 242–243. Philip Forth, the eldest son of William Forth of Hadleigh and Dorothy Harvey Forth, was a cousin of Governor Winthrop's first wife, Mary Forth.

tunyte of this Messenger my kinseman Sonne to Mr. Edward Bemont one of owr Alldemen of the Corporation of Ha[dleigh] who haue verie oftine shewed me many kinde Fau[ors] inciteth me to be Sutor to you in the behalf of his Sonne that you woold be pleased on sit[*torn*] and reding theese Lynes to impart and frelie vouchsafe and grant unto him the Extent of all your Firtherance and Freindship auaileable for his good and benefitt during all the time of his residence and Abode in your partes: He [is] of an honest playn and religious disposition which I knowe will preuaile to obteyn from you what I haue peticioned you in his behalf: For which as I haue good cause I doe and will euer remayn your obliged Seruant and kinseman

PHILIP FOORTHE

HADLEITH the xxth of Aprill 1637

I salute your beloued wife, my good Cossen your Sonne and all the rest my kyndred Freinds and Contrymen with you to whom I pray and wishe all happynes as vnto

PHILIP FOORTHE

PRISCILLA PAYNTER TO JOHN WINTHROP[1]

To my much honoured brother John Winthrope Esquire at his howse in Boston
New Ingland deliver

MY MUCH HONORED AND DERE BROTHER, I doe much reioyce to heare of your helth and prosterity and doe hartyly thanke you for your kind remembrance of vs at last after so many sad thoughts supposing my selfe to be forgotten of my derest frinds whom I trust that nether Prosperity nor aduersty shall euer make me vnmindfull of though the later may and doth offen hinder the mafastation of derest affections as it hath done with me four seuerall times when our nebours cam from us: as first the death of my dere sonne next the sikenes of my louing husband and thirdly the death of my beloued and honest harted daughter mary, and last of all the death of my honred father all these haue bin no small afflickcions neither is the smart of them yet worne away but my soule hath them still in remembrance and is humbled for them but yet god is good and I cannot but make knowen to my dere brother his goodnes and maruelous louing kindnes towards me in a strang citye for through his marcy I inioy a uery godly louing and tender harted husband

---

[1] W. 4. 27; 5 *Collections*, I. 72–73.

and much loue from my nue frinds here in exon   but aboue all we yet inioy
the ordance of god the meanes of grace in a most powerfull and plentyfull
maner but it is otherwise in sum parts of our land and whildes the flame is so
vilent we cannot but aprehend the danger we stand in and how soone we may
be with you or wish our selfes with you god only knowes: the experence I haue
had of your and my dere sister former loue makes me not to dout of our welcom to you when the lord shall call us thervnto and these with the remembranc of my dereest respets to your selfe my worthy and truly beloued sister
and all your intreating your Prayers for vs and our land which if you doe not
labour to strengthen vs withall you will be gilty of the weakneing of your
natife country forgit vs not therfore in your dayly prayers, nor me your much
obleged

Pris: Paynter

Exon Aprill the 20, 1637

JEFFREY CUTTING TO JOHN WINTHROP[1]

To the Right Wor[shi]pful Mr. Wentrop governor of the plantation of in New England

RYGHT WOR[SHI]PFULL AND WORTHY SIR, my humble servyce vnto you
Remembered   haveing now soe fytt and convenient a messenger as this my
freind and Neyghbour the bearer heerof I could not omytt to wryt by him
vnto your wor[shi]p partly to acknowleg my thankfullnes vnto you for your
love to me and others of that worthy plantation (which I dayly pray god to
prosper) as allsoe concerning some mony due vnto your selffe to the some of
Eyght powndes for my passage for my wyff and my selffe wherof fowre
powndes I paid to your selffe at your howse at growton and forty shillings to
your son at London and soe 40*s* is yeat remayning behynd   yeat notwithstanding my great crosses and losses I sustayned in that voyage god haveing
blessed me with a settled estate I thinke my selff in consyence bownd to paye
that yff that shall please your wor[shi]p to requyre yt off me and therfore yff
you please to apoynt any man heer to Receiue yt off me and to gyve me a
sufficyent discharge for the same I shalbe willing to paye the same vnto you
or whome you shall deput for same purpose   thus much I thought good to
certefye vnto your wor[shi]p for the discharge of my consyence praying god to
blesse you and that whole plantation in whose prosperitye I shall ever much

---

[1] W. I. 119.

reioyce to heer offe comend you and all yours vnto the mercyfull protection of allmyghtye god I doe Rest Your wor[shi]ps in all servyce

JEOFFRY CUTTINGE

DUBLIN in Irland this xxvth of Aprell 1637

—— —— TO JOHN WINTHROP[1]

To the worshipfull Mr. Wintropp, at his house in Boston in New England, these be delivered

WORSHIPFULL AND MUCH HONOURED SIR, my selfe with many others are daily petitioners to god for his grace to abound towards you in New England, that you may encrease in fayth, wisedome, humility, loue, zeale, patience, brotherly kindenes etc. inioying such a competency of outward prosperity as may make you to liue in the seruice of the Lord the more comfortably. And we are exceedingly gladd to heare of your wellfare, and especially your growths in holines.

Now for myne owne particular, I haue bin much moued of late, as obseru-ing some passages both in your and our England, to write my slender aduice to some prudent man among you and one gracious with the plantations, and thereby able to giue counsell to them and to prevayle with them in things conducing to gods glory and your owne prosperities.

First, I haue red and heard of sundry lettres written from some with you vnto others with vs (and I feare there haue bin very many such sent ouer to vs into diuerse parts of our land,) wherein there are many weake and some dangerous passages, which if they should come to the eyes or eares of any one of many thousands of your aduersaries, it would afford them matter enough to attempt your vndoing what in them did lye. And it is gods mercy that they are not made knowen, if at least they are not. As, namely, there came ouer not long since a lettre from you to a friend with vs, which, I feare, through indiscretion, the eies and eares of many haue bin made priuy to, to this effect, that whereas it is reported there will be a Gouernour and a Bishopp sent ouer vnto you, he hopeth (or else it was, we hope) that god will giue you grace to stand for his truth, which words will carry a strange construction with our state, howeuer it might not be soe meant by him that wrote it, and it would redound to the preiudice of you all. Another among you writes, that he

---

[1] W. 2. 158; 4 *Collections,* VI. 442–451.

knowes no newse to acquainte his friend withall, but that you are like to haue warrs the next yeere with old England. Others haue written as freely and vnaduisedly about your discipline, writing ouer to vs formes thereof, and the opinions and tenents which you hold, whyther all of them as they relate, or not, we know not, which hath caused a wonderfull disaffection in very many towards you, and which is most grieuous, in many such as are the deare children of god, insomuch that there is like to be, if it be not maturely healed, a greate rent in affection betweene you and them, that though we are like to see sadd times, yet there are, till they be otherwise informed, who are resolued to vndergoe much misery heere rather then euer to remoue hence. And one not of meane ranck and of long approued holines, hearing of your renouncing vs to be a Church, and that you mainteine the opinions of the seperacion contrary to your declaracion at your first going ouer, professed secretely to one that told it me, that he could scarce tell how to pray for you. Not that I (for perhaps not himselfe in cold blood doth) approue such vncharitable speeches, but my Intention is to shew what a rent and alienation there is like to be, and how sadd both myne owne and others harts haue bin made about thes things, not a little fearing the evill consequences that will come heereby both to you and vs from others, and to you and vs from ourselues, that soe, if it be possible as much as in you lyeth, you may endeauour a prevention of them. Besides, the whole kingdome begins, or rather proceeds, to be full of preiudice against you, and you are spoken of disgracefully and with bitternes in the greatest meetings in the kingdome, the Pulpitts sound of you both at Visitacions and Assises, and the Judges begin to mention you in theyre charges. The Judg in his circuite now lately, in giuing his charge and speaking of Recusants, rancked them into two sorts, some Papists and others of the seperacion, and those of the seperacion were such, he sayd, as preferred Amsterdam before London, and N. England before old. And for these last, he gaue a speciall charge that they should be lookt after, and to that end, that they should take notice of such as inclined towards N. England for they were the causes of error and faction in Church and State. And much more there is, 'tis likely, that neuer came to my knowledg. I know that the wise among you doe not expect protection from god without a mixture of the serpents wisedome with the doues innocency, and that is as much wisedome (the serpent being the subtilest of the beasts of the field) as may consist with innocency; and as much innocency (the doue being the simplest of the fowles of the ayre) as may consist with wisedome.

Now giue me leaue to propose some few things, of which some perhaps, if not all, may doe you good. 1. You may please in some publike meeting to disclayme all such lettres tending to the purpose first mentioned, and withall to establish an order against any that shall euer be known to indite and send ouer such lettres to vs, and against any that shall speake among you to such or the like purpose; that soe if any quæstion be made at any time of these things against you by any in our state, (as iustly they may and will if they meete with it) your order and penalty to be inflicted on such offenders may secure you. 2. You may please to haue further cautions giuen in euery plantacion touching writing ouer to vs about your discipline, and how any be censorious of vs heere in theyre lettres to vs, not calling any of vs, as I vnderstand some haue done, doggs and swine, especially those of the profaner sort among vs, nor questioning our ministry and calling to it, as another with you did in a lettre written ouer to a godly minister and friend both of the parties and myne; for your disclaymings of these and the like odious things shall much aduantage you to the preseruation of Brotherly affections and peace with your friends in old E[ngland]. As you may gather heereby, that your dis- clayming of Mr. William's opinions and your dealing with him soe as we heare you did, tooke off much preiudice from you with vs, and hath stopt the mouths of some. Moreouer, you may please that Items be giuen in Planta- cions that whosoeuer of them shall at any time come ouer from you to vs, as most yeeres many doe, they would spare to speake of any such or the like matters as aforesayd, yea though they are prouoked, for I heare of one of your men now with vs that disclaymes our Church for a true Church, and shews I know not what booke or bookes to that purpose, which if it be soe, as I heare it reported, it may doe both you and vs exceeding greate hurt. Likewise that all commers ouer from you to vs be aduised to carry themselues meekely and humbly, and not somewhat highly and disdeignefully, as slighting vs in com- parison of you, as some haue bin noted to doe. 3. That any with you be aduised how they doe answeare the lettres (such as they may be) of theire friends sent ouer from vs to you; for we heare of a letter that Mr. Cotton should write (how true the report is, I knowe not yet) in answere to a lettre written to him by one Mr. Bernard of Botcombe in Sommersetshire, a man though vpright in the mayne, yet of very greate weaknesses; wherein, as we heare, Mr. Cotton should write, that we are a true Church Implicitè but not Explicitè, which if it be soe (as you may soone vnderstand) will doe not a little hurt among vs, for besides that much fauour will be graunted vs by the strict- est of the seperacion, and might haue bin graunted our church in the dayes of King H[enry] the 8th, or of Q[ueen] Mary, which will be the common exception against that distinction by the most among vs; yet suppose the dis- tinction admitted, we doe wonder if a reuerend and wise minister of Christ should vpon the letter, or perhaps prouocation of Mr. Bernard, or indeed of any, send ouer your opinions to vs in such a point, which can doe vs little or noe good, your selues very much disadvantage many wayes. 4. That your ministers, especially they of chiefest note, be persuaded to please to write ouer theire kind letters to theire friends with vs, especially to the chiefest of the ministry with vs in the seuerall parts of the Kingdome, for the preseruacion of Brotherly loue, which otherwise will decay apace, and it is conceiued by many that there is a greate alienacion in you of affeccion towards vs. 5. Aduise may be giuen that any with you be wary how they receaue some such bookes as haue of late bin written in our land which haue more stirred the state then euer I knew it, and after which bookes there is greate inquiry made, and many haue bin bound ouer to the Assises about them, others imprisoned, and not a few are now, as I heare, in the Starr-chamber about them, and if once it be perceaued that the bookes goe likewise ouer vnto you, it will double the Preiudice against you. Of these bookes there are especially two, the one intituled Newse from Ipswitch, the other conteining the Judgments of God which within this two or three yeeres he hath shewen on profaneners of the Lord's day. For the first of which, it is a Booke of extreame bitternes and farr enough off from the spirit of Christ, wherein the Libeller (for soe he is generally termed) speakes of the Bishops, that which the Ark-Angell would not speake vnto the Diuell; besides that he makes in it an Apostophe to our king, to whom he speakes very vnreuerently; and he pretends the name of Matthew White, and the newse to be sent from Ipswitch, which is noe better then Lying, and pretends, in the frontispice, a third Edition etc. For the other booke, There are very many remarkeable Judgments mentioned in it shewen of late on profaneners of the Lords day, for the Lord hath bin knowen among vs by the Judgments that he hath executed, but the booke is carryed but weakely in the penning, for it is feared that there is a greate fayling in many and chiefe circumstances in the Instances alleaged, if some few of them alsoe were not taken too suddenly on trust and heare-say without well looking after the truth, insomuch that the Judg now lately in open Assises boldly affirmed that all the Instances were eyther altogether or in part lyes, and bad any one in the Audience to say the contrary, if he could. Moreouer there is a Post-script added to the booke touching the remarkeable hand of god on Mr. Noy, which taxeth the whole Starr-chamber, and digresseth farr from the quæstion of the book; and this latter is noe lesse, but rather more heinously taken then the other. The greatest Clothier in England one Mr. Ash of Sommersetshire, a man reputed for honest, is now in quæstion for receauing and dispersing 150 of these bookes.[1] He was bound ouer for it by his Bishop to the Assises, and about 20 more of ministers and others, and besides much spoken by the Judg vnto him and of this matter. He told him that he pittyed him, being one that did soe much good in his Countrey, as setting a 1000 poore people on worke, but he would be made an example to the whole kingdome.

These things I am bold to certify you of, that in your wisedome you may doe that which shall most make for gods glory and your prosperities. Especially our hope is that if euer any bookes should be penn'd by you, they will be farr from bitternes or weakenes, and such as may much profite gods people and not iustly preiudice you; but I suppose your Imployments take you vp otherwise. Lastly, this one thing more, that whereas the hand of God hath lyen vpon vs aboue these two yeeres by a grieuous kind of pox generall through the kingdome, killing many of the ageder as well as others of the yonger sort, and likewise whereas the pestilence hath reigned for aboue this yeere and killed betweene 12 and 20 thousand in London and the suburbs, and euen layd wast New Castle in the North, and is like yet further to continew; by meanes whereof there hath bin a greate stoppage in trading, and much misery throughout all the kingdome, for the Lord is highly displeased with vs, and there is some feare likewise of scarcity, (Oh our sins are exceeding greate!) that you would be pleased to procure a generall publike Fast throughout your plantations for vs, for we stand in greate need of it, afford vs, for the Lords sake, the help and pitty of Brethren, and how doe you know what fauour this may winne you both with god and men? And how would such a pious course answeare for you to very many (and some of them your brethren) who thinke you are gone from vs in affection and brotherly kindenes, as well as in place. And let me speake freely to you, that if soe iust a motion as this should find noe place with you, I feare that God will be angry with you. And O that some pourefull sermon that would endure the reading in old E[ngland], preached with you vpon such a day, might come to our hands heere, how ioyfully should we read it, and prayse our God, and how readily should we obiect it to all such as eyther condemne or suspect you of vncharitablenes, and vnnaturall affections!

And now perhaps you may thinke (at least I know many among you would, for I am well acquainted with the spiritts of many with you in this thing)

---

[1] John Ash was one of those (including William Prynne and Henry Burton) against whom an action was filed in the Court of Star Chamber in April, 1637, "for the publication of various libellous books," including *Newes from Ipswich* and *A Divine Tragedy Lately Acted*, "with intent to move the people to discontent against the King's ecclesiastical government." *Calendar of State Papers, Domestic, 1637*, 49.

that all these things sauour of feare, vnbeliefe and ouer much discretion. But I would answere them, that what I thus write, it is for theyre sakes, and well may I shew loue, but why feare for theyre sakes, I meane distrustfull feare? And whereas my spirit is naturally farr from pragmaticall, inclining rather to the other extreme, I haue bin much moued of late thus to write, and yet whither euer I shall come ouer vnto you, I know not, for I desire to doe the worke of God, and to glorify him heere or there, liuing and dying; and I haue found the Lords speciall presence with me now of late (praise be to his name for euer) in such remarkeable manner, as I neuer found the like before, and I can but inioy his presence in any part of the world. Onely this I say, that if god send me to you, for I wayte vpon him, I shall not vnwillingly goe, and whereas he hath pleased to open a doore of liberty with you for many that haue bin streightned heere, my desire is to vse all iust wayes to keepe it open, both for your and our sakes, and, apprehending you to be our deare brethren, to prevent all such inconveniences, as (without greate mercy from God, who yet will be wayted vpon in the vse of meanes) I plainely see approching towards you. Howeuer you conceiue of me, my endeauour is heerein with Jethro to giue aduise to the people of God in the wildernes, for whom my prayers daily are. And soe long as you hold any correspondence with vs, haue any dependance vpon vs, stand in that relation to vs which you can neuer breake, nor all the waters betweene you and vs wash away, I cannot but thinke my aduise though weake, yet such as may doe you good. There be other things that I might haue written, but I shall be gladd if these may be accepted. I haue not subscribed heerevnto, not knowing whither my lettre may not miscarry. The bearer perhaps can tell you of me. Now the Lord in his Infinite mercy be with your plantacions and his churches with you, and with your selfe in particular, to blesse you and your posterityes after you to the worlds end.

[No signature]¹

[*Ca.* May, 1637]

SIR, I humbly entreate you to conceale it, that any with vs hath thus written vnto you. There is another thing that I haue noted since I wrote the inclosed lettre, that many in your plantacions discouer much pride, as appeareth by the lettres we receaue from them, wherein some of them write

---

¹ The only clue to the identity of the writer is that he refers to himself (page 403, below) as a neighbor of a member of the Massachusetts Bay Company who has been identified here as Sir John Young. The subject matter of the letter is in itself sufficient to explain why no signature was appended.

ouer to vs for lace, though of the smaller sort, going as farr as they may, for we heare that you prohibite them any other; and this they say hath very good vent with you, non benè ripae creditur. They write ouer likewise for cutt-worke coifes; and others, for deep stammell dyes; and some of your owne men tell vs that many with you goe finely cladd, though they are free from the fantasticalnes of our land.

There is likewise another thing which I haue not mentioned in the lettre enclosed, which I suppose you are not altogether ignorant of, that your Patent is called in and condemned, and the Patentees haue renounced, and they are outlawed that haue not, till they come in and make theyre peace; of whom one of them is my neighbour, and is now riding to London about it.[1] You know, I beleeue, the causes heereof, but what the effects of it will be, we are ignorant, but doubt and feare, onely we looke vp to God. I hope you striue to keepe close with the Lord. How earnestly can I pray that you may, and that you may all mind holines, and the things that are aboue, and grow vp in fayth, loue, humility and self-denyall; and that you may be of an Euangelicall spiritt. For if once Pride, Couetousnes, opposicion and contention etc. destroy the poure of holines among you, yea or your being cast into a new frame of discipline take you vp for the most part, diuerting your minds, meditacions and practises from all holy Conuersacion and Godlines, there will soone grow a strangenes betweene you and God, who will then surely bring affliccions vpon you to draw you nearer to himselfe. The good Lord in his infinite mercy be gracious to you. Oh how doe I desire it! I can noe more forget you then my selfe. And the Almighty god vouchsafe that both your Doctrine and discipline worke mightily and effectually vpon your hearts and liues, to meeken and sanctify them throughout. If you please to write any thing back to me, the bearer heereof can tell you how it may be sent and deliuered to me. The Lord be with your spirit. Amen.

[*Endorsed by Governor Winthrop:*] Spec. Lettre ab ignot.

---

[1] Sir John Young of Colyton, Devon, one of the members of the Massachusetts Bay Company in England, appeared in the *quo warranto* proceedings against the Company's charter in Easter Term (April 15–May 8), 1637.

JOHN HIGGINSON TO JOHN WINTHROP[1]

For the right worshipfull and much honoured in the Lord Mr. Jo: Winthrop Esquire and Deputie Gouernour these with speed

RIGHT WORSHIPFULL AND MUCH HONOURED IN THE LORD, my due service and respect remembred and having giuen full information to the Governour of the manner of the Lords Proceeding with vs here, I spare to write therof vnto your selfe. Onely I make bould to present you with my weak and feeble thoughts concerning the same which you may be pleased to consider of as you see cause.

First whether now the Lord begins not to send (as shephards vse to doe their dogs to fetch in their stragling sheep so he) the Indians vpon his servants, to make them cleaue more close togither, and prize each other, to prevent contentions of Brethren which may proue as hard to break as Castle barres, and stop their now beginning breaches before they be as the letting out of many waters that cannot be gathered in againe, etc. O that as this is the Lords meaning so it may be the vse that all his servants may make therof, that he may haue the praise in Jesus Christ forever more.

Secondly whether the Lord intends not in his dealings here with vs a gratious warning to all the English in the land that shall ever haue to doe with Indians againe in this kinde: For it hath been a common conceit but is in truth a dangerous errour, Indians are afrayd of pieces, etc. 10 English will make a 100 Indians fly: some dare venture (happily now) with 20 40 60 men among a 1000 Armed Pequots (for that, if not many more, in probabilitie is their number) etc. etc. but if the passages here be well considered, and the Lord be pleas'd to sanctifie our punishments to be warnings to the wise; I hope it may be a means to roote out that deeply-rooted securitie, and confidence in our owne supposed strength (2 English diseases and dangerous wormes that vse to breed and grow in abused peace or slighted liberties), that so the loss of these, and danger of our selues may be the saftie and preservation of many others.

Thirdly, whether now the Lord calls not by all these sad alarums and heauenly warnings from hence, to all his servants lowder and lowder etc. more seriously to intend this warre then yet they seeme to doe.

For if that our condition here, to haue 10 lustie men out of so little a number

---

[1] W. 3. 109; 4 *Collections*, VII. 394–399. For John Higginson, see 2 *Proceedings*, XVI. 478–521; *D.A.B.*

as ours is so cruelly slayne, others crying and roaring out through extremitie of the paine of wounds, others gasping and dying and breathing out their last, our selues beleaguerd by the same blood thirstie, and hemmed in by those who daily seek our liues, etc. etc. If this I say were the case of the servants of the Lord in the Bay their hearts would be affected, their purses opened and their hands enlarged to defend (not so much their liues and liberties, to say nothing of them) as the glorious gospell of Jesus Christ, which hath shined amongst vs hitherto, and may doe yet if it be not our owne fault.

And yet this may be the condition of those pretious servants of the Lord vp this river we know not how soone; vnless the Lord be pleas'd as he hath done hitherto and I hope he will make salvation vnto them for walls and bulwarks round about. For had not the Lord in abundant mercy to them, kept the many hundreds of our enimies in a serious and furious beleaguering of vs here, and restraind them from attempting any thing there as yet as they have vpon our selues, I see not how they could haue been preseru'd without a miracle.

And let not Boston Roxburie etc. thinke warre is farre enough from them, for this seems to be an vniversall deluge creeping and encroaching on all the English in the land: The multitudes of our enimies daily encrease, by the falling of Mohigoners, Nepmets (who liue not many miles from the bay) Niantucuts at Narrohigganset and their malice is not to be questiond, their cruelty diuers of ours haue felt. Their experience in warlike affaires (being men of warre from their youth) their advantages against vs, in agilitie and armes, their industrious sedulitie plying and attending the warre against the English as their mainest busines, provideing retreats at long Iland, fortifying vpon the maine, gathering new supplyes of forces, confœderating with former enimies, giuing large rewards to those amongst them, who are most skilfull to destroy, etc. (which we hear of from Plantations aboue, and they from Indians) doe farre exceed the preparations and provisions of the English against them, who yet haue farre more cause to seek to defend their liues and liberties and gospell, then such bloodthirstie wretches haue to invade destroy and take away the same.

And add to the former also this, that now the eyes of all the Indians in the countrey are vpon the English, to see what they will doe; and All may be assured of this, that if some serious and verie speedie course be not taken to tame the pride and take down the insolencie of these now-insulting Pequots though with charge and loss and damage for the present, we are like to haue all the Indians in the countrey about our ears, and then their will be worke enough, etc.

In all these respects and many more I desire it may be considered whither the serious and speedie prosecution of this warre be not the greatest busines New England hath.   For it cannot be conceiued that either building planting fishing trading colledges etc. or in a word the good of either Church or Commonweal can flourish, and goe forward, without a timely remouing and preventing the warres that now begin. For these are but the beginnings of warre, the progress hath been something sad, what the Issue will be the Lord he onely knowes.

Now the Lord be pleased to raise vp the publick spirits of his servants (and where they are not to create them) that every heart and head and hand may be stirring and working in this case; for the strength and sinnewes of these warres I take to lye in the combined abilities and vnited hearts and hands of all the servants of the Lord etc. (To omit that it cannot be expected that ever warres should prosper abroad, if ciuill (nay worse and religious) dissentions abound at home) yet all pertaking in the good and benifit of peace and in the danger and damage of a common warre should also be every way enlarged to their vtmost for the procuring and preserving the one, removing and preventing of the other.

Three places and presidents in scripture I onely make bould to present your w[orshi]pp with and so I end. Judges 20, 1, 2, 8: Ezra 10, 3, 4: Hag. 2, 4. Hence may be collected this in brief, that (after serious reconciliation with the Lord of armies and Indians himselfe) It belongeth firstly and chiefly to you the much honoured magistrates that as you haue hitherto not been wanting according as the Lord hath called, so now yow will arise be serious be speedie, be strong, and be couragious in the Lord, etc.

That also our much honoured the ministers and watchmen of the Lord will not be wanting to press vpon the conscience, charge as a dutie, command in the name of the Lord from heaven, etc. the serious and speedie prosecution of this warre.

That also all the people of the land should be seriously rouzed vp to open their purses and enlarge their hands offer their persons etc. to doe what service they can to help the Lord against the mighty.

And O that the heavie curse of Merosh may never fall vpon any of the Lords. And O that the disposition of this bearer and others also lately come out of the bay, who are sensibly affected with things here etc. might runne through all the land viz. they would willingly lay downe halfe they haue to serue this way, and yet less then a halfe a quarter a tenth would doe that now which herafter all the world cannot recouer, etc. But I fear I am to bold; I entreat you therfore pardon my weaknes, and consider the things and tho I it may be am afraid to die, our men here fearfull, melancholy, etc. yet the Lord help all his servants to consider what his will and pleasure is in all these sad occurrences hitherto: He be pleased to counsell and direct and bless from heaven all intended enterprizes in Jesus Christ. (In great hast) I rest Yours engaged in many bonds in all due service most devoted

JO: HIGGINSON

[*Ca.* May, 1637]

The necessitie of Mr. Dixes stay hath been very great hitherto; partly to fit our ordnance partly to be a safegard to vs in respect of weaknes and fewnes of our number, etc. etc. etc. and for ought I know his stay hath been the preservation of vs all: I hope it will be considered, etc.

THOMAS HOOKER TO JOHN WINTHROP[1]

To his much honored freind John Wyntrop Esquier his house at Boston deliver

MUCH HONORED IN OUR BLESSED SAVIOUR, When I first heard of those heavy distractions which have risen so vnexpectedly: I did reioyce from the root of my heart, that the Lord did, and hath gratiously kept you from any taynt of those new-coyned conceits: The Lord strenghthen and establish you in every holy word and work: In a good cause he hath given you gratious abilityes to do him much service, and I am perswaded he will blesse you in such indeavors. you know my playnnesse: you cannot keepe your comfort, nor an honorable respect in Christ in the hearts of his more then in keeping closse to the truth: you shall have what interest I have in heaven to help you in that work: How the Pequoyts have made an inrode by a suddayne surprisall vpon some of our brethren of Watertowne,[2] slayyng weomen and children who were sent out carelessly without watch and guard, this bearer will tell you:

Though we feele nether the tyme nor our strenght fitt for such a service, yet the Indians here our frends were so importunate with vs to make warr presently that vnlesse we had attempted some thing we had delivered our persons vnto contempt of base feare and cowardise, and caused them to turne enemyes agaynst vs: Agaynst our mynds, being constrayned by necessity, we

---

[1] Connecticut Historical Society; 4 *Collections*, VI. 388–389.

[2] For Winthrop's account of the surprise attack at Wethersfield, see *Journal*, I. 213; see also Sherman W. Adams and Henry R. Stiles, *The History of Ancient Wethersfield, Connecticut*, I (New York, 1904), 60–70.

have sent out a company, taking some Indians for guides with vs: What is done you will better heare it by report, then I shall relate it by penn, for our men went downe as these pynaces came to vs: Only we heare, ther is six of the Pequoyts slayne by our Indians not far from the fort. I hope you see a necessity to hasten execution, and not to do this work of the Lords revenge slackly: I shall commend the cause to your love and wisdome, and your self to the rich mercy of our God in Christ, and in all thankfulnes for all your love rest Yours in all due-respect

T: HOOKER

[*Ca.* May, 1637]

THOMAS SHEPARD TO JOHN WINTHROP[1]

To right Wor[shipfu]ll John Winthrop Esquire at Boston

SIR, My occasions will not permit me this day to be at Boston with yow my selfe and therefore I would intreat yow to deliuer to Mr. Harlakenden the 30*li* which (I thanke yow) yow promised vnto me for my brother; I dare not presse your readines to helpe me to the rest of the 100*li* yet if yow could with conueniency do it herafter, it would be thankfully taken from yow, euery way; tis much desired, that our cuntrymens blood might not rest vnsatisfyed for; our eyes are much vpon yow and the Lord in yow to deuise some speedy execution which may end with honour and quiet to the state and terrour to all the rest of them: the God of all wisdom grace and glory fill yow and direct yow: my respect remembred to yours   in hast I rest Yours in the Lord J[esus]

THO. SHEPARD

[*Ca.* May, 1637]

ISAAC LOVELL TO JOHN WINTHROP[2]

*To the Wor[shi]p[fu]ll Mr. Winthurup at his houce in the plantation of niw Ingland
I pray deliuer this*

SIR, after the humble remembrance of our loues vnto your selfe your wife and children

Forasmutch as God (who is the cause of our earthly being and hath re-

¹ W. 3. 71; 4 *Collections*, VII. 265–266. For Shepard, see *D.A.B.*
² W. 4. 87; 5 *Collections*, I. 243–244.

deamed vs in his sonne the Lord Jeasus Christ vnto a celestial habitation) hath
commanded vs to loue on another, hauing this fit oportunity vppon occasion
of our louing frind Mr. John Hales pasing for niw Ingland (who for his time is
an approued seruant of Gods and frind vnto his people) by him in wrighting
in obeadienc vnto God I am bould (in a few lines) to be trublesum in the
manifesting of my Christian loue vnto you and yours which was longe since
begun betweene our parents Sir John Tindal and his virtious Lady your
Wiues Father and Moother and your good Father and my Father Mr. Thomas
Louell in his life time a long time minister of Gods word in great Waldingfild,
and my selfe, for my selfe and mine and so for you and yours doe desire of the
Lord that aboue all things wee may inioye the ritches of his mercies by being
in Christ Jesus his only begoten sonne and so mutch of temporals as may be
for his glory and our good. Sir I haue within these few years vndergon many
grete troubels so as if mine and my wiues desired purpose take efect for Niw
Ingland wee shall not be so ritchly prouided for the viadge as many of our
bretheren, yet by reason of the opressions that are imposed and greater like
to be (for ought wee can see) wee shall content our selues with the portion
God bestoweth on vs My imployment hath beene about the space of fiue
years in the States of Hollands wars. you know Sir whether in that waye my
exsperience may doe you seruice. It would mutch reioyce me to receiue a line
or too to certifie me of your wellfars. Thus commending your wor[shi]p vnto
the Holy Lord our God with your virtuous wife (my ould acquaintance whose
moother was one of the witnesses at my baptisme) and your children etc: I
humbly take my [leaue] Your Wor[shi]ps in the Lord Jeasus Christ to the
vtmost of my power

                                                    ISAACK LOUELL

From Andriw Hubards in LONDON May the ij 1637

FRANCIS KIRBY TO JOHN WINTHROP[1]

*To the right worshipfull John Winthrop Esquire at his house at Boston this deliver
in New England*

                                        LONDON this 10th of May 1637

SIR, I wrote you lately per the Hector wherin I sent a runlet marked with
your marke contayneinge some things your son did write to me to send him.

---

[1] W. 3. 8; 4 *Collections*, VII. 19–20.

John Wood masters mate did promise mee and James Downeinge that he would be carfull of it and deliver it to you.

These are now to intreat you that you would be assistante to the bearer herof (Thomas Hale my neer kinsman),[1] in your councell and aduise to put him in the way how and where to settle himselfe in a hopefull way of subsisteinge with his family. he hath brought with him all his estate which he hath heer or can haue dureinge the life of his mother my sister   he had almost 200*li* when he began to make his provision for this voyage   I suppose the greatest halfe is expended in his transportion and in such necessaries as will be spent by him and his family in the first vse, the lesser halfe I suppose he hath in mony and vendible goods to provide him a Cottage to dwell in, and a milshe Cow for his Childrens sustenance. I suppose his way will be to hire a house or part of a house for the first year vntill he can looke out and buy or build him a dwellinge, wherin as in other things I shall intreat you to direct him, and the Courtesy that you shall do him therin I shall acknowledge as done to myselfe, and I shall be redy (deo assistante) to endeuour to requite it in any seruice which I can performe for you heer. Thus for this present I commit you all to the protection of the almighty and shall euer rest Your lo[ving] frend

FRA: KIRBY

·I desire to be remembred to Mrs. Winthrop to your son Mr. Jo: and his wife and the rest of yours, also to my Cosen Mary and Su: Downeinge.

My bro: Downeinge will hasten to you, the next springe will be farthest God willinge, for he seeth that euery year bringeth forth new difficulties. my nephew can tell you how they haue met with many interuptions prohibitions and such like, which Mr. Peirce and others that went since Mr. Peirce were not troubled withall.

ROGER WILLIAMS TO THE GOVERNOR OF MASSACHUSETTS[2]

For his much honoured Mr. Gov[erno]r, or, Mr. Deputie Gov[erno]r these with speede

This last of the present weeke in the morning [May 13, 1637][3]

SIR, Miantunnommu with a great Traine arrived the same day that

---

[1] See Robert S. Hale, "Thomas Hale of Newbury, Mass., 1637, His English Origin and Connections," *N. E. Historical and Genealogical Register*, XXXV. 367–376.

[2] W. 2. 96; 4 *Collections*, VI. 189–191; *N.C.*, VI. 23–26.

[3] The context of this letter shows it to have been written within the first two weeks of May, 1637. There is good reason to place the date as Saturday, May 13, rather than Saturday, May 6,

Anthony Dike departed hence with his sad tidings, and confirmeth with the most, the report of Anthony.

The Nanihiggonsicks are at present doubtfull of Realitie in all our promises: I haue alleadged the best Arguments I haue heard or could invent to perswade Realitie of purpose and speedie performance, as allso reasons of delay.

Miantunnummu and his best Councell here with him, haue requested me earnestly to make this proffer to you. The Pequts are scarce of provision and therefore (as vsually so now especially) they are in some numbers come downe to the sea side (and 2 Ilands by name *Munnawtawkit and Manittuwond* especially) to take sturgeon and other fish as allso to make new fields of Corne in case the English should destroy their fields at home.

Miantunnommu desires to goe himselfe with one *Wequash* the Pequt of whome I haue formerly writ here at present with him, in this pinnace here left by Anthony or any other that shall take him in at the Nanhiggonsick.

He will put in 40 or 50 or more as the vessell will stow.

He will put in Vitailes himselfe for his men. He will direct the Pinnace to the Places and in the Night land his men, despoile them of their Canowes, cut of the men he finds (the greatest number being women and children, which for the most of them he would cut of) as allso spoile their fields.

And this he proffers to doe without landing an English man with whome he will remaine aboord in English Cloths which he desires for himselfe.

John, a seaman aboord, calls the Iland *Plum Iland* and is very willing to goe on the designe and thincks as allso Miantunnommu doth, that if within 2 or 3 dayes they went forth they would be here againe within 4 or 5 or less.

Sir for my selfe I dare not advice: but if my thoughts be asked: I shall (with all due submission) say this.

It will at present wedge them in from any starting aside, vntill your forces shall follow.

If they speede it will weaken the Enemie and distresse them, being put by their hopes: as allso much enrage the Pequts for euer against them, a thing much desirable.

Beside the charge or danger of the English will be none vnles Miantunnommues Course Cloths and a large Coate for *Wequash* the Pequt guide a man of great vse. The most holy and only wise be pleased to smile vpon the face of the English that be his, (we haue all if euer Cause to examine our selues, our Errands and Worck) in the face of Jesus Christ:

since it was Winthrop, who was elected Governor on May 17, who endorsed the letter as having come from Williams. Had the letter been written on the earlier date, it would presumably have been delivered while Vane was Governor.

While I write a Messenger is come to Miantunnommu from Neepemut reporting a farr greater slaughter then that Anthony brought word of and since the for[mer] a great number at the Plantacions and some persons are mencioned, but I will not name either, but hope and long to heare it countermanded.

In case that Anthony or other seamen can not be gotten suddenly, here is one with vs willing to make vp a third man (to the other 2 left with the pinnace) to carrie the vessell, though I iudge Anthony himselfe the fittest.

Sir, Miantunnommu desird me to giue you a hint that the 6 fathom of Beades which he gaue for the slaying of Audsah be repaid him and sent now if it may be. his warrs keepe him bare. Your Wor[ship]s vnfaignedly respectiue

ROGER WILLIAMS

For any gratuities or tokens Caunonicus desires Sugar and Miantunnommu powder. My humble respects to all my lo[ving] friends.

Sir, Miantunnommu is close in this his proiect, and therefore I thinck the messenger is sent only for the Beades: it is very convenient that Miantunnommues cloths and Wequash his Coate be sent by him.

ROGER WILLIAMS TO SIR HENRY VANE AND JOHN WINTHROP[1]

For his much honoured Mr. Governour, and Mr. Winthrop, Deputy Governour of the Massachusetts, these

NEW PROVIDENCE this 2d of the week [May 15, 1637]

SIR, The latter end of the last week I gave notice to our neighbour princes of your intentions and preparations against the common enemy, the Pequts. At my first coming to them, Caunounicus (morosus æque ac barbarus senex) was very sour, and accused the English and myself for sending the plague amongst them, and threatening to kill him especially.

---

[1] Original not located; 3 *Collections*, I. 159–161; *N.C.*, VI. 16–20. Two others of the letters from Roger Williams to John Winthrop which are printed in this volume (those on pages 488–490 and 502–503) were also printed in 3 *Collections*, I. None of the originals came to the Society with the Winthrop Papers. Since that volume of the *Collections* appeared in 1825, and since James Savage was a member of the Publication Committee that year, it is safe to assume that Savage had these letters in his possession and that they were destroyed in the fire which occurred in his Boston office on November 10, 1825. All three letters, accordingly, have been reprinted exactly as Savage edited them.

Such tidings (it seems) were lately brought to his ears by some of his flatterers and our ill-willers. I discerned cause of bestirring myself, and staid the longer, and at last (through the mercy of the Most High) I not only sweetened his spirit, but possest him, that the plague and other sicknesses were alone in the hand of the one God, who made him and us, who being displeased with the English for lying, stealing, idleness and uncleanness, (the natives' epidemical sins,) smote many thousands of us ourselves with general and late mortalities.

Miantunnomu kept his barbarous court lately at my house,[1] and with him I have far better dealing. He takes some pleasure to visit me, and sent me word of his coming over again some eight days hence.

They pass not a week without some skirmishes, though hitherto little loss on either side. They were glad of your preparations, and in much conference with themselves and others, (fishing de industria for instructions from them,) I gathered these observations, which you may please (as cause may be) to consider and take notice of:

1. They conceive that to do execution to purpose on the Pequts, will require not two or three days and away, but a riding by it and following of the work to and again the space of three weeks or a month, that there be a falling off and a retreat, as if you were departed, and a falling on again within three or four days, when they are returned again to their houses securely from their flight.

2. That if any pinnaces come in ken, they presently prepare for flight, women and old men and children, to a swamp some three or four miles on the back of them, a marvellous great and secure swamp, which they called Ohomowauke, which signifies owl's nest, and by another name, Cuppacommock, which signifies a refuge or hiding place, as I conceive.

3. That therefore Nayantaquit (which is Miantunnomue's place of rendezvous) be thought on for the riding and retiring to of vessel or vessels, which place is faithful to the Nanhiggonticks and at present enmity with the Pequts.

4. They also conceive it easy for the English, that the provisions and munition first arrive at Aquednetick, called by us Rode-Island, at the Nanhiggontick's mouth, and then a messenger may be despatched hither, and so to the bay, for the soldiers to march up by land to the vessels, who otherwise might spend long time about the cape and fill more vessels than needs.

5. That the assault would be in the night, when they are commonly more

---

[1] Cf. the references to "Miantunnomu with a great Traine" and "Miantonnumu and his best Councell here with him" in Williams's letter to Winthrop, *ca.* May 13, 1637 (pages 410–411).

secure and at home, by which advantage the English, being armed, may enter the houses and do what execution they please.

6. That before the assault be given, an ambush be laid behind them, between them and the swamp, to prevent their flight, etc.

7. That to that purpose such guides as shall be best liked of be taken along to direct, especially two Pequts, viz. Wequash and Wuttackquiackommin, valiant men, especially the latter, who have lived these three or four years with the Nanhiggonticks, and know every pass and passage amongst them, who desire armour to enter their houses.

8. That it would be pleasing to all natives, that women and children be spared, etc.

9. That if there be any more land travel to Qunnihticutt, some course would also be taken with the Wunhowatuckoogs, who are confederates with and a refuge to the Pequts.

Sir, if any thing be sent to the princes, I find that Canounicus would gladly accept of a box of eight or ten pounds of sugar, and indeed he told me he would thank Mr. Governour for a box full.

Sir, you may please to take notice of a rude view, how the Pequts lie:

River Qunnihticut.
_____

     ○ a fort of the Nayantaquit men, confederate with the Pequts.
Mohiganic
_____

River.
    Wein ○ shauks, where   Ohom ││││ owauke, the swamp,
Sasacous the chief Sachim is.   three or four miles from———
    Mis ○ tick, where is Mamoho, another chief sachim.

River.
    Nayanta ○ quit, where is Wepiteammock and our friends.

River.

Thus, with my best salutes to your worthy selves and loving friends with you, and daily cries to the Father of mercies for a merciful issue to all these enterprises, I rest Your worship's unfeignedly respective

ROGER WILLIAMS

THOMAS SHEPARD TO JOHN WINTHROP[1]

To the Right Wor[shipfu]ll Mr. Winthrop Gouernour

MUCH HONOURED IN OUR BLESSED SAUIOUR, I haue looked vpon the Rod (your Suruey) yow have made to whip the Remonstrants[2] back: my dim eyes can find no fault with it but that which yow fear may be on, vizt. that it wants twigs enough: but yet it may be, they may mend by this which if it fall out, the mistake is mine; howeuer it be, your reward of such loue to the Lord and his truth and his people by stepping your selfe betwene them and the blow, shall not be forgotten another day in a better woorld; nor yet I beleeue in this, of all those that know yow and these labours of your loue for the vse and safety of these churches and cuntry: for my own part I am not a little glad to see how the Lord hath helped yow also in this Suruey: I will only leaue these things to be considered of by yow.

  1. Pag: 1: In your preface your charity is sweet and good, if yow had to deale with another author of the Apologie then him that indeed yow combat withall: For yow seeme to make him a good man in zeale of a conceiued good cause; who is so notoriously known to be the prime craftsman of forging all our late nouelties, the Sheba of our distractions, and that in this very Apollogye hath cunningly and slyly layd down the principle and sown the seed of the confusion of this and all states in the world; and whom the vigilant eye of judicious obseruers haue noted to cut out all his courses and carriages in so diuerse colours: and vntill we see his repentence and returne why shall our charity couer his craft, and yet tell the woorld he may be an honest man: I do beleeue yow do aime at others as well as he to be authors of his Apology, and so may truly speake as yow do; but I leaue it to your wisdom to consider, if hauing this occasion and cause to speake it would not be fit to leaue others out, and single out him and set your brand vpon him, that it may be is now hatching euill agaynst this place, and by his colours more fit to delude vs then any man else: Admiration of persons yow know hath carryed on great stroke in this cause; and of him among the rest; its our wisdom therefore to make there wickednes and guile manifest to all men that they may goe no farther, and then they will sinke of themselues.

---

[1] W. 3. 71; 4 *Collections*, VII. 266–268.

[2] This was the term applied to those who in March, 1636/37, signed the "Remonstrance" against the action taken by the Massachusetts General Court against the Reverend John Wheelwright. The Wheelwright controversy flared up again when the General Court met in May. At that time Winthrop wrote in his Journal (I. 26): "Divers writings were now published about these differences." His "Survey" may have been one of these writings.

2. agayne yow say a faythfull seruant is not so stiled in an act of his vnfayth-fulnes; as in Moses and Aaron: Answ. Doubtles the contrary may be found in scripture, ex: gr: 1 Kings 15: 14: Gen: 20: where Abram had told a ly, yet Pss. 7: he is called by god himselfe a prophet: to call him a Prophet, neither his practise deserues it nor yet doe the churches call at this day any men prophets vsually but those that were extraordinary: its the Jesuits craft at this day to put fayre names on fowle things and so to beat religion with its own weapon. He dazles the eyes of the woorld by opposing a prophet of god agaynst the Elders of churches.

Pag. 4: His maxime that a sentence giuen by the major part of the Court when another doe dissent is a nullity: I desire 2 things concerning it if your prudence thinke it fit: 1: that herein yow would lay down more reasons agaynst it and shew more particularly to what it leads, and from what spirit it came; for its as monstrous deuillish hellish a birth as euer wickednes could bring foorth and as yow well note enough to ruine vs and all states in the woorld. 2: To answer his arguments more fully woud seeme to be to haue colour of strength but that of the witnesses dissenting: which if you opend more clearly would be pleasing to many; witnesses answer de facto: Judges sentence is de Jure: if the major part of the Court haue jus with them, i: any law of god or Diduct from it the law must judge: if the lesser part Haue the law of god on there side that law should judge.

Pag: 11: Sedition and Murther are sins; Now tho sin in generall be a trans-gression of the law yet this or that particular sin is according to the seuerall externall circumstances, time place persons etc. and in all morall acts good or evill externall circumstances ad to the internall being and formallity of euery sin, and h[ence] Mr. Vanes addition of deuiding in the good wherein they ought [to] be vnited is not nothing: for yourselfe make Adition, where mens minds are made feirce. Now if yow had not added by an euill act which is an externall thing yet internall to sedition, Paul and the apostles as they truly say had bin seditious when they preached the truth. Yow seeme also to say that hatred is the formall cause of murther, which is a degree only to it; and to kill a man out of hatred because he crosseth gods will is not mur-der but Justice: I also question whether that can be the end of sedition also.

I haue not had time exactly to view euery particular woord, because all did so well sute with me that I could not desire to blame any th[ing]; Thus in extreame hast with many thankes for this and all your loue to this cuntry and these churches and my selfe, I leaue yow in his arms that loues yow. Your

T. S.

[*Ca.* May 20, 1637]

JOHN WINTHROP TO WILLIAM BRADFORD[1]

Sir, The Lord hauing so disposed, as that your letters to our late Gou[er-nou]r is fallen to my lott to make answer vnto; I could haue wished I might haue been at more freedome of time, and thoughts also, that I might haue done It more to your, and my owne satisfaction. But what shall be wanting now, may be supplyed hearafter. for the matters which from your selfe, and counsell, were propounded, and objected to vs; we thought not fitte to make them so publicke as the cognizance of our generall courte. But as they haue been considered by those of our counsell; this answer we thinke fitt to return vnto you. (1) Wereas you signifie your willingnes to joyne with vs, in this warr against the pequents, though you cannot Ingage your selues, without the con-sente of your generall courte; we acknowledg your good affection towards vs (which we neuer had cause to doubt of) and are willing to attend your full resolution, when it may most seasonably be ripened. (2ly) Wheras you make this warr, to be our peopls; and not to conceirne your selues, otherwise then by consequence, we do in parte consente to you therin; yet we suppose, that in case of perill, you will not stand vpon such terms, as we hope, we should not doe towards you; and withall we conceiue that you looke at the pequents, and all other Indeans, as a commone enimie, who though he may take occa-sion, of the begining of his rage, from some one parte of the English, yet if he preuaile, will surly pursue his aduantage, to the rooting out of the whole nation; therfore when we desired your help, we did it not without respecte to your owne saftie, as ours. (3ly) wheras you desire we should be Ingaged to aide you, vpon all like occasions; we are perswaded, you doe not doubte of it; yet as we now deale with you, as a free people, and at libertie, so as we can-not draw you into this warr with vs, otherwise then as reason may guid, and prouock you; so we desire we may be at the like freedome, when any occasion may call for help from vs. And wheras it is objected to vs, that we refused to aide you, against the french; we conceiue the case was not alicke; yet we can-not wholy excuse our failing in that matter.

(4ly) Weras you objecte that we began the warr, without your priuitie, and managed it contrary to your aduise, The truth is, that our first Inten-tions being only against Block Iland, and the Interprice seeming of small

---

[1] Original not located; Bradford, *History of Plymouth* (facsimile edition, London, 1896), 423–427; (1912), II. 244–246; *L. and L.*, II. 194–197. For Winthrop's account of the negotiations between the Massachusetts Bay and Plymouth colonies concerning the latter's participation in the war against the Pequots, see *Journal*, I. 213–214.

difficultie, we did not so much as consider of taking aduise, or looking out for
aide abroad. And when we had resolued vpon the pequents, we sent presently, or not long after, to you aboute it; but the answer receiued, it was not
seasonable for vs to chaing our counsells, excepte we had seen, and waighed
your grounds, which might haue out wayed our owne.

(5ly) for our peoples trading at Kenebeck, we assure you (to our knowledge)
it hath not been by any allowance from vs; and what we haue prouided in
this and like cases, at our last Courte, Mr. E[dward] W[inslow] can certifie
you.

And (6ly) wheras you objecte to vs that we should hold trade and corre-
spondancie with the french your enemise; we answer you are misinformed,
for besids some letters which hath passed betweene our late Gou[ernou]r and
them, to which we were priuie, we have neither sente nor Incouraged ours to
trade with them, only one vessell or tow, for the better conueance of our
letters, had licens from our Gou[erno]r to sayle thither.[1]

diuerce other things haue been priuatly objected to vs by our worthy freind,
whervnto he receiued some answer; but most of them concerning the appre-
hentions of perticuler discurteseis, or Injueries from some perticuler persons
amongst vs; It concernes us not to giue any other answer to them, then this;
that if the offenders shall be brought forth, in a right way, we shall be ready
to doe Justice as the case shall require. In the meane time, we desire you to
rest assured, that such things are without our priuity, and not a litle greeueous
to vs.

Now for the joyning with vs in this warr, which indeed concerns vs no
other wise, then it may your selues, viz: the releeuing of our freinds, and
christian Breethren, who are now first in the danger. Though you may thinke
us able to make it good without you, (as if the lord please to be with us, we
may) yet 3 things we offer to your consideration which (we conceiue) may
haue some waight with you. (first) that If we should sinck vnder this burden,
your opportunitie of seasonable help would be lost in 3 respects. 1. You cannot recouer vs, or secure your selues ther, with 3 times the charge and hazard
which now ye may. 2ly The sorrowes, which we should lye vnder (If through
your neglect) would much abate of the acceptablenes of your help afterwards.
3ly, Those of yours, who are now full of courage, and forwardnes, would be
much damped, and so less able to vndergoe so great a burden The (2) thing
is this, that it concernes vs much to hasten this warr to an end before the end

---

[1] Bradford's marginal comment on this statement by Winthrop is: "But by this means they did
furnish them, and have still continued to doe."

of this sommer; other wise the newes of it will discourage both your and our freinds from coming to vs next year, with what further hazard and losse it may expose vs vnto, your selues may judge.

The (3) thing is this, that if the lord shall please to blesse our endeaours, so as we end the warr, or put it in a hopefull way without you; It may breed such ill thoughts in our people towards yours, as will be hard to entertaine such oppinione of your good will towards vs, as were fitt to be nurished among such neigbours and brethren as we are. And what Ill consequences may follow, on both sids, wise men may fear, and would rather preuente, then hope to redress so with my harty salutations to you selfe, and all your counsell, and other our good freinds with you, I rest Yours most Assured in the lord

                                                        Jo: Winthrop

Boston, the 20 of the 3 month 1637

EDWARD WINSLOW TO JOHN WINTHROP[1]

To the right Wor[shi]pp[fu]ll his much honored Friend John Winthrop Esqr. Governer of the Massachusetts these be delivered

Much honored Sir, Your many and undeserued kindnesses as formerly so more especially at my being last with you tie me if possible yet neerer in heart and affeccion towards you and yours whom I salute in the Lord. At our comming home by the goodnes of our God there was an Indian newly commen from Tittacutt to advertise us that they had that day being the day of our travell and 2d of the weeke discovered the track and footing of a party of Indians which could not be lesse in number then an hundred which made either towards Duxburrow or your parts, advising us to be in readines to receiue them not knowing what their intent might be. Thomas Willet is commen from the Dutch, your son Mr. Stephen in good health, who hath written to you by him. Capt. Vnderhill and the Company at the Fort in health, he hath violently taken an Pecoat woman from the Dutch which was a Sachims wife and hath her prisoner, knows nothing of what we heare concerning Capt. Mason, but onely that he was exspected downe with ninety men. Mr. Gardner it seems much discourageth common men by extolling the valor of your adversaries preferring them before the Spaniards. Your Sachim of the Massachusets is in some jealousie amongst others because say they he was at

---

[1] W. 2. 89; 4 *Collections*, VI. 163–164.

Narrohigganset and saw the willingnes of the multitude to become your enemies when the head was brought and did not acquaint you. The Pecoats follow their fishing and planting as if they had no enemies: Their weomen of esteeme and children are gone to long Island with a strong gard at Pecoat. They professe there you shall find them, and as they were there borne and bred there their bones shall be buried and rott in despight of the English: but if the lord be on our side, their braggs will soone fall. The truth is if onece they be routed we know their courage will faile: ergo feare not. I pray you when the questions are once stated for the conference let us haue a coppy of them: My letters heer but newly deliuered. The lord in mercy goe along with you. I durst not lose this opportunity, nor can I write more being called on to seale. Yours assured to his power

EDW: WINSLOW

May 22, 1637

I pray you salute your Assistants also mr. Wilson mr. Peeters mr. Shepheard etc. let my hast excuse me.

LUCY DOWNING TO JOHN WINTHROP[1]

To her very good brother Jhon winthrop esqr. present this

MY DEAR BROTHER, I hope you haue heard ere this by msr. [*blank*] of gods mercy to me in giuinge me safe deliuery: and health againe to this present: and to all our famylie wich is noe small blessinge this contagious time: I pray as I know wee pertake in your prayers, so be pleasd to assist vs in thankfullnes: I cannot yet present you with more then formerly of our cominge to you: wich is next and next springs or falles: but so many haue mist that I now grow incredulous: yet beleeue me, I doe not aprehend it aduantagious to vs to be apon such vncertainties either for soule or body. I could earnestly wish a more settled condition in new or ould, but what shall I saye. It hath bine the lot of many, far more deseruing then my selfe, to be in greater exigents, then I haue yet felt: and this is a far less cros, then I deserue: yet I cannot wish to suffer in a way of indiscretion: but I hope god will dispose of vs for the best, in his good time: and wee desire you to commend vs to god in this respect for the work is great: and our wisdome and power very small: and very perfidious

---

[1] W. 4. 6; 5 *Collections*, I. 21–22.

and diffident is my hart I am suer: god perswade it to that condiction, that may be most pleasinge to him: I doupt not but you will hear how things goe with vs hear: the difficuties to newe engl: are not all vanisht: nor the motiues neither: and it wear well if peac and truth might prosper in your littell sosietie: but, it is feard, as the ould prouerb: the diuell will haue a chapell whear god hath a church: and what pollicy or wisdom can preuent that epidemicall diseas: our frinds att groton and att graces and charter howes are resonable well: but msr. tindall hath buryed his elldest daughter,[1] wich is a great tryall to them: I should be very glad, if whilst wee are hear, wee might doe you seruis hear: wee make noe scruple of troublinge you: theerfore I pray be as free with vs and you shall therby oblige your sister that desiers your prosperity.

                                                          LUCIE DOWNINGE

May 23, [1637]

DANIEL PATRICK TO JOHN WINTHROP[2]

To the Right Worshipfull Mr. Winthrope Gouernour giue this

RIGHT WORSHIP[FU]LL SIR, Wee are all saflye arriued at the pinnis, only 3 or 4 of our horsses gott from vs in the night which wee lay by the waye, and hoope they are returnde home bye this time. oure prouisions beinge butt shorte, wee hoope supplye will not tarrye longe. wee shall greatlye want a shallop. Captayne Vnderhill and Captayne Massonn with 80 souldiers in 2 pinnaces are heer in the baye and a 100 Indeans from the Riuer at there disposinge. as soone as I came, I dispatcht an Indean to them, intendinge to peece in with them, if I should heer of the Illanders remoouall. I will if possible send constant word of our proceedings. Your worships to Commaunde

                                                          DANI. PATTRICKE

PROUIDEN this 23 May 1637

Mr. Williams informs your worship at large.

---

[1] Cf. Herbert Pelham to John Winthrop, April 19, 1637 (pages 393–394, above).
[2] W. 3. 87; 4 *Collections*, VII. 321–322. For Patrick, see 4 *Collections*, VII. 321*n*.

THOMAS MARRIOTT TO JOHN WINTHROP[1]

To his worthy freinde the right wor[shi]pfull Mr. John Waintrope this be delivered
Boastonn New Ingland

Frome WAPPING the 26 of May 1637

MR. WINTROPE, SER, my remembred vnto you giving you many Thankes for your Loue and kindnes shewed vnto me and to vs all when we ware with you nott knowing whi[c]h way I shall any way reqit your kind Loue: I would intrett you as for to exsept of a few netts tungs thatt I haue sent you by mr. Robert Lov his ship called the Increse this within on the Cases for mr. wenttope ther should be fouer dosen I wold intreatt you to doe me the Favour as for to remember my seruis to mr. Cotten and the Gentellman that was gouernor the last yeir and you wold be pl[ea]sed for to send to them tow one dossen of the tungs and for to keep the other thre for your selfe so Com[it]-ting you all to the protexsion of him whom I doubt nott but with a spe[c]aill hand doth watch ouer you your se[rva]nt to command in what I may

THO. MARRIOTT

A DECLARATION IN DEFENSE OF AN ORDER OF COURT MADE IN MAY, 1637[2]

A Declaration of the Intent and Equitye of the Order made at the last Court, to this
effect, that none should be received to inhabite within this Jurisdiction but such
as should be allowed by some of the Magistrates

For clearing of such scruples as have arisen about this order, it is to be considered, first, what is the essentiall forme of a common weale or body

---

[1] W. 15. 20. The writer of this letter, who is obviously not the person of that name who was one of the early settlers of Cambridge, has not been identified.

[2] Original not located; *Hutchinson Papers* (1769), 67–71; (1865), I. 79–83; *L. and L.*, II. 182–186. The Massachusetts General Court, as an aftermath of the proceedings against Wheelright in March, 1636/37, passed an order at the May session "to keep out all such persons as might be dangerous to the commonwealth, by imposing a penalty upon all such as should retain any, etc., above three weeks, which should not be allowed by some of the magistrates; for it was very probable, that they [the Antinomians] expected many of their opinion to come out of England from Mr. Brierly his church, etc." *Journal*, I. 219. The protests of those against whom the order was really directed were so strenuous that this defense of the Court's action was drawn up. It has been universally attributed to Governor Winthrop. In due time there appeared an answer, commonly attributed to Vane, entitled "A briefe Answer to a certaine declaration, made of the intent and equitye of the order of court, that none should be received to inhabite within this jurisdiction but such as should be allowed

politic such as this is, which I conceive to be this—The consent of a certaine companie of people, to cohabite together, under one government for their mutual safety and welfare.

In this description all these things doe concurre to the well being of such a body, 1 Persons, 2 Place, 3 Consent, 4 Government or Order, 5 Wellfare.

It is clearly agreed, by all, that the care of safety and wellfare was the original cause or occasion of common weales and of many familyes subjecting themselves to rulers and laws; for no man hath lawfull power over another, but by birth or consent, so likewise, by the law of proprietye, no man can have just interest in that which belongeth to another, without his consent.

From the premises will arise these conclusions.

1. No common weale can be founded but by free consent.

2. The persons so incorporating have a public and relative interest each in other, and in the place of their co-habitation and goods, and laws etc. and in all the means of their wellfare so as none other can claime priviledge with them but by free consent.

3. The nature of such an incorporation tyes every member thereof to seeke out and entertaine all means that may conduce to the wellfare of the bodye, and to keepe off whatsoever doth appeare to tend to theire damage.

4. The wellfare of the whole is to be put to apparent hazard for the advantage of any particular members.

From these conclusions I thus reason.

1. If we heere be a corporation established by free consent, if the place of our cohabitation be our owne, then no man hath right to come into us etc. without our consent.

2. If no man hath right to our lands, our government priviledges etc., but by our consent, then it is reason we should take notice of before we conferre any such upon them.

3. If we are bound to keepe off whatsoever appears to tend to our ruine or damage, then we may lawfully refuse to receive such whose dispositions suite not with ours and whose society (we know) will be hurtfull to us, and therefore it is lawfull to take knowledge of all men before we receive them.

4. The churches take liberty (as lawfully they may) to receive or reject at their discretion; yea particular towns make orders to the like effect; why then should the common weale be denied the like liberty, and the whole more restrained than any parte?

---

by some of the magistrates." *Hutchinson Papers* (1769), 71–83; (1865), 1. 84–96. This, in turn, evoked a further statement, also attributed to Winthrop, which is printed below (pages 463–476).

5. If it be sinne in us to deny some men place etc. amongst us, then it is because of some right they have to this place etc. for to deny a man that which he hath no right unto, is neither sinne nor injury.

6. If strangers have right to our houses or lands etc., then it is either of justice or of mercye; if of justice let them plead it, and we shall know what to answer: but if it be only in way of mercye, or by the rule of hospitality etc., then I answer 1st a man is not a fit object of mercye except he be in miserye. 2d. We are not bound to exercise mercye to others to the ruine of ourselves. 3d. There are few that stand in neede of mercye at their first coming hither. As for hospitality, that rule doth not bind further than for some present occasion, not for continual residence.

7. A family is a little common wealth, and a common wealth is a greate family. Now as a family is not bound to entertaine all comers, no not every good man (otherwise than by way of hospitality) no more is a common wealth.

8. It is a generall received rule, *turpius ejicitur quam non admittitur hospes*, it is worse to receive a man whom we must cast out againe, than to denye him admittance.

9. The rule of the Apostle, John 2. 10. is, that such as come and bring not the true doctrine with them should not be received to house, and by the same reason not into the common weale.

10. Seeing it must be granted that there may come such persons (suppose Jesuits etc.) which by consent of all ought to be rejected, it will follow that by this law (being only for notice to be taken of all that come to us, without which we cannot avoyd such as indeed are to be kept out) is no other but just and needfull, and if any should be rejected that ought to be received, that is not to be imputed to the law, but to those who are betrusted with the execution of it. And herein is to be considered, what the intent of the law is, and by consequence, by what rule they are to walke, who are betrusted with the keeping of it. The intent of the law is to preserve the wellfare of the body; and for this ende to have none received into any fellowship with it who are likely to disturbe the same, and this intent (I am sure) is lawful and good. Now then, if such to whom the keeping of this law is committed, be persuaded in theire judgments that such a man is likely to disturbe and hinder the publick weale, but some others who are not in the same trust, judge otherwise, yet they are to follow their owne judgments, rather than the judgments of others who are not alike interested: As in tryall of an offender by jury; the twelve men are satisfied in their consciences, upon the evidence given, that the party deserves death: but there are 20 or 40 standers by, who conceive otherwise, yet is the jury bound to condemn him according to their owne consciences,

and not to acquit him upon the different opinion of other men, except theire reasons can convince them of the errour of their consciences, and this is according to the rule of the Apostle. Rom. 14. 5. Let every man be fully persuaded in his own mynde.

If it be objected, that some prophane persons are received and others who are religious are rejected, I answer 1st, It is not knowne that any such thinge has as yet fallen out. 2. Such a practice may be justifiable as the case may be, for younger persons (even prophane ones) may be of lesse danger to the common weale (and to the churches also) than some older persons, though professors of religion: for our Saviour Christ when he conversed with publicans etc. sayeth that such were nearer the Kingdom of heaven than the religious pharisees, and one that is of large parts and confirmed in some erroneous way, is likely to doe more harme to church and common weale, and is of lesse hope to be reclaymed, than 10 prophane persons, who have not yet become hardened, in the contempt of the meanes of grace.

Lastly, Whereas it is objected that by this law, we reject good christians and so consequently Christ himselfe: I answer 1st. It is not knowne that any christian man hath been rejected. 2. a man that is a true christian, may be denyed residence among us, in some cases, without rejecting Christ, as admitt a true christian should come over, and should maintain community of goods, or that magistrates ought not to punish the breakers of the first table, or the members of churches for criminal offences: or that no man were bound to be subject to those lawes or magistrates to which they should not give an explicite consent, etc. I hope no man will say, that not to receive such an one were to reject Christ; for such opinions (though being maintained in simple ignorance, they might stand with a state of grace yet) they may be so dangerous to the publick weale in many respects, as it would be our sinne and unfaithfullness to receive such among us, except it were for tryall of theire reformation. I would demand then in the case in question (for it is bootlesse curiosity to refrayne openesse in things publick) whereas it is sayd that this law was made of purpose to keepe away such as are of Mr. Wheelwright his judgment (admitt it were so which yet I cannot confesse) where is the evill of it? If we conceive and finde by sadd experience that his opinions are such, as by his own profession cannot stand with externall peace, may we not provide for our peace, by keeping of such as would strengthen him and infect others with such dangerous tenets? and if we finde his opinions such as will cause divisions, and make people looke at their magistrates, ministers and brethren as enemies to Christ and Antichrists etc., were it not sinne and unfaithfullness in us, to receive more of those opinions, which we already finde the evill fruite of: Nay, why doe not those who now complayne joyne with us in keeping out of such, as well as formerly they did in expelling Mr. Williams for the like, though lesse dangerous? Where this change of theire judgments should arise I leave them to themselves to examine, and I earnestly entreat them so to doe, and for this law let the equally mynded judge, what evill they finde in it, or in the practice of those who are betrusted with the execution of it.

[*Ca.* June, 1637]

ROGER WILLIAMS TO JOHN WINTHROP[1]

New Providence this 6th of this present
weeke, toward midnight [*ca.* June 2, 1637]

Sir, By John Throckmorton I was bold to advertize of the late mercifull Successe it hath pleased the Father of Mercies to vouchsafe to the first attempts of our Countrimen against these Barbarous.

After his departure toward you I went over to the Nanhiggonsick partly for Intelligence and partly to encourage the Nanhiggonsicks in case the sad newes of all their men and yours defeated were true.

I found the first newes of the Cutting of the whole Fort of the Pequts at Mistick to be certaine and vnquestionably true as I sent, with litle or no Variation, of which hereafter.

The Newes of the Cutting of 3 hundreth Nanhiggonsicks and all the English held still for Currant, and confirmed that they were opprest with multitudes their provision being spent and the English wanting powder and shot and the Nanhiggonsicks Arrowes.

I gaue the best reasons I could to perswade that they were all either gone togeather to Qunnihticut for provision or vpon some second assault vpon the other of the Pequt Forts.

As allso I was bold to promise (in Mr. Gov[ernou]rs name) that allthough all these or more were cut of yet there should be fresh Supplies of the English who would never sheath their swords etc.

This 5th day past toward night I haue receaved tidings (blessed for euer be the Lord of Hosts) that the Nanhiggonsicks are all came safe home yesternight (at noone I came from thence) and brought word that the English were all safe but the first 3 slaine at the Fort with 2 of their owne.

---

1 W. 2. 97; 4 *Collections*, VI. 191–194; *N.C.*, VI. 27–30.

As allso that indeede they fought thrice that day of their first Victorie with no losse of their side and with the losse of 2 Pequts more.

That themselues and the English prepard next day after for their other Forts, found all fled, made themselues Lords of one in which both English and Nanhiggonsicks now keepe.

That Maumanadtuck one of their biggest with great Troops (as before he gaue out he could) is gone to Wunnashowatuckqut (the further Neepmucks.)

That Sasacous said he would to Long Iland, and thither is gone or hid in the Swampes but not a Pequt is to be found.

That Miantunnommu is come from Pequt to Nayantaquit and was re-solved homeward to send out to Wunnashowatuckqut where the Enemie shelters and haue Forts.

Now Sir, considering the worck is effected (through the mercie of the most High) in these parts and that the Qunnihticut English togeather with Capt: Patrick and his are sufficient to mainteine what they haue gotten and pursue Sasacous in all his Motions thereabouts: I conceaved (with Submission) that it might saue the Countrey no small charge and hazard and losse timely to advertize and give Intelligence.

The Wunnashowatuckoogs and Pequts with them are about the distance from you that we are: on them I conceaue and vnderstand the Nanhiggon-sicks next fall.

If you see Cause and grounds to make a Stop for a day or 2, if the Lord please, the 2nd day or 3d of the next weeke I hope to acquaint you with Miantunnomues and Caunonnicus their advice and desire, which it may be will be to meete his Companies at the hither Neepmucks and none to come this way, or some the one way and some the other   This morning I goe over (if the Lord please) to consult with them, hoping to be at home (if possible) to morrow Evening and so to dispatch some Messenger the 2nd in the morning.

Sir, your late message to the Neepmucks (through the Lords mercy) hath wrought this Effect, that whereas they staggerd as nevters they brought this present weeke divers basketts of their Nokehick and Chesnuts to Canounicus towards his wars.

Sir I vnderstand that the Cause why the English hurt so many of the Nanhiggonsicks was want of signes or marcks   You may please therefore to prouide some yellow or red for their heads: the Qunnihticut English had yellow but not enough.

Thus beseeching the God of Peace to be at Peace with vs, that all the fruit may be the taking away of our Sinn, (which if not remooved will vnstop worse vialls) to guid your Consultations and prosper your Expeditions to the prayse of his owne most holy name I rest Your Wo[rshi]ps faythfull and affectionate in all civill bonds

ROGER WILLIAMS

EDWARD WINSLOW TO JOHN WINTHROP[1]

RIGHT WO[RSHI]PP[FU]LL, Being newly rysen from Court I was requested by our Gov[erno]r who cannot at present write, to dispatch a messenger to you partly to informe you that we haue this day by solemne act of Court ingaged our selves to take part with you and our brethren of Coneetacut in the war against the Pecoats, purposing to sett fourth thirty men for the land service besides the mannaging of the vessels which we conceiue will not be lesse than forty; now we fear it will be longer then we willingly would for want of Coats or Coslets which are very scarce with us, unles you can furnish us for which we would willingly pay as also some other necessaries thereunto belonging. Tomorrow we shall know who are the men goe with them but heereof our Gov[erno]r will write at large (who desireth to salute you once more by my pen) so soone as our Court is ended and opportunity is offered. Another maine end of our sending is in regard we haue heard no more, till since we rose this evening of the last expedicion of our brethren of Coneetacut and Capt. Vnderhill, and that is by Capt. Standish his Indian who was sent this morning to Namasket and saith the defeat of the Fort is true and that onely three English were slaine in the taking of it. As also that the foresaid English and Capt. Patrick are still at Narrohigganset and haue been daies which makes us jealous and shall be till we heare from you, and the rather because you heard nothing from any of them by letter when John Jenny came away. I pray you therefore let us heare, and let not this (though true) discourage the sending of your 160 men but take such revenge as may be a service to after times for any the barbarians to rise against us. If any letters be commen from Engl. I pray you send them by the bearer, or such news as is worth the sending. I am sorry for the carriages of your people   God sanctefie his hand and fit us for such trials as he hath appointed. Thus with my loue to you and prayers for you and yours desiring you to salute my christian friends with you take leave remayning Yours till death

EDWA: WINSLOW

PLYM. the 5th of the 4 mo. 1636 [1637]

---

[1] Massachusetts Archives, CCXL. 29; *Hutchinson Papers* (1769), 60–61; (1865), I. 67–69.

JOHN HUMFREY TO JOHN WINTHROP[1]

June 7th 1637

MUCH HONOURED, Hitherto the lord hath beene with us, blessed for ever be his ever blessed name. Our nation, the gospel, the blood of those murthered persons of ours seems to triump in the present successe; now I onely desire to suggest it to your wise and deeper considerations whether it be not probable the confederates of the Pequots will not be glad to purchase a secure and fear-less condition to themselves, by delivering up those men or their heads, who have wrought and brought so much miserie upon themselves and theirs. Or if not so, whither (if they give good assurance by hostages etc.) the blood shed by them may not seeme to be sufficiently expiated by so great an in-equalitie on their sides. Hitherto the honour and terrour of our peeple to all the natives is abundantly vendicated and made good. If providence for our humbling (as in regard of myselfe I much feare) should flesh them [   ] by some new cruelties upon anie of ours, how low wee may be laide both in their, and the eyes of our confederate Indians, and to how great daunger to us, yea possiblie our posterities, I leave to your graver thoughts, if it be worth the consideration. Onely to my shallownes it seemes considerable whither it were not safe pawsing to see what effect this will or may work upon such a demaund. 2dly whither not best to rest in certaine victorie and honour ac-quired, upon so small a losse. 3dly whither, (if wee carrie away the greatest glory of these poore barbarous people in our triumphs over them,) the losse of three men more (if we should not exceede) may not be paraleld with so manie hundreds more of theirs. 4thly whither we must not be forced at last (and it may be in worse circumstances) to take this course unlesse divine iustice will miraculously shew it selfe in bringing them all into our net, which according to reason is not likely. 5thly, whether the dreadfulnes of our maine Battallion (as it were) be better to be measured by their feares raised on this last, then to see, say or thinke, that our former victorie was not so much of valour as accident which we ourselves do acknowledge providence. 6thly, if we refuse to give or take such conditions now, they may not be likely to hold us to worse, or necessitate us to a perpetual war if for our owne ease wee after seeke them, and when they see us (as they may) afraide in like manner.

Much more, and to as little purpose might be saide. But if you continue your resolutions to proceede according to former intentions you may please to consider whither these bottles to be used granado wise, may not be of some

---

[1] Original not located; Mather, *Early History of New England*, 288–289.

use; and whither (if the fort be so difficile as it is reported, into which they shall for their last refuge retire) it were not operæ pretium to prepare a petar or two to command entrance. Thus laying my low thoughts and myself at your feete to be kicked out or admitted as you see good, being glad to hope of the continuance of your purpose to see us in your way to Ipswich, With my service to you and yours I rest yet and ever yours (anie thing) to serve you.

Jo: HUMFREY

DANIEL PATRICK TO THE GOVERNOR AND COUNCIL OF WAR IN MASSACHUSETTS[1]

To the honnorable the Gouernore and the Rest of the Councell of war in Massechusets theese be delivered

HONNORABLE GENTLEMEN, Your Commissione I receiude at narregansets the 17 daye of June, requiringe me to narregansets, or be sure of a sufficient reasone for the Contrarye. at narregansets I was, but goe backe to saybrooke this 19 of June, to fetch the Companye, yet but to meat Mr. Stoughtone at Pequote, or if oportunitie be offerd to venter your fauour as well as my owne lyfe, for to make anny thinge sure in ware cannot bee. what may stand with good reasone, Prouidence may cross, therefore as the lord shall dereckt, beinge tirde to be tide to Saybrooke soe longe, and heering a ruemore of Pequots dispersione, alsoe hauinge taken some Cannoes laden with all sorts of Indean howsell stuff passinge by the riuers mouth I guest a probbabillitie of it, and resolude to take 10 men with the pinace and goe obserue the motione and posture of Pequote riuer, but before I went Cobbine beets and 2 or 3 more weare cut of cominge downe in a shallop from Quenechtequed, the Dutch yacht broght vs worde, whoe had bine to carry home our captiue mades. Captane Vnderhill and I went out and founde the shallope ruinated, and the Indeans fled. next day being come home, one of the slane menn came driuinge by saybrooke, stuck with 3 or 4 arrows, his cloths one, his bandeleors about hime, and his sworde vnder his arme readye drawne, being one of Mr. Michaels men. this was dune 6 mile from sayebrooke. to pequot as I intended I came, and found all gone though I knew not where. then I argued if the Indeans be gone, what need such Chardg from the baye, therfore to Narregansets, where I found William Quicke. I landed and dealt with the

---

[1] W. 3. 88; 4 *Collections*, VII. 322–324.

Narreganset Sachems, whoe blamde the baye of procrastinatione, informd vs of the Pequots desertinge there Cuntrye, as neuer to returne in there Judgments, of there flight at present to Quinnopiage, which I witnes to, hauinge seene, and as I sayd taken 2 of there Cannoes, but then not acquanted with there intended proggress, that ther cheyfe eandeuor for a while till after waye made to the mowhoake. the opertunitye I spake of maye bee to surprise them there by night, with some Nareganset if I cann drawe them to runn the venter, venter I say of loosinge soe much time as marchinge to and froe, for I am not certane whether they will be gone before wee come or whether danger at home will forbide our frinds to come downe the riuer or Captn. Vnderhill will doe any thinge in the Case, but if I can get them to runn the venter which is smale to them, then times fore locke woulde be taken houlde of, and a fare farwell giuen them at partinge. 40 or 50 Pequots remayne at longe Iland, 300 fitt for fight at quinnopiage. Nowe if those at Quinnopiage avoyde to the Mowhoake, or if but 50 mile aboue the Riuer townes, as some thinke, what will you doe with or where will you imploye our 200 men   I barely propounde it, and soe leaue it. our frinds at Quenechtequod resolue to joyne with you possessinge the Pequots Cuntrye   for that, and the manner, I leaue till farther order, onely for the present if noe better seruice fale out, if at my returne to the Riuers mouth quinnopiage fayle, and they will and are readye to set downe at Pequot, Ile be doinge with them in possessione. a cale of your worships cann fetch mee of when you will, but if sounde reasone not for quenopiage, nor possessinge of Pequote will permite, then accordinge to Comissione, I hoope shortly to returne to Narreganset where Ile leaue a Coppy of this letter for Mr. Stoughtone to make vse of as he shall thinke good. Thus after seruice in all due Respeckt, I leaue you to the lord and rest yours to commaunde

DANI. PATTRICKE

NARREGANSETs this 19 of June 1637

Pequots and Naantucke is rich lande full of good Corne   a Coate and a pare of shoes the Indeane is to haue   Capt. Vnderhill is gone vp the Riuer to the plantations   the Narregansets propound for some smale interrest and priueledg in Pequot Cuntrye, but reffer them selus to you.

Williame Quicke hath bine heere this 10 dayes but none but hee is yet come.

PETITION OF THE INHABITANTS OF IPSWICH[1]

To our much honored Gouv[erno]r and Counsello[rs] att Boston deliver

Our humble duties and respects premised: vnderstanding there is an Intention to call Mr. Winthrop Junr. from vs and to committ the Custody of the Castle to him, we could not out of the entire affection we beare to him and his welfare but become earnest petitioners to your worships that you would not depriue our Church and Towne of one whose presence is so gratefull and vsefull to vs. It was for his sake that many of vs came to this place and without him we should not haue come, his abode with vs hath made our abode here much more comfortable then otherwise it would haue bene: Mr. Dudleys leaving vs hath made vs much more desolate and weake then we were, and if we should lose another magistrate it would be too great a greif to vs and breach vpon vs: and not a magistrate only but our Lieutenant Colonell so beloued of our Souldiours and military men that this remote Corner would be left so destitute and desolate; neither can we conceiue but that his removall from vs will much preiudice and vnsetle him, the place he is chosen vnto we feare will neither mayntaine him and his company comfortably nor proue certaine to him, but vpon sundry occasions mutable. It would be very vncomfortable to him as we suppose to live vpon others maintenance, or to neglect that portion of land and loue which God hath giuen him amongst vs. the improvall of his estate here we hope will proue a better and surer support then a yearly stipend from the Country which hath groaned much vnder the burthen of that fort already. We find his affections great and constant to our Towne and we hope ours shall never faile towards him and his. We therfore humbly beseech you that we may still inioy him and that you would not expose him to so solitary a life and a place where we hope there will not be much vse of him: nor vs to the losse and want of one so much desired of vs. The distance we are sett in hath made vs earnest for the company of able men and as loath to loose them when we haue obtained them. Thus hoping you will please to consider and tender our Condition we humbly take our leaues resting your Wor[shi]ps in all due serviss

June 21, 1637

NATHL. WARDE   MICAELL CATHERICK
RICHARD SALTONSTALL   HENRI PINNDER
JOHN NORTON   SAMUELL SHARMAN

---

[1] Essex Institute; 2 *Proceedings*, III. 198–199. The text of this petition is in the handwriting of Nathaniel Ward.

Daniell Denison	Jhon Jhonson
Samuell Appleton	Thomas French
Thomas Bressye	W: Hubbard
Robertt Andrewes	Jonathan Wade
Joseph Morse	William White
Christopher Osgood	John Pirkines senar
John Perkins, Jouner	George Car
Richard Jacob	John Tuttell
Philip Fouler	Richard Haffeild
William Goodhue	George Giddings
Roger Lanckton	Edward Gardner
Thomas Dorman	John Satchwell
Joseph Medcalfe	John Saunders
Thomas Borman	John Severnes
John Webster	Antony Colby
Robert Lord	Robert Mussy
Thomas Wells	John Peekins
John Gassett	Nathaniell Bishop
John Coggswell	John Couentun
Humfrie Brodstree	Allen Perley
Thomas Cooke	John Procter
Heugh Sherratt	Thomas Howlitt
Edward Katcham	William Fuller
Thomas Clark	Alexander Knight
John Gage	Thomas Hardy
William Barthollmew	

ROGER WILLIAMS TO JOHN WINTHROP[1]

For his much honoured Mr. Governour these   Mr. Stoughton or Capt. Traske
on their way may please to reade this

New Providence this 4th of the weeke, *manè* [*ca*. June 21, 1637]

Sir, John Gallop (blessed be the Lord) is safely arrived at our dores and hath brought from the Lord and you a mercifull refreshing to vs: he be graciously pleased to recompence it a thoughsand fold to the whole land and your selues especially.

---

[1] American Antiquarian Society; 4 *Collections*, vi. 194–195; *N.C.*, vi. 32–34.

He relates that there is now riding below 3 pinnaces (the names of the M[aste]rs Quick, Jiglies and Robinson):[1] and the 2 Shalops as allso that the other whereof —— Jackson of Salem is m[aste]r was in Company with them the night before and waighed anchor togeather but being not able to turne about was faigne to chop to an anchor againe but they hope is in by this time.

Sir I heare our lo[ving] friends Mr. Stoughton Mr. Traske etc. are on their way and 160 (the intended number) with them. I hope the Continuance of the number will be seasonable, if not for Pursuit of Sasacous and the Pequts (of whome it is said that they are gone farr and finally) yet for the quelling of their Confederates the Wunnashowatuckoogs and Monashackotoogs etc. who liue neerer to you on the westward etc.

Some 200 of these (since the slaughter at the Fort) came in revenge vpon the Nanhiggonsicks: which the Nanhiggonsicks themselues knew not till three Pequts (now fallen to them) related it: for it pleased the Lord to send a great mist that morning, that they durst not fight, and so returned: so that there is Cause to take some Course with them, and especially if it be possible for the Clearing of land passage to Qunnihticut.

I vnderstand it would be very gratefull to our neighbours that such Pequts as fall to them be not enslaved, like those which are taken in warr: but (as they say is their generall Custome) be vsed kindly, haue howses and goods and fields given them: because they voluntarily choose to come in to them and if not receaved will to the Enemie or turne wild Irish themselues: but of this more as I shall vnderstand: thus in hast with best Salutacions to Mrs. Wintrop and all yours with my poore desires to the Lord for yours I rest Your wo[rshi]ps vnfaigned

ROGER WILLIAMS

My best respects to Mr. Deputie Mr. Bellingham theirs and other lo[ving] friends.

---

[1] Cf. Captain Patrick's letter written on June 19, two days before this, in which he says that only Captain Quick had arrived (page 431, above).

ISRAEL STOUGHTON TO JOHN WINTHROP[1]

To the Right Wor[shipfu]ll the Gouernour of the Massachusets these present

HONORED SIR, By this Pinnace being Giggles, you shall Receiue 48 or 50 women and Children, vnlesse there stay any here to be helpfull etc. Concerning which, there is one I formerly mentioned that is the fairest and largest that I saw amongst them to whome I haue giuen a coate to cloath her: It is my desire to haue her for a servant if it may stand with your good likeing: ells not. There is a little Squa that Steward Calacot desireth, to whom he hath giuen a coate. Lifetenant Damport allso desireth one, to witt a tall one that hath 3 stroakes vpon her stummach thus —|||+: he desireth her if it will stand with your good likeing: Solomon the indian desireth a young little squa which I know not. But I leaue all to your dispose: He had one here for one of his men.

At present Mr. Haynes, Mr. Ludlo, Capteyne Mason and 30 men are with us in Pequid Riuer, and we shall the next weeke joyne in seeing what we can do against Sasacos, and an other great Sagamore: Momomattuck: Here is yet good ruff worke to be done. And how deere it will cost is vnknowne: Sasacos is resolud to sell his life and so the other with their Company as deere as they cann: but we doubt not but god will giue him to vs; we are in a faire way. one of the former that we tooke (or that were taken to our hands in a great measure) is a great Sachim, the 3d of the pequids: whom we reserue for a help, and find Gods prouidence directed it well, for we are all cleere he is like to do vs good: yet we are farr from giuing him any assurance of life we see so much worke behind that we dare not dismiss more men yet:

we hope to find a way to bring them in plentifully, and to get the Murderers too: and to make their assosiats tributory if they still adhære to them: for we heare of a great Number up the Country among the Neepenetts: but we shall not deale with them without your advice, vnless more remotely.

we haue settled on a place for our randavooze: not full to our Content but the best we could for the present: vpon the Mouth of Pequid Riuer, on the Noanticot side, where we haue 200 acres corne if not 2 or 300 neere at hand, and a curious spring of water within our pallazado, and may by great Gunns Command the Riuer.

So the Charg of keeping this fort need not be great, seeing Corne, water and wood are so neere at hand: and fishing etc.

---

[1] New York Public Library; *Proceedings*, LI. 285–286; Mather, *Early History of New England*, 285–286.

I pray lett not provisions be neglegted with the first, such as the Country
affordeth shall content vs: only when we haue frends, as now, we could be-
teeme them a peece of Beefe etc: if we had it. The Ru[n]dlet of Sack we haue
is some comfort and Credit: but many hands make light worke: and in cases
of fayntings, sicknes etc. among a many, It cannot be but occasions will
happen of some expence of such things as are a little better then ordinary.

Thus with my deerest Respects remembered to your self with the Councell
etc. I take leaue Resting Yours as in duty I am bound

ISRAEL STOUGHTON

[*Ca.* June 28, 1637][1]

[*Endorsed by Governor Winthrop*:] Mr. Stoughton Received 5. 6.

ROGER WILLIAMS TO JOHN WINTHROP[2]

For his much honoured Mr. Gouernour these

NEW PROVIDENCE this 6t instantis [*ca.* June 30, 1637][3]

MUCH HONOURED SIR, It having againe pleased the most High to put into
your hands another miserable droue of Adams degenerate seede, and our
brethren by nature: I am bold (if I may not offend in it) to request the keeping and bringing vp of one of the Children. I haue fixed mine eye on this
litle one with the red about his neck, but I will not be peremptory in my
choice but will rest in your loving pleasure for him or any etc.

Sir, Capt. Patrick giues me a hint of the likely returne of most of youer
forces (Sasacous and about a score of men with him and other Companies,
4 score in one, surviving) I shall humbly propound whether it be not considerable, that better now then hereafter the Pursuit be continued.

1st Because it may stop a Conglutination betweene them and the Mowhauogs, which longer time is like to make.

2ndly Longer time will put many opportunities of occasionall revenge into

---

[1] Stoughton, in his next letter to Governor Winthrop, says that this letter was written "about
the end of June." It must have been written long enough before the end of the month to have made
it possible for the pinnace which conveyed it to convey also the letter which Roger Williams wrote
Winthrop from Providence on June 30, printed immediately following.

[2] W. 2. 98; 4 *Collections*, VI. 195–196; *N.C.*, VI. 35–36.

[3] In view of Williams's common practice of dating his letters as of "this present week," it is
assumed that he intended that here, rather than "this present month." Furthermore, the date June
30 seems to accord completely with the chronology of other letters of this period and with the cor-
responding entries in Winthrop's Journal.

their hand, as we see in the 3 last cut of vpon Qunnihticut river, after the fort cut of.

Capt. Patrick allso informes me of a great Itch vpon the Souldiers to fall fowle vpon our Neighbours: Litle sparkes proue great fires. The God of Peace, who is only wise be pleased to guide vs: Capt. Patrick confesseth that they were the chiefe Actors in the last Captiues, and had taken all by a wile and slaine 2 before the English came: I heare no speech at present about inæqualitie, but Content and affection toward vs.

I must reioice that (as he sayth) some of the chiefe at Qunnihticut (Mr. Heynes and Mr. Ludlow) are almost averse from killing women and children. Mercie outshines all the worckes and Atributes of him who is the Father of mercies, vnto whome with earnest supplications for you and yours I rest Your w[orshi]ps vnfeined

Roger Williams

My best respects to good Mrs. Wintrop, Mr. Deputie Mr. Bellingham and theirs.

EDWARD WINSLOW TO JOHN WINTHROP[1]

Right Worshippfull, Although you cannot but be overburthened with busines of divers kinds yet I am bold once more to trouble you, giving thanks for your last remembrance in sending the coppy to me,[2] which I haue sent againe, not knowing whether you haue any other, but hope we shall never be troubled with the reallity thereof. If such a thing be, I perswade my selfe it never was without my old neighbour Isaack,[3] whose head is alwaies full of such projects, and hath too great familiarity with our common adversaries: but were he as well knowne to yours as us, they would rather haue kept him heer then any way haue incouraged his going over: but what I write I would not haue made publick; but the truth is he loveth neither you nor us.

We heare there is a noble man commen over vnto you,[4] but cannot beleeue till we can receiue more credible informacon. If you could spare us a line you should further obliege us. I am sorry to heare the differences are as great as

---

[1] Pilgrim Society; 4 *Collections*, vi. 164–165.

[2] "We had news of a commission granted in England to divers gentlemen here for the governing of New England. . . . As for the commission from the king, we received only a copy of it, but the commission itself staid at the seal for want of paying the fees." *Journal*, i. 224.

[3] Isaac Allerton.

[4] Lord Ley, son and heir of the Earl of Marlborough. *Journal*, i. 223–224, 228, 229.

ever, but glad that our good God hath sent over men of such abilities to helpe in his cawse. I pray you salute your brother Peeters, Mr. Damport (unknowne) also Mr. Eaton and Mr. Hopkins. If I be not too bold with you, and if you heare from Mr. Stoughton and Mr. Wilson I beseech you let us know how things stand. Thus with my prayers for you and yours take leaue remayning Yours assured to his power

EDW: WINSLOW

PLYM. the 1 of the 5th mo. 1637

ROGER WILLIAMS TO JOHN WINTHROP[1]

NEW PROVIDENCE 2ndo 7manae instantis[2] [July 3, 1637]

SIR, I haue nothing certaine to acquaint you with at present: there haue bene reports these 10 dayes, that the Pequts are entred leauge by the hire of 3 or 4 bushells of beades (black and white) with the Mauquawogs or Mohowawogs which signifies Men Eaters in their language: These Caniballs haue bene all the talke these 10 dayes, and the Nanhiggonsicks are much troubled at them.

2 dayes since came tidings that these Mauquawogs and Pequts haue slaine many both English and Natiues at Qunnihticut plantations. as yet I beleeue it not, and hope in the Lords mercy it is false yet since you please to make such good vse of (Poyson) bad and lying newes, (which for that End to awaken people I confesse) I sent the last: I would not conceale this: I hope to send better in like manner after this; yet I sadly feare if the Lord please to let loose these mad dogs, their practice will render the Pequts Canibals too and 2ndly (at the least) cut of all hopes of safe residence at Qunnihticut, and yet they are an 100 mile to the westward of Qunnihticut Plantations: I hope it will please the Most High to put his hooke into their nose etc. as allso to giue wisedome in the managing of the warr, that if it be possible a leauge may rather be firmely strooke with them: they are most savage, their weapons more dangerous and their crueltie dreadfull, rosting aliue etc.

Sir, I heare of the danger of the Innovation of your Government. The God of heaven be pleased to giue you faythfullnes and Courage in his feare: I feare not so much iron and steele as the cutting of our Throats with golden kniues. I meane that vnder the pleasing baits of Execution of Justice to the

---

[1] W. 2. 107; 4 *Collections*, VI. 239–240; *N.C.*, VI. 14–16.
[2] I.e., the second day of the present week.

Eastward and Enlargment of Authoritie, beyond all question, lies hid the hooke to catch your vnvaluable Liberties.[1] Better an honorable death then a slaves life.

Sir I may not forget due thanckes for your intended Requitalls of my poore Endeavours toward the Barbarous: if it please the Lord to vse (with any good Success) so dull a toole, Satis Superque etc.

One kindnes (yet according to true Justice) let me be bold to request. I haue not yet got a peny of those 2 vnfaythfull ones James and Tho. Haukins of Boston, concerning whome my selfe and wife haue formerly troubled you. Mr. Coxall hath long had their Bills: agreement of mitigation hath bene made since by Arbitrators but to no purpose: Their great Earnings (if I had not lovingly released them) were mine owne: my owne debts lye vnpaid, dayly calld for, and I heare for certaine (though they can flatter and lye) they haue spent lavishly and fared daintily of my purse while my selfe would haue bene glad of a Crust of their Leavings, though yet I haue not wanted through his loue that feedes the Ravens etc. John Throckmorton hath often demaunded but in vaine   he will now attend your lo[ving] helpefullnes, and he who is most holy and blessed all mercy and all pitie helpe you mercifully to steere (by his holy Compasse and allso with his owne most holy hand) in the ocean of Troubles and Trialls wherein we saile: It is no small favour that once againe (though the occasions are sad) we may sale and speake togeather, but the Harbour (safe and large) will pay for all: Thus praying for our meeting with best salutes to Mrs. Wintrop and all yours and my true respects to Mr. Deputie Mr. Bellingham and other lo[ving] friends I rest Your Wo[rshi]ps vnfaigned

ROGER WILLIAMS

BOND OF FERDINANDO ADAMS[2]

Noverint universi per presentes me Ferdinandam Adams nuper de Gibvico in Com[itatu] Suffolk shoemaker teneri et firmiter obligari Johanni Winthrop

---

[1] "We had news of a commission granted in England to divers gentlemen here for the governing of New England, etc.; but instead thereof we received a commission from Sir Ferdinando Gorges to govern his province of New Somersetshire, which is from Cape Elizabeth to Sagadahoc, and withal to oversee his servants and private affairs; which was observed as a matter of no good discretion, but passed in silence." *Journal* (June 26, 1637), I. 224.

[2] W. I. 141. The body of the document is in the handwriting of Governor Winthrop. Ferdinando Adams, who settled in Dedham in 1637, has been described as "a person of factious and schismatical disposition." He was formerly a shoemaker of Ipswich, Suffolk, where he was churchwarden of St. Mary at the Tower. He and his fellow warden were exccommunicated because "they had not according to order removed certain seats from the east wall of the chancel of that church, and placed

de Boston in Massachusetts in Nova Anglia armiger[o] in ducentis libris legalis monete Anglie Soluendis eidem Joh[anni] vel suo Certo Atturnato executoribus vel Assignatis suis Ad quam quidem solutionem bene et fideli-[ter] faciendam obligo me heredes Executores et Administratores meos firmiter per presentes Sigillo meo sigillat[as] dat[as] 5to die Julij Anno regno dom[ini] n[ost]ri Caroli Anglie etc. decimo tertio.

The Condition of this Obligation is such that whereas the said Adams is reported at his departure out of England to have been vnder question in some of his ma[jes]ties Courts for matter of Contempt or misdemeanor, for which some engagement may lye vpon others there, for his departure, or some dis-pleasure or damage may arise to the magistrates or others heere for receivinge of him: If theref[ore] the said Ferdinando Adams shall take suche order whereby all and everye of his friends in Englande shall from tyme to tyme be sufficiently saved harmeless from all damage that may arise to them by occasion of his departure thence, and whereby the magistrates and others heere may be likewise saved harmeless from all trouble or damage that may come to them, for his receiving heere: and shalbe likewise be readye at all tymes to make his personall appearance in any of his ma[jes]ties Courts if he shalbe so required, there to answeare to suche matter as shalbe obiected against him, then this present obligation to be voyde, otherwise to remaine in full force and effecte.

FERDINANDO ADAM

Seald and delivered in the presence of
    Jo: UNDERHILL
    STEPHEN WINTHROP

DANIEL PATRICK TO INCREASE NOWELL[1]

To his Worthye and verry much respeckted Frinde Mr. Encrease Nowell at his howse in Charles Towne giue theese

WORTHY SIR, all due respeckt vnto you. our common newes for the present I suppoose you haue hearde, yet moore to your self Ile saye. The Narregansets woulde be the onelye lords of Indeans; the Inglish if god will, may, I doubt

---

the Lord's table next the said wall; and also, that they had not removed from the said church an in-scription from Mark XI. 17, and put up in its place certain words from Deuteronomy I. 17." *Calendar of State Papers, Domestic, 1635–1636*, 565.

[1] W. 3. 88; 4 *Collections*, VII. 324–325.

not, receiue tribbute of all but Narregansets. what our articles with them are,
must bee, but if wee be tide to make peace with none of ther ennymies but
with ther consent, then still troublde shall wee be as wee haue bine much
about that poynte alreadye. Sassecous is at longe Ilande, and mamenatucke
at quenepiage, or latelye gone to the Mowhoake. Moheegins and Narregansets I doubt will not longe agree, nor will Neantucke next to Narregansets
willinglye be brought vnder his subiectione; wee goe the first winde for longe
Ilande to sallute Sassecous. youer prayres wee desire. my loue to Captayne
Segwicke and Mr. Caine of bostone. I leaue you to the lorde and in hast rest
yours to commaunde

DANIELL PATTRICKE

From PEQUOTT this 6 of Julye 1637

Good Sir, remember mee since I cannot help myselfe, the Confirmatione
of Shae sheene 300 ackers for Mr. Payne, which I soulde hime, elce loose I
20 pounde which indeed I am not able to beare. The Gennoral Courte maye
considder for whome I am imployde; how suddenly I was sent awaye, and
ther prommise to further it when I was gone. I leaue it to them, hoopinge by
your means noe longer to be kept from that which soe longe since was prom-
misd. once moor as before.

ISRAEL STOUGHTON TO JOHN WINTHROP[1]

To the Right Wor[shipfu]ll The Gouernor in Massachusets These Present

HONORED SIR, My last bearing date about the end of June sent by the
pinnace with the Captiues together with the former, may giue you intelligence
of the most materiall passages to that day.

Since, we with our Company and Mr. Haynes and Mr. Ludlo and their
Company haue beene together in pequid, and haue acted nothing but ordinary, our time haueing beene much spent in Councell etc: as various objects
haue occasioned; winds, and weather, and some other things concurring to
detayne vs from procecuting intentions.

In this time we are informed, and do gather out the Narragansets dealings
with vs (I meane our state) not to be faire: but very prejudiciall in some
points. Not faire: for they keepe not the articles they subscribed: for 1st they
frequently receiue wampam of our Enemies without advising with vs which

---

[1] W. I. 125.

our enemies giue them to obtayne peace, etc. yea they utterly conceale it from vs, and evade things manifest. 2ly and whereas we had 10 men from them for guides, Spies etc., and expected their attendance, they for their owne ends with draw them at their pleasure. Yea the truth is they are so eagerly sett vpon their owne ends, to gett booty etc. and to augment their owne King-dome etc., that vpon the matter they vse us as their stalking horse: and if god do not help vs to diuert the streame into an other Channell with wisedome and honesty (from which I would be loath to swerve) I feare our being here will not be to that purpose as was desired.

I cannot relate all their dealings. Ile giue you a tast in one principall. There sent a Squa-Sachem 2 daies since, (that is of long island, and hath 200 men) to desire peace with vs, declaring that shee nor hers haue never shed any English blood: and we find it true by all informations from pequids, from Mohiggens, from Narragansetts, and from myantonimo himself: only the pequids haue forst treasure from her by exaction. Af[t]er this information, we sent her word Thus, That prouided what she affirmd was true, and that she and hers would submitt to the English, and do no harme to the English hereafter, Then the English should not hurt her: and so appointed her a time of meeting: for shee promised her utmost aid to compass Sasacous now resident in long Iland.

So we lookt vpon this as a great prouidence of God for good toward us, and as a leading case to bring in other Indians.

But now we find Myantonimo little pleasd hereat, and hath first sought to Compass her goods and subjects to himself: for she bringing 30 fadom of wam-pam as a present, 10 for Myanto: 10 for Cannonicus, and 10 for the English, to make way for a treaty of peace: Myantonimo takes all to himself, and tells her lett him alone for the English, (or the like) But when he sees this will not do: (God inclyning her hart to send directly to the English besides his desires) now he comes in person to vs (that before would not without sending for) to prejudice us against her etc. that we might fall foule with her, albeit he can shew in truth no cause. She by sicknes cannot come unto vs, but hath sent a Narraganset Sachem to effect her and our desires at Long Iland, shee being at this Narragansets house, and intending marriag with him, the which is not pleasing to the 2 great Sachems of Narra: for they affect not others greatnes. an other thing we find Myantonimo is growne into disaffection with one of his men (that is by nature a pecot)[1] meerely for the respect the English haue giuen him, which he hath deserved; and he hath withdrawne him from us:

---

[1] I.e., Wequash.

and tis doubted his life wilbe betrayed. Lately Myant: sent a message to vs, to haue the pecot country, and corne diuided that they might haue their part etc: But we returnd this Ans: we are now in pursuing the Enimie: Let us first subdue him, and talke of that after wards: yea we told him his mynd was so much vpon the spoyle, that he too much neglegted the mayne worke. since, his company haue kild as they say 11 pecots, they brought one head to vs. Our Captiues say and we told it him playnely, That were it not for the English the Pecots would not yet feare the Narra: but would take their Country, and annoy him as much as ever. And when they submitt to the Narraganset they say it is meerly for the English sake, and because they conceiue that the way, and know no other meanes to procure the Englishs favour: So the Narra: do pil and pole them all that ever they haue, and giue the poore soules hope that the English will shew them mercy: and then they bring them to the Engl: and leaue vs the hangmans worke: in effect, yea expressly requiring it of vs: shewing anger and impatience that the delay it. All this is true in the Sachem we haue captive:

Such like matters as these haue putt vs to serious thoughts for redresse: and allbeit we are tender of offending them justly, and so of increasing enimies: yet we are loath to be as carelesse of your Honor and advantages, as they are carefull of theirs But would gladly obtayne the present end (namely these enimies to be subdud) with present honor (so farr as honesty allowes it) and future safety.

Which to effect we cannot declare all the meanes that we take (memory and oportunitie will not permit) yet this for a tast.

1 For the Narra: we leaue the pecots gifts (and booty etc.) to sleepe with them for the present, (because we will make no disturbance: only we take notis of what we can learne out because we conceiue that for gifts intended for peace especially, they may and ought to [*torn*] led to account about them in convenient time) and animate them to the worke of bringing under the open Enimie.

2 Then for the poor Pecots such as are inclynable to submission etc. we do [*torn*] diuulge this amongst them. 1st That they shall find the English as propence to merc[y] as the Narra: 2ly If any pecots desire mercy from the English they shall soonest obtayne by comming directly unto vs, which we purpose to make good as amply as we may to this Squa Sachem and hers, for example and incouragment to all the Rest. Thus much for the present.

I confesse we haue a service in hand full of difficulty to be well done: I feare our specially my owne weakenes will much hinder: Only we rely vpon the lords help and his and your favorable acceptance according to the talent we haue receiued not requiring more. And if you find defects (as I know you can do no other) you may please to supply it either by your aduice, or otherwise as you may see Cause. But if our God giue vs help to do more or less to your content Let his holy name haue all the honor now and Ever Amen: To whome I Leaue you and yours and all your waighty affaires desiring to be remembered to your self, the Deputy, Mr. Bellengam Mr. Nowell etc. I pray pardon all my abrupt and imperfect writing: for I profess my self a Child and altogether to learne in these State affaires, besides the distracted condition we are in doth greatly disable my disabilitie. Yours to be Commanded

ISRAEL STOUGHTON

[*Ca.* July 6, 1637][1]

One thing allmost forgott, the Narragansetts doings hath made Chicchomikin desire to returne home with his men: which we redily yeeld to: for the Heathen shall not say our dependence is on them. So we looke up to God. Chicchomikin will not so much as leaue an interpreter. The Narra: haue and do manifest emulation against the Mohiggen speciall helps in this service, and are like to do vs displeasure that way too:

[*Endorsed by Governor Winthrop:*] [S]toughton about the Narra. bad dealinge.

ROGER WILLIAMS TO JOHN WINTHROP[2]

NEW PROVIDENCE this 2nd 7næ [July 10, 1637]

SIR, Concerning your prisoners taken at Block Iland I haue informed the Sachims of your care not to iniure them and desire to haue them cleared:[3] accordingly Cutshamaquene (now come from pursuing Sasacous, who is fled Southerly farr out of reach) I say he hath receaved testimonie from the Sachims Princes that they are Nayantaquit men (Wepiteammocks men) and so all are Nanhiggonsick men: and so indeede Sir I had thought to send you

---

[1] A comparison of this letter with that of Roger Williams to Governor Winthrop, July 15, 1637, indicates clearly that Williams's letter was a reply to inquiries made by Winthrop as a result of the information Stoughton here presents. Stoughton must, therefore, have written about July 6, in order to have made possible this interchange of correspondence.

[2] W. 2. 98; 4 *Collections*, VI. 197–198; *N.C.*, VI. 37–39.

[3] The Governor writes in his Journal (I. 225) under the date of July 5, 1637: "A pinnace, returning, took a canoe with four Indians near Block Island. We sent to Miantunnomoh to know what they were, and after we discharged all save one, who was a Pequod, whom we gave Mr. Cutting to carry into England."

word at this present, had not I receaved your letter, for it was continually affirmed to me for truth by all the Nanhiggonsick men occasionally being here.

Sir The last messenger that caried letters from you to Pequat, related to the Sachims at Nanhiggonsick, that you were displeased that the Captiues brought to the Bay lately, were taken by the English from the Nanhiggon-sicks, as allso the spoile vpon them, which was given to the English Souldiers: I haue answered that I thinck it was not so, but I shall vnderstand the truth shortly: and therefore Sir be pleased in your next to intimate a word: that I may satisfie them, for though I would not feare a Jarr with them yet I would fend of from being fowle, and deale with them wisely as with wolues endewed with mens braines.

The last weeke is a battell fought betweene the hither Neepmucks and the further the Wunnashowatuckoogs etc. the Successe is not yet knowne: it will be of Consequence, for it is said they fortifie ioyning with scattered Pequts.

Sir The last day of the weeke Wequash the Pequt guide neere hand slue his Country man Sassawwaw a Pequt allso Miantunnomues speciall darling and a kind of Generall of his forces. There was yesterday some tumult about it because Wequash liues with Canounicus and Miantunnomu pursues the Revenge and Justice etc.

By the way although Wequash it may be haue treacherously allmost slaine him, yet I see the righteous hand of the most High Judge, thus: Sassawwaw turnd to the Nanhiggonsicks and againe pretends a returne to the Pequts, gets them forth the last yeare against the Nanhiggonsicks, and spying advan-tage, slue the chiefe Pequt Capt[ain] and whips of his head and so againe to the Nanhiggonsick: their treacheries exceede Machiavills etc.

Sir Capt. Stoughton left sick at my howse one Souldier, a Boston man Tho: Roberts, his m[aste]r is absent, and Mr. Harding hath charge of him I haue sent to him etc. The man was neere death. through the Lords mercy my wife hath gott him vpon his legs, though very weake, only his hearing is quite gone and I should be glad to receaue any helpe for him in that great losse: So with my respectiue Salutacions to Mr. Deputie Mr. Bellingham yours and theirs and other lo[ving] friends, and my poore sighes to heaven to meete you there if not here below I rest Your Wor[shi]ps vnworthy yet vnfaigned

ROGER WILLIAMS

ROGER WILLIAMS TO JOHN WINTHROP[1]

For his most honou[red] Governour these. The second letter

SIR, In the morning I wrote by John Throckmorton, what I heard and thought in generall. It hath pleased the Lord now this afternoone to send this Messenger (Assotemuit) with Varietie and Plentie and Strangenes of Newes and Tidings, I hope true and for ought I can discerne, true, blessed be the holy name of the most High who breakes the Bow and cuts the spear etc. Psal. 46.

This man was sent this morning from Miantunnomu and Caunounicus (as I conceaue allso from all their chiefs in Councell) with charge to bring relacion to my selfe of what hath lately happened amongst the Pequts: as allso that with my letter he should make Speede to your selfe with Tidings.

He relates that a Pequat man and some 5 Pequt women came 2 dayes since to the Nanhiggonsick and with their ordinary submission begd their liues, and libertie to declare in the name of many others what had happened amongst them: before that Pequt came one squaw and a second came but was questioned much for their Truth, but vpon the comming and report of the old Pequat, he saith, they all take his report for true.

This man himselfe Assotemuit is a noted messenger from the Sachims and one whome Miantunnomu hath commended to me for an especiall Messenger from him.

This Pequt and the women report that (as I allso heard before) all the Pequts were assembled some 10 dayes since with Sasacous in Councell: some perswaded to fight and fall first vpon the Nanhiggonsicks (this allso I heard before) the greater part dissented and were for Remoovall: Sasacous and about 4 score resolved for Mauquowkit alias Waukhegannick where the Men Eaters are: a hundreth more for Long Island; another Company the least for Qunnihticut some part of it with purpose to take finall leaue of their Countrey.

70 men women and children (of men betweene 20 and thirtie) resolved for the Nanhiggonsicks to beg their liues etc.

Sasacous and his Company were wroth with these resolved for the Nanhiggonsick and a skirmish past betweene them where some were wounded, but away they got, and each Company packt vp and departed their intended iourneyes.

---

[1] W. 2. 99; 4 *Collections*, VI. 198–202; *N.C.*, VI. 40–44.

Miantunnomu sent word to this Company remayning in the mid way betweene Pequatit and Nayantakick that he was in leauge with Mr. Governour and therefore of himselfe would say nothing, but desired them there to rest (at Cuppunaugunnit) in the mid way vntill he sent to Mr. Governour, and what he said that he would assent vnto.

They tould Miantunnomu that they had brought 3 guns with them   He sent the women for the guns who fetcht them from that place Cuppunnaugunnit, and there they are with him: Only he claimes a promise of one to himselfe which he desires may be out of these 3, as allso some powder and shot to it as indeede was promised when Mr. Vane was Governour. I haue much laboured with this man to find if it were possible any deceit or falsehood, but as he himselfe and the Sachims question not the Pequt man and women so I can not question him.

I aske him (in discourse) what he thincks were best to be done   he answereth that as Miantunnomu himselfe when he sent to Canounicus to speake his minde and Caunounicus refusing sent to him to speake first, Miantunnomu would say nothing, but would say as Mr. Governour said so himselfe would likewise say nothing   Yet in discourse I fisht out divers hints of their owne desire and good liking.

As first that there is not amongst these any Sachim or any of those who were Murtherers of the English: if there were they should die.

2ndly That if Mr. Governour were so minded, they incline to mercy and to giue them their liues: and I doubt not but your owne breasts are farr more tender, like the mercifull Kings of Israell.

3rdly That divers more beside these remaine in the woods and resolve to come in and submit if these be accepted.

4. For the disposing of them I propounded what if Mr. Governour did desire to send for some of them into the Bay; leaue some at the Nanhiggonsick and so scatter and disperse them: this he liked well that they should liue with the English and themselues as Slaues: I then propounded that if they lived amongst the English or themselues they might hereafter be false to the English etc. and what if therefore they were appointed and limited to liue vpon Nayantacawnick or some other Iland: and this he thought allso well of if not best, because they were most of them families.

5. That they desire you would please to send some English to take possession of the Pequt Countrey and there to inhabite.

6. That for their owne hunting sake Miantunnomu desires that the English would inhabite that part neerest Qunnihticut and that Mistick which is neerest and where the slaughter was and thereabout might be free for them.

I told him that they might hunt in the woods as they doe at Massachusett and here, notwithstanding the English did generally inhabite: and this satisfied.

7. That they desire the Pequts Corne might be enioyed by the English and themselues as Mr. Governour please.

8. That the Wunnashowatuckoogs are also afraid and fled so that there is hope of a safe passage to Qunnihticut by land.

9. That there is no hope that the Mauquawogs or any other people will euer assist Sasacous or any of the Pequts against the English, because he is now as it were turned Slaue to beg his life.

If all this be true (as I hope it is) we may all see the God of Heaven delights in mercy and to draw by loue and pitie then by fury and wrath: I hope Sir, now that troubles may arise from other parts his holy Ma[jest]ie is pleased to quench these neerer fires. He be pleased to confirme this newes and tune all hearts to his prayses in the ordering of our Conversation aright. So I rest praying Your Wo[rshi]ps vnfained

ROGER WILLIAMS

[July 10, 1637]

This man relates that yesterday the Lords day in the morning a Pinnace arriued but he knowes not yet what she is.

I pray Sir forget not to reward this messenger with a Coate as allso some Powder for Miantunnomu.

My lo[ving] respects to Mrs. Wintrop, Mr. Deputie Mr. Bellingham, and theirs etc.

ROGER WILLIAMS TO JOHN WINTHROP[1]

For his much honoured Mr. Governour these

This 3rd 7æ [July 11, 1637]

SIR, Yesterday by our neighbour Throckmorton I wrote concerning those Nayantaquit men your pinnace tooke. This bearer Jvanemo[2] (one of the chiefe Sachims of that place and chiefe souldier) came last night with neere a score of his men to enquire after them. He was very desirous of a letter to you: I told him I hoped he would find his men at libertie. He hath brought a musket and a barrell of a leue piece which his men tooke from the Pequts.

---

[1] Original not located; 4 *Collections*, VII. 202–203.

[2] Ninigret. Winthrop records in his Journal (I. 227) under the date of July 11, 1637, Ninigret's arrival in Boston with seventeen men.

There was a speach that 3 of these men were Nayantakoogs and one a Pequat: it seemes he is a Pequt borne, but hath long since bene theirs, fallen to them, and done good service in their warrs against the Pequts.

Sir, this Jvanemo is a notable instrument amongst them etc. your wisedome, I know therefore, will lay hold of this his visit, to engage him the more to you.

Thus humbly begging mercies from the God of heaven for you and yours in all affaires, I rest, in hast Your Worships vnfaigned

ROGER WILLIAMS

All due respects and salutacions, etc.

WILLIAM HILTON TO JOHN WINTHROP[1]

To the Right wor[shi]p[fu]ll John Winthrop esqire Gouernor of the Masachsets giue these

PASCATAQUE, July the 14th 1637

SER, My humble duty remembred the bearer hereof beeing Sonne to Passaconoway[2] is in debted vnto mr. Vane, three skines which hee desighreth to pay but hee is affread to come to pay them by reason that the Sagamo[re] of Aguawam serteffieth him that if hee come in to the bay you will take awey his head   hee hath desighred mee to write in his beehalffe that hee may come and pay his debts and likewise that you would bee pleased to bid him welcome and soe desighring the lord to blese you and yours I humbly rest Your worships to command to his poure

WILLIAM HILTON

Ser this beearer desighreth mee to serteyffie in his behalffe that the Eanglish haue awais bin verry welcome vnto him   I am able to testeffie that hee hath euer since I knew him bin a verry loving Indean.

[1] W. I. 119; 2 *Proceedings*, x. 362.
[2] Possibly this was Wonnalansit, who was the eldest son of Passaconaway, the great sachem of the Merrimac River region.

HUGH PETER TO JOHN WINTHROP[1]

To our noble Gouernour John Winthrop Esqr. these deliver Boston

Sir, Mr. Endecot and my selfe salute you in the Lord Jesus etc. Wee haue heard of a diuidence of women and children in the bay and would bee glad of a share viz: a yong woman or girle and a boy if you thinke good: I wrote to you for some boyes for Bermudas, which I thinke is considerable.

Besides wee are bold to impart our thoughts about the Corne at Pequoit, which wee wish were all cut downe, or left to the Naragansicks rather than for vs to take it, for wee feare it will proue a snare thus to hunt after their goods, whilst wee come forth pretending only the doing of Justice, and wee beleeue it would strike more terror into the Indians so to doe: It will neuer quit cost for vs to keepe it.

Wee are not well at ease some of vs viz: Mr. Endecot and my selfe, but wee haue a strong God to whom wee commend you and my deere and much honourd sister, tendering all our respects vnto you vnfaynedly I rest Yours vnworthy of you

HUGH PETER

Salem, last day [*ca.* July 15, 1637]

ROGER WILLIAMS TO JOHN WINTHROP[2]

New Providence this 15th of the 5t [1637]

Sir, For the Captiues and bootie I never heard any of these Natiues question the Acts of the English only that Natiue who brought letters to you from Capt. Patrick, and was twice at Boston, related so much as I wrote of in my former,[3] at his returne to the Nanhiggonsick, viz. that your selfe should be angry with the English etc. I met since with him and he sayth he had it not from your selfe but an English man at Roxbury: I thought good to cleare your name and remooue suspicions from Mr. Stoughton etc.

Wequash is aliue, so is allso the other like to recover of his wound: I never heard that Miantunnomu was displeased with Wequash for any Service to the English, but that Wequash was suspected to deale falsely when he went to hunt for the Pequts at the rivers mouth: Tis true there is no feare of God

---

[1] W. 2. 51; 4 *Collections*, VI. 95.
[2] W. 2. 100; 4 *Collections*, VI. 203–204; *N.C.*, VI. 46–49.
[3] See the second paragraph of Williams's letter to Winthrop, July 10, 1637 (above, page 445).

before their eye, and all the Cords that euer bound the Barbarous to For-
reiners were made of Selfe and Covetuousnes: Yet if I mistake not I obserue
in Miantunnomu some sparkes of true Friendshipp. could it be deepely im-
printed into him that the English never intended to despoile him of the
Countrey I probably coniecture his friendship would appeare in attending of
vs with 500 men (in case) against any forreigne Enemie.

The Neepmucks are returned with 3 heads of the Wunnashoatuckoogs.
they slue 6, wounded many, and brought home 20 Captiues.

Those Inlanders are fled vp toward the Mowhauogs: so they say is Sasacous:
Our friends at Qunnihticut are to cast a iealous eye at that people: they say
(vnles they are belied) that they are to warre with the English etc.

Truely Sir to speake my thoughts in your Eare freely, I blesse the Lord for
your mercifull dealing etc. but feare that some innocent blood cryes at
Qunnihticut. Many things may be spoken to proue the Lords perpetuall warr
with Amalek extraordinary and misticall: but the 2 Kings 14: 5. 6. is a bright
Light discovering the ordinary path wherein to walke and please him. If the
Pequts were Murtherers (though pretending revenge for Sasacous his Fathers
Death, which the Dutch affirmed was from Mr. Governour) yet not comparable to those treacherous servants that slue their Lord and king Joash K[ing]
of Judah, and tipe of Jesus, yet the Fathers only perish in their Sinn in the
place quoted etc. The blessed Lambe of God wash away Iniquitie and receaue vs graceously.

Thus with best Salutes to your lo[ving] selfe and yours Mr. Deputie Mr.
Bellingham and other lo[ving] friends with them and dayly Cryes to the
Father of mercie for you I rest Your Wor[shi]ps vnfaigned

ROGER WILLIAMS

Postscript. Sir to yours brought by Ivanemo on the Lords day[1] I could
haue litle speech with him: but concerning Miantunnomu I haue not heard
as yet of any vnfaythfullnes toward vs: I know they bely each other: and I
obserue our Country men haue allmost quite forgotten our great pretences
to K[ing] and State and all the world concerning their soules etc. I shall desire to attend with my poore helpe to discover any perfidious dealing: and
shall desire the revenge of it for a common good and peace though my selfe
and mine should perish by it: yet I feare the Lords quarrell is not ended, for
which the warr began viz. the litle sence (I speake for the generall that I can
heare of) of their soules Condicion and our large protestations that way etc.

---

[1] July 16, 1637.

The generall speech is, all must be rooted out etc. The body of the Pequin men yet liue, and are onely remooved from their dens: the good Lord grant, that the Mowhaugs and they, and the wh[ole] at the last vnite not. For mine owne Lot I can [not be] without suspicions of it.

Sir I thanckfully expect a litle of your helpe (in a way of Justice and æquitie) concerning another vn[just] debtour of mine, Mr. Ludlow, from whome allso (in mine absence) I h[aue] much suffered. The good Lord smile vpon you and yours in the face of his annointed. Your Wo[rshi]ps vnworthy

R. W.

RICHARD DAVENPORT TO HUGH PETER[1]

For his Reuerend Pastor Mr. Hugh Peeter at Salem

DEARE AND HONORED IN THE LORD, To whom (for christ and in him) I owe not onely any seruise but my selfe allso: and the desire of my soule is that hee in whom is my breath and beeing will helpe mee to walke worthy of this fellowship in Christ our hope: since my last letter to you (as before) soe since wee haue had still experence of gods blessed presence and grace with vs and shining vpon vs: it pleased our god 3 days after our Brother Graften left vs to direct our Course to Sea-brook fort to joyne with our Brethren of Conetecutt who stayd for vs there the same eueing being the sixt day of the weeke wee went toward Long Iland and sent in a shallop with an Indian to espy our enemy Sasacoos: but hee not beeing there wee had a Sachem came aboord vs who tould vs hee was gone thence to Quenepiacke and that himselfe would goe to bee our guide to find him out: which motion wee accepted of hee allso promising his willingnes that as Long Iland had payd tribute to Sasacas hee would procure it to vs. the next day being the lords day wee came to a harbour about 3 leagus short of quenepiak where wee lay that day that morning 4 Indians went out for spyes who tooke 2 pecott Indians whom after examination with 2 prisoners more wee put to death that night and called the place Sacheme head:[2] the second day of the weeke wee came to que-ne-piacke and comming into the harbour wee saw a smoake on the shore and speedily landed and sent out spys who speedily returned and tould vs the weere Conetecutt Indians and brought downe 4 Indians with them: vpon the nuse wee repayrd to the barks.

---

[1] W. 4. 88; 5 *Collections*, I. 244–248. For Davenport, see 5 *Collections*, I. 244n.
[2] In the margin: "one of them was a Sachem."

Yet the Counsell thought meet to send my selfe with 20 men to see the truth: which a little before day I did   vpon one side of the Riuer found noe signe of Indians but wading ouer the Riuer after 2 houres seeking wee found som scouting pecotts   it pleased god to deliuer to our hands 7 of them one sachem   5 wee slew 2 women wee brought aboard haueing taken all by Runing and in an extreame Raine.

as soone as wee gott aboard that day about 12 of Clocke wee were all landed on the other side to pursue Sasacoos that afternoone; the next day and the 5th day wee marched after them and haueing found the base Cowardlines of the Indians being out of hope of the enemy wee fell to cutting downe all the Corne in which time wee took in the corne a Pecott man very poore and weake   hee tould vs of som squaws that weere not farr of: at the same instant some of our Indians tould vs they heard som cutting wood another way: whervpon part of the Company went to the one and part to the other: it pleased god to lead my Captain one way and my selfe another way with Captain Patricke: and Leiutenant Seilley with my Captain: it was our day to lead and after 2 miles march wee came where they were and soddenly coming to the place theire wigwams being vpon the edge of the swamp as soone as euer they saw vs they tooke the swamp. it pleased god it was not very great, and our Company did surround it:

For my part I judged best while the terrour was vpon them to fall in vpon them and calling a file of men entered the swamp: overtooke a man and a sachems Child and thrust him through with my pike twise: going further, I perseaued I had but 3 men with mee and soddenly one of [them] cryed out Leiutenant they kill mee they kill mee: with that I saw him haueing four stout Rougus vpon him downe   the lord helped mee soone to make three of them repent their Closing, the fourth held him still and soe sheltred himselfe with the Englishman that I could not come to make a thrust at him yet after som tryall the lord gaue him his wound in the belly and soe left his prey: all which time a Crew stood shooting vpon mee at 12 foot distance   they stook eleuen arroos in my Coat and hat and Cloths and flesh: onely 2 in my flesh: now all had left mee but god stood to mee and after this they left mee and runn and I retreated hauing onely a halfe pike and my Cutles: upon our shooting the Rest of our Company came thither and found vs about the swamp and the Indians in it: then the gott a Pecott and came to parley Sasacuos was gone: and all their women came out about ninescore   it was and is lamentable to see into what condicion they haue brought themselus all seeking one anothers Ruine and euery one crying out of each other: then weere wee that were hurt sent to the pinaces about six leagus: and comming againe with them wee found the Company all well: many Indians killd and som runn away in the night: by what default I know not: yet I hope in mercy.

my owne wounds are one in the left arme through the arme close in the arme pitt which head was taken out in the vnder side my Arme with great paine   the other is on the right side my brest which was through my Coat: which is not deepe   3 dayes I was in exeeding paine haueing the mussles hurt: but blessed bee god who hath not left mee but as hee hath giuen my life soe hee giueth mee now wonderfull amendment.

the souldiers that are hurt are two of Ipswich Tho: Sherman and Jon. Wedgwood whom god saued by mee the other Edw: Shorthose of Charlestowne   my humble Request to you is that you remember my case and soule to the lord that hee that teacheth his people to profitt will teach mee how to vse this speciall deliuerance and a second Request that you cheere vp the spirit of my poore wife who I feare will apprehend worse then the thing is: if you shall bee pleased to accept of this rude intellegence to your selfe I doubt not but you will declare the somme of it to the Church: wee are now in the way to Pecott with allmost 100 Indian women and Children aboord Goodman Jackson and 45 souldiers   when I know more you shall heare more: my Captain and Tho: Lauthoup salute you and the Church: thus with my humble Respects to my Colonell mr. Sharp and Ensign and all theirs and yours and all mine I rest Yours while I am

RICHARD DAUENPORT

[*Ca.* July 17, 1637]

Conetecut men haue had their equall share in women and treys   the princes treasurers are run from him with his wampum and hee and Momonottuk with 20 men are fled to the Mowhoak: wee haue Momonotuk squaw and childeren [*several words obliterated*].

I pray tell my Colonell Mr. Ludlow is well who was at this business and narrowly mist a shott with an arrow.

ROGER WILLIAMS TO JOHN WINTHROP[1]

For his much honoured Mr. Governour these

New Providence 21 of 5t month [1637]

Much honoured Sir, My vnfaigned loue and respect to your Soules eternall Comfort, and firme perswasion of your Levelling at the highest white haue imboldned me once more to tell you of some poore thought of mine owne pend and sent to some friends amongst you; which happily (if the good Lord so please) may some way conduct to your Soules Satisfaction in the midst of all your troubles.

I haue bene long requested to write my grounds against the English preaching etc. and especially my answeres to some reasons of Mr. Robinsons[2] for hearing.

In the midst of a multitude of barbarous distractions I haue fitted some thing to that purpose: and being not able at present to transcribe the whole: yet having bene long sollicited by Mr. Buckley (from whome I receaved some Obiections) and by many others, and of late by my worthy friend Mr. Peters [*torn*] sight of them, I haue thought good to send so much as I haue transcribed to the hand of my lo[ving] friend Mr. Buckly.

Sir I am bold to giue you this Intimacion because in these first loose leaues, handling the state of a Nationall church from the 38 page I haue enlarged the differences betweene Israell and all other States. I know and am perswaded that your misguidings are great and lamentable, and the further you pass in your way, the further you wander, and haue the further to come back, and the end of one Vexation will be but the beginning of another, till Conscience be permitted (though Erronious) to be free amongst you.

I am sorry my straights are such that I can not transcribe the remaynder and especially, what concernes the matter, most concerning your deare selfe, and therein especially the assoiling of some Obiections, but if the Lord please I liue I shall endeavour the rest and thanckfully receaue any Intimacion from your selfe yea from the least, whereby I might my selfe returne from any wandrings The Lord Jesus be to you and me the Way, the Truth, and he will be the Life allso. So prayes Your Wor[shi]ps most vnfained

Roger Williams

---

[1] W. 2. 99; 4 *Collections*, vi. 205–207; *N.C.*, vi. 49–52.

[2] The Reverend John Robinson (d 1625) of Leyden. This may refer to *A Treatise of the Lawfulnesse of Hearing of the Ministers in the Church of England*, printed posthumously in 1634, presumably in Amsterdam.

I haue no newes, but from Qunnihticut, the receaving of Sasacous, his present and Company by the Mawhauogs, and some promises of theirs to him to setle him againe at Pequt: This weeke Souwonckquawsir old Sequins Sonn, cut of 20 Pequt women and children in their passage to the Mowhauogs allso one Sachim who 3 yeares agoe was with you in the Bay with a present.

JOHN WINTHROP TO WILLIAM BRADFORD[1]

WORTHY SIR, I receiued your louing letter, and am much prouocked to express my affections towards you, but straitnes of time forbids me, for my desire is to acquainte you, with the lords greate mercies towards vs, in our preuailing against his, and our enimies; that you may rejoyce, and praise his name with vs. About 80 of our men haueing costed along towards the dutch plantation, (some times by water, but most by land) mett hear, and ther, with some pequents, whom they slew or tooke prisoners. 2 sachems they tooke, and beheaded And not hearing of Sassacous (the cheefe sachem) they gaue a prisoner his life, to goe and find him out. He wente and brought them word wher he was, but Sassacouse suspecting him to be a spie, after he was gone fled away, with some 20 more, to the Mowakes; so our men missed of him. yet deviding them selues, and ranging vp and downe, as the providence of God guided them (for the Indeans were all gone, saue 3 or 4 And they knew not whither to guid them, or els would not) vpon the 13 of this month, they light vpon a great company of them viz. 80 strong men, and 200 women, and children, in a small Indean towne, fast by a hideous swamp, which they all slipped Into before our men could gett to them. Our captains were not then come togeither, but ther was mr. Ludlow, and Captaine Masson, with some 10 of their men, and Captaine Patrick with some 20 or more of his; who shooting at the Indeans, Captaine Trask with 50 more came soone in at the noyse; then they gaue order to surround the swampe, it being aboute a mile aboute; but Leuetenante Dauenporte, and some 12 more, not hearing that cammand, fell into the swampe among the Indeans. the swampe was so thicke with shrub woode, and so boggie with all, that some of them stuck fast, and receiued many shott. Leuetenant Dauenport was dangerously wounded about his armehole, and another shott in the head, so as fainting, they were in great danger to haue been taken by the Indeans; but Sargante Rigges, and Jeffery

---

[1] Original not located; Bradford, *History of Plymouth* (facsimile edition, London, 1896), 431–435; (1912), II. 253–257; *L. and L.*, II. 197–200.

and 2 or 3 more rescued them, and slew diuerse of the Indeans, with their swords. After they were drawne out, the Indeans desired parley; and were offered (by Thomas Stanton, our Interpretour) that if they would come out, and yeeld them selues, they should haue their liues all that had not their hands in the English blood; whervpon the sachem of the place came forth, and an old man or 2 and their wiues and chilldren; and after that some other women and children, and so they spake 2 howers, till it was night. then Thomas Stanton was sente into them againe, to call them forth; but they said, they would selle their liues their, and so shott at him so thicke, as If he had not cried out, and been presently rescued, they had slaine him. Then our men cutt of a place of the swampe with their swords, and cooped the Indeans into so narrow a compass, as they could easier kill them throw the thikets; so they continued all the night, standing aboute 12 foote one from an other, and the Indeans coming close vp to our men, shot their arrows so thicke, as they peirced their hatte brimes, and their sleeues and stockins, and other parts of their cloaths, yet so miraculously did the lord preserue them, as not one of them was wounded, saue those 3 who rashly went into the swampe. When it was nere day, It grue very darke, so as those of them which were left, dropt away betweene our men, though they stood but 12 or 14 foote assunder; but were presenly discouered, and some killed in the pursute. Vpon searching of the swampe the next morning, they found 9 slaine, and some they pulled vp, whome the Indeans had buried in the mire; so as they doe thinke that, of all this company, not 20 did escape, for they after found some, who dyed in their flight, of their wounds receiued. The prisoners were devided, some to those of the riuer, and the rest to vs; of these we send the male children to Bermuda, by mr. William Peirce, and the women and maid children are disposed aboute in the townes. Ther haue been now slaine and taken in all aboute 700. The rest are dispersed, and the Indeans in all quarters so terrified, as all their freinds are affraid to receiue them. 2 of the Sachems of long Iland came to mr. Stoughton and tendered them selues to be tributaries, vnder our protec-tion. And 2 of the Neepnett Sachems haue been with me to seeke our frend-ship. Amonge the prisoners we haue the wife and children of Mononotto, a womon of a very modest countenance and behauiour. It was by her media-tion that they 2 English maids were spared from death, and were kindly vsed by her; so that I haue taken charge of her. One of her first requests was that the English would not abuse her body and that her children might not be taken from her. Those which were wounded were fetched of soone by John Galopp who came with his shalop in a happie houre, to bring them victuals, and to carrie their wounded men to the pinnass, wher our cheefe surgeon was, with mr. Willson, being aboute 8 leagues of. Our people are all in health (the lord be praised) and allthough they had marched in their armes all the day, and had been in fight all the night, yet they professed they found them selues so fresh as they could willingly haue gone to such another bussines.

This is the substance of that which I receiued, though I am forced to omite many considerable circomstances. So being in much straitnes of time (the ship being to departe within this 4 days, and in them the Lord Lee and mr. Vane) I heer breake of, and with harty saluts to, etc. I rest Yours assured

Jo: WINTHROP

the 28 of the 5 month 1637

The captains reporte, we haue slaine 13 sachems; but Sassacouse and Monotto are yet liuing.

ROGER WILLIAMS TO JOHN WINTHROP[1]

NEW PROVIDENCE the 2nd of present weeke [July 31, 1637]

MUCH HONOURED SIR,. I am bold to interpose (in all humble respect) a word or 2 concerning the bearer Mr. Greene: Being at Salem this last weeke to take order about the sale of his howse etc. comming away, an ancient acquaintance meetes him (Ed: Batter) and questions whether he would come and liue there againe vnto which he answered, how could he vnles he might enioy the freedome of his Soule and Conscience. Ed. Batter replied he might so: to which he again replied, he knew that could not be for the power of the Lord Jesus was in the hand of civill authoritie: vpon this came by Mr. Endicot, calls Ed: Batter and questions him (as himselfe related to Mr. Greene) what was their Conference: the Summe whereof being told Mr. Endicot warnd Mr. Greene to appeare at this generall Court.[2]

Sir For my selfe I have no partiall respect to Mr. Greene nor relation, but of neighbours togeather: Only for the better following of Peace (euen when

---

[1] W. 2. 102; 4 *Collections*, VI. 212–214; *N.C.*, VI. 52–55.

[2] John Greene was, on August 1, 1637, bound over to the Court of Assistants by the Massachusetts General Court in one hundred marks for having "spoken against the magistrates contemptuously," and on September 19 was fined £20, committed until the fine should be paid, and banished from the colony. *Records of Massachusetts*, I. 200, 203. When later, upon his return to Providence, Greene protested in writing that the action taken against him by the Massachusetts authorities was a usurpation of "the power of Christ over the churches and mens consciences," the General Court, in March, 1637/38, reaffirmed its sentence of banishment. *Ibid.*, 224.

it flies from vs) I am bold to acquaint with passages of Truth (as I can not but hope) before hand: I shall grieue much that any Molestation or trouble should arise vnto you from hence, or that there be the appearance of any further Jarr: Sir I know to whome I speake, Mr. Endicot had neede haue a true Compasse for he makes great way etc: the Father of Lights and Spirits mercifully be pleased to guide all our steerings.

Mr. Greene here is peaceable, a peacemaker, and a lover of all English that visits vs. I conceaue he would not disturbe peace in relating his Judgment to his friend (if I may so call him) demaunding it first allso of him, or els I presume he should not haue heard a word of such matters, if I know Mr. Greene.

Sir I here yet not of any of the runnaway Captiues amongst our neighbours   yesterday I heard that 2 scapt from them to the Pequt: If any be or doe come amongst them I suppose they shall be speedily returned, or I shall certifie where the default is.

Sir I desire to be truely thanckfull for the Boy intended: his Father was of Sasquankit where the last fight was: and fought not with the English as his mother (who is with you and 2 children more) certi[fi]ed me: I shall endeavour his good and the common, in him. I shall appoint some to fetch him: only I request that you would please to giue a name to him.

Sir concerning Captiues (pardon my wonted boldnes) the Scripture is full of mysterie, and the old Testament of Types.

If they have deserved Death, tis Sinn to spare:

If they haue not deserved Death then what punishments? Whether perpetuall slaverie.

I doubt not but the Enemie may lawfully be weakned and despoild of all Comfort of wife and children etc: but I beseech you well weigh if after a due time of trayning vp to labour, and restraint, they ought not to be set free: yet so as without danger of adioyning to the Enemie   Thus earnestly looking vp to heaven for you and all yours I rest Your wo[rshi]ps vnfaigned

ROGER WILLIAMS

My best respect to Mrs. Wintrop Mr. Deputie Mr. Bellingham etc.

JOHN UNDERHILL TO JOHN WINTHROP[1]

To the honourable gouerner John Winthrupp att his howse in Boston give these

SIR, Yow knowe how powerfully our Lord Jesus hath lately appeared in the ministrye exhorting vs to passe by personall wrongs: nay though they were such as mightt greately redounde to the dishonour of a mans Calling, yett as Moses mekely [to] overlooke them. And to the ende deare and honoured ser, that we mightt once more (if itt be the will of god) enjoye our wonted hermonye without any alieonation in affection, I presume to acquaint yow with certaine objeckts which for the preasentt doe hinder the free passage of thatt Christian Love, thatt should [be] founde amongst vs. Ser yow know I once tould yow in regarde of my inward troubles and myne absence three moneths I was almost a nuter betwene booth, nott well knowing where the differences lay, further then god was pleased to teach me by his word and spiritt. And therefore was the more silentt, hopinge that god in his owne tyme would lighten the minds of men soe as to be convinsed of the trueth, att leastt some, for though Israell were [as] the sand, yett a remnant shall returne. And the god of peace now begininge to appeare amongst vs to cause peace to abounde amongst vs booth in Church and Comunewealth, giue me leaue a litle to sertifie yow of the speach of people, nay should I make itt my humblest request I should expresse noe more then the earnest desire of my hearte: and thatt [*torn*] first to putt yow in mynde thatt Mr. Whelewrightt being con-v[ented] before the Judgementt seate, in the behalfe of Christ and the peace of his church which of vs all is much desired, thatt yow would sweetely lett his censure faull, and manifest the forbearance of god in that particular the matter now depending but in poyntt of honour: yow knowe Contempt con-se[rn]es your persons and sopose yow should be offended that way which I see nott soe to be yett passe itt by: for prefering the honour of Christ and his spouses peace, and I dare say itt wilbe safer to forfitt your honour then pro-seede to disunion for sedition: yow see he intented noe disturbance amongst vs, how ever accidentally all this shaking followed vpon itt, for we may easilie disscerne thatt where the sworde of the worde comes sharpened itt seperats a man from himselfee, therefore lett this suffice thatt itt hath donne more good then evill, many haue endeavored to manifest there vnion more

---

[1] W. 3: 43; 4 *Collections*, VII. 170–174. For Underhill, see L. Effingham de Forest and Anne L. de Forest, *Captain John Underhill, Gentleman, Soldier of Fortune* (New York, 1934); Henry C. Shelley, *John Underhill, Captain of New England and New Netherland* (New York, 1932); *D.A.B.* This letter is not in Underhill's handwriting.

and more, and because god onely can bringe good outt of evill giue him
leaue to ta[ke his] owne way: which doubteles we must doe we whatt we
cann. Ser giue me leaue to make a serious protestation for yow withoutt any
Ins[*torn*]ation. I haue seene thatt in yow thatt hath confirmed me that yow
are as deare to god as the Aple of his eye, though these late passages haue
much stumbled me, yett I hould yow the same man as before as deare to god
as ever, though perhaps for the tyme being yow were left to temptation as
Hezechia to see whatt was [*torn*] yow therefore good ser goe on in pursueing
peace to pur[*torn*]se itt. Ser to an vnmortified heartt my bouldnesse might
seem teadyous, espetially your selfe being Gouernour and generall of our
forces: and my selfe butt a meane Captaine, butt when I meete with the
spiritt of Christ I dare be the boulder.

2. My second request is yow would be pleased in the bowells of mercie
alike to consider the estate of Stephen Greenesmith:[1] yow partly knowe the
infirmityes of the man which I hope will moove yow to a serious pondering of
his præsentt Condition. remember itt is a day of Jubille wherein we are to
lett the oppressed goe free.

Yow knowe itt is nott an offence against Christ, butt the Callings of men,
and I hope for peace sake god will moove your hearte to preferre the peace of
his Church before the rightt of your owne Cause.

3. my third request is that yow would soe farre respectt the glory of god
and the safetie of vs all as to pardon thatt same vnaduised speach of his in
Corte and that by his sodaine returne to England he may stopp the Clamors
may there be rased. ser I doubte nott if the man had vnderstood him selfe
he would nott haue vttered such provoakeing speaches, for he might himselfe gesse that the kings eare will not be opne to resceiue every Clamour. for
my owne partt I am aptt to thinke he lookes att itt as a part of his honour to
haue such a people vnder his soueraintye and soe much the rather seeing he is
not charged by vs and we acknowledge him our Kinge, and therefore good
ser consider the mans Ignorance which is pardonable from all lawes booth of
heauen and earth. Itt is the first offence of this nature [he] ever fell into, and
being the man came hether to seeke after Christ, and [*torn*] his corse he hath
ronne vpon this shelfe, lett itt suf[*torn*] the po[*torn*] that is past, least if he lye
longe in prisson, booth [he] and others [who] are vpon the poynte of closinge

---

¹ The Massachusetts General Court had taken strong action against Stephen Greensmith in
March, 1637, "for affirming that all the ministers (except Mr. Cotton, Mr. Wheelwright, and he
thought Mr. Hooker) did teach a covenant of works." His case hung fire until August, when, in spite
of his appeal to the King, the General Court ordered him to be put in prison. *Records of Massachusetts*, I. 189, 196, 200; *Journal*, I. 211, 228.

with Christ, be driuen [*torn*] much sorrowe the treasure of Christ be sand swallowed, [*torn*] shipwrack be made of Cause and persons booth att once. Therefore ser be pleased in the behalfe of Christ to release the prisoner and to let [the] oppressed goe free which is the true purtrature of a solomn fast. Es[ai. 5]8. 6. otherwise to be zealous for god with neglectt of mercie will prooue noe lesse dangerous then sinfull Eccl. 7. 16. mercie and pittie espetially [to] Ignorantes which by reason of that infirmity are gone oute of the way is soe approved booth of god and Nature as thatt Alexander could sing the prases of these prinses that ruled a free people with a spiritt of mercie, nay further Cirus an hethen prince yett in regarde of thatt mercie and Cleamencie he showed to his Captiues, they were forsed to blesse the god of heauen, Thatt seing they were fallen [*torn*] that itt was there happ to fall into the hands of soe kinde [*torn*] Therefore thatt all may be att peace manifested by the [*torn*] day of humilliation,[1] lett me once more craue your Ch[*torn*] and afforde me your Juditious eare, in these propositions which till [*torn*] be [*torn*] my spiritt will remaine still burthened. And the first [is] whether [yow] thinke itt according to rule to deale in Corte with an officer as [*torn*] were [*torn*] to doe. To chose me to the place of a muster master, and come to [*torn*] hopefull way of subsistance and then because it appeared thatt a muster masters place was more superior then the former had almost broughtt me to noethinge when yow all pretended my aduancement. ser I knowe not myne owne heartt, butt suer I am itt is proane to all evill, natural as [*torn*] is to fall downeward, which Judgementt is just from god vpon the asp[*torn*]d beames of pride, butt yett I hope the Lord will mortifie [and] treade downe Sathan vnder all our feete shortely: therefore blame me nott for speaking, butt vpon whatt just grownde yow should be soe fearefull [to] aduance me I knowe nott when as yow haue had soe many pledges of my fidellity.

1. as first my deepe ingagementt in Corte openly promissing to stand for the libertie of gods ordenances against all vnlawfull powers.

2. My returne from my Natiue Cuntrye and refusinge profers of prefermentt there. Thirdly my open subscribing the last yeare to repell all vnlawfull power that should come against vs. Ser I haue ever professed your enemyes to be myne, And will yow yett be afeard of me. I professe ser till I know the Cause I shall nott be satisfied, butt I hope god will subdew me to his will, yett this I say thatt such handeling of officers in forraine parts hath soe farre subuerted some of them as to cause them turne publique rebbells against theire

---

[1] "A day of humiliation" to be observed in all the churches was set by the elders and magistrates for August 24, 1637. *Journal*, I. 230.

state and kingdome, which god forbid should ever be founde once soe much as to appeare in my breast, for as for personall wrongs and Impedyments to Callings are nott soe much to be stood vpon. Butt make itt your owne Case, would itt nott trouble your spiritt, to spend all your dayes aboute a Callinge and hauing noething else to liue vpon, and yett booth to be slighted: and such as never serued onely [adu]ansed. nay would itt nott be a greater tryall to haue [*torn*]ge castt in a mans dish to his dishonour. I pray yow [c]ons[ider] of itt, and judge charitablye of my expressions. And further (good ser) lett me tell yow the trueth of my hearte, to avoyd those desperate temptations I haue hereby bene exposed too, since I haue bene the lands seruantt, I would farre rather lay downe my place then be exposed to such miseries, as I haue knowne many Commanders faull into. Thus humblye craving pardon for my Rudenesse, I leaue you to god and resting yours att commande

JOHN VNDERHILL

[*Ca.* August, 1637]

A REPLY IN FURTHER DEFENSE OF AN ORDER OF COURT MADE IN MAY, 1637[1]

A Reply to an Answer made to a Declaration of the Intent and Equity of the Order made at the Court in May last, whereby none are to be received etc. but by allowance of the Magistrates

Contentions among brethren are sad spectacles, among the churches of Christ, especially when they come once to favour of bitternesse, which would have discouraged me from publishing the former declaration, if I could have expected such an answer: And in that respect I should willingly have sitten downe under my reproach, if the cause of truth and justice had not called me againe to this taske; wherein, if I deale more sharply, than myne owne disposition leads me, the blame must fall upon him, who puts such occasions upon me, as I cannot otherwise shunne.

---

[1] Original not located; *Hutchinson Papers* (1769), 84–100; (1865), 1. 96–113. For the circumstances which gave rise to this document, see note 2, page 422, above. *A Short Story of the Rise, Reign, and Ruine of the Antinomians* (London, 1644), in its account of this reply, states that it was made public for the first time at the November session of the General Court. It had been written "above six weeks since but was kept in upon expectation that the late Assembly [i.e., the Synod, which was in session from August 30 to September 22, 1637] would have had some good effect in clearing the points in controversie, and reconciling the minds of the adverse party. . . ." Charles Francis Adams, *Antinomianism in the Colony of Massachusetts Bay, 1636–1638* (Prince Society, Boston, 1894), 138–139.

Many faults doth the Answerer find in my declaration, which I must examine as thay come in order. The "1st is, that in describing a common wealth (such as ours is) I do not describe it, as it is christian, nor as it is founded upon the grant of our King."

To this I replye 1st, the defininition or description of the genus may be applyed to all the species, reserving the specificall differences: To define a man to be a reasonable creature is a true definition of any man, whether rich or poor, christian or heathen: and when I describe a common wealth in general or in a more civil or politicke respecte, the churches or christians which are in it, fall not into consideration, as to the being of it, for it may be a true body politicke, though there be neither church nor christian in it.

The like may be sayd for the forme of government, whether it be by patent or otherwise yet it is a government, and so the description is safe and true.

2d. The description which I make doth include all that which he doth complaine to be wanting. The words are these. A company of people, consenting to cohabite under one government, for their mutual safety and wellfare. Now let ours be layd to this description and the truth will appeare. We A. B. C. etc. consented to cohabite in the Massachusetts, and under the government set up among us by his Majesty's patent or grant for our mutual safety and wellfare, we agreed to walke according to the rules of the gospell. And thus you have both a christian common weale and the same founded upon the patent, and both included within my description.

I will adde only what I conceive from this and other like passages in his answer, viz. that he makes this exception rather to shelter himself under pretence of his tenderness of the kings honour and right, than out of any ignorance of the true latitude of my description; and withall he discovers how little he regardeth what jealousyes he put us under, so he may shelter his owne parties. The Lord give him to see his secret underminings, that it may be forgiven him. Having thus faulted my description, he taketh upon him to teach me a better; and for this he refers me, by a marginal quotation to Proverb 8. 5. the text is this, Oh ye simple understand wisdome and ye fools be ye of an understanding heart; and to Isai. 6. 7. And he layd it upon my mouth and sayd loe this hath touched thy lipps etc. How these places will prove his description of a christian common wealth, founded upon the kings patent is beyond my reach, but it suits well with a practise now in use, to speak nothing but what they bring scripture for; so scripture be alledged it matters not how impertinent they be.

As for your description it self, I have no more to say against it, but that it was not requisite, to that which I projected, to expresse those particulars;

and our lawyers will tell you that *expressio eorum quæ tacitè infunt nihil operatur*: My intent was to prove the proprietye and priviledges of a common weale which may also belong to such government among Turkes and Pagans, so far as they may fall within my description without any prejudice to the most christian government, that is, as if I speake of one that is an honest man, and say that he goeth upright, speakes, laughs, etc. when a Turke or a Pagan doth the same.

His next exception is, that I say "that such a body politic may use all meanes, which may conduce to their wellfare, and do not restrain it to lawful meanes."

To this I reply, that it is according to scripture phrase, and our common speach. When we call upon a sicke man, to use meanes for his recoverye, we are well enough understood, though we put not the word lawful: I may do all things, saith Paul, and give all diligence saith Peter, without expressing lawful, which the Answerer would have understood well enough, if he had not beene minded to seeke a knot in a rush; only I see not why he should passe over those many things which he saith are questionable in my ground worke, and take up those which will afford so little advantage.

Then he proceeds to examine the reasons which I layd downe to prove the equitie of this law.

The first reason is this, "If we be a corporation established by free consent, if the place of our habitation be our owne—then no man hath right to come in to us, without our consent."

To this he answers, that "he knoweth not how we who stand a corporation by the Kings patent can thus argue." To this I replye then. I will tell him, that which the King is pleased to bestow upon us, and we have accepted, is truly our owne.

2. He denyeth the consequence by a distinction of a consent regulated, and a vast and illimited consent.

Replye: To speake of consent in general, implyeth always a consent suitable to the power or interest of him who is to give it; as when we say, a child may not marrye without consent of parents, we know it is regulated, yet when a father pleads it, he doth not neede to expresse all the limitations.

Thus he runs on in a frivolous discourse, and in the end falls upon this false conclusion, "An unlawful dissent can hinder no man," So that if he had need to borrow my horse, and I ought by the rule of love to lend him to him, though I refuse to consent to his request herein, yet he may take him, because my dissent is unlawfully; so by this conclusion a wife, a childe, a servant may doe any thinge that is lawfull, though the husband, father, or maister deny their consent. If this speed well, the next conclusion will be an anarchie.

After this discourse I expected somewhat to have taken away the consequence of my argument, but I finde not a word to that purpose, he is suddainly fallen upon my second reason, which is this,

"If no man hath right to our land, etc. but by our consent, then it is reason we should take nottice of men, before we conferre any such upon them."

This he partly grants, but complaines of the change of the question, to which I replye that I did not propound any reasons in a syllogisticall frame, but by way of discourse, and that which this argument tends unto was only to shew why some were not presently allowed, but a time taken, wherein we might gayne some nottice and tryall of them, and there was no need why the answerer should so often complaine of the change of the question; for if he takes my reasons together he cannot denye but the question itselfe is argued and concluded, as will appeare by the sequell, I will therefore passe by all that he strives about, upon this supposed fallacie, and joyne with him in the question, as he states it, viz.

Whether the admitting or rejecting of persons should depend upon the discretions of men, which he calls an unlimitted and unsafe rule and their discretion not regulated, though they should be magistrates.

To this I replye, or rather answere, first, That which he takes for granted, and wherein lyes the whole strength of his defence is untrue, viz. That the magistrates will and discretion in our case is not regulated, for 1st, the magistrates are members of the churches here and, by that covenant, are regulated to direct all their wayes by the rule of the gospell, and if they faile in any thinge, they are subject to the churches correction. 2dly. As they are freemen, they are regulated by oath, to direct their aymes to the wellfare of this civill body. 3dly. As they are magistrates, they are sworne to doe right to all, and regulated by their relation to the people, to seeke their wellfare in all things; so as here is no such irregulated discretion as is supposed, and it seems to me an improper speech and favouring of contradiction; for discretion alwayes implyes a rule for its guide. And herein I have occasion to take in his answere so my 4th reason drawne from the practice of our churches, and some towns where matters of admitting or rejecting are ordered by discretion. And here it is made a wonder that I shew so much ignorance. I must confesse my ignorance is greate, and I cannot hide it, being exposed so much as I am to publick view: Yet that will not cover the answerers blindness, from prejudice in this greate wonder, which is such as he cannot discerne the voyce and will of Christ dispenced in the discretion of his servants and people, and yet tells us not how it should be knowne otherwise. Did he never heare, that our practise is, that none are propounded to the congregation, except they be first allowed by the elders, and is not this to admitt or reject by discretion? Did he never heare of a christian man rejected by the church, or put off at least, because a brother hath professed want of satisfaction? Hath he never heard that the dissent of some few brethren may, by rule, (as hath beene sayd) cause the rejection of a man, whom all the rest of the brethren shall approve of? And where is Christs voyce to be heard now, if he will have discretion shut out of the church. So says the instance of townes matters (which he wisely declines and gives no answer to) he well knowes that within the towne of Boston it is an established order, that none should be received into cohabitation there, except they be allowed by certain men appointed to judge of their fitness for church-fellowship. And so, whereas the way of God hath alwayes beene to gather his churches out of the world; now, the world, or civill state, must be raised out of the churches. And yet the answerer can finde nothing of wonder of ignorance here. And if he had enquired of our neighbours at Plymouth, they could have told him that their practice hath beene upon the like law, for many yeares, I mean in referring it to the discretion of the magistrates to receive and reject such as come to them. And if he had considered of a rule in the law of Moses, he should finde that there is power given to a husband or father to allow or make void any vow of a wife or childe at their discretion, yet I hope he will not call this a vast and unlimitted rule.

But because the word discretion seems so offensive and unsafe, let us trye it by the ballance of the sanctuarye, if we can finde it to hold weight there, sure it will prove a good measure for civill affaires.

The word in scripture is sometymes taken for sound reason, as Psal. 112. 5. He will order his affaires by discretion; so Pro. 11. 12. Sometymes for skill, as Pro. 2. 11. Pro. 3. 21. Sometymes for judgment, Phill. 1. 9. And in all places in a good fence, for it is a gift of God wherein he despenseth his own wisdome in all the affairs of men, both in church and common wealth; all lawes are made by discretion, and the equitie of them is found out and ap-plyed to particular cases by discretion; by it (being guided by the spirit of God) the mynde and will of God is found out in his word, Acts 5. 8 and Acts 8. 23. Acts 15. 38. Acts 21, 23. Levit. 27. 8, 12. So for judgment in civil causes; by discretion did Solomon judge betweene the harlots. It is not possible to provide a law that in the letter of it shall reach every case which may fall out, as we see by the law of God it selfe in the same place of Levit. 27. 8. then it must rest in the discretion of the judge to discerne, so doth the Lord himselfe appointe, Deut. 17. 8, 9. etc. they are to do as the judge shall determine, and that which he shall declare for law, that must they obey, otherwise there could be no determination in hard and doubtful cases. As for these scriptures which the Answerer alledgeth about Christ his souerainty, etc. they are nothing to the question; for the prerogative authority of Christ in all affaires in church and common wealth, doth not hinder the manner of his dispensations of the ministry of his servants, and in the improvement of such gifts of his, of wisdome, discretion, etc. as he is pleased to exercise his authority in, according to the rule of his word.

My 5th reason is, that it is no sinne or injury to deny a man that which he hath no right unto, therefore we may denye some men place amongst us. In the answer, there is againe complainte of changing the question, because I go about to prove that some men may be rejected, which he seemeth to grant, and if so then that which he maketh the maine question will easily be cleared, for if we may reject some, then the care of this must be committed to some persons, for to speak of discerning Christ his authority in church or common wealth, otherwise than as it is dispensed in the ministry of men, is a meer idea or fantasye. If then it must be committed to some persons, to whom may it more properly than to the fathers of the common wealth? And if it cannot be foreseene who are to be received and who to be rejected, those persons must be trusted with the tryall of them, and if no certaine rule can be set downe which may be sufficient to discerne of every man, then must it be committed to their discretion, regulated by the word of God, and the dutye of their place, which they are bound to observe. And whereas the Answerer cryes out against this course as vast, illimitted, sinefull and injurious, and yet will not (and cannot) prescribe us a better, neither in his answer, nor at the court when he opposed the makeing of this law, may we not safely judge that such opposition and those reproachful termes as are cast from it, upon an ordinance of God, in the faces of those whom he would have to be had in honor for his sake, proceed rather from distemper of minde, than from any just cause of offence?

Now here I might strike him with his owne weappon, for when he seekes to prove that any of the kings subjects have right by our patent to come and plant in places not inhabited, he changes the question indeed, for both the law and our dispute have beene about entertaining into houses and townes, and not into places not inhabited. That question may fall to be discussed upon some other occasion.

Againe (that we may take notice how his zeale for the cause outrunes his judgment) he gives to all the kings christian subjects a right to plant among us, by vertue of our patent, and such a right as by misusage whereof they may forfeit the patent, and here he might fitly have brought in his vast and illimitted termes, had he not misplaced them, for hast, for there was never seene such a vast patent of incorporation as should comprehend all the kings christian subjects, which is as large as if he had said all his subjects.

But that others may see his errour, if he himselfe will not, let the patent be perused, and there it will be found, that the incorporation is made to certaine persons by name, and unto such as they shall associate to themselves, and all this tract of land is granted to them and their associates: And after this he gives leave to any of his subjects to depart out of other dominions to this place: So then the case standeth thus, the 10 men of Boston allow a strainger to sit downe among them, yet this gives him no right to any mans house or land, nor to any lot in the towne, till it be granted him, nor to any privilege there till he be made free; we must have a new fort of reason to make this a good argument; the King gives a man leave to inhabite in the incorporate colony of the Massachusets, *ergo*, he hath hereby right to the lands there. His discourse about the matter of general right by patent is so confused and irrational, as I should but waste tyme and paper to follow him in it, *valeat ut valere potest*. I finde nothing in it which may endainger my argument, except it be put out of countenance, by a false clamour of robbery, vexation, oppression, etc. as if the state here went about to take from men their lawful right and expell them from their houses, etc.

The 6th reason is this, if straingers have right to our houses, etc. then it is either of justice or of mercye, etc.

The answerer, after his wonted prejudice of change of the question, undertakes to prove, "that some straingers have right in justice by the Kings patent," only he restraineth it to cohabitation and sojourning (which will conclude nothing for him, seeing this law doth not shutt out all straingers) The reasons he bringeth are three, the 1st, because they are fellow-subjects, 2dly, because they are of the same nation, 3dly, because they are christians.

To this I replye, that I have alreadye cleared this pointe in laying open the extent and meaneing of the patent, and this I may say further, that I have reade over all the lawes of England and all the general customes and privileges of the Kings subjects there, but I have not found any thinge that may give the least colour for such a priviledge as is pretended.

As for that of christianitye I have granted in my declaration that there is a right of hospitalitye, but for other right of cohabitation or sojourning it must be considered in such special cases, as may fall out and cannot be provided for by general rule.

My 7th reason is drawne from the proportion or resemblance that a common-wealth hath to a familye, which is not bound to entertaine all comers, no not every good man, otherwise than by way of hospitalitye.

The answerer (his complainte of changing the question premised) seekes to disprove the proportion, by "distinguishing between the right which the maister of a familye hath to his house, etc. and the right which this common wealth hath to all the houses, etc. within this patent." This he amplyfyes by particular instances. "1. in power of bequeathing them to his wife and children. 2. In regard of the King's right. 3. In respect of such as are no members, etc. and yet have right to their houses, etc. 4. In regard to such as have protested against this law."

To this I replye, that it is not needful they should hold proportion in all respects: It is sufficient if they hold in that which is intended, viz. libertye to receive or reject; which beinge knowne to all and confessed by the answerer, in granting that some may be rejected, is sufficient to make good the argument drawne from this similitude: yet to make it more cleare, I replye to these instances.

To the first I say, that a bodye politicke may leave their houses, etc. to their successors, which are in the place of their children. 2. For the Kings right, that being paramount, hinders no more in a common-wealth than it doth in a familye, for he hath the same interest in the houses, etc. of the father of a familye. 3. For such as are no members they are as sojourners in a familye, who though they have right to be in the familye themselves, yet may not receive in any to reside in their particular chambers, without consent of the matter of the familye. 4. For such as protested against this law, that protestation cometh too late (except they first convince us of the injustice of the law) seeing they formerly gave an implicite consent to all the wholesome lawes and orders of the body; neither need we feare to proclaime our right to our houses, etc. against all intruders, more than particular persons and corporations may do in England, notwithstanding his Majesties interest in them also. Such objections are not worth any answer.

In his answer to my 8th reason, viz. "*Turpius eijcitur quam non admittititur* [sic] *hospes*," he saith it is of humaine authority, and that my conclusions are farr from the marke.

To this I replye, that though this sentence be humaine, yet the equitye of it is strengthened by divine truths: It had been lesse griefe to Abraham not to have received Hagar to his bed then it was after to cast her out; and it was *turpius* for Tobija and his stuffe to be cast out of the temple, then it would if he had not been received in. Now that it may appear how farre my conclusion is from the marke, I will thus lay downe the argument. That law which shuts out such as being received in, shall be worthy to be cast out is honest and of good reporte, but this law doth so, *ergo*, etc.

The major proposition is proved by the examples of Hagar and Tobija, the minor I prove thus; the law provides to have such kept out as will disturbe the peace here, rightly established by the rules of Gods word, *ergo*, etc. except the argument may be avoyded, the conclusion will hitt the marke.

But the Answerer saith that, "1. Such ones as are intended to be kept out, are no disturbers of our peace. 2. That the law doth not declare who are to be kept out and who not."

To these I replye first, for brevitys sake let the apologie and the remonstrance, with the coppie of the whole sermon (which himselfe delivered into the court) be compared and examined, and they shall decide the question, if you will stand to it.

To the second I replye, that yourselfe confesses who the law intended to keepe out; and though such a preamble as might have expressed the full intent, was (for want of time) omitted (which was indeed a defect) yet such as were of the court, and did well know, can make no such advantage of it, seeing the magistrates have other rules to guide them in the execution of it; and so it is warranted by scripture examples as that of our saviour Math. 16. 19. and 18. 18. whatsoever you binde on earth shall be bound in heaven etc. yet he doth not there tell them, who they ought to binde or loose.

The 9th argument is taken from that of the 2 John 10. Such as bring not the true doctrine are not to be received to house, and consequently not into the common wealth.

The Answerer (after his usual complainte of the change of the question) acknowledgeth, that if the order had been made against such it would not have been opposed; but affirmeth that it appears (by the same expressions in the court, and by the execution of the law in part) that this law is made to keepe out such as bring the true doctrine of the gospell, so that now he hath brought the question to this state, whether the opinions spread in the country, and opposed by the magistrates and elders, be the doctrines of the gospell or not, which seeing it is to be decyded by the synod assembled, it will be best to attend the issue thereof.

In his answer to the 10th reason, he doth only discourse and finde fault with a conclusion which is of his own framing (for I do not conclude that the law was only for taking notice of such as come to us, but I add also the ende of such notice, viz. for avoyding such as are to be kept out) which being all included in one parentesis, it is more than a slip thus to mistake it.

And whereas he chargeth me, as if I grounded the law upon no better foundation than a good intent, the reader may easily judge that it is a meere slander: For I lay down the order of the law to be, that such should not be received into our fellowship who are likely to disturbe the same; and thence I inferre that this intent is lawfull and good.

The like cast he hath at the persuasion and conscience of such as are to execute this law: And here I must make bold to aske him this question, viz. Seeing you are bound by your oath in all causes wherein you are to give your vote for elections, etc. to goe according to your conscience, if then one be propounded to be chosen a magistrate, and you are persuaded in your conscience, by the best knowledge you can get of him, that he is not fitt for that place, whether are you to give your vote for him or not? When you have answered this question, I will replye further to you: And with all I desyre the answerer to take this along with him; that this law concerning the freemens oath, whereunto all the godly of this common-wealth consented, (and which referrs the judgment of persons and churches in that cause to the conscience and persuasion of christian men) was never yet held to be a vast and illimitted rule.

The Answerer proceeds to the objections, and least his arguments should not reach his ayme, he speakes to prejudice the readers judgment, by averring much unsoundnes, etc. beforehand, but I must intreate him to make a better discovery ere it be yeelded.

The 1st objection is, that some profane persons are received and others who are religious are rejected.

The answerer disclaymes this objection as none of theirs, which matters not greatly. I know from whome I heard it, though he did not; yet he might as well owne it, as offer to prove that such as are truly and christianly religious have been rejected, except he will denye such to be religious: But I affirme still, as I did before, that I know of none such, who have been rejected, nor any such blasphemers or quarrellers (as he speakes of) to have been received.

In his answer to my solution of this objection, I only observe this, that whereas my argument is by way of comparison "betweene a younge prophaine person and an elder professor confirmed in some errour," he gainesaith the comparison by introduction of Abraham, who was a blessing to others; but alledgeth not any opposite member; but sure he was in a greate streight, otherwise he would not have held forth the father of the faithfull as such an one, as he must produce to answer my comparison; but it well accords with his owne tenent, that he must have leave to advance his owne partie, whatever danger or damage befall others by it.

After this he takes upon him to prove, "that all such as are confirmed in any way of errour, are not to be denyed cohabitation, but are to be pittyed and reformed, for this he alledgeth two places of scripture, Jude 22, 23. Gen. 16. 17."

To this I replye 1st, Let it be observed how this answers my argument. I endeavoured to prove that some professors were to be denyed cohabitation, rather than some prophaine ones, for this reason, viz. because they may be more dangerous. His answer is, that all such as are confirmed in any way of errour are not to be denyed, etc. and omitts that wherein the weight of the argument lies, viz. their being dangerous to publick peace. 2dly, I denye that these scriptures prove his proposition, for that in Jude speakes nothinge of cohabitation, or confirmation in errour, nor speakes he to magistrates, or such as had power, to receive or reject, etc. and if he will bring that place to his purpose it will inferre this conclusion, that no compassion is to be had of such as we may denye cohabitation unto. As for that, Gen. 16. 12. it is as little to the purpose. Ismaell dwelt in the house of his brethren, but not among them; so, by our law, such as we hold not fitt to dwell among us are not denyed to dwell by us.

Another objection is, "that by this law we reject true christians, and so consequently Christ himselfe."

The solution of this objection is, that in some cases a man that is a true christian may be rejected or denyed residence, and yet Christ not rejected; for proof whereof I instance in diverse particulars, all which he passeth by, without any direct answer; but concludes, that is nothing to the law; which I must leave to the reader to judge of, seeing he brings neither reason nor scripture against it, to which I may replye.

After this he comes to the particular occasion of the law, and here he layes about him in earnest, and strikes all that come in his way, magistrates, elders, and all that doe walk in that way which Mr. Wheelewright hath described to be a way of a covenant of workes, and holds them forth as Antichrists; and for proof hereof alledges that in 1 John 4. 1, 2, 3. where the Apostle, giving a rule to discover false spirits by, gives this as the marke, they confesse not that Jesus Christ came in the flesh, and such a spirit is of Antichrist. How this place proves his assertion I am not able to discerne: Sure I am that such, as he casts under a covenant of workes, doe confesse that Christ is come in the flesh, but then I see that hereby he hath brought the cause, which he is so zealous for, into such a toyle as all the skill he hath cannot extricate, unlesse (as before) he will draw in Abraham into the same estate of antichristianism; seeing by that doctrine he walked in the same way of a covenant of workes, 14 yeares together, viz. while he kept Hagar, etc.

For his answer in defence of Mr. Wheelewright his opinions, I will make no replye, but waite the successe of the conference among the churches now assembled.

In the last place he bringeth diverse reasons to prove "that this law is most wicked and sinnefull."

His 1st reason is, this law giveth that, without limitation, to men, which is proper to God; and so is a ground of grosse popery; for proofe he cites Deut. 1. 17. and 17. 9, 10, 11.

To which I answer, that I have proved already that the magistrates are limitted both by their church covenant and by their oath, and by the dutye of theire places, to square all their proceedings by the rule of Gods word, for the advancement of the gospell and the weale publick; neither doth it crosse either of the places mentioned, for whatsoever sentence the magistrate gives, according to these limittations, the judgment is the Lords, though he do it not by any rule particularly prescribed by civill authority. As for that other place in Deut. 17. 9. it strengthens our law, and reflects sharply upon such as doe oppose it; for it streightly commands all persons to submitt to the sentence of the judge, and to receive the exposition of the law from his mouth; so as such gainesayers stand guilty of presumption in opposeing the sentence of the judges, before they have clearly convinced them that their sentence is contrary to the law of God.

As for that aspersion of popery, etc. it will draw no blood; his earnestnes in the cause makes him thus to cast dirt upon his opposers, when he hath spent his shott.

2. His 2d reason against this law is, that it gives libertye to the magistrates to expell and reject those who are most eminent christians, if they suite not with the magistrates disposition; and thence concludes that Christ and his members will finde worse entertainment among us than the Israelites did among the Egyptians and Babilonians, than Abraham and Isaack among the Philistines, than Lott among the Sodomites, etc.

To this I answer, 1. His earnestnes confounds his memorye; he knows well, that this law gives no power to expell any, neither doth it make the magistrates disposition the rule for rejecting any; but this slander hath beene confuted before. 2. For a brother in church covenant and a fellow member of such a civill body as ours, to conclude so peremptorily of his fellow brethren, favours of much arogance and desperate prejudice. If his charity can hope no better of us, but that we will deale worse with Gods people than the Pagans (and that before he hath seene any experience of it) it is no marvaile if he favour such as have ranked us with the same before; onely herein he deales fairely with us, in giving us tymely warneing what to expect from the imbittered mynde of such a brother; but for his argument it selfe thus it stands: The Egyptians, etc. gave leave to Gods people, to sett downe amongst them; But the magistrates will not give leave, etc. *ergo*, they are worse than the Egyptians, etc.

I answer, howsoever the magistrates cannot stopp his fury, yet we shall free the law from the force of his argument: For except he had assumed thus, the magistrates must or may etc. for it is nothing to the law, that they will doe so, seeing a magistrates will may transgresse a good law, and if they should doe so, yet I denye that it is by the liberty of the law, which I shall not need further to prove, seeing my denyall will bear as much weight as his affirmation.

3. His 3d reason is, this law doth crosse many lawes of Christ. This he proves by enumeration of 3 particulars, Matt. 22. 21. Heb. 13. 2. Gal. 6. 10.

To this I answer, and 1. to that of Matt. 22. 21. Give unto Cesar the things which are Cesars. The reason lyes thus: The King hath right to plant any of his subjects among us; but we denye to let him plant some of his subjects among us, unlesse they please us; *ergo*, we denye to Cesar, etc. The proposition is false; for I have proved before, that the King haveing given all the land within certaine limitts to the patentees and their associates, cannot send others to possesse that which he hath granted before.

2. As for that in Heb. 13. it is nothing to the purpose: This law of the court hinders not the entertainment of straingers so farre as the rule of hospitalitye requires; and there is no other intended in that place.

3. For that in Gal. 6. I confesse the houshold of faith are principally to be regarded; and it is apparent that the care of their wellfare was the only occasion and ground (next the glory of God) of the making of this law: For, the court, taking nottice how the hearts of the faithfull were sadded by the spreading of diverse new and unsound opinions, and the uncharitable censures which they laye under by occasion of them, how brotherly love and communion decayed, how the ordinances of religion were neglected, and the faithfull dispensers thereof (sometimes more precious than fine gold) slighted and reproached, throughout the whole countrey, they found it needfull to provide remedye in tyme, that it might goe well with the houshold of faith, and though the execution of this law should turne to the damage of some of this houshold, yet better it is some member should suffer the evill they bring upon themselves, than that, by indulgence towards them, the whole familye of God in this countrey should be scattered, if not destroyed.

His last argument (by which we may see that he ment not to quitt the cause, so long as his breath would hold) is this, This law dasheth against many other lawes of Christ *ergo*, it is more wicked and sinnefull.

To which my answer may be short, and yet sufficient to withstand the force of his argument. This law dasheth not against any law of Christ; *ergo*, it is just and good.

[*Ca.* August, 1637]

JOHN BLACKLEACH TO JOHN WINTHROP[1]

Greate and many are the Reasons (Right Worshipfull) that mooued vpon the vast and trobled Ocean Sea, to study, and commit to writinge, this followinge discourse:

For first consideringe the estate and condicion of some particular Cases of Conscience which weare dependinge and not thoroughlie resolued, when I left the Confines of America, to saile into Engelande:

And allsoe consideringe the sad, many, and lamentable breaches, that haue bene, and continued, in some other partes of the worlde, not onely betwene Churches, but allsoe betwene deare and louinge freindes.

Theise and other thinges beinge taken into consideracion, I deemed my tyme not vnprofitably spent, to enquire booth diligently and exactly, booth what might be the true resolution of those Cases then dependinge.

And allsoe what might be the ocasion of those many breaches before spoken of.

Togeather with the motiues aforesaide, I takinge into Consideracion my owne estate and Condicion, togeather with the estate and Condicion of many poore Soules, which haue to theire great Hazard, and expences, trauelled into theise parts of the vast willdernesse in America:

For theise aforesaide causes I haue (with some difficulty) enquired and searched into the Holy scriptures: to see if that (by the assistance of Gods hoely spirit) I might finde out the way of peace.

Which after I had diligently endeuoured truely and plainely to resolue some Cases of Conscience, and had endeauoured likewise truely and plainely (as the place, tyme, and Gods assistance would) to shew the originall of the aforesaide breaches, and the way to preuent the future that might arise.

---

[1] W. 3. 37; 4 *Collections*, VII. 146–149. For Blackleach, see 4 *Collections*, VII. 146*n*.

I was forced further to resolue this question, in what Cases, and how far wee may differ in iudgement, and yet neuerthelesse Cohabitation, peace, and loue may (accordinge to the Rule of the Hoely Scriptures), continue amongst us.

The Cause that mooued mee to present theise my laboures to your veiue in the first and principall place; is for many and (as I conceiue) very weightie reasons:

To instance in one or two moouinge Causes.

First in regarde that I haue obserued, (soe far as I coulde) that the Greate God hath enriched you, with a large portion of Spirituall Graces, wheareby (I hope and pray) that God will direct you vprightlie, wisely, and thorough-lie, to scann, and peruse the contents of this treatise:

2ly. For that Cause because that God haueinge preferred you aboue many of your brethren, in place of Gouernement, you haue theireby occasion to doe much good, to many a poore Soule.

I vmblie pray you let not the truth be dispiced, allthough the person that tendereth it be weake. I hope God hath giuen you wisdome to receiue the truth, in loue of the truth, not hauinge respecte of or to persons: in such Cases:

Try all thinges, refuse the bad hould fast the truth to the death: remember (I pray you) that not many wisemen (accordinge to the worlde) doe vnder-stande the hid mistery of the Gospell:

The Bereans are commended (for that they did not reiect, but they tryed the truth diligently), and a blessinge from God was vpon them, theirefore many of them beleeued.

These followinge notes haue cost mee much paines, and some tyme, to gather them togeather, and to commit them to writinge.

I pray you let it not be greiuous to you aduisedly to read them: it may bee that somethinge hearein may seeme harsh (I am but a mortall man, theirefore subiect to error) yet I beleeue what I haue written, to be truth, otherwaies I would not haue tendered it to your conscideracion:

And allthough the troblesomenesse of the sease, togeather with the short-nesse of my tyme, haue not suffered mee to explaine my selfe soe fully, as I desired: Yet I beleeue the truth of euery parte (that is of moment) doth playnely appeare.

Weare it soe that the matter hearin contained, weare such as did allto-geather runn with the Current of the tymes, I beleeue that I should get more grounde, with lesse tyme, and with lesse paines.

but in regarde that I am forced to goe vphill, I shall haue the more difficulty, and purchase lesse grounde then other waies, howeuer, my lyfe is not deare vnto mee, I must runn or goe the rase that is set before mee:

And this I doe ensure you (in the presence of him that is my lyfe and cheifest ioy) that (soe far as I knowe my owne heart) my ende, and onely ende, in what I haue written in this treatise, is the Glory of God, the benefitt of his people, and the discharge of my owne duety: I durst doe noe lesse.

it is not in him that willeth, nor in him that runneth, but in God that giueth the successe.

I pray you in loue couer my infirmities, and let your fauorable helpe bee to assist mee.

Beloued ser, be stronge in the Lorde, and in the powre of his might, take vnto you (which I pray God to bestow vpon you and to girde fast vnto you) the whole Armore of God, That soe you may be in this worlde, an instrument of his Glory, and after this shorte, brittle, and unconstant life is ended, you for euer may behould the bewty of his Countenance, and the brightnesse of his face, the knowledge of whome is lyfe eternall:

He that dwelleth in loue, dwelleth in God, and God in him. Yours as you are Christs

J: B:

[August 3, 1637]

I vmblie pray you that when you haue perused the followinge treatise,[1] that you will restore it to mee againe.

[*Endorsed by Governor Winthrop:*] Mr. Blackleach 3 of mo: 6: 1637.

ISRAEL STOUGHTON TO JOHN WINTHROP[2]

Honourable Sir, It hath pleased God further to crowne our poore endeavours with success graciously, as you shall largely and punctually understand by Capt. Patrick, to whome I leave the relation wholly, seeing a lively voyce will do it: and therefore I entreat your favour for this omission; specially because it is late in the night and a faire wind attends us. Surely there have been so many singular providences as are worthy of due observance and eternall prayse. And allbeit we have not the whole of our desires, yet O that

---

[1] Blackleach's manuscript has not been preserved.
[2] Original not located; *Hutchinson Papers* (1769), 61–63; (1865), I. 69–70.

we could extoll him for what we have and waite for more. Much is done, but not all, and if aught be well done, I desire we be not weary thereof, but proceed as God shall minister new occasions. Capt. Patrick can informe you of our intentions for the future: both for Block Island, Long Island, Indians beyond Puillipioak etc. Allso if it shall appear usefull and pleasing to you we will some of us come march through Neepenet: I earnestly desire the work may be thoroughly done, and see we and our friends will suffer much by scattered wretches, if they be not closely followed. But I shall write more fully suddenly, and do desire to understand your pleasures: For we will prefer your minds before ours: But 'tis clear some must reside here or hereabouts. It is beyond my abilities for the present to resolve you which is best in all things, or particularly about planting Pecot. For tho' the place be subsistable, and an excellent harbour, and abundance of corne, and the same ground ready for English grayne forthwith, which is a great help to planters, yet the providence of God guided us to so excellent a country at Quaillipioak river, and so all along the coast as we travelled, as I am confident we have not the like in English possession as yet, and probable 'tis the Dutch will seaze it if the English do not. It is conceived generally far more worthy than Pequid notwithstanding the former considerations. It is too good for any but friends; Capt. Patrick can informe you the full.

I heartely thank you for your loving care of us about necessaries and do acknowledge your kind acceptance of our poore imperfect indeavours, craving your prayers for more grace that we may so increase in loyal faithfullness and fruitfullness, such as may be God's honor and the fullfilling of your and our joy through Jesus Christ our Lord; and so, with my due respect to yourself with the councell and majestrates I take leave, Yours as in duty I am bound

ISRAEL STOUGHTON

POSSESSION HOUSE IN PEQUID, the 4th day of the 5th weeke of our warrfare about midnight [August 9, 1637]

ROGER WILLIAMS TO JOHN WINTHROP[1]

NEW PROVIDENCE this last of the weeke [*ca.* August 12, 1637]

SIR, I am much desired by Yotaash (the bearer hereof Miantunnomues

---

[1] Original in private possession; 4 *Collections*, VI. 241.

brother) to interprete his Message to you viz: that Miantunnomu requests you to bestow a Pequt squaw upon him.

I obiect, he had his share sent him. he answeres that Caunounicus receaved but a few women and keepes them: and yet he sayth his brother hath more right: for, himselfe and his brothers men first laid hold vpon that Company.

I obiect, that all are disposed of he answeres, if so, he desires to buy one or 2 of some English man.

I obiect that here are many runn away, which I haue desired himselfe might convey home to you: he replies, they haue bene this fortnight busie (that is keeping of a kind of Christmas): and 2ndly at present Miantunnomues father in law lyes a dying:[1] as allso that some of the Runnawayes perished in the woods: 3 are at the Nanhighonsick, and 3 within 10 mile of this place: which I thinck may best be fetcht by 2 or 3 Massachuset Indians who may here get some one or 2 more to accompany and helpe.

Sir you were pleased some while since to intimate some breach of leauge in Miantunnomu. I would not disharten this man from comming by my speech any way: but I could wish you would please to intimate your mind fully to him as allso that if there be any iust exception which they cannot well answere that vse be made of it (if it may be with the Safetie of the Common Peace) to get the bit into their mouthes[2] especially if there be good assurance from the Mowhauges so with my best salutes and earnest sighes to heaven I rest Your Wo[rshi]ps vnworthy

ROGER WILLIAMS

ISRAEL STOUGHTON
TO THE GOVERNOR AND COUNCIL OF MASSACHUSETTS[3]

To his much honored in the Lord, the Governour and Council of the Massachusetts, these present

SIR, Yours by Robinson we have received, and careful we shall be (I trust) to observe your instructions, and to hasten home as fast as the cause will permit. We are now in a readiness for Block Island; only we wait for a fair wind. We are informed of many Indians there; so we expect the toughest work we

---

[1] In the margin: "both are true."

[2] In the margin: "I meane the bit of awfull respect that now they fall not into mutinies at home etc."

[3] Original not located; Savage (1825) I. 398–401; (1853), I. 478–481.

have yet met. But we are assured our cause is good, and so we commend ourselves to God's mercy and power. By reason you sent for Mr. Wilson to come with Mr. Hooker, we being willing to show our loyalty to you, and love to the common cause, we have, without gainsaying, dismissed him, albeit we conceived we had special interest in him, and count ourselves naked without him, and therefore expect supply, if we be required to abide by it. Upon consideration that Mr. Wilson going along in the vessel to Connecticut might the more engage Mr. Hooker and expedite his journey to you, and for that, being to go to Block Island, we could enjoy him but one Sabbath more, we dismissed him at first view of your letter.

We do thankfully acknowledge your care and tenderness toward us, signified by your writings, and sending my provisions, etc., and desire we may deserve it. For the hardship you conceive you put us to, and pity us for, for my part, what I endure is so little thought of, that it is not worthy pity, neither doth it trouble me, and therefore I desire it may trouble none of my friends. It is what I have been acquainted with in part before; and if I be never more put to it for God's cause sake, it is much less than I have expected. Whiles we enjoy part in what is there to be had, I hope we shall be satisfied.

We hear not of Miantonimo, nor any of the Narrigansets nor Nianticks that were with you, concerning the Pequids they have, or any thing else, albeit we have sent for Miantonimo to come to us. The last day of the week, (being to go to Block Island, and) wanting a guide, we sent Tho. Stanton and twenty men, with Lieut. How, towards the Narragansets to get one, who found divers people in Pequid corn, and desired speech with some of them, but by no means could not obtain it, for they ran all away. Still they endeavored after it, and to know the reason of their running, especially seeing we had formerly expressly told them, they must not use that, for we should then take them for Pequids. At length, they told, that Englishmen had some of them in prison in the bay, and they knew not what Englishmen meant towards them. But we were also told by a squaw, that they were mixt, Pequids and Narragansets together; and were besides signs of two rendezvous; she said, one was the Pequids. So, there being twenty canoes, ours brought two away, with one kettle and beans, that were at the Pequids' rendezvous, but told them, let them come hither, and, if they were Narragansets, they should have all without any damage.

We conceive you do well, in keeping them to strict, just terms, as also in that you refer them to us in the matters specified; for we conceive, being in the field, with our swords in our hands, we shall do better with them than when the sword is sheathed, and all peace.

Concerning Pequids harbored by them, we have thoughts (after return from Block Island) to require every one of them from those that have them, for these reasons:

1. Their flying to them is no submission to us, but of purpose to avoid it; so that they bear the same good will to us as formerly; that is, they stand enemies, only use the Narragansetts and others as their covering.

2. Standing thus, we can expect no other but that they will do us mischiefs as opportunity serves; and, besides, be as spurs to the Narragansetts to provoke them to it, and as captains to aid and strengthen them in it, when, etc.

3. Under the vizor of a Narragansett, they will come amongst us, and do us mischiefs.

4. And when a mischief is done, then it will be fathered upon some renegado Pecot, that will have no master to own him; but it will be said, such a one did it, or such a one, etc.

Therefore, if they will not deliver all to us, according to their covenant, we cannot think their intentions to be good toward us, and shall accordingly declare ourselves towards them; though we will not so use like faith with them, but first advise with you, unless we be constrained. And if God do harden their hearts, I doubt not but it will be to their perdition. Only I pray for the contrary, if it be the Lord's will.

For Wequash, we fear he is killed; and if he be, 'tis a mere wicked plot, and, seeing he showed faithfulness to us, and for it is so rewarded, it is hard measure to us-ward; and what is meet to be done therein, is difficult to me to conclude; I shall therefore desire your speedy advice.

After return from Block Island, we shall fall upon destroying corn. Near to us it fails much by the weeds, and far from us it will do us little good. The Naragansetts do gather beans in abundance, and we are silent at it; yet, if they should turn enemy, it would be to our great damage. But my opinion is, that they will be twice advised before they will fall out with us. Only they will let us bear their injuries as long as we will, and, if they see us in good earnest, I believe they will think upon it, especially whiles the terror of our sword and our God's doings is upon them.

There be many Pequids yet living, and such as will do much mischief. It will be found therefore necessary for one pinnace, one shallop, and some sixty men, to abide here, to take opportunities, partly at Long Island, and elsewhere upon the coasts, (for they lie mostly upon the coast, except such as are under the wing of other Indians). Else I see not many need stay. For, for this place, it is scarce worthy much cost. As for plantation, here is no meadow I see or hear of near; the upland good, but rocky and unfit for ploughs for the most part. Indeed, were there no better, 'twere worthy the best of us, the upland being, as I judge, stronger land than the bay upland.

But if you would enlarge the state, and provide for the poor servants of Christ, that are yet unprovided, (which I esteem a worthy work,) I must speak my conscience. I confess the place and places whither God's providence carried us, that is, to Quillipeage River, and so beyond to the Dutch, is before this, or the bay either, (so far as I can judge,) abundantly. But unless great necessity, or approved policy, require such undertakings, I would be loath to have a hand in, or that my pen should further them, for I affect not scattering, but would rather part stakes at home; yet, so far as it may tend to public utility, and the enlargement of Christ's kingdom, I hope I should not hinder so good a work, though it be to self's disadvantage. It seems to me, God hath much people to bring hither, and the place is too strait, most think. And if so, then, considering, 1st, the goodness of the land, 2d, the fairness of the title, 3d, the neighborhood of Connecticut, 4th, the good access that may be thereto, wherein it is before Connecticut, even in the three forementioned considerations, (for the land Connecticut men so judge,) and, 5th, that an ill neighbor may possess it, if a good do not,—I should readily give it my good word, if any good souls have a good liking to it.

I am willing, for my own particular, to stay here so long as yourself and the council, or general court, shall see just cause to require me. Yet I also am as willing to be at home so soon as it may be permitted; and, for my part, when some few things more are over, I see nothing against but that I may come home, and therefore shall wait to know your minds therein.

Thus, with my due respect remembered to yourself, the honored council, and the rest of the magistrates, desiring your prayers, I humbly commend you to God. Yours, as in duty I am bound

ISRAEL STOUGHTON

From PEQUID, the 2d day of the 6th week of our warfare [August 14, 1637]

JOHN ENDECOTT TO JOHN WINTHROP[1]

To the right Wor[shipfu]ll John Winthrop Esqr. Gouernour deliver

DEAREST SIR, The bearer heereof Francis Felmingham being husband to the eldest daughter of Beniamyn Cooper deceased who (as you haue already

---

[1] W. 2. 69; 4 *Collections*, VI. 132–133.

beene informed) dyed intestate in the way overbound to this place, doeth in the right of his wiefe and sonne clayme his right in the goods and chattells of the said Beniamyn: the rather for that the said Beniamyn gaue him no portion with his daughter. I therefore haue addressed him to your selfe to giue him some satisfaccion in that behalfe: I haue caused the order made in this particular to be put in practise that the goods may not come to dammage, and that the younger daughter be prouided for.[1] But I conceaue that Scruggs with whom the younger daughter is, will not be a convenent Guardian for her, both in regard of his Judgement, and his and his wifs breedinge and therefore to take some other when we shall meete. The wiefe of this Francis Felmingham (as I ame informed) is one that feares God. And her Father brought her husband and her over vppon his owne chardge and did intend to prouide for them heere. Having nothing else at present but my due respects vnto your deare wiefe I leaue you to the Almighties guidance and blessing resting Yours if any thing

Jo: Endecott

Salem this 15 of the 6th moneth 1637

HENRY JACIE TO JOHN WINTHROP, JR.[2]

To the Worsh[ipfu]ll his very good friend John Winthrop the Yonger Esquier, in New Ipswich in New England. Leave these with the Right Worsh[ipfu]ll Mr. Winthrop of Boston

London 6th mon. 18th day [1637]

Good Mr. Winthrop, Though about 2 or 3 months ago I writ to you, yet it seeming that that letter is not yet sent away, and now there being further opportunity of sending, I desire what in me lies, to make some satisfaction for my former neglect or at least, not so oft performing it in this kind, as love and respect I ow bind me. Now to acquaint you with our affaires: S. Mat:[3] having (by the L[ord]s good provision) obteined a most meet helper, as one of the same heart mind and spirit, remaining this 12 month within 20 miles of London, in a place 5 miles from the Parish Church, hath enjoyed great freedome: but now of late the clouds gather fast towards à storme, their ship

---

[1] For the subsequent story of Rebecca Cooper, see Lawrence S. Mayo, *John Endecott* (Cambridge, 1936), 108–109.

[2] W. 2. 160; 4 *Collections*, VI. 459–464.

[3] Sir Matthew Boynton, who was living at Hedgely House, near Uxbridge.

is like to be filled with waves, but they seeking to awaken Christ for their help, they there desire to expect all help. As for me, the Lord having discovered the necessity and beauty of being under Christs Govern[ment] and refrained some time, hoping the last spring to haue come with them to N. E. Now seing they ar yet stayed and ar like to stay I know not how long, til they be satisfied: I could not so be content, tho I enjoyd so great priviledges there, bodily and spiritual: but having been sued unto and oft provoked by that society wher Mr. Lathr[op] was, and long sought, and at last obteined ful satisfaction for uniting to them, the Lord removing divers lets, and providing so wel for the place I supplied, I am now come to Lon[don] to them, though not undertaking any office, though now urged to it, desiring first to hear from some in N. E. to whom I writ about half a yeer ago. Letters to me may be directed as before to be left with Mr. Overton in Popes head Alley.

Touching Mr. Burton etc. He having preached Novemb. 5 on Prov. 24. 21; My son, fear G[od] and the K[ing] and meddle not with them that ar given to Change, Then urged his people to take notice of many Changes of late in books allowed, and in Practise, as Altars etc. and being charged to answere before the High Commission, he appealed to the K[ing]. Being asked why he did so, he answered, Because I would not have mine adversaries be my judges. Hence being forced thro danger to keep his house, he writ to the K[ing] the Grounds hereof tog[ether] with his 2 sermons, as also to the Judges etc. which he appointed that vpon his apprehension should be delivered to the Counsel as they sate, by his wiffe, which was performed. She ergo was imprisond for a time, then released upon petition. He remaind close prisoner in the Fleet, as Mr. Prynn in the Towr, and Dr. Bastwick at Gatehouse, divers books being by stealth printed and divulged, (as News from Ipswich, of that Bishop Wrens Acts etc.) Judgments on Sabbath breakers of late, therin a Story of Mr. Noys death; Dr. Bastwick printing Πραξεις των Ἐπισχόπων, conteining ther Acts in their proceedings against him for some passages against Lord B[ishop]s in his book of reply in justifying the K[ing]s supremacy against the Bishop of Rome, he having had many confronts here by a p[a]p[is]t in that point. Then (as the Star Chamber bil saith) he writ a book cald a Leitany wherin were many scandaulous passages, as, From Bishops, Pri[est]s, and Deac[on]s, Good L[ord] deliver us. Also this, he therin in his wives Name entreats Father William of Cant[erbury] his holines (so is his stile) and Father William of London, Magnificus Rector of the Treasury, to be Godfa[ther]s to her child, not doubting but that her husb[and] should procure the Whoor of Babylon their old Mrs. with whom they had so long committed Adultery, to be Godmother. And then (s[ays] he) we shal have such a Christening as

hath not been in Europe this many a blessed day, etc. Mr. Burtons books being spread by divers persons known. Also Mr. Wakelin Esq. when the Church-
wardens of Bures enquird whether their Comunion Table should be placed
Altar wise and pailed in as others are, he answered Its no matter, its but a
dance before Popery: he being rebuked by others there, answered You may
say what you wil. The King hath a wife, and he loves her wel, and she is a
p[a]p[is]t and we must al be of her Religion, and thats the thing the Bishops
aime at, etc. as the bil hath it.

Those 3 ergo with Mr. Wakelin and about 16 more, were al joind together
in a Starchamber bil, as such as ar combind together in their practises: the
one doing or speaking so by the procurement abetting etc. of the rest.

These 3 came to their ans[wer] neer the end of June, whose speaches then
were taken by some, showing how they were hindred from giving answers,
being close prisoners, and Counsels not comming, and ther own answers not
admitted, and now Mr. Pryn would give his, on oath. But now no answere
to be admitted, but their guilt taken pro confesso, they were censured at
5000*li* a peece, and perpetual imprisonment. Mr. Burton being first degraded
they al to stand on the pillory then to loose their Eares in Westm[inster]
pallace. Mr. Pryn also to be branded with S. L. for Seditious Libeller, which
was performed Jun. last (and their spea[che]s then ar recorded by some
writers.) Some say S. L. is for Syons Lawyer. The morning they suffred, Mr.
Burton said thus to his sad wife. Good wife, let me not see a tear in thine eyes,
nor hear a Groane from thy heart. I have had 2 very joyful dayes, the first
when I married my former wife, the latter when I married thee: and it was a
joyful time indeed: yet nothing comparable to this day. This day the L[ord]
puts greatest honour upon me. And he so fils me with comfort, that I am not
able to keep it in, and I long to be at the work I am cald to, etc. (or to this
effect). Then presently the Officers came for him. Dr. Bas[twick] and Mr.
Pryn were set on one Pillory: who sweetly embraced one another. Mr. Burton
soon after was brought to the other pillory somwhat lower. Many thousands of
peo[ple] were there, al generally pitying or applauding them and oft laffing
and clapping and shouting for joy to see so great courage and comfort and
undauntednes in each of them: they 2 spake to Mr. Bur[ton] he to them, the
peo[ple] to each of them; encouraging and comforting them, al this without
any controll except by one or 2 officers, as one observed, that went round
about to observe the peo[ple]s dispositions. One woman indeed, that was
wondrous free in her speaches to them and to the people going up and down
encouraging them to suffer: speaking of the Ene[mie]s Cruelty, an officer

overheard and laid hold, and chargd a halbertman to cary her away. She passing a litle way on, said to him, Friend I have nothing to say to you; and smiled on him, and so went among the rest, and he let her go.

There without any interruption, first Dr. Bas[twick] then Mr. Pryn, then Mr. Burton, make large speaches to the peo[ple] declaring the cause of their suffrings, and what comfort they had in it, against the Prelates. Mr. Pryn said the Statute was thus, made in Q[ueen] Eliz[abeths] reigne. That if one usd libels against the K[ing] or Q[ueen] ther should be 2 months imprisonment and 300*li* fine, (which had been I take it, but 1 month, and 100*li* in Q[ueen] Ma[rys] rei[gn]) but for want of paying that fine, such punishment as seemed proportionable. Wheras now see the change of times (s[aid] he) when they say we ar libellers against the Prelates (yet prove it not,) we ar fined 5000*li* a man, and perpetual imprisonment and besides that, to h[ave] this corporal punishment, etc.

They were to stand on the pillory (I think) 3 hours: some there observd that the handle on the clock was set backward, sometimes ½ an hour at a time. So having joyfully and triumphantly suffred, despising the (intended) shame, they were had, each to the place whence they came, where they were very much visited by al sorts, except black coates (for none (or scarce any) of them, visited, or were at their pillory suffrings, or accompanied them toward the places whither they were adjudged to be caried, as thousands did) which was one part of their Censure, Dr. Bas[twick] to a Castle in Cornewal, Mr. Burton to Lancaster, Mr. Pryn into a Castle in Wales, which was performed about 3 weeks after; one 3 or 4 days after the other, with abundance of people and happy he or she that could get them by the hand, or but touch their Coat (as one said, Wel I toucht his coat once more). Divers had writ letters to their Christian friends that dwelt neer the way towards these 3 Castles, and many people met them in several places, and so went alongst with them, til others came in. Dr. Bast[wick] we hear hath a very poor hole to lodge in (and so Mr. Burton) (where the Countrey Rogues were wont to be it seemes.) We hear not yet of Mr. Pryns place, what it is. By these devices, the Prelates hoped to have more prevailed; but its feared they have lost greatly by it. The poor credit they had with the vulgar is almost quite lost. Every wrech, and swearing and drunken beast almost, is ready on the least speach, to cry out on them, which makes many consider Mal. 2. 8, 9. Bec[ause] you h[ave] departed you have caused many to stumble, ergo have I made you contemptible. Good Sir sympathise with our Land, with our vis[ible] Church. I want time to write to many friends. Salute Mr. and Mrs. Saltons[tall], William

Spaf[ford], with Robert etc. Accept hereof instead of many letters from Your faithful tho unworthy friend

H. JACIE

ROGER WILLIAMS TO JOHN WINTHROP[1]

For his much honoured Mr. Governour, these

NEW PROVIDENCE, 20th of the 6th [1637]

MUCH HONOURED SIR, Yours by Yotaash (Miantunnomue's brother) received. I accompanied him to the Nanhiggonticks, and having got Canounicus and Miantunnomu with their council together, I acquainted them faithfully with the contents of your letter, both grievances and threatenings; and to demonstrate, I produced the copy of the league, (which Mr. Vane sent me,) and with breaking of a straw in two or three places, I showed them what they had done.

In sum their answer was, that they thought they should prove themselves honest and faithful, when Mr. Governour understood their answers; and that (although they would not contend with their friends) yet they could relate many particulars, wherein the English had broken (since these wars) their promises, etc.

First then, concerning the Pequt squaws, Canounicus answered, that he never saw any, but heard of some that came into these parts, and he bad carry them back to Mr. Governour, but since he never heard of them till I came, and now he would have the country searched for them. Miantunnomu answered, that he never heard of but six, and four he saw which were brought to him, at which he was angry, and asked why they did not carry them to me, that I might convey them home again. Then he bid the natives that brought them to carry them to me, who departing brought him word, that the squaws were lame, and they could not travel. Whereupon he sent me word, that I should send for them. This I must acknowledge, that this message I received from him, and sent him word, that we were but few here, and could not fetch them, nor convey them, and therefore desired him to send men with them, and to seek out the rest. Then, saith he, we were busy ten or twelve days together, as indeed they were in a strange kind of solemnity, wherein the sachims eat nothing but at night, and all the natives round about the country

---

[1] Original not located (see note 1, page 412, above); 3 *Collections*, I. 162–164; *N.C.*, VI. 55–58.

were feasted. In which time, saith he, I wished some to look to them, which notwithstanding, in this time, they scaped; and now he would employ men instantly to search all places for them, and within two or three days to convey them home. Besides he profest that he desired them not, and was sorry the governour should think he did. I objected, that he sent to beg one. He answered, that Sassamun, being sent by the governour with letters to Pequt, fell lame, and laying at his house, told him of a squaw he saw, which was a sachim's daughter, who while he lived was his, Miantunnomue's, great friend. He therefore desired, in kindness to his dead friend, to beg her, or redeem her.

Concerning his departure from the English, and leaving them without guides, he answered, first, that they had been faithful, many hundreds of them, (though they were solicited to the contrary,) that they stuck to the English in life or death, without which they were persuaded that Okace and the Mohiganeucks had proved false, (as he fears they will yet,) as also that they never had found a Pequt, and therefore, saith he, sure there was some cause. I desired to know it. He replied in these words, Chenock eiuse wetompatimucks? that is, Did ever friends deal so with friends? I urging wherein, he told me this tale: that his brother, Yotaash, had seized upon Puttaquppuunck-Quame and twenty Pequts and three-score squaws, they killed three and bound the rest, watching them all night, and sending for the English, delivered them to them in the morning. Miantunnomu (who according to promise came by land with two hundred men, killing ten Pequts in their march) was desirous to see the great sachim, whom his brother had taken, being now in the English houses, but (saith he) I was thrust at with a pike many times, that I durst not come near the door. I objected, he was not known. He and others affirmed, he was, and asked, if they should have dealt so with Mr. Governour. I still denied, that he was known, etc. Upon this, he saith, all my company were disheartened, and they all and Cutshamoquene desired to be gone; and yet, saith he, two of my men (Wagonckwhut and Maunamoh) were their guides to Sesquankit from the river's mouth.

Sir, I dare not stir coals, but I saw them to [be] much disregarded by many, which their ignorance imputed to all, and thence came the misprision, and blessed be the Lord, things were not worse.

I objected, they received Pequts and wampom without Mr. Governour's consent. Caunounicus replied, that although he and Miantunnomu had paid many hundred fathom of wampom to their soldiers, as Mr. Governour did, yet he had not received one yard of beads nor a Pequt. Nor, saith Miantunnomu, did I but one small present from four women of Long Island, which were no Pequts, but of that isle, being afraid, desired to put themselves under my protection.

By the next I shall add something more of consequence, and which must cause our loving friends at Qunnihticut to be very watchful, as also, if you please, their grievances, which I have laboured already to answer, to preserve the English name; but now end abruptly with best salutes and earnest prayers for your peace with the God of peace and all men. So praying, I rest Your worship's unfeigned

ROGER WILLIAMS

All loving respects to Mrs. Winthrop and yours, as also to Mr. Deputy, Mr. Bellingham, theirs, and Mr. Wilson, etc.

RICHARD DAVENPORT TO JOHN WINTHROP[1]

To the Right Worthyly Honored Gouernor of Massachusets these present

POSSESION HOUSE[2] this 4th day of the week: Mo: 6th [*ca.* August 23, 1637]

HONORED SIR, My most humble and due respect to your worsh[i]p, Mr. Deputy, my colonell, with all the rest of our noble worthyes. Sir, the mesenger staying for vs I must make hast. How God hath dealt with vs, I doubt not but your worship, h[avin]g full intelligence by them from Block Iland; now since their departure, there came some Mohegens to the house, and brought the [hands] of a great Sachem, as they said greater then Sasacus, hee beeing Momonotuk Samm, a mighty fellow for curradge, and one that I know by some experience his desperatenes in the swamp: for as I gather by the description of him, and also the Indians report that slew him, that hee sayd hee kild one in the swamp, shooting him in the belley; and another he killd with arrows, which was my selfe, but, blessed be God, wee all liue. 2 days after this, the same Indians kild another, who was then runn away from Sasacus: hee sayd hee thought that Sasacus was kild; for that Monowhoak had beset

---

[1] Connecticut State Library; 5 *Collections*, I. 248–250; 5 *Collections*, IX. 1–3. At the time this volume was in preparation, the original manuscript of this letter (the latter portion of which is in a mutilated condition) was, due to the exigencies of wartime, not accessible. The two versions of the letter previously printed in the *Collections* vary in some details, although both are obviously taken from the same manuscript. The text as given here is taken from 5 *Collections*, I, except for the endorsement, which is found only in the version printed in 5 *Collections*, IX.

[2] "Possession House" was the house built by Stoughton on or near what was later the site of Fort Trumbull in New London.

the wigwam where they weere, and soe fell vpon them, and this man lying at the doore rann away: but what creditt to giue to it wee knew not. 2 days since I went vp to the head of this river with 20 men to cut corne or gather beans, and comming thither I found a great company of Mohegens, who were returned to their countrey, about 500 of men, wo[men] and children. They were som what fearefull at first, but after spoke with vs and loueingly intertained vs. They tell for certaine that Sasacus is killd, as the former suspected, and 40 men with him, and som women. 6 men are escaped, whereof Momoonotuk is one. I perseaue the Indians would bee glad to make women[1] of all the Pecotts now, except the sachems and capt. and murtherers: but them they would kill. They seeme to feare the Naregansick men, but hope the English will not suffer them to be wronged. Capt. Stoughton is gone a weeke since to Conetecutt Plantations, and I heare that the sachems of Long Iland doe now wayt for him, with their tribute, at the riuer mouth: I suppose, vnder fauour, this place will not proue good for a plantation, so farr as I can judge, haueing seene the greatest part of the countrey, but I must extoll Qenepiake and Marriadge Poynt; but this I know you heare of. I see not what busines heere will bee for many men long. I know not Capt. Stoughtons mind, till his returne, about marching by the Nipnets home. My capt. and my selfe are for it.

[*torn*] of our souldiers haue noe mind to worke, and how they would fight I know not, the[y] murmure much for butter and cheese, etc: but I hope God will giue so much wisdome to indeauor their passifieing: I confesse some spirits heere will trouble a patient man.

My capt. humbly saluts you with the counsell; for my selfe, deare Sir, I blesse God I too am wholly recouered of my hurts, onely some strength I want. My capt. desireth some goose shott by the first.

I h[o]pe we shall take order that the Indians shall gather the corne that is heere to halfes. Thus with my pr[a]ye[rs for] your wors[hi]p and [k]ind respect to [Mr. W]illson, I humbly cease [   ] euer at [y]our wors[hi]ps com[mand]

RICHARD DAUENPORT

The Naregansik com not [   ]: onely one which I tooke when the compa[ny] was at Blok Il[and] going downe the R[   ] on vs and makin[g] [   ].

[*Endorsed:*] Received 6. 25. 1637.

---

[1] In the margin: "slaves."

SIR FERDINANDO GORGES TO SIR HENRY VANE,
JOHN WINTHROP, AND OTHERS[1]

To my much respected freindes Henry Vane, John Winthropp, John Haines,
John Humfrey and John Dudley Esquiers give theis with speed[2]

MAIE IT PLEASE YOU, having receaved severall lettres from my Servant
Vines, and others, of the generall dislike conceaved against Mr. Cleeves for
having to doe with anie my affaires, by reason (as it is affirmed) of the miscarriage of him, as well towardes myselfe in particuler, as the wronges hee
offered them by his misreports to mee of theire miscarriage in theire places,
whereby hee hath intruded himselfe into my good opinion soe far forth, as to
bee joyned with you in matters of soe great trust being soe vnworthey: which
complaint of theires hath so far forth prevailed with mee (if it bee soe) as to
desire your favourable excuse, and to give my order to my Servant Vines for
the righting of mee; and vindicating of himselfe, and the rest, taking an ordinary Course for the farther questioning thereof, and to proceed therein
according as it shalbee found of more, or lesse, consequence, which I referr
vnto your Judgments (to whome hee is to adresse himselfe for Justice) to
censure as to you it shall seeme good, vppon a full hearing, and due prooffe
made thereof. As for Vines I know his honesty to bee such as I could not
abandon him out of my affeccion as formerly I haue written, yet I conceived
itt not amisse to rancke him with the rest in the generall discharge, that it
might appeare there was noe partiallity vsed, nor respecte of persons, for
therein I spared not my Nephewe, whome I esteeme next my owne Children.
As for Vines, I intend hee shall still continue Deputie Governour, and soe
doe pray you to settle him as before hee was, and to joyne with him my
Nephewe Champernowne, and such others, as you shall receave notice to bee
fittest for such service. That thereby you maie avoid the troubles you may
otherwise bee put vnto by the maney trobbles that maie arise soe farr distant
from you. What resteth more to bee done in this, I referr to your best resolu-
cions, as tyme and occasion serves, wherein I feare I haue too much trenched
vppon your favours. But my trust is, as shall bee my endeavours, that I maie
attaine to the oppertunity to make you some kind of requitall, and that in
some nature to your good likinges. In the meane while let mee tell you, that

---

[1] W. 3. 90; 4 *Collections*, VII. 329–332. For Gorges, see *D.N.B.*; 4 *Collections*, VII. 329n.
[2] Vane, Winthrop, Haynes, Humfrey, and Dudley (Thomas, not John) had been designated
by Gorges as commissioners to govern his province of New Somersetshire in Maine and to manage his
servants and private affairs. *Journal*, I. 224.

being at London this last Terme, and daiely in Companey with the Lordes, I heard nothing of the Commission Cleeves assured mee was afoote, contrary to the expectacion I had thereof, vppon Confidence of Mr. Cleeves reporte to mee. By which meanes I was (I fear mee drawne to abuse you vnwillingly) by my certificate in his behalfe. But a little to excuse him therein, for that it might bee hee was soe perswaded vppon such promises as Moorton his Agent assured him, who since is wholely casheerd from intermedlinge with anie our affaires hereafter; but this I write to you in perticuler that you maie take private notice thereof, and howe much I am offended with my selfe for being over credulous of another, neither needes it seeme strang it should bee soe, Consideracion being had to the sincerity of one, and the fraude of others. But I will forbeare to say more in this Subiecte, and onely leave all to tyme and oppertunity, desiring the Assistance of the Most Highest to give mee power to doe what shall make most for his glorie, and the publique good of his Church, to whose sacred proteccion I committ you, with the assurance that I will approve my selfe Your true freind to serve yow

FERDE: GORGES

AISHTON PHILLIPPES 23° Augustij 1637

SIR MATTHEW BOYNTON TO JOHN WINTHROP[1]

To my uerie worthy friende John Winthorpe esqr. att Boston in the Masachusetts Bay in New England present this

SIR, itt will be a great deale of charg to send ouer more seruants or to make such prouisions as you speke of for Carts and Oxen and theyrfor I thinke that will be my best way which you propound to lett out my Cattle reseruing the whole increase for that I desire to preserue. Sir I will wholie relye upon you for your direction, since you haue giuen me leaue to be soe bould with you, and what you would chuse to doe for your selfe if your case were mine, is that which I desire you would direct for me, and if the Lord giue me leaue to see your Contrie I shall then endeauour my selfe to acknowledg all your kindnesses: in the meane while I rest Your much engaged friend

MATT. BOYNTON

Sep. 9th [1637]

William Spofferd I hope will be carefull ouer the Cattle if they be letten forth as you thinke itt will be conuenient.

---

[1] W. 3. 42; 4 *Collections*, VII. 168.

ROGER WILLIAMS TO JOHN WINTHROP[1]

For his much honoured Mr. Governour these

MUCH HONOURED SIR, I was fearefull that those dead hands were no pleasing sight (otherwise then a remarkeable vengance had seazed vpon the first murtherer of the English, Wauphanck) yet I was willing to permit what I could not aproue, least if I had buried the present myselfe, I should haue incurd suspicion of pride and wronged my betters, in the natiues and others eyes: I haue alwaies showne dislike to such dismembring the dead and now the more, (according to your desire) in your name.

I was allso fearefull that mine owne hand (having no commission from my heart (which is not in mine hand but in the hand of its Maker, the Most High) to write you ought of mine owne returne in spiritualls) I say fearefull that mine owne might not be so gratefull and pleasing to you: but being calld vpon by your message and your loue, (your paper), I am emboldened.

Concerning the Pequts, the souldiers here related to me that Okace the Mohiganie Sachim had about 300 men with him on Pequt river, some 16 mile from the howse, which I belieue are most of them Pequts and their confederates the Wunnashowatuckoogs and their Inlanders (whome he charged vnder paine of death not to come to Canounicus) and with whome he hath made himselfe great. This man is but a litle Sachim, and hath not aboue 40 or 50 Mohiganeucks which as the English told me were all he could make.

It is generally confirmed that Thomas Stanton (as himselfe allso confest to me at my howse) was grossly cousend and deluded by one Wequashcuck (a Nayantaquit Sachim) who sheltred 4 Pequts Sachims and 60 Pequts at Long Iland where now they are, where peace was made with promise from the natiues not to permit one Pequt: yet Wequashcuck marrying Sasacous his mother hath thus deceaved you. This Wequashcuck was the man (to my knowledge) that sheltred Audsah, the murthrer of Mr. Oldham, and kept his head so long vpon his shoulders: yet to this man Thomas Stanton (as it appeares) did to much listen, slighting, I feare, to much the Nanhiggonsicks.

I find our Neighbours very eager to pursue these 4 Sachims and the 60 Pequts there. I presse them to patience till Mr. Governours mind be knowne, and Miantunnomu (to my knowledge) doth all he can to restreine them, or els long since they had bene there. They plead that Mr. Governour may please to accompanie, or send himselfe against them, but can not by any

---

[1] Original not located; 4 *Collections*, VI. 207–210; *N.C.*, VI. 60–65.

article in the leauge bind them to suffer so many of their enemies in a knot so neere them.

I presse them to humane consideracion of so much blood spilt, they answere if they haue the Sachims heads they will make the rest Nanhiggonsicks, and for the Long Ilanders themselues and Wequashcuck, they will not medle with them, because of the peace Mr. Stoughton made with them.

Concerning the ketles: Miantunnomu answeres, that he hath bene much wronged by the reports of enemies and false friends to whom some of vs (as he saith) haue hearkned before himselfe.

He saith he never knew of more then 2, one of which the English vsed at the howse, and the other as he heares is at the Fort still: he sayth he hath many of his owne, and in deede when I came first hiether I saw neere 10 or 12 which himselfe and Canounicus had.

He repaid me with a grievance about a Pequt canow which he desired might be ordred by your owne hearing, but it was denyed him: his plea seemes very faire: thus this brother Yoteash having taken the great Sachim (Puttaquappuonckquame who was kept in the pinnace aliue sometime) tooke his canow, which, sayth he, the English Captaines sitting all togeather were very willing vnto: this canow Mr. Stoughton afterwards brought about homeward: Miantunnomu and his brother claime it: twas denyed: he requested that it might be left at my howse till Mr. Governours mind was knowne. Capt. Stoughton would not yeald, but desired him to go along to me, but sayth he, I would not trust my selfe with him, seing he would not stand to Mr. Governours determination about the canow: I would not haue mencioned this least it might provoke Mr. Stoughton or any: but I know to whome I intimate it: and I haue prettie well appeased the matter allready.

He answeres all I can obiect to him with this: let Mr. Governour haue the hearing of it: I will rest in his word, and obiecting to him in the particular before divers, that the English complaine he was proud, he desired that I would present to Mr. Governour these particulars, that he had cause to mainteine his right, because, the Qunnihticut English equalld Okace and the Mohiganeucks with himselfe and his men.

Whereas sayth he these Mohiganeucks are but as a twig, we are as a great tree.

They fell to the English but last yeare, we haue bene euer friends etc.

Okace and his men had a hand in the death of all the English and fought against the Rivers mouth (at Qunnihticut) we never kild nor consented to the death of an English man.

When the Dutchmen and we fought with the Pequts the Mogianeucks ioyned against vs.

When Capt. Endicot came against the Pequts the Mohiganeucks receaved the Pequt women and children and kept them, while the men fought with him etc.

Okace brought presents to Canounicus, and Miant[unnomu], yet at the same time kild 2 of his women treacherously.

They fell to the English this yeare in feare or other policie, and we, (sayth he) haue continued friendship and loue euer since they landed. Thus he pleaded etc., and yet proud and covetous and filthy they are etc. only I was willing to gratifie him in this, because as I know your owne heart studies peace, and their soules good, so your wisedome may make vse of it vnto others who happily take some more pleasure in warrs: The blessed God of Peace be pleased to giue you peace within, at home, and round about you abroad, So prayes Your worships vnfainedly respectiue

ROGER WILLIAMS

[September 9, 1637]

To Mrs. Wintrop, Mr. Deputie, Mr. Bellingham etc. all respectiue salutacions.

I haue at present returned Rich. Collicuts Pequt girle which Miantunnomu found out, and desired me to send home,[1] with promise of further enquiring.

[*Endorsed:*] Mr. Williams, 7: 9: 1637.

ROGER WILLIAMS TO RICHARD COLLICOTT[2]

For his kind friend Mr. Richard Collicut, these

KIND FRIEND, I lately wrote vnto you: once when I sent home your boy, and againe when I sent the girle: Concerning either of them, if you be minded to put either of them away, I desire to giue you your desire: otherwise I wish you much Comfort in the keeping of them.

As I am many wayes indebted, so I haue many debts comming to me   I take it very lovingly that you please to helpe me concerning Mr. Ludlow   I

---

[1] Cf. Roger Williams to Richard Collicott, September 12, 1637, immediately following.
[2] Library of Congress; 4 *Collections*, VI. 211; *N.C.*, VI. 59.

haue accordingly sent you power to deale in it   In 3 respects I request you to be serious and punctuall.

1st It is now an old debt, especially my Cow was mine left behind 4 yeares agoe for me in Virginia and some goats.

2ndly I have requested the last yeare divers to helpe me and gaue them power, but all failed me, so that I shall haue cause to be thanckfull to you aboue others.

3rdly If his payment like you I shall request you first to satisfie your selfe, and shall remaine Yours most vnfained

ROGER WILLIAMS

[September 12, 1637]

I shall gladly satisfie not only your charge, but allso your time and paines in dealing with Mr. Ludlow.

POWER OF ATTORNEY FROM ROGER WILLIAMS TO RICHARD COLLICOTT[1]

MEMORAND: that I, Roger Williams of New Providence, doe constitute and ordaine Richard Collicut of Dorchester my true and lawfull Atturney, for me and in my name to aske or demaund, sue or arrest, acquit or release George Ludlow of all such summes of money or goods as are due unto me from him. per me

ROGER WILLIAMS

This 12th of the 7th mon. (commonly calld) 1637

WILLIAM HOOKE AND THOMAS BRADBURY TO JOHN WINTHROP[2]

To the Right Wor[shi]p[fu]ll John Winthop Esqr. Gouernour of the Masichewsetts these present be delivered in Baye

Wee haue found it written (Right Worshipfull) that where noe vision is the people perrish. The Consederation where of forceth vs to become humble

---

[1] Original not located; 4 *Collections*, VI. 211; *N.C.*, VI. 60.
[2] W. 3. 51; 4 *Collections*, VII. 195–196. For Hooke and Bradbury, see 4 *Collections*, VII. 195n.

sutours to your worshipp, to solicite in our behalfe some godly Minister, to pitty the miserable estate and Condicion wee are in for want of those blessed meanes which the lord hath appointed to the fortherance of our saluation: hoping he will stirre vp your hart with all conueniant speede to supply (out of your abundance) vs his poore people heere whoe are almost starued for want of the spirituall foode of our soules. Wee shall not neede to vse many arguments to moue you; whoe canne better apprehend our misery, then wee expresse itt. Maye it please you Mr. Blackstone haeth formerly promised to come and liue with vs, but wee nowe finde by his answers to some, that his hopes are fedd with the expectation of farre greater profitt by his husbandry there; then hee should haue had by his ministry here, which God only knowes. Nowe Sir for the accommodation of a Minister thus farr wee canne goe at present; hee shall haue a very good howse, with an Inclosure to it for the planting of corne, and allsoe a stipend of 20*li* per annum; which wee hope in a short time wilbe doubled if not trebled. Neather will wee seeke to tye him to any other manor of dissipline then what shalbe found approueable out of word of God: which must be the touchtone and triall of all our actions. good Sir lett not any former scandals which haue beene (partly iust and partly vniust raysed vppon vs) be any obstacles to hinder the good and proffitt which by this meanes may through Gods blessinge betide our poore soules heere after. What wee haue spoken vouchsafe to take into your serious Consideration: and affectually answer vs by the ferst opportunity; soe shall wee praye for a continuall increse of Gods fauour towards you, in derecting all your accions to his glory to home wee leaue you and rest Your humble Suppliants euer to command

WILLIAM HOOKE
THOMAS BRADBURY

ACCOMENTICUS the 13th day of September Anno 1637

THOMAS HOOKER TO JOHN WINTHROP[1]

To the right worship[full] John Wynthropp Esquier Governour [of] Matheshusetts,
deliver

RIGHT WORSHIP[FULL] AND MUCH HONERD IN OUR BLESSED SAVIOUR, By returne of our speciall freinds, I could not but returne a thankfull acknowl-

---

[1] W. Au. 68; 2 *Proceedings*, VI. 425.

edgment of all your former kyndenesses, and your last loving entertayne-
ment, and also to give you an account of such businesses, which were in part
commended to our care, touching the ripenin[g of] such passages of the
Synod,[1] which were of wayt and worthy record and consideration: you may
[be] pleased therfore to vnderstand, that Mr. Higgynson, who was the scribe
in assembly, hath imployd his tyme since his coming, to transcribe such
things which were of vse, but because the things were many and his tyme
short, our freinds returning so speedily, he could not accomplish much, but
hath taken his papers with him downe to the mouth of the river, whither his
occasions call him for the present, and from whence he will send you such
particulars as he shall perfectly write out, and that by the soonest conveyance   The good Lord prosper these begynnings for the setling of peace and
truth with you in all his churches. I dayly expect many stratagems of Satan
to be plotted and practised: All that I would crave leave to present to your
iudicious apprehension is that in short: I have ever iudged it, in cases of difficulty which must come to scanning, most safe, to attend nothing for ground
of determination, but that which will cary an undeniable evidence to an im-
partiall iudge: he that desires multitude of arguments to cary a cause, and
therfore take [*illegible*] the weaknes of some dishonor and [*illegible*] the wayt of
the rest: For execution let it be so secret and suddayne that it cannot be
prevented, so resolute and vncontrolable that it may tak off hope from the
adversary that it can be resisted: and this damps opposition and prevents
hazard. men will not attempt resistance when ther is no expectation to
attayne what they do attempt, whereas opennes and fayntnes of resolution
provokes men to oppose and to adventure vpon hazard in opposition: you
will not be offended that I shot my bolts, your loving acceptance adds encoragement in this kynd. The Lord steare your course for you and give a
blessing to all your indeavors and godly proceedings   So he wisheth who
rests in all thankfulnes Yours in all due respect

T. HOOKER

[*Ca.* October, 1637]

---

[1] The Synod called by the Massachusetts General Court to consider the Antinomian controversy was held in Cambridge from August 30 to September 22, 1637.

AGREEMENT BETWEEN JOHN WINTHROP, JR., AND SAMUEL DUDLEY[1]

An agreement made betweene John Winthrop of Ipswich
Esqr: and Sam: Dudley for the wintring of nyne Cowes

It is agreed that Sam: Dudley shall winter nine cowes of Sir Mathew
Boitons, with good hay and howsing at Chebacco; and for the consideration
of the same he is to receive three cow calfes: after this manner following: that
if the nyne cowes shall have but 3 cow calfes, then the said Sam: Dudley is to
haue them; but if more then three the said Sam: is to haue the three worst:
but if the cowes haue not 3 cow calfes; then to haue 2 bul cafes instead of a
cow calfe: and it is further agreed that when these calfes shall haue eight or
nyne weekes sucked: then to be divided: In witnes whereof the parties aboue
haue set to their hands.

                                                    JOHN WINTHROP
8: 18: 1637   SAM: DUDLEY
Witness
    SAMUEL SYMONDS
    MATH: ROGERS

ROGER WILLIAMS TO JOHN WINTHROP[2]

To his much honoured Mr. Governour these

SIR, Some while since you were pleased to desire me to signifie to the
Sachims, the promise of the Block Ilanders to your selues, and therefore their
exemption from all other Submission and Tribute. Their answere was that
as they had left them to Mr. Governour formerly vpon Mr. Oldames death
so haue they done since, and haue had no other dealing with them then for
the getting of the head of Audsah the chiefe murtherer: as allso that they
vnderstand the 100 fathom of beades to be yearely paid to Mr. Governour,
in which respect they haue bene farr from desiring a bead from them, and doe
acknowledge them to be wholy Mr. Governours Subiects.

Sir I heard that there is now at Pequat with the Monahiganeucks one
William (Baker I thinck his name is) who was pursued, as is said, by the Eng-

---

[1] Essex Institute.
[2] W. 2. 102; 4 *Collections*, VI. 214–217; *N.C.*, VI. 66–69.

lish of Qunnihticut for vncleanenes with an Indian Squaw, who is now with
child by him. He hath there gotten another Squaw and lies close vnknowne
to the English   They say he came from a trading howse which Plymmouth
men haue at Qunnihticut, and can speake much Indian: If it be he, when I
lived at Plymmouth, I heard the Plymmouth men speake much of his evill
Course that way with the Natiues.

The occasion that our neighbours know of him was this: Some 8 dayes
since 6 Nanhiggonsick men were comming from Qunnihticut, and by the
way fell vpon some Pequts who were rescued out of their hands by the
Monahiganeucks, who allso bound those 6 Nanhiggonsicks many dayes togeather at Monahiganick (vpon Pequat river where this William was) and
spoild them of their Coats and what els they had.

The Sachims and the men are greatly incensed, affirming that they can
not but revenge this abuse offerd to their men; yet haue I got this promise
that they will not doe ought without Mr. Governours advice.

Sir I haue long heard, and these 6 men affirme, that there are many of the
scattered Pequts randevouzed with Okace the Monahiganic Sachim and
Wequash the Pequt, who being employed as one of the guides to the English
in their late Warrs, is growne rich and a Sachim with the Pequts: and hath 5
or 6 runnawayes. There are all the Runnawayes harboured (which vpon long
and diligent inquirie) I am certaine and confident of, and can giue good
assurance that there is not one amongst all the Nanhiggonsicks.

Mr. Stoughton hath bene long assured that *Meiksah* Canounicus eldest Sonn
hath his Squaw, but having enquired it out I find she was never at the Nanhiggonsicks, but is married to one *Meiksomp* a Sachim of Nayantaquit, which
being neerer to Pequt is more friendly to the Pequts: and where as I heare
that Wequashcuck (who long sheltred Audsah and so grossly deluded Tho:
Stanton in the late warrs) hath filled many baskets with beades from Pequts
Sachims and 120 Pequts which he sheltreth now at Nayantaquit.

Okace the Monahiggon and Wequashcuck were lately at Long Iland, from
whence some few dayes since Okace caried away 40 Pequts to Monahiganick
and Wequashcuck 30 to Nayantaquit.

While I write, Miantunnomu is come to my howse and affirmeth the same:
professing if I would advise him he would goe over to Mr. Governour to
acquaint the Governour that Caunonicus and himselfe haue no hand in
these passages. He askes me often if he may safely goe, and I assure him if he
haue an honest heart he neede not feare any deceit or Treacherie amongst the
English: So I thinck within a day or 2 he will be comming towards you.

He tells me what I had not heard that of those Pequts to whome at the

first by my hand you were pleased to giue life, but 7 came to them of which
5 allso long since are gone to Monahiganick.

Sir I forget not your loving remembrance of me concerning Mr. Ludlowes
debt: I yet know not where that Tobacco is: but desire if Mr. Cradocks
Agent Mr. Jolly would accept it, that it may be delivered to him in part of
some payments for which I haue made over my howse to Mr. Mayhew.

Sir your servant Repriue lodged here 2 nights, and Miantunnomu tells me
that 5 dayes since he lay a night with him and is gone to Block Iland: He is
very hopefully improoved since I first saw him: and am bold to wish that he
might now take his last farewell of his friends, to whome you would be rather
pleased to giue leaue to visit him at Boston, for you can not belieue how hard
it is for him to escape much evill and especially vncleanenes while he is with
them. The good Lord be pleased to blesse him to you, and to make you a
blessing to him and many others. [*Torn*] runn headlong (without once hearing
of it) into [*torn*] everlasting burnings. So prayes dayly Your Wo[rshi]ps
vnfaigned

R: WILLIAMS

[*Ca.* October 26, 1637]

To Mrs. Wintrop Mr. Deputie Mr. Bellingham and theirs respectiue
Salutacions.

ROGER WILLIAMS TO JOHN WINTHROP[1]

For his much honoured Mr. Gouvernour, these

The last of the week, I think the 28th of the 8th [1637]

SIR, This bearer, Miantunnomu, resolving to go on his visit, I am bold to
request a word of advice from you concerning a proposition made by Caunounicus and himself to me some half year since. Caunounicus gave an island
in this bay to Mr. Oldam, by name Chibachuwese, upon condition, as it
should seem, that he would dwell there near unto them. The Lord (in whose
hands all hearts are) turning their affections towards myself, they desired me
to remove thither and dwell nearer to them. I have answered once and again,
that for present I mind not to remove; but if I have it from them, I would
give them satisfaction for it, and build a little house and put in some swine, as
understanding the place to have store of fish and good feeding for swine. Of

---

[1] Original not located (see note 1, page 412, above); 3 *Collections*, I. 165; *N.C.*, VI. 70–71.

late I have heard, that Mr. Gibbons, upon occasion, motioned your desire and his own of putting some swine on some of these islands, which hath made me since more desire to obtain it, because I might thereby not only benefit myself, but also pleasure yourself whom I more desire to pleasure and honour. I spake of it now to this sachim, and he tells me, that because of the store of fish, Caunounicus desires that I would accept half, (it being spectaclewise, and between a mile or two in circuit, as I guess,) and he would reserve the other; but I think, if I go over, I shall obtain the whole. Your loving counsel, how far it may be inoffensive, because it was once (upon a condition not kept) Mr. Oldam's.[1] So, with respective salutes to your kind self and Mrs. Winthrop, I rest Your worship's unfeigned, in all I may,

ROGER WILLIAMS

PETITION OF JOHN UNDERHILL TO THE GOVERNOR AND ASSISTANTS OF MASSACHUSETTS[2]

To the righte Wor[shipful] the Gouernour and Assistants in this present Courte

I am sorry that there is so iust occasion of offence giuen in this Patten by them of Salem, not only vnto vs, which are Inferiour vnto the Gouernour and Assistantes, but allso vnto the whole Courte, and the Authoritie that belonges vnto you, in that they haue appropriated vnto themselues without order that which properly belonges vnto you, as may appeare by the relation of this petition. To lett you vnderstand the circumstance of the offence, it is this. How they haue of their owne appoyntment made them a Captaine, Lieutennant, and Ensigne, and after such a manner as neuer was hearde of in any Schoole of warre; nor in no Kingedome vnder heauen; the Company standeinge togither, as they were ordered, the Constable comes vp to the Company takeinge the Authoritie of the maiestrate vpon him; delivers the partisan to Mr. Turner and tells him, that he is chosen Lieutennant to this Company and so bids, God giue him joye; Mr. Turner vnderstandinge himselfe better then he that broughte it, would not accepte of the place without order of Courte; Wee may thinke it strange that theire should be suche officers made in the Patten, without order, eyther from the Gouernour, or from the Courte;

---

[1] Miantunnomoh and Canonicus sold Chibbachuweset (Prudence Island) to Williams and Winthrop on November 1, 1637, for twenty fathom of wampum and two coats. *Collections of the Rhode Island Historical Society*, III. 29.

[2] W. 3. 43; 4 *Collections*, VII. 175–177.

Intreatinge the Courte to take it into their wise Considerations: For my parte, if there should not be a reformation in this disordered practise, I would not acknowledge such Officers. If Officers should be of no better esteeme then for Constables to place them, and martiall discipline to proceede disorderly, I would rather lay downe my Commande then to shame so noble a Prince, from whome wee came; thus Intreatinge the Courte, that they woulde both satisfie themselus and vs in rightinge this Cause, I rest Yours at Command in the Lord

CAPTAINE VNDERHILL

I desire to giue one touche withall concerninge your forgetfullnes of the Gouernour in not vpholdinge him, and supplyinge him with a watche, which may tend to the preseruation of his life, and all our good, besydes his further Encouragement. The Course which you mighte take in this Case may be this, without any great diffyculty to send a Coople from Charlestowne, a Coople from Rockesberry, and Boston to make vp the compleat number. I thinke I am in Conscience bounde to enforce this vpon the Courte seeinge it tendes to his preseruation and further Encouragement, his life beinge more pretious to vs then many others and therfore the care of it to be preferd before so little labour and trouble as such a busines imports. Such was the Care of the Children of Israell towards their Gouernour, that they esteemed his life worth tenn thousand of the common people; secondly the practise of other Countries commends this Course vnto vs, who are so prouydent in such Cases for the vpholdinge of there gouermente with peace and safety; I desire to putt you in minde of theise thinges, leaste wee smarte for our securitie, not know-inge what time may bringe forthe; and thirdly wee may take an example from our neighbours of Plimmoth that are not negligent in theise affaires:[1] and so I leaue theise thinges to your Consideration, desireinge to be excused in any thinge that you may except againste, and Intreateinge the Lord that he would direct your heartes in all thinges for the best, and prosper what shall be vndertaken for his glory, and the good of this people.

[*Ca.* November, 1637]

[*Endorsed by Governor Winthrop:*] Capt. Vnderhill his Petition etc.

---

[1] The Plymouth General Court had ordered on June 7, 1637, that "there shalbe a guard of twelue musketiers to attend the person of the Gouernor on the Lords day, and other tymes when it shalbe required." *Records of the Colony of New Plymouth*, Nathaniel B. Shurtleff, Editor, 1 (Boston, 1855), 62. The Massachusetts General Court took a similar step on November 15, 1637, when if

JOHN WINTHROP'S ESSAY
AGAINST THE POWER OF THE CHURCH
TO SIT IN JUDGMENT ON THE CIVIL MAGISTRACY[1]

That a Church hath not power to Call any Civill Magistrate, to give Account of his Juditiall proceedinge in any Court of Civill Justice: and what the Church may doe in such Causes.

1: The Scripture affords neither Rule nor example of any such power in the Church, but diverse against it: for Christ disclameth it, where he asketh who made him a Judge of dividing Inheritances But if they should have this power, they must of necessitye, be Judges of such thinges: for putt Case, a Magistrate give sentence against a member of a Church, vpon a title of Inheritance, or in an Action of debt or Trespasse, and he beinge offended with the magistrate for it (as supposing it to be vniust) bringes him to the Church for it, then must the Church trye this title, and examine the matter of debt or Trespasse, with all the circumstances of it de integro: else how shall they be able to Judge, whither the magistrate hath given offence to his brother or not?

2: By occasion heerof the Church should become the supreame Court in the Jurisdiction, and capable of all Appeales, and so in trueth meerly Antichrist, by beinge exalted aboue all, that is called God etc:

3: If this were allowed, then the Church should have power to Judge, where it wants meanes to finde out the Trueth: for the Churche cannot call in forrein witnesses: nor examine witnesses vpon Oath, nor require the view of the Records of the Court: all which may be needfull for findinge out the trueth in many Cases.

4: To examine a Civill businesse, in a waye of Judicature (though it ayme not at outward punishment) is an exercise of such Aut[horit]ye as Christ forbidds his disciples: the Lords of the Gentiles exercise Aut[horit]ye etc.: but you shall not doe so.

---

ordered that "two sufficient men should be kept in armes to guard and attend the Governor at the charge of the country." *Records of Massachusetts*, 1. 209.

[1] W. 1. 121; *L. and L.*, 11. 211–214. The Governor wrote in his Journal (1. 256), after his account of the sentencing of Wheelwright and Mrs. Hutchinson in November, 1637, as follows: "After this, many of the church of Boston, being highly offended with the governor for this proceeding, were earnest with the elders to have him called to account for it; but they were not forward in it, and himself, understanding their intent, thought fit to prevent such a public disorder, and so took occasion to speak to the congregation to this effect." The occasional parallels between certain phrases in the abstract Winthrop gives of his speech and those of the document here printed suggest that the two were composed at about the same time.

5: Christ his kingdome is not of this world, therefore his officers in this king-dome, cannot Juditially enq[uir]e into affaires of this world.

6: Such power would confounde those Jurisdictions, which Christ hath made distinct: for as he is Kinge of Kings and Lord of Lords he hath sett up another kingdome in this worlde, wherein <u>magistrates are his officers, and they are to</u> <u>be accountable to him, for their miscarriages in the waye and order of this</u> <u>kingdome.</u>

7: This would sett Christ against himselfe in his owne Ordinances, without any ordinary meanes of redress and so there must needs be a defecte in his dispensation which cant be: for if the Church (supposinge the Civill magis-trate had intrenched vpon Christs sp[irit]uall Kingdome) should excom-[munica]te them: and againe the magistrate (supposinge the Officers of the Church had vsurped vpon his Civill Aut[horit]ye) should imprison or banishe them: now is Christs kingdom divided, one Ordinance against another, not to moderation but to destruction: and heere is no menes to reconcile them: but if the Rule of Christ be observed, Resist not evill, and submitt yourselues to the higher powers, now is the honor and safetye of . . . .[1]

It was Luthers Counsell to the Anabaptists (from the example of himself and others of those Churches) that thoughe their magistrates did oppresse and iniure them, yet they should praye for them, and Commende them, and seeke to winne them by gentlenesse etc, and when the Church shall binde kings in chaines and nobles in fetters of iron (ps: 149) (which cannot be meant of Church Censures, for it shalbe in vengeance and Judgment foretold against the heathen) then the meek shalbe beautified with salvation: then Kinges shalbe their nursinge fathers etc: (Esay 49.23) they shall bowe downe to hir and licke the dust of her feet: and none shall hurt or destroye in all the holy mountaine (Isay 65.25): So that the wisdome, piety, and meeknesse of the Church shall winne the hearts of Kinges etc: and binde them so to her in the power of the Gospell, as they shall love the verye earth she treads on; they shall beare that Reverence to her, as she shall need feare no hurt from them, no more than a Child doth from the nurse: therefore no need to binde them by Churche Censures: they were other kinges whom he sayth the people should curse in the dayes of their Calamitye; and yet when they should Curse their Kings, he sayth they should Curse their God allso. (Esay 8.21:) a man may not say to a Kinge, thou art wicked: nor call Princes vngodly. (Job: 34.18).

I denye not but that a private person may privatly reprooue a magistrate

---

[1] At this point there is at least one leaf of text missing.

offendinge, but he may not doe it publ[icly]: except he be publ[icly] called, to beare witnesse to the Trueth, as Stephen was.

I Consent allso, that magistrates should beare with the faylinges of their christian brethren, when in tender care of the publ[ic] good and their honor and comfort, they chance to exceede the Limitts of their lib[er]ty: but such breth[ren] must then see, and not Justifie their faylings: for Christ bidds us not, forgive our brother, till he saye, it repenteth him.

[*Ca.* November, 1637]

JOHN WINTHROP TO MARGARET WINTHROP[1]

For Mrs. Winthrop at Boston

MY SWEET WIFE, I prayse God I am in good health, peace be to thee and our familye, so I kisse thee, and hope shortly to see thee: farewell.
Hasten the sendinge awaye Skarlett, and gatheringe the Turnips.

[JOHN WINTHROP]

[*Ca.* November, 1637]

JOHN WINTHROP TO MARGARET WINTHROP[2]

for Mrs. Winthrop at Boston

MY SWEET WIFE, So fitt an occasion must not passe without a token to thee. I prayse God I am well: the Lord blesse thee and all ours, so I kisse thee the second tyme farewell.

[JOHN WINTHROP]

[*Ca.* November, 1637]

JOHN WINTHROP TO MARGARET WINTHROP[3]

For mrs. Winthrop at her howse in Boston

SWEET HEART, I was unwillingly hindred from comminge to thee, nor am I like to see thee before the last daye of this weeke: therefore I shall want a

---

1 W. Au. 69; *L. and L.*, II. 217; Twichell, 185.
2 W. Au. 69; *L. and L.*, II. 217; Twichell, 186.
3 W. I. 120; *L. and L.*, II. 216; Twichell, 183–184.

band or 2 and cuffes. I pray thee also send me 6 or 7 leaues of Tobacco dried, and powdred. have care of thy selfe this colde weather, and speake to the folkes to keepe the goates well out of the Garden, and if my brother Peter hath not fetched awaye the sheepe ramme, let them looke him up and giue him meate, the green pease in the Garden etc. are good for him: If any lettres be come for me send them by this bearer. I will trouble thee no further. the Lorde blesse and keepe thee my sweet wife and all our familye: and send us a comfortable meetinge, so I kisse thee and loue thee euer and rest Thy faithfull husband

JO: WINTHROP

This 6th of the 9th 1637

ROGER WILLIAMS TO JOHN WINTHROP[1]

SIR, I acquainted this Indian Miantunnomu, with the Contents of your letter sent by him, who rests well perswaded that if it breake not first with them, the leauge is firme and lasting, and the English are vnfaigned.

I haue bought and paid for the Iland:[2] and because I desired the best Confirmacion of the purchase to your selfe that I could, I was bold to insert your name in the Originall here inclosed.

The 10 fathom of beades and one Coate you may please at leasure to deliver to Mr. Throckmorton: who will allso be serviceable in the Conveyance of Swine this way.

Your Natiue, Repriue, requests me to write a word for himselfe and another for the Sachim of Block Iland, Jacquontu.

For himself, he tells me when he departed hence being alone he wandred toward Neepmuck: At Nayantuquit Jvanemo said he was a spie from Mr. Governour and threatned to kill him, denied that there was Pequts saying (though Repriue saw many himselfe) that they were all gone to Monahiganick: So he came back in feare of his life to Wepiteammock (Miantunnomues brother in law) who lent him a Canow to Block Iland where he staid but 6 dayes.

From Jaquauntu, Block Iland Sachim, that he is preparing 13 fathom of white and 2 of blew to present you with about the 1st Month.

That they are greatly in feare of the Nayantaquit men who threaten them, in case the English fall vpon Nayantaquit.

---

[1] W. 2. 103; 4 *Collections*, VI. 217–219; *N.C.*, VI. 78–81.
[2] Prudence Island. See above, note 1, page 503.

I am glad to see this poore fellow Repriue carefull to please you, for he sayth you gaue him leaue for 28 dayes and though he could stay but 6 dayes where he desired to stay longest, yet he will not lye.

He sayth his brother goes along with him to stay some while, till the spring.

Sir There are 2 Pequt Squaus, brought by the Nanhiggansick allmost starued: viz: Mr. Coles his Natiue, and one guirle from Winisimmit: there was a 3rd (I thinck Mr. Blackstones) who had scapt before to Nayantaquit.

I promised these, if they would stay at my howse and not run away I would write that they might be vsed kindly. The biggest Mr. Coles his natiue complaines that she of all the natiues in Boston is vsed worst: is beaten with fire-sticks and especially by some of the Servants.

The litle one makes no Complaint of vsage, but sayth she was inticed by that other Squaw which I thinck was Mr. Blackstones.

I asked the biggest, who burnt her and why, she told me, Mr. Pen, because a fellow lay with her, but she saith, for her part she refused.

My humble desire is that all that haue those poore wretches might be ex-horted as to walke wisely and iustly towards them, so to make mercy eminent, for in that Attribute the Father of mercy most shines to Adams miserable of-spring.

Sir I feare I am tædious, yet I must craue leaue for a line more: I receaued a letter from some in Charlestowne (in speciall from one Benjamin Hubbard) intimating his and others desire (with my helpe and furtherance) to be my neighbours in some place neere adioyning: Mr. James hath not declared him-selfe to be one, but I guesse he is inclining to accompanye them.

On the Nanhiggonsick side, the natiues are populous on the side to Massa-chusetward Plymmouth men challenge, so that I presume if they come to the place where first I was Plymmouth will call them theirs: I know not the per-sons, yet in generall could wish (if it be either with Countenance or Conniv-ance) that these wayes might be more trod into these inland parts, and that amongst the multitudes of the Barbarous, the neighbourhood of some Eng-lish Plantation (especially of men desiring to feare God) might helpe and strengthen. I shall be thanckfull for a word of Advice, and beseeching the most holy and only wise ir mercy and goodnes to know and guide the Soules of his in this remote willdernes, and in this materiall desart, to discover gra-ciously the misticall where 1200 and 3 score dayes his S[ain]ts are hid. Revel. 12. I rest Your Wo[rshi]ps, sorry that I am not more yours, and neither of vs more the Lords.

R. WILLIAMS

To Mrs. Wintrop all respectiue remembrance.

I shall beg (this winter in some leasure) your helpe with my bad debtours James and Tho: Haukins, from whome as yet I get nought but words.

10th of the 9th [1637]

MARGARET WINTHROP TO JOHN WINTHROP[1]

To hir Honered husban these be delivered

DEARE IN MY THOUGTS, I blush to thinke howe much I have neclected the opertunytye of presenting my loue to you. sad thougts posses my sperits, and I cannot repulce them which makes me vnfit for any thinge wondringe what the lord meanes by all these troubles amounge us. shure I am that all shall worke to the best, to them that loue god, or rather are loued of hime. I know he will bring light out of obcuritye, and make his rituusnesse shine forth as clere as the noune daye. yet I finde in my selfe an aferce spiret, and a tremblinge hart, not so wilinge to submit to the will of god as i desyre. thear is a time to plant and a time to pul vp that which is planted, which I could desyre mite not be yet. but the lord knoweth what is best, and his wilbe done. but i will write no more, hopeinge to see thee to morro my best affections beinge commended to your selfe, the rest of our frends at Nuetone, I commit thee to god, Your louinge wife

                                                        MARGARET W.

Sad BOSTON [*ca.* November 15, 1637]

JOHN WINTHROP TO MARGARET WINTHROP[2]

For Mrs. Winthrop at Boston

DEARE [*torn*], I am still de[tai]ned from thee, but it is by the Lord, who hath a greater interest in me then thy selfe. when his worke is doone he will restore me to thee againe to our mutuall comfort: Amen. I thanke thee for thy sweet Lettre   my heart was with thee to have written to thee everye daye, but businesse would not permitt me. I suppose thou hearest much newes from hence: it may be some greiueous to thee: but be not troubled. I assure thee thinges goe well, and they must needs doe so, for God is with us, and

---

[1] W. 7A. 59; Savage (1825), I. 393; (1853), I. 471–472; *L. and L.*, II. 178–179; Twichell, 180–181.
[2] W. I. 119; *L. and L.*, II. 179; Twichell, 182.

thou shalt see a happy issue. I hope to be with thee to morrowe and a frende or 2 I suppose. so I kisse my sweet wife and rest Thine

Jo: WINTHROP

This 6: daye [*ca.* November 17, 1637]

ROGER WILLIAMS TO JOHN WINTHROP[1]

20th of the 9th [1637]

SIR, I rest thanckfully satisfied in your propounding of my Motion to the Court, and the Answere. (The earth is Jehovahs, and the Plenitude of it.) I am not a little glad that the Lot is fallen vpon a Branch of that Roote, in whose good (present and æternall both of Roote and Branches) I reioice. For his sake I wish it Ground and Grasse, and Trees, yet what vse so euer he please to make of it I desire he would not spare to make vse of me in any Service toward the Natiues on it or about it.

Miantunnomu in his Relations of passages in the Bay with you, thanckfully acknowledges to my selfe and others your loving Cariage to him and promiseth to send forth word to all Natiues to cease from Prudence Trees[2] etc. Since your letter I travelled vp to Nayantaquit by Land where I heard Repriue was: There the Sachim (to whome he adheres Wepiteammock) and the people related that he was gone to his wife to Monhiggin: Allso that he Wepiteammock had sent to Onkas advising and vrging their Returne but he could not prevaile, and that if Repriue come within his Reach he will send him (though alone without his wife) howeuer.

I travelled to Monhiggin and vnderstood that they were all at Pequt Nayantaquit, but Onkas not being at home (but at Newhaven) I could not doe ought.

Sir I haue often called vpon your debtour Joshua, but his ill advisednes of refusing my service and spending of his time vpon a howse and ground hath disabled him. Vpon this occasion of your louing proffer of the halfe of the debt (8*li*) to my selfe, I shall be vrgent with him to seeke some course of payment of the whole to your selfe from whome in recompence of any paines etc. I desire no other Satisfaction but your louing and wonted acceptation, yea, although the busines had bene effected: Sir I had almost bene bold to say my Thoughts what I would doe in this case were the Runnawayes mine, but I

---

[1] W. 2. 103; 4 *Collections*, VI. 220–221; *N.C.*, VI. 82–83.
[2] I.e., trees on Prudence Island, recently purchased from the Narragansetts by Williams and Winthrop.

will not more at present. If you shall please to require account of what my observacion hath taught me I shall readily yeald it in my next, euer begging Mercy and Truth to you and yours and my lo[ving] friends with you: The Lord Jesus returne vs all (poore Runnawayes) with weeping and supplications to seeke him that was nailed to the Gallowes, in him I desire to be (and mourne I am not) more Your Wo[rshi]ps vnfaigned

ROGER WILLIAMS

Sir I receaued 6 fathom of beades from Mr. Throcmorton, which though I will not returne, yet I account them yours in my keeping.

Sir I pray my respectiue remembrance to Mrs. Wintrop.

EMMANUEL DOWNING TO JOHN WINTHROP[1]

To the Ho[noura]ble his verie loving brother John Winthrop Governour of the Massachusetts in New Engl[and]

GOOD BROTHER, Its noe small Comfort to me that I haue hope ere long to enioy your Companie. I purpose God willing to sett forth hence in the begynning of Aprill at furthest, and to take your sonne hence with me.

For my provision of Corne I purpose to buy yt there. If you feare the rising of the prise, I pray buy some for me and promise payment in money at my Landing. Here hath been great Joy for your great victories, but farr more for vanquishing your erronious opinions then for conquering the Pequoits. Our best and worthyest men doe much mervile you did not banishe Whee[l]wright and Hutchinsons wife, but suffer them to sowe more sedition among you; Mr. Vanes ill behaviour there hath lost all his reputation here. I heare he is about to travaile into Germanie.

The Nobility, gentry and Comons of Scotland are in Confederatie and combyned soe strong togeather that they will admitt of noe Conformity to our good B[isho]ps orders. they haue throwne out the holy booke of Comon prayer, beaten theire B[isho]ps and torne theire sirplisses of the backs of the Ministers, and manie more outrages in this kinde wee heare of dayly.

The Dutch haue taken in Breda.

In August last mr. Tyndall paid me one hundreth pounds.

I follow your Councell in coming to the bay before I resolve where to pitche. I pray helpe me to hire or buy some howse (soe as I may sell yt againe if I shall remove) in some plantation about the Bay   thus for present I take

---

[1] W. 2. 25; 4 *Collections*, VI. 48–49.

leave and rest leaving you and your affayres to the blessed proteccion of the Almighty. Your assured loving brother

EM. DOWNINGE

21 9br 1637

I can give noe answ[er] to my Cosen Winthrops letter yet for his monie from the lords. I pray salute him and all my freinds.

ACKNOWLEDGMENT OF SAMUEL COLE AND OTHERS[1]

Whereas I Joyned in Preferring to the Court a Writing Called a Remonstrance, or Petition, I acknowledge it was ill done, and vnwarrantably, as Transgressing therein the Rule of due honour to Authority, and of Modesty, and Submission in Private Persons, and therefore I desire my name may be Put out of it.

SAMUELL COLE	THOMAS OLIVER
JOHN+BUTTON	OLIVER MELLOWES
ISACKE GROSSE	RICHARD FAYERBANKS
JOHN+BIGGS	JOHN OLIVER
THOMAS WARDELL	THOMAS MATSON
HENRY ELKIN	JOHN+DAVIS
ROBERT HULL	WILLIAM DINELEY
HUNG GUNDISON[2]	RICHARD COOKE
GEORGE BURDEN	ZAKEUS BOSWORTH
WM.+WARDELL	MATHIAS+FANCE
RICH. GRIDLYE[3]+	JAMES JOHNSON
WILLM.+TOWNSEND	ROBERT ROYS

[Ca. November 22, 1637]

---

[1] W. 4. 166; 5 *Collections*, I. 486. The document referred to in this and the following six acknowledgments is the "Remonstrance or Petition" submitted to the Massachusetts General Court in March, 1636/37, in behalf of the Reverend John Wheelwright, who was then on trial on charges of sedition arising out of his Fast-Day Sermon. On November 20, 1637, the General Court ordered that all those who had signed "the seditious libell" and had not hitherto recanted should, before the thirtieth of the month, be disarmed, surrendering "all such guns, pistols, swords, powder, shot, and match as they shalbee owners of, or have in their custody," unless they should "acknowledg their sinn in subscribing the seditious libell, or do not iustify it, but acknowledg it evill to two magistrates. . . ." All those whose acknowledgments are here printed were, with the exception of Ralph Hudson, included among those specifically designated to be disarmed. *Records of Massachusetts*, I. 211–212. The records of the General Court do not mention these acknowledgments.

[2] The handwriting of this signature appears to be the same as that of Robert Hull, just above. It is unlike that of another Hugh Gunnison signature in the Winthrop manuscripts.

[3] The handwriting of this signature is that of Governor Winthrop.

ACKNOWLEDGMENT OF EDWARD RAINSFORD AND OTHERS[1]

Whereas we ioyned in a writinge called a Remonstrance or Petition, wherin we did take vpon vs to censure the proceedings of the Court, we acknowledge we did ill and vnwarrantably therin, and humbly desire pardon therof

ED: RAYNSFORD
JACOB ELIOT
JOHN ODLIN

[*Ca.* November 22, 1637]

ACKNOWLEDGMENT OF JOHN CLARKE AND NICHOLAS PARKER[2]

For the writing called a petition which hath given Offence to the Court we had no hand in it, nor doe knowe the contents of it: and for the Aut[horit]y heere sett ouer vs: we acknowledge it to be of God, and that we are bound to be subiect therto while we live under it and that it were sinfull in vs to resist the same, or to goe about by any violent course to stoppe the Course of Justice.

JOHN CLARKE
NICHOLAS PARKER

[*Ca.* November 22, 1637]

ACKNOWLEDGMENT OF JAMES PENNIMAN AND OTHERS[3]

I doe affirme that I never consented to have my hande sett to the Petition which gave offence to the Court, neither doe I allowe of it but doe think it was doone without warrant.

JAMES PANIMAN
RICHARD WAITE

---

[1] W. 4. 166; 5 *Collections*, 1. 486. This acknowledgment, written on the verso of the document immediately preceding, is in the handwriting of Governor Winthrop. Immediately above it, also in the Governor's handwriting, is the following draft of another form of acknowledgment: "Whereas we had our hands to a writing called a Remonstrance or Petition, we acknowledge we did ill and vnwarrantably therin, as taking vpon us to censure the proceedings of the Court, which is not lawfull for private persons so to doe."

[2] W. 1. 118. This document is in the handwriting of Governor Winthrop.

[3] W. 1. 118. This document is in the handwriting of Governor Winthrop.

I never sawe the said Petition, and I doe disalowe of it as evill and vnwarrantable.

JAMES BROWNE

[*Ca.* November 22, 1637]

ACKNOWLEDGMENT OF RALPH HUDSON[1]

Whereas I Joyned in preferring to the Court a writeing Called a Remonstrance or petition I doe acknowledge it was Ill Done, and vnwarrantably as Transgressinge therein the Rule of due honor to Authoritie and of modestye, and submission In a privaite persone.

per me RAIPH HUDSON

[*Ca.* November 22, 1637]

ACKNOWLEDGMENT OF WILLIAM PELL[2]

My hand being at the petition, (haueing considered of it,) I am convinced of the vnlawfullnesse of the Action; for I did it Rashly without aduice, allso, Ignorantly not Knowing what I did: For had I knowen it had beene against the Rule, or would haue beene offensiuely taken, or that I had expressed any disrespect or vnreverentness to Authority in the leaste measure I would not haue done it, For it goeing vnder the name of a Petition (being Ignorant in things of that nature) I set my hand to it without any scruple: But God hath let me see that herein I haue sinned, and therfore my disire is, that my hand may be withdrawne from it.

WILLIAM PELL

[*Ca.* November 22, 1637]

ACKNOWLEDGMENT OF THOMAS SAVAGE[3]

Wheareas I ioyned in presenting to the corte a writing called a petition ore remonstrance, in which some exspresyons did iustly giue ofence to our honoured magestrats, these are thearefor to intreate your worships to consider that it is and hath bene and through the asistance of the lord I hope euer

---

[1] W. 1. 118. [2] W. 1. 110.
[3] W. 4. 165; 5 *Collections*, 1. 485–486.

shall be contrary to my sperite and Judgmente to cast the lest dishonor vpon athorytie whom god hath commanded vs to honour, and intreate your wor-ships to consider that it was onely the cause for which I did petition, which I alone loke at, and those exspresyons in it as besem not the place of a priuat person I humbly craue pardon for   as for the word remonstrance at which ofenc was taken I vnderstod not what it meante.

THOMAS SAUAGE

[*Ca.* November 22, 1637]

JAMES LUXFORD TO JOHN WINTHROP[1]

RIGHT WOR[SHIPFUL], I haue sent downe this morninge soome butter and other things such as wee haue. time will not giue me leaue to coome to your wor[ship] since I came from Concod, but I haue not yet drawd to a full con-clusion with them because of soome of the cheefe of them beinge absent, and I could not stay all night as soome desired mee, because of my imployments at home which did require my speedy returne, but I perceiue that the towne will grant a reasonable lott in the towne;[2] Furthermore, my purpose is the lord assistinge of mee to goe on with all conuenyent speed in buildinge a house for your wor[ship] at Bostone, accordinge as I propounded to your wor[ship] desiringe this on thinge of your wor[ship] that you will be pleased to leaue the ordering of it in soome kind to mee, to the end that I may doe it for your best aduantage either to sell or keepe. I know that your wor[ship] doth delite in playnnesse, and I shall not willingly digresse from that rule, contriuinge it soe as that, if occasion be offered it may giue content to those that delite in commodious neatnesse, not exceedinge in cost, but if for a matter of ten pound charge a man may make it happely 50*li* better it weare cost Ill saued, beside men doe now build, as lokinge on a setled Commonwelth, and there-fore, wee looke at posteryty and what may be vsefull or profitable for them, neither haue I any purpose to be sumtuous, or at any superfluous charge, but as may be I hope for your wor[ship's] best content; beinge the best im-ployment soe far as I conceiue, that for the present I can settle on wherby to furnish your wor[ship] with mony, for if the lord be pleased to blesse my Indeuors, I hope to haue it a house habitable either for your wor[ship] or

---

[1] W. 4. 49; 5 *Collections*, I. 127–128. For James Luxford, see 5 *Collections*, I. 127*n*.; 2 *Proceedings*, VII. 127–140.

[2] The land that Winthrop subsequently acquired on the Concord River came to him not through a grant from the town but through a grant from the General Court, May 2, 1638. *Records of Massachusetts*, I. 229.

your frend in the springe. neither I trust shall it at all hinder my other proceedings, nor be a matter of any great charge to your wor[ship] in the conclusion for as it hath been to this day, soe I trust it shall be my care to reckon
the cost of what I vndertake, and to cast how to accomplish it, and in an
honest way to rayse the charge   neither doe I much question but that I shall
rayse neare inought from the wood this yeare to accomplish it, and because
when I coome to digg the sellers, a draught will be of soome vse for mee I had
thought to haue a draught ther this winter, which I doe conceiue may be
much for my furtherance, saue that Mr. Jeffery hath sould his house and is
cominge to bostone, and purposes to keepe a draught there, and is now in
hand with me for 500 load of wood which if he by, then it may detayne mee
from cominge Else not, for as these times are it is good to vse all lawfull
meanes in a way of god for the accomplishment of those things that are necessary. But I will now trouble your wor[ship] noe farther: but bend my selfe
the Lord asistinge me to proceed in such a way as may giue your wor[ship]
content.

[JAMES LUXFORD]

[*Ca.* December, 1637]

[*Endorsed by Governor Winthrop:*] Jeames Luxford.

JOHN HARRISON, JR., TO JOHN WINTHROP, JR.[1]

To kisse the hands of his honoured freind John Winthrop esquire humbly present these
Ipswitch

SIR, so good an oportunity presenting it selfe vnto mee, I could not without
the brand of ingratitude but by these present my servise to ye; I am through
Gods mercy and Mr. Paines pitty of mee (pricked on with his owne feare)
arived at Salem, where acording to your commaunds I haue presented your
letters, together with the portraiture of your engine, to the terror of all woods.
I am now in haste going to Boston. I should else further presume vpon your
patience, but not doubting of a kind acceptance of your freinds servise I shall
rest desireing to bee, Your humble servant

JO: HARRISON

SALEM 7 Dec: Ann: Dom: 1637

---

[1] W. 4. 46; 5 *Collections,* I. 119. John Harrison, Jr., as it appears from a later letter to Governor
Winthrop, was at this time under age. He subsequently returned to England and was a student at the
Inner Temple. He was called to the bar on May 20, 1647. *Calendar of Inner Temple Records,* II. 276.

SAMUEL SYMONDS TO JOHN WINTHROP, JR.[1]

SIR, after I had dispatched my letters and busines to you by my father Peter, it soe came to passe that a kinde neighbour and an vnderstandeing man came into the howse where I was and after some discourse about imploying of servants this winter tyme, and of my particuler case about my sendeing any servants to Ipswich, I resolved to take the oportunity of my fathers Barke now at Boston to send certaine necessarie things by it as far as Salem that soe by some meanes or other they may be gotten to Argilla.[2] I have alsoe sent Daniell[3] and two men to sett forward (what they can) my businesse there. They are rawe planters as yet they want experience but we doubt not but you will be pleased to councell, and order them in their businesses. while the hard weather last, I suppose that their worke wilbe to deale in woodworke, as stubbing of trees cleareing of grounds etc. and as soone as any open weather come not to omit breakeing vp of grounds for Indian corne this yeare. Its indiferent to me whether they cleare in the mowed plow ground or in the other, onely this I take it to be best to begin wheare most grownde may easliest and spediest be cleared. I would faine get as much corne growing this yeare as I can, and then seed being gotten into ground we shall attend breaking vp and tilling of ground for next yeare. They will want direccions alsoe I feare for their lodgeings to be warme for provideing besides Indian corne some other cheape provition as garden things fish etc. Albeit I shalbe glad to find some good entrance made in my businesse against my comeing yet if with a litle matter done it please god that I meet them in health I hope I shall rest well content. The lord god prosper all our enterprises. amen. vale. Yours ever in all brotherly affeccion

S: SYMONDS

Dec: 14th 1637

ROBERT KEAYNE TO JOHN WINTHROP, JR.[4]

DEAR SIR, I haue receaued yor louinge letter abowt Mr. Hall and that debt which is made ouer to me from Mr. Dixon, who should haue payd me mony in London, and doth now wright to me to take this hear. I should be ready

[1] W. 3. 32; 4 *Collections*, VII. 121–122. For Symonds, see 4 *Collections*, VII. 118n.
[2] The name of the farm at Ipswich which John Winthrop, Jr., sold to Symonds.
[3] Daniel Epes.
[4] W. 4. 91; 5 *Collections*, I. 254–255. For Keayne, see 5 *Collections*, I. 254n.

to doe him what Curtesie I could not wronginge my selfe. Therfor I hope he
will strayne him selfe the more to giue me satisfaction as soon as he cane. for
the offer of thear seruice, and your comendation of them, I canot but take
well yet my wife thinkes thay are both to fine to take any greate paynes and
soe may be the more vnlowly to subiect them selues to the cond[ition] of seruants, and I neede one that is able not only [*torn*] and ouerlooke seruants in my
absence but alsoe [by his] owne example to incowrage, and draw the rest
[*torn*] full labour, and orderinge things to my best aduan[tage] [*torn*] Prouerb
runns of a good Husband indeed, that [*torn*] doe such a thing but come and
let vs doe such a thing [*torn*]. Since your selfe and I had any speech abowt
him, I [*torn*] a frend in England the offer of a very good Husbandman [and
his] wife to liue at my Farme, for whom I haue sent letters to come this next
somer; which yet it is possible may not come, therefor I am willinge to treate
with Mr. Hall vpon thease Termes if he will come ouer shortly to me, and we
may pitch vpon the wages: he and his wife may come early to the farme in the
springe, only thus if this man should come from England then he must be
content to dispose of him selfe otherways only I will giue them a qwarter of a
years time to prouide them selues, and than it wilbe no preiudice, and besides
though I will prouide nothinge, yet if I should aproue of his faythfullnes and
dilligence to my likinge, it may be thear may be longer continuance and I may
dispose of the other some other way: yet both my selfe and wife maruell how
he beinge a yownge man and withowt charge: and haue had such helpes and
haue made away this parcell of goods, and yet be behind hand, and not able
to liue, whare others that come ouere very poor doe grow pretty rich and before hand and yet mayntayne a wife and 3 or 4 children by thear owne labor.
thus desiring yow to present owr due respects to your selfe wife, Mr. and Mrs.
Norton, your Brother Dudlye etc. I rest Your louinge frend

ROBERT KEAYNE

December 15th 1637

ADDENDUM

. .

THE CHURCH AT HARTFORD TO JOHN WINTHROP[1]

MUCH HONORED SIR, The sight of your worthy messengers our welbeloved freinds, did exceedingly refresh our hearts, but ther message both unexpected and sad, we know not, wether it did more afflict then the other did refresh: We have putt our selves into your place and stead in our owne apprehensions, as being the only way to work a fellow-feeling with Bretheren in the same fayth: Those heavy distractions, had they assaulted our weaknes, we should have conceaved them vnsupportable and therfore we could not but conclude them exceeding uncomfortable vnto your selves, though gratiously furnished with sweet supplyes from the good hand of God: We could have wished, that our teares and prayers, which we have, and do desire to send vp to heaven in your behalfs, might have excused our sending vpon this occasion: The tymes are dangerous, our begynnings raw, our encumberances great necessityes many, our helps few, and those few weake, the little oyle in the creuse not sufficient to refresh our owne faynting spirits, all those presented themselves before vs, and pleaded with vs. But when we weighed whose was the cause vpon whom lay the hazard from [whom] came the request, the cause of Christ to be at- tended, the churches of Christ to be sur[*torn*] the m[em]bers of Christ call for that little help [*torn*] hands: [*torn*] or [*torn*] loves [*obliterated*] deare, to do the duty of [*torn*] to [*torn*] Jesus and to your selves in him and for him vnder whose wing we were first sheltered when we were [*obliterated*] into this westerne cor- ner of the world, and are willing therfore not only to do what you desired, but may be more then you did expect, having resolved and purposed to send both our elders in the next fitt season, to be serviceable to you to the vtmost of ther ability, in the wayty occasions which now be offered to consideration, vnlesse some overruling hand of providence appeare beyond that which in an ordi- nary course of common conceaving we do expect: the severall passages which came into our consultations in the debate of the busines, and the conclusion which issued therfrom, touching the season of our coming, we leave to the re-

---

[1] W. 1. 156. The body of the document is in the handwriting of Thomas Hooker. From the con- text it appears that this letter refers to the Synod which convened at Cambridge on August 30, 1637, to deliberate on the questions arising out of the Antinomian controversy.

lation of these our beloved brethren the messengers of the churches, and the glory of Christ: and your selves and them and the cause to the guidance and blessing of our good God, in whom we rest: Yours in the truth truly

TH: HOOKER

HARTFORD the [*blank*] of 5th month [1637]   SAM: STONE

WILL. GOODWIN

In the name and with the consent of the wholl church

INDEX

NOTE

Places are in Massachusetts unless otherwise stated.

Names of ships are grouped under the heading "Ships, shipbuilding, etc."

Names of individual Indians are grouped under the heading "Indians."

Names of Indian tribes are grouped under the heading "Indians, tribes."

INDEX

Video Content and Resources from Dr. Tebbetts

DVD 1

■ **Breast Augmentation: A Masterclass Curriculum**

1.1   Introduction – Redefining Patient Outcomes
1.2   Requirements for Optimal Patient Outcomes
1.3   Evolution of Tissue-based Implant Selection Systems
1.4   Five Critical Decisions and Measurements
1.5   Clinical Application of the High Five™ Systems
1.6   Implant Selection Principles and Processes
1.7   Preoperative Marking
1.8   Premedications and Anesthesia
1.9   Surgical Processes and Techniques
1.10 Prospective Hemostasis Principles
1.11 Pocket Dissection Sequence
1.12 Incision and Pocket Access
1.13 Inferiomedial (Zone 2) Pocket Dissection
1.14 Transition to the Lateral Pocket Dissection (Zone 3 and 4)
1.15 Medial Pocket (Zone 5) Dissection
1.16 Implant Insertion and Positioning
1.17 Incision Closure
1.18 Postoperative Adjuncts
1.19 Recovery and PACU Care
1.20 Postoperative Care for the 24-hour Recovery
1.21 Redefining the Patient Experience

Running time = 97 minutes

DVD 2 INCLUDING RESOURCES FOLDER

■ **Instrumentation, Anesthesia, and Postoperative Care**

2.1   Surgical Instrumentation for Augmentation
2.2   Anesthesia for Augmentation
2.3   IMF Augmentation in Real Time
2.4   PACU Management Post Augmentation
2.5   Patient in Step Down Immediately Pre Discharge
2.6   Instructions to Patient Caregiver
2.7   Phone Call to Patient Afternoon of Surgery

Running time = 142 minutes

RESOURCES FOLDER

The Resources Folder located on Disk 2 is only accessible o̶ ̶ ̶ ̶ ̶ ̶not on standard DVD players. To access the Resources folder on a computer, r̶ ̶ ̶ ̶ ̶select "Open" (Windows and Macintosh).

00.   **Accessing Materials in the Resourc̶**

01.   **Tebbetts Published Papers in Pl̶**

1.01 What is Adequate F̶i̶l̶ ̶ ̶mplant? (June, 1996)
1.02 Patient Acceptanc̶e̶ ̶ ̶ely Filled Implants (July, 2000)
1.03 Greatest Myths in Brea̶s̶t̶ ̶ugmentation (June, 2001)
1.04 Informed Consent Article (Sept, 2002)
1.05 TEPID System Implant Selection by Tissues (April, 2002)
1.06 High Five™ Augmentation Decision System (Dec, 2005)
1.07 24-hour Augmentation Recovery Part 1 (Jan, 2002)
1.08 24-hour Augmentation Recovery Part 2 (Jan, 2002)
1.09 Dual Plane Augmentation (April, 2001)
1.10 Out Points Criteria for Breast Implant Removal (Oct, 2004)
1.11 BASPI Decision and Management Algorithms (Oct, 2004)
1.12 Wishes and Tissues - Concerns about Dimensional Systems (Jan, 2006)
1.13 Axillary Endoscopic Breast Augmentation - a 28-year Experience (Dec, 2006)
1.14 Zero Percent Reoperation rate at 3 years (Nov, 2006)

02.   **Tebbetts Informed Consent Materials**

2.1   Patient Education and Informed Consent
2.2   Common Questions and Answers
2.3   Patient Images Analysis with Surgeon Dialogue

03.   **Patient Images Analysis and Surgeon Dialogue**

3.1   Patient Images Analysis with Surgeon Dialogue
3.2   Patient Images Analysis without Surgeon Dialogue

04.   **High Five™ System Form and Clinical Evaluation Sheet**

4.1   High Five™ System Measurements Techniques Illustrated
4.2   Five Critical Decisions in Breast Augmentation
4.3   High Five™ Comprehensive Clinical Evaluation Sheet

05.   **Surgical Scripts for Inframammary and Axillary Breast Augmentation**

5.1   Axillary Breast Augmentation Script
5.2   Inframammary Breast Augmentation Script

06.   **Requirements for Out-to-Dinner Augmentation and 24-hour Recovery**

07.   **Dr. Tebbetts' Course Handout - Processes that Redefine a Practice**

08.   **Integrated Anesthesia PACU and Stepdown Protocol**

09.   **Augmentation Instruments and Equipment**

10.   **Post-op Instructions – Dr. Tebbetts' Recipe for Augmentation Recovery**

11.   **FDA PMA Studies and Tebbetts Published Data Comparison Table**

Please see inside back cover for DVDs 3 & 4.